A HISTORY OF
WESTERN SOCIETY

A HISTORY OF WESTERN SOCIETY

THIRD EDITION

VOLUME II: FROM ABSOLUTISM TO THE PRESENT

JOHN P. McKAY

BENNETT D. HILL

JOHN BUCKLER

University of Illinois at Urbana-Champaign

HOUGHTON MIFFLIN COMPANY   BOSTON

Dallas   Geneva, Illinois

Lawrenceville, New Jersey   Palo Alto

Copyright © 1987 by Houghton Mifflin Company.

All rights reserved. No part of this work may be reproduced or transmitted in any form or by any means, electronic or mechanical, including photocopying and recording, or by any information storage or retrieval system, except as may be expressly permitted by the 1976 Copyright Act or in writing by the publisher. Requests for permission should be addressed in writing to Houghton Mifflin Company, One Beacon Street, Boston, Massachusetts 02108.

Printed in the U.S.A.

Library of Congress Catalog Card Number: 86–81469

ISBN: 0-395-36917-7

ABCDEFGHIJ-RM-89876

About the Authors

John P. McKay Born in St. Louis, Missouri, John P. McKay received his B.A. from Wesleyan University (1961), his M.A. from the Fletcher School of Law and Diplomacy (1962), and his Ph.D. from the University of California, Berkeley (1968). He began teaching history at the University of Illinois in 1966 and became a professor there in 1976. John won the Herbert Baxter Adams Prize for his book *Pioneers for Profit: Foreign Entrepreneurship and Russian Industrialization, 1885–1913* (1970). He has also written *Tramways and Trolleys: The Rise of Urban Mass Transport in Europe* (1976) and has translated Jules Michelet's *The People* (1973). His research has been supported by fellowships from the Ford Foundation, the Guggenheim Foundation, the National Endowment for the Humanities, and IREX. His articles and reviews have appeared in numerous journals, including *The American Historical Review, Business History Review, The Journal of Economic History,* and *Slavic Review.* He edits *Industrial Development and the Social Fabric: An International Series of Historical Monographs.*

Bennett D. Hill A native of Philadelphia, Bennett D. Hill earned an A.B. at Princeton (1956) and advanced degrees from Harvard (A.M., 1958) and Princeton (Ph.D., 1963). He taught history at the University of Illinois at Urbana, where he was department chairman from 1978 to 1981. He has published *English Cistercian Monasteries and Their Patrons in the Twelfth Century* (1968) and *Church and State in the Middle Ages* (1970); and articles in *Analecta Cisterciensia, The New Catholic Encyclopaedia, The American Benedictine Review,* and *The Dictionary of the Middle Ages.* His reviews have appeared in *The American Historical Review, Speculum, The Historian, The Catholic Historical Review,* and *Library Journal.* He has been a fellow of the American Council of Learned Societies and has served on committees for the National Endowment for the Humanities. Now a Benedictine monk at St. Anselm's Abbey, Washington, D.C., he is also a Lecturer at the University of Maryland at College Park.

John Buckler Born in Louisville, Ky., John Buckler received his B.A. from the University of Louisville in 1967. Harvard University awarded him the Ph.D. in 1973. From 1984 to 1986 he was the Alexander von Humboldt Fellow at Institut für Alte Geschichte, University of Munich. He is currently an associate professor at the University of Illinois, and is serving on the Subcommittee on Cartography of the American Philological Association. In 1980 Harvard University Press published his *The Theban Hegemony, 371–362 B.C.* His articles have appeared in journals both here and abroad, like the *American Journal of Ancient History, Classical Philology, Rheinisches Museum für Philologie, Classical Quarterly, Wiener Studien,* and *Symbolae Osloenses.*

CONTENTS

30
THE RECOVERY OF EUROPE AND THE AMERICAS   957

31
LIFE IN THE POSTWAR ERA   991

32
THE RECENT PAST, 1968 TO THE PRESENT   1015

MAPS

TIMELINES / GENEALOGIES

PREFACE

A HISTORY OF WESTERN SOCIETY grew out of the authors' desire to infuse new life into the study of Western civilization. We knew full well that historians were using imaginative questions and innovative research to open up vast new areas of historical interest and knowledge. We also recognized that these advances had dramatically affected the subject of European economic, intellectual, and, especially, social history, while new research and fresh interpretations were also revitalizing the study of the traditional mainstream of political, diplomatic, and religious development. Despite history's vitality as a discipline, however, it seemed to us that both the broad public and the intelligentsia were generally losing interest in the past. The mathematical economist of our acquaintance who smugly quipped "What's new in history?"—confident that the answer was nothing and that historians were as dead as the events they examine—was not alone.

It was our conviction, based on considerable experience introducing large numbers of students to the broad sweep of Western civilization, that a book reflecting current trends could excite readers and inspire a renewed interest in history and our Western heritage. Our strategy was twofold. First, we made social history the core element of our work. Not only did we incorporate recent research by social historians, but also we sought to re-create the life of ordinary people in appealing human terms. At the same time we were determined to give the great economic, political, intellectual, and cultural developments the attention they unquestionably deserve. We wanted to give individual readers and instructors a balanced, integrated perspective, so that they could pursue on their own or in the classroom those themes and questions that they found particularly exciting and significant. In an effort to realize fully the potential of our fresh yet balanced approach, we made many changes, large and small, in the second edition.

In preparing the third edition we have worked hard to keep our book up-to-date and to make it still more effective. First, every chapter has been carefully revised to incorporate recent scholarship. Many of our revisions relate to the ongoing explosion in social history, and once again important findings on such subjects as class relations, population, women, and the family have been integrated into the text. New scholarship also led to substantial revisions on many other questions, such as the Neolithic agricultural revolution, political and economic growth in ancient Greece, the rise and spread of Christianity, the Germanic nobility, medieval feudalism, the origins of the Renaissance, Louis XIV and the French nobility, eighteenth-century absolutism, the French Revolution and Napoleon, nationalism, life in the postwar era, and events of the recent past. We believe that the incorporation of newer interpretations of the main political developments in the medieval, early modern, and French revolutionary periods is a particularly noteworthy change in this edition. Better integration of political and social development contributes to this improvement.

Second, we have carefully examined each chapter for organization and clarity. Chapters 7, 8, 9, 11, 14, and 15 have been thoroughly reorganized, while Chapters 17, 18, 21, and 23 have been reordered to a lesser extent. The result of these changes is a more logical presentation of material and a clearer chronological sequence. Similarly, the reorganization of Chapters 30 and 31 and the addition of Chapter 32 have permitted a more complete discussion of changes since World War Two and an innovative interpretation of this complicated era. We have also taken special care to explain terms and concepts as soon as they are introduced.

Third, we have added or expanded material on previously neglected topics to help keep our work fresh and appealing. Coverage of religious developments, with special emphasis on their popular and social aspects, now extends from ancient to modern times and includes several new sections. The reader will also find new material on many other topics, notably the Minoans, Greek and Roman wars, medieval Germany, the Hanseatic League, the African slave trade, Hume and d'Holbach, the pre-revolutionary French elite, Mill, and events since the late 1960s.

Finally, the illustrative component of our work has been completely revised. There are many new illustrations, including a tripling of the color plates that let both great art and earlier times come alive. Twenty new maps containing social as well as political material have also been added, while maps from the second edition have been re-edited and placed in a more effective format. As in earlier editions, all illustrations have been carefully selected to complement the text, and all carry captions that enhance their value. Artwork remains an integral part of our book, for the past can speak in pictures as well as words.

Distinctive features from earlier editions remain in the third. To help guide the reader toward historical understanding we have posed specific historical questions at the beginning of each chapter. These questions are then answered in the course of the chapter, each of which concludes with a concise summary of the chapter's findings. The timelines added in the second edition have proved useful, and still more are found in this edition.

We have also tried to suggest how historians actually work and think. We have quoted extensively from a wide variety of primary sources and have demonstrated in our use of these quotations how historians sift and weigh evidence. We want the reader to realize that history is neither a list of cut-and-dried facts nor a senseless jumble of conflicting opinions. It is our further hope that the primary quotations, so carefully fitted into their historical context, will give the reader a sense that even in the earliest and most remote periods of human experience history has been shaped by individual men and women, some of them great aristocrats, others ordinary folk.

Each chapter concludes with carefully selected suggestions for further reading. These suggestions are briefly described in order to help readers know where to turn to continue thinking and learning about the Western world. The chapter bibliographies have been revised and expanded in order to keep them current with the vast and complex new work being done in many fields.

Western civilization courses differ widely in chronological structure from one campus to another. To accommodate the various divisions of historical time into intervals that fit a two-quarter, three-quarter, or two-semester period, *A History of Western Society* is being published in three versions, each set embracing the complete work:

One-volume hardcover edition, A HISTORY OF WESTERN SOCIETY; two-volume paperback, A HISTORY OF WESTERN SOCIETY *Volume I: From Antiquity to the Enlightenment* (Chapters 1–17), *Volume II: From Absolutism to the Present* (Chapters 16–32); three-volume paperback, A HISTORY OF WESTERN

SOCIETY *Volume A: From Antiquity to the Reformation* (Chapters 1–13), *Volume B: From the Renaissance to 1815* (Chapters 12–21), *Volume C: From the Revolutionary Era to the Present* (Chapters 21–32).

Note that overlapping chapters in both the two- and the three-volume sets permit still wider flexibility in matching the appropriate volume with the opening and closing dates of a course term. Furthermore for courses beginning with the Renaissance rather than antiquity or the medieval period, the reader can begin study with Volume B.

Learning and teaching ancillaries, including a *Study Guide, Computerized Study Guide, Instructor's Manual, Test Items, Computerized Test Items,* and *Map Transparencies,* also contribute to the usefulness of the text. The excellent *Study Guide* has been revised by Professor James Schmiechen of Central Michigan University. Professor Schmiechen has been a tower of strength ever since he critiqued our initial prospectus, and he has continued to give us many valuable suggestions and his warmly appreciated support. His *Study Guide* contains chapter summaries, chapter outlines, review questions, extensive multiple-choice exercises, self-check lists of important concepts and events, and a variety of study aids and suggestions. One innovation in the *Study Guide* that has proved useful to the student is the step-by-step Reading with Understanding exercises, which take the reader by ostensive example through reading and studying activities like underlining, summarizing, identifying main points, classifying information according to sequence, and making historical comparisons. To enable both students and instructors to use the *Study Guide* with the greatest possible flexibility, the guide is available in two volumes, with considerable overlapping of chapters. Instructors and students who use only Volumes A and B of the text have all the pertinent study materials in a single volume, *Study Guide, Volume 1* (Chapters 1–21); likewise, those who use only Volumes B and C of the text also have all the necessary materials in one volume, *Study Guide, Volume 2* (Chapters 12–32). The multiple-choice sections of the *Study Guide* are also available in a computerized version that provides the student with tutorial instruction.

The *Instructor's Manual,* prepared by Professor Philip Adler of East Carolina University, contains learning objectives, chapter synopses, suggestions for lectures and discussion, paper and class activity topics, and lists of audio-visual resources. The accompanying *Test Items,* also by Professor Adler, offers more than 1100 multiple-choice and essay questions and approximately 500 identification terms. The test items are available to adopters on computer tape and disk. In addition, a set of forty color map transparencies is available on adoption.

It is a pleasure to thank the many instructors who have read and critiqued the manuscript through its development: James W. Alexander, University of Georgia; Susan D. Amussen, Connecticut College; Jack M. Balcer, Ohio State University; Ronald M. Berger, State University College at Oneonta, New York; Charles R. Berry, Wright State University; Shirley J. Black, Texas A & M University; John W. Bohnstedt, California State University at Fresno; Paul Bookbinder, University of Massachusetts—Boston, Harbor Campus; Jerry H. Brookshire, Middle Tennessee State University; Thomas S. Burns, Emory University; Robert Clouse, Indiana State University; Norman H. Cooke, Rhode Island College; Charles E. Daniel, University of Rhode Island; Gary S. Cross, Pennsylvania State University; Lawrence G. Duggan, University of Delaware; J. Rufus Fears, Indiana University; John B. Freed, Illinois State University; James Friguglietti, Eastern Montana College; Charles L. Geddes, University of Denver; James Gump, University of San Diego; Charles D. Hamilton, San Diego State University; Barbara Hanawalt, Indiana University; Thomas J. Heston, West Chester State College; Edward J. Kealey, College of the Holy Cross; Isabel F. Knight, Pennsylvania State University; Charles A. Le Guin, Portland State University; Richard Lyman, Simmons College; Rhoda McFadden, Montgomery County Community College; Christian D. Nokkentved, University of Illinois at Chicago; John E. Roberts, Jr., Lincoln Land Community College; William J. Roosen, Northern Arizona University; Lawrence Silverman, University of Colorado; Armstrong Starkey, Adelphi University; Robert E. Stebbins, Eastern Kentucky University; Bailey S. Stone, University of Houston; C. Mary Taney, Glassboro State College; Allen M. Ward, University of Connecticut; and Donald Wilcox, University of New Hampshire.

Many of our colleagues at the University of Illinois kindly provided information and stimulation for our book, often without even knowing it. N. Frederick Nash, Rare Book Librarian, gave freely of his time and made many helpful suggestions for illustrations. The World Heritage Museum at the University continued to allow us complete access to its sizable holdings. James Dengate kindly supplied information on objects from the museum's collection. Caroline Buckler took many excellent photographs of the museum's objects and generously helped us at crucial moments in production. Such wide-ranging expertise was a great asset for which we are very appreciative. Bennett Hill wishes to express his sincere appreciation to Ramón de la Fuente of Washington, D.C., for his support, encouragement, and research assistance in the preparation of this third edition. John Buckler extends his thanks to Elke Bernlocher.

Each of us has benefited from the generous criticism of his co-authors, although each of us assumes responsibility for what he has written. John Buckler has written the first six chapters; Bennett Hill has continued the narrative through Chapter 16; and John McKay has written Chapters 17 through 32. Finally, we continue to welcome from our readers comments and suggestions for improvements, for they have helped us greatly in this ongoing endeavor.

JOHN P. MCKAY
BENNETT D. HILL
JOHN BUCKLER

INTRODUCTION

THE ORIGINS OF MODERN WESTERN SOCIETY

 *T*HE ORIGINS of modern western society lie in the ancient and medieval past. Scholars trace the roots of Western culture to Mesopotamia in the Middle East, the area bound by the Tigris and Euphrates rivers. The civilizations that successively flourished there between roughly 7000 and 500 B.C.—Mesopotamian, Egyptian, and Hittite—each made notable achievements. These achievements became the legacies that were absorbed and utilized by later cultures, Hebraic, Greek, and Roman. The Middle Ages built on the Greek and Roman past. Similarly, the European intellectual and religious movements often called the Renaissance and the Reformation derive from the medieval past. History, the study of change over time, reveals that each age has re-interpreted the cultural legacy of its predecessors in the effort to meet its own demands. The modern world exists as the product of all that has gone before.

THE ANCIENT WORLD

The ancient world provided several cultural elements that the modern world has inherited. First came the beliefs of the Hebrews (Jewish forebears) in one God and in a chosen people with whom God had made a covenant. The book known as the Scriptures, or "sacred writings," embodied Hebraic law, history, and culture. Second, Greek architectural, philosophical, and scientific ideas have exercised a profound influence on Western thought. Rome subsequently gave the West language and law. The Latin language became the instrument of verbal and written communication for over a thousand years; Roman concepts of law and government molded Western ideas of political organization. Finally, Christianity, the spiritual faith and ecclesiastical organization that derived from the Palestinian Jew, Jesus of Nazareth (ca 3 B.C.–A.D. 29), also conditioned Western religious, social, and moral values and systems.

The Hebrews

The Hebrews probably originated in northern Mesopotamia. Nomads who tended flocks of sheep, they were forced by drought to follow their patriarch Abraham into the Nile Delta in Egypt. The Egyptians enslaved them and put them to work on various agricultural and building projects. In the crucial event in early Jewish history, the lawgiver Moses, in response to God's command, led the Hebrews out of Egypt into the promised land (Palestine) in the thirteenth century B.C. At that time, the Hebrews consisted of twelve disunited tribes made up of families. They all believed themselves descendants of a common ancestor, Abraham. The family was their primary social institution, and most families engaged in agricultural or pastoral pursuits. Under the pressure of a series of wars for the control of Palestine, the twelve independent Hebrew tribes were united into a centralized political force under one king. Kings Saul, David, and especially Solomon (ca 965–925 B.C.) built the Hebrew nation with its religious center at Jerusalem, the symbol of Jewish unity.

The Hebrews developed their religious ideas in the Scriptures, also known as the Old Testament. In their migrations, the Jews had come in contact with many peoples, such as the Mesopotamians and the Egyptians, who had many gods. The Jews, however, were monotheistic: their God was the one and only God, he had created all things, his presence filled the universe, and he took a strong personal interest in the individual. During the Exodus from Egypt, God had made a covenant with the Jews. He promised to protect them as his chosen people and to give them the land; in return, they must worship only him and obey the Ten Commandments that he had given Moses. The Ten Commandments comprise an ethical code of behavior, forbidding the Jews to steal, lie, murder, or commit adultery. This covenant was to prove a constant force in Jewish life. The Old Testament also contains detailed legal proscriptions, books of history, concepts of social and familial structure, wisdom literature, and prophecies of a Messiah to come. Parts of the Old Testament show the Hebraic debt to other cultures. For example, the Books of Proverbs and Sirach reflect strong Egyptian influences. The Jews developed an emotionally satisfying religion whose ideals shaped not only later faiths, such as Christianity and Islam, but also the modern world.

The Greeks

While ancient Middle Eastern peoples such as the Hebrews interpreted the origins, nature, and end of man in religious or theological terms, the Greeks treated these issues in terms of reason. In the fifth century B.C., small independent city-states (poleis) dotted the Greek peninsula. Athens, especially, created a brilliant culture that greatly influenced Western civilization. Athens developed a magnificent architecture whose grace, beauty, and quiet intensity still speak to humankind. In their comedies and tragedies, the Athenians Aeschylus, Sophocles, and Euripedes were the first playwrights to treat eternal problems of the human condition. Athens also experimented with the political system we call democracy. All free adult males participated directly in the making of laws and in the government of the polis. Since a large part of the population—women and slaves—were not allowed to share in the activity of the Assembly, and since aristocrats held most important offices in the polis, Athenian democracy must not be confused with modern democratic practices. The modern form of democracy, moreover, is representative rather than direct: citizens express their views and wishes through elected representatives. Nevertheless, in their noble experiment in which the people were the government, and in their view that the state existed for the good of the citizen, Athenians served to create a powerful political ideal.

Classical Greece of the fifth and fourth centuries B.C. also witnessed an incredible flowering of philosophical ideas. The Greeks were not the first people to speculate about the origins and nature of man and the universe. The outstanding achievement of the Greeks, rather, was their interest in treating these questions in rational instead of religious terms. Hippocrates, the "father of medicine," taught that natural means—not magical or religious ones—could be found to fight disease. He based his opinions on observation and experimentation. Hippocrates also insisted that medicine was a branch of knowledge separate from philosophy. This distinction between natural science and philosophy was supported by the sophists, who traveled the Greek world teaching young men that human beings were the proper subject for study. They laid great emphasis on logic and the meaning of words and criticized traditional beliefs, religion, even the laws of the polis.

Building on the approach of the sophists, Socrates (ca 470–399 B.C.) spent his life questioning and investigating. Socrates held that human beings and their environments represent the essential subject for philosophical inquiry. He taught that excellence could be learned and, by seeking excellence through knowledge, human beings could find the highest good and ultimately true happiness. Socrates' pupil, Plato (427–347 B.C.), continued his teacher's work. Plato wrote down his thoughts, which survive in the form of dialogues. He founded a school, the Academy, where he developed the theory that visible, tangible things are unreal, archetypes of "ideas" or "forms" that are constant and indestructible. In *The Republic,* the first literary description of a utopian society, Plato discusses the nature of justice in the ideal state. In *The Symposium,* he treats the nature and end of love.

Aristotle (384–322 B.C.), Plato's student, continued the philosophical tradition in the next generation. The range of his subjects of investigation is vast. He explores the nature of government in *Politics,* ideas of matter and motion in *Physics* and *Metaphysics,* outer space in *On the Heavens,* conduct in the *Nichomachian Ethics,* and language and literature in *Rhetoric.* In all his works, Aristotle emphasizes the importance of the direct observation of nature; he insists that theory must follow fact. Aristotle had one of the most inquiring and original minds that Western civilization has ever produced, and his ideas later profoundly shaped both Muslim and Roman Catholic theology. The Greeks originated medicine, science, philosophy, and other branches of knowledge. They asked penetrating questions and came up with immortal responses.

These phenomenal intellectual advances took place against a background of constant warfare. The long and bitter struggle between the cities of Athens and Sparta called the Peloponnesian War (459–404 B.C.), described in the historian Thucydides' classic, *The Histories,* ended in Athens' defeat. Shortly afterward, Sparta, Athens, and Thebes contested for hegemony in Greece, but no single state was strong enough to dominate the others. Taking advantage of the situation, Philip II (359–336 B.C.) of Macedon, a small kingdom comprising part of modern Greece and Yugoslavia, defeated a combined Theban-Athenian army in 338 B.C. Unable to resolve their domestic quarrels, the Greeks lost their freedom to the Macedonian invader.

In 323 B.C. Philip's son, Alexander of Macedonia, died at the ripe age of 32. During the twelve short years of his reign, Alexander had conquered an empire stretching from Macedonia in the present-day Balkans across the Middle East into Asia as far as India. Because none of the generals who succeeded him could hold together such a vast territory, it disintegrated into separate kingdoms. Scholars label the period dating from ca 800 B.C. to 323 B.C., in which the polis predominated, the Hellenic Age. The time span from Alexander's death in 323 B.C. to the collapse of Egypt to Rome in 30 B.C., which was characterized by independent kingdoms, is commonly called the Hellenistic Age.

The Hellenistic period witnessed two profoundly significant developments: the diffusion of Greek culture through Asia Minor, and the further advance of science, medicine, and philosophy. As Alexander advanced eastward, he established cities and military colonies in strategic spots. Militarily, these helped to secure his supply line and control the countryside. Culturally, as Greek immigrants poured into the East, they served as powerful instruments in the spread of Hellenism. Though the Greeks were a minority in the East, the dominant language, laws, and institutions became Greek. Thus, a uniform culture spread throughout the East. Greek culture linked the East and the West, and this cultural bond later helped Roman efforts to impose unity on the Roman world.

Hellenistic scientific progress likewise had enormous consequences. Aristarchus of Samos (ca 310–230 B.C.) rejected Aristotle's idea that the earth is the center of the universe, and using only the naked eye, advanced the heliocentric theory that the earth and other planets revolve around the sun. The Alexandrian mathematician Euclid (ca 300 B.C.) compiled a textbook, *Principles of Geometry,* which has been studied by school boys and girls for centuries and has proved basic to education in the West. Archimedes of Syracuse studied the principles of mechanics governing instruments such as the lever and invented numerous practical devices, including the catapult and

Archimedan screw. Hellenistic physicians dissected the human body, enabling better knowledge of anatomy and improvements in surgery. The mathematician Eratosthenes (285–ca 204 B.C.), who directed the library of Alexandria—the greatest seat of learning in the Hellenistic world—calculated the earth's circumference geometrically at 24,675 miles; it is actually 24,860 miles. In philosophy Hellenistic thinkers continued the rational approach of the Greeks. Stoicism, so called from the building where its earliest proponents taught (the *Stoa*), represents the greatest philosophical development of the Hellenistic period. Stressing the efficacy of inner strength, or patience, in facing life's difficulties, the Stoics originated the concept of natural law. Since all men are brothers and all good men live in harmony with nature (reason) and the universe, one law—the natural law—governs all. The Stoics advocated a universal state government: not a political state but an ethical one based on individual behavior. These ideas strongly attracted the Romans, who used the ideal of a universal state as a rationale for extending their empire over peoples of diverse political laws and institutions.

ROME

The city of Rome, situated near the center of the boot-shaped peninsula of Italy, conquered all of what it considered the civilized world. Rome's great achievement, however, rested in its ability not only to conquer peoples but to incorporate them into the Roman way of life. Rome created a world state that embraced the entire Mediterranean basin. It bequeathed to the Middle Ages and the modern world three great legacies: Roman law, the Latin language, and flexible administrative practices.

According to tradition, Rome was founded in the mid-eighth century B.C. Obscure Etruscans from the north and waves of Greek immigrants from the south influenced its early history. In 509 B.C. Rome expelled the Etruscan king, Tarquin the Proud, and founded a republic. Scholars customarily divide Roman history into two stages: the Republic (ca 509–31 B.C.), during which Rome grew from a small city-state to an empire, and the Empire, the period when the old republican constitution fell to a consti-

tutional monarchy. Between 509 and 290 B.C. Rome subdued all of Italy, and between 282 and 146 B.C. slowly acquired an overseas empire. The dominant feature of the social history of the early Republic was the clash between patrician aristocrats and plebeian commoners.

While the Greeks speculated about the ideal state, the Romans pragmatically developed methods of governing themselves and their empire. Their real genius lay in government and law. Because the Romans continually faced concrete challenges, change was a constant feature of their political life. The senate acted as the most important institution of the Republic. Composed of aristocratic elders, it initially served to advise the other governing group, the magistrates. As the senate's prestige increased, its advice came to have the force of law. Roman law, called the *ius civilis* or "civil law," consisted of statutes, customs, and forms of procedure. The goal of the *ius civilis* was to protect citizens' lives, property, and reputations. As Rome expanded, first throughout Italy, then the Mediterranean basin, legal devices had to be found to deal with disputes among foreigners or between foreigners and Romans. Sometimes, magistrates adopted parts of other (foreign) legal systems. On other occasions, they used the law of equity: with no precedent to guide them, they made decisions on the basis of what seemed fair to all parties. Thus with flexibility the keynote in dealing with specific cases and circumstances, a new body of law, the *ius gentium* or "law of the peoples," evolved. This law was applicable to both Romans and foreigners.

Law was not the only facet of Hellenistic culture to influence the Romans. Indeed, Hellenistic thought and lifestyles so thoroughly permeated Roman life that the poet Horace (68–8 B.C.) could write "Captive Greece captured her rough conquerors and introduced the arts into rustic Latium." The Roman conquest of the Hellenistic East led to the wholesale confiscation of Greek sculpture and paintings to adorn Roman temples. Greek literary and historical classics were translated into Latin; Greek philosophy was studied in the Roman schools; Greek plays were adapted to the Roman stage; educated people learned Greek as a matter of course. Public baths based on the Greek model—with exercise rooms, swimming pools, reading rooms, and snack bars—served not only as centers for recreation and exercise but as centers of Roman public life. Rome assimilated the Greek achievement, and Hellenism became an enduring feature of Roman life.

With territorial conquests Rome also acquired serious problems, which surfaced by the late second century B.C. Characteristically, the Romans responded practically with a system of provincial administration that placed at the head of local, provincial governments appointed state officials, who were formally incorporated into the Republic's constitution. The Romans devised an efficient system of tax collecting as well. Overseas warfare required armies of huge numbers of men for long periods of time. A few officers gained fabulous wealth, but most soldiers did not and returned home to find their farms in ruins. Those with cash to invest bought up small farms, creating vast estates called *latifundia.* Since the law forbade landless men to serve in the army, most veterans migrated to Rome seeking work. Victorious armies had already sent tens of thousands of slaves to Rome, and veterans could not compete in the labor market with slaves. A huge unemployed urban proletariat resulted. Its demands for work and political reform were bitterly resisted by the aristocratic senate, and civil war characterized the first century B.C.

Out of the violence and disorder emerged Julius Caesar (100–44 B.C.), a victorious general, shrewd politician, and highly popular figure. He took practical steps to end the civil war, such as expanding citizenship and sending large numbers of the urban poor to found colonies in Gaul, Spain, and North Africa. These settlements spread Roman culture. Fearful that Caesar's popularity and ambition would turn Rome into a monarchy, a group of aristocratic conspirators assassinated him in 44 B.C. Civil war was renewed. Ultimately, in 31 B.C. Caesar's adopted son Octavian, known as Augustus, defeated his rivals and became master of Rome.

The reign of Augustus (31 B.C.–A.D. 14) marked the end of the Republic and the beginning of what historians call the Empire. Augustus continued Caesar's work. By fashioning a means of cooperation in government among the people, magistrates, senate, and army, Augustus established a constitutional monarchy that replaced the Republic. His own power derived from the various magistracies he held and the power granted him by the senate. Thus, as commander of the Roman army, he held the title of *imperator,* which later came to mean "emperor" in the modern sense of sovereign power. Augustus ended domestic turmoil and secured the provinces. He founded new colonies, mainly in the western Mediterranean basin, which promoted the spread of Greco-Roman culture and the Latin language to the West. Colonists with latifundia exercised authority in their regions as representatives of Rome. (Later, after the Empire disintegrated, they continued to exercise local power.) Augustus extended Roman citizenship to all freemen. A system of Roman roads and sea lanes united the empire. For two hundred years the Mediterranean world experienced the *pax Romana* —a period of piece, order, harmony, and flourishing culture.

In the third century this harmony collapsed. Rival generals backed by their troops contested the imperial throne. In the disorder caused by the civil war that ensued, the frontiers were left unmanned, and Germanic invaders poured across the borders. Throughout the Empire, civil war and barbarian invasions devastated towns and farms, causing severe economic depression. The emperors Diocletian (A.D. 285–305) and Constantine (A.D. 306–337) tried to halt the general disintegration by reorganizing the Empire, expanding the state of bureaucracy, and imposing heavier taxation. For administrative purposes, Diocletian divided the Empire into a western half and an eastern half. Constantine established the new capital city of Constantinople in Byzantium. The two parts drifted further apart in the fourth century, when the division became permanent. Diocletian's unrealistic attempt to curb inflation by arbitrarily freezing wages and prices failed. In the early fifth century the borders collapsed entirely, and various Germanic tribes completely overran the western provinces. In 410 and again in 455, Rome itself was sacked by the barbarians.

After the Roman Empire's decline, the rich legacy of Greco-Roman culture was absorbed by the medieval world and ultimately the modern world. The Latin language remained the basic medium of communication among educated people for the next thousand years; for almost two thousand years, Latin literature formed the core of all Western education. Roman roads, buildings, and aqueducts remained in use. Roman law left its mark on the legal and political systems of most European countries. Rome had preserved the best of ancient culture for later times.

CHRISTIANITY

The ancient world also left behind a powerful religious legacy, Christianity. Christianity derives from the life, teachings, death, and resurrection of the Galilean Jew, Jesus of Nazareth (ca 3 B.C.–A.D. 29). Thoroughly Jewish in his teaching, Jesus preached the coming of the kingdom of God, a "kingdom not of this world," but one of eternal peace and happiness. He urged his followers and listeners to reform their lives according to the commandments, especially that stating, "You shall love the Lord your God with your whole heart, your whole mind, and your whole soul, and your neighbor as yourself." Thus, the heart of Christian teaching is love of God and love of neighbor. Some Jews believed that Jesus was the long-awaited Messiah. Others, to whom Jesus represented a threat to ancient traditions, hated and feared him. Though Jesus did not preach rebellion against the Roman governors, the Roman prefect of Judea, Pontius Pilate, feared that the popular agitation surrounding Jesus could lead to revolt against Rome. When Jewish leaders subsequently delivered Jesus to the Roman authorities, to avert violence Pilate sentenced him to death by crucifixion—the usual method for common criminals. Jesus' followers maintained that he rose from the dead three days later.

Those followers might have remained a small Jewish sect but for the preaching of the Hellenized Jew, Paul of Tarsus (ca A.D. 5–67). Paul taught that Jesus was the Son of God, that he brought a new law of love, and that Jesus' message was to be proclaimed to all people, Greek and Jew, slave and free, male and female. He traveled between and wrote letters to the Christian communities at Corinth, Ephesus, Thessalonica, and other cities. As the Roman Empire declined, Christianity spread throughout the Roman world. Because it welcomed people of all social classes, offered a message of divine forgiveness and salvation, and taught that every individual has a role to play in the building of the kingdom of God, thereby fostering a deep sense of community in many of its followers, Christianity won thousands of adherents. Roman efforts to crush Christianity failed. The emperor Constantine legalized Christianity, and in 392 the emperor Theodosius made it the state religion of the Empire. Carried by settlers, missionaries, and merchants to Gaul, Spain, North Africa, and Britain, Christianity formed a fundamental element of Western civilization.

THE MIDDLE AGES

Fourteenth-century writers coined the term "Middle Ages," meaning a middle period of Gothic barbarism between two ages of enormous cultural brilliance— the Roman world of the first and second centuries, and their own age, the fourteenth century, which these writers thought had recaptured the true spirit of classical antiquity. Recent scholars have demonstrated that the thousand-year period between roughly the fourth and fourteenth centuries witnessed incredible developments: social, political, intellectual, economic, and religious. The men and women of the Middle Ages built on the cultural heritage of the Greco-Roman past and made phenomenal advances in their own right.

THE EARLY MIDDLE AGES

The time period that historians mark off as the early Middle Ages, extending from about the fifth to the tenth century, saw the emergence of a distinctly Western society and culture. The geographical center of that society shifted northward from the Mediterranean basin to western Europe. While a rich urban life and flourishing trade had characterized the ancient world, the Germanic invasions led to the decline of cities and the destruction of commerce. Early medieval society was rural and local, with the farm or latifundium serving as the characteristic social unit. Several ingredients went into the making of European culture. First, Europe became Christian. Christian missionary activity led to the slow, imperfect Christianization of the Germanic peoples who had overrun the Roman Empire. Christianity taught the barbarians a higher code of morality and behavior and served as the integrating principle of medieval society. Christian writers played a powerful role in the conservation of Greco-Roman thought. They used Latin as their medium of communication, thereby preserving it. They copied and transmitted classical texts. Writers such as St. Augustine of Hippo (354–430) used Roman rhetoric and Roman history to defend Christian theology. In so doing, they assimilated classical culture to Christian teaching.

Second, as the Germanic tribes overran the Roman Empire, they intermarried with the old Gallo-Roman aristocracy. The elite class that emerged held the dominant political, social, and economic power in early—and later—medieval Europe. Germanic custom and tradition, such as ideals of military prowess and bravery in battle, became part of the mental furniture of Europeans.

Third, in the seventh and eighth centuries, Muslim military conquests carried Islam, the religion inspired by the prophet Mohammed (?570–632) across North Africa, the Mediterranean Sea, and Spain into southern France. The Arabs eventually translated many Greek texts. When, beginning in the ninth century, those texts were translated from Arabic into Latin, they came to play a role in the formation of European scientific, medical, and philosophical thought.

In the eighth century, also, the Carolingian dynasty, named after its most illustrious member, Charles the Great, or Charlemagne (768–814), gradually acquired a broad hegemony over much of what is today France, Germany, and northern Italy. Charlemagne's coronation by the pope at Rome in a ceremony filled with Latin anthems represented a fusion of classical, Christian, and Germanic elements. This Germanic warrior-king supported Christian missionary efforts and encouraged both classical and Christian scholarship. For the first time since the decay of the Roman Empire, Western Europe had achieved a degree of political unity. Similarly, the culture of Carolingian Europe blended Germanic, Christian, and Greco-Roman elements.

Its enormous size proved to be the undoing of the Carolingian empire, and Charlemagne's descendants could not govern it. Attacks by Viking (early Scandinavian), Muslim, and Magyar (early Hungarian) marauders led to the collapse of centralized power. The new invaders wreaked more destruction than had the Germans in the fifth and sixth centuries. Real authority passed into the hands of local strongmen. Political authority was completely decentralized. Scholars describe the society that emerged as feudal and manorial: a small group of military leaders held public political power. They gave such protection as they could to the people living on their estates. They held courts. They coined money. And they negotiated with outside powers. The manor or local estate was the basic community unit. Serfs on the manor engaged in agriculture, which everywhere was the dominant form of economy. Since no feudal lord could exercise authority or provide peace over a very wide area, political instability, violence, and chronic disorder characterized Western society.

THE HIGH AND LATER MIDDLE AGES

By the beginning of the eleventh century, the European world showed distinct signs of recovery, vitality, and creativity. Over the next two centuries that recovery and creativity manifested itself in every facet of culture—economic, social, political, intellectual, and artistic. A greater degree of peace paved the way for these achievements.

The Viking and Magyar invasions gradually ended. Warring knights supported ecclesiastical pressure against violence, and disorder declined. Improvements in farming technology, such as the use of the horse collar, led to an agricultural revolution. Old land was better utilized and new land brought under cultivation. Agricultural productivity increased tremendously. These factors led to considerable population growth.

Increased population contributed to some remarkable economic and social developments. A salient manifestation of the recovery of Europe and of the vitality of the High Middle Ages was the rise of towns and concurrent growth of a new commercial class. Surplus population and the search for new economic opportunities led to the expansion of old towns, such as Florence, Paris, London, and Cologne, and the foundation of completely new ones, such as Munich and Berlin. A new artisan and merchant class, frequently called the "middle class," appeared. In medieval sociology, just three classes existed: the clergy, who prayed; the nobility, who fought; and the peasantry, who tilled the land. The middle class, engaging in manufacturing and trade, seeking freedom from the jurisdiction of feudal lords, and pursuing wealth with a fiercely competitive spirit, fit none of the standard categories. Townspeople represented a radical force for change.

The twelfth and thirteenth centuries witnessed an enormous increase in the volume of local and international trade. For example, Italian merchants traveled to the regional fairs of France and Flanders to exchange silk from China and slaves from the Crimea for English woolens, French wines, and Flemish textiles. Merchants adopted new business techniques. They had a strongly capitalistic spirit and were eager to invest surplus capital to make more money. These developments added up to what scholars have termed a commercial revolution, a major turning point in the economic and social life of the West. The High Middle Ages saw the transformation of Europe from a rural and agrarian society into an urban and industrial one.

The High Middle Ages also saw the birth of the modern centralized state. Rome had bequeathed to Western civilization the concepts of the state and the law, but for centuries after the disintegration of the Roman Empire the state as a reality did not exist. With the possible exception of the Carolingian experience, no early medieval government exercised authority over a wide area; real political power rested in the hands of local strongmen. Beginning in the twelfth century, kings worked to establish means of communication with all their peoples, to weaken the influence of feudal lords and thus to strengthen their own authority, and to build efficient bureaucracies. Kings often created courts of law, which served not only to punish criminals and reduce violence but also to increase royal income. In France, Spain, Italy, and Germany courts applied principles of Roman law. The Roman *ius civilis* was thus preserved through its use in the development of states. The law courts strengthened royal influence. People began to extend their primary loyalty to the king rather than to the "international" church or the local feudal lord. By the end of the thirteenth century, the kings of France and England had achieved a high degree of unity and laid the foundations of modern centralized states. In Italy, Germany, and Spain, however, strong independent local authorities continued to predominate.

In the realm of government and law, the Middle Ages made other powerful contributions to the modern world. The use of law to weaken feudal barons and to strengthen royal authority worked to increase respect for the law itself. Following a bitter dispute with his barons, King John of England (1199–1216) was forced to sign the document known as Magna Carta. Magna Carta contains the principle that there is an authority higher than the king to which even he

is responsible: the law. The idea of the "rule of law" became embedded in the Western political consciousness. English kings following John recognized this common law, a law that their judges applied throughout the country. Exercise of common law often involved juries of local people to answer questions of fact. The common law and jury system of the Middle Ages have become integral features of Anglo-American jurisprudence. In the fourteenth century, kings also summoned meetings of the leading classes in their kingdoms, and thus were born representative assemblies, most notably the English parliament.

In their work of consolidation and centralization, kings increasingly used the knowledge of university-trained officials. Universities first emerged in Western Europe in the thirteenth century. Medieval universities were educational guilds that produced educated and trained officials for the new bureaucratic states. The universities at Bologna in Italy and Montpellier in France, for example, were centers for the study of Roman law. After Aristotle's works had been translated from Arabic into Latin, Paris became the leading university for the study of philosophy and theology. Medieval scholastics (as philosophers and theologians were called because they belonged to schools) sought to harmonize Greek philosophy with Christian teaching. They wanted to use reason to deepen the understanding of what was believed on faith. At the University of Paris, Thomas Aquinas (1225–1274) recorded a brilliant synthesis of Christian revelation and Aristotelian philosophy in his *Summa Theologica*. Medieval universities developed the basic structures familiar to modern students: colleges, universities, examinations, and degrees. Colleges and universities represent a major legacy of the Middle Ages to the modern world.

Under the leadership of the Christian church, Christian ideals permeated all aspects of medieval culture. The village priest blessed the fields before the spring planting and the fall harvesting. Guilds of merchants sought the protection of patron saints and held elaborate public celebrations on the saints' feast days. University lectures and meetings of parliaments began with prayers. Kings relied on the services of bishops and abbots in the work of the government. Around the parish church not only the religious life but the social, political, and often economic life of the community centered. The twelfth and thirteenth centuries witnessed a remarkable outburst of Christian piety, as the crusades (or "holy wars" waged against the Muslims for control of Jerusalem) and Gothic cathedrals reveal. More stone was quarried for churches in medieval France than had been mined in ancient Egypt, where the Great Pyramid alone consumed 40.5 million cubic feet of stone. Churches and cathedrals were visible manifestations of community civic pride. But ideals can rarely be achieved. As centuries passed, abuses in the church multiplied; so did cries for reform.

The high level of energy and creativity that characterized the twelfth and thirteenth centuries could not be sustained indefinitely. In the fourteenth century, every conceivable disaster struck western Europe. Drought or excessive rain destroyed harvests, causing widespread famine. The bubonic plague (or Black Death) swept across the continent, taking a terrible toll on population. England and France became deadlocked in a long and bitter struggle known as the Hundred Years' War (1337–1453). Schism in the Catholic church resulted in the simultaneous claim by two popes of jurisdiction. Many parts of Europe experienced a resurgence of feudal violence and petty warfare. Out of this misery, disorder, and confusion, a new society gradually emerged.

EARLY MODERN EUROPE

The period frequently labeled early modern Europe, extending from about 1400 to 1600, was an age of great change in European society. Men and women of the Renaissance and the Reformation laid the foundations of a new Europe. But Europe remained very different from our modern contemporary world. The industrial and the French revolutions, the growth of nationalism, and the profound secularization of culture occurred in the eighteenth and nineteenth centuries; these forces unleashed what we mean when we speak of the "modern world." By late twentieth-century standards, fifteenth- and sixteenth-century Europe remained—in its class structure, economic life, technology, and methods of communication—closer to imperial Rome than to present-day Europe and America.[1] Our emphasis,

[1] Eugene F. Rice, *The Foundations of Early Modern Europe, 1460–1559*, W. W. Norton & Co., New York, 1970, p. x.

therefore, rests on *early* modern Europe, which nevertheless saw phenomenal development. The Renaissance, the Reformation, and the expansion of Europe overseas drastically altered European attitudes, values, and lifestyles.

THE RENAISSANCE

While war, famine, disease, and death swept across northern Europe in the fourteenth century, a new culture was emerging in Italy. Italian society underwent great changes. In the fifteenth century, these phenomena spread beyond Italy and gradually influenced northern Europe. These cultural changes have collectively been called the Renaissance. The Italian Renaissance evolved in two broad and overlapping stages. In the first period, which dated from about 1050 to 1300, a new economy emerged, based on Venetian and Genoese shipping and long-distance trade and on Florentine banking and cloth manufacturing. At the end of the thirteenth century, Florentine bankers gained control of the papal banking. From this position as tax collectors for the papacy, Florentine mercantile families began to dominate European banking on both sides of the Alps. They had offices in London, Bruges, Barcelona, Tunis, Naples, and Rome. Profits from loans and investments were pumped back into urban industries, especially the woolen industry. Florence bought the highest quality wool from England and Spain, developed techniques for its manufacture, and employed tens of thousands of workers to turn it into cloth. Florentine cloth brought the highest prices in the fairs, markets, and bazaars of Europe, Africa, and Asia. The wealth so produced brought into existence a new urban and aristocratic class.

In the industrial cities of Venice and Florence, this new aristocratic class governed as oligarchs: they maintained the façade of republican government in which political power theoretically resides in the people and is exercised by their chosen representatives, but, in fact, they ruled. In cities with strong agricultural bases, such as Verona, Mantua, and Ferrara, despots predominated. In the fifteenth century, political power and elite culture centered at the princely courts of oligarchs and despots. At his court the Renaissance prince displayed his patronage of the arts and learning.

The second stage of the Italian Renaissance, which lasted from about 1300 to 1600, was characterized by extraordinary manifestations of intellectual and artistic energies. Scholars commonly use the French term *renaissance* ("rebirth") to describe the cultural achievements of the fourteenth through sixteenth centuries. As an intellectual movement the Renaissance possessed certain hallmarks that held profound significance for the evolution of the modern world.

Fourteenth- and fifteenth-century Italians had the self-conscious awareness that they were living in new times. They believed that theirs was a golden age of creativity, an age of rebirth of classical antiquity. They identified with the philosophers and artists of Greek and Roman antiquity, copied the lifestyles of the ancients, and expressed contempt for their immediate medieval past. Second, the Renaissance manifested a new attitude toward men, women, and the world, an attitude often described as individualism. Individualism stressed personality, uniqueness, genius, the fullest possible development of human potential. Artist, athlete, sculptor, scholar, whatever —a person's potential should be stretched until fully realized. The thirst for fame, the burning quest for glory was a central component of Renaissance individualism.

Closely connected with individualism was a deep interest in the Latin classics. This feature of the Renaissance became known as "the new learning," or simply "humanism." The terms "humanism" and "humanist" derive from the Latin *humanitas,* which the ancient Roman orator Cicero used to describe the literary culture needed by anyone who would be considered educated or civilized. Humanists studied the Latin classics to discover past insights into human nature.

A new secular spirit constitutes another basic feature of the Italian Renaissance. Secularism involves a greater regard for, and interest in, the things of this world, rather than in otherworldly concerns. Medieval people certainly pursued financial profits ruthlessly, and Renaissance men and women had deep spiritual concerns. In the Middle Ages, however, the dominant ideals focused on life after death. The fourteenth and fifteenth centuries witnessed the slow and steady growth of secularism in Italy. Economic changes, preoccupation with money-making, and the rising prosperity of the Italian cities precipitated a fundamental change in the attitudes and values of the urban aristocracy and bourgeoisie.

Renaissance art, which some scholars consider the period's greatest achievement, differed markedly from medieval art. In the Renaissance the individual portrait emerged as a distinct artistic genre. Whereas medieval artists had depicted the nude human body only in a spiritualizing or moralizing context, Renaissance artists such as Donatello (1386–1466) revived the classical figure with its balance and self-awareness; in so doing, they revealed the secular spirit of the age. The new style was characterized by greater realism, narrative power, and more effective use of light and shadow. In addition, the artist Brunelleschi (1377–1466) pioneered perspective in painting, the linear representation of distance and space on a flat surface.

The age also saw profound social changes that have enormously influenced the modern world. The invention of the printing press in the mid-fifteenth century revolutionized communication. Printing made governmental propaganda possible, bridged the gap between oral and written cultures, and stimulated the literacy of lay people. Whereas women in the Middle Ages often had great responsibilities, and with responsibility, power, in the Renaissance their purpose came to be decorative—to grace the courts of princes and aristocrats. Women's status in society accordingly declined. As servants and slaves black people entered Europe during the Renaissance in sizable numbers for the first time since the collapse of the Roman Empire. In northern Europe urban merchants and rural gentry allied with rising monarchies. With the newly levied taxes paid by businesspeople, kings provided a greater degree of domestic peace and order. In Spain, France, and England, rulers also emphasized royal dignity and authority; they used the tough ideas of the Italian political theorist Machiavelli to ensure the preservation and continuation of their governments. Feudal monarchies gradually evolved in the direction of nation-states.

As the intellectual features of the Renaissance spread outside Italy, they affected the culture of all Europe. A secular attitude toward life has become one of the dominant features of the modern world. Its germ was planted in the attitudes and approaches of the Italian humanists. Those humanists studied classical literature to understand human nature and to strengthen their interest in the world around them. Similarly, a strong belief in the complete realization of individual potential has become an abiding component of our world-view.

THE REFORMATION

The idea of reform is as old as Christianity itself. Jesus had preached the coming of the kingdom of God through the reform of the individual, and through the centuries his cry had been repeated. The need for the reform of the individual Christian and of the institutional church is central to the Christian faith. Christian humanists of the fifteenth and sixteenth centuries urged the reform of the church on the pattern of the early Christian communities.

The sixteenth century was a deeply religious age. While almost all people were sincere believers and religious practices and observances pervaded their lives, the institutional church showed serious signs of disorder. Clerical immorality, ignorance, and pluralism (the simultaneous holding of two or more church offices by a priest) constituted widespread abuses. The Renaissance princes who ruled the church made only feeble efforts at reform. Informed and intelligent laypeople, especially in the cities, condemned the clergy's tax-exempt and privileged social position.

In 1517 Martin Luther (1483–1546), a professor of Scripture at a minor German university, launched an attack on certain church practices. Asked to recant, Luther rejected church authority itself. The newly invented printing press swept Luther's prolific ideas across Germany and Europe. He and other reformers soon won the support of northern German princes who embraced Luther's reforming or "Protestant" ideas. Some of the princes coveted church lands and revenues. Others resented the authority of the strongly Catholic Holy Roman Emperor, Charles V. By accepting Luther's religious ideas—and thereby denying orthodox Catholic doctrine—the princes also rejected the emperor's political authority. In a world that insisted on the necessity of religious unity for political order and social stability, the adoption of the new faith implied political opposition. In England, largely because the papacy would not approve his request for a divorce, King Henry VIII (1509–1547) broke with Rome and established the English Church. Kings and princes, political and economic issues played the decisive role in the advance of the Reformation.

In the first half of the sixteenth century, perhaps a fourth of the population of Western Europe accepted some version of Protestantism. Besides northern Germany, all of Scandinavia, England, Scotland, and the cities of Geneva and Zurich in Switzerland and Strasbourg in Germany rejected the religious authority of the Roman church and adopted new faiths. The number of Protestant sects proliferated, but the core of Protestant doctrine, consisting of three fundamental ideas remained. First, Protestants believe that salvation comes by faith alone, not from faith and good works, as Catholic teaching asserts. Second, authority in the Christian church resides in the Scriptures alone, not in tradition or papal authority (which all Protestants rejected). The church itself consists of the community of all believers; medieval churchmen had tended to identify the church with the clergy.

In the later sixteenth century, the Roman church worked to clean up its house. The Council of Trent, meeting intermittently from 1545 to 1563, suppressed pluralism and the sale of church offices, redefined doctrine, made provision for the education of all the clergy, and laid the basis for general spiritual renewal. New religious orders, such as the Society of Jesus (or Jesuits), sought to re-convert Protestants. A new church department, the Holy Office, tried to impose doctrinal uniformity everywhere.

The break with Rome and the rise of Lutheran, Anglican, Calvinist, and other faiths shattered the unity of Europe as an organic Christian society. On the other hand, religious belief remained exceedingly strong. In fact, the strength of religious convictions caused political fragmentation. In the later sixteenth and throughout most of the seventeenth centuries, religion and religious issues continued to play a major role in the lives of individuals and in the policies and actions of governments. Religion, whether Protestant or Catholic, decisively influenced the evolution of national states. Though most reformers rejected religious toleration, they helped pave the way for the toleration and pluralism that characterize the modern world.

OVERSEAS EXPANSION

In the sixteenth and seventeenth centuries, Europeans for the first time gained access to large parts of the globe. Overseas expansion broadened Europe's geographical horizons and brought its states into confrontation with ancient civilizations in Africa, Asia, and the Americas. These confrontations led first to conquest, then to exploitation, and finally to profound social changes in both Europe and the conquered territories. At the same time, the consequences of the Renaissance and the Reformation drastically altered intellectual, political, religious, and social life within Europe. War and religious issues dominated the political life of European states. Though religion was commonly used to rationalize international conflicts, wars were fought for power and territorial expansion.

Europeans had a variety of motives for overseas exploration and conquest. Some desired to Christianize Muslims and pagan peoples. Many others, finding economic and political advancement limited at home, emigrated abroad in search of fresh opportunities. The governments of Portugal, Spain, Holland, and England sponsored and encouraged voyages of exploration. Spices—pepper, nutmeg, mace, cinnamon, ginger—were another incentive. Spices, which added flavor and variety to a monotonous diet, also yielded high profits. The basic reason for European exploration and expansion was the quest for material profit. As the Portuguese navigator Bartholomew Diaz, the first man to round the Cape of Good Hope and open the road to India, put it, his motives were "to serve God and His Majesty, to give light to those who were in darkness and to grow rich as all men desire to do."

Sixteenth- and seventeenth-century Europeans had the intellectual curiosity, driving ambition, and scientific technology to attempt feats that were as difficult and expensive then as going to the moon is today. The exploration and exploitation of parts of South America, Africa, and Asia increased the standard of living of the colonists, who were now able to enjoy spices and Asian luxury goods; through the corresponding influx of South American silver and gold, it also led to considerable international inflation. Governments, the upper classes, and the peasantry were badly hurt by the inflation. Meanwhile, the middle class of bankers, shippers, financiers, and manufacturers prospered for much of the seventeenth century.

European expansion and colonization overseas took place against a background of religious conflict and rising national consciousness. The seventeenth century was by no means a secular period. Though the medieval religious framework had broken down, people still thought largely in religious terms. Europeans explained what they did politically and economically in terms of religious doctrine. Religious ideology served as a justification for many goals: the opposition of the French nobility to the crown, the Dutch struggle for political and economic independence from Spain. In Germany religious pluralism and the intervention of the French and the Swedes led to the long and devastating Thirty Years' War (1618–1648). After 1648 the divisions between Protestants and Catholics in Germany tended to become permanent. In France the bitter civil wars between the Catholic monarchy and Protestant nobility contributed to the growth of religious skepticism. The religious pluralism and skepticism that mark modern society are largely the legacy of this age of religious struggle.

ABSOLUTISM AND CONSTITUTIONALISM IN WESTERN EUROPE
(CA 1589–1715)

*T*HE SEVENTEENTH century was a period of revolutionary transformation. Some of its most profound developments were political: it has been called the century when government became modern. The sixteenth century had witnessed the emergence of the nation-state. The long series of wars fought in the name of religion—actually contests between royal authority and aristocratic power—brought social dislocation and agricultural and commercial disaster. Increasingly, strong national monarchy seemed the only solution. Spanish and French monarchs gained control of the major competing institution in their domains, the Roman Catholic church. Rulers of England and some of the German principalities, who could not completely regulate the church, set up national churches. In the German empire, the Treaty of Westphalia placed territorial sovereignty in the princes' hands. The kings of France, England, and Spain claimed the basic loyalty of their subjects. Monarchs made laws, to which everyone within their borders was subject. These powers added up to something close to sovereignty.

A state may be termed *sovereign* when it possesses a monopoly over the instruments of justice and the use of force within clearly defined boundaries. In a sovereign state no system of courts, such as ecclesiastical tribunals, competes with state courts in the dispensation of justice; and private armies, such as those of feudal lords, present no threat to royal authority because the state's army is stronger. Royal law touches all persons within the country. Sovereignty had been evolving during the late sixteenth century. Seventeenth-century governments now needed to address the problem of *which* authority within the state would possess sovereignty—the crown or the nobility.

In the period between roughly 1589 and 1715, two basic patterns of government emerged in Europe: absolute monarchy and the constitutional state. Almost all subsequent governments have been modeled on one of these patterns. In what sense were they "modern"? How did these forms of government differ from the feudal and dynastic monarchies of earlier centuries? Which Western countries most clearly illustrate the new patterns of political organization? This chapter will be concerned with these political questions.

ABSOLUTISM

In the *absolutist* state, sovereignty is embodied in the person of the ruler. The ruler is not restrained by legal authority. Absolute kings claim to rule by divine right, meaning they are responsible to God alone. (Medieval kings governed "by the grace of God," but invariably they acknowledged that they had to respect and obey the law.) Absolute monarchs in the seventeenth and eighteenth centuries had to respect the divine law and the fundamental laws of the land. But they were not checked by national assemblies. Estates general and parliaments met at the wish and in response to kings' needs. Because these meetings provided opportunities for opposition to the crown to coalesce, absolute monarchs eventually stopped summoning them.

Absolute rulers effectively controlled all competing jurisdictions, institutions, or interest groups in their territories. They regulated religious sects. They abolished the liberties long held by certain areas, groups, or provinces. Absolute kings also secured mastery over the one class that historically had posed the greatest threat to monarchy, the nobility. Medieval governments, restrained by the church, the feudal nobility, and their own financial limitations, had been able to do none of these.

In some respects, the key to the power and success of absolute monarchs lay in how they solved their financial problems. Kings frequently found temporary financial support through bargains with the nobility: the nobility agreed to an ad hoc grant in return for freedom from future taxation. The absolutist solution was the creation of new state bureaucracies, which directed the economic life of the country in the interests of the king, either increasing taxes ever higher or devising alternative methods of raising revenue.

Bureaucracies were composed of career officials, appointed by and solely accountable to the king. The backgrounds of these civil servants varied. Absolute monarchs sometimes drew on the middle class, as in France, or utilized members of the nobility, as in Spain and eastern Europe. Where there was no middle class or an insignificant one, as in Austria, Prussia, Spain, and Russia, the government of the absolutist state consisted of an interlocking elite of monarchy, aristocracy, and bureaucracy.

Royal agents in medieval kingdoms had used their public offices and positions to benefit themselves and their families. In England, for example, crown servants from Thomas Becket to Thomas Wolsey had treated their high offices as their private property and reaped considerable profit from them. The most striking difference between seventeenth-century bureaucracies and their medieval predecessors was that seventeenth-century civil servants served the state as represented by the king. Bureaucrats recognized that the offices they held were public, or state, positions. The state paid them salaries to handle revenues that belonged to the crown, and they were not supposed to use their positions for private gain. Bureaucrats gradually came to distinguish between public duties and private property.

Absolute monarchs also maintained permanent standing armies. Medieval armies had been raised by feudal lords for particular wars or campaigns, after which the troops were disbanded. In the seventeenth century, monarchs alone recruited and maintained armies—in peacetime as well as during war. Kings deployed their troops both inside and outside the country in the interests of the monarchy. Armies became basic features of absolutist, and modern, states. Absolute rulers also invented new methods of compulsion. They concerned themselves with the private lives of potentially troublesome subjects, often through the use of secret police.

Rule of absolute monarchs was not all-embracing, because they lacked the financial and military resources and the technology to make it so. Thus the absolutist state was not the same as a totalitarian state. *Totalitarianism* is a twentieth-century phenomenon; it seeks to direct all facets of a state's culture—art, education, religion, the economy, and politics—in the interests of the state. By definition totalitarian rule is *total* regulation. By twentieth-century standards, the ambitions of an absolute monarch were quite limited: he sought the exaltation of himself as the embodiment of the state. Whether or not Louis XIV of France actually said, "L'état, c'est moi!" ("I am the state!"), the remark expresses his belief that he personified the French nation. Yet the absolutist state did foreshadow recent totalitarian regimes in two fundamental respects: in the glorification of the state over all other aspects of the state's culture, and in the use of war and an expansionist foreign policy to divert attention from domestic ills.

All of this is best illustrated by the experience of France, aptly known as the model of absolute monarchy.

THE FOUNDATIONS OF ABSOLUTISM IN FRANCE: HENRY IV AND SULLY

The ingenious Huguenot-turned-Catholic Henry IV (pages 477–478) ended the French religious wars with the Edict of Nantes. The first of the Bourbon dynasty, and probably the first French ruler since Louis IX in the thirteenth century genuinely to care about the French people, Henry IV and his great minister Sully (1560–1641) laid the foundations of later French absolutism. Henry denied influence on the royal council to the nobility, which had harassed the countryside for half a century. Maintaining that "if we are without compassion for the people, they must succumb and we all perish with them," Henry also lowered the severe taxes on the overburdened peasantry.

Sully proved himself a financial genius. He not only reduced the crushing royal debt but began to build up the treasury. He levied an annual tax, the *paulette,* on people who had purchased financial and judicial offices and had consequently been exempt from royal taxation. One of the first French officials to appreciate the significance of overseas trade, Sully subsidized the Company for Trade with the Indies. He started a countrywide highway system and even dreamed of an international organization for the maintenance of peace.

In twelve short years, Henry IV and Sully restored public order in France and laid the foundations for economic prosperity. By late sixteenth-century standards, Henry IV's government was progressive and promising. His murder in 1610 by a crazed fanatic led to a severe crisis.

THE CORNERSTONE OF FRENCH ABSOLUTISM: LOUIS XIII AND RICHELIEU

After the death of Henry IV, the queen-regent Marie de' Medici led the government for the child-king Louis XIII (1610–1643), but in fact feudal nobles and princes of the blood dominated the political scene. In 1624 Marie de' Medici secured the appointment of Armand Jean du Plessis—Cardinal Richelieu (1585–1642)—to the council of ministers. It was a remarkable appointment. The next year Richelieu became president of the council, and after 1628 he was first minister of the French crown. Richelieu used his strong influence over King Louis XIII to exalt the French monarchy as the embodiment of the French state. One of the greatest servants of the French state, Richelieu set in place the cornerstone of French absolutism, and his work served as the basis for France's cultural domination of Europe in the later seventeenth century.

Richelieu's policy was the total subordination of all groups and institutions to the French monarchy. The French nobility, with its selfish and independent interests, had long constituted the foremost threat to the centralizing goals of the crown and to a strong national state. Therefore, Richelieu tried to break the power of the nobility. He leveled castles, long the symbol of feudal independence. He crushed aristocratic conspiracies with quick executions. For example, when the duke of Montmorency, the first peer of France and the godson of Henry IV, became involved in a revolt in 1632, he was summarily put to death.

The constructive genius of Cardinal Richelieu is best reflected in the administrative system he established. He extended the use of the royal commissioners called intendants. France was divided into thirty-two *généralités* ("districts"), in each of which a royal intendant had extensive responsibility for justice, police, and finances. The intendants were authorized "to decide, order and execute all that they see good to do." Usually members of the upper middle class or minor nobility, the intendants were appointed directly by the monarch, to whom they were solely responsible. The intendants recruited men for the army, supervised the collection of taxes, presided over the administration of local law, checked up on the local nobility, and regulated economic activities —commerce, trade, the guilds, marketplaces—in their districts. They were to use their power for two related purposes: to enforce royal orders in the généralités of their jurisdiction and to weaken the power and influence of the regional nobility. The system of government by intendants derived from Philip Augustus's baillis and seneschals, and ultimately from Charlemagne's missi dominici. As the intendants' power grew during Richelieu's administration, so did the power of the centralized state.

Though Richelieu succeeded in building a rational and centralized political machine in the intendant system, he was not the effective financial administrator Sully had been. France lacked a sound system of taxation, a method of raising sufficient revenue to meet the needs of the state. Richelieu reverted to the old device of selling offices. He increased the number of sinecures, tax exemptions, and benefices that were purchasable and inheritable. In 1624 this device brought in almost 40 percent of royal revenues.

The rising cost of foreign and domestic policies led to the auctioning of *tax farms,* a system whereby a man bought the right to collect taxes. Tax farmers kept a very large part of the receipts they collected. The sale of offices and this antiquated system of tax collection were improvisations that promoted confusion and corruption. Even worse, state offices, once purchased, were passed on to heirs, which meant that a family that held a state office was eternally exempt from taxation. Richelieu's inadequate and temporary solutions created grave financial problems for the future.

The cardinal perceived that Protestantism all too often served as a cloak for the political intrigues of ambitious lords. When the Huguenots revolted in 1625, under the duke of Rohan, Richelieu personally supervised the siege of their walled city, La Rochelle, and forced it to surrender. Thereafter, fortified places of security were abolished. Huguenots were allowed to practice their faith, but they no longer possessed armed strongholds or the means to be an independent party in the state. Another aristocratic prop was knocked down.

French foreign policy under Richelieu was aimed at the destruction of the fence of Habsburg territories that surrounded France. Consequently Richelieu supported the Habsburgs' enemies. In 1631 he signed a treaty with the Lutheran king Gustavus Adolphus, promising French support against the Catholic Habsburgs in what has been called the Swedish phase of the Thirty Years' War (page 485). French influence became an important factor in the political future of the German empire. Richelieu acquired for France extensive rights in Alsace in the east and Arras in the north.

Richelieu's efforts at centralization extended even to literature. In 1635 he gave official recognition to a group of philologists who were interested in grammar and rhetoric. Thus was born the French Academy. With Richelieu's encouragement, the Academy began the preparation of a dictionary to standardize the French language; it was completed in 1694. The French Academy survives as a prestigious learned society, whose membership has been broadened to include people outside the field of literature.

Richelieu personified the increasingly secular spirit of the seventeenth century. Though a bishop of the Roman Catholic church, he gave his first loyalty to the French state. Though a Roman Catholic cardinal, he gave strong support to the Protestant Lutherans of Germany.

Richelieu had persuaded Louis XIII to appoint his protegé Jules Mazarin (1602–1661) as his successor. An Italian diplomat of great charm, Mazarin served on the Council of State under Richelieu, acquiring considerable political experience. He became a cardinal in 1641 and a French citizen in 1643. When Louis XIII followed Richelieu to the grave in 1643 and a regency headed by Queen Anne of Austria governed for the child-king Louis XIV, Mazarin became the dominant power in the government. He continued the antifeudal and centralizing policies of Richelieu, but his attempts to increase royal revenues led to the civil wars known as the "Fronde."

The word *fronde* means "slingshot" or "catapult," and a *frondeur* was originally a street urchin who threw mud at the passing carriages of the rich. The term came to be used for anyone who opposed the policies of the government. Richelieu had stirred up the bitter resentment of the aristocracy, who felt its constitutional status and ancient privileges threatened. He also bequeathed to the crown a staggering debt, and when Mazarin tried to impose financial reforms, the monarchy incurred the enmity of the middle classes. Both groups plotted against Anne and Mazarin. Most historians see the Fronde as the last serious effort by the French nobility to oppose the monarchy by force. When in 1648 Mazarin proposed new methods for raising income, bitter civil war ensued between the monarchy on the one side and the frondeurs (the nobility and the upper-middle classes) on the other. Riots and public turmoil wracked Paris and the nation. The violence continued intermittently for almost twelve years. Factional disputes among the nobles led to their ultimate defeat.

The conflicts of the Fronde had two significant results for the future: a badly disruptive effect on the French economy and a traumatic impact on the young Louis XIV. The king and his mother were frequently threatened and sometimes treated as pris-

Philippe de Champaigne: Cardinal Richelieu This portrait, with its penetrating eyes, expression of haughty and imperturable cynicism, and dramatic sweep of red robes, suggests the authority, grandeur, and power that Richelieu wished to convey as first minister of France. *(Reproduced by courtesy of the Trustees, The National Gallery, London)*

oners by aristocratic factions. On one occasion a mob broke into the royal bedchamber to make sure the king was actually there; it succeeded in giving him a bad fright. Louis never forgot such humiliations. The period of the Fronde formed the cornerstone of his political education and of his conviction that the sole alternative to anarchy was absolute monarchy.

Coysevox: Louis XIV (1687–1689) The French court envisioned a new classical age with the Sun King as emperor and his court a new Rome. This statue depicts Louis in a classical pose, clothed (except for the wig) as for a Roman military triumph. *(Caisse Nationale des Monuments Historiques et des Sites, Paris)*

THE ABSOLUTE MONARCHY OF LOUIS XIV

According to the court theologian Bossuet, the clergy at the coronation of Louis XIV in Rheims Cathedral asked God to cause the splendors of the French court to fill all who beheld it with awe. God subsequently granted that prayer. In the reign of Louis XIV (1643–1715), the longest in European history, the French monarchy reached the peak of absolutist development. In the magnificence of his court, in his absolute power, in the brilliance of the culture over which he presided and which permeated all of Europe, and in his remarkably long life, the "Sun King" dominated his age. No wonder scholars have characterized the second half of the seventeenth century as the "Grand Century," the "Age of Magnificence," and echoing the eighteenth-century philosopher Voltaire, the "Age of Louis XIV."

Who was this phenomenon, of whom it was said that when Louis sneezed, all Europe caught cold? Born in 1638, king at the age of five, he entered into personal, or independent, rule in 1661. One of the first tales recorded about him gained wide circulation during his lifetime. Taken as a small child to his father's deathbed, he identified himself as *Louis Quatorze* ("Louis the fourteenth"). Since neither Louis nor his father referred to themselves with numerals, the story is probably untrue. But it reveals the incredible sense of self that contemporaries, both French and foreign, believed that Louis possessed throughout his life.

In old age, Louis claimed that he had grown up learning very little, but recent historians think he was being modest. True, he knew little Latin and only the rudiments of arithmetic and thus by Renaissance standards was not well educated. On the other hand, he learned to speak Italian and Spanish fluently; he spoke and wrote elegant French; he knew some French history and more European geography than the ambassadors accredited to his court. He imbibed the devout Catholicism of his mother, Anne of Austria, and throughout his long life scrupulously performed his religious duties. Religion, Anne, and Mazarin all taught Louis that God had established kings as his rulers on earth. The royal coronation consecrated him to God's service, and he was certain—to use Shakespeare's phrase—that there was a divinity that doth hedge a king. Though kings were a race apart, they could not do as they pleased: they must obey God's laws and rule for the good of the people.

Louis's education was more practical than formal. Under Mazarin's instruction, he studied state papers as they arrived, and he attended council meetings and sessions at which French ambassadors were dispatched abroad and foreign ambassadors received. He learned by direct experience and gained professional training in the work of government. Above all, the misery he suffered during the Fronde gave Louis an eternal distrust of the nobility and a profound sense of his own isolation. Accordingly, silence, caution, and secrecy became political tools for the achievement of his goals. His characteristic answer to requests of all kinds became the enigmatic "Je verrai" ("I shall see").

Louis grew up with an absolute sense of his royal dignity. Tall and distinguished in appearance, he was inclined to heaviness because of the gargantuan meals in which he indulged. Seduced by one of his mother's maids when he was sixteen, the king matured into a highly sensual man easily aroused by an attractive female face and figure. It is to his credit, however, that neither his wife, Queen Maria Theresa, whom he married as the result of a diplomatic agreement with Spain, nor his mistresses ever possessed any political influence. One contemporary described him this way: "He has an elevated, distinguished, proud, intrepid, agreeable air . . . a face that is at the same time sweet and majestic. . . . His manner is cold; he speaks little except to people with whom he is familiar . . . (and then) he speaks well and effectively,

and says what is apropos. . . . he has natural goodness, is charitable, liberal, and properly acts out the role of king."[1] Louis XIV was a consummate actor, and his "terrifying majesty" awed all who saw him. He worked extremely hard and succeeded in being "every moment and every inch a king." Because he so relished the role of monarch, historians have had difficulty distinguishing the man from the monarch.

Recent scholarship indicates that Louis XIV introduced significant governmental innovations: the most significant was his acquisition of absolute control over the French nobility. Indeed it is often said that Louis achieved complete "domestication of the nobility." In doing so, Louis XIV turned the royal court into a fixed institution. In the past, the king of France and the royal court had traveled constantly, visiting the king's properties, the great noblemen, and his *bonnes villes* or "good towns." Since the time of Louis IX, or even Charlemagne, rulers had traveled to maintain order in distant parts of the realm, to impress humbler subjects with the royal dignity and magnificence, and to bind the country together through loyalty to the king. Since the early Middle Ages, the king's court had consisted of his family, trusted advisers and councilors, a few favorites, and servants. Except for the very highest officials of the state, members of the council had changed constantly.

Louis XIV installed the court at Versailles, a small town ten miles from Paris. He required all the great nobility of France, at the peril of social, political, and sometimes economic disaster, to come live at Versailles for at least part of the year. Today Versailles stands as the best surviving museum of a vanished society on earth. In the seventeenth century, it became a model of rational order, the center of France and thus the center of Western civilization, the perfect symbol of the king's absolute power.

Louis XIII began Versailles as a hunting lodge, a retreat from a queen he did not like. His son's architects, Le Nôtre and Le Vau, turned what Saint-Simon called "the most dismal and thankless of sights" into a veritable paradise. Wings were added to the original building to make the palace U-shaped. Everywhere at Versailles the viewer had a sense of grandeur, vastness, and elegance. Enormous state rooms became display galleries for inlaid tables, Italian marble statuary, Gobelin tapestries woven at the state factory in Paris, silver ewers, and beautiful (if uncomfortable) furniture. If genius means attention to detail, Louis XIV and his designers had it: the décor was perfected down to the last doorknob and keyhole. In the gigantic Hall of Mirrors, later to reflect so much of German as well as French history, hundreds of candles illuminated the domed ceiling, where allegorical paintings celebrated the king's victories.

The Ambassador's Staircase was of brilliantly colored marble, with part of the railing gold-plated. The staircase was dominated by a great bust of the king, which, when completed, so overwhelmed a courtier that he exclaimed to the sculptor, Bernini, "Don't do anything more to it, it's so good I'm afraid you might spoil it." The statue, like the staircase—and the entire palace—succeeded from the start in its purpose: it awed.

The formal, carefully ordered, and perfectly landscaped gardens at Versailles express at a glance the spirit of the age of Louis XIV. Every tree, every bush, every foot of grass, every fountain, pool, and piece of statuary within three miles is perfectly laid out. The vista is of the world made rational and absolutely controlled. Nature itself was subdued to enhance the greatness of the king.

The art and architecture of Versailles served as fundamental tools of state policy under Louis XIV. Architecture was another device the king used to overawe his subjects and foreign visitors. Versailles was seen as a reflection of French genius. Thus the Russian tsar Peter the Great imitated Versailles in the construction of his palace, Peterhof, as did the Prussian emperor Frederick the Great in his palace at Potsdam outside Berlin.

As in architecture, so too in language. Beginning in the reign of Louis XIV, French became the language of polite society and the vehicle of diplomatic exchange. French also gradually replaced Latin as the language of international scholarship and learning. The wish of other kings to ape the courtly style of Louis XIV and the imitation of French intellectuals and artists spread the language all over Europe. The royal courts of Sweden, Russia, Poland, and Germany all spoke French. In the eighteenth century, the great Russian aristocrats were more fluent in French than in Russian. In England, the first Hanoverian king, George I, spoke fluent French, halting English. France inspired a cosmopolitan European culture in the late seventeenth century, and that culture was inspired by the king. That is why the French today revere Louis XIV as one of their greatest national heroes: because of the culture that he inspired and symbolized.

Against this background of magnificent splendor, as Saint-Simon describes him, Louis XIV

reduced everyone to subjection, and brought to his court those very persons he cared least about. Whoever was old enough to serve did not dare demur. It was still another device to ruin the nobles by accustoming them to equality and forcing them to mingle with everyone indiscriminately. . . .

To keep everyone assiduous and attentive, the King personally named the guests for each festivity, each stroll through Versailles, and each trip. These were his rewards and punishments. He knew there was little else he could distribute to keep everyone in line. He substituted idle rewards for real ones and these operated through jealousy, the petty preferences he showed many times a day, and his artfulness in showing them. . . .

Upon rising, at bedtime, during meals, in his apartments, in the gardens of Versailles, everywhere the courtiers had a right to follow, he would glance right and left to see who was there; he saw and noted everyone; he missed no one, even those who were hoping they would not be seen. . . .

Louis XIV took great pains to inform himself on what was happening everywhere, in public places, private homes, and even on the international scene. . . . Spies and informers of all kinds were numberless. . . .

But the King's most vicious method of securing information was opening letters. [2]

Though this passage was written by one of Louis's severest critics, all agree that the king used court ceremonial to undermine the power of the great nobility. By excluding the highest nobles from his councils, he destroyed their ancient right to advise the king and to participate in government; they became mere instruments of royal policy. Operas, fetes, balls, gossip, and trivia occupied the nobles' time and attention. Through painstaking attention to detail and precisely calculated showmanship, Louis XIV emasculated the major threat to his absolute power. He separated power from status and grandeur: the nobility enjoyed the status and grandeur in which they lived; the king alone held the power.

Louis dominated the court, and in his scheme of things, the court was more significant than the government. In government Louis utilized several councils of state, which he personally attended, and the intendants, who acted for the councils throughout France. A stream of questions and instructions flowed between local districts and Versailles, and under Louis XIV a uniform and centralized administration was imposed on the country. In 1685 France was the strongest and most highly centralized state in Europe.

Councilors of state and intendants came from the recently ennobled or the upper-middle class. Royal service provided a means of social mobility. These professional bureaucrats served the state in the person of the king, but they did not share power with him. Louis stated that he chose bourgeois officials because he wanted "people to know by the rank of the men who served him that he had no intention of sharing power with them."[3] If great ones were the king's advisers, they would seem to share the royal authority; professional administrators from the middle class would not.

Throughout his long reign and despite increasing financial problems, he never called a meeting of the Estates General. The nobility, therefore, had no means of united expression or action. Nor did Louis have a first minister, freeing him from worry about the inordinate power of a Richelieu. Louis's use of terror—a secret police force, a system of informers, and the practice of opening private letters—foreshadowed some of the devices of the modern state. French government remained highly structured, bureaucratic, centered at Versailles, and responsible to Louis XIV.

FINANCIAL AND ECONOMIC MANAGEMENT UNDER LOUIS XIV: COLBERT

Finance was the grave weakness of Louis XIV's absolutism. An expanding professional bureaucracy, the court of Versailles, and extensive military reforms (see above) cost a great amount of money. The French method of collecting taxes consistently failed to produce enough revenue. Tax farmers pocketed the difference between what they raked in and what they handed over to the state. Consequently, the tax farmers profited, while the government got far less than the people paid. Then, by an old agreement between the crown and the nobility, the king could freely tax the common people, provided he did not tax the nobles. The nobility thereby relinquished a role in government: since they did not pay taxes, they could not legitimately claim a say in how taxes were spent. Louis, however, lost enormous potential revenue. The middle classes, moreover, secured many tax exemptions. With the rich and prosperous classes exempt, the tax burden fell heavily on those least able to pay, the poor peasants.

The king named Jean-Baptiste Colbert (1619–1683), the son of a wealthy merchant-financier of Rheims, as controller-general of finances. Colbert came to manage the entire royal administration and proved himself a financial genius. Colbert's central principle was that the wealth and the economy of France should serve the state. He did not invent the system called "mercantilism," but he rigorously applied it to France.

Mercantilism is a collection of governmental policies for the regulation of economic activities, especially commercial activities, by and for the state. In seventeenth- and eighteenth-century economic theory, a nation's international power was thought to be based on its wealth, specifically its gold supply. To accumulate gold, a country should always sell abroad more than it bought. Colbert believed that a successful economic policy meant more than a favorable balance of trade. He insisted that the French sell abroad and buy *nothing* back. France should be self-sufficient, able to produce within its borders everything the subjects of the French king needed. Consequently, the outflow of gold would be halted, debtor states would pay in bullion, and with the wealth of the nation increased, its power and prestige would be enhanced.

Colbert attempted to accomplish self-sufficiency through state support for both old industries and newly created ones. He subsidized the established cloth industries at Abbeville, Saint-Quentin, and Carcassonne. He granted special royal privileges to the rug and tapestry industries at Paris, Gobelin, and Beauvais. New factories at Saint-Antoine in Paris manufactured mirrors to replace Venetian imports. Looms at Chantilly and Alençon competed with English lacemaking, and foundries at Saint-Etienne made steel and firearms that cut Swedish imports. To ensure a high-quality finished product, Colbert set up a system of state inspection and regulation. To ensure order within every industry, he compelled all craftsmen to organize into guilds, and within every guild he gave the masters absolute power over their workers. Colbert encouraged skilled foreign craftsmen and manufacturers to immigrate to France, and he gave them special privileges. To improve communications, he built roads and canals, the most famous linking the Mediterranean and the Bay of Biscay. To protect French goods, he abolished many domestic tariffs and enacted high foreign tariffs, which prevented foreign products from competing with French ones.

Colbert's most important work was the creation of a powerful merchant marine to transport French goods. He gave bonuses to French ship owners and builders and established a method of maritime conscription, arsenals, and academies for the training of sailors. In 1661 France possessed 18 unseaworthy vessels; by 1681 it had 276 frigates, galleys, and ships of the line. Colbert tried to organize and regulate the entire French economy for the glory of the French state as embodied in the king.

Colbert hoped to make Canada—rich in untapped minerals and some of the best agricultural land in the world—part of a vast French empire. He gathered four thousand peasants from western France and shipped them to Canada, where they peopled the province of Quebec. (In 1608, one year after the English arrived at Jamestown, Virginia, Sully had established the city of Quebec, which became the capital of French Canada.) Subsequently, the Jesuit Marquette and the merchant Joliet sailed down the Mississippi River and took possession of the land on both sides, as far south as present-day Arkansas. In 1684 the French explorer La Salle continued down the Mississippi to its mouth and claimed vast territories and the rich delta for Louis XIV. The area was called, naturally, "Louisiana."

How successful were Colbert's policies? His achievement in the development of manufacturing was prodigious. The textile industry, especially in woolens, expanded enormously, and "France. . . had become in 1683 the leading nation of the world in industrial productivity."[4] The commercial classes prospered, and between 1660 and 1700 their position steadily improved. The national economy, however, rested on agriculture. Although French peasants did not become serfs, as did the peasants of eastern Europe, they were mercilessly taxed. After 1685 other hardships afflicted them: poor harvests, continuing deflation of the currency, and fluctuation in the price of grain. Many peasants emigrated. With the decline in population and thus in the number of taxable people (the poorest), the state's resources fell. A totally inadequate tax base and heavy expenditure for war in the later years of the reign nullified Colbert's goals.

THE REVOCATION OF THE EDICT OF NANTES

We now see with the proper gratitude what we owe to God . . . for the best and largest part of our subjects of the so-called reformed religion have embraced Catholicism, and now that, to the extent that the execution of the Edict of Nantes remains useless, we have judged that we can do nothing better to wipe out the memory of the troubles, of the confusion, of the evils that the progress of this false religion has caused our kingdom . . . than to revoke entirely the said Edict.[5]

Thus in 1685, Louis XIV revoked the Edict of Nantes, by which his grandfather Henry IV had granted liberty of conscience to French Huguenots. The new law ordered the destruction of churches, the closing of schools, the Catholic baptism of Huguenots, and the exile of Huguenot pastors who refused to renounce their faith. Why? There had been so many mass conversions during previous years (many of them forced) that Madame de Maintenon, Louis's second wife, could say that "nearly all the Huguenots were converted." Some Huguenots had emigrated. Richelieu had already deprived French Calvinists of political rights. Why, then, did Louis, by revoking the Edict, persecute some of his most loyal and industrially skilled subjects, force others to flee abroad, and provoke the outrage of Protestant Europe?

Recent scholarship has convincingly shown that Louis XIV was basically tolerant. He insisted on religious unity not for religious but for political reasons. His goal was "one king, one law, one faith." He hated division within the realm and insisted that religious unity was essential to his royal dignity and to the security of the state. The seventeenth century, moreover, was not a tolerant one. While France in the early years of Louis's reign permitted religious liberty, it was not a popular policy. Revocation was solely the king's decision, and it won him enormous praise. "If the flood of congratulation means anything, it . . . was probably the one act of his reign that, at the time, was popular with the majority of his subjects."[6]

The Spider and the Fly In reference to the insect symbolism (upper left), the caption on the lower left side of this illustration states, "The noble is the spider, the peasant the fly." The other caption (upper right) notes, "The more people have, the more they want. The poor man brings everything—wheat, fruit, money, vegetables. The greedy lord sitting there ready to take everything will not even give him the favor of a glance." This satirical print summarizes peasant grievances. *(New York Public Library)*

While contemporaries applauded Louis XIV, scholars since the eighteenth century damned him for the adverse impact that revocation had on the economy and foreign affairs. Tens of thousands of Huguenot craftsmen, soldiers, and businesspeople emigrated, depriving France of their skills and tax revenues and carrying their bitterness to Holland, England, and Prussia. Modern scholarship has greatly modified this picture. While Huguenot settlers in northern Europe aggravated Protestant hatred for Louis, the revocation of the Edict of Nantes had only minor and scattered effects on French economic development.[7]

FRENCH CLASSICISM

Scholars characterize the art and literature of the age of Louis XIV as "French classicism." By this they mean that the artists and writers of the late seventeenth century deliberately imitated the subject matter and style of classical antiquity; that their work resembled that of Renaissance Italy; and that French art possessed the classical qualities of discipline, balance, and restraint. Classicism was the official style of Louis's court. In painting, however, French classicism had already reached its peak before 1661, the beginning of the king's personal government.

Poussin: The Rape of the Sabine Women Considered the greatest French painter of the seventeenth century, Poussin in this dramatic work (ca 1636) shows his complete devotion to the ideals of classicism. The heroic figures are superb physical specimens, but hardly life-like. *(Metropolitan Museum of Art, New York [Dick Fund, 1946])*

Nicholas Poussin (1593–1665) is generally considered the finest example of French classicist painting. Poussin spent all but eighteen months of his creative life in Rome because he found the atmosphere in Paris uncongenial. Deeply attached to classical antiquity, he believed that the highest aim of painting was to represent noble actions in a logical and orderly, but not realistic, way. His masterpiece, "The Rape of the Sabine Women," exhibits these qualities. Its subject is an incident in Roman history; the figures of people and horses are ideal representations, and the emotions expressed are studied, not spontaneous. Even the buildings are exact architectural models of ancient Roman structures.

While Poussin selected grand and "noble" themes, Louis Le Nain (1593–1648) painted genre scenes of peasant life. At a time when artists favored Biblical and classical allegories, Le Nain's paintings are unique for their depiction of peasants. The highly realistic group assembled in "The Peasant Family" has great human dignity. The painting itself is reminiscent of portrayals of peasants by seventeenth-century Dutch painters.

Le Nain and Poussin, whose paintings still had individualistic features, did their work before 1661. After Louis's accession to power, the principles of absolutism molded the ideals of French classicism. Individualism was not allowed, and artists' efforts were directed to the glorification of the state as personified by the king. Precise rules governed all aspects of culture, with the goal of formal and restrained perfection.

Contemporaries said that Louis XIV never ceased playing the role of grand monarch on the stage of his court. If the king never fully relaxed from the pressures and intrigues of government, he did enjoy music and theater and used them as a backdrop for court ceremonial. Louis favored Jean-Baptiste Lully (1632–1687), whose orchestral works combine lively animation with the restrained austerity typical of French classicism. Lully also composed court ballets, and his operatic productions achieved a powerful influence throughout Europe. Louis supported François Couperin (1668–1733), whose harpsichord and organ works possess the regal grandeur the king loved, and Marc-Antoine Charpentier (1634–1704), whose solemn religious music entertained him at meals. Charpentier received a pension for the *Te Deums,* hymns of thanksgiving, he composed to celebrate French military victories.

Louis XIV loved the stage, and in the plays of Molière and Racine his court witnessed the finest achievements in the history of the French theater. When Jean-Baptiste Poquelin (1622–1673), the son of a prosperous tapestry maker, refused to join his father's business and entered the theater, he took the stage name "Molière." As playwright, stage manager, director, and actor, Molière produced comedies that exposed the hypocrisies and follies of society through brilliant caricature. *Tartuffe* satirized the religious hypocrite, *Le Bourgeois Gentilhomme (The Would-Be Gentleman)* attacked the social parvenu, and *Les Femmes Savantes (The Learned Women)* mocked the fashionable pseudo-intellectuals of the day. In structure Molière's plays followed classical models, but they were based on careful social observation. Molière made the bourgeoisie the butt of his ridicule; he stopped short of criticizing the nobility, thus reflecting the policy of his royal patron.

While Molière dissected social mores, his contemporary Jean Racine (1639–1699) analyzed the power of love. Racine based his tragic dramas on Greek and Roman legends, and his persistent theme is the conflict of good and evil. Several plays—*Andromache, Berenice, Iphigenie,* and *Phèdre*—bear the names of women and deal with the power of passion in women. Louis preferred *Mithridates* and *Britannicus* because of the "grandeur" of their themes. For sim-

plicity of language, symmetrical structure, and calm restraint, the plays of Racine represent the finest examples of French classicism. His tragedies and Molière's comedies are still produced today.

LOUIS XIV'S WARS

Just as the architecture and court life at Versailles served to reflect the king's glory, and as the economy of the state under Colbert was managed to advance the king's prestige, so did Louis XIV use war to exalt himself above the other rulers and nations of Europe. He visualized himself as a great military hero. "The character of a conqueror," he remarked, "is regarded as the noblest and highest of titles." Military glory was his aim. In 1666 Louis appointed François le Tellier (later marquis of Louvois) as secretary of war. Louvois created a professional army, which was modern in the sense that the French state, rather than private nobles, employed the soldiers. The king himself took personal command of the army and directly supervised all aspects and details of military affairs.

A commissariat was established to feed the troops, in place of their ancient practice of living off the countryside. An ambulance corps was designed to look after the wounded. Uniforms and weapons were standardized. Finally, a rational system of recruitment, training, discipline, and promotion was imposed. With this new military machine, for the first time in Europe's history one national state, France, was able to dominate the politics of Europe.

Louis continued on a broader scale the expansionist policy begun by Cardinal Richelieu. In 1667, using a dynastic excuse, he invaded Flanders, part of the Spanish Netherlands, and Franche-Comté in the east. In consequence he acquired twelve towns, including the important commercial centers of Lille and Tournai (see Map 16.1). Five years later, Louis personally led an army of over a hundred thousand men into Holland, and the Dutch ultimately saved themselves only by opening the dikes and flooding the countryside. This war, which lasted six years and eventually involved the Holy Roman Empire and Spain, was concluded by the Treaty of Nijmegen (1678). Louis gained additional Flemish towns and the whole of Franche-Comté.

Encouraged by his successes, by the weakness of the German Empire, and by divisions among the other European powers, Louis continued his aggression. In 1681 he seized the city of Strasbourg and three years later sent his armies into the province of Lorraine. At that moment the king seemed invincible. In fact, Louis had reached the limit of his expansion at Nijmegen. The wars of the 1680s and 1690s brought him no additional territories. In 1689 the Dutch prince William of Orange, a bitter foe of Louis XIV, became king of England. William joined the League of Augsburg—which included the Habsburg emperor, the kings of Spain and Sweden, and the electors of Bavaria, Saxony, and the Palatinate—adding British resources and men to the alliance. Neither the French nor the league won any decisive victories. The alliance served instead as preparation for the long-expected conflict known as the War of the Spanish Succession.

This struggle (1701–1713), provoked by the territorial disputes of the past century, also involved the dynastic question of the succession to the Spanish throne. It was an open secret in Europe that the king of Spain, Charles II (1665–1700), was mentally defective and sexually impotent. In 1698 the European powers, including France, agreed by treaty to partition, or divide, the vast Spanish possessions between the king of France and the Holy Roman emperor, who were Charles II's brothers-in-law. When Charles died in 1700, however, his will left the Spanish crown and the worldwide Spanish empire to Philip of Anjou, Louis XIV's grandson. While the will specifically rejected union of the French and Spanish crowns, Louis was obviously the power in France, not his seventeen-year-old grandson. Louis reneged on the treaty and accepted the will.

The Dutch and the English would not accept French acquisition of the Spanish Netherlands and of the rich trade with the Spanish colonies. The union of the Spanish and French crowns, moreover, would have totally upset the European balance of power. The Versailles declaration that "the Pyrenees no longer exist" provoked the long-anticipated crisis. In 1701 the English, Dutch, Austrians, and Prussians formed the Grand Alliance against Louis XIV. They claimed that they were fighting to prevent France from becoming too strong in Europe, but during the previous half-century, overseas maritime rivalry among France, Holland, and England had created serious international tension. The secondary motive of the allied powers was to check France's expanding commercial power in North America, Asia, and Africa. In the ensuing series of conflicts, two great soldiers dominated the alliance against France: Eu-

gene, prince of Savoy, representing the Holy Roman Empire, and the Englishman John Churchill, subsequently duke of Marlborough. Eugene and Churchill inflicted a severe defeat on Louis in 1704 at Blenheim in Bavaria. Marlborough followed with another victory at Ramillies near Namur in Brabant.

The war was finally concluded at Utrecht in 1713, where the principle of partition was applied. Louis's grandson Philip remained the first Bourbon king of Spain on the understanding that the French and Spanish crowns would never be united. France surrendered Newfoundland, Nova Scotia, and the Hudson Bay territory to England, which also acquired Gibraltar, Minorca, and control of the African slave trade from Spain. The Dutch gained little because Austria received the former Spanish Netherlands.

The Peace of Utrecht had important international consequences. It represented the balance-of-power principle in operation, setting limits on the extent to which any one power, in this case France, could expand. The treaty completed the decline of Spain as a great power. It vastly expanded the British Empire. Finally, Utrecht gave European powers experience in international cooperation, thus preparing them for the alliances against France at the end of the century.

The Peace of Utrecht marked the end of French expansionist policy. In Louis's thirty-five-year quest for military glory, his main territorial acquisition was Strasbourg. Even revisionist historians, who portray the aging monarch as responsible in negotiation and moderate in his demands, acknowledge "that the widespread misery in France during the period was in part due to royal policies, especially the incessant wars."[8] To raise revenue for the wars, forty thousand additional offices had been sold, thus increasing the number of families exempt from future taxation. Constant war had disrupted trade, which meant the state could not tax the profits of trade. Widespread starvation in the provinces provoked peasant revolts, especially in Brittany. In 1714 France hovered on the brink of financial bankruptcy. Louis had exhausted the country without much compensation. It is no wonder that when he died on September 1, 1715, Saint-Simon wrote, "Those . . . wearied by the heavy and oppressive rule of the King and his ministers, felt a delighted freedom. . . . Paris . . . found relief in the hope of liberation. . . . The provinces . . . quivered with delight . . . [and] the people, ruined, abused, despairing, now thanked God for a deliverance which answered their most ardent desires."[9]

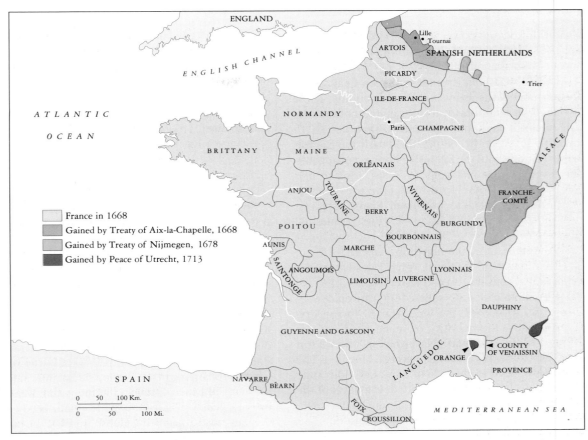

MAP 16.1 The Acquisitions of Louis XIV, 1668–1713 The desire for glory and the weakness of his German neighbors encouraged Louis' expansionist policy. But he paid a high price for his acquisitions.

THE DECLINE OF ABSOLUTIST SPAIN IN THE SEVENTEENTH CENTURY

Spanish absolutism and greatness had preceded that of the French. In the sixteenth century, Spain (or, more precisely, the kingdom of Castile) had developed the standard features of absolute monarchy: a permanent bureaucracy staffed by professionals employed in the various councils of state, a standing army, and national taxes, the *servicios,* which fell most heavily on the poor.

France depended on financial and administrative unification within its borders; Spain had developed an international absolutism on the basis of silver bullion from Peru. Spanish gold and silver, armies, and glory had dominated the Continent for most of the sixteenth century, but by the 1590s the seeds of disas-

ter were sprouting. While France in the seventeenth century represented the classic model of the modern absolute state, Spain was experiencing steady decline. Fiscal disorder, political incompetence, population decline, intellectual isolation, and psychological malaise—all combined to reduce Spain, by 1715, to the rank of a second-rate power.

The fabulous and seemingly inexhaustible flow of silver from Mexico and Peru had led Philip II (page 482) to assume the role of defender of Roman Catholicism in Europe. In order to humble the Protestant Dutch and to control the Spanish Netherlands, Philip believed that England, the Netherlands' greatest supporter, had to be crushed. He poured millions of Spanish ducats and all of Spanish hopes into the vast fleet that sailed in 1588. When the "Invincible Armada" went down in the North Sea, a century of

Spanish pride and power went with it. After 1590 a spirit of defeatism and disillusionment crippled almost all efforts at reform.

Philip II's Catholic crusade had been financed by the revenues of the Spanish-Atlantic economy. These included, in addition to silver and gold bullion, the sale of cloth, grain, oil, and wine to the colonies. In the early seventeenth century, the Dutch and English began to trade with the Spanish colonies, cutting into the revenues that had gone to Spain. Mexico and Peru themselves developed local industries, further lessening their need to buy from Spain. Between 1610 and 1650, Spanish trade with the colonies fell 60 percent.

At the same time, the native Indians and African slaves, who worked the South American silver mines under conditions that would have disgraced the ancient Egyptian pharaohs, suffered frightful epidemics of disease. Moreover, the lodes started to run dry. Consequently, the quantity of metal produced for Spain steadily declined. Nevertheless, in Madrid royal expenditures constantly exceeded income. The remedies applied in the face of a mountainous state debt and declining revenues were devaluation of the coinage and declarations of bankruptcy. In 1596, 1607, 1627, 1647, and 1680, Spanish kings found no solution to the problem of an empty treasury other than to cancel the national debt. Given the frequency of cancellation, naturally public confidence in the state deteriorated.

Spain, in contrast to the other countries of western Europe, had only a tiny middle class. Disdain for money, in a century of increasing commercialism and bourgeois attitudes, reveals a significant facet of the Spanish national character. Public opinion, taking its cue from the aristocracy, condemned money-making as vulgar and undignified. Those with influence or connections sought titles of nobility and social prestige. Thousands entered economically unproductive professions and became priests, monks, and nuns: there were said to be nine thousand monasteries in the province of Castile alone. The flood of gold and silver had produced severe inflation, pushing the costs of production in the textile industry higher and higher, to the point that Castilian cloth could not compete in colonial and international markets. Many manufacturers and businessmen found so many obstacles in the way of profitable enterprise that they simply gave up.[10]

Velazquez: The Maids of Honor The Infanta Margarita painted in 1656 with her maids and playmates has invaded the artist's studio, while her parents' image is reflected in the mirror on the back wall. Velazquez (extreme left), who powerfully influenced nineteenth-century impressionist painters, imbued all of his subjects, including the pathetic dwarf (right, in black) with a sense of dignity. *(Giraudon)*

Spanish aristocrats, attempting to maintain an extravagant lifestyle they could no longer afford, increased the rents on their estates. High rents and heavy taxes in turn drove the peasants from the land. Agricultural production suffered and the peasants departed for the large cities, where they swelled the ranks of unemployed beggars.

Their most Catholic majesties, the kings of Spain, had no solutions to these dire problems. If one can discern personality from pictures, the portraits of Philip III (1598–1622), Philip IV (1622–1665), and Charles II hanging in the Prado, the Spanish national museum in Madrid, reflect the increasing weakness of the dynasty. Their faces—the small, beady eyes, the long noses, the jutting Habsburg jaws, the pathetically stupid expressions—tell a story of excessive inbreeding and decaying monarchy. The Spanish kings all lacked force of character. Philip III, a pallid, melancholy, and deeply pious man "whose only virtue appeared to reside in a total absence of vice," handed the government over to the lazy duke of Lerma, who used it to advance his personal and familial wealth. Philip IV left the management of his several kingdoms to Count Olivares.

Olivares was an able administrator. He did not lack energy and ideas; he devised new sources of revenue. But he clung to the grandiose belief that the solution to Spain's difficulties rested in a return to the imperial tradition. Unfortunately, the imperial tradition demanded the revival of war with the Dutch, at the expiration of a twelve-year truce in 1622, and a long war with France over Mantua (1628–1659). Spain thus became embroiled in the Thirty Years' War. These conflicts, on top of an empty treasury, brought disaster.

In 1640 Spain faced serious revolts in Naples and Portugal, and in 1643 the French inflicted a crushing defeat on a Spanish army in Belgium. By the Treaty

of the Pyrenees of 1659, which ended the French-Spanish wars, Spain was compelled to surrender extensive territories to France. This treaty marked the end of Spain as a great power.

Seventeenth-century Spain was the victim of its past. It could not forget the grandeur of the sixteenth century and look to the future. The bureaucratic councils of state continued to function as symbols of the absolute Spanish monarchy. But because those councils were staffed by aristocrats, it was the aristocracy that held the real power. Spanish absolutism had been built largely on slave-produced gold and silver. When the supply of bullion decreased, the power and standing of the Spanish state declined.

The most cherished Spanish ideals were military glory and strong Roman Catholic faith. In the seventeenth century, Spain lacked the finances and the manpower to fight the expensive wars in which it foolishly got involved. Spain also ignored the new mercantile ideas and scientific methods, because they came from heretical nations, Holland and England. The incredible wealth of South America destroyed the tiny Spanish middle class and created contempt for business and manual labor.

The decadence of the Habsburg dynasty and the lack of effective royal councilors also contributed to Spanish failure. Spanish leaders seemed to lack the will to reform. Pessimism and fatalism permeated national life. In the reign of Philip IV, a royal council was appointed to plan the construction of a canal linking the Tagus and Manzanares rivers in Spain. After interminable debate, the committee decided that "if God had intended the rivers to be navigable, He would have made them so."

In the brilliant novel *Don Quixote,* the Spanish writer Cervantes (1547–1616) produced one of the great masterpieces of world literature. *Don Quixote* —on which the modern play *The Man of La Mancha* is based—delineates the whole fabric of sixteenth-century Spanish society. The main character, Don Quixote, lives in a world of dreams, traveling about the countryside seeking military glory. From the title of the book, the English language has borrowed the word *quixotic.* Meaning "idealistic but impractical," the term characterizes seventeenth-century Spain. As a leading scholar has written, "The Spaniard convinced himself that reality was what he felt, believed, imagined. He filled the world with heroic reverberations. Don Quixote was born and grew."[11]

CONSTITUTIONALISM

The seventeenth century, which witnessed the development of absolute monarchy, also saw the appearance of the constitutional state. While France and later Prussia, Russia, and Austria solved the question of sovereignty with the absolutist state, England and Holland evolved toward the constitutional state. What is constitutionalism? Is it identical to democracy?

Constitutionalism is the limitation of government by law. Constitutionalism also implies a balance between the authority and power of the government on the one hand and the rights and liberties of the subjects on the other. The balance is often very delicate.

A nation's constitution may be written or unwritten. It may be embodied in one basic document, occasionally revised by amendment or judicial decision, like the Constitution of the United States. Or a constitution may be partly written and partly unwritten and include parliamentary statutes, judicial decisions, and a body of traditional procedures and practices, like the English and Canadian constitutions. Whether written or unwritten, a constitution gets its binding force from the government's acknowledgment that it must respect that constitution—that is, that the state must govern according to the laws. Likewise, in a constitutional state, the people look on the law and the constitution as the protectors of their rights, liberties, and property.

Modern constitutional governments may take either a republican or a monarchial form. In a constitutional republic, the sovereign power resides in the electorate and is exercised by the electorate's representatives. In a constitutional monarchy, a king or queen serves as the head of state and possesses some residual political authority, but again the ultimate or sovereign power rests in the electorate.

A constitutional government is not, however, quite the same as a democratic government. In a complete democracy, *all* the people have the right to participate either directly, or indirectly through their elected representatives, in the government of the state. Democratic government, therefore, is intimately tied up with the *franchise* (the vote). Most men could not vote until the late nineteenth century. Even then, women—probably the majority in Western societies —lacked the franchise; they gained the right to vote only in the twentieth century. Consequently, although constitutionalism developed in the seventeenth century, full democracy was achieved only in very recent times.

The Decline of Royal Absolutism in England (1603–1649)

In the late sixteenth century the French monarchy was powerless; a century later, the king's power was absolute. In 1588 Queen Elizabeth I of England exercised very great personal power; by 1689 the English monarchy was severely circumscribed. Change in England was anything but orderly. Seventeenth-century England displayed as much political stability as some modern African states. It executed one king, experienced a bloody civil war, experimented with military dictatorship, then restored the son of the murdered king, and finally, after a bloodless revolution, established constitutional monarchy. Political stability came only in the 1690s. How do we account for the fact that, after such a violent and tumultuous century, England laid the foundations for constitutional monarchy? What combination of political, socioeconomic, and religious factors brought on a civil war in 1642 to 1649 and then the constitutional settlement of 1688 to 1689?

The extraordinary success of Elizabeth I had rested on her political shrewdness and flexibility, her careful management of finances, her wise selection of ministers, her clever manipulation of Parliament, and her sense of royal dignity and devotion to hard work. The aging queen had always refused to discuss the succession. After her Scottish cousin James Stuart succeeded her as James I (1603–1625), Elizabeth's strengths seemed even greater than they actually had been. The Stuarts lacked every quality Elizabeth had possessed.

King James was well educated and learned but lacking in common sense—he was once called "the wisest fool in Christendom." He also lacked the common touch. Urged to wave at the crowds who waited to greet their new ruler, James complained that he was tired and threatened to drop his breeches "so they can cheer at my arse." Having left barbarous and violent Scotland for rich and prosperous England, James believed he had entered the "Promised Land." As soon as he got to London, the new English king went to see the crown jewels.

Abysmally ignorant of English law and of the English Parliament, but sublimely arrogant, James was devoted to the theory of the divine right of kings. He expressed his ideas about divine right in his essay "The Trew Law of Free Monarchy." According to James I, a monarch has a divine (or God-given) right to his authority and is responsible only to God. Rebellion is the worst of political crimes. If a king orders something evil, the subject should respond with passive disobedience but should be prepared to accept any penalty for noncompliance.

James substituted political theorizing and talk for real work. He lectured the House of Commons: "There are no privileges and immunities which can stand against a divinely appointed King." This notion, implying total royal jurisdiction over the liberties, persons, and properties of English men and women, formed the basis of the Stuart concept of absolutism. Such a view ran directly counter to the long-standing English idea that a person's property could not be taken away without due process of law. James's expression of such views before the English House of Commons constituted a grave political mistake.

The House of Commons guarded the state's pocketbook, and James and later Stuart kings badly needed to open that pocketbook. Elizabeth had bequeathed to James a sizable royal debt. Through prudent management the debt could have been gradually reduced, but James I looked on all revenues as a happy windfall to be squandered on a lavish court and favorite courtiers. In reality, the extravagance displayed in James's court, as well as the public flaunting of his male lovers, weakened respect for the monarchy.

Elizabeth had also left to her Stuart successors a House of Commons that appreciated its own financial strength and intended to use that strength to acquire a greater say in the government of the state. The knights and burgesses who sat at Westminster in the late sixteenth and early seventeenth centuries wanted to discuss royal expenditures, religious reform, and foreign affairs. In short, the Commons wanted what amounted to sovereignty.

Profound social changes had occurred since the sixteenth century. The English House of Commons during the reigns of James I and his son Charles I (1625–1649) was very different from the assembly Henry VIII had terrorized into passing his Reformation legislation. A social revolution had brought about the change. The dissolution of the monasteries and the sale of monastic land had enriched many people. Agricultural techniques like the draining of wasteland and the application of fertilizers improved the land and its yield. Old manorial common land had been enclosed and turned into sheep runs; breeding was carefully supervised, and the size of the flocks increased. In these activities, as well as in renting and leasing parcels of land, precise accounts were kept.

Many men invested in commercial ventures at home, such as the expanding cloth industry, and in partnerships and joint stock companies engaged in foreign enterprises. They made prudent marriages. All these developments led to a great deal of social mobility. Both in commerce and in agriculture, the English in the late sixteenth and early seventeenth centuries were capitalists, investing their profits to make more money. Though the international inflation of the period hit everywhere, in England commercial and agricultural income rose faster than prices. Wealthy country gentry, rich city merchants, and financiers invested abroad.

The typical pattern was for the commercially successful to set themselves up as country gentry, thus creating an elite group that possessed a far greater proportion of land and of the national wealth in 1640 than had been the case in 1540. Small wonder that in 1640 someone could declare in the House of Commons, probably accurately, "We could buy the House of Lords three times over." Increased wealth had also produced a better-educated and more articulate House of Commons. Many members had acquired at least a smattering of legal knowledge, and they used that knowledge to search for medieval precedents from which to argue against the king. The class that dominated the Commons wanted political power corresponding to its economic strength.

In England, unlike France, there was no social stigma attached to paying taxes. Members of the House of Commons were willing to tax themselves provided they had some say in the expenditure of those taxes and in the formulation of state policies. The Stuart kings, however, considered such ambitions intolerable presumption and a threat to their divine-right prerogative. Consequently, at every parliament between 1603 and 1640, bitter squabbles erupted between the crown and the wealthy, articulate, and legal-minded Commons. Charles I's attempt to

govern without Parliament (1629–1640), and to finance his government by arbitrary nonparliamentary levies, brought the country to a crisis.

An issue graver than royal extravagance and Parliament's desire to make law also disturbed the English and embittered relations between the king and the House of Commons. That problem was religion. In the early seventeenth century, increasing numbers of English people felt dissatisfied with the Church of England established by Henry VIII and reformed by Elizabeth. Many Puritans (see Chapter 14) believed that Reformation had not gone far enough. They wanted to "purify" the Anglican church of Roman Catholic elements—elaborate vestments and ceremonial, the position of the altar in the church, even the giving and wearing of wedding rings.

It is very difficult to establish what proportion of the English population was Puritan. According to the present scholarly consensus, the dominant religious groups in the early seventeenth century were Calvinist and Protestant; their more zealous members were Puritans. It also seems clear that many English men and women were attracted by the socioeconomic implications of John Calvin's theology. Calvinism emphasized hard work, sobriety, thrift, competition, and postponement of pleasure, and tended to link sin and poverty with weakness and moral corruption. These attitudes fit in precisely with the economic approaches and practices of many (successful) businessmen and farmers. These values have frequently been called the "Protestant," "middle class," or "capitalist ethic." While it is hazardous to identify capitalism and progress with Protestantism—there were many successful Catholic capitalists—the "Protestant virtues" represented the prevailing values of members of the House of Commons.

James I and Charles I both gave the impression of being highly sympathetic to Roman Catholicism. Charles supported the policies of William Laud, archbishop of Canterbury (1573–1645), who tried to impose elaborate ritual and rich ceremonial on all churches. Laud insisted on complete uniformity of church services and enforced that uniformity through an ecclesiastical court called the "Court of High Commission." People believed the country was being led back to Roman Catholicism. When in 1637 Laud attempted to impose a new prayer book, modeled on the Anglican Book of Common Prayer, on the Presbyterian Scots, the Scots revolted. In order to finance an army to put down the Scots, King Charles was compelled to summon Parliament in November 1640.

For eleven years Charles I had ruled without Parliament, financing his government through extraordinary stopgap levies, considered illegal by most English people. For example, the king revived a medieval law requiring coastal districts to help pay the cost of ships for defense, but levied the tax, called "ship money," on inland as well as coastal counties. When the issue was tested in the courts, the judges, having been suborned, decided in the king's favor.

Most members of Parliament believed that such taxation without consent amounted to arbitrary and absolute despotism. Consequently, they were not willing to trust the king with an army. Accordingly, this parliament, commonly called the "Long Parliament" because it sat from 1640 to 1660, proceeded to enact legislation that limited the power of the monarch and made arbitrary government impossible.

In 1641 the Commons passed the Triennial Act, which compelled the king to summon Parliament every three years. The Commons impeached Archbishop Laud and abolished the House of Lords and the Court of High Commission. It went further and threatened to abolish the institution of episcopacy. King Charles, fearful of a Scottish invasion—the original reason for summoning Parliament—accepted these measures. Understanding and peace were not achieved, however, partly because radical members of the Commons pushed increasingly revolutionary propositions, partly because Charles maneuvered to rescind those he had already approved. An uprising in Ireland precipitated civil war.

Ever since Henry II had conquered Ireland in 1171, English governors had mercilessly ruled the Irish, and English landlords had ruthlessly exploited them. The English Reformation had made a bad situation worse: because the Irish remained Catholic, religious differences became united with economic and political oppression. Without an army, Charles I could neither come to terms with the Scots nor put down the Irish rebellion, and the Long Parliament remained unwilling to place an army under a king it did not trust. Charles thus instigated military action against parliamentary forces. He recruited an army drawn from the nobility and their cavalry staff, the rural gentry, and mercenaries. The parliamentary army was composed of the militia of the city of Lon-

THE LAMENTABLE COMPLAINTS OF NICK FROTH the Tapſter, and RVLEROST the Cooke. Concerning the reſtraint lately ſet forth, againſt drinking, potting, and piping on the Sabbath day, and againſt ſelling meate.

Printed in the yeare, 1641.

Puritan Ideals Opposed The Puritans preached sober living and abstention from alcoholic drink, rich food, and dancing. This pamphlet reflects the common man's hostility to such restraints. "Potting" refers to tankards of beer; "piping" means making music. *(The British Museum)*

don, country squires with business connections, and men with a firm belief in the spiritual duty of serving.

The English civil war (1642–1646) tested whether sovereignty in England was to reside in the king or in Parliament. The civil war did not resolve that problem, although it ended in 1649 with the execution of King Charles on the charge of high treason—a severe blow to the theory of divine right monarchy. The period between 1649 and 1660, called the "Interregnum" because it separated two monarchial periods, witnessed England's solitary experience of military dictatorship.

The House of Commons This seal of the Commonwealth shows the small House of Commons in session with the speaker presiding: the legend "in the third year of freedom" refers to 1651, three years after the abolition of the monarchy. In 1653, however, Cromwell abolished this "Rump Parliament"—so-called because it consisted of the few surviving members elected before the Civil War—and he and the army governed the land. *(The British Museum)*

PURITANICAL ABSOLUTISM IN ENGLAND: CROMWELL AND THE PROTECTORATE

The problem of sovereignty was vigorously debated in the middle years of the seventeenth century. In *Leviathan,* the English philosopher and political theorist Thomas Hobbes (1588–1679) maintained that sovereignty is ultimately derived from the people, who transfer it to the monarchy by implicit contract. The power of the ruler is absolute, but kings do not hold their power by divine right. This view pleased no one in the seventeenth century.

When Charles I was beheaded on January 30, 1649, the kingship was abolished. A *commonwealth,* or republican form of government, was proclaimed. Theoretically, legislative power rested in the surviving members of Parliament and executive power in a council of state. In fact, the army that had defeated the royal forces controlled the government, and Oliver Cromwell controlled the army. Though called the "Protectorate," the rule of Cromwell (1653–1658) constituted military dictatorship.

Oliver Cromwell (1599–1658) came from the country gentry, the class that dominated the House of Commons in the early seventeenth century. He himself had sat in the Long Parliament. Cromwell rose in the parliamentary army and achieved nationwide fame by infusing the army with his Puritan convictions and molding it into the highly effective military machine, called the "New Model Army," that defeated the royalist forces.

Parliament had written a constitution, the Instrument of Government (1653), that invested executive power in a lord protector (Cromwell) and a council of state. The instrument provided for triennial parliaments and gave Parliament the sole power to raise taxes. But after repeated disputes, Cromwell tore the document up. He continued the standing army and proclaimed quasi-martial law. He divided England into twelve military districts, each governed by a major general. The major-generals acted through the justices of the peace, though they sometimes overrode them. On the issue of religion, Cromwell favored broad toleration, and the Instrument of

Government gave all Christians, except Roman Catholics, the right to practice their faith. Toleration meant state protection of many different Protestant sects, and most English people had no enthusiasm for such a notion; the idea was far ahead of its time. Cromwell identified Irish Catholicism with sedition. In 1649 he crushed rebellion there with merciless savagery, leaving a legacy of Irish hatred for England that has not yet subsided. The state rigorously censored the press, forbade sports, and kept the theaters closed.

Cromwell's regulation of the nation's economy had features typical of seventeenth-century absolutism. The lord protector's policies were mercantilist, similar to those Colbert established in France. Cromwell enforced a navigation act requiring that English goods be transported on English ships. The navigation act was a great boost to the development of an English merchant marine and brought about a short but successful war with the commercially threatened Dutch. Cromwell also welcomed the immigration of Jews, because of their skills, and they began to return to England in larger numbers after four centuries of absence.

Absolute government collapsed when Cromwell died in 1658 because the English got fed up with military rule. They longed for a return to civilian government, restoration of the common law, and social stability. Moreover, the strain of creating a community of puritanical saints proved too psychologically exhausting. Government by military dictatorship was an unfortunate experiment that the English never forgot nor repeated. By 1660 they were ready to restore the monarchy.

THE RESTORATION OF THE ENGLISH MONARCHY

The Restoration of 1660 re-established the monarchy in the person of Charles II (1660–1685), eldest son of Charles I. At the same time both houses of Parliament were restored, together with the established Anglican church, the courts of law, and the system of local government through justices of the peace. The Restoration failed to resolve two serious problems. What was to be the attitude of the state toward Puritans, Catholics, and dissenters from the established church? And what was to be the constitutional position of the king—that is, what was to be the relationship between the king and Parliament?

About the first of these issues, Charles II, a relaxed, easygoing, and sensual man, was basically indifferent. He was not interested in doctrinal issues. Parliamentarians were, and they proceeded to enact a body of laws that sought to compel religious uniformity. Those who refused to receive the sacrament of the Church of England could not vote, hold public office, preach, teach, attend the universities, or even assemble for meetings, according to the Test Act of 1673. These restrictions could not be enforced. When the Quaker William Penn held a meeting of his Friends and was arrested, the jury refused to convict him.

In politics, Charles II was determined "not to set out in his travels again," which meant that he intended to get along with Parliament. Charles II's solution to the problem of the relationship between the king and the House of Commons had profound importance for later constitutional development. Generally good rapport existed between the king and the strongly royalist Parliament that had restored him. This rapport was due largely to the king's appointment of a council of five men who served both as his major advisers and as members of Parliament, thus acting as liason agents between the executive and the legislature. This body—known as the "Cabal" from the names of its five members (Clifford, Arlington, Buckingham, Ashley-Cooper and Lauderdale)—was an ancestor of the later cabinet system (see page 532). It gradually came to be accepted that the Cabal was answerable in Parliament for the decisions of the king. This development gave rise to the concept of ministerial responsibility: royal ministers must answer to the Commons.

Harmony between the crown and Parliament rested on the understanding that Charles would summon frequent parliaments and that Parliament would vote him sufficient revenues. However, although Parliament believed Charles had a virtual divine right to govern, it did not grant him an adequate income. Accordingly, in 1670 Charles entered into a secret agreement with Louis XIV. The French king would give Charles £200,000 annually, and in return Charles would relax the laws against Catholics, gradually re-Catholicize England, and support French policy against the Dutch.

When the details of this secret treaty leaked out, a great wave of anti-Catholic fear swept England. This fear was compounded by a crucial fact: although Charles had produced several bastards, he had no legitimate children. It therefore appeared that his brother and heir, James, duke of York, who had publicly acknowledged his Catholicism, would inaugurate a Catholic dynasty. The combination of hatred for the French absolutism embodied in Louis XIV, hostility to Roman Catholicism, and fear of a permanent Catholic dynasty produced virtual hysteria. The Commons passed an exclusion bill denying the succession to a Roman Catholic, but Charles quickly dissolved Parliament and the bill never became law.

James II (1685–1688) did succeed his brother. Almost at once the worst English anti-Catholic fears, already aroused by Louis XIV's revocation of the Edict of Nantes, were realized. In direct violation of the Test Act, James appointed Roman Catholics to positions in the army, the universities, and local government. When these actions were tested in the courts, the judges, whom James had appointed, decided for the king. The king was suspending the law at will and appeared to be reviving the absolutism of his father and grandfather. He went further. Attempting to broaden his base of support with Protestant dissenters and nonconformists, James issued a declaration of indulgence granting religious freedom to all.

Two events gave the signals for revolution. First, seven bishops of the Church of England petitioned the king that they not be forced to read the declaration of indulgence because of their belief that it was an illegal act. They were imprisoned in the Tower of London but subsequently acquitted amid great public enthusiasm. Second, in June 1688 James's second wife produced a male heir. A Catholic dynasty seemed assured. The fear of a Roman Catholic monarchy, supported by France and ruling outside the law, prompted a group of eminent persons to offer the English throne to James's Protestant daughter, Mary, and her Dutch husband, Prince William of Orange. In November 1688 James II, his queen, and their infant son fled to France and became pensioners of Louis XIV.

THE TRIUMPH OF ENGLAND'S PARLIAMENT: CONSTITUTIONAL MONARCHY AND CABINET GOVERNMENT

The English call the events of 1688 the "Glorious Revolution." The revolution was indeed glorious in the sense that it replaced one king with another with a minimum of bloodshed. It also represented the de-struction, once and for all, of the idea of divine-right monarchy. William and Mary accepted the English throne from Parliament and in so doing explicitly recognized the supremacy of Parliament. The revolution of 1688 established the principle that sovereignty, the ultimate power in the state, rested in Parliament and that the king ruled with the consent of the governed.

The men who brought about the revolution quickly framed their intentions in the Bill of Rights, the cornerstone of the modern British constitution. The basic principles of the Bill of Rights were formulated in direct response to Stuart absolutism. Law was to be made in Parliament; once made, it could not be suspended by the crown. Parliament had to be called at least every three years. Both elections to and debate in Parliament were to be free, in the sense that the Crown was not to interfere in them; this aspect of the bill was widely disregarded in the eighteenth century. Judges would hold their offices "during good behavior," which assured the independence of the judiciary. No longer could the crown get the judicial decisions it wanted by threats of removal. There was to be no standing army in peacetime—a limitation designed to prevent the repetition of either Stuart or Cromwellian military government. The Bill of Rights granted "that the subjects which are Protestants may have arms for their defense suitable to their conditions and as allowed by law,"[12] meaning that Catholics could not possess firearms because the Protestant majority feared them. Additional legislation granted freedom of worship to Protestant dissenters and nonconformists and required that the English monarch always be Protestant.

The Glorious Revolution found its best defense in the political philosopher John Locke's "Second Treatise on Civil Government" (1690). Locke (1632–1704) maintained that men set up civil governments in order to protect their property. The purpose of government, therefore, is to protect life, liberty, and property. A government that oversteps its proper function—protecting the natural rights of life, liberty, and property—becomes a tyranny. (By "natural" rights, Locke meant rights basic to all men because all have the ability to reason.) Under a tyrannical government, the people have the natural right to rebellion. Rebellion can be avoided if the government carefully respects the rights of citizens and if the people zealously defend their liberty. Recognizing the close relationship between economic

The Rise of Western Absolutism and Constitutionalism

1581	Formation of the United Provinces of the Netherlands
1588	Defeat of the Spanish Armada
1589–1610	Reign of Henry IV of France; economic reforms help to restore public order, lay foundation for absolutist rule
1598	Edict of Nantes: Henry IV ends the French Wars of Religion
1608	France establishes its first Canadian settlement, at Quebec
1609	Philip III of Spain recognizes Dutch independence
1610–1650	Spanish trade with the New World falls by 60 percent
1618–1648	Thirty Years' War
1624–1643	Richelieu dominates French government
1625	Huguenot revolt in France; siege of La Rochelle
1629–1640	Eleven Years' Tyranny: Charles I attempts to rule England without the aid of Parliament
1640–1660	Long Parliament in England
1642–1646	English Civil War
1643–1661	Mazarin dominates France's regency government
1643–1715	Reign of Louis XIV
1648–1660	The Fronde: French nobility opposes centralizing efforts of monarchy
1648	Peace of Westphalia confirms Dutch independence from Spain
1649	Execution of Charles I; beginning of the Interregnum in England
1653–1658	The Protectorate: Cromwell heads military rule of England
1659	Treaty of the Pyrenees forces Spain to cede extensive territories to France, marks end of Spain as a great power
1660	Restoration of the English monarchy: Charles II returns from exile
1661	Louis XIV enters into independent rule
ca 1663–1683	Colbert directs Louis XIV's mercantilist economic policy
1673	Test Act excludes Roman Catholics from public office in England
	France invades Holland
1678	Treaty of Nijmegen: Louis XIV acquires Franche-Comté
1680	Treaty of Dover: Charles II secretly agrees with Louis XIV to re-catholicize England
1681	France acquires Strasbourg
1685	Revocation of the Edict of Nantes
1685–1688	James II rules England, attempts to restore Roman Catholicism as state religion
1688–1689	The Glorious Revolution establishes a constitutional monarchy under William III in England; enactment of the Bill of Rights
1701–1713	War of the Spanish Succession
1713	Peace of Utrecht ends French territorial acquisitions, expands the British Empire

and political freedom, Locke linked economic liberty and private property with political freedom. Locke served as the great spokesman for the liberal English revolution of 1689 and for representative government. His idea, inherited from ancient Greece and Rome (see page 120), that there are natural or universal rights, equally valid for all peoples and societies, played a powerful role in eighteenth-century Enlightenment thought. His ideas on liberty and tyranny were especially popular in colonial America.

The events of 1688 to 1690 did not constitute a *democratic* revolution. The revolution placed sovereignty in Parliament, and Parliament represented the upper classes. The great majority of English people acquired no say in their government. The English revolution established a constitutional monarchy; it also inaugurated an age of aristocratic government, which lasted at least until 1832 and probably until 1914.

In the course of the eighteenth century, the cabinet system of government evolved. The term *cabinet* refers to the small private room in which English rulers consulted their chief ministers. In a cabinet system, the leading ministers, who must have seats in and the support of a majority of the House of Commons, formulate common policy and conduct the business of the country. During the administration of one royal minister, Sir Robert Walpole (1721–1742), the idea developed that the cabinet was responsible to the House of Commons. The Hanoverian king George I (1714–1727) normally presided at cabinet meetings throughout his reign, but his son and heir George II (1727–1760) discontinued the practice. The influence of the crown in decision making accordingly declined. Walpole enjoyed the favor of the monarchy and of the House of Commons and came to be called the king's first, or "prime," minister. In the English cabinet system, both legislative and executive power are held by the leading ministers, who form the government.

THE DUTCH REPUBLIC IN THE SEVENTEENTH CENTURY

The seventeenth century witnessed an unparalleled flowering of Dutch scientific, artistic, and literary achievement. In this period, often called the "golden age of the Netherlands," Dutch ideas and attitudes played a profound role in shaping a new and modern world-view. At the same time, the Republic of the United Provinces of the Netherlands represents another model of the development of the modern state.

In the late sixteenth century, the seven northern provinces of the Netherlands, of which Holland and Zeeland were the most prosperous, succeeded in throwing off Spanish domination. This success was based on their geographical lines of defense, the wealth of their cities, the brilliant military strategy of William the Silent, the preoccupation of Philip II of Spain with so many other concerns, and the northern provinces' vigorous Calvinism. In 1581 the seven provinces of the Union of Utrecht had formed the United Provinces (page 520). Philip II continued to try to crush the Dutch with the Armada, but in 1609 his son Philip III agreed to a truce that implicitly recognized the independence of the United Provinces. At the time neither side expected the peace to be permanent. The Peace of Westphalia in 1648, however, confirmed the Dutch republic's independence.

Within each province an oligarchy of wealthy merchants called "regents" handled domestic affairs in the local Estates. The provincial Estates held virtually all the power. A federal assembly, or States General, handled matters of foreign affairs, such as war. But the States General did not possess sovereign authority, since all issues had to be referred back to the local Estates for approval. The States General appointed a representative, the *stadholder,* in each province. As the highest executive there, the stadholder carried out ceremonial functions and was responsible for defense and good order. The sons of William the Silent, Maurice and William Louis, held the office of stadholder in all seven provinces. As members of the House of Orange, they were closely identified with the struggle against Spain and Dutch patriotism. The regents in each province jealously guarded local independence and resisted efforts at centralization. Nevertheless, Holland, which had the largest navy and the most wealth, dominated the republic and the States General. Significantly, the Estates assembled at Holland's capital, The Hague.

The government of the United Provinces fits none of the standard categories of seventeenth-century political organization. The Dutch were not monarchial, but fiercely republican. The government was controlled by wealthy merchants and financiers. Though rich, their values were not aristocratic but strongly

Vermeer: Young Woman with a Water Jug The mystery of light fascinated seventeenth-century scientists and artists, perhaps the Dutch painter Vermeer most of all. His calm quiet scenes of ordinary people performing everyday tasks in rooms suffused with light has given him the title "poet of domesticity." The map on the wall suggests curiosity about the wider world. *(Metropolitan Museum of Art)*

Amsterdam Harbor, 1663 Amsterdam's great wealth depended on the presence of a relatively large number of people with capital for overseas investment *and* on its fleet, which brought goods from all over the world. As shown here, because the inner docks were often jammed to capacity, many ships had to be moored outside the city. *(Scheepvaart Museum, Amsterdam)*

middle class, emphasizing thrift, hard work, and simplicity in living. The Dutch republic was not a strong federation but a confederation—that is, a weak union of strong provinces. The provinces were a temptation to powerful neighbors, yet the Dutch resisted the long Spanish effort at reconquest and withstood both French and English attacks in the second half of the century. Louis XIV's hatred of the Dutch was proverbial. They represented all that he despised —middle-class values, religious toleration, and political independence.

The political success of the Dutch rested on the phenomenal commercial prosperity of the Netherlands. The moral and ethical bases of that commercial wealth were thrift, frugality, and religious toleration. John Calvin had written, "From where do the merchant's profits come except from his own diligence and industry." This attitude undoubtedly encouraged a sturdy people who had waged a centuries-old struggle against the sea.

Alone of all European peoples in the seventeenth century, the Dutch practiced religious toleration. Peoples of all faiths were welcome within their borders. It is a striking testimony to the urbanity of Dutch society that in a century when patriotism was closely identified with religious uniformity, the Calvinist province of Holland allowed its highest official, Jan van Oldenbarneveldt, to continue to practice his Roman Catholic faith. As long as a businessman conducted his religion in private, the government did not interfere with him.

Toleration also paid off: it attracted a great deal of foreign capital and investment. Deposits at the Bank of Amsterdam were guaranteed by the city council, and in the middle years of the century the bank became Europe's best source of cheap credit and commercial intelligence and the main clearing-house for bills of exchange. Men of all races and creeds traded in Amsterdam, at whose docks on the Amstel River five thousand ships, half the merchant marine of the United Provinces, were berthed. Joost van den Vondel, the poet of Dutch imperialism, exulted:

God, God, the Lord of Amstel cried, hold every conscience free;
And Liberty ride, on Holland's tide, with billowing sails to sea,
And run our Amstel out and in; let freedom gird the bold,
And merchant in his counting house stand elbow deep in gold.[13]

The fishing industry was the cornerstone of the Dutch economy. For half the year, from June to December, fishing fleets combed the dangerous English coast and the North Sea, raking in tiny herring. Profits from herring stimulated shipbuilding, and even before 1600 the Dutch were offering the lowest shipping rates in Europe. Although Dutch cities became famous for their exports—diamonds, linen from Haarlem, pottery from Delft—Dutch wealth depended less on exports than on transport. The merchant marine was the largest in Europe.

In 1602 a group of the regents of Holland formed the Dutch East India Company, a joint stock company. Each investor received a percentage of the profits proportional to the amount of money he had put in. Within half a century, the Dutch East India Company had cut heavily into Portuguese trading in the Far East. The Dutch seized the Cape of Good Hope, Ceylon, and Malacca and established trading posts in each place. In the 1630s the Dutch East India Company was paying its investors about a 35-percent annual return on their investments. The Dutch West India Company, founded in 1621, traded extensively with Latin America and Africa.

Although the initial purpose of both companies was commercial—the import of spices and silks to Europe—the Dutch found themselves involved in the imperialistic exploitation of large parts of the Pacific and Latin America. Amsterdam, the center of a worldwide Dutch empire, became the commercial and financial capital of Europe. During the seventeenth century, the Dutch translated their commercial acumen and flexibility into political and imperialist terms with striking success. But war with France and England in the 1670s hurt the United Provinces. The long War of the Spanish Succession, in which the Dutch supported England against France, was a costly drain on Dutch manpower and financial resources. The peace signed in 1715 to end the war marked the beginning of Dutch economic decline.

nessed the emergence of the fully absolutist state. The king commanded all the powers of the state: judicial, military, political, and to a great extent, ecclesiastical. France developed a centralized bureaucracy, a professional army, a state-directed economy, all of which Louis personally supervised. For the first time in history all the institutions and powers of the national state were effectively controlled by a single person. The king saw himself as the representative of God on earth, and it has been said that "to the seventeenth century imagination God was a sort of image of Louis XIV."[14]

As Louis XIV personifies absolutism, so Stuart England exemplifies the evolution of the first modern constitutional state. The conflicts between Parliament and the first two Stuart rulers, James I and Charles I, tested where sovereign power would rest in the state. The resulting civil war did not solve the problem. The Instrument of Government, the document produced in 1653 by the victorious parliamentary army, provided for a balance of governmental authority and recognition of popular rights; as such, the Instrument has been called the first modern constitution. Unfortunately, it lacked public support. James II's absolutist tendencies brought on the Revolution of 1688, and the people who made that revolution settled three basic issues. Sovereign power was divided between king and Parliament, with Parliament enjoying the greater share. Government was to be based on the rule of law. And the liberties of English people were made explicit in written form, in the Bill of Rights. The framers of the English constitution left to later generations the task of making constitutional government work.

The models of governmental power established by seventeenth-century England and France strongly influenced other states then and ever since. As the American novelist William Faulkner wrote, "The past isn't dead; it's not even past."

NOTES

According to Thomas Hobbes, the central drive in every man is "a perpetual and restless desire of Power, after Power, that ceaseth only in Death." The seventeenth century solved the problem of sovereign power in two fundamental ways: absolutism and constitutionalism. The France of Louis XIV wit-

1. Cited in John Wolf, *Louis XIV,* W. W. Norton & Co., New York, 1968, p. 115.
2. S. de Gramont, ed., *The Age of Magnificence: Memoirs of the Court of Louis XIV by the Duc de Saint-Simon,* Capricorn Books, New York, 1964, pp. 141–145.

3. Cited in Wolf, p. 146.

4. Cited in Andrew Trout, *Jean-Baptiste Colbert,* Twayne Publishers, Boston, 1978, p. 128.

5. Cited in Wolf, p. 394.

6. Ibid.

7. See Warren C. Scoville, *The Persecution of the Huguenots and French Economic Development: 1680–1720,* University of California Press, Berkeley, 1960.

8. See William F. Church, *Louis XIV in Historical Thought: From Voltaire to the Annales School,* W. W. Norton & Co., New York, 1976, p. 92.

9. S. de Gramont, ed., *The Age of Magnificence,* p. 183.

10. J. H. Elliott, *Imperial Spain, 1469–1716,* Mentor Books, New York, 1963, pp. 306–308.

11. See Bartolome Bennassar, *The Spanish Character: Attitudes and Mentalities from the Sixteenth to the Nineteenth Century,* trans. Benjamin Keen, University of California Press, Berkeley, 1979, p. 125.

12. C. Stephenson and G. F. Marcham, *Sources of English Constitutional History,* Harper & Row, New York, 1937, p. 601.

13. Cited in D. Maland, *Europe in the Seventeenth Century,* Macmillan, New York, 1967, pp. 198–199.

14. Cited in Carl J. Friedrich and Charles Blitzer, *The Age of Power,* Cornell University Press, Ithaca, N.Y., 1957, p. 112.

SUGGESTED READING

Students who wish to explore the problems presented in this chapter in greater depth will easily find a rich and exciting literature, with many titles available in paperback editions. The following surveys all provide good background material. G. Parker, *Europe in Crisis, 1598–1618* (1980), provides a sound introduction to the social, economic, and religious tensions of the period. R. S. Dunn, *The Age of Religious Wars, 1559–1715,* 2nd ed. (1979), examines the period from the perspective of the confessional strife between Protestants and Catholics, but there is also stimulating material on absolutism and constitutionalism. T. Aston, ed., *Crisis in Europe, 1560–1660* (1967), contains essays by leading historians. P. Anderson, *Lineages of the Absolutist State* (1974), is a Marxist interpretation of absolutism in western and eastern Europe. M. Beloff, *The Age of Absolutism* (1967), concentrates on the social forces that underlay administrative change. H. Rosenberg, "Absolute Monarchy and Its Legacy," in *Early Modern Europe, 1450–1650,* ed. N. F. Cantor and S. Werthman (1967), is a seminal study. The classic treatment of constitutionalism remains that of C. H. McIlwain, *Constitutionalism: Ancient and Modern* (1940), written by a great scholar during the rise of German fascism. S. B. Crimes, *English Constitutional History* (1967), is an excellent survey with useful chapters on the sixteenth and seventeenth centuries.

Louis XIV and his age have predictably attracted the attention of many scholars. J. Wolf, *Louis XIV* (1968), remains the best available biography. Two works of W. H. Lewis, *The Splendid Century* (1957) and *The Sunset of the Splendid Century* (1963), make delightful light reading, especially for the beginning student. The advanced student will want to consult W. F. Church, *Louis XIV in Historical Thought: From Voltaire to the Annales School* (1976), an excellent historiographical analysis. Perhaps the best work of the Annales school on the period is P. Goubert, *Louis XIV and Twenty Million Frenchmen* (1972), and his heavily detailed *The Ancien Regime: French Society, 1600–1750,* 2 vols. (1969–1973), which contains invaluable material on the lives and work of ordinary people. For the French economy and financial conditions, the old study of C. W. Cole, *Colbert and a Century of French Mercantilism,* 2 vols. (1939), is still valuable but should be supplemented by R. Bonney, *The King's Debts: Finance and Politics in France, 1589–1661* (1981); A. Trout, *Jean-Baptiste Colbert* (1978); and especially W. Scoville, *The Persecution of the Huguenots and French Economic Decline, 1680–1720* (1960), a significant book in revisionist history. For Louis XIV's foreign policy and wars, see R. Hatton, "Louis XIV: Recent Gains in Historical Knowledge," *Journal of Modern History* 45 (1973), and her edited work *Louis XIV and Europe* (1976), an important collection of essays. Hatton's *Europe in the Age of Louis XIV* (1979) is a splendidly illustrated survey of many aspects of seventeenth-century European culture. O. Ranum, *Paris in the Age of Absolutism* (1968), describes the geographical, political, economic, and architectural significance of the cultural capital of Europe, while V. L. Tapie, *The Age of Grandeur: Baroque Art and Architecture* (1960), also emphasizes the relationship between art and politics with excellent illustrations.

For Spain and Portugal, see J. H. Elliott, *Imperial Spain, 1469–1716,* rev. ed. (1977), a sensitively written and authoritative study; B. Bennassar, *The Spanish Character: Attitudes and Mentalities from the Sixteenth to the Nineteenth Century* (trans. B. Keen, 1979); and M. Defourneaux, *Daily Life in Spain in the Golden Age* (1976), which are highly useful for an understanding of ordinary people and of Spanish society; and C. R. Phillips, *Ciudad Real, 1570–1750: Growth, Crisis, and Readjustment in the Spanish Economy* (1979), a significant case study.

The following works all offer solid material on English political and social issues of the seventeenth century: M. Ashley, *England in the Seventeenth Century*, rev. ed. (1980) and *The House of Stuart: Its Rise and Fall* (1980); C. Hill, *A Century of Revolution* (1961); J. P. Kenyon, *Stuart England* (1978); and K. Wrightson, *English Society, 1580–1680* (1982). Perhaps the most comprehensive treatment of Parliament is C. Russell, *Crisis of Parliaments, 1509–1660* (1971) and *Parliaments and English Politics, 1621–1629* (1979). On the background of the English civil war, L. Stone, *The Crisis of the Aristocracy* (1965) and *The Causes of the English Revolution* (1972) are standard works, while both B. Manning, *The English People and the English Revolution* (1976), and D. Underdown, *Revel, Riot, and Rebellion* (1985), discuss the extent of popular involvement; Underdown's is the more sophisticated treatment. For English intellectual currents, see J. O. Appleby, *Economic Thought and Ideology in Seventeenth Century England* (1978); and C. Hill, *Intellectual Origins of the English Revolution* (1966) and *Society and Puritanism in Pre-Revolutionary England* (1964).

For the several shades of Protestant sentiment in the early seventeenth century, see P. Collinson, *The Religion of Protestants* (1982). C. M. Hibbard, *Charles I and the Popish Plot* (1983), treats Roman Catholic influence; like Collinson's work, it is an excellent, fundamental reference for religious issues, though the older work of W. Haller, *The Rise of Puritanism* (1957), is still valuable. For women, see R. Thompson, *Women in Stuart England and America* (1974), and A. Fraser, *The Weaker Vessel* (1985). For Cromwell and the Interregnum, C. Firth, *Oliver Cromwell and the Rule of the Puritans in England* (1956), C. Hill, *God's Englishman* (1972), and A. Fraser, *Cromwell, The Lord Protector* (1973), are all valuable. J. Morrill, *The Revolt of the Provinces*, 2nd ed. (1980), is the best study of neutralism, while C. Hill, *The World Turned Upside Down* (1972), discusses radical thought during the period.

For the Restoration and the Glorious Revolution, see A. Fraser, *Royal Charles: Charles II and the Restoration* (1979), a highly readable biography; R. Ollard, *The Image of the King: Charles I and Charles II* (1980), which examines the nature of monarchy; J. Miller, *James II: A Study in Kingship* (1977); J. Childs, *The Army, James II, and the Glorious Revolution* (1980); J. R. Jones, *The Revolution of 1688 in England* (1972); and L. G. Schwoerer, *The Declaration of Rights, 1689* (1981), a fine assessment of that fundamental document. The ideas of John Locke are analyzed by J. P. Kenyon, *Revolution Principles: The Politics of Party, 1689–1720* (1977). R. Hutton, *The Restoration, 1658–1667* (1985), is a thorough if somewhat difficult narrative.

On Holland, K. H. D. Haley, *The Dutch Republic in the Seventeenth Century* (1972), is a splendidly illustrated appreciation of Dutch commercial and artistic achievements, while J. L. Price, *Culture and Society in the Dutch Republic During the Seventeenth Century* (1974), is a sound scholarly work. R. Boxer, *The Dutch Seaborne Empire* (1980), and the appropriate chapters of D. Maland, *Europe in the Seventeenth Century* (1967), are useful for Dutch overseas expansion and the reasons for Dutch prosperity. The following works focus on the economic and cultural life of the leading Dutch city: V. Barbour, *Capitalism in Amsterdam in the Seventeenth Century* (1950), and D. Regin, *Traders, Artists, Burghers: A Cultural History of Amsterdam in the Seventeenth Century* (1977). J. M. Montias, *Artists and Artisans in Delft: A Socio-Economic Study of the Seventeenth Century* (1982), examines another major city. The leading statesmen of the period may be studied in these biographies: H. H. Rowen, *John de Witt, Grand Pensionary of Holland, 1625–1672* (1978); S. B. Baxter, *William the III and the Defense of European Liberty, 1650–1702* (1966); and J. den Tex, *Oldenbarnevelt*, 2 vols. (1973).

Many facets of the lives of ordinary French, Spanish, English, and Dutch people are discussed by P. Burke, *Popular Culture in Early Modern Europe* (1978), an important and provocative study.

17

**ABSOLUTISM IN
EASTERN EUROPE
TO 1740**

*T*HE SEVENTEENTH century witnessed a struggle between constitutionalism and absolutism in eastern Europe. With the notable exception of the kingdom of Poland, monarchial absolutism was everywhere triumphant in eastern Europe; constitutionalism was decisively defeated. Absolute monarchies emerged in Austria, Prussia, and Russia. This was a development of great significance: these three monarchies exercised enormous influence until 1918, and they created a strong authoritarian tradition that is still dominant in eastern Europe.

Although the monarchs of eastern Europe were greatly impressed by Louis XIV and his model of royal absolutism, their states differed in several important ways from their French counterpart. Louis XIV built French absolutism on the heritage of a well-developed medieval monarchy and a strong royal bureaucracy. And when Louis XIV came to the throne, the powers of the nobility were already somewhat limited, the French middle-class was relatively strong, and the peasants were generally free from serfdom. Eastern absolutism rested on a very different social reality: a powerful nobility, a weak middle class, and an oppressed peasantry composed of serfs.

These differences in social conditions raise three major questions. First, why did the basic structure of society in eastern Europe move away from that of western Europe in the early modern period? Second, how and why, in their different social environments, did the rulers of Austria, Prussia, and Russia manage to build powerful absolute monarchies, which proved more durable than that of Louis XIV? Finally, how did the absolute monarchs' interaction with artists and architects contribute to the splendid achievements of baroque culture? These are the questions that will be explored in this chapter.

LORDS AND PEASANTS IN EASTERN EUROPE

When absolute monarchy took shape in eastern Europe in the seventeenth century, it built on social and economic foundations laid between roughly 1400 and 1650. In those years, the princes and the landed nobility of eastern Europe rolled back the gains made by the peasantry during the High Middle Ages and reimposed a harsh serfdom on the rural masses. The nobility also reduced the importance of the towns and the middle classes. This process differed profoundly from developments in western Europe at the same time. In the west, peasants won greater freedom and the urban capitalistic middle class continued its rise. Thus, the east that emerged contrasted sharply with the west—another aspect of the shattered unity of medieval Latin Christendom.

THE MEDIEVAL BACKGROUND

Between roughly 1400 and 1650, nobles and rulers re-established serfdom in the eastern lands of Bohemia, Silesia, Hungary, eastern Germany, Poland, Lithuania, and Russia. The east—the land east of the Elbe River in Germany, which historians often call "East Elbia"—gained a certain social and economic unity in the process. But eastern peasants lost their rights and freedoms. They became bound first to the land they worked and then, by degrading obligations, to the lords they served.

This development was a tragic reversal of trends in the High Middle Ages. The period from roughly 1050 to 1300 had been a time of general economic expansion characterized by the growth of trade, towns, and population. Expansion also meant clearing the forests and colonizing the frontier beyond the Elbe River. Anxious to attract German settlers to their sparsely populated lands, the rulers and nobles of eastern Europe had offered potential newcomers attractive economic and legal incentives. Large numbers of incoming settlers obtained land on excellent terms and gained much greater personal freedom. These benefits were also gradually extended to the local Slavic populations, even those of central Russia. Thus by 1300 there had occurred a very general improvement in peasant conditions in eastern Europe. Serfdom all but disappeared. Peasants bargained freely with their landlords and moved about as they pleased. Opportunities and improvements east of the Elbe had a positive impact on western Europe, where the weight of serfdom was also reduced between 1100 and 1300.

After about 1300, however, as Europe's population and economy both declined grievously, mainly because of the Black Death, the east and the west went in different directions. In both east and west there occurred a many-sided landlord reaction, as lords sought to solve their tough economic problems by more heavily exploiting the peasantry. Yet this reaction generally failed in the west. In many western areas by 1500 almost all of the peasants were completely free, and in the rest of western Europe serf obligations had declined greatly. East of the Elbe, however, the landlords won. By 1500 eastern peasants were well on their way to becoming serfs again.

Throughout eastern Europe, as in western Europe, the drop in population and prices in the fourteenth and fifteenth centuries caused severe labor shortages and hard times for the nobles. Yet rather than offer better economic and legal terms to keep old peasants and attract new ones, eastern landlords used their political and police power to turn the tables on the peasants. They did this in two ways.

First, the lords made their kings and princes issue laws that restricted or eliminated the peasants' precious, time-honored right of free movement. Thus, a peasant could no longer leave to take advantage of better opportunities elsewhere without the lord's permission, and the lord had no reason to make such concessions. In Prussian territories by 1500, the law required that runaway peasants be hunted down and returned to their lords; a runaway servant was to be nailed to a post by one ear and given a knife to cut himself loose. Until the middle of the fifteenth century, medieval Russian peasants had been free to move wherever they wished and seek the best landlord. Thereafter this freedom was gradually curtailed, so that by 1497 a Russian peasant had the right to move only during a two-week period after the fall harvest. Eastern peasants were losing their status as free and independent men and women.

Second, lords steadily took more and more of their peasants' land and imposed heavier and heavier labor obligations. Instead of being independent farmers paying reasonable, freely negotiated rents, peasants tended to become forced laborers on the lords' estates. By the early 1500s, lords in many territories could command their peasants to work for them without pay as many as six days a week. A German writer of the mid-sixteenth century described peasants in eastern Prussia who "do not possess the heritage of their holdings and have to serve their master whenever he wants them."[1]

The gradual erosion of the peasantry's economic position was bound up with manipulation of the legal system. The local lord was also the local prosecutor, judge, and jailer. As a matter of course, he ruled in his own favor in disputes with his peasants. There were no independent royal officials to provide justice or uphold the common law.

THE CONSOLIDATION OF SERFDOM

Between 1500 and 1650, the social, legal, and economic conditions of peasants in eastern Europe continued to decline. Free peasants lost their freedom and became serfs. In Poland, for example, nobles gained complete control over their peasants in 1574, after which they could legally inflict the death penalty on their serfs whenever they wished. In Prussia a long series of oppressive measures reached their culmination in 1653. Not only were all the old privileges of the lords reaffirmed, but peasants were assumed to be in "hereditary subjugation" to their lords unless they could prove the contrary in the lords' courts, which was practically impossible. Prussian peasants were serfs tied to their lords as well as to the land.

In Russia the right of peasants to move from a given estate was "temporarily" suspended in the 1590s and permanently abolished in 1603. In 1649 a new law code completed the process. At the insistence of the lower nobility, the Russian tsar lifted the nine-year time limit on the recovery of runaways. Henceforth runaway peasants were to be returned to their lords whenever they were caught, as long as they lived. The last small hope of escaping serfdom was gone. Control of serfs was strictly the lords' own business, for the new law code set no limits on the lords' authority over their peasants. Although the political development of the various eastern states differed, the legal re-establishment of permanent hereditary serfdom was the common fate of peasants in the east by the middle of the seventeenth century.

The consolidation of serfdom between 1500 and 1650 was accompanied by the growth of estate agriculture, particularly in Poland and eastern Germany. In the sixteenth century, European economic expansion and population growth resumed after the great declines of the late Middle Ages. Prices for agricultural commodities also rose sharply as gold and silver flowed in from the New World. Thus Polish and German lords had powerful economic incentives to increase the production of their estates. And they did.

Lords seized more and more peasant land for their own estates and then demanded and received ever more unpaid serf labor on those enlarged estates.

Punishing Serfs This seventeenth-century illustration from Olearius's famous *Travels to Moscovy* suggests what eastern serfdom really meant. The scene is set in eastern Poland. There, according to Olearius, a common command of the lord was, "Beat him till the skin falls from the flesh." *(Photo: Caroline Buckler)*

Even when the estates were inefficient and technically backward, as they generally were, the great Polish nobles and middle-rank German lords squeezed sizable, cheap, and thus very profitable surpluses out of their impoverished peasants. These surpluses in wheat and timber were easily sold to big foreign merchants, who exported them to the growing cities of the west. The poor east helped feed the much wealthier west.

The re-emergence of serfdom in eastern Europe in the early modern period was clearly a momentous human development, and historians have advanced a variety of explanations for it. As always, some scholars have stressed the economic interpretation. Agricultural depression and population decline in the fourteenth and fifteenth centuries led to a severe labor shortage, they have argued, and thus eastern landlords naturally tied their precious peasants to the land. With the return of prosperity and the development of export markets in the sixteenth century, the landlords finished the job, grabbing the peasants' land and making them work as unpaid serfs on the enlarged estates. This argument by itself is not very convincing, for almost identical economic developments "caused" the opposite result in the west. Indeed, some historians have maintained that labor shortage and subsequent expansion were key factors in the virtual disappearance of Western serfdom.

It seems fairly clear, therefore, that political rather than economic factors were crucial in the simultaneous rise of serfdom in the east and decline of serfdom in the west. Specifically, eastern lords enjoyed much greater political power than their western counterparts. In the late Middle Ages, when much of eastern

Europe experienced innumerable wars and general political chaos, the noble landlord class greatly increased its political power at the expense of the ruling monarchs. There were, for example, many disputed royal successions, so that weak kings were forced to grant political favors to win the support of the nobility. Thus while strong "new monarchs" were rising in Spain, France, and England and providing effective central government, kings were generally losing power in the east. Such weak kings could not resist the demands of the lords regarding their peasants.

Moreover, most eastern monarchs did not want to resist even if they could. The typical king was only first among equals in the noble class. He, too, thought mainly in private rather than public terms. He, too, wanted to squeeze as much as he could out of *his* peasants and enlarge *his* estates. The western concept and reality of sovereignty, as embodied in a king who protected the interests of all his people, was not well developed in eastern Europe before 1650.

The political power of the peasants was also weaker in eastern Europe and declined steadily after about 1400. Although there were occasional bloody peasant uprisings against the oppression of the landlords, they never succeeded. Nor did eastern peasants effectively resist day-by-day infringements on their liberties by their landlords. Part of the reason was that the lords, rather than the kings, ran the courts—one of the important concessions nobles extorted from weak monarchs. It has also been suggested that peasant solidarity was weaker in the east, possibly reflecting the lack of long-established village communities on the eastern frontier.

Finally, with the approval of weak kings, the landlords systematically undermined the medieval privileges of the towns and the power of the urban classes. Instead of selling their products to local merchants in the towns, as required in the Middle Ages, the landlords sold directly to big foreign capitalists. For example, Dutch ships sailed up the rivers of Poland and eastern Germany to the loading docks of the great estates, completely short-circuiting the local towns. Moreover, "town air" no longer "made people free," for the eastern towns lost their medieval right of refuge and were compelled to return runaways to their lords. The population of the towns and the importance of the urban middle classes declined greatly. This development both reflected and promoted the supremacy of noble landlords in most of eastern Europe in the sixteenth century.

THE RISE OF AUSTRIA AND PRUSSIA

Despite the strength of the nobility and the weakness of many monarchs before 1600, strong kings did begin to emerge in many lands in the course of the seventeenth century. War and the threat of war aided rulers greatly in their attempts to build absolute monarchies. There was an endless struggle for power, as eastern rulers not only fought each other but also battled with hordes of Asiatic invaders. In this atmosphere of continuous wartime emergency, monarchs reduced the political power of the landlord nobility. Cautiously leaving the nobles the unchallenged masters of their peasants, the absolutist monarchs of eastern Europe gradually gained and monopolized political power in three key areas. They imposed and collected permanent taxes without consent. They maintained permanent standing armies, which policed their subjects in addition to fighting abroad. And they conducted relations with other states as they pleased.

As with all general historical developments, there were important variations on the absolutist theme in eastern Europe. The royal absolutism created in Prussia was stronger and more effective than that established in Austria. This advantage gave Prussia a thin edge over Austria in the struggle for power in east-central Europe in the eighteenth century. That edge had enormous long-term political significance, for it was a rising Prussia that unified the German people in the nineteenth century and imposed on them a fateful Prussian stamp.

AUSTRIA AND THE OTTOMAN TURKS

Like all the peoples and rulers of central Europe, the Habsburgs of Austria emerged from the Thirty Years' War (pages 483–489) impoverished and exhausted. The effort to root out Protestantism in the German lands had failed utterly, and the authority of the Holy Roman Empire and its Habsburg emperors had declined almost to the vanishing point. Yet defeat in central Europe also opened new vistas. The Habsburg monarchs were forced to turn inward and eastward in the attempt to fuse their diverse holdings into a strong unified state.

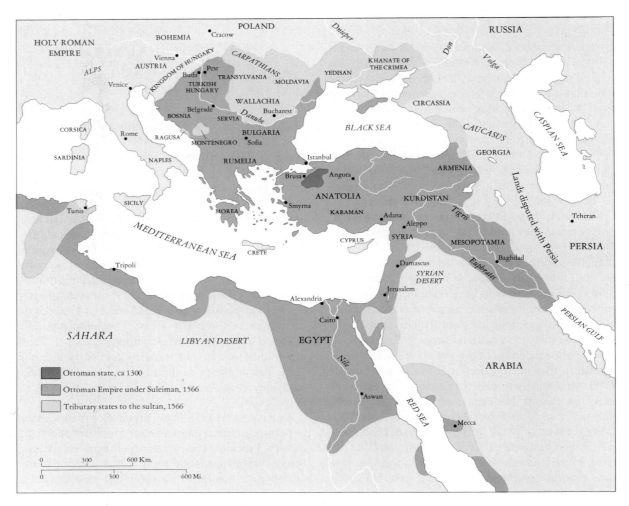

MAP 17.1 The Ottoman Empire at Its Height, 1566 The Ottomans, like their great rivals the Habsburgs, rose to rule a far-flung dynastic empire encompassing many different peoples and ethnic groups. The army and the bureaucracy served to unite the disparate territories into a single state.

An important step in this direction had actually been taken in Bohemia during the Thirty Years' War. Protestantism had been strong among the Czechs of Bohemia, and in 1618 the Czech nobles who controlled the Bohemian Estates—the semiparliamentary body of Bohemia—had risen up against their Habsburg king. Not only was this revolt crushed, but the old Czech nobility was wiped out as well. Those Czech nobles who did not die in 1620 at the Battle of the White Mountain (page 484), a momentous turning point in Czech history, had their estates confiscated. The Habsburg king, Ferdinand II (1619–

1637), then redistributed the Czech lands to a motley band of aristocratic soldiers of fortune from all over Europe.

In fact, after 1650, 80 to 90 percent of the Bohemian nobility was of recent foreign origin and owed everything to the Habsburgs. With the help of this new nobility, the Habsburgs established strong direct rule over reconquered Bohemia. The condition of the enserfed peasantry worsened: three days per week of unpaid labor—the *robot*—became the norm, and a quarter of the serfs worked for their lords every day but Sundays and religious holidays. Serfs also paid

The Ottoman Slave Tax This contemporary drawing shows Ottoman officials rounding up male Christian children in the Balkans. The children became part of a special slave corps, which served the sultan for life as soldiers and administrators. The slave tax and the slave corps were of great importance to the Ottoman Turks in the struggle with Austria. *(The British Museum)*

the taxes, which further strengthened the alliance between the Habsburg monarch and the Bohemian nobility. Protestantism was also stamped out, in the course of which a growing unity of religion was brought about. The reorganization of Bohemia was a giant step toward absolutism.

After the Thirty Years' War, Ferdinand III centralized the government in the old hereditary provinces of Austria proper, the second part of the Habsburg holdings. For the first time, under Ferdinand was created a permanent standing army, which stood ready to put down any internal opposition. The Habsburg

monarchy was then ready to turn toward the vast plains of Hungary, which it claimed as the third and largest part of its dominion, in opposition to the Ottoman Turks.

The Ottomans came out of the Anatolia, in present-day Turkey, to create one of history's greatest military empires. At their peak in the middle of the sixteenth century under Suleiman the Magnificent (1520–1566), they ruled the most powerful empire in the world. Their possessions stretched from western Persia across North Africa and up into the heart of central Europe (see Map 17.1). Apostles of Islam, the

Ottoman Turks were old and determined foes of the Catholic Habsburgs. Their armies had almost captured Vienna in 1529, and for more than 150 years thereafter the Ottomans ruled all of the Balkan territories, almost all of Hungary, and part of southern Russia.

The Ottoman Empire was originally built on a fascinating and very non-European conception of state and society. There was an almost complete absence of private landed property. All the agricultural land of the empire was the personal hereditary property of the sultan, who exploited the land as he saw fit according to Ottoman political theory. There was, therefore, no security of landholding and no hereditary nobility. Everyone was dependent on the sultan and virtually his slave.

Indeed, the top ranks of the bureaucracy were staffed by the sultan's slave corps. Every year the sultan levied a "tax" of one to three thousand male children on the conquered Christian populations in the Balkans. These and other slaves were raised in Turkey as Muslims and trained to fight and to administer. The most talented slaves rose to the top of the bureaucracy; the less fortunate formed the brave and skillful core of the sultan's army, the so-called janissary corps.

As long as the Ottoman Empire expanded, the system worked well. As the sultan won more territory, he could impose his slave tax on larger populations. Moreover, he could amply reward loyal and effective servants by letting them draw a carefully defined income from conquered Christian peasants on a strictly temporary basis. For a long time, Christian peasants in eastern Europe were economically exploited less by the Muslim Turks than by Christian nobles, and they were not forced to convert to Islam. After about 1570, however, the powerful, centralized Ottoman system slowly began to disintegrate as the Turks' western advance was stopped. Temporary landholders became hard-to-control permanent oppressors. Weak sultans left the glory of the battlefield for the delights of the harem, and the army lost its dedication and failed to keep up with European military advances.

Yet in the late seventeenth century, under vigorous reforming leadership, the Ottoman Empire succeeded in marshaling its forces for one last mighty blow at Christian Europe. After wresting territory from Poland, fighting a long inconclusive war with Russia, and establishing an alliance with Louis XIV of France, the Turks turned again on Austria. A huge Turkish army surrounded Vienna and laid siege to it in 1683. But after holding out against great odds for two months, the city was relieved by a mixed force of Habsburg, Saxon, Bavarian, and Polish troops, and the Ottomans were forced to retreat. Soon the retreat became a rout. As their Russian and Venetian allies attacked on other fronts, the Habsburgs conquered all of Hungary and Transylvania (part of present-day Rumania) by 1699 (see Map 17.2).

The Turkish wars and this great expansion strengthened the Habsburg army and promoted some sense of unity in the Habsburg lands. The Habsburgs moved to centralize their power and make it as absolute as possible. These efforts to create a fully developed, highly centralized, absolutist state were only partly successful.

The Habsburg state was composed of three separate and distinct territories—the old "hereditary provinces" of Austria, the kingdom of Bohemia, and the kingdom of Hungary. These three parts were tied together primarily by their common ruler—the Habsburg monarch. Each part had its own laws and political life, for the three noble-dominated Estates continued to exist, though with reduced powers. The Habsburgs themselves were well aware of the fragility of the union they had forged. In 1713 Charles VI (1711–1740) proclaimed the so-called Pragmatic Sanction, which stated that the Habsburg possessions were never to be divided and were always to be passed intact to a single heir, who might be female since Charles had no sons. Charles spent much of his reign trying to get this principle accepted by the various branches of the Habsburg family, by the three different Estates of the realm, and by the states of Europe. His fears turned out to be well founded.

The Hungarian nobility, despite its reduced strength, effectively thwarted the full development of Habsburg absolutism. Time and again throughout the seventeenth century, Hungarian nobles—the most numerous in Europe, making up 5 to 7 percent of the Hungarian population—rose in revolt against the attempts of Vienna to impose absolute rule. They never triumphed decisively, but neither were they ever crushed and replaced, as the Czech nobility had been in 1620.

Hungarians resisted because many of them were Protestants, especially in the area long ruled by the more tolerant Turks, and they hated the heavy-handed attempts of the conquering Habsburgs to re-

The Siege of Vienna, 1683 The Turks dreamed of establishing a western Muslim Empire in the heart of Europe. But their army of nearly 300,000 men failed to pierce the elaborate fortifications that protected the old city walls from cannon fire and underground mines. *(BBC Hulton Pictures Library/The Bettmann Archive)*

Catholicize everyone. Moreover, the lords of Hungary often found a powerful military ally in Turkey. Finally, the Hungarian nobility, and even part of the peasantry, had become attached to a national ideal long before most of the peoples of Europe. They were determined to maintain as much independence and local control as possible. Thus when the Habsburgs were bogged down in the War of the Spanish Succession (page 520), the Hungarians rose in one last patriotic rebellion under Prince Francis Rakoczy in 1703. Rakoczy and his forces were eventually defeated, but this time the Habsburgs had to accept a definitive compromise. Charles VI restored many of the traditional privileges of the Hungarian aristocracy in return for Hungarian acceptance of hereditary Habsburg rule. Thus Hungary, unlike Austria or Bohemia, never came close to being fully integrated into a centralized, absolute Habsburg state.

PRUSSIA IN THE SEVENTEENTH CENTURY

After 1400 the status of east German peasants declined steadily; their serfdom was formally spelled out in the early seventeenth century. While the local princes lost political power and influence, a revitalized landed nobility became the undisputed ruling class. The Hohenzollern family, which ruled through its senior and junior branches as the electors of Brandenburg and the dukes of Prussia, had little real princely power. The Hohenzollern rulers were nothing more than the first among equals, the largest landowners in a landlord society.

Nothing suggested that the Hohenzollerns and their territories would ever play an important role in European or even German affairs. The elector of Brandenburg's right to help choose the Holy Roman

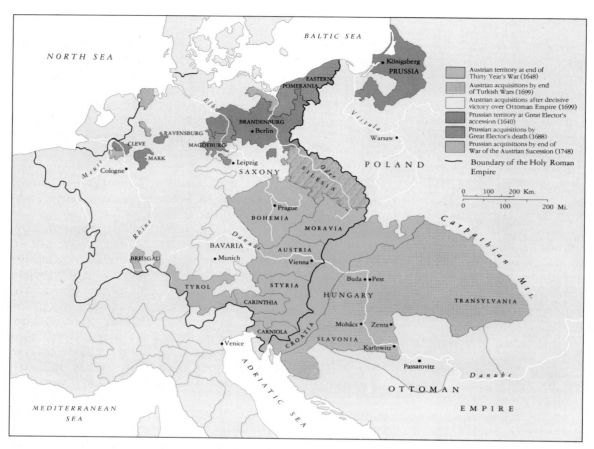

MAP 17.2 The Growth of Austria and Brandenburg-Prussia to 1748 Austria expanded
to the southwest into Hungary and Transylvania at the expense of the Ottoman Empire.
It was unable to hold the rich German province of Silesia, however, which was
conquered by Brandenburg-Prussia.

emperor with six other electors was of little practical
value, and the elector had no military strength whatsoever. The territory of his cousin, the duke of Prussia, was actually part of the kingdom of Poland.
Moreover, geography conspired against the Hohenzollerns. Brandenburg, their power base, was completely cut off from the sea (see Map 17.2). A tiny
part of the vast north European plain that stretches
from France to Russia, Brandenburg lacked natural
frontiers and lay open to attack from all directions.
The land was poor, a combination of sand and
swamp. Contemporaries contemptuously called
Brandenburg the "sand-box of the Holy Roman Empire."[2]

Brandenburg was a helpless spectator in the Thirty
Years' War, its territory alternately ravaged by Swedish and Habsburg armies. Population fell drastically,

and many villages disappeared. The power of the Hohenzollerns reached its lowest point. Yet the devastation of the country prepared the way for Hohenzollern absolutism, because foreign armies dramatically
weakened the political power of the Estates—the representative assemblies of the realm. This weakening
of the Estates helped the very talented young elector
Frederick William (1640–1688), later known as the
"Great Elector," to ride roughshod over traditional
parliamentary liberties and to take a giant step toward royal absolutism. This constitutional struggle,
often unjustly neglected by historians, was the most
crucial in Prussian history for hundreds of years,
until that of the 1860s.

When he came to power in 1640, the twenty-year-
old Great Elector was determined to unify his three
quite separate provinces and to add to them by diplo-

macy and war. These provinces were historic Brandenburg, the area around Berlin; Prussia, inherited in 1618 when the junior branch of the Hohenzollern family died out; and completely separate, scattered holdings along the Rhine in western Germany, inherited in 1614 (see Map 17.2). Each of the three provinces was inhabited by Germans; but each had its own Estates, whose power had increased until about 1600 as the power of the rulers declined. Although the Estates had not met regularly during the chaotic Thirty Years' War, they still had the power of the purse in their respective provinces. Taxes could not be levied without their consent. The Estates of Brandenburg and Prussia were dominated by the nobility and the landowning classes, known as the "Junkers." But it must be remembered that this was also true of the English Parliament before and after the civil war. Had the Estates successfully resisted the absolutist demands of the Great Elector, they, too, might have evolved toward more broadly based constitutionalism.

The struggle between the Great Elector and the provincial Estates was long, complicated, and intense. After the Thirty Years' War, the representatives of the nobility zealously reasserted the right of the Estates to vote taxes, a right the Swedish armies of occupation had simply ignored. Yet first in Brandenburg in 1653 and then in Prussia between 1661 and 1663, the Great Elector eventually had his way.

To pay for the permanent standing army he first established in 1660, Frederick William forced the Estates to accept the introduction of permanent taxation without consent. Moreover, the soldiers doubled as tax collectors and policemen, becoming the core of the rapidly expanding state bureaucracy. The power of the Estates declined rapidly thereafter, for the Great Elector had both financial independence and superior force. He turned the screws of taxation: the state's total revenue tripled during his reign. The size of the army leaped about tenfold. In 1688 a population of one million was supporting a peacetime standing army of thirty thousand. Many of the soldiers were French Huguenot immigrants, whom the Great Elector welcomed as the talented, hardworking citizens they were.

In accounting for the Great Elector's fateful triumph, two factors appear central. As in the formation of every absolutist state, war was a decisive factor. The ongoing struggle between Sweden and Poland for control of the Baltic after 1648 and the wars of Louis XIV in western Europe created an atmosphere of permanent crisis. The wild Tartars of southern Russia swept through Prussia in the winter of 1656 to 1657, killing and carrying off as slaves more than fifty thousand people, according to an old estimate. This invasion softened up the Estates and strengthened the urgency of the elector's demands for more money for more soldiers. It was no accident that, except for commercially minded Holland, constitutionalism won out only in England, the only major country to escape devastating foreign invasions in the seventeenth century.

Second, the nobility had long dominated the government through the Estates, but only for its own narrow self-interest. When the crunch came, the Prussian nobles proved unwilling to join the representatives of the towns in a consistent common front against royal pretensions. The nobility was all too concerned with its own rights and privileges, especially its freedom from taxation and its unlimited control over the peasants. When, therefore, the Great Elector reconfirmed these privileges in 1653 and after, even while reducing the political power of the Estates, the nobility growled but did not bite. It accepted a compromise whereby the bulk of the new taxes fell on towns, and royal authority stopped at the landlords' gates. The elector could and did use naked force to break the liberties of the towns. The main leader of the urban opposition in the key city of Königsberg, for example, was simply arrested and imprisoned for life without trial.

THE CONSOLIDATION OF PRUSSIAN ABSOLUTISM

By the time of his death in 1688, the Great Elector had created a single state out of scattered principalities. But his new creation was still small and fragile. All the leading states of Europe had many more people—France with 20 million was fully twenty times as populous—and strong monarchy was still a novelty. Moreover, the Great Elector's successor, Elector Frederick III, "the Ostentatious" (1688–1713), was weak of body and mind.

Like so many of the small princes of Germany and Italy at the time, Frederick III imitated Louis XIV in every possible way. He built his own very expensive version of Versailles. He surrounded himself with cultivated artists and musicians and basked in the praise of toadies and sycophants. His only real politi-

Molding the Prussian Spirit Discipline was strict and punishment brutal in the Prussian army. This scene, from an eighteenth-century book used to teach school children, shows one soldier being flogged while another is being beaten with canes as he walks between rows of troops. The officer on horseback proudly commands. *(Photo: Caroline Buckler)*

cal accomplishment was to gain the title of king from the Holy Roman emperor, a Habsburg, in return for military aid in the War of the Spanish Succession, and in 1701 he was crowned King Frederick I.

This tendency toward luxury-loving, happy, and harmless petty tyranny was completely reversed by Frederick William I, "the Soldiers' King" (1713–1740). A crude, dangerous psychoneurotic, Frederick William I was nevertheless the most talented reformer ever produced by the Hohenzollern family. It was he who truly established Prussian absolutism and

gave it its unique character. It was he who created the the best army in Europe, for its size, and who infused military values into a whole society. In the words of a leading historian of Prussia:

For a whole generation, the Hohenzollern subjects were victimized by a royal bully, imbued with an obsessive bent for military organization and military scales of value. This left a deep mark upon the institutions of Prussiandom and upon the molding of the "Prussian spirit."[3]

Frederick William's passion for the army and military life was intensely emotional. He had, for example, a bizarre, almost pathological love for tall soldiers, whom he credited with superior strength and endurance. Austere and always faithful to his wife, he confided to the French ambassador: "The most beautiful girl or woman in the world would be a matter of indifference to me, but tall soldiers—they are my weakness." Like some fanatical modern-day basketball coach in search of a championship team, he sent his agents throughout both Prussia and all of Europe, tricking, buying, and kidnapping top recruits. Neighboring princes sent him their giants as gifts to win his gratitude. Prussian mothers told their sons: "Stop growing or the recruiting agents will get you."[4]

Profoundly military in temperament, Frederick William always wore an army uniform, and he lived the highly disciplined life of the professional soldier. He began his work by five or six in the morning; at ten he almost always went to the parade ground to drill or inspect his troops. A man of violent temper, Frederick William personally punished the most minor infractions on the spot: a missing button off a soldier's coat quickly provoked a savage beating with his heavy walking stick.

Frederick William's love of the army was also based on a hardheaded conception of the struggle for power and a dog-eat-dog view of international politics. Even before ascending the throne, he bitterly criticized his father's ministers: "They say that they will obtain land and power for the king with the pen; but I say it can be done only with the sword." Years later he summed up his life's philosophy in his instructions to his son: "A formidable army and a war chest large enough to make this army mobile in times of need can create great respect for you in the world, so that you can speak a word like the other powers."[5] This unshakable belief that the welfare of king and state depended on the army above all else reinforced Frederick William's personal passion for playing soldier.

The cult of military power provided the rationale for a great expansion of royal absolutism. As the king himself put it with his characteristic ruthlessness: "I must be served with life and limb, with house and wealth, with honour and conscience, everything must be committed except eternal salvation—that belongs to God, but all else is mine."[6] To make good these extraordinary demands, Frederick William cre-

A Prussian Giant Grenadier Frederick William I wanted tall handsome soldiers, and he dressed them in tight bright uniforms to distinguish them from the peasant population from which most soldiers emerged. Grenadiers wore the distinctive mitre cap instead of an ordinary hat so that they could hurl their heavy hand grenades unimpeded by a broad brim. *(Royal Library, Windsor)*

ated a strong centralized bureaucracy. More commoners probably rose to top positions in the civil government than at any other time in Prussia's history. The last traces of the parliamentary Estates and local self-government vanished.

The king's grab for power brought him into considerable conflict with the noble landowners, the Junkers. In his early years, he even threatened to destroy them; yet in the end, the Prussian nobility was not destroyed but enlisted—into the army. Responding to a combination of threats and opportunities, the Junkers became the officer caste. By 1739 all but 5 of 245 officers with the rank of major or above were aristocrats, and most of them were native Prussians. A new compromise had been worked out, whereby the proud nobility imperiously commanded the peasantry in the army as well as on its estates.

Coarse and crude, penny-pinching and hardworking, Frederick William achieved results. Above all, he built a first-rate army on the basis of third-rate resources. The standing army increased from 38,000 to 83,000 during his reign. Prussia, twelfth in Europe in population, had the fourth largest army by 1740. Only the much more populous states of France, Russia, and Austria had larger forces, and even France's army was only twice as large as Prussia's. Moreover, soldier for soldier, the Prussian army became the best in Europe, astonishing foreign observers with its precision, skill, and discipline. For the next two hundred years, Prussia and then prussianized Germany would almost always win the crucial military battles.

Frederick William and his ministers also built an exceptionally honest and conscientious bureaucracy, which not only administered the country but tried with some success to develop it economically. Finally, like the miser he was, living very frugally off the income of his own landholdings, the king loved his "blue boys" so much that he hated to "spend" them. This most militaristic of kings was, paradoxically, almost always at peace.

Nevertheless, the Prussian people paid a heavy and lasting price for the obsessions of the royal drillmaster. Civil society became rigid and highly disciplined. Prussia became the "Sparta of the North"; unquestioning obedience was the highest virtue. As a Prussian minister later summed up, "To keep quiet is the first civic duty."[7] Thus the policies of Frederick William I combined with harsh peasant bondage and Junker tyranny to lay the foundations for probably the most militaristic country of modern times.

THE DEVELOPMENT OF RUSSIA

One of the favorite parlor games of nineteenth-century Russian (and non-Russian) intellectuals was debating whether Russia was a western European or a nonwestern Asiatic society. This question was particularly fascinating because it was unanswerable. To this day Russia differs fundamentally from the West in some basic ways, though Russian history has paralleled that of the West in other ways. A good case can be made for either position: thus the hypnotic attraction of Russian history.

The differences between Russia and the West were particularly striking before 1700, when Russia's overall development began to draw progressively closer to that of its western neighbors. These early differences and Russia's long isolation from Europe explain why little has so far been said here about Russia. Yet it is impossible to understand how Russia has increasingly influenced and been influenced by western European civilization since roughly the late seventeenth century without looking at the course of early Russian history. Such a brief survey will also help explain how, when absolute monarchy finally and decisively triumphed under the rough guidance of Peter the Great in the early eighteenth century, it was a quite different type of absolute monarchy from that of France or even Prussia.

THE VIKINGS AND THE KIEVAN PRINCIPALITY

In antiquity the Slavs lived as a single people in central Europe. With the start of the mass migrations of the late Roman Empire, the Slavs moved in different directions and split into three groups. Between the fifth and ninth centuries, the eastern Slavs, from whom the Ukrainians, the Russians, and the White Russians descend, moved into the vast and practically uninhabited area of present-day European Russia and the Ukraine (see Map 17.3).

This enormous area consisted of an immense virgin forest to the north, where most of the eastern Slavs settled, and an endless prairie grassland to the south. Probably organized as tribal communities, the eastern Slavs, like many North American pioneers much later, lived off the great abundance of wild game and a crude "slash and burn" agriculture. After clearing a piece of the forest to build log cabins, they burned the stumps and brush. The ashes left a rich deposit of potash and lime, and the land gave several good crops before it was exhausted. The people then moved on to another untouched area and repeated the process.

In the ninth century, the Vikings, those fearless warriors from Scandinavia, appeared in the lands of the eastern Slavs. Called "Varangians" in the old Russian chronicles, the Vikings were interested primarily in international trade, and the opportunities were good, since the Muslim conquests of the eighth century had greatly reduced Christian trade in the Mediterranean. Moving up and down the rivers, the Vikings soon linked Scandinavia and northern Europe with the Black Sea and the Byzantine Empire with its capital at Constantinople. They built a few strategic forts along the rivers, from which they raided the neighboring Slavic tribes and collected tribute. Slaves were the most important article of tribute, and *Slav* even became the word for "slave" in several European languages.

In order to increase and protect their international commerce, the Vikings declared themselves the rulers of the eastern Slavs. According to tradition, the semilegendary chieftain Ruirik founded the princely dynasty about 860. In any event, the Varangian ruler Oleg (878–912) established his residence at Kiev. He and his successors ruled over a loosely united confederation of Slavic territories—the Kievan state—until 1054. The Viking prince and his clansmen quickly became assimilated into the Slavic population, taking local wives and emerging as the noble class.

Assimilation and loss of Scandinavian ethnic identity was speeded up by the conversion of the Vikings and local Slavs to Eastern Orthodox Christianity by missionaries from the Byzantine Empire. The written language of these missionaries, Slavic—church Slavonic—was subsequently used in all religious and nonreligious documents in the Kievan principality. Thus the rapidly slavified Vikings left two important legacies for the future. They created a loose unification of Slavic territories under a single ruling prince and a single ruling dynasty. And they imposed a basic religious unity by accepting Orthodox Christianity, as opposed to Roman Catholicism, for themselves and the eastern Slavs.

Even at its height under Great Prince Iaroslav the Wise (1019–1054), the unity of the Kievan principality was extremely tenuous. Trade, rather than government, was the main concern of the rulers. Moreover, the slavified Vikings failed to find a way of peacefully transferring power from one generation to the next. In medieval western Europe this fundamental problem of government was increasingly resolved by resort to the principle of primogeniture: the king's eldest son received the crown as his rightful inheritance when his father died. Civil war was thus averted; order was preserved. In early Kiev, however, there were apparently no fixed rules and much strife accompanied each succession.

Possibly to avoid such chaos, before his death in 1054 Great Prince Iaroslav divided the Kievan principality among his five sons, who in turn divided their properties when they died. Between 1054 and 1237, Kiev disintegrated into more and more competing units, each ruled by a prince claiming to be a descendant of Ruirik. Even when only one prince was claiming to be the great prince, the whole situation was very unsettled.

The princes divided their land like private property because they thought of it as private property. A given prince owned a certain number of farms or landed estates and had them worked directly by his people, mainly slaves, called *kholops* in Russian. Outside of these estates, which constituted the princely domain, the prince exercised only very limited authority in his principality. Excluding the clergy, two kinds of people lived there: the noble *boyars* and the commoner peasants.

The boyars were the descendants of the original Viking warriors, and they also held their lands as free and clear private property. And although the boyars normally fought in princely armies, the customary law declared they could serve any prince they wished. The ordinary peasants were also truly free. The peasants could move at will wherever opportunities were greatest. In the touching phrase of the times, theirs was "a clean road, without boundaries."[8] In short, fragmented princely power, private property, and personal freedom all went together.

THE MONGOL YOKE AND THE RISE OF MOSCOW

The eastern Slavs, like the Germans and the Italians, might have emerged from the Middle Ages weak and politically divided, had it not been for a development of extraordinary importance—the Mongol conquest of the Kievan state. Wild nomadic tribes from

SIBERIA →

BARENTS SEA

NORWAY

SWEDEN

FINLAND

• Stockholm

• Helsinki

ESTONIA

BALTIC SEA

• Riga

LATVIA

LITHUANIA

Dvina

Danzig

• Königsberg

• Vilna

POLAND

• Minsk

• Warsaw

• Brest

• Pinsk

Vistula

CARPATHIAN MTS.

BESSARABIA

HUNGARY

• Belgrade

WALLACHIA

Danube

OTTOMAN

EMPIRE

• Athens

• Ankara

• Constantinople

CRIMEA

BLACK SEA

• Arkhangelsk

N. Dvina

L. Onega

L. Ladoga

St. Petersburg

Neva

N O V G O R O D

• Novgorod

• Pskov

• Smolensk

Volga

GREAT RUSSIANS

Tver

• Moscow

• Vladimir

• Nizhni Novgorod

• Ryazan

UKRAINIANS

• Chernigov

Kiev

Dniester

Dnieper

✕ Poltava

COSSACKS

Don

Tsaritsyn

• Saratov

Volga

Kama

Ural

COSSACKS

• Samara

Uralsk

KIRGHIZ

• (New) Saray

• Saray

• Astrakhan

U R A L   M T S.

Ob

ARAL SEA

CASPIAN SEA

• Tiflis

GEORGIA

ARMENIA

Principality of Moscow, ca 1300

Acquisitions by Ivan III's accession (1462)

Acquisitions under Ivan III (1462-1505)

Acquisitions by death of Ivan the Terrible (1584)

Acquisitions by Peter the Great's accession (1689)

Acquisitions under Peter the Great (1689-1725)

| 0 | 200 | 400 Km. |

| 0 | 200 | 400 Mi. |

✕ Major Battle

MAP 17.3 The Expansion of Russia to 1725 After the disintegration of the Kievan state and the Mongol conquest, the princes of Moscow and their descendants gradually extended their rule over an enormous territory.

present-day Mongolia, the Mongols were temporarily unified in the thirteenth century by Jenghiz Khan (1162–1227), one of history's greatest conquerors. In five years his armies subdued all of China. His successors then wheeled westward, smashing everything in their path and reaching the plains of Hungary victorious before they pulled back in 1242. The Mongol army—the Golden Horde—was savage in the extreme, often slaughtering the entire populations of cities before burning them to the ground. En route to Mongolia, Archbishop John of Plano Carpini, the famous papal ambassador to Mongolia, passed through Kiev in southern Russia in 1245 to 1246 and wrote an unforgettable eyewitness account:

The Mongols went against Russia and enacted a great massacre in the Russian land. They destroyed towns and fortresses and killed people. They besieged Kiev which had been the capital of Russia, and after a long siege they took it and killed the inhabitants of the city. For this reason, when we passed through that land, we found lying in the field countless heads and bones of dead people; for this city had been extremely large and very populous, whereas now it has been reduced to nothing: barely two hundred houses stand there, and those people are held in the harshest slavery.[9]

Having devastated and conquered, the Mongols ruled the eastern Slavs for more than two hundred years. They built their capital of Saray on the lower Volga (see Map 17.3). They forced all the bickering Slavic princes to submit to their rule and to give them tribute and slaves. If the conquered peoples rebelled, the Mongols were quick to punish with death and destruction. Thus, the Mongols unified the eastern Slavs, for the Mongol khan was acknowledged by all as the supreme ruler.

The Mongol unification completely changed the internal political situation. Although the Mongols conquered, they were quite willing to use local princes as their obedient servants and tax collectors. Therefore they did not abolish the title of great prince, bestowing it instead on the prince who served them best and paid them most handsomely.

Beginning with Alexander Nevsky in 1252, the previously insignificant princes of Moscow became particularly adept at serving the Mongols. They loyally put down popular uprisings and collected the khan's harsh taxes. By way of reward, the princes of Moscow emerged as hereditary great princes. Eventually the Muscovite princes were able to destroy their princely rivals and even to replace the khan as supreme ruler. In this complex process, two princes of Moscow after Alexander Nevsky—Ivan I and Ivan III—were especially noteworthy.

Ivan I (1328–1341) was popularly known as Ivan the Moneybag. A bit like Frederick William of Prussia, he was extremely stingy and built up a large personal fortune. This enabled him to buy more property and to increase his influence by loaning money to less frugal princes to pay their Mongol taxes. Ivan's most serious rival was the prince of Tver, whom the Mongols at one point appointed as great prince.

In 1327 the population of Tver revolted against Mongol oppression, and the prince of Tver joined his people. Ivan immediately went to the Mongol capital of Saray, where he was appointed commander of a large Russian-Mongol army, which then laid waste to Tver and its lands. For this proof of devotion, the Mongols made Ivan the general tax collector for all the Slavic lands they had subjugated and named him great prince. Ivan also convinced the metropolitan of Kiev, the leading churchman of all eastern Slavs, to settle in Moscow; Ivan I thus gained greater prestige, while the church gained a powerful advocate before the khan.

In the next hundred-odd years, in the course of innumerable wars and intrigues, the great princes of Moscow significantly increased their holdings. Then, in the reign of Ivan III (1462–1505), the long process was largely completed. After purchasing Rostov, Ivan conquered and annexed other principalities, of which Novgorod with its lands extending as far as the Baltic Sea was most crucial (see Map 17.3). Thus, more than four hundred years after Iaroslav the Wise had divided the embryonic Kievan state, the princes of Moscow defeated all the rival branches of the house of Ruirik to win complete princely authority.

Another dimension to princely power developed. Not only were the princes of Moscow the *unique* rulers, they were the *absolute* ruler, the autocrat, the *tsar*—the Slavic contraction for "caesar," with all its connotations. This imperious conception of absolute power is expressed in a famous letter from the aging Ivan III to the Holy Roman Emperor Frederick III (1440–1493). Frederick had offered Ivan the title of king in conjunction with the marriage of his daughter to Ivan's nephew. Ivan proudly refused:

We by the grace of God have been sovereigns over our domains from the beginning, from our first forebears, and our right we hold from God, as did our forebears. . . . As in the past we have never needed appointment from anyone, so now do we not desire it.[10]

The Muscovite idea of absolute authority was powerfully reinforced by two developments. First, about 1480 Ivan III stopped acknowledging the khan as his supreme ruler. There is good evidence to suggest that Ivan and his successors saw themselves as khans. Certainly they assimilated the Mongol concept of kingship as the exercise of unrestrained and unpredictable power.

Second, after the fall of Constantinople to the Turks in 1453, the tsars saw themselves as the heirs of both the caesars and Orthodox Christianity, the one true faith. All the other kings of Europe were heretics: only the tsars were rightful and holy rulers. This idea was promoted by Orthodox churchmen, who spoke of "holy Russia" as the "Third Rome." As the monk Pilotheus stated: "Two Romes have fallen, but the third stands, and a fourth there will not be."[11] Ivan's marriage to the daughter of the last Byzantine emperor further enhanced the aura of an eastern imperial inheritance for Moscow. Worthy successor to the mighty khan and the true Christian emperor, the Muscovite tsar was a king above all others.

TSAR AND PEOPLE TO 1689

By 1505 the great prince of Moscow—the tsar—had emerged as the single hereditary ruler of "all the Russias"—all the lands of the eastern Slavs—and he was claiming unrestricted power as his God-given right. In effect, the tsar was demanding the same kind of total authority over all his subjects that the princely descendants of Ruirik had long exercised over their slaves on their own landed estates. This was an extremely radical demand.

While peasants had begun losing their freedom of movement in the fifteenth century, so had the noble boyars begun to lose power and influence. Ivan III pi-

oneered in this regard, as in so many others. When Ivan conquered the principality of Novgorod in the 1480s, he confiscated fully 80 percent of the land, executing the previous owners or resettling them nearer Moscow. He then kept more than half of the confiscated land for himself and distributed the remainder to members of a newly emerging service nobility. The boyars had previously held their land as hereditary private property and been free to serve the prince of their choosing. The new service nobility held the tsar's land on the explicit condition that they serve in the tsar's army. Moreover, Ivan III began to require boyars outside of Novgorod to serve him if they wished to retain their lands. Since there were no competing princes left to turn to, the boyars had to yield.

The rise of the new service nobility accelerated under Ivan IV (1533–1584), the famous Ivan the Terrible. Having ascended the throne at age three, Ivan had suffered insults and neglect at the hands of the haughty boyars after his mother mysteriously died, possibly poisoned, when he was just eight. At age sixteen he suddenly pushed aside his hated boyar advisers. In an awe-inspiring ceremony, complete with gold coins pouring down on his head, he majestically crowned himself and officially took the august title of tsar for the first time.

Selecting the beautiful and kind Anastasia of the popular Romanov family for his wife and queen, the young tsar soon declared war on the remnants of Mongol power. He defeated the faltering khanates of Kazan and Astrakhan between 1552 and 1556, adding vast new territories to Russia. In the course of these wars Ivan virtually abolished the old distinction between hereditary boyar private property and land granted temporarily for service. All nobles, old and new, had to serve the tsar in order to hold any land.

The process of transforming the entire nobility into a service nobility was completed in the second part of Ivan the Terrible's reign. In 1557 Ivan turned westward, and for the next twenty-five years Muscovy waged an exhausting, unsuccessful war primarily with the large Polish-Lithuanian state, which controlled not only Poland but much of the Ukraine in the sixteenth century. Quarreling with the boyars over the war and blaming them for the sudden death of his beloved Anastasia in 1560, the increasingly cruel and demented Ivan turned to strike down all who stood in his way.

Above all, he struck down the ancient Muscovite boyars with a reign of terror. Leading boyars, their relatives, and even their peasants and servants were executed en masse by a special corps of unquestioning servants. Dressed in black and riding black horses, they were forerunners of the modern dictator's secret police. Large estates were confiscated, broken up, and reapportioned to the lower service nobility. The great boyar families were severely reduced. The newer, poorer, more nearly equal service nobility, still less than .5 percent of the total population, was totally dependent on the autocrat.

Ivan also took giant strides toward making all commoners servants of the tsar. His endless wars and demonic purges left much of central Russia depopulated. It grew increasingly difficult for the lower service nobility to squeeze a living for themselves out of the peasants left on their landholdings. As the service nobles demanded more from the remaining peasants, more and more peasants fled toward the wild, recently conquered territories to the east and south. There they formed free groups and outlaw armies known as "Cossacks." The Cossacks maintained a precarious independence beyond the reach of the oppressive landholders and the tsar's hated officials. The solution to this problem was to complete the tying of the peasants to the land, making them serfs perpetually bound to serve the noble landholders, who were bound in turn to serve the tsar.

In the time of Ivan the Terrible, urban traders and artisans were also bound to their towns and jobs, so that the tsar could tax them more heavily. Ivan assumed that the tsar owned Russia's trade and industry, just as he owned all the land. In the course of the sixteenth and seventeenth centuries, the tsars therefore took over the mines and industries and monopolized the country's important commercial activities. The urban classes had no security in their work or property, and even the wealthiest merchants were basically dependent agents of the tsar. If a new commercial activity became profitable, it was often taken over by the tsar and made a royal monopoly. This royal monopolization was in sharp contrast to developments in western Europe, where the capitalist middle classes were gaining strength and security in their private property. The tsar's service obligations checked the growth of the Russian middle classes, just as they led to decline of the boyars, rise of the lower nobility, and the final enserfment of the peasants.

St. Basil's Cathedral in Moscow, with its steeply sloping roofs and proliferation of multicolored onion-shaped domes, was a striking example of powerful Byzantine influences on Russian culture. According to tradition, an enchanted Ivan the Terrible blinded the cathedral's architects to ensure that they would never duplicate their fantastic achievement. *(The New York Public Library)*

Ivan the Terrible's system of autocracy and compulsory service struck foreign observers forcibly. Sigismund Herberstein, a German traveler to Russia, wrote in 1571: "All the people consider themselves to be *kholops,* that is slaves of their Prince." At the same time, Jean Bodin, the French thinker who did so much to develop the modern concept of sovereignty, concluded that Russia's political system was fundamentally different from those of all other European monarchies and comparable only to that of the Turkish empire. In both Turkey and Russia, as in other parts of Asia and Africa, "the prince is become lord of the goods and persons of his subjects . . . governing them as a master of a family does his slaves."[12] The Mongol inheritance weighed heavily on Russia.

As has so often occurred in Russia, the death of an iron-fisted tyrant—in this case, Ivan the Terrible in 1584—ushered in an era of confusion and violent struggles for power. Events were particularly chaotic after Ivan's son Theodore died in 1598 without an heir. The years 1598 to 1613 are aptly called the "Time of Troubles."

The close relatives of the deceased tsar intrigued against and murdered each other, alternately fighting and welcoming the invading Swedes and Poles, who even occupied Moscow. Most serious for the cause of autocracy, there was a great social upheaval as Cossack bands marched northward, rallying peasants and slaughtering nobles and officials. The mass of Cossacks and peasants called for the "true tsar," who would restore their freedom of movement and allow them to farm for whomever they pleased, who would reduce their heavy taxes and lighten the yoke imposed by the landlords.

This social explosion from below, which combined with a belated surge of patriotic opposition to Polish invaders, brought the nobles, big and small, to their senses. In 1613 they elected Ivan's sixteen-year-old grand-nephew, Michael Romanov, the new hereditary tsar. Then they rallied around him in the face of common internal and external threats. Michael's election was a real restoration, and his reign saw the gradual re-establishment of tsarist autocracy. Michael was understandably more kindly disposed toward the supportive nobility than toward the sullen peasants. Thus, while peasants were completely enserfed in 1649, Ivan's heavy military obligations on the nobility were relaxed considerably. In the long reign of Michael's successor, the pious Alexis (1645–1676), this asymmetry of obligations was accentuated. The nobility gained more exemptions from military service, while the peasants were further ground down.

The result was a second round of mass upheaval and protest. In the later seventeenth century, the unity of the Russian Orthodox church was torn apart by a great split. The surface question was the religious reforms introduced in 1652 by the patriarch Nikon, a dogmatic purist who wished to bring "corrupted" Russian practices of worship into line with the Greek Orthodox model. The self-serving church hierarchy quickly went along, but the intensely religious common people resisted. They saw Nikon as the anti-Christ, who was stripping them of the only thing they had—the true religion of "holy Russia."

Great numbers left the church and formed illegal communities of Old Believers, who were hunted down and persecuted. As many as twenty thousand people burned themselves alive, singing the "halleluyah" in their chants three times rather than twice as Nikon had demanded and crossing themselves in the old style, with two rather than three fingers, as they went down in flames. After the great split, the Russian masses were alienated from the established church, which became totally dependent on the state for its authority.

Again the Cossacks revolted against the state, which was doggedly trying to catch up with them on the frontiers and reduce them to serfdom. Under Stenka Razin they moved up the Volga River in 1670 and 1671, attracting a great undisciplined army of peasants, murdering landlords and high church officials, and proclaiming freedom from oppression. This rebellion to overthrow the established order was finally defeated by the government. In response, the thoroughly scared upper classes tightened the screws of serfdom even further. Holding down the peasants, and thereby maintaining the tsar, became almost the principal obligation of the nobility until 1689.

THE REFORMS OF PETER THE GREAT

It is now possible to understand the reforms of Peter the Great (1689–1725) and his kind of monarchial absolutism. Contrary to some historians' assertions, Peter was interested primarily in military power and not in some grandiose westernization plan. A giant for his time, at six feet seven inches, and possessing enormous energy and willpower, Peter was determined to redress the defeats the tsar's armies had occasionally suffered in their wars with Poland and Sweden since the time of Ivan the Terrible.

To be sure, these western foes had never seriously threatened the existence of the tsar's vast kingdom, except perhaps when they had added to the confusion of civil war and domestic social upheaval in the Time of Troubles. Russia had even gained a large mass of the Ukraine from the kingdom of Poland in 1667 (see Map 17.3). And tsarist forces had completed the conquest of the primitive tribes of all Siberia in the seventeenth century. Muscovy, which had been as large

"The Bronze Horseman" This equestrian masterpiece of Peter the Great, finished for Catherine the Great in 1783, dominates the center of St. Petersburg (modern Leningrad). The French sculptor Falconnet has captured the tsar's enormous energy, power, and determination. *(Courtesy of the Courtauld Institute of Art)*

as all the rest of Europe combined in 1600, was three times as large as the rest of Europe in 1689 and by far the largest kingdom on earth. But territorial expansion was the soul of tsardom, and it was natural that Peter would seek further gains. The thirty-six years of his reign knew only one year of peace.

When Peter came to the throne, the heart of his army still consisted of cavalry made up of boyars and service nobility. Foot soldiers played a secondary role, and the whole army served on a part-time basis. The Russian army was lagging behind the professional standing armies being formed in Europe in the seventeenth century. The core of such armies was a highly disciplined infantry—an infantry that fired and refired rifles as it fearlessly advanced, until it charged with bayonets fixed. Such a large permanent army was enormously expensive and could be created only at the cost of great sacrifice. Given the desire to conquer more territory, Peter's military problem was serious.

Peter's solution was, in essence, to tighten up Muscovy's old service system and really make it work. He put the nobility back in harness with a vengeance. Every nobleman, great or small, was once again required to serve in the army or in the civil administration—for life. Since a more modern army and government required skilled technicians and experts, Peter created schools and even universities. One of his most hated reforms required five years of compulsory education away from home for every young nobleman. Peter established an interlocking military-civilian bureaucracy with fourteen ranks, and he decreed that all must start at the bottom and work toward the top. More people of nonnoble origins rose to high positions in the embryonic meritocracy. Peter searched out talented foreigners—twice in his reign he went abroad to study and observe—and placed them in his service. These measures combined to make the army and government more powerful and efficient.

The Rise of Absolutism in Eastern Europe

1050–1300	Increasing economic development in eastern Europe encourages decline in serfdom
1054	Death of Great Prince Iaroslav the Wise, under whom the Kievan principality reached its height of unity
1054–1237	Kiev is divided into numerous territories ruled by competing princes
1237–1240	Mongol invasion of Russia
1252	Alexander Nevsky, Prince of Moscow, recognizes Mongol overlordship
1327–1328	Suppression of the Tver revolt; Mongol khan recognizes Ivan I as great prince
1400–1650	The nobility reimposes serfdom in eastern Europe
ca 1480	Ivan III rejects Mongol overlordship and adopts the title of tsar
1520–1566	Rule of Suleiman the Magnificent: Ottoman Empire reaches its height
1533–1584	Rule of Tsar Ivan IV (the Terrible): defeat of the khanates of Kazan and Astrakhan; subjugation of the boyar aristocracy
1574	Polish nobles receive the right to inflict the death penalty on their serfs
1598–1613	"Time of Troubles" in Russia
1613	Election of Michael Romanov as tsar: re-establishment of autocracy
1620	Battle of the White Mountain in Bohemia: Ferdinand II initiates Habsburg confiscation of Czech estates
1640–1688	Rule of Frederick William, the Great Elector, who unites Brandenburg, Prussia, and western German holdings intu one state, Brandenburg-Prussia
1649	Tsar Alexis lifts the nine-year limit on the recovery of runaway serfs
1652	Patriarch Nikon's reforms split the Russian Orthodox church
1653	Principle of peasants' "hereditary subjugation" to their lords affirmed in Prussia
1670–1671	Cossack revolt of Stenka Razin in Russia
1683	Siege of Vienna by the Ottoman Turks
1683–1699	Habsburg conquest of Hungary and Transylvania
1689–1725	Rule of Tsar Peter the Great
1700–1721	Great Northern War between Russia and Sweden, resulting in Russian victory and territorial expansion
1701	Elector Frederick III crowned king of Prussia
1703	Foundation of St. Petersburg
	Rebellion of Prince Francis Rakoczy in Hungary
1713	Pragmatic Sanction: Charles VII guarantees Maria Theresa's succession to the Austrian Empire
1713–1740	Rule of King Frederick William I in Prussia

Peter also greatly increased the service requirements of the commoners. He established a regular standing army of more than 200,000 soldiers, made up mainly of peasants commanded by officers from the nobility. In addition, special forces of Cossacks and foreigners numbered more than 100,000. The departure of a drafted peasant boy was celebrated by his family and village almost like a funeral, as indeed it was, since the recruit was drafted for life. The peasantry also served with its taxes, which increased threefold during Peter's reign, as people—"souls"—replaced land as the primary unit of taxation. Serfs were also arbitrarily assigned to work in the growing number of factories and mines. Most of these industrial enterprises were directly or indirectly owned by the state, and they were worked almost exclusively for the military. In general, Russian serfdom became more oppressive under the reforming tsar.

The constant warfare of Peter's reign consumed 80 to 85 percent of all revenues but brought only modest territorial expansion. Yet the Great Northern War with Sweden, which lasted from 1700 to 1721, was crowned in the end by Russian victory. After initial losses, Peter's new war machine crushed the smaller army of Sweden's Charles XII in the Ukraine at Poltava in 1709, one of the most significant battles in Russian history. Sweden never really regained the offensive, and Russia eventually annexed Estonia and much of present-day Latvia (see Map 17.2), lands that had never before been under Russian rule. Russia became the dominant power on the Baltic Sea and very much a European Great Power. If victory or defeat is the ultimate historical criterion, Peter's reforms were a success.

There were other important consequences of Peter's reign. Because of his feverish desire to use modern technology to strengthen the army, many Westerners and Western ideas flowed into Russia for the first time. A new class of educated Russians began to emerge. At the same time, vast numbers of Russians, especially among the poor and weak, hated Peter's massive changes. The split between the enserfed peasantry and the educated nobility thus widened, even though all were caught up in the endless demands of the sovereign.

A new idea of state interest, distinct from the tsar's personal interests, began to take hold. Peter himself fostered this conception of the public interest by claiming time and again to be serving the common good. For the first time a Russian tsar attached explanations to his decrees in an attempt to gain the confidence and enthusiastic support of the populace. Yet, as before, the tsar alone decided what the common good was. Here was a source of future tension between tsar and people.

In sum, Peter built on the service obligations of old Muscovy. His monarchial absolutism was truly the culmination of the long development of a unique Russian civilization. Yet the creation of a more modern army and state introduced much that was new and western to that civilization. This development paved the way for Russia to move much closer to the European mainstream in its thought and institutions during the Enlightenment, especially under that famous administrative and sexual lioness, Catherine the Great.

ABSOLUTISM AND THE BAROQUE

The rise of royal absolutism in eastern Europe had many consequences. Nobles served their powerful rulers in new ways, while the great inferiority of the urban middle classes and the peasants was reconfirmed. Armies became larger and more professional, while taxes rose and authoritarian traditions were strengthened. Nor was this all. Royal absolutism also interacted with baroque culture and art, baroque music and literature. Inspired in part by Louis XIV of France, the great and not-so-great rulers called on the artistic talent of the age to glorify their power and magnificence. This exaltation of despotic rule was particularly striking in the lavish masterpieces of architecture.

Baroque Art and Music

Throughout European history, the cultural tastes of one age have often seemed quite unsatisfactory to the next. So it was with the baroque. The term *baroque* itself may have come from the Portuguese word for an "odd-shaped, imperfect pearl" and was commonly used by late eighteenth-century art critics as an expression of scorn for what they considered an overblown, unbalanced style. The hostility of these critics, who also scorned the Gothic style of medieval cathedrals in favor of a classicism inspired by antiquity and the Renaissance, has long since passed. Specialists agree that the triumphs of the baroque marked one of the high points in the history of Western culture.

The early development of the baroque is complex, but most scholars stress the influence of Rome and the revitalized Catholic church of the later sixteenth century. The papacy and the Jesuits encouraged the growth of an intensely emotional, exuberant art. These patrons wanted artists to go beyond the Renaissance focus on pleasing a small, wealthy cultural elite. They wanted artists to appeal to the senses and thereby touch the souls and kindle the faith of ordinary churchgoers, while proclaiming the power and confidence of the reformed Catholic church. In addition to this underlying religious emotionalism, the baroque drew its sense of drama, motion, and ceaseless striving from the Catholic Reformation. The interior of the famous Jesuit Church of Jesus in Rome

—the Gesù—combined all these characteristics in its lavish, shimmering, wildly active decorations and frescoes.

Taking definite shape in Italy after 1600, the baroque style in the visual arts developed with exceptional vigor in Catholic countries—in Spain and Latin America, Austria, southern Germany, and Poland. Yet baroque art was more than just "Catholic art" in the seventeenth century and the first half of the eighteenth. True, neither Protestant England nor the Netherlands ever came fully under the spell of the baroque, but neither did Catholic France. And Protestants accounted for some of the finest examples of baroque style, especially in music. The baroque style spread partly because its tension and bombast spoke to an agitated age, which was experiencing great violence and controversy in politics and religion.

In painting, the baroque reached maturity early with Peter Paul Rubens (1577–1640), the most outstanding and representative of baroque painters (see color insert IV). Studying in his native Flanders and in Italy, where he was influenced by masters of the High Renaissance such as Michelangelo, Rubens developed his own rich, sensuous, colorful style, which was characterized by animated figures, melodramatic contrasts, and monumental size. Although Rubens excelled in glorifying monarchs such as Queen Mother Marie de' Medici of France, he was also a devout Catholic. Nearly half of his pictures treat Christian subjects. Yet one of Rubens's trademarks was fleshy, sensual nudes, who populate his canvasses as Roman goddesses, water nymphs, and remarkably voluptuous saints and angels.

Rubens was enormously successful. To meet the demand for his work, he established a large studio and hired many assistants to execute his rough sketches and gigantic murals. Sometimes the master artist added only the finishing touches. Rubens's wealth and position—on occasion he was given special diplomatic assignments by the Habsburgs—attest that distinguished artists continued to enjoy the high social status they had won in the Renaissance.

In music, the baroque style reached its culmination almost a century later in the dynamic, soaring lines of the endlessly inventive Johann Sebastian Bach (1685–1750), one of the greatest composers the Western world has ever produced. Organist and choirmaster of several Lutheran churches across Germany, Bach was equally at home writing secular concertos and sublime religious cantatas. Bach's organ music, the greatest ever written, combined the baroque spirit of invention, tension, and emotion in an unforgettable striving toward the infinite. Unlike Rubens, Bach was not fully appreciated in his lifetime, but since the early nineteenth century his reputation has grown steadily.

PALACES AND POWER

As soaring Gothic cathedrals expressed the idealized spirit of the High Middle Ages, so dramatic baroque palaces symbolized the age of absolutist power. By 1700 palace building had become a veritable obsession for the rulers of central and eastern Europe. These baroque palaces were clearly intended to overawe the people with the monarch's strength. The great palaces were also visual declarations of equality with Louis XIV and were therefore modeled after Versailles to a greater or lesser extent. One such palace was Schönbrunn, an enormous Viennese Versailles, begun in 1695 by Emperor Leopold to celebrate Austrian military victories and Habsburg might. Charles XI of Sweden, having reduced the power of the aristocracy, ordered the construction in 1693 of his Royal Palace, which dominates the center of Stockholm to this day. Frederick I of Prussia began his imposing new royal residence in Berlin in 1701, a year after he attained the title of king.

Petty princes also contributed mightily to the palace-building mania. Frederick the Great of Prussia noted that every descendant of a princely family "imagines himself to be something like Louis XIV. He builds his Versailles, has his mistresses, and maintains his army."[13] The not-very-important elector-archbishop of Mainz, the ruling prince of that city, confessed apologetically that "building is a craze which costs much, but every fool likes his own hat."[14] The archbishop of Mainz's own "hat" was an architectural gem, like that of another churchly ruler, the prince-bishop of Würzburg.

In central and eastern Europe, the favorite noble servants of royalty became extremely rich and powerful, and they, too, built grandiose palaces in the capital cities. These palaces were in part an extension of the monarch, for they surpassed the buildings of less-favored nobles and showed all the high road to fame and fortune. Take, for example, the palaces of Prince Eugene of Savoy. A French nobleman by birth and education, Prince Eugene entered the service of Leopold I with the relief of the besieged Vienna in 1683,

Rubens: The Education of Marie One of twenty-one pictures celebrating episodes from the life of Marie de' Medici, the influential widow of France's Henri IV, Rubens's painting is imbued with sensuous vitality. The three muses inspiring the studious young Marie dominate the canvas. *(Louvre/Giraudon/Art Resource)*

The Benedictine Abbey of Melk Rebuilt in the eighteenth century, this masterpiece of the Austrian baroque stands majestically on the heights above the Danube River. *(Archiv/Photo Researchers)*

and he became Austria's most outstanding military hero. It was he who reorganized the Austrian army, smashed the Turks, fought Louis XIV to a standstill, and generally guided the triumph of absolutism in Austria. Rewarded with great wealth by his grateful royal employer, Eugene called on the leading architects of the day, J. B. Fischer von Erlach and Johann Lukas von Hildebrandt, to consecrate his glory in stone and fresco. Fischer built Eugene's Winter (or Town) Palace in Vienna, and he and Hildebrandt collaborated on the prince's Summer Palace on the city's outskirts.

The Summer Palace was actually two enormous buildings, the Lower Belvedere and the Upper Belvedere, completed in 1713 and 1722 respectively and joined by one of the most exquisite gardens in Europe. The Upper Belvedere, Hildebrandt's masterpiece, stood gracefully, even playfully, behind a great sheet of water. One entered through magnificent iron gates into a hall where sculptured giants crouched as pillars and then moved on to a great staircase of dazzling whiteness and ornamentation. Even today the emotional impact of this building is great: here art and beauty create a sense of immense power and wealth.

Palaces like the Upper Belvedere were magnificent examples of the baroque style. They expressed the baroque delight in bold, sweeping statements, which were intended to provide a dramatic emotional experience. To create this experience, baroque masters dissolved the traditional artistic frontiers: the architect permitted the painter and the artisan to cover his undulating surfaces with wildly colorful paintings, graceful sculptures, and fanciful carvings. Space was used in a highly original way, to blend everything together in a total environment. These techniques shone in all their glory in the churches of southern Germany and in the colossal entrance halls of palaces like that of the prince-bishop of Würzburg (see color insert IV). Artistic achievement and political statement reinforced each other.

ROYAL CITIES

Absolute monarchs and baroque architects were not content with fashioning ostentatious palaces. They remodeled existing capital cities, or even built new ones, to reflect royal magnificence and the centralization of political power. Karlsruhe, founded in 1715 as the capital city of a small German principality, is one extreme example. There, broad, straight avenues radiated out from the palace, so that all roads—like all power—were focused on the ruler. More typically, the monarch's architects added new urban areas alongside the old city; these areas then became the real heart of the expanding capital.

The distinctive features of these new additions were their broad avenues, their imposing government buildings, and their rigorous mathematical layout. Along these major thoroughfares the nobles built elaborate baroque townhouses; stables and servants' quarters were built on the alleys behind. Wide avenues also facilitated the rapid movement of soldiers through the city to quell any disturbance (the king's planners had the needs of the military constantly in mind). Under the arcades along the avenues appeared smart and very expensive shops, the first department stores, with plate-glass windows and fancy displays.

The new avenues brought reckless speed to the European city. Whereas everyone had walked through the narrow, twisting streets of the medieval town, the high and mighty raced down the broad boulevards in their elegant carriages. A social gap opened between the wealthy riders and the gaping, dodging pedestrians. "Mind the carriages!" wrote one eighteenth-century observer in Paris:

Here comes the black-coated physician in his chariot, the dancing master in his coach, the fencing master in his surrey—and the Prince behind six horses at the gallop as if he were in the open country. . . . The threatening wheels of the overbearing rich drive as rapidly as ever over stones stained with the blood of their unhappy victims.[15]

Speeding carriages on broad avenues, an endless parade of power and position: here was the symbol and substance of the baroque city.

THE GROWTH OF ST. PETERSBURG

No city illustrated better than St. Petersburg the close ties among politics, architecture, and urban development in this period. In 1700, when the Great Northern War between Russia and Sweden began, the city did not exist. There was only a small Swedish fortress on one of the water-logged islands at the mouth of the Neva River, where it flows into the Baltic Sea. In 1702 Peter the Great's armies seized this desolate outpost. Within a year the reforming tsar had decided to build a new city there and to make it, rather than ancient Moscow, his capital.

Since the first step was to secure the Baltic coast, military construction was the main concern for the next eight years. A mighty fortress was built on Peter Island, and a port and shipyards were built across the river on the mainland, as a Russian navy came into being. The land was swampy and uninhabited, the climate damp and unpleasant. But Peter cared not at all: for him, the inhospitable northern marshland was a future metropolis, gloriously bearing his name.

After the decisive Russian victory at Poltava in 1709 greatly reduced the threat of Swedish armies, Peter moved into high gear. In one imperious decree after another, he ordered his people to build a city that would equal any in the world. Such a city had to be Western and baroque, just as Peter's army had to be Western and permanent. From such a new city, his "window on Europe," Peter also believed it would be easier to reform the country militarily and administratively.

These general political goals matched Peter's architectural ideas, which had been influenced by his travels in western Europe. First, Peter wanted a comfortable, "modern" city. Modernity meant broad, straight, stone-paved avenues, houses built in a uniform line and not haphazardly set back from the street, large parks, canals for drainage, stone bridges, and street lighting. Second, all building had to conform strictly to detailed architectural regulations set down by the government. Finally, each social group—the nobility, the merchants, the artisans, and so on—was to live in a certain section of town. In short, the city and its population were to conform to a carefully defined urban plan of the baroque type.

St. Petersburg, ca 1760 Rastrelli's remodeled Winter Palace, which housed the royal family until the Russian Revolution of 1917, stands on the left along the Neva River, near the ministries of the tsar's government. The Navy Office with its famous golden spire is in the center. Russia became a naval power and St. Petersburg a great port. *(From G. H. Hamilton,* Art and Architecture in Russia, *Penguin Books, 1954)*

Peter used the traditional but reinforced methods of Russian autocracy to build his modern capital. The creation of St. Petersburg was just one of the heavy obligations he dictatorially imposed on all social groups in Russia. The peasants bore the heaviest burdens. Just as the government drafted peasants for the army, it also drafted twenty-five to forty thousand men each summer to labor in St. Petersburg for three months, without pay. Every ten to fifteen peasant households had to furnish one such worker each summer and then pay a special tax in order to feed that worker in St. Petersburg.

Peasants hated this forced labor in the capital, and each year one-fourth to one-third of those sent risked brutal punishment and ran away. Many peasant construction workers died each summer from hunger, sickness, and accidents. Many also died because peasant villages tended to elect old men or young boys to labor in St. Petersburg, since strong and able-bodied men were desperately needed on the farm in the busy summer months. Thus beautiful St. Peters-

burg was built on the shoveling, carting, and paving of a mass of conscripted serfs.

Peter also drafted more privileged groups to his city, but on a permanent basis. Nobles were summarily ordered to build costly stone houses and palaces in St. Petersburg and to live in them most of the year. The more serfs a noble possessed, the bigger his dwelling had to be. Merchants and artisans were also commanded to settle and build in St. Petersburg. These nobles and merchants were then required to pay for the city's avenues, parks, canals, embankments, pilings, and bridges, all of which were very costly in terms of both money and lives because they were built on a swamp. The building of St. Petersburg was, in truth, an enormous direct tax levied on the wealthy, who in turn forced the peasantry to do most of the work. The only immediate beneficiaries were the foreign architects and urban planners. No wonder so many Russians hated Peter's new city.

Yet the tsar had his way. By the time of his death in 1725, there were at least six thousand houses and numerous impressive government buildings in St. Petersburg. Under the remarkable women who ruled Russia throughout most of the eighteenth century, St. Petersburg blossomed fully as a majestic and well-organized city, at least in its wealthy showpiece sections. Peter's youngest daughter, the quick-witted, sensual beauty, Elizabeth (1741–1762), named as her chief architect Bartolomeo Rastrelli, who had come to Russia from Italy as a boy of fifteen in 1715. Combining Italian and Russian traditions into a unique, wildly colorful St. Petersburg style, Rastrelli built many palaces for the nobility and all the larger government buildings erected during Elizabeth's reign. He also rebuilt the Winter Palace as an enormous, aqua-colored royal residence, now the Hermitage Museum. There Elizabeth established a flashy, luxury-loving, and slightly crude court, which Catherine in turn made truly imperial. All the while St. Petersburg grew rapidly, and its almost 300,000 inhabitants in 1782 made it one of the world's largest cities. Peter and his successors had created out of nothing a magnificent and harmonious royal city, which unmistakably proclaimed the power of Russia's rulers and the creative potential of the absolutist state.

From about 1400 to 1650, social and economic developments in eastern Europe increasingly diverged from those in western Europe. In the east, peasants and townspeople lost precious freedoms, while the nobility increased its power and prestige. It was within this framework of resurgent serfdom and entrenched nobility that Austrian and Prussian monarchs fashioned absolutist states in the seventeenth and early eighteenth centuries. Thus monarchs won absolutist control over standing armies, permanent taxes, and legislative bodies. But they did not question the underlying social and economic relationships. Indeed, they enhanced the privileges of the nobility, which furnished the leading servitors for enlarged armies and growing state bureaucracies.

In Russia, the social and economic trends were similar, but the timing of political absolutism was different. Mongol conquest and rule was a crucial experience, and a harsh, indigenous tsarist autocracy was firmly in place by the reign of Ivan the Terrible in the sixteenth century. More than a century later,

Peter the Great succeeded in tightening up Russia's traditional absolutism and modernizing it by reforming the army, the bureaucracy, and the defense industry. In Russia and throughout eastern Europe, war and the needs of the state in time of war weighed heavily in the triumph of absolutism.

Triumphant absolutism interacted spectacularly with the arts. Baroque art, which had grown out of the Catholic Reformation's desire to move the faithful and exalt the true faith, admirably suited the secular aspirations of eastern rulers. They built grandiose baroque palaces, monumental public squares, and even whole cities to glorify their power and majesty. Thus baroque art attained magnificent heights in eastern Europe, symbolizing the ideal and harmonizing with the reality of imperious royal absolutism.

NOTES

1. Quoted by F. L. Carsten, *The Origins of Prussia*, Clarendon Press, Oxford, 1954, p. 152.
2. Ibid., p. 175.
3. H. Rosenberg, *Bureaucracy, Aristocracy, and Autocracy: The Prussian Experience, 1660–1815*, Beacon Press, Boston, 1966, p. 38.
4. Quoted by R. Ergang, *The Potsdam Führer: Frederick William I, Father of Prussian Militarism*, Octagon Books, New York, 1972, pp. 85, 87.
5. Ibid., pp. 6–7, 43.
6. Quoted by R. A. Dorwart, *The Administrative Reforms of Frederick William I of Prussia*, Harvard University Press, Cambridge, Mass., 1953, p. 226.
7. Quoted by Rosenberg, p. 40.
8. Quoted by R. Pipes, *Russia Under the Old Regime*, Charles Scribner's Sons, New York, 1974, p. 48.
9. Quoted by N. V. Riasanovsky, *A History of Russia*, Oxford University Press, New York, 1963, p. 79.
10. Quoted by I. Grey, *Ivan III and the Unification of Russia*, Collier Books, New York, 1967, p. 39.
11. Quoted by Grey, p. 42.
12. Both quoted by Pipes, pp. 65, 85.
13. Quoted by Ergang, p. 13.
14. Quoted by J. Summerson, in *The Eighteenth Century: Europe in the Age of Enlightenment,* ed. A. Cobban, McGraw-Hill, New York, 1969, p. 80.
15. Quoted by L. Mumford, *The Culture of Cities,* Harcourt Brace Jovanovich, New York, 1938, p. 97.

SUGGESTED READING

All of the books cited in the Notes are highly recommended. F. L. Carsten's *The Origin of Prussia* (1954) is the best study on early Prussian history, and H. Rosenberg, *Bureaucracy, Aristocracy, and Autocracy: The Prussian Experience, 1660–1815* (1966), is a masterful analysis of the social context of Prussian absolutism. In addition to R. Ergang's exciting and critical biography of ramrod Frederick William I, *The Potsdam Führer* (1972), there is G. Ritter, *Frederick the Great* (1968), a more sympathetic study of the talented son by one of Germany's leading conservative historians. G. Craig, *The Politics of the Prussian Army, 1640–1945* (1964), expertly traces the great influence of the military on the Prussian state over three hundred years. R. J. Evans, *The Making of the Habsburg Empire, 1550–1770* (1979), and R. A. Kann, *A History of the Habsburg Empire, 1526–1918* (1974), analyze the development of absolutism in Austria, as does A. Wandruszka, *The House of Habsburg* (1964). J. Stoye, *The Siege of Vienna* (1964), is a fascinating account of the last great Ottoman offensive, which is also treated in the interesting study by P. Coles, *The Ottoman Impact on Europe, 1350–1699* (1968). The Austro-Ottoman conflict is also a theme of L. S. Stavrianos, *The Balkans Since 1453* (1958), and D. McKay's fine biography, *Prince Eugene of Savoy* (1978). A good general account is provided in D. McKay and H. Scott, *The Rise of the Great Powers, 1648–1815* (1983).

On Eastern peasants and serfdom, J. Blum, "The Rise of Serfdom in Eastern Europe," *American Historical Review 62* (July 1957):807–836, is a good point of departure, while R. Mousnier, *Peasant Uprisings in Seventeenth-Century France, Russia, and China* (1970), is an engrossing comparative study. J. Blum, *Lord and Peasant in Russia from the Ninth to the Nineteenth Century* (1961), provides a good look at conditions in rural Russia, and P. Avrich, *Russian Rebels, 1600–1800* (1972), treats some of the violent peasant upheavals those conditions produced. R. Hellie, *Enserfment and Military Change in Muscovy* (1971), is outstanding, as is A. Yanov's provocative *Origins of Autocracy: Ivan the Terrible in Russian History* (1981). In addition to the fine surveys by Pipes and Riasanovsky cited in the Notes, J. Billington, *The Icon and the Axe* (1970), is a stimulating history of early Russian intellectual and cultural developments, such as the great split in the church. M. Raeff, *Origins of the Russian Intelligentsia* (1966), skillfully probes the mind of the Russian nobility in the eighteenth century. B. H. Sumner, *Peter the Great and the Emergence of Russia* (1962), is a fine brief introduction, which may be compared with the brilliant biography by Russia's greatest prerevolutionary historian, V. Klyuchevsky, *Peter the Great* (trans. 1958), and with N. Riasanovsky, *The Image of Peter the Great in Russian History and Thought* (1985). G. Vernadsky and R. Fisher, eds., *A Source Book of Russian History from Early Times to 1917*, 3 vols. (1972), is an invaluable, highly recommended collection of documents and contemporary writings.

Three good books on art and architecture are E. Hempel, *Baroque Art and Architecture in Central Europe* (1965); G. Hamilton, *The Art and Architecture of Russia* (1954); and N. Pevsner, *An Outline of European Architecture*, 6th ed. (1960). Bach, Handel, and other composers are discussed intelligently by M. Bufkozer, *Music in the Baroque Era* (1947).

18

TOWARD A NEW
WORLD-VIEW

MOST PEOPLE are not philosophers, but nevertheless they have a basic outlook on life, a more or less coherent world-view. At the risk of oversimplification, one may say that the world-view of medieval and early modern Europe was primarily religious and theological. Not only did Christian or Jewish teachings form the core of people's spiritual and philosophical beliefs, but religious teachings also permeated all the rest of human thought and activity. Political theory relied on the divine right of kings, for example, and activities ranging from marriage and divorce to eating habits and hours of business were regulated by churches and religious doctrines.

In the course of the eighteenth century, this religious and theological world-view of the educated classes of western Europe underwent a fundamental transformation. Many educated people came to see the world primarily in secular and scientific terms. And while few abandoned religious beliefs altogether, many became openly hostile toward established Christianity. The role of churches and religious thinking in earthly affairs and in the pursuit of knowledge was substantially reduced. Among many in the upper and middle classes, a new critical, scientific, and very "modern" world-view took shape. Why did this momentous change occur? How did this new outlook on life affect society and politics? This chapter will focus on these questions.

THE SCIENTIFIC REVOLUTION

The foremost cause of the change in world-view was the scientific revolution. Modern science—precise knowledge of the physical world based on the union of experimental observations with sophisticated mathematics—crystallized in the seventeenth century. Whereas science had been secondary and subordinate in medieval intellectual life, it became independent and even primary for many educated people in the eighteenth century.

The emergence of modern science was a development of tremendous long-term significance. A noted historian has even said that the scientific revolution of the late sixteenth and seventeenth centuries "outshines everything since the rise of Christianity and reduces the Renaissance and Reformation to the rank of mere episodes, mere internal displacements, within the system of medieval Christendom." The scientific revolution was "the real origin both of the modern world and the modern mentality."[1] This statement is an exaggeration, but not much of one. Of all the great civilizations, only that of the West developed modern science. It was with the scientific revolution that Western society began to acquire its most distinctive traits.

Though historians agree that the scientific revolution was enormously important, they approach it in quite different ways. Some scholars believe that the history of scientific achievement in this period had its own basic "internal" logic and that "nonscientific" factors had quite limited significance. These scholars write brilliant, often highly technical, intellectual studies, but they neglect the broader historical context. Other historians stress "external" economic, social, and religious factors, brushing over the scientific developments themselves. Historians of science now realize that these two approaches need to be brought together, but they are only beginning to do so. It is best, therefore, to examine the milestones on the fateful march toward modern science first and then to search for nonscientific influences along the route.

SCIENTIFIC THOUGHT IN 1500

Since developments in astronomy and physics were at the heart of the scientific revolution, one must begin with the traditional European conception of the universe and movement in it. In the early 1500s, traditional European ideas about the universe were still based primarily on the ideas of Aristotle, the great Greek philosopher of the fourth century B.C. These ideas had gradually been recovered during the Middle Ages and then brought into harmony with Christian doctrines by medieval theologians. According to this revised Aristotelian view, a motionless earth was fixed at the center of the universe. Around it moved ten separate, transparent, crystal spheres. In the first eight spheres were embedded, in turn, the moon, the sun, the five known planets, and the fixed stars. Then followed two spheres added during the Middle Ages to account for slight changes in the positions of the stars over the centuries. Beyond the tenth sphere was heaven, with the throne of God and the souls of the saved. Angels kept the spheres moving in perfect circles.

Aristotle's views, suitably revised by medieval philosophers, also dominated thinking about physics and motion on earth. Aristotle had distinguished sharply between the world of the celestial spheres and that of the earth—the sublunar world. The spheres consisted of a perfect, incorruptible "quintescence," or fifth essence. The sublunar world, however, was made up of four imperfect, changeable elements. The "light" elements—air and fire—naturally moved upward, while the "heavy" elements—water and earth—naturally moved downward. The natural directions of motion did not always prevail, however, for elements were often mixed together and could be affected by an outside force such as a human being. Aristotle and his followers also believed that a uniform force moved an object at a constant speed and that the object would stop as soon as that force was removed.

Aristotle's ideas about astronomy and physics were accepted with minor revisions for two thousand years, and with good reason. First, they offered an understandable, common-sense explanation for what the eye actually saw. Second, Aristotle's science, as interpreted by Christian theologians, fit neatly with Christian doctrines. It established a home for God and a place for Christian souls. It put human beings at the center of the universe and made them the critical link in a "great chain of being" that stretched from the throne of God to the most lowly insect on earth. Thus science was primarily a branch of theology, and it reinforced religious thought. At the same time, medieval "scientists" were already providing closely reasoned explanations of the universe, explanations they felt were worthy of God's perfect creation.

THE COPERNICAN HYPOTHESIS

The desire to explain and thereby glorify God's handiwork led to the first great departure from the medieval system. This departure was the work of the Polish clergyman and astronomer Nicolaus Copernicus (1473–1543). As a young man, Copernicus studied church law and astronomy in various European universities. He saw how professional astronomers were still dependent for their most accurate calculations

Ptolemy's System This 1543 drawing shows how the changing configurations of the planets moving around the earth form the twelve different constellations, or "signs," of the zodiac. The learned astronomer on the right is using his knowledge to predict the future for the king on the left. *(Mary Evans Picture Library)*

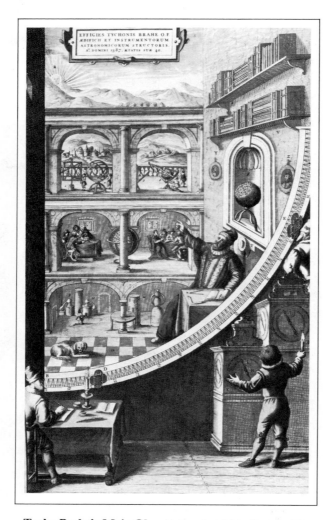

Tycho Brahe's Main Observatory Lavishly financed by the king of Denmark, Brahe built his magnificent observatory at Uraniborg between 1576 and 1580. For twenty years he studied the heavens and accumulated a mass of precise but undigested data. *(The British Library)*

on the work of Ptolemy, the last great ancient astronomer, who had lived in Alexandria in the second century A.D. Ptolemy's achievement had been to work out complicated rules to explain the minor irregularities in the movement of the planets. These rules enabled stargazers and astrologers to track the planets with greater precision. Many people then (and now) believed that the changing relationships between planets and stars influenced and even determined an individual's future.

The young Copernicus was uninterested in astrology and felt that Ptolemy's cumbersome and occasionally inaccurate rules detracted from the majesty of a perfect Creator. He preferred an old Greek idea being discussed in Renaissance Italy: that the sun rather than the earth was at the center of the universe. Finishing his university studies and returning to a church position in east Prussia, Copernicus worked on his hypothesis from 1506 to 1530. Never questioning the Aristotelian belief in crystal spheres or the idea that circular motion was most perfect and divine, Copernicus theorized that the stars and planets, including the earth, revolve around a fixed sun. Yet Copernicus was a cautious man. Fearing the ridicule of other astronomers, he did not publish his *On the Revolutions of the Heavenly Spheres* until 1543, the year of his death.

Copernicus's theory had enormous scientific and religious implications, many of which the conservative Copernicus did not anticipate. First, it put the stars at rest, their apparent nightly movement simply a result of the earth's rotation. Thus it destroyed the main reason for believing in crystal spheres capable of moving the stars around the earth. Second, Copernicus's theory suggested a universe of staggering size. If in the course of a year the earth moved around the sun and yet the stars appeared to remain in the same place, then the universe was unthinkably large or even infinite. Finally, by characterizing the earth as just another planet, Copernicus destroyed the basic idea of Aristotelian physics—that the earthly world was quite different from the heavenly one. Where, then, was the realm of perfection? Where was heaven and the throne of God?

The Copernican theory quickly brought sharp attacks from religious leaders, especially Protestants. Hearing of Copernicus's work even before it was published, Martin Luther spoke of him as the "new astrologer who wants to prove that the earth moves and goes round. . . . The fool wants to turn the whole art of astronomy upside down." Luther noted that "as the Holy Scripture tells us, so did Joshua bid the sun stand still and not the earth." Calvin also condemned Copernicus, citing as evidence the first verse of Psalm 93: "The world also is established that it cannot be moved." "Who," asked Calvin, "will venture to place the authority of Copernicus above that of the Holy Spirit?"[2] Catholic reaction was milder at first. The Catholic church had never been hypnotized by literal interpretations of the Bible, and not until 1616 did it officially declare the Copernican theory false.

This slow reaction also reflected the slow progress of Copernicus's theory for many years. Other events were almost as influential in creating doubts about traditional astronomical ideas. In 1572 a new star appeared and shone very brightly for almost two years. The new star, which was actually a distant exploding star, made an enormous impression on people. It seemed to contradict the idea that the heavenly spheres were unchanging and therefore perfect. In 1577 a new comet suddenly moved through the sky, cutting a straight path across the supposedly impenetrable crystal spheres. It was time, as a typical scientific writer put it, for "the radical renovation of astronomy."[3]

From Tycho Brahe to Galileo

One astronomer who agreed was Tycho Brahe (1546–1601). Born into a leading Danish noble family and earmarked for a career in government, Brahe was at an early age tremendously impressed by a partial eclipse of the sun. It seemed to him "something divine that men could know the motions of the stars so accurately that they were able a long time beforehand to predict their places and relative positions."[4] Completing his studies abroad and returning to Denmark, Brahe established himself as Europe's leading astronomer with his detailed observations of the new star of 1572. Aided by generous grants from the king of Denmark, which made him one of the richest men in the country, Brahe built the most sophisticated observatory of his day. For twenty years he meticulously observed the stars and planets with the naked eye. An imposing man who had lost a piece of his nose in a duel and replaced it with a special bridge of gold and silver alloy, a noble who exploited his peasants arrogantly and approached the heavens humbly, Brahe's great contribution was his mass of data. His limited understanding of mathematics prevented him, however, from making much sense out of his data. Part Ptolemaic, part Copernican, he believed that all the planets revolved around the sun and that the entire group of sun and planets revolved in turn around the earth-moon system.

It was left to Brahe's brilliant young assistant, Johannes Kepler (1571–1630), to go much further.

Kepler was a medieval figure in many ways. Coming from a minor German noble family and trained for the Lutheran ministry, he long believed that the universe was built on mystical mathematical relationships and a musical harmony of the heavenly bodies. Working and reworking Brahe's mountain of observations in a staggering sustained effort after the Dane's death, this brilliant mathematician eventually went beyond mystical intuitions.

Kepler formulated three famous laws of planetary motion. First, building on Copernican theory, he demonstrated in 1609 that the orbits of the planets around the sun are elliptical rather than circular. Second, he demonstrated that the planets do not move at a uniform speed in their orbits. Third, in 1619 he showed that the time a planet takes to make its complete orbit is precisely related to its distance from the sun. Kepler's contribution was monumental. Whereas Copernicus had speculated, Kepler proved mathematically the precise relations of a sun-centered (solar) system. His work demolished the old system of Aristotle and Ptolemy, and in his third law he came close to formulating the idea of universal gravitation.

While Kepler was unraveling planetary motion, a young Florentine named Galileo Galilei (1564–1642) was challenging all the old ideas about motion. Like so many early scientists, Galileo was a poor nobleman first marked for a religious career. However, he soon became fascinated by mathematics. A brilliant student, Galileo became a professor of mathematics in 1589 at age twenty-five. He proceeded to examine motion and mechanics in a new way. Indeed, his great achievement was the elaboration and consolidation of the modern experimental method. Rather than speculate about what might or should happen, Galileo conducted controlled experiments to find out what actually *did* happen.

In his famous acceleration experiment, he showed that a uniform force—in this case, gravity—produced a uniform acceleration. Here is how Galileo described his pathbreaking method and conclusion in his *Two New Sciences:*

A piece of wooden moulding . . . was taken; on its edge was cut a channel a little more than one finger in breadth. Having made this groove very straight, smooth and polished, and having lined it with parchment, also as smooth and polished as possible, we rolled along it a

Galileo Explains the two new sciences, astronomy and mechanics, to an eager young visitor to his observatory in this artist's reconstruction. After his trial for heresy by the papal Inquisition, Galileo spent the last eight years of his life under house arrest. *(The Mansell Collection)*

hard, smooth and very round bronze ball. . . . Noting . . . the time required to make the descent . . . we now rolled the ball only one-quarter the length of the channel; and having measured the time of its descent, we found it precisely one-half of the former. . . . In such experiments [over many distances], repeated a full hundred times, we always found that the spaces traversed were to each other as the squares of the times, and that this was true for all inclinations of the plane.[5]

With this and other experiments, Galileo also formulated the law of inertia. That is, rather than rest being the natural state of objects, an object continues in motion forever unless stopped by some external force. Aristotelian physics was in a shambles.

In the tradition of Brahe, Galileo also applied the experimental method to astronomy. His astronomical discoveries had a great impact on scientific development. On hearing of the invention of the telescope in Holland, Galileo made one for himself and trained it on the heavens. He quickly discovered the first four moons of Jupiter, which clearly suggested that Jupiter could not possibly be embedded in any impenetrable crystal sphere. This discovery provided new evidence for the Copernican theory, in which Galileo already believed.

Galileo then pointed his telescope at the moon. He wrote in 1610 in *Siderus Nuncius:*

*I feel sure that the moon is not perfectly smooth, free
from inequalities, and exactly spherical, as a large
school of philosophers considers with regard to the moon
and the other heavenly bodies. On the contrary, it is full
of inequalities, uneven, full of hollows and protuber-
ances, just like the surface of the earth itself, which is
varied. . . . The next object which I have observed is the
essence or substance of the Milky Way. By the aid of a
telescope anyone may behold this in a manner which so
distinctly appeals to the senses that all the disputes which
have tormented philosophers through so many ages are
exploded by the irrefutable evidence of our eyes, and we
are freed from wordy disputes upon the subject. For the
galaxy is nothing else but a mass of innumerable stars
planted together in clusters. Upon whatever part of it you
direct the telescope straightway a vast crowd of stars
presents itself to view; many of them are tolerably large
and extremely bright, but the number of small ones is
quite beyond determination.*[6]

Reading these famous lines, one feels that a crucial
corner in Western civilization is being turned. The
traditional religious and theological world-view,
which rested on determining and then accepting the
proper established authority, is beginning to give way
in certain fields to a critical, "scientific" method.
This new method of learning and investigating was
the greatest accomplishment of the entire scientific
revolution, for it has proved capable of great extension. A historian investigating documents of the past,
for example, is not much different from a Galileo
studying stars and rolling balls.

Galileo was employed in Florence by the Medici
grand dukes of Tuscany, and his work eventually
aroused the ire of some theologians. The issue was
presented in 1624 to Pope Urban VII, who permitted
Galileo to write about different possible systems of
the world, as long as he did not presume to judge
which one actually existed. After the publication in
Italian of his widely read *Dialogue on the Two Chief
Systems of the World* in 1632, which too openly lampooned the traditional views of Aristotle and Ptolemy and defended those of Copernicus, Galileo was
tried for heresy by the papal Inquisition. Imprisoned
and threatened with torture, the aging Galileo re-
canted, "renouncing and cursing" his Copernican
errors. Of minor importance in the development of
science, Galileo's trial later became for some writers
the perfect symbol of the inevitable conflict between
religious belief and scientific knowledge.

NEWTON'S SYNTHESIS

The accomplishments of Kepler, Galileo, and other
scientists had taken effect by about 1640. The old astronomy and physics were in ruins, and several fundamental breakthroughs had been made. The new
findings had not, however, been fused together in a
new synthesis, a single explanatory system that
would comprehend motion both on earth and in the
skies. That synthesis, which prevailed until the twentieth century, was the work of Isaac Newton (1642–
1727).

Newton was born into lower English gentry and attended Cambridge University. A great genius who
spectacularly united the experimental and theoreti-
cal-mathematical sides of modern science, Newton
was also fascinated by alchemy. He sought the elixir
of life and a way to change base metals into gold and
silver. Not without reason did the twentieth-century
economist John Maynard Keynes call Newton the
"last of the magicians." Newton was intensely religious. He had a highly suspicious nature, lacked all interest in women and sex, and in 1693 suffered a ner-
vous breakdown from which he later recovered. He
was far from being the perfect rationalist so endlessly
eulogized by writers in the eighteenth and nineteenth
centuries.

Of his intellectual genius and incredible powers of
concentration there can be no doubt, however. Arriving at some of his most basic ideas about physics in
1666 at age twenty-four, but unable to prove these
theories mathematically, he attained a professorship
and studied optics for many years. In 1684 Newton
returned to physics for eighteen extraordinarily intensive months. For weeks on end he seldom left his
room except to read his lectures. His meals were sent
up but he usually forgot to eat them, his mind fas-
tened like a vise on the laws of the universe. Thus did
Newton open the third book of his immortal *Mathematical Principles of Natural Philosophy*, published
in Latin in 1687 and generally known as the *Principia*, with these lines:

*In the preceding books I have laid down the principles of
philosophy [that is, science]. . . . These principles are the
laws of certain motions, and powers or forces, which
chiefly have respect to philosophy. . . . It remains that
from the same principles I now demonstrate the frame of
the System of the World.*

Newton made good his grandiose claim. His towering accomplishment was to integrate in a single explanatory system the astronomy of Copernicus, as corrected by Kepler's laws, with the physics of Galileo and his predecessors. Newton did this by means of a set of mathematical laws that explain motion and mechanics. These laws of dynamics are complex, and it took scientists and engineers two hundred years to work out all their implications. Nevertheless, the key feature of the Newtonian synthesis was the law of universal gravitation. According to this law, every body in the universe attracts every other body in the universe in a precise mathematical relationship, whereby the force of attraction is proportional to the quantity of matter of the objects and inversely proportional to the square of the distance between them. The whole universe—from Kepler's elliptical orbits to Galileo's rolling balls—was unified in one majestic system.

CAUSES OF THE SCIENTIFIC REVOLUTION

With a charming combination of modesty and self-congratulation, Newton once wrote: "If I have seen further [than others], it is by standing on the shoulders of Giants."[7] Surely the path from Copernicus to Newton confirms the "internal" view of the scientific revolution as a product of towering individual genius. The problems of science were inherently exciting, and solution of those problems was its own reward for inquisitive, high-powered minds. Yet there were certainly broader causes as well.

The long-term contribution of medieval intellectual life and medieval universities to the scientific revolution was much more considerable than historians unsympathetic to the Middle Ages once believed. By the thirteenth century, permanent universities with professors and large student bodies had been established in western Europe. The universities were supported by society because they trained the lawyers, doctors, and church leaders society required. By 1300 philosophy had taken its place alongside law, medicine, and theology. Medieval philosophers developed a limited but real independence from theologians and a sense of free inquiry. They nobly pursued a body of knowledge and tried to arrange it meaningfully by means of abstract theories.

Within this framework, science was able to emerge as a minor but distinct branch of philosophy. In the fourteenth and fifteenth centuries, first in Italy and then elsewhere in Europe, leading universities established new professorships of mathematics, astronomy, and physics (natural philosophy) within their faculties of philosophy. The prestige of the new fields was still low among both professors and students. Nevertheless, this pattern of academic science, which grew out of the medieval commitment to philosophy and did not change substantially until the late eighteenth century, undoubtedly promoted scientific development. Rational, critical thinking was applied to scientific problems by a permanent community of scholars. And an outlet existed for the talents of a Galileo or a Newton: all the great pathbreakers either studied or taught at universities.

The Renaissance also stimulated scientific progress. One of the great deficiencies of medieval science was its rather rudimentary mathematics. The recovery of the finest works of Greek mathematics—a by-product of Renaissance humanism's ceaseless search for the knowledge of antiquity—greatly improved European mathematics well into the early seventeenth century. The recovery of more texts also showed that classical mathematicians had had their differences, and Europeans were forced to try to resolve these ancient controversies by means of their own efforts. Finally, the Renaissance pattern of patronage, especially in Italy, was often scientific as well as artistic and humanistic. Various rulers and wealthy businessmen supported scientific investigations, just as the Medicis of Florence supported those of Galileo.

The navigational problems of long sea voyages in the age of overseas expansion were a third factor in the scientific revolution. Ship captains on distant shores needed to be able to chart their positions as accurately as possible, so that reliable maps could be drawn and the risks of international trade reduced. As early as 1484, the king of Portugal appointed a commission of mathematicians to perfect tables to help seamen find their latitude. This resulted in the first European navigation manual.

The problem of fixing longitude was much more difficult. In England, the government and the great capitalistic trading companies turned to science and scientific education in an attempt to solve this pressing practical problem. When the famous Elizabethan financier Sir Thomas Gresham left a large amount of money to establish Gresham College in London, he stipulated that three of the college's seven professors had to concern themselves exclusively with scientific

State Support Governments supported scientific research because they thought it might be useful. Here Louis XIV visits the French Royal Academy of Sciences in 1671 and examines a plan for better military fortifications. The great interest in astronomy, anatomy, and geography is evident. *(Bibliothèque Nationale, Paris)*

subjects. The professor of astronomy was directed to teach courses on the science of navigation. A seventeenth-century popular ballad took note of the new college's calling:

This college will the whole world measure
Which most impossible conclude,
And navigation make a pleasure
By finding out the longitude.[8]

At Gresham College scientists had, for the first time in history, an important, honored role in society. They enjoyed close ties with the top officials of the Royal Navy and with the leading merchants and shipbuilders. Gresham College became the main center of scientific activity in England in the first half of the seventeenth century. The close tie between practical men and scientists also led to the establishment in 1662 of the Royal Society of London, which published scientific papers and sponsored scientific meetings.

Navigational problems were also critical in the development of many new scientific instruments, such as the telescope, the barometer, the thermometer, the pendulum clock, the microscope, and the air pump. Better instruments, which permitted more accurate observations, often led to important new knowledge. Galileo with his telescope was by no means unique.

Better instruments were part of the fourth factor, the development of better ways of obtaining knowledge about the world. Two important thinkers, Francis Bacon (1561–1626) and René Descartes (1596–1650), represented key aspects of this improvement in scientific methodology.

The English politician and writer Francis Bacon was the greatest early propagandist for the new experimental method, as Galileo was its greatest early practitioner. Rejecting the Aristotelian and medieval method of using speculative reasoning to build general theories, Bacon argued that new knowledge had to be pursued through empirical, experimental research. That is, the researcher who wants to learn more about leaves or rocks should not speculate about the subject but rather collect a multitude of specimens and then compare and analyze them. Thus freed from sterile medieval speculation, the facts will speak for themselves, and important general principles will then emerge. Knowledge will increase. Bacon's contribution was to formalize the empirical method, which had already been used by scientists like Brahe and Galileo, into the general theory of inductive reasoning known as *empiricism.*

Bacon claimed that the empirical method would result not only in more knowledge, but in highly practical, useful knowledge. According to Bacon, scientific discoveries like those so avidly sought at Gresham College would bring about much greater control over the physical environment and make people rich and nations powerful. Thus Bacon helped provide a radically new and effective justification for private and public support of scientific inquiry.

The French philosopher René Descartes was a true genius who made his first great discovery in mathematics. As a twenty-three-year-old soldier serving in the Thirty Years' War, he experienced on a single night in 1619 a life-changing intellectual vision. What Descartes saw was that there was a perfect correspondence between geometry and algebra and that geometrical, spatial figures could be expressed as algebraic equations and vice versa. A great step forward in the history of mathematics, Descartes' discovery of analytic geometry provided scientists with an important new tool. Descartes also made contributions to the science of optics, but his greatest achievement was to develop his initial vision into a whole philosophy of knowledge and science.

Like Bacon, Descartes scorned traditional science and had great faith in the powers of the human mind. Yet Descartes was much more systematic and mathematical than Bacon. He decided it was necessary to doubt everything that could reasonably be doubted and then, as in geometry, to use deductive reasoning from self-evident principles to ascertain scientific laws. Descartes' reasoning ultimately reduced all substances to "matter" and "mind"—that is, to the physical and the spiritual. His view of the world as consisting of two fundamental entities is known as *Cartesian dualism.* Descartes was a profoundly original and extremely influential thinker.

It is important to realize that the modern scientific method, which began to crystallize in the late seventeenth century, has combined Bacon's inductive experimentalism and Descartes' deductive, mathematical rationalism. Neither of these extreme approaches was sufficient by itself. Bacon's inability to appreciate the importance of mathematics and his obsession with practical results clearly showed the limitations of antitheoretical empiricism. Likewise, some of

Descartes' positions—he believed, for example, that it was possible to deduce the whole science of medicine from first principles—aptly demonstrated the inadequacy of rigid, dogmatic rationalism. Significantly, Bacon faulted Galileo for his use of abstract formulas, while Descartes criticized the great Italian for being too experimental and insufficiently theoretical. Thus the modern scientific method has typically combined Bacon and Descartes. It has joined precise observations and experimentalism with the search for general laws that may be expressed in rigorously logical, mathematical language.

Finally, there is the question of science and religion. Just as some historians have argued that Protestantism led to the rise of capitalism, others have concluded that Protestantism was a fundamental factor in the rise of modern science. Protestantism, particularly in its Calvinist varieties, supposedly made scientific inquiry a question of individual conscience and not of religious doctrine. The Catholic church, on the other hand, supposedly suppressed scientific theories that conflicted with its teachings and thus discouraged scientific progress.

The truth of the matter is more complicated. *All* religious authorities—Catholic, Protestant, and Jewish—opposed the Copernican system to a greater or lesser extent until about 1630, by which time the scientific revolution was definitely in progress. The Catholic church was initially less hostile than Protestant and Jewish religious leaders. This early Catholic toleration and the scientific interests of Renaissance Italy help account for the undeniable fact that Italian scientists played a crucial role in scientific progress right up to the trial of Galileo in 1633. Thereafter the Counter-Reformation church became more hostile to science, which helps account for the decline of science in Italy (but not in Catholic France) after 1640. At the same time, some Protestant countries became quite "pro-science," especially if the country lacked a strong religious authority capable of imposing religious orthodoxy on scientific questions.

This was the case with England after 1630. English religious conflicts became so intense that it was impossible for the authorities to impose religious unity on anything, including science. It is significant that the forerunners of the Royal Society agreed to discuss only "neutral" scientific questions, so as not to come to blows over closely related religious and political disputes. The work of Bacon's many followers during

René Descartes dismissed the scientific theories of Aristotle and his medieval disciples as outdated dogma. A brilliant philosopher and mathematician, he formulated rules for abstract, deductive reasoning and the search for comprehensive scientific laws. *(Royal Museum of Fine Arts, Copenhagen)*

Cromwell's commonwealth helped solidify the neutrality and independence of science. Bacon advocated the experimental approach precisely because it was open-minded and independent of any preconceived religious or philosophical ideas. Neutral and useful, science became an accepted part of life and developed rapidly in England after about 1640.

SOME CONSEQUENCES OF THE SCIENTIFIC REVOLUTION

The rise of modern science had many consequences, some of which are still unfolding. First, it went hand in hand with the rise of a new and expanding social group—the scientific community. Members of this community were linked together by learned societies, common interests, and shared values. Expansion of knowledge was the primary goal of this community, and scientists' material and psychological rewards depended on their success in this endeavor. Thus science became quite competitive, and even more scientific advance was inevitable.

Second, the scientific revolution introduced not only new knowledge about nature but also a new and revolutionary way of obtaining such knowledge—the modern scientific method. In addition to being both theoretical and experimental, this method was highly critical, and it differed profoundly from the old way of getting knowledge about nature. It refused to base its conclusions on tradition and established sources, on ancient authorities and sacred texts.

The scientific revolution had few consequences for economic life and the living standards of the masses until the late eighteenth century at the very earliest. True, improvements in the techniques of navigation facilitated overseas trade and helped enrich leading merchants. But science had relatively few practical economic applications, and the hopes of the early Baconians were frustrated. The close link between theoretical, or pure, science and applied technology, which we take for granted today, simply did not exist before the nineteenth century. Thus the scientific revolution of the seventeenth century was first and foremost an intellectual revolution. It is not surprising that for more than a hundred years its greatest impact was on how people thought and believed.

THE ENLIGHTENMENT

The scientific revolution was the single most important factor in the creation of the new world-view of the eighteenth-century Enlightenment. This world-view, which has played a large role in shaping the modern mind, was based on a rich mix of ideas, sometimes conflicting, for intellectuals delight in playing with ideas just as athletes delight in playing games. Despite this diversity, three central concepts stand out.

The most important and original idea of the Enlightenment was that the methods of natural science could and should be used to examine and understand all aspects of life. This was what intellectuals meant by *reason,* a favorite word of Enlightenment thinkers. Nothing was to be accepted on faith. Everything was to be submitted to the rational, critical, "scientific" way of thinking. This approach brought the Enlightenment into a head-on conflict with the established churches, which rested their beliefs on the special authority of the Bible and Christian theology. A second important Enlightenment concept was that the scientific method was capable of discovering the laws of human society as well as those of nature. Thus was social science born. Its birth led to the third key idea, that of progress. Armed with the proper method of discovering the laws of human existence, Enlightenment thinkers believed it was at least possible to create better societies and better people. Their belief was strengthened by some genuine improvements in economic and social life during the eighteenth century (see Chapters 19 and 20).

The Enlightenment was therefore profoundly secular. It revived and expanded the Renaissance concentration on worldly explanations. In the course of the eighteenth century, the Enlightenment had a profound impact on the thought and culture of the urban middle and upper classes. It did not have much appeal for the poor and the peasants.

THE EMERGENCE OF THE ENLIGHTENMENT

The Enlightenment did not reach its maturity until about 1750. Yet it was the generation that came of age between the publication of Newton's masterpiece in 1687 and the death of Louis XIV in 1715 that tied the crucial knot between the scientific revolution and a new outlook on life.

Talented writers of that generation popularized hard-to-understand scientific achievements for the educated elite. The most famous and influential popularizer was a versatile French man of letters, Bernard de Fontenelle (1657–1757). Fontenelle practically invented the technique of making highly complicated scientific findings understandable to a broad nonscientific audience. He set out to make science witty and entertaining, as easy to read as a novel. This was a tall order, but Fontenelle largely succeeded.

His most famous work, *Conversations on the Plurality of Worlds* of 1686, begins with two elegant figures walking in the gathering shadows of a large park. One is a woman, a sophisticated aristocrat, and the other is her friend, perhaps even her lover. They gaze at the stars, and their talk turns to a passionate discussion of . . . astronomy! He confides that "each star may well be a different world." She is intrigued by his novel idea: "Teach me about these stars of yours." And he does, gently but persistently stressing how error is giving way to truth. At one point he explains:

There came on the scene a certain German, one Copernicus, who made short work of all those various circles, all those solid skies, which the ancients had pictured to themselves. The former he abolished; the latter he broke in pieces. Fired with the noble zeal of a true astronomer, he took the earth and spun it very far away from the center of the universe, where it had been installed, and in that center he put the sun, which had a far better title to the honor.[9]

Rather than tremble in despair in the face of these revelations, Fontenelle's lady rejoices in the advance of knowledge. Fontenelle thus went beyond entertainment to instruction, suggesting that the human mind was capable of making great progress.

This idea of progress was essentially a new idea of the later seventeenth century. Medieval and Reformation thinkers had been concerned primarily with sin and salvation. The humanists of the Renaissance had emphasized worldly matters, but they had been backward-looking. They had believed it might be possible to equal the magnificent accomplishments of the ancients, but they did not ask for more. Fontenelle and like-minded writers had come to believe that, at least in science and mathematics, their era had gone far *beyond* antiquity. Progress, at least intellectual progress, was clearly possible. During the eighteenth century, this idea would sink deeply into the consciousness of the European elite.

Fontenelle and other literary figures of his generation were also instrumental in bringing science into conflict with religion. Contrary to what is often assumed, many seventeenth-century scientists, both Catholic and Protestant, believed that their work exalted God. They did not draw antireligious implications from their scientific findings. The greatest scientist of them all, Isaac Newton, was a devout if unorthodox Christian who saw all of his studies as directed toward explaining God's message. Newton devoted far more of his time to angels and biblical prophecies than to universal gravitation, and he was convinced that all of his inquiries were equally "scientific."

Fontenelle, on the other hand, was skeptical about absolute truth and cynical about the claims of organized religion. Since such unorthodox views could not be stated openly in Louis XIV's France, Fontenelle made his point through subtle editorializing about science. His depiction of the cautious Copernicus as a self-conscious revolutionary was typical. In his *Eulogies of Scientists,* Fontenelle exploited with endless variations the basic theme of rational, progressive scientists versus prejudiced, reactionary priests. Time and time again Fontenelle's fledgling scientists attended church and studied theology; then, at some crucial moment, each was converted from the obscurity of religion to the clarity of science.

The progressive and antireligious implications that writers like Fontenelle drew from the scientific revolution reflected a very real crisis in European thought at the end of the seventeenth century. This crisis had its roots in several intellectual uncertainties and dissatisfactions, of which the demolition of Aristotelian-medieval science was only one.

A second uncertainty involved the whole question of religious truth. The destructive wars of religion had been fought, in part, because religious freedom was an intolerable idea in the early seventeenth century. Both Catholics and Protestants had believed that religious truth was absolute and therefore worth fighting and dying for. It was also generally believed that a strong state required unity in religious faith. Yet the disastrous results of the many attempts to impose such religious unity, such as Louis XIV's expulsion of the French Huguenots in 1685, led some people to ask if ideological conformity in religious matters was really necessary. Others skeptically asked if religious truth could ever be known with absolute certainty and concluded that it could not.

The most famous of these skeptics was Pierre Bayle (1647–1706), a French Huguenot who took refuge in Holland. A teacher by profession and a crusading journalist by inclination, Bayle critically examined the religious beliefs and persecutions of the past in his *Historical and Critical Dictionary,* published in 1697. Demonstrating that human beliefs had been extremely varied and very often mistaken, Bayle concluded that nothing can ever be known beyond all doubt. In religion as in philosophy, humanity's best hope was open-minded toleration. Bayle's skeptical views were very influential. Many eighteenth-century writers mined his inexhaustible vein of critical skepticism for ammunition in their attacks on superstition and theology. Bayle's four-volume *Dictionary* was found in more private libraries of eighteenth-century France than any other book.

Popularizing Science The frontispiece illustration of Fontenelle's *Conversations on the Plurality of Worlds* invites the reader to share the pleasures of astronomy with an elegant lady and an entertaining teacher. *(University of Illinois)*

The rapidly growing travel literature on non-European lands and cultures was a third cause of uncertainty. In the wake of the great discoveries, Europeans were learning that the peoples of China, India, Africa, and the Americas all had their own very different beliefs and customs. Europeans shaved their faces and let their hair grow. The Turks shaved their heads and let their beards grow. In Europe a man bowed before a woman to show respect. In Siam a man turned his back on a woman when he met her, because it was disrespectful to look directly at her. Countless similar examples discussed in the travel accounts helped change the perspective of educated Europeans. They began to look at truth and morality in relative rather than absolute terms. Anything was possible, and who could say what was right or wrong? As one Frenchman wrote: "There is nothing that opinion, prejudice, custom, hope, and a sense of honor cannot do." Another wrote disapprovingly of religious skeptics who were corrupted "by extensive travel and lose whatever shreds of religion that remained with them. Every day they see a new religion, new customs, new rites."[10]

A fourth cause and manifestation of European intellectual turmoil was John Locke's epoch-making *Essay Concerning Human Understanding.* Published in 1690—the same year Locke published his famous *Second Treatise on Civil Government* (page 530)— Locke's essay brilliantly set forth a new theory about how human beings learn and form their ideas. In doing so, he rejected the prevailing view of Descartes, who had held that all people are born with certain basic ideas and ways of thinking. Locke insisted that all ideas are derived from experience. The human mind is like a blank tablet (*tabula rasa*) at birth, a tablet on which environment writes the individual's understanding and beliefs. Human development is therefore determined by education and social institutions, for good or for evil. Locke's *Essay Concerning Human Understanding* passed through many editions and translations. It was, along with Newton's *Principia,* one of the dominant intellectual inspirations of the Enlightenment.

The Philosophes and Their Ideas

By the death of Louis XIV in 1715, many of the ideas that would soon coalesce into the new world-view had been assembled. Yet Christian Europe was still strongly attached to its traditional beliefs, as witnessed by the powerful revival of religious orthodoxy in the first half of the eighteenth century. By the outbreak of the American Revolution in 1775, however, a large portion of western Europe's educated elite had embraced many of the new ideas. This acceptance was the work of one of history's most influential groups of intellectuals, the *philosophes.* It was the philosophes who proudly and effectively proclaimed that they, at long last, were bringing the light of knowledge to their ignorant fellow creatures in a great Age of Enlightenment.

Philosophe is the French word for "philosopher," and it was in France that the Enlightenment reached its highest development. The French philosophes were indeed philosophers. They asked fundamental philosophical questions about the meaning of life, about God, human nature, good and evil, and cause and effect. But, in the tradition of Bayle and Fontenelle, they were not content with abstract arguments or ivory-tower speculations among a tiny minority of scholars and professors. They wanted to influence and convince a broad audience.

The philosophes were intensely committed to reforming society and humanity, yet they were not free to write as they wished, since it was illegal in France to criticize openly either church or state. Their most radical works had to circulate in France in manuscript form, very much as critical works are passed from hand to hand in unpublished form in dictatorships today. Knowing that direct attacks would probably be banned or burned, the philosophes wrote novels and plays, histories and philosophies, dictionaries and encyclopedias, all filled with satire and double meanings to spread the message.

One of the greatest philosophes, the baron de Montesquieu (1689–1755), brilliantly pioneered this approach in *The Persian Letters,* an extremely influential social satire published in 1721. Montesquieu's work consisted of amusing letters supposedly written by Persian travelers, who see European customs in unique ways and thereby cleverly criticize existing practices and beliefs.

Having gained fame using wit as a weapon against cruelty and superstition, Montesquieu settled down on his family estate to study history and politics. His interest was partly personal for, like many members of the high French nobility, he was dismayed that royal absolutism had triumphed in France under

Bust of Voltaire Voltaire first gained fame as a poet and playwright, but today his odes and dramas are remembered largely by scholars. The sparkling short stories he occasionally dashed off still captivate the modern reader, however. *Candide* is the most famous of these witty tales. *(The Fine Arts Museums of San Francisco, Mr. and Mrs. E. John Magnin Gift)*

Louis XIV. But Montesquieu was also inspired by the example of the physical sciences, and he set out to apply the critical method to the problem of government in *The Spirit of Laws* (1748). The result was a complex comparative study of republics, monarchies, and despotisms—a great pioneering inquiry in the emerging social sciences.

Showing that forms of government were related to history, geography, and customs, Montesquieu focused on the conditions that would promote liberty and prevent tyranny. He argued that despotism could be avoided if political power were divided and shared by a diversity of classes and orders holding unequal rights and privileges. A strong, independent upper class was especially important, according to Montes-

quieu, because in order to prevent the abuse of power, "it is necessary that by the arrangement of things, power checks power." Admiring greatly the English balance of power among the king, the houses of Parliament, and the independent courts, Montesquieu believed that in France the thirteen high courts —the *parlements*—were front-line defenders of liberty against royal despotism. Clearly no democrat and apprehensive about the uneducated poor, Montesquieu's theory of separation of powers had a great impact on France's wealthy, well-educated elite. The constitutions of the young United States in 1789 and of France in 1791 were based in large part on this theory.

The most famous and in many ways most representative philosophe was François Marie Arouet, who was known by the pen name of Voltaire (1694–1778). In his long career, this son of a comfortable middle-class family wrote over seventy witty volumes, hobnobbed with kings and queens, and died a millionaire because of shrewd business speculations. His early career, however, was turbulent. In 1717 Voltaire was imprisoned for eleven months in the Bastille in Paris for insulting the regent of France. In 1726 a barb from his sharp tongue led a great French nobleman to have him beaten and arrested. This experience made a deep impression on Voltaire. All his life he struggled against legal injustice and class inequalities before the law.

Released from prison after promising to leave the country, Voltaire lived in England for three years. Sharing Montesquieu's enthusiasm for English institutions, Voltaire then wrote various works praising England and popularizing English scientific progress. Newton, he wrote, was history's greatest man, for he had used his genius for the benefit of humanity. "It is," wrote Voltaire, "the man who sways our minds by the prevalence of reason and the native force of truth, not they who reduce mankind to a state of slavery by force and downright violence . . . that claims our reverence and admiration."[11] In the true style of the Enlightenment, Voltaire mixed the glorification of science and reason with an appeal for better people and institutions.

Yet, like almost all of the philosophes, Voltaire was a reformer and not a revolutionary in social and political matters. Returning to France, he was eventually appointed royal historian in 1743, and his *Age of Louis XIV* portrayed Louis as the dignified leader of his age. Voltaire also began a long correspondence with Frederick the Great, and he accepted Frederick's flattering invitation to come brighten up the Prussian court in Berlin. The two men later quarreled, but Voltaire always admired Frederick as a free thinker and an enlightened monarch.

Unlike Montesquieu, Voltaire pessimistically concluded that the best one could hope for in the way of government was a good monarch, since human beings "are very rarely worthy to govern themselves." Nor did he believe in social equality in human affairs. The idea of making servants equal to their masters was "absurd and impossible." The only realizable equality, Voltaire thought, was that "by which the citizen only depends on the laws which protect the freedom of the feeble against the ambitions of the strong."[12]

Voltaire's philosophical and religious positions were much more radical. In the tradition of Bayle, his voluminous writings challenged—often indirectly—the Catholic church and Christian theology at almost every point. Though he was considered by many devout Christians to be a shallow blasphemer, Voltaire's religious views were influential and quite typical of the mature Enlightenment. The essay on religion from his widely read *Philosophical Dictionary* sums up many of his criticisms and beliefs:

I meditated last night; I was absorbed in the contemplation of nature; I admired the immensity, the course, the harmony of these infinite globes which the vulgar do not know how to admire.

I admired still more the intelligence which directs these vast forces. I said to myself: "One must be blind not to be dazzled by this spectacle; one must be stupid not to recognize its author; one must be mad not to worship the Supreme Being."

I was deep in these ideas when one of those genii who fill the intermundane spaces came down to me . . . and transported me into a desert all covered with piles of bones. . . . He began with the first pile. "These," he said, "are the twenty-three thousand Jews who danced before a calf, with the twenty-four thousand who were killed while lying with Midianitish women. The number of those massacred for such errors and offences amounts to nearly three hundred thousand.

"In the other piles are the bones of the Christians slaughtered by each other because of metaphysical disputes. . . ."

"What!" I cried, "brothers have treated their brothers like this, and I have the misfortune to be of this brotherhood! . . . Why assemble here all these abominable monuments to barbarism and fanaticism?"

"To instruct you. . . . Follow me now.". . .

I saw a man with a gentle, simple face, who seemed to me to be about thirty-five years old. From afar he looked with compassion upon those piles of whitened bones, through which I had been led to reach the sage's dwelling place. I was astonished to find his feet swollen and bleeding, his hands likewise, his side pierced, and his ribs laid bare by the cut of the lash. "Good God!" I said to him, "is it possible for a just man, a sage, to be in this state? . . . Was it . . . by priests and judges that you were so cruelly assassinated?"

With great courtesy he answered, "Yes."

"And who were these monsters?"

"They were hypocrites."

"Ah! that says everything; I understand by that one word that they would have condemned you to the cruelest punishment. Had you then proved to them, as Socrates did, that the Moon was not a goddess, and that Mercury was not a god?"

"No, it was not a question of planets. My countrymen did not even know what a planet was; they were all arrant ignoramuses. Their superstitions were quite different from those of the Greeks."

"Then you wanted to teach them a new religion?"

"Not at all; I told them simply: 'Love God with all your heart and your neighbor as yourself, for that is the whole of mankind's duty.' Judge yourself if this precept is not as old as the universe; judge yourself if I brought them a new religion." . . .

"Did you not say once that you were come not to bring peace, but a sword?"

"It was a scribe's error; I told them that I brought peace and not a sword. I never wrote anything; what I said can have been changed without evil intention."

"You did not then contribute in any way by your teaching, either badly reported or badly interpreted, to those frightful piles of bones which I saw on my way to consult with you?"

"I have only looked with horror upon those who have made themselves guilty of all these murders."

. . . [Finally] I asked him to tell me in what true religion consisted.

"Have I not already told you? Love God and your neighbor as yourself." . . .

"Well, if that is so, I take you for my only master."[13]

Voltaire was a prodigious worker. This painting shows him dictating to his secretary from the very moment he hops out of bed. *(Bulloz)*

This passage requires careful study, for it suggests many Enlightenment themes of religion and philosophy. As the opening paragraphs show, Voltaire clearly believed in a God. But the God of Voltaire and most philosophes was a distant, deistic God, a great Clockmaker who built an orderly universe and then stepped aside and let it run. Finally, the philosophes hated all forms of religious intolerance. They believed that people had to be wary of dogmatic certainty and religious disputes, which often led to fanaticism and savage, inhuman action. Simple piety and human kindness—the love of God and the golden rule—were religion enough, even Christianity enough, as Voltaire's interpretation of Christ suggests.

The ultimate strength of the philosophes lay, however, in their numbers, dedication, and organization. The philosophes felt keenly that they were engaged in a common undertaking that transcended individuals. Their greatest and most representative intellectual achievement was, quite fittingly, a group effort —the seventeen-volume *Encyclopedia: The Rational Dictionary of the Sciences, the Arts, and the Crafts,* edited by Denis Diderot (1713–1774) and Jean le Rond d'Alembert (1717–1783). Diderot and d'Alembert made a curious pair. Diderot began his career as a hack writer, first attracting attention with a skeptical tract on religion that was quickly burned by the judges of Paris. D'Alembert was one of Europe's leading scientists and mathematicians, the orphaned and illegitimate son of celebrated aristocrats. Moving in different circles and with different interests, the two men set out to find coauthors who would examine the rapidly expanding whole of human knowledge. Even more fundamentally, they set out to teach people how to think critically and objectively about all matters. As Diderot said, he wanted the *Encyclopedia* to "change the general way of thinking."[14]

The editors of the *Encyclopedia* had to conquer innumerable obstacles. After the appearance in 1751 of the first volume, which dealt with such controversial subjects as atheism, the soul, and blind people—all words beginning with *a* in French—the government temporarily banned publication. The pope later placed it on the Index and pronounced excommunication on all who read or bought it. The timid publisher mutilated some of the articles in the last ten volumes without the editors' consent in an attempt to appease the authorities. Yet Diderot's unwavering belief in the importance of his mission held the encyclopedists together for fifteen years, and the enormous work was completed in 1765. Hundreds of thousands of articles by leading scientists and famous writers, skilled workers and progressive priests, treated every aspect of life and knowledge.

Not every article was daring or original, but the overall effect was little short of revolutionary. Science and the industrial arts were exalted, religion and immortality questioned. Intolerance, legal injustice, and out-of-date social institutions were openly criticized. More generally, the writers of the *Encyclopedia* showed that human beings could use the process of reasoning to expand human knowledge. Encyclopedists were convinced that greater knowledge would result in greater human happiness, for knowledge was useful and made possible economic, social, and political progress. The *Encyclopedia* was widely read and extremely influential in France and throughout western Europe as well. It summed up the new world-view of the Enlightenment.

The Later Enlightenment

After about 1770, the harmonious unity of the philosophes and their thought began to break down. As the new world-view became increasingly accepted by the educated public, some thinkers sought originality by exaggerating certain ideas of the Enlightenment to the exclusion of others. These latter-day philosophes often built rigid, dogmatic systems.

In his *System of Nature* (1770) and other works, the wealthy, aristocratic Baron Paul d'Holbach (1723–1789) argued that human beings were machines completely determined by outside forces. Free will, God, and immortality of the soul were foolish myths. D'Holbach's aggressive atheism and determinism, which were coupled with deep hostility toward Christianity and all other religions, dealt the unity of the Enlightenment movement a severe blow. *Deists* such as Voltaire, who believed in God but not in established churches, were repelled by the inflexible atheism they found in the *System of Nature*. They saw in it the same dogmatic intolerance they had been fighting all their lives.

D'Holbach published his philosophically radical works anonymously to avoid possible prosecution, and in his lifetime he was best known to the public as the generous patron and witty host of writers and intellectuals. At his twice-weekly dinner parties, an inner circle of regulars who knew the baron's secret exchanged ideas with aspiring philosophes and distinguished visitors. One of the most important was the Scottish philosopher David Hume (1711–1776), whose carefully argued skepticism had a powerful long-term influence.

Building on John Locke's teachings on learning (page 585), Hume argued that the human mind is really nothing but a bundle of impressions. These impressions originate only in sense experiences and our habits of joining these experiences together. Since our ideas ultimately reflect only our sense experiences, our reason cannot tell us anything about questions like the origin of the universe or the existence of God, questions that cannot be verified by sense experience (in the form of controlled experiments or mathematics). Paradoxically, Hume's rationalistic inquiry ended up undermining the Enlightenment's faith in the very power of reason itself.

Another French aristocrat, the marquis Marie-Jean de Condorcet (1743–1794), transformed the Enlightenment belief in gradual, hard-won progress into fanciful utopianism. In his *Progress of the Human Mind,* written in 1793 during the French Revolution, Condorcet tracked the nine stages of human progress that had already occurred and predicted that the tenth would bring perfection. Ironically, Condorcet wrote this work while fleeing for his life. Caught and condemned by revolutionary extremists, he preferred death by his own hand to the blade of the guillotine.

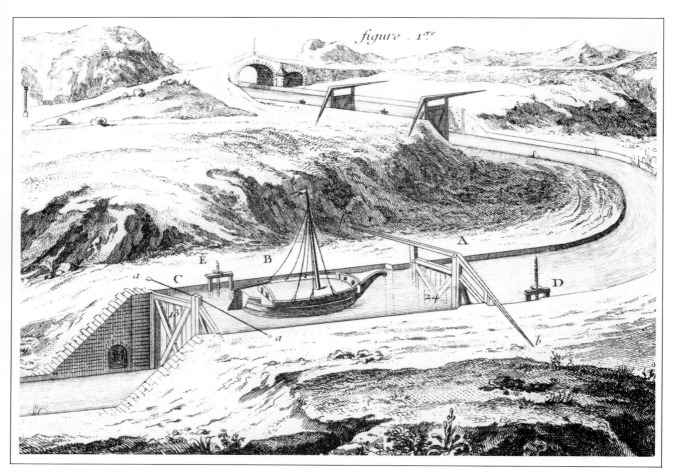

figure 1.re

Canal with Locks The articles on science and the industrial arts in the *Encyclopedia* carried lavish explanatory illustrations. This typical engraving from the section on water and its uses shows advances in canal building and reflects the encyclopedists' faith in technical progress. *(University of Illinois)*

Other thinkers and writers after about 1770 began to attack the Enlightenment's faith in reason, progress, and moderation. The most famous of these was the Swiss Jean-Jacques Rousseau (1712–1778), a brilliant but difficult thinker, an appealing but neurotic individual. Born into a poor family of watchmakers in Geneva, Rousseau went to Paris and was greatly influenced by Diderot and Voltaire. Always extraordinarily sensitive and suspicious, Rousseau came to believe his philosophe friends were plotting against him. In the mid-1750s he broke with them personally and intellectually, living thereafter as a lonely outsider with his uneducated common-law wife and going in his own highly original direction.

Like other Enlightenment thinkers, Rousseau was passionately committed to individual freedom. Un-like them, however, he attacked rationalism and civilization as destroying rather than liberating the individual. Warm, spontaneous feeling had to complement and correct the cold intellect. Moreover, the individual's basic goodness had to be protected from the cruel refinements of civilization. These ideas greatly influenced the early romantic movement (see Chapter 23), which rebelled against the culture of the Enlightenment in the late eighteenth century.

Applying his heartfelt ideas to children, Rousseau had a powerful impact on the development of modern education. In his famous treatise *Emile* (1762), he argued that education must shield the naturally unspoiled child from the corrupting influences of civilization and too many books. According to Rousseau, children must develop naturally and spontane-

Sugar Cane Mill Enlightenment thinkers were keenly interested in non-European societies and in the comparative study of human development. This engraving depicts an aspect of sugar production with slave labor in the Americas. *(Courtesy of the University of Minnesota Libraries)*

ously, at their own speed and in their own way. It is eloquent testimony to Rousseau's troubled life and complicated personality that he placed all five of his own children in orphanages.

Rousseau also made an important contribution to political theory in the *Social Contract* (1762). His fundamental ideas were the general will and popular sovereignty. According to Rousseau, the general will is sacred and absolute, reflecting the common interests of the people, who have displaced the monarch as the holder of the sovereign power. The general will is not necessarily the will of the majority, however, although minorities have to subordinate themselves to it without question. Little noticed before the French Revolution, Rousseau's concept of the general will appealed greatly to democrats and nationalists after

1789. The concept has also been used since 1789 by many dictators, who have claimed that they, rather than some momentary majority of the voters, represent the general will and thus the true interests of democracy and the sovereign masses.

THE SOCIAL SETTING OF THE ENLIGHTENMENT

The philosophes were splendid talkers as well as effective writers. Indeed, sparkling conversation in private homes spread Enlightenment ideas to Europe's upper-middle class and aristocracy. Paris set the example, and other French cities and European capitals followed. In Paris a number of talented and often rich

Madame Geoffrin's Salon In this stylized group portrait a famous actor reads to a gathering of leading philosophes and aristocrats in 1755. Third from the right presiding over her gathering, is Madame Geoffrin, next to the sleepy ninety-eight-year-old Bernard de Fontenelle. *(Malmaison Chateau/Giraudon/Art Resource)*

women presided over regular social gatherings of the great and near-great in their elegant drawing rooms, or *salons*. There a d'Alembert and a Fontenelle could exchange witty, uncensored observations on literature, science, and philosophy with great aristocrats, wealthy middle-class financiers, high-ranking officials, and noteworthy foreigners. These intellectual salons practiced the equality the philosophes preached. They were open to all men and women with good manners, provided only that they were famous or talented, rich or important. More generally, the philosophes championed greater rights and expanded education for women, arguing that the subordination of females was an unreasonable prejudice and the sign of a barbaric society.

One of the most famous salons was that of Madame Geoffrin, the unofficial godmother of the *Encyclopedia*. Having lost her parents at an early age, the future Madame Geoffrin was married at fifteen by her well-meaning grandmother to a rich and boring businessman of forty-eight. It was the classic marriage of convenience—the poor young girl and the rich old man—and neither side ever pretended that love was a consideration. After dutifully raising her children, Madame Geoffrin sought to break out of her gilded cage as she entered middle age. The very proper businessman's wife became friendly with a neighbor, the marquise de Tencin. In her youth this aristocratic beauty had been rather infamous as the mistress of the regent of France, but she had settled down to run a salon that counted Fontenelle and the philosopher Montesquieu among its regular guests.

When the marquise died in 1749, Madame Geoffrin tactfully transferred these luminaries to her spacious mansion for regular dinners. At first Madame Geoffrin's husband loudly protested the arrival of this horde of "parasites." But his wife's will was much stronger than his, and he soon opened his purse and even appeared at the twice-weekly dinners. "Who was that old man at the end of the table who never said anything?" an innocent newcomer asked one evening. "That," replied Madame Geoffrin without the slightest emotion, "was my husband. He's dead."[15]

When Monsieur Geoffrin's death became official, Madame Geoffrin put the large fortune and a spacious mansion she inherited to good use. She welcomed the encyclopedists—Diderot, d'Alembert, Fontenelle, and a host of others. She gave them generous financial aid and helped to save their enterprise from collapse, especially after the first eight volumes were burned by the authorities in 1759. She also corresponded with the king of Sweden and Catherine the Great of Russia. Madame Geoffrin was, however, her own woman. She remained a practicing Christian and would not tolerate attacks on the church in her house. It was said that distinguished foreigners felt they had not seen Paris unless they had been invited to one of her dinners. The plain and long-neglected Madame Geoffrin managed to become the most renowned hostess of the eighteenth century.

There were many other hostesses, but Madame Geoffrin's greatest rival, Madame du Deffand, was one of the most interesting. While Madame Geoffrin was middle-class, pious, and chaste, Madame du Deffand was a skeptic from the nobility, who lived fast and easy, at least in the early years. Another difference was that women—mostly highly intelligent, worldly members of the nobility—were fully the equal of men in Madame du Deffand's intellectual salon. Forever pursuing fulfillment in love and life, Madame du Deffand was an accomplished and liberated woman. An exceptionally fine letter writer, she carried on a vast correspondence with leading men and women all across Europe. Voltaire was her most enduring friend.

Madame du Deffand's closest female friend was Julie de Lespinasse, a beautiful, talented young woman whom she befriended and made her protégée. The never-acknowledged illegitimate daughter of noble parents, Julie de Lespinasse had a hard youth, but she flowered in Madame du Deffand's drawing room—so much so that she was eventually dismissed by her jealous patroness.

Once again Julie de Lespinasse triumphed. Her friends gave her money so that she could form her own salon. Her highly informal gatherings—she was not rich enough to supply more than tea and cake—attracted the keenest minds in France and Europe. As one philosophe wrote:

She could unite the different types, even the most antagonistic, sustaining the conversation by a well-aimed phrase, animating and guiding it at will. . . . Politics, religion, philosophy, news: nothing was excluded. Her circle met daily from five to nine. There one found men of all ranks in the State, the Church, and the Court, soldiers and foreigners, and the leading writers of the day.[16]

Thus in France the ideas of the Enlightenment thrived in a social setting that graciously united members of the intellectual, economic, and social elites. Never before and never again would social and intellectual life be so closely and so pleasantly joined. In such an atmosphere, the philosophes, the French nobility, and the upper-middle class increasingly influenced one another. Critical thinking became fashionable and flourished alongside hopes for human progress through greater knowledge.

THE EVOLUTION OF ABSOLUTISM

How did the Enlightenment influence political developments? To this important question there is no easy answer. On the one hand, the philosophes were primarily interested in converting people to critical "scientific" thinking and were not particularly concerned with politics. On the other hand, such thinking naturally led to political criticism and interest in political reform. Educated people, who belonged mainly to the nobility and middle class, came to regard political change as both possible and desirable. A further problem is that Enlightenment thinkers had different views on politics. Some, led by the nobleman Montesquieu, argued for curbs on monarchial power in order to promote liberty, and some French judges applied such theories in practical questions.

Until the American Revolution, however, most Enlightenment thinkers believed that political change could best come from above—from the ruler —rather than from below, especially in central and eastern Europe. There were several reasons for this essentially moderate belief. First, royal absolutism was a fact of life, and the kings and queens of Europe's leading states clearly had no intention of giving up their great powers. Therefore the philosophes realistically concluded that a benevolent absolutism offered the best opportunities for improving society. Critical thinking was turning the art of good government into an exact science. It was necessary only to educate and "enlighten" the monarch, who could then make good laws and promote human happiness. Second, philosophes turned toward rulers because rulers seemed to be listening, treating them with respect, and seeking their advice. Finally, although the philosophes did not dwell on this fact, they distrusted the masses. Known simply as "the people" in the eighteenth century, the peasant masses and the urban poor were, according to the philosophes, still enchained by religious superstitions and violent passions. No doubt the people were maturing, but they were still children in need of firm parental guidance.

Encouraged and instructed by the philosophes, several absolutist rulers of the later eighteenth century tried to govern in an "enlightened" manner. Yet, because European monarchs had long been locked in an intense international competition, a more enlightened state often meant in practice a more effective state, a state capable of expanding its territory and defeating its enemies. Moreover, reforms from above had to be grafted onto previous historical developments and existing social structures. Little wonder, then, that the actual programs and accomplishments of these rulers varied greatly. Let us therefore examine the evolution of monarchial absolutism at close range before trying to form any overall judgment regarding the meaning of what historians have often called the "enlightened absolutism" of the later eighteenth century.

THE "GREATS": FREDERICK OF PRUSSIA AND CATHERINE OF RUSSIA

Just as the French culture and absolutism of Louis XIV provided models for European rulers in the late seventeenth century, the Enlightenment teachings of the French philosophes inspired European monarchs in the second half of the eighteenth century. French was the international language of the educated classes, and the education of future kings and queens across Europe lay in the hands of French tutors espousing Enlightenment ideas. France's cultural leadership was reinforced by the fact that it was still the wealthiest and most populous country in Europe. Thus, absolutist monarchs in several west German and Italian states, as well as in Spain and Portugal, proclaimed themselves more enlightened. By far the most influential of the new-style monarchs were Frederick II of Prussia and Catherine II of Russia, both styled "the Great."

FREDERICK THE GREAT. Frederick II (1740–1786), also known as Frederick the Great, built masterfully on his father's work. This was somewhat surprising for, like many children with tyrannical parents, he rebelled against his family's wishes in his early years. Rejecting the crude life of the barracks, Frederick embraced culture and literature, even writing poetry and fine prose in French, a language his father detested. He threw off his father's dour Calvinism and dabbled with atheism. After trying unsuccessfully to run away at age eighteen in 1730, he was virtually imprisoned and even compelled to watch his companion in flight beheaded at his father's command. Yet, like many other rebellious youths, Frederick eventually reached a reconciliation with his father, and by the time he came to the throne ten years later he was determined to use the splendid army his father had left him.

When, therefore, the emperor of Austria, Charles VI, also died in 1740 and his young and beautiful daughter, Maria Theresa, became ruler of the Habsburg dominions, Frederick suddenly and without warning invaded her rich, all-German province of Silesia. This action defied solemn Prussian promises to respect the Pragmatic Sanction, which guaranteed Maria Theresa's succession, but no matter. For Frederick, it was the opportunity of a lifetime to expand the size and power of Prussia. Although Maria Theresa succeeded in dramatically rallying the normally quarrelsome Hungarian nobility, her multinational army was no match for Prussian precision. In 1742, as other greedy powers were falling on her lands in the general European War of the Austrian Succession (1740–1748), she was forced to cede all of Silesia to

Maria Theresa and her husband pose with eleven of their sixteen children at Schön-brunn palace. Joseph, the heir to the throne, stands at the center of the star pattern. Wealthy women often had very large families, in part because they seldom nursed their babies as poor women usually did. *(Kunsthistorisches Museum, Vienna)*

Prussia. In one stroke, Prussia doubled its population to 6 million people. Now Prussia unquestionably towered above all the other German states and stood as a European Great Power.

Successful in 1742, Frederick had to spend much of his reign fighting against great odds to save Prussia from total destruction. Maria Theresa was determined to regain Silesia, and when the ongoing competition between Britain and France for colonial empire brought renewed conflict in 1756, her able chief minister fashioned an aggressive alliance with France and Russia. The aim of the alliance was to conquer Prussia and divide up its territory, just as Frederick II and other monarchs had so recently sought to partition the Austrian Empire. Frederick led his army brilliantly, striking repeatedly at vastly superior forces invading from all sides. At times he believed all was lost, but he fought on with stoic courage. In the end, he was miraculously saved: Peter III came to the Russian throne in 1762 and called off the attack against Frederick, whom he greatly admired.

In the early years of his reign, Frederick II had kept his enthusiasm for Enlightenment culture strictly separated from a brutal concept of international politics. He wrote:

Of all States, from the smallest to the biggest, one can safely say that the fundamental rule of government is the principle of extending their territories. . . . The passions of rulers have no other curb but the limits of their power. Those are the fixed laws of European politics to which every politician submits.[17]

Catherine the Great Intelligent, pleasure-loving, and vain, Catherine succeeded in bringing Russia closer to western Europe than ever before. *(John R. Freeman)*

But the terrible struggle of the Seven Years' War tempered Frederick and brought him to consider how more humane policies for his subjects might also strengthen the state.

Thus Frederick went beyond a superficial commitment to Enlightenment culture for himself and his circle. He tolerantly allowed his subjects to believe as they wished in religious and philosophical matters. He promoted the advancement of knowledge, improving his country's schools and universities.

Second, Frederick tried to improve the lives of his subjects more directly. As he wrote his friend Voltaire, "I must enlighten my people, cultivate their manners and morals, and make them as happy as human beings can be, or as happy as the means at my disposal permit." The legal system and the bureaucracy were Frederick's primary tools. Prussia's laws were simplified, and judges decided cases quickly and impartially. Prussian officials became famous for their hard work and honesty. After the Seven Years' War ended in 1763, Frederick's government also energetically promoted the reconstruction of agriculture and industry in his war-torn country. In all this Frederick set a good example. He worked hard and lived modestly, claiming that he was "only the first servant of the state." Thus Frederick justified monarchy in terms of practical results and said nothing of the divine right of kings.

Frederick's dedication to high-minded principles went only so far, however. He never tried to change Prussia's existing social structure. True, he condemned serfdom in the abstract, but he accepted it in practice and did not even free the serfs on his own estates. He accepted and extended the privileges of the nobility, which he saw as his primary ally in the defense and extension of his realm. It became practically impossible for a middle-class person to gain a top position in the government. The Junker nobility remained the backbone of the army and the entire Prussian state.

CATHERINE THE GREAT. Catherine the Great of Russia (1762–1796) was one of the most remarkable rulers who ever lived, and the philosophes adored her. Catherine was a German princess from Anhalt-Zerbst, a totally insignificant principality sandwiched between Prussia and Saxony. Her father commanded a regiment of the Prussian army, but her mother was related to the Romanovs of Russia, and that proved to be her chance.

Peter the Great had abolished the hereditary succession of tsars so that he could name his successor and thus preserve his policies. This move opened a period of palace intrigue and a rapid turnover of rulers until Peter's youngest daughter Elizabeth came to the Russian throne in 1741. A crude, shrewd woman noted for her hard drinking and hard loving —one of her official lovers was an illiterate shepherd boy—Elizabeth named her nephew Peter heir to the throne and chose Catherine to be his wife in 1744. It was a mismatch from the beginning. The fifteen-year-old Catherine was intelligent and attractive; her husband was stupid and ugly, his face badly scarred by smallpox. Ignored by her childish husband, Catherine carefully studied Russian, endlessly read writers like Bayle and Voltaire, and made friends at court. Soon she knew what she wanted. "I did not care about Peter," she wrote in her *Memoirs,* "but I did care about the crown."[18]

As the old empress Elizabeth approached death, Catherine plotted against her unpopular husband. A dynamic, sensuous woman, Catherine used her sexuality to good political advantage. She selected as her new lover a tall, dashing young officer named Gregory Orlov, who with his four officer brothers commanded considerable support among the soldiers stationed in St. Petersburg. When Peter came to the throne in 1762, his decision to withdraw Russian troops from the coalition against Prussia alienated the army. Nor did Peter III's attempt to gain support from the Russian nobility by freeing it from compulsory state service succeed. At the end of six months, Catherine and the military conspirators deposed Peter III in a palace revolution. Then the Orlov brothers murdered him. The German princess became empress of Russia.

Catherine had drunk deeply at the Enlightenment well. Never questioning the common assumption that absolute monarchy was the best form of government, she set out to rule in an enlightened manner. One of her most enduring goals was to bring the sophisticated culture of western Europe to backward Russia. To do so, she imported Western architects, sculptors, musicians, and intellectuals. She bought masterpieces of Western art in wholesale lots and patronized the philosophes. An enthusiastic letter writer, she corresponded extensively with Voltaire and praised him as the "champion of the human race." When the French government banned the *Encyclopedia,* she offered to publish it in St. Petersburg.

She discussed reform with Diderot in St. Petersburg; and when Diderot needed money, she purchased his library for a small fortune but allowed him to keep it during his lifetime. With these and countless similar actions, Catherine skillfully won a good press for herself and for her country in the West. Moreover, this intellectual ruler, who wrote plays and loved good talk, set the tone for the entire Russian nobility. Peter the Great westernized Russian armies, but it was Catherine who westernized the thinking of the Russian nobility.

Catherine's second goal was domestic reform, and she began her reign with sincere and ambitious projects. Better laws were a major concern. In 1767 she drew up enlightened instructions for the special legislative commission she appointed to prepare a new law code. No new unified code was ever produced, but Catherine did restrict the practice of torture and allowed limited religious toleration. She also tried to improve education and strengthen local government. The philosophes applauded these measures and hoped more would follow.

Such was not the case. In 1773 a simple Cossack soldier named Emelian Pugachev sparked a gigantic uprising of serfs, very much as Stenka Razin had done a century earlier (page 558). Proclaiming himself the true tsar, Pugachev issued "decrees" abolishing serfdom, taxes, and army service. Thousands joined his cause, slaughtering landlords and officials over a vast area of southwestern Russia. Pugachev's untrained hordes eventually proved no match for Catherine's noble-led regular army. Betrayed by his own company, Pugachev was captured and savagely executed.

Pugachev's rebellion was a decisive turning point in Catherine's domestic policy. On coming to the throne she had condemned serfdom in theory, but she was smart enough to realize that any changes would have to be very gradual or else she would quickly follow her departed husband. Pugachev's rebellion put an end to any illusions she might have had about reforming serfdom. The peasants were clearly dangerous, and her empire rested on the support of the nobility. After 1775 Catherine gave the nobles absolute control of their serfs. She extended serfdom into new areas, such as the Ukraine. In 1785 she formalized the nobility's privileged position, freeing them forever from taxes and state service. She also confiscated the lands of the Russian Orthodox church and gave them to favorite officials. Under

Catherine, the Russian nobility attained its most exalted position, and serfdom entered its most oppressive phase.

Catherine's third goal was territorial expansion, and in this respect she was extremely successful. Her armies subjugated the last descendants of the Mongols, the Crimean Tartars, and began the conquest of the Caucasus.

Her greatest coup by far was the partitioning of Poland. Poland showed the dangers of failing to build a strong absolutist state. For decades all important decisions had required the unanimous agreement of every Polish noble, which meant that nothing could ever be done. When between 1768 and 1772 Catherine's armies scored unprecedented victories against the Turks and thereby threatened to disturb the balance of power between Russia and Austria in eastern Europe, Frederick of Prussia obligingly came forward with a deal. He proposed that Turkey be let off easily, and that Prussia, Austria, and Russia each compensate itself by taking a gigantic slice of Polish territory. Catherine jumped at the chance. The first partition of Poland took place in 1772. Two more partitions, in 1793 and 1795, gave all three powers more Polish territory, and the kingdom of Poland simply vanished from the map (see Map 18.1).

Expansion helped Catherine keep the nobility happy, for it provided her vast new lands to give to her faithful servants. Expansion also helped Catherine reward her lovers, of whom twenty-one have been definitely identified. On all these royal favorites she lavished large estates with many serfs, as if to make sure there were no hard feelings when her interest cooled. Until the end this remarkably talented woman—who always believed that, in spite of her domestic setbacks, she was slowly civilizing Russia—kept her zest for life. Fascinated by a new twenty-two-year-old flame when she was a roly-poly grandmother in her sixties, she happily reported her good fortune to a favorite former lover: "I have come back to life like a frozen fly; I am gay and well."[19]

Absolutism in France and Austria

The Enlightenment's influence on political developments in France and Austria was complex. In France, the monarchy maintained its absolutist claims, and some philosophes like Voltaire believed that the king was still the best source of needed reform. At the same time, discontented nobles and learned judges drew on thinkers such as Montesquieu for liberal arguments, and they sought with some success to limit the king's power. In Austria, two talented rulers did manage to introduce major reforms, although traditional power politics were more important than Enlightenment teachings.

LOUIS XV OF FRANCE. In building French absolutism, Louis XIV successfully drew on the middle class to curb the political power of the nobility. As long as the Grand Monarch lived, the nobility could only grumble and, like the duke of Saint-Simon in his *Memoirs,* scornfully lament the rise of "the vile bourgeoisie." But when Louis XIV finally died in 1715, to be succeeded by his five-year-old great-grandson, Louis XV (1715–1774), the Sun King's elaborate system of absolutist rule was challenged in a general reaction. Favored by the duke of Orléans, who governed as regent until 1723, the nobility made a strong comeback.

Most importantly, the duke restored to the high court of Paris—the Parlement—the right to "register" and thereby approve the king's decrees. This was a fateful step. The judges of the Parlement of Paris had originally come from the middle class, and their high position reflected the way that Louis XIV (and earlier French monarchs) had chosen to use that class to build the royal bureaucracy so necessary for an absolutist state. By the eighteenth century, however, these "middle-class" judges had risen to become hereditary nobles for, although Louis XIV had curbed the political power of the nobility, he had never challenged its enormous social prestige. Thus, high position in the government continued to bestow the noble status that middle-class officials wanted, either immediately or after three generations of continuous service. The judges of Paris, like many high-ranking officials, actually owned their government jobs and freely passed them on as private property from father to son. By supporting the claim of this well-entrenched and increasingly aristocratic group to register the king's laws, the duke of Orléans sanctioned a counterweight to absolute power.

These implications became clear when the heavy expenses of the War of the Austrian Succession plunged France into financial crisis. In 1748 Louis

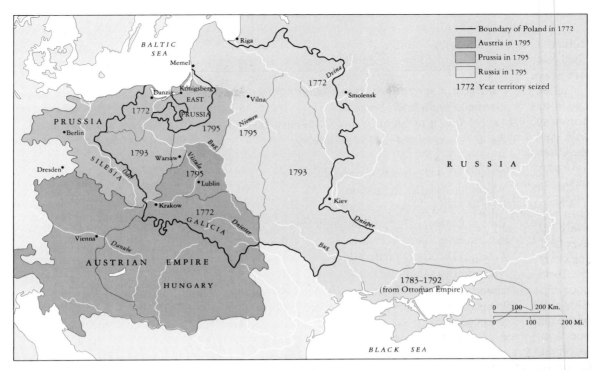

MAP 18.1 The Partition of Poland and Russia's Expansion, 1772–1795 Though all three of the great eastern absolutist states profited from the division of large but weak Poland, Catherine's Russia gained the most.

XV appointed a finance minister who decreed a 5 percent income tax on every individual, regardless of social status. Exemption from most taxation had long been a hallowed privilege of the nobility, and other important groups—the clergy, the large towns, and some wealthy bourgeoisie—had also gained special tax advantages over time. The result was a vigorous protest from many sides, and the Parlement of Paris refused to ratify the tax law. The monarchy retreated; the new tax was dropped.

Following the disastrously expensive Seven Years' War, the conflict re-emerged. The government tried to maintain emergency taxes after the war ended. The Parlement of Paris protested and even challenged the basis of royal authority, claiming that the king's power must necessarily be limited to protect liberty. Once again the government caved in and withdrew the wartime taxes in 1764. Emboldened by its striking victory and widespread support from France's educated elite, the judicial opposition in

Paris and the provinces pressed its demands. In a barrage of pamphlets and legal briefs, it asserted that the king could not levy taxes without the consent of the Parlement of Paris acting as the representative of the entire nation.

Indolent and sensual by nature, more interested in his many mistresses than in affairs of state, Louis XV finally roused himself for a determined defense of his absolutist inheritance. "The magistrates," he angrily told the Parlement of Paris in a famous face-to-face confrontation, "are my officers. . . . In my person only does the sovereign power rest."[20] In 1768 Louis appointed a tough career official named René de Maupeou as chancellor and ordered him to crush the judicial opposition.

Maupeou abolished the Parlement of Paris and exiled its members to isolated backwaters in the provinces. He created a new and docile parlement of royal officials, and he began once again to tax the privileged groups. A few philosophes like Voltaire ap-

THE ENLIGHTENMENT

1686	Fontenelle, *Conversations on the Plurality of Worlds*
1687	Newton, *Principia Mathematica*
1690	Locke, *Essay Concerning Human Understanding* and *Second Treatise on Civil Government*
1697	Bayle, *Historical and Critical Dictionary*
1715–1774	Rule of Louis XV in France
1721	Montesquieu, *The Persian Letters*
1740–1748	War of the Austrian Succession
1740–1780	Rule of Maria Theresa in Austria
1740–1786	Rule of Frederick II (the Great) in Prussia
1742	Austria cedes Silesia to Prussia
1743	Voltaire, *The Age of Louis XIV*
1748	Montesquieu, *The Spirit of the Laws*
	Hume, *An Enquiry Concerning Human Understanding*
1751–1765	Publication of the *Encyclopedia,* edited by Diderot and d'Alembert
1756–1763	Seven Years' War
1762	Rousseau, *The Social Contract*
1762–1796	Rule of Catherine II (the Great) in Russia
1767	Catherine the Great appoints commission to prepare a new law code
1770	D'Holbach, *The System of Nature*
1771	Maupeou, Louis XV's chancellor, abolishes Parlement of Paris
1772	First partition of Poland among Russia, Prussia, and Austria
1774	Ascension of Louis XVI in France: restoration of Parlement of Paris
1780–1790	Rule of Joseph II in Austria
1781	Abolition of serfdom in Austria
1785	Catherine the Great issues the Russian Charter of Nobility, which guarantees the servitude of the peasants
1790–1792	Rule of Leopold II in Austria: serfdom is re-established
1793	Second partition of Poland
	Condorcet, *The Progress of the Human Mind*
1795	Third partition of Poland, which completes its absorption

plauded these measures: the sovereign was using his power to introduce badly needed reforms that had been blocked by a self-serving aristocratic elite. Most philosophes and educated public opinion as a whole sided with the old parlements, however, and there was widespread dissatisfaction with royal despotism. Yet the monarchy's power was still great enough for Maupeou to simply ride over the opposition, and Louis XV would probably have prevailed—if he had lived to a very ripe old age.

But Louis XV died in 1774. The new king, Louis XVI (1774–1792), was a shy twenty-year-old with good intentions. Taking the throne, he is reported to have said: "What I should like most is to be loved."[21] The eager-to-please monarch decided to yield in the face of such strong criticism from so much of France's elite. He dismissed Maupeou and repudiated the strong-willed minister's work. The old Parlement of Paris was reinstated, as enlightened public opinion cheered and hoped for moves toward repre-

ART: A MIRROR OF SOCIETY

Art reveals the interests and values of society and frequently gives intimate and unique glimpses of how people actually lived. In portraits and statues, whether of saints, generals, philosophers, popes, poets, or merchants, it preserves the memory and fame of men and women who shaped society. In paintings, drawings, and carvings, it also shows how people worked, played, relaxed, suffered, and triumphed. Art, therefore, is extremely useful to the historian, especially for periods when written records are scarce. Every work of art and every part of it has meaning and has something of its own to say.

Art also manifests the changes and continuity of European life; as values changed in Europe, so did major artistic themes. Europeans of the sixteenth and seventeenth centuries remained deeply religious and showed a new interest in the world around them; their middle-class attitudes and experiences and their appreciation of agricultural life replaced the activities and interests of a small, wealthy, cultural elite as the subject matter of art. The scenes of everyday life presented in seventeenth-century genre painting were considered interesting in themselves and, as the works following by Siberechts and Van Ostade support, worthy of high art.

Just as Renaissance princes had used art to memorialize themselves, so in the later seventeenth century all the arts were organized to exalt and glorify the Sun King, Louis XIV. As the following painting by Lebrun, *Louis XIV's Visit to the Gobelin Factory,* demonstrates, art served the image of the French absolute monarch as the personification of the French state. Art thereby reflected the political ideal of the times. Known as the court baroque style, it spread throughout France, England, Germany, Italy, and Spain. Politics had triumphed over other expressions of cultural life.

In painting the baroque reached maturity early with Peter Paul Rubens. Court painter to James I and Charles I of England and to Louis XIII and Marie de' Medici of France, Rubens also illustrated many classical and rural subjects. In *Country Fair* (1635), below, against an immense landscape twilight descends, bringing to a close the peasants' day of celebration. (Cliché des Musées Nationaux-Paris.)

The Anatomy Lesson *(above)* Rembrandt (ca 1632). In the seventeenth century science became modern, in the sense that it was based on direct observation and experimentation. This highly dramatic scene, one of the earliest of Rembrandt (who painted it at age 25), shows his masterful control of light and shade, borne out by the tense atmosphere of the laboratory, and the expressions of deep curiosity on the students' faces. *(Rijksmuseum, Amsterdam)*

A Woman Weighing Gold *(above)* Vermeer (ca 1657). Vermeer painted pictures of middle-class women involved in ordinary activities in the quiet interiors of their homes. Unrivaled among Dutch masters for his superb control of light, in this painting Vermeer illuminates the pregnant woman weighing gold on her scales, as Christ in the painting on the wall weighs the saved and the damned. *(National Gallery of Art, Washington; Widener Collection)*

Louis XIV's Visit to the Gobelin Factory *(left, above)* Lebrun (1663–1675). World-famous for its superb tapestries, the Gobelin factory was a state-owned industry under Colbert's supervision. It produced everything needed for furnishing the royal palaces. The king (left, holding his hat) gazes around, while the tapestry above celebrates Alexander the Great's triumphs, considered a model of Louis XIV's. *(Haeseler/Art Resource)*

Saint Mark's Square: Looking South-East *(above)* Canaletto (1697–1768). The Venetian Canaletto worked primarily for wealthy aristocrats. His most enthusiastic patrons were English nobles, who became enamoured of his magnificent views of historic Venice while making the continental "grand tour" that topped off the education of the English upper class. This lively scene, showing much a visitor would wish to remember, features Saint Mark's on the left, the Ducal Palace, ships in the lagoon, and market stalls. *(National Gallery, Washington)*

Gersaint's Shop *(left, below)* Watteau. In reaction to the rigid and pompous spirit of Louis XIV's Versailles, Watteau's paintings captured the grace and informality of aristocratic life during the early reign of Louis XV. Here the viewer steps from the cobblestoned streets directly into Gersaint's salesroom with its busy assistants and rich patrons. A clerk (left) packs away a portrait of Louis XIV, reflecting the end of an era, while the seductive figures in many paintings on the walls suggest the new rococo frivolity. *(Staatliche Museen zu Berlin)*

The Ford *(left, below)* Jan Siberechts (1627–1703). Most seventeenth-century artists specialized. The Flemish painter Siberechts concentrated on water-logged landscapes of his native Flanders, which he peopled with peaceful, hardworking peasants absorbed in their daily tasks. Viewing this scene, one feels the slow, difficult movement of beasts and goods along a flooded road, as well as the solid virtues of the little milkmaid and the young peasant woman. *(Niedersächsisches Landesmuseum, Hannover)*

The Spinners *(above)* Diego Velázquez (1599–1660). Spain's master of realism captures women workers in a tapestry workshop and three ladies inspecting a tapestry in the background. Or so people long believed. Modern critics see a mythological weaving competition between the low-born Arachne on the right and the goddess of arts and crafts on the left. (The gutsy Arachne lost and was turned into a spider.) Art historians also have their debates and conflicting interpretations. *(Museo del Prado, Madrid)*

Rustic Interior *(left, above)* Adriaen Van Ostade (1610–1685). Peasant life was also the theme of the Dutch painter Van Ostade. But Van Ostade did not idealize his peasants, who usually lounge in the midst of modest possessions and sport a comical, not-quite-sober air. Pictures of ordinary life, like those of Van Ostade and Siberechts, were small in size, sharply detailed, and well adapted for the living rooms of the Dutch middle class. *(Rijksmuseum, Amsterdam)*

Herrenchiemsee, the Hall of Mirrors by Candlelight *(above)* The splendor of Louis XIV's palace at Versailles long served as a model of royal elegance for European monarchs. Ludwig II of Bavaria built his version of Versailles and its famous Hall of Mirrors on a large lake in southern Germany in the nineteenth century. In the summer season the visitor can still savour the full beauty of Ludwig's Hall of Mirrors at evening concerts by candlelight. *(Werner Neumeister/George Rainbird/Robert Harding)*

sentative government. Such moves were not forth-coming. Instead, a weakened but unrepentant monarchy faced a judicial opposition that claimed to speak for the entire French nation. Increasingly locked in stalemate, the country was drifting toward renewed financial crisis and political upheaval.

THE AUSTRIAN HABSBURGS. Joseph II (1780–1790) was a fascinating individual. For an earlier generation of historians he was the "revolutionary emperor," a tragic hero whose lofty reforms were undone by the landowning nobility he dared to challenge. More recent scholarship has revised this romantic interpretation and stressed how Joseph II continued the state-building work of his mother, the empress Maria Theresa, a remarkable but old-fashioned absolutist.

Maria Theresa's long reign (1740–1780) began with her neighbors, led by Frederick II of Prussia, invading her lands and trying to dismember them (see page 594). Emerging from the long War of the Austrian Succession in 1748 with only the serious loss of Silesia, Maria Theresa and her closest ministers were determined to introduce reforms that would make the state stronger and more efficient. Three aspects were most important in these reforms. First, Maria Theresa introduced measures to bring relations between church and state under government control. Like some medieval rulers, the most devout and very Catholic Maria Theresa aimed at limiting the papacy's political influence in her realm. Second, a whole series of administrative reforms strengthened the central bureaucracy, smoothed out some provincial differences, and revamped the tax system, taxing even the lands of nobles without special exemptions. Finally, the government sought to improve the lot of the agricultural population, cautiously reducing the power of lords over both their hereditary serfs and partially free peasant tenants.

Coregent with his mother from 1765 onward and a strong supporter of change, Joseph II moved forward rapidly when he came to the throne in 1780. He controlled the established Catholic church even more closely, in an attempt to ensure that it produced better citizens. He granted religious toleration and civic rights to Protestants and Jews—a radical innovation that impressed this contemporaries. In even more spectacular peasant reforms, Joseph abolished serfdom in 1781, and in 1789 he decreed that all peasant labor obligations be converted into cash payments.

This ill-conceived measure was violently rejected not only by the nobility but by the peasants it was intended to help, since their primitive barter economy was woefully lacking in money. When a disillusioned Joseph died prematurely at forty-nine, the entire Habsburg Empire was in turmoil. His brother Leopold (1790–1792) was forced to cancel Joseph's radical edicts in order to re-establish order. Peasants lost most of their recent gains, and once again they were required to do forced labor for their lords, as in the 1770s under Maria Theresa.

AN OVERALL EVALUATION

Having examined the evolution of monarchial absolutism in four leading states, it is possible to look for meaningful generalizations and evaluate the overall influence of Enlightenment thought on politics. That thought, it will be remembered, was clustered in two distinct schools: the liberal critique of unregulated monarchy promoted by Montesquieu and the defenders of royal absolutism led by Voltaire.

It is clear that France diverged from its eastern neighbors in its political developments in the eighteenth century. Thus, while neither the French monarchy nor the eastern rulers abandoned the absolutist claims and institutions they had inherited, the monarch's capacity to govern in a truly absolutist manner declined substantially in France, which was not the case in eastern Europe. The immediate cause of this divergence was the political resurgence of the French nobility after 1715 and the growth of judicial opposition, led by the Parlement of Paris. More fundamentally, however, the judicial and aristocratic opposition in France achieved its still rather modest successes because it received major support from educated public opinion, which increasingly made the liberal critique of unregulated royal authority its own. In France, then, the proponents of absolute monarchy were increasingly on the defense, as was the French monarchy itself.

The situation in eastern Europe was different. The liberal critique of absolute monarchy remained an intellectual curiosity, and proponents of reform from above held sway. Moreover, despite their differences, the leading eastern monarchs of the later eighteenth century all claimed that they were acting on the principles of the Enlightenment. The philosophes generally agreed with this assessment and cheered them on. Beginning in the mid-nineteenth century, histo-

Frederick the Great of Prussia Embracing the elegant, intellectual, and international culture of the Enlightenment, Frederick II was also a composer and accomplished musician. This painting shows Frederick playing the flute for family and friends with a chamber orchestra at his favorite retreat, the palace he called *Sans Souci* ("Free from Care"). *(The Mansell Collection)*

rians developed the idea of a common "enlightened despotism" or "enlightened absolutism," and they canonized Frederick, Catherine, and Joseph as its most outstanding examples. More recent research has raised doubts about this old interpretation and has led to a fundamental re-evaluation.

First, there is general agreement that these absolutists, especially Catherine and Frederick, did encourage and spread the cultural values of the Enlightenment. Perhaps this was their greatest achievement. Skeptical in religion and intensely secular in basic orientation, they unabashedly accepted the here and now and sought their happiness in the enjoyment of it. At the same time, they were proud of their intellectual accomplishments and good taste, and they sup-ported knowledge, education, and the arts. No wonder the philosophes felt the monarchs were kindred spirits.

Historians also agree that the absolutists believed in change from above and tried to enact needed reforms. Yet the results of these efforts brought only very modest improvements, and the life of the peasantry remained very hard in the eighteenth century. Thus some historians have concluded that these monarchs were not really sincere in their reform efforts. Others disagree, arguing that powerful nobilities determined to maintain their privileges blocked the absolutists' genuine commitment to reform. (The old interpretation of Joseph II as the tragic "revolutionary emperor" forms part of this argument.)

The emerging answer to this confusion is that the later eastern absolutists were indeed committed to reform, but that humanitarian objectives were of quite secondary importance. Above all, the absolutists wanted reforms that would strengthen the state and allow them to compete militarily with their neighbors. Modern scholarship has stressed, therefore, how Catherine, Frederick, and Joseph were in many ways simply continuing the state building of their predecessors, reorganizing their armies and expanding their bureaucracies to raise more taxes and troops. The reason for this continuation was simple. The international political struggle was brutal, and the stakes were high. First Austria under Maria Theresa, and then Prussia under Frederick the Great, had to engage in bitter fighting to escape dismemberment, while decentralized Poland was coldly divided and eventually liquidated.

Yet, in their drive for more state power, the later absolutists were also innovators, and the idea of an era of enlightened absolutism retains a certain validity. Sharing the Enlightenment faith in critical thinking and believing that knowledge meant power, these absolutists really were more enlightened because they put their state-building reforms in a new, broader perspective. Above all, they considered how more humane laws and practices could help their populations become more productive and satisfied, and thus able to contribute more substantially to the welfare of the state. It was from this perspective that they introduced many of their most progressive reforms, tolerating religious minorities, simplifying legal codes, and promoting practical education.

The primacy of state as opposed to individual interests—a concept foreign to North Americans long accustomed to easy dominion over a vast continent—also helps to explain some puzzling variations in social policies. For example, Catherine the Great took measures that worsened the peasants' condition because she looked increasingly to the nobility as her natural ally and sought to strengthen it. Frederick the Great basically favored the status quo, limiting only the counter-productive excesses of his trusted nobility against its peasants. On the other hand, Joseph II believed that greater freedom for peasants was the means to strengthen his realm, and he acted accordingly. Each enlightened absolutist sought greater state power, but each believed a different policy would attain that end.

In conclusion, the eastern absolutists of the later eighteenth century combined old-fashioned state building with the culture and critical thinking of the Enlightenment. In doing so, they succeeded in expanding the role of the state in the life of society. Unlike the successors of Louis XIV, they perfected bureaucratic machines that were to prove surprisingly adaptive and capable of enduring into the twentieth century.

This chapter has focused on the complex development of a new world-view in Western civilization. This new view of the world was essentially critical and secular, drawing its inspiration from the Scientific Revolution and crystallizing in the Enlightenment.

The decisive breakthroughs in astronomy and physics in the seventeenth century, which demolished the imposing medieval synthesis of Aristotelian philosophy and Christian theology, had only limited practical consequences despite the expectations of scientific enthusiasts like Bacon. Yet the impact of new scientific knowledge on intellectual life became great. Interpreting scientific findings and Newtonian laws in an antitraditional, antireligious manner, the French philosophes of the Enlightenment extolled the superiority of rational, critical thinking. This new method, they believed, promised not just increased knowledge but even the discovery of the fundamental laws of human society. Although they reached different conclusions when they turned to social and political realities, the philosophes nevertheless succeeded in spreading their radically new world-view. That was a momentous accomplishment.

NOTES

1. H. Butterfield, *The Origins of Modern Science,* Macmillan, New York, 1951, p. viii.
2. Quoted by A. G. R. Smith, *Science and Society in the Sixteenth and Seventeenth Centuries,* Harcourt Brace Jovanovich, New York, 1972, p. 97.

3. Quoted by Butterfield, p. 47.

4. Quoted by Smith, p.100.

5. Ibid., pp. 115–116.

6. Ibid., p. 120.

7. A. R. Hall, *From Galileo to Newton, 1630–1720*, Harper & Row, New York, 1963, p. 290.

8. Quoted by R. K. Merton, *Science, Technology and Society in Seventeenth-Century England*, rev. ed., Harper & Row, New York, 1970, p. 164.

9. Quoted by P. Hazard, *The European Mind, 1680–1715*, Meridian Books, Cleveland, 1963, pp. 304–305.

10. Ibid., pp.11–12.

11. Quoted by L. M. Marsak, ed., *The Enlightenment*, John Wiley & Sons, New York, 1972, p. 56.

12. Quoted by G. L. Mosse et al., eds., *Europe in Review*, Rand McNally, Chicago, 1964, p. 156.

13. M. F. Arouet de Voltaire, *Oeuvres complètes*, Firmin-Didot Frères, Fils et Cie, Paris, 1875, VIII, 188–190.

14. Quoted by P. Gay, "The Unity of the Enlightenment," *History* 3 (1960): 25.

15. Quoted by G. P. Gooch, *Catherine the Great and Other Studies*, Archon Books, Hamden, Conn., 1966, p. 112.

16. Ibid., p. 149.

17. Quoted by L. Krieger, *Kings and Philosophers, 1689–1789*, W. W. Norton, New York, 1970, p. 257.

18. Ibid., p. 15.

19. Ibid., p. 53.

20. Quoted by R. R. Palmer, *The Age of Democratic Revolution*, Princeton University Press, Princeton, N. J., 1959, 1.95–1.96.

21. Quoted by G. Wright, *France in Modern Times*, Rand McNally, Chicago, 1960, p. 42.

SUGGESTED READING

The first three authors cited in the Notes—H. Butterfield, A. G. R. Smith, and A. R. Hall—have written excellent general interpretations of the scientific revolution. Another good study is M. Boas, *The Scientific Renaissance, 1450–1630* (1966), which is especially insightful on the influence of magic on science and on Galileo's trial. T. Kuhn, *The Copernican Revolution* (1957), is the best treatment of the subject; his *The Structure of Scientific Revolutions* (1962) is a challenging, much-discussed attempt to understand major breakthroughs in scientific thought over time. Two stimulating books on the ties between science and society in history are R. Merton, *Science, Technology and Society in Seventeenth-Century England*, rev. ed. (1970), and J. Ben-David, *The Scientist's Role in Society* (1971). E. Andrade, *Sir Isaac Newton* (1958), is a good short biography, which may be compared with F. Manuel, *The Religion of Isaac Newton* (1974).

P. Hazard, *The European Mind, 1680–1715* (1963), is a classic study of the formative years of Enlightenment thought, and his *European Thought in the Eighteenth Century* (1954) is also recommended. A famous, controversial interpretation of the Enlightenment is that of C. Becker, *The Heavenly City of the Eighteenth Century Philosophes* (1932), which maintains that the worldview of medieval Christianity continued to influence the philosophes greatly. Becker's ideas are discussed interestingly in R. O. Rockwood, ed., *Carl Becker's Heavenly City Revisited* (1958). P. Gay has written several major studies on the Enlightenment: *Voltaire's Politics* (1959) and *The Party of Humanity* (1971) are two of the best. I. Wade, *The Structure and Form of the French Enlightenment* (1977), is a recent major synthesis. F. Baumer's *Religion and the Rise of Skepticism* (1969), H. Payne's *The Philosophes and the People* (1976), K. Rogers's *Feminism in Eighteenth-Century England* (1982), and J. B. Bury's old but still exciting *The Idea of Progress* (1932) are stimulating studies of important aspects of Enlightenment thought. Above all, one should read some of the philosophes and let them speak for themselves. Two good anthologies are C. Brinton, ed., *The Portable Age of Reason* (1956), and F. Manuel, ed., *The Enlightenment* (1951). Voltaire's most famous and very amusing novel *Candide* is highly recommended, as are S. Gendzier, ed., *Denis Diderot: The Encyclopedia: Selections* (1967), and A. Wilson's biography, *Diderot* (1972).

In addition to the works mentioned in the Suggested Reading for Chapters 16 and 17, the monarchies of Europe are carefully analyzed in C. Tilly, ed., *The Formation of National States in Western Europe* (1975), and in J. Gagliardo, *Enlightened Despotism* (1967), both of which have useful bibliographies. M. Anderson, *Historians and Eighteenth-Century Europe* (1979), is a valuable introduction to recent scholarship. Other recommended studies on the struggle for power and reform in different countries are: F. Ford, *Robe and Sword* (1953), which discusses the resurgence of the French nobility after the death of Louis XIV; R. Herr, *The Eighteenth-Century Revolution in Spain* (1958), on the impact of Enlightenment thought in Spain; and P. Bernard, *Joseph II* (1968). In addition to I. de Madariaga's masterful *Russia in the Age of Catherine the Great* (1981) and D. Ransel's solid *Politics of Catherinean Russia* (1975), the ambitious reader should look at A. N. Radishchev, *A Journey from St. Petersburg to Moscow* (trans. 1958), a famous 1790 attack on Russian serfdom and an appeal to Catherine the Great to free the serfs, for which Radishchev was exiled to Siberia.

The culture of the time may be approached through A. Cobban, ed., *The Eighteenth Century* (1969), a richly illustrated work with excellent essays, and C. B. Behrens, *The Ancien Régime* (1967). C. Rosen, *The Classical Style: Haydn, Mozart, Beethoven* (1972), brilliantly synthesizes music and society, as did Mozart himself in his great opera *The Marriage of Figaro*, where the count is the buffoon and his servant the hero.

19

THE EXPANSION OF EUROPE IN THE EIGHTEENTH CENTURY

*T*HE WORLD of absolutism and aristocracy, a combination of raw power and elegant refinement, was a world apart from that of ordinary men and women. For the overwhelming majority of the population in the eighteenth century, life remained a struggle with poverty and uncertainty, with the landlord and the tax collector. In 1700 peasants on the land and artisans in their shops lived little better than had their ancestors in the Middle Ages. Only in science and thought, and there only among a few intellectual leaders, had Western society succeeded in going beyond the great achievements of the High Middle Ages, achievements that in turn owed so much to Greece and Rome.

Everyday life was a struggle because European societies, despite their best efforts, still could not produce very much by modern standards. Ordinary people might work like their beasts in the fields, and they often did, but there was seldom enough good food, warm clothing, and decent housing. Life went on; history went on. The wars of religion ravaged Germany in the seventeenth century; Russia rose to become a Great Power; the kingdom of Poland simply disappeared; monarchs and nobles continuously jockeyed for power and wealth. In 1700 or even 1750, the idea of progress—of substantial improvement in the lives of great numbers of people—was still only the dream of a small elite in fashionable salons.

Yet the economic basis of European life was beginning to change. In the course of the eighteenth century, the European economy emerged from the long crisis of the seventeenth century, responded to challenges, and began to expand once again. Some areas were more fortunate than others. The rising Atlantic powers—Holland, France, and above all England—and their colonies led the way. Agriculture and industry, trade and population, began a surge comparable to that of the eleventh- and twelfth-century springtime of European civilization. Only this time, development was not cut short. This time the response to new challenges led toward one of the most influential developments in human history, the Industrial Revolution, considered in Chapter 22. What were the causes of this renewed surge? Why were the fundamental economic underpinnings of European society beginning to change, and what were the dimensions of these changes? How did these changes affect people and their work? These are the questions this chapter will address.

AGRICULTURE AND THE LAND

At the end of the seventeenth century, the economy of Europe was agrarian, as it had been for several hundred years. With the possible exception of Holland, at least 80 percent of the people of all western European countries drew their livelihoods from agriculture. In eastern Europe the percentage was considerably higher.

Men and women lavished their attention on the land, plowing fields and sowing seed, reaping harvests and storing grain. The land repaid these efforts, year after year yielding up the food and most of the raw materials for industry that made life possible. Yet the land was stingy. Even in a rich agricultural region like the Po valley in northern Italy, every bushel of wheat sown yielded on average only five or six bushels of grain at harvest during the seventeenth century. The average French yield in the same period was somewhat less. Such yields were barely more than those attained in fertile, well-watered areas in the thirteenth century or in ancient Greece. By modern standards, output was distressingly low. (For each bushel of wheat seed sown today on fertile land with good rainfall, an American or French farmer can expect roughly forty bushels of produce.) In 1700 European agriculture was much more ancient and medieval than modern.

If the land was stingy, it was also capricious. In most regions of Europe in the sixteenth and seventeenth centuries, harvests were poor, or even failed completely, every eight or nine years. The vast majority of the population who lived off the land might survive a single bad harvest by eating less and drawing on their reserves of grain. But when the land combined with persistent bad weather—too much rain rotting the seed or drought withering the young stalks—the result was catastrophic. Meager grain reserves were soon exhausted, and the price of grain soared. Provisions from other areas with better harvests were hard to obtain.

In such crisis years, which periodically stalked Europe in the seventeenth and even into the eighteenth century, a terrible tightening knot in the belly forced people to tragic substitutes—the "famine foods" of a desperate population. People gathered chestnuts and stripped bark in the forests; they cut dandelions and grass; and they ate these substitutes to escape starvation. In one community in Norway in the early 1700s

Farming the Land Agricultural methods in Europe changed very slowly from the Middle Ages to the early eighteenth century. This realistic picture from Diderot's *Encyclopedia* has striking similarities with agricultural scenes found in medieval manuscripts. *(University of Illinois)*

people were forced to wash dung from the straw in old manure piles in order to bake a pathetic substitute for bread. Even cannibalism occurred in the seventeenth century.

Such unbalanced and inadequate food in famine years made people weak and extremely susceptible to illness and epidemics. Eating material unfit for human consumption, such as bark or grass, resulted in dysentery and intestinal ailments of every kind. Influenza and smallpox preyed with particular savagery on populations weakened by famine. In famine years, the number of deaths soared far above normal. A third of a village's population might disappear in a year or two. The 1690s were as dismal as many of the worst periods of earlier times. One county in Finland, probably typical of the entire country, lost fully 28 percent of its inhabitants in 1696 and 1697. Certain well-studied villages in the Beauvais region of northern France suffered a similar fate. In preindustrial Europe, the harvest was the real king, and the king was seldom generous and often cruel.

To understand why Europeans produced barely enough food in good years and occasionally agonized through years of famine throughout the later seventeenth century, one must follow the plowman, his wife, and his children into the fields to observe their battle for food and life. There the ingenious pattern of farming that Europe had developed in the Middle Ages, a pattern that allowed fairly large numbers of people to survive but could never produce material abundance, was still dominant.

THE OPEN-FIELD SYSTEM

The greatest accomplishment of medieval agriculture was the open-field system of village agriculture developed by European peasants (page 284). That system divided the land to be cultivated by the peasants into a few large fields, which were in turn cut up into long narrow strips. The fields were open, and the strips were not enclosed into small plots by fences or hedges. An individual peasant family—if it were fortunate—held a number of strips scattered throughout the various large fields. The land of those who owned but did not till, primarily the nobility, the clergy, and wealthy townsmen, was also in scattered strips. The peasant community farmed each large field as a community, with each family following the same pattern of plowing, sowing, and harvesting in accordance with tradition and the village leaders.

The ever-present problem was exhaustion of soil. If the community planted wheat year after year in a field, the nitrogen in the soil was soon depleted and crop failure was certain. Since the supply of manure for fertilizer was limited, the only way for the land to recover its life-giving fertility was for a field to lie fallow for a period of time. In the early Middle Ages, a year of fallow was alternated with a year of cropping, so that half the land stood idle in a given year. With time, three-year rotations were introduced, especially on more fertile lands. This system permitted a year of wheat or rye to be followed by a year of oats or beans, and only then by a year of fallow. Even so, only awareness of the tragic consequences of continuous cropping forced undernourished populations to let a third (or half) of their land lie constantly idle, especially when the fallow had to be plowed two or three times a year to keep down the weeds.

Traditional rights reinforced the traditional pattern of farming. In addition to rotating the field crops in a uniform way, villages maintained open meadows for hay and natural pasture. These lands were "common" lands, set aside primarily for the draft horses and oxen so necessary in the fields, but open to the cows and pigs of the village community as well. After the harvest, the people of the village also pastured their animals on the wheat or rye stubble. In many places such pasturing followed a brief period, also established by tradition, for the gleaning of grain. Poor women would go through the fields picking up the few single grains that had fallen to the ground in the course of the harvest. The subject of a great nineteenth-century painting, *The Gleaners* by Jean François Millet, this backbreaking work by hardworking but impoverished women meant quite literally the slender margin of survival for some people in the winter months.

In the age of absolutism and nobility, state and landlord continued to levy heavy taxes and high rents as a matter of course. In so doing they stripped the peasants of much of their meager earnings. The level of exploitation varied. Conditions for the rural population were very different in different areas.

Generally speaking, the peasants of eastern Europe were worst off. As we have seen in Chapter 17, they were still serfs, bound to their lords in hereditary service. Though serfdom in eastern Europe in the eighteenth century had much in common with medieval serfdom in central and western Europe, it was, if anything, harsher and more oppressive. In much of

Millet: The Gleaners Poor French peasant women search for grains and stalks the harvesters (in the background) have missed. The open-field system seen here could still be found in parts of Europe in 1857, when this picture was painted. Millet is known for his great paintings expressing social themes. *(Cliché des Musées Nationaux, Paris)*

eastern Europe there were few limitations on the amount of forced labor the lord could require, and five or six days of unpaid work per week on the lord's land was not uncommon. Well into the nineteenth century, individual Russian serfs and serf families were regularly sold with and without land. Serfdom was often very close to slavery. The only compensating factor in much of eastern Europe was that, as with slavery, differences in well-being among serfs were slight. In Russia, for example, the land available to the serfs for their own crops was divided among them almost equally.

Social conditions were considerably better in western Europe. Peasants were generally free from serfdom. In France and western Germany, they owned land and could pass it on to their children. Yet life in the village was unquestionably hard, and poverty was the great reality for most people. For the Beauvais region of France at the beginning of the eighteenth century, it has been carefully estimated that in good years and bad only a tenth of the peasants could live satisfactorily off the fruits of their landholdings. Owning less than half of the land, the peasants had to pay heavy royal taxes, the church's tithe, and dues to the lord, as well as set aside seed for the next season. Left with only half of their crop for their own use, they had to toil and till for others and seek work far afield in a constant scramble for a meager living. And this was in a country where peasants were comparatively well off. The privileges of the ruling elites weighed heavily on the people of the land.

AGRICULTURAL REVOLUTION

The social conditions of the countryside were well entrenched. The great need was for new farming methods that would enable Europeans to produce more and eat more. The idle fields were the heart of the matter. If peasants could replace the fallow with crops, they could increase the land under cultivation by 50 percent. So remarkable were the possibilities and the results that historians have often spoken of the progressive elimination of the fallow, which occurred slowly throughout Europe from the late seventeenth century on, as an agricultural revolution.

This agricultural revolution, which took longer than historians used to believe, was a great milestone in human development. The famous French scholar Marc Bloch, who gave his life in the resistance to the Nazis in World War Two, summed it up well: "The history of the conquest of the fallow by new crops, a fresh triumph of man over the earth that is just as moving as the great land clearing of the Middle Ages, [is] one of the noblest stories that can be told."[1]

Because grain crops exhaust the soil and make fallowing necessary, the secret to eliminating the fallow lies in alternating grain with certain nitrogen-storing crops. Such crops not only rejuvenate the soil even better than fallowing, but give more produce as well. The most important of these land-reviving crops are peas and beans, root crops such as turnips and potatoes, and clovers and grasses. In the eighteenth century, peas and beans were old standbys; turnips, potatoes, and clover were newcomers to the fields. As time went on, the number of crops that were systematically rotated grew, and farmers developed increas-

Enclosing the Fields This remarkable aerial photograph captures key aspects of the agricultural revolution. Though the long ridges and furrows of the old open-field system still stretch across the whole picture, hedge rows now cut through the long strips to divide the land into several enclosed fields. *(Cambridge University Collection)*

ingly sophisticated patterns of rotation to suit different kinds of soils. For example, farmers in French Flanders near Lille in the late eighteenth century used a ten-year rotation, alternating a number of grain, root, and hay crops on a ten-year schedule. Continuous experimentation resulted in more scientific farming.

Improvements in farming had multiple effects. The new crops made ideal feed for animals. Because peasants and larger farmers had more fodder—hay and root crops—for the winter months, they could build up their small herds of cattle and sheep. More animals meant more meat and better diets for the people. More animals also meant more manure for fertilizer, and therefore more grain for bread and porridge. The vicious cycle in which few animals meant inadequate manure, which meant little grain and less fodder, which led to fewer animals, and so on, could be broken. The cycle became positive: more animals meant more manure, which meant more grain and more fodder, which meant more animals, which meant better diets.

Technical progress had its price, though. The new rotations were scarcely possible within the traditional framework of open fields and common rights. A farmer who wanted to experiment with new methods would have to control the village's pattern of rotation. To wait for the entire village to agree might mean waiting forever. The improving, innovating agriculturalist needed to enclose and consolidate his scattered holdings into a compact, fenced-in field. In doing so, he would also seek to enclose his share of the natural pasture, the common. Yet the common rights were precious to many rural people. Thus when the small landholders and the poor could effectively oppose the enclosure of the open fields, they did so. Only powerful social and political pressures could overcome the traditionalism of rural communities.

The old system of unenclosed open fields and the new system of continuous rotation coexisted in Europe for a very long time. In large parts of central Russia, for example, the old system did not disappear until after the Communist Revolution in 1917. It could also be found in much of France and Germany in the early years of the nineteenth century. Indeed, until the end of the eighteenth century, the promise of the new system was extensively realized only in the Low Countries and in England.

THE LEADERSHIP OF THE LOW COUNTRIES AND ENGLAND

The new methods of the agriculture revolution originated in the Low Countries. The vibrant, dynamic middle-class society of seventeenth-century republican Holland was the most advanced in Europe in many areas of human endeavor. In shipbuilding and navigation, in commerce and banking, in drainage and agriculture, the people of the Low Countries, especially the Dutch, provided models the jealous English and French sought to copy or to cripple.

By the middle of the seventeenth century, intensive farming was well established throughout much of the Low Countries. Enclosed fields, continuous rotation, heavy manuring, and a wide variety of crops—all these innovations were present. Agriculture was highly specialized and commercialized. The same skills that grew turnips produced flax to be spun into linen for clothes and tulip bulbs to lighten the heart with their beauty. The fat cattle of Holland, so beloved by Dutch painters, gave the most milk in Europe. Dutch cheeses were already world renowned.

The reasons for early Dutch leadership in farming were basically threefold. In the first place, since the end of the Middle Ages the Low Countries had been one of the most densely populated areas in Europe. Thus, in order to feed themselves and provide employment, the Dutch were forced at an early date to seek maximum yields from their land and to increase it through the steady draining of marshes and swamps. Even so, they had to import wheat from Poland and eastern Germany.

The pressure of population was connected with the second cause, the growth of towns and cities in the Low Countries. Stimulated by commerce and overseas trade, Amsterdam grew from 30,000 to 200,000 in its golden seventeenth century. The growth of urban population provided Dutch peasants with good markets for all they could produce and allowed each region to specialize in what it did best.

Finally, there was the quality of the people. Oppressed by neither grasping nobles nor war-minded monarchs, the Dutch could develop their potential in a free and capitalistic society. The Low Countries became "the Mecca of foreign agricultural experts who came . . . to see Flemish agriculture with their own eyes, to write about it and to propagate its methods in their home lands."[2]

Harvesting This harvest scene by Pieter Brueghel the Elder (ca 1525–1569) suggests how the relatively prosperous Low Countries might take the lead in agricultural development. Brueghel was a master at depicting everyday peasant life. *(Nelson Gallery–Atkins Museum, Kansas City, Mo., Nelson Fund)*

The English were the best students. Indeed, they were such good students that it is often forgotten that they had teachers at all. Drainage and water control was one subject in which they received instruction. Large parts of seventeenth-century Holland had once been sea and sea marsh, and the efforts of centuries had made the Dutch the world's leaders in the skills of drainage. In the first half of the seventeenth century, Dutch experts made a great contribution to draining the extensive marshes, or fens, of wet and rainy England.

The most famous of these Dutch engineers, Cornelius Vermuyden, directed one large drainage project in Yorkshire and another in Cambridgeshire. The project in Yorkshire was supported by Charles I and financed by a group of Dutch capitalists, who were to receive one-third of all land reclaimed in return for

their investment. Despite local opposition, Vermuyden drained the land by means of a large canal—his so-called Dutch river—and settlers cultivated the new fields in the Dutch fashion. In the Cambridge fens, Vermuyden and his Dutch workers eventually reclaimed forty thousand acres, which were then farmed intensively in the Dutch manner. Although all these efforts were disrupted in the turbulent 1640s by the English civil war, Vermuyden and his countrymen largely succeeded. A swampy wilderness was converted into thousands of acres of some of the best land in England. On such new land, where traditions and common rights were not established, farmers introduced new crops and new rotations fairly easily.

Dutch experience was also important to Viscount Charles Townsend (1674–1738), one of the pioneers of English agricultural improvement. This lord from

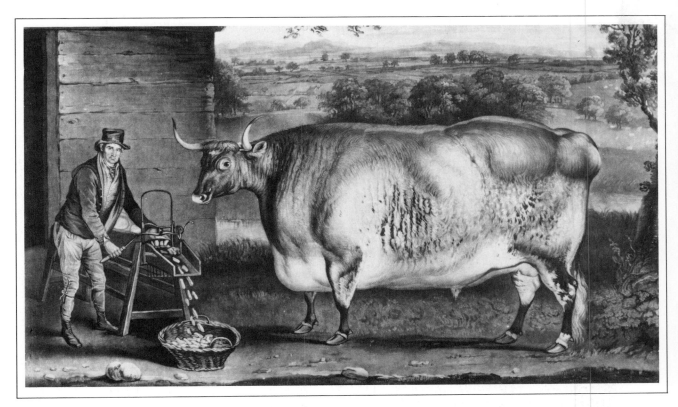

Selective Breeding meant bigger livestock and more meat on English tables. This gigantic champion, one of the new improved shorthorn breed, was known as the Newbus Ox. Such great fat beasts were pictured in the press and praised by poets. *(Institute of Agricultural History and Museum of English Rural Life, University of Reading)*

the upper reaches of the English aristocracy learned about turnips and clover while serving as English ambassador to Holland. In the 1710s, he was using these crops in the sandy soil of his large estates in Norfolk in eastern England, already one of the most innovative agricultural areas in the country. When Lord Charles retired from politics in 1730 and returned to Norfolk, it was said that he spoke of turnips, turnips, and nothing but turnips. This led some wit to nickname his lordship "Turnip" Townsend. But Townsend had the last laugh. Draining extensively, manuring heavily, and sowing crops in regular rotation without fallowing, the farmers who leased Townsend's lands produced larger crops. They and he earned higher incomes. Those who had scoffed reconsidered. By 1740 agricultural improvement in various forms had become something of a craze among the English aristocracy.

Jethro Tull (1674–1741), part crank and part genius, was another important English innovator. A true son of the early Enlightenment, Tull constantly tested accepted ideas about farming in an effort to develop better methods through empirical research. He was especially enthusiastic about using horses for plowing, in preference to slower-moving oxen. He also advocated sowing seed with drilling equipment, rather than scattering it by hand. Drilling distributed seed evenly and at the proper depth. There were also improvements in livestock, inspired in part by the earlier successes of English country gentlemen in breeding ever-faster horses for the races and fox hunts that were their passions. Selective breeding of ordinary livestock was a marked improvement over the old pattern, which has been graphically described as little more than "the haphazard union of nobody's son with everybody's daughter."

By the mid-eighteenth century, English agriculture was in the process of a radical and desirable transformation. The eventual result was that by 1870 English farmers produced 300 percent more food than they had produced in 1700, although the number of people working the land had increased by only 14 percent. This great surge of agricultural production provided food for England's rapidly growing urban population. It was a tremendous achievement.

THE DEBATE OVER ENCLOSURE

To what extent was technical progress a product of social injustice? There are sharp differences of opinion among historians. The oldest and still widely accepted view is that the powerful ruling class, the English landowning aristocracy, enclosed the open fields and divided up the common pasture in such a way that poor people lost their small landholdings and were pushed off the land. The large landowners controlled Parliament, which made the laws. They had Parliament pass hundreds of "enclosure acts," each of which authorized the fencing of open fields in a given district and abolished common rights there. Small farmers who had little land and cottagers who had only common rights could no longer make a living. They lost position and security and had to work for a large landowner for wages or else move to town in search of work. This view, popularized by Karl Marx in the nineteenth century, has remained dear to many historians to this day.

There is some validity to this idea, but more recent studies have shown that the harmful consequences of enclosure in the eighteenth century have often been exaggerated. In the first place, as much as half of English farmland was already enclosed by 1750. A great wave of enclosure of English open fields into sheep pastures had already occurred in the sixteenth and early seventeenth centuries, in order to produce wool for the thriving textile industry. In the later seventeenth and early eighteenth centuries, many open fields were enclosed fairly harmoniously by mutual agreement among all classes of landowners in English villages. Thus parliamentary enclosure, the great bulk of which occurred after 1760 and particularly during the Napoleonic wars early in the nineteenth century, only completed a process that was in full swing. Nor did an army of landless farm laborers appear only in the last years of the eighteenth century.

Much earlier, and certainly by 1700, there were perhaps two landless agricultural workers in England for every self-sufficient farmer. In 1830, after the enclosures were complete, the proportion of landless laborers on the land was not much greater.

Indeed, by 1700 a highly distinctive pattern of landownership existed in England. At one extreme were a few large landowners, at the other a large mass of laborers who held little land and worked for wages. In between stood two other groups: small, self-sufficient farmers who owned their own land and substantial tenant farmers who rented land from the big landowners and hired wage laborers. Yet the small, independent English farmers were already declining in number by 1700, and they continued to do so in the eighteenth century. They could not compete with the profit-minded, market-oriented tenant farmers.

The tenant farmers, many of whom had formerly been independent owners, were the key to mastering the new methods of farming. Well financed by the large landowners, the tenant farmers fenced fields, built drains, and improved the soil with fertilizers. Such improvements actually increased employment opportunities for wage workers in the countryside. So did new methods of farming, for land was farmed more intensively without the fallow, and new crops like turnips required more care and effort. Thus enclosure did not force people off the land by eliminating jobs. By the early nineteenth century, rural poverty was often greatest in those areas of England where the new farming techniques had not been adopted.

THE BEGINNING OF THE POPULATION EXPLOSION

There was another factor that affected the existing order of life and forced economic changes in the eighteenth century. This was the remarkable growth of European population, the beginning of the "population explosion." This population explosion continued in Europe until the twentieth century, by which time it was affecting non-Western areas of the globe. What caused the growth of population, and what did the challenge of more mouths to feed and more hands to employ do to the European economy?

LIMITATIONS ON POPULATION GROWTH

Many commonly held ideas about population in the past are wrong. One such mistaken idea is that people always married young and had large families. A related error is the belief that past societies were so ignorant that they could do nothing to control their numbers and that population was always growing too fast. On the contrary, until 1700 the total population of Europe grew slowly much of the time, and by no means constantly (see Figure 19.1). There were very few occurrences of the frightening increases found in many poor countries today.

In seventeenth-century Europe, births and deaths, fertility and mortality, were in a crude but effective balance. The birthrate—annual births as a proportion of the population—was fairly high, but far lower than it would have been if all women between ages fifteen and forty-five had been having as many children as biologically possible. The death rate in normal years was also high, though somewhat lower than the birthrate. As a result, the population grew modestly in normal years at a rate of perhaps .5 to 1 percent, or enough to double the population in 70 to 140 years. This is, of course, a generalization encompassing many different patterns. In areas like Russia and colonial New England, where there was a great deal of frontier to be settled, the annual rate of increase might well exceed 1 percent. In a country like France, where the land had long been densely settled, the rate of increase might be less than .5 percent.

Although population growth of even 1 percent per year is fairly modest by the standards of many African and Latin American countries today—some of which are growing at about 3 percent annually—it will produce a very large increase over a long period. An annual increase of even 1 percent will result in sixteen times as many people in three hundred years. Such gigantic increases simply did not occur in agrarian Europe before the eighteenth century. In certain abnormal years and tragic periods, many more people died than were born. Total population fell sharply, even catastrophically. A number of years of modest growth would then be necessary to make up for those who had died in an abnormal year. Such savage increases in deaths helped check total numbers and kept the population from growing rapidly for long periods.

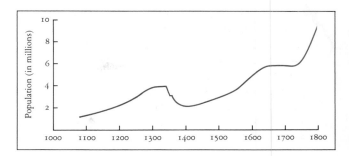

FIGURE 19.1 The Growth of Population in England 1000–1800 England is a good example of both the uneven increase of European population before 1700 and the third great surge of growth, which began in the eighteenth century. *(Source: E. A. Wrigley,* Population and History, *McGraw-Hill, New York, 1969)*

The grim reapers of demographic crisis were famine, epidemic disease, and war. Famine, the inevitable result of poor farming methods and periodic crop failures, was particularly murderous because it was accompanied by disease. With a brutal one-two punch, famine stunned and weakened a population, and disease finished it off. Disease could also ravage independently, even in years of adequate harvests. Bubonic plague returned again and again in Europe for more than three hundred years after the ravages of the Black Death in the fourteenth century. Not until the late 1500s did most countries have as many people as in the early 1300s. Epidemics of dysentery and smallpox also operated independently of famine.

War was another scourge. The indirect effects were more harmful than the organized killing. War spread disease. Soldiers and camp followers passed venereal disease through the countryside to scar and kill. Armies requisitioned scarce food supplies for their own use and disrupted the agricultural cycle. The Thirty Years' War (pages 483–489) witnessed all possible combinations of distress. In the German states, the number of inhabitants declined by more than *two-thirds* in some large areas and by at least one-third almost everywhere else. The Thirty Years' War reduced total German population by no less than 40 percent. But numbers inadequately convey the dimensions of such human tragedy. One needs the vision of the artist. The great sixteenth-century artist, Albrecht Dürer, captured the horror of demographic crisis in his chilling woodcut *The Four Horsemen of*

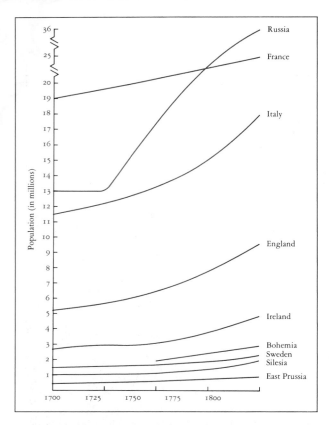

FIGURE 19.2 The Increase of Population in Europe in the Eighteenth Century France's large population continued to support French political and intellectual leadership. Russia emerged as Europe's most populous state because natural increase was complemented by growth from territorial expansion.

the Apocalypse (page 384). Death, accompanied by his trusty companions War, Famine, and Disease, takes his merciless ride of destruction. The narrow victory of life over death that prevails in normal times is being undone.

THE NEW PATTERN OF THE EIGHTEENTH CENTURY

In the eighteenth century, the population of Europe began to grow markedly. This increase in numbers occurred in all areas of Europe—western and eastern, northern and southern, dynamic and stagnant. Growth was especially dramatic after about 1750, as Figure 19.2 shows.

Although it is certain that Europe's population grew greatly, it is less clear why. Recent painstaking and innovative research in population history has shown that, because population grew everywhere, it

is best to look for general factors and not those limited to individual countries or areas. What, then, caused fewer people to die or, possibly, more babies to be born? In some kinds of families women may have had more babies than before. Yet the basic cause was a decline in mortality—fewer deaths.

The bubonic plague mysteriously disappeared. Following the Black Death in the fourteenth century, plagues had remained a part of the European experience, striking again and again with savage force, particularly in towns. As a German writer of the early sixteenth century noted, "It is remarkable and astonishing that the plague should never wholly cease, but it should appear every year here and there, making its way from one place to another. Having subsided at one time, it returns within a few years by a circuitous route."[3]

As late as 1720, a ship from Syria and the Levant, where plague was ever-present, brought the monstrous disease to Marseilles. In a few weeks, forty thousand of the city's ninety thousand inhabitants died. The epidemic swept southern France, killing one-third, one-half, even three-fourths of those in the larger towns. Once again an awful fear swept across Europe. But the epidemic passed, and that was the last time plague fell on western and central Europe. The final disappearance of plague was due in part to stricter measures of quarantine in Mediterranean ports and along the Austrian border with Turkey. Human carriers of plague were carefully isolated. Chance and plain good luck were more important, however.

It is now understood that bubonic plague is, above all, a disease of rats. More precisely, it is the black rat that spreads major epidemics, for the black rat's flea is the principal carrier of the plague bacillus. After 1600, for reasons unknown, a new rat of Asiatic origin—the brown, or wander, rat—began to drive out and eventually eliminate its black competitor. In the words of a noted authority, "This revolution in the animal kingdom must have gone far to break the lethal link between rat and man."[4] Although the brown rat also contracts the plague, another kind of flea is its main parasite. That flea carries the plague poorly and, for good measure, has little taste for human blood.

Advances in medical knowledge did not contribute much to reducing the death rate in the eighteenth century. The most important advance in preventive medicine in this period was inoculation against smallpox. Yet this great improvement was long confined mainly to England and probably did little to reduce deaths throughout Europe until the latter part of the century. Improvements in the water supply and sewerage promoted somewhat better public health and helped reduce such diseases as typhoid and typhus in some urban areas of western Europe. Yet those early public-health measures had only limited general significance. In fact, changes in the rat population helped much more than did doctors and medical science in the eighteenth century.

Human beings were more successful in their efforts to safeguard the supply of food and protect against famine. The eighteenth century was a time of considerable canal and road building in western Europe. These advances in transportation, which were among the more positive aspects of strong absolutist states, lessened the impact of local crop failure and famine. Emergency supplies could be brought in. The age-old spectacle of localized starvation became less frequent. Wars became more gentlemanly and less destructive than in the seventeenth century and spread fewer epidemics. New foods, particularly the potato, were introduced. Potatoes served as an important alternative source of vitamins A and C for the poor, especially when the grain crops were skimpy or failed. In short, population grew in the eighteenth century primarily because years of abnormal death rates were less catastrophic. Famines, epidemics, and wars continued to occur, but their severity moderated.

The growth of population in the eighteenth century cannot be interpreted as a sign of human progress, however. Plague faded from memory, transport improved, people learned to eat potatoes; yet for the common people, life was still a great struggle. Indeed, it was often more of a struggle than ever, for in many areas increasing numbers led to overpopulation. A serious imbalance between the number of people and the economic opportunities available to them developed. There was only so much land available, and tradition slowed the adoption of better farming methods. Therefore agriculture could not provide enough work for the rapidly growing labor force. Everyone might work steadily during planting and harvesting, when many hands were needed, but at other times rural people were often unemployed or underemployed.

Doctor in Protective Clothing Most doctors believed, incorrectly, that poisonous smells carried the plague. This doctor has placed strong-smelling salts in his "beak" to protect himself against deadly plague vapors. *(Germanisches Nationalmuseum, Nuremberg)*

Women Working This mother and her daughters may well be knitting, lace-making, and spinning for some merchant capitalist. The close ties between cottage industry and agriculture are well illustrated in this summer scene. *(Photo: Caroline Buckler)*

Growing numbers increased the challenge of poverty, especially the severe poverty of the rural poor. People in the countryside had to look for new ways to make a living. Even if work outside of farming paid poorly, small wages were better than none. Thus in the eighteenth century, growing numbers of people and acute poverty were even more influential than new farming methods as forces for profound change in agrarian Europe.

THE GROWTH OF COTTAGE INDUSTRY

The growth of population contributed to the development of industry in rural areas. The poor in the countryside were eager to supplement their earnings from agriculture with other types of work, and capitalists from the city were eager to employ them, often at lower wages than urban workers commanded. Manufacturing with hand tools in peasant cottages grew markedly in the eighteenth century. Rural industry became a crucial feature of the European economy.

To be sure, peasant communities had always made some clothing, processed some food, and constructed some housing for their own use. But in the High Middle Ages, peasants did not produce manufactured goods on a large scale for sale in a market; they were not handicraft workers as well as farmers and field laborers. Industry in the Middle Ages was dominated and organized by urban craft guilds and urban merchants, who jealously regulated handicraft production and sought to maintain it as an urban monopoly. By the eighteenth century, however, the pressures of rural poverty and the need for employment in the countryside had proved too great, and a new system

The Linen Industry in Ireland Many steps went into making textiles. Here the women are beating away the coarse woody part of the flax plant so that the man can draw the soft part through a series of combs. The fine flax fibers will then be spun into thread and woven into cloth by this family enterprise. *(The Mansell Collection)*

was expanding lustily. The new system had many names. Sometimes referred to as "cottage industry" or "domestic industry," it has often been called the "putting-out system."

THE PUTTING-OUT SYSTEM

The two main participants in the putting-out system were the merchant-capitalist and the rural worker. The merchant loaned or "put out" raw materials—raw wool, for example—to several cottage workers. Those workers processed the raw material in their own homes, spinning and weaving the wool into cloth in this case, and returned the cloth to the merchant. The merchant paid the outworkers for their work by the piece and proceeded to sell the finished product. There were endless variations on this basic relationship. Sometimes rural workers would buy their own materials and work as independent pro-

ducers before they sold to the merchant. The relative importance of earnings from the land and from industry varied greatly for handicraft workers. In all cases, however, the putting-out system was a kind of capitalism. Merchants needed large amounts of capital, which they held in the form of goods being worked up and sold in distant markets. They sought to make profits and increase their capital in their businesses.

The putting-out system was not perfect, but it had definite advantages. It increased employment in the countryside and provided the poor with additional income. Since production in the countryside was unregulated, workers and merchants could change procedures and experiment as they saw fit. Because they did not need to meet rigid guild standards, which maintained quality but discouraged the development of new methods, cottage industry became capable of producing many kinds of goods. Textiles, all

Rural Industry in Action This French engraving suggests just how many things could be made in the countryside with simple hand tools. These men are making inexpensive but long-lasting wooden shoes, which were widely worn by the poor. *(University of Illinois)*

manner of knives, forks, and housewares, buttons and gloves, clocks and musical instruments could be produced quite satisfactorily in the countryside. Luxury goods for the rich, such as exquisite tapestries and fine porcelain, demanded special training, close supervision, and centralized workshops. Yet such goods were as exceptional as those who used them. The skills of rural industry were sufficient for everyday articles.

Rural manufacturing did not spread across Europe at an even rate. It appeared first in England and developed most successfully there, particularly for the spinning and weaving of woolen cloth. By 1500 half of England's textiles were being produced in the countryside. By 1700 English industry was generally more rural than urban and heavily reliant on the putting-out system. Continental countries developed rural industry more slowly.

In France at the time of Louis XIV, Colbert had revived the urban guilds and used them as a means to control the cities and collect taxes (page 515). But the pressure of rural poverty proved too great. In 1762 the special privileges of urban manufacturing were

abolished in France, and the already-developing rural industries were given free rein from then on. The royal government in France had come to believe that the best way to help the poor peasants was to encourage the growth of cottage manufacturing. Thus in France, as in Germany and other areas, the later part of the eighteenth century witnessed a remarkable expansion of rural industry in certain densely populated regions. The pattern established in England was spreading to the Continent.

THE TEXTILE INDUSTRY

Throughout most of history, until at least the nineteenth century, the industry that has employed the most people has been textiles. The making of linen, woolen, and eventually cotton cloth was the typical activity of cottage workers engaged in the putting-out system. A look inside the cottage of the English rural textile worker illustrates a way of life as well as an economic system.

The rural worker lived in a small cottage, with tiny windows and little space. Indeed, the worker's cottage was often a single room that served as workshop, kitchen, and bedroom. There were only a few pieces of furniture, of which the weaver's loom was by far the largest and most important. That loom had changed somewhat in the early eighteenth century, when John Kay's invention of the flying shuttle enabled the weaver to throw the shuttle back and forth between the threads with one hand. Aside from that improvement, however, the loom was as it had been for much of history. In the cottage there were also spinning wheels, tubs for dyeing cloth and washing raw wool, and carding pieces to comb and prepare the raw material.

These different pieces of equipment were necessary because cottage industry was first and foremost a family enterprise. All the members of the family helped in the work, so that "every person from seven to eighty (who retained their sight and who could move their hands) could earn their bread," as one eighteenth-century English observer put it.[5] While the women and children prepared the raw material and spun the thread, the man of the house wove the cloth. There was work for everyone, even the youngest. After the dirt was beaten out of the raw cotton, it had to be thoroughly cleaned with strong soap in a tub, where tiny feet took the place of the agitator in a washing machine. George Crompton, the son of Samuel Crompton, who in 1784 invented the mule for cotton spinning, recalled that "soon after I was able to walk I was employed in the cotton manufacture. . . . My mother tucked up my petticoats about my waist, and put me into the tub to tread upon the cotton at the bottom."[6] Slightly older children and aged relatives carded and combed the cotton or wool, so that the woman and the older daughter she had taught could spin it into thread. Each member had a task. The very young and very old worked in the family unit as a matter of course.

There was always a serious imbalance in this family enterprise: the work of four or five spinners was needed to keep one weaver steadily employed. Therefore, the wife and the husband had constantly to try to find more thread and more spinners. Widows and unmarried women—those "spinsters" who spun for their living—were recruited by the wife. Or perhaps the weaver's son went off on horseback to seek thread. The need for more thread might even lead the weaver and his wife to become small capitalist employers. At the end of the week, when they received the raw wool or cotton from the merchant-manufacturer, they would put out some of this raw material to other cottages. The following week they would return to pick up the thread and pay for the spinning—spinning that would help keep the weaver busy for a week until the merchant came for the finished cloth.

Relations between workers and employers were not always harmonious. In fact, there was continuous conflict. An English popular song written about 1700, called "The Clothier's Delight, or the Rich Men's Joy and The Poor Men's Sorrow," has the merchant boasting of his countless tricks used to "beat down wages":

We heapeth up riches and treasure great store
Which we get by griping and grinding the poor.
And this is a way for to fill up our purse
Although we do get it with many a curse.[7]

There were constant disputes over weights of materials and the quality of the cloth. Merchants accused workers of stealing raw materials, and weavers complained that merchants delivered underweight bales. Both were right; each tried to cheat the other, even if only in self-defense.

There was another problem, at least from the merchant-capitalist's point of view. Rural labor was cheap, scattered, and poorly organized. For these reasons it was hard to control. Cottage workers tended to work in spurts. After they got paid on Saturday afternoon, the men in particular tended to drink and carouse for two or three days. Indeed, Monday was called "holy Monday" because inactivity was so religiously observed. By the end of the week the weaver was probably working feverishly to make his quota. But if he did not succeed, there was little the merchant could do. When times were good and the merchant could easily sell everything produced, the weaver and his family did fairly well and were particularly inclined to loaf, to the dismay of the capitalist. Thus, in spite of its virtues, the putting-out system in the textile industry had definite shortcomings. There was an imbalance between spinning and weaving. Labor relations were often poor, and the merchant was unable to control the quality of the cloth or the schedule of the workers. The merchant-capitalist's search for more efficient methods of production became intense.

BUILDING THE ATLANTIC ECONOMY

In addition to agricultural improvement, population pressure, and expanding cottage industry, the expansion of Europe in the eighteenth century was characterized by the growth of world trade. Spain and Portugal revitalized their empires and began drawing more wealth from renewed development. Yet once again, the countries of northwestern Europe—the Netherlands, France, and above all Great Britain—benefited most. Great Britain (formed in 1707 by the union of England and Scotland in a single kingdom), gradually became the leading maritime power. In the eighteenth century, British ships and merchants succeeded in dominating long-distance trade, particularly the fast-growing intercontinental trade across the Atlantic Ocean. The British played the critical role in building a fairly unified Atlantic economy, which offered remarkable opportunities for them and their colonists.

MERCANTILISM AND COLONIAL WARS

Britain's commercial leadership in the eighteenth century had its origins in the mercantilism of the seventeenth century (page 515). European mercantilism was a system of economic regulations aimed at increasing the power of the state. As practiced by a leading advocate like Colbert under Louis XIV, mercantilism aimed particularly at creating a favorable balance of foreign trade in order to increase a country's stock of gold. A country's gold holdings served as an all-important treasure chest, to be opened periodically to pay for war in a violent age.

Early English mercantilists shared these views. As Thomas Mun, a leading merchant and early mercantilist, wrote in *England's Treasure by Foreign Trade* (1630, published 1664): "The ordinary means therefore to increase our wealth and treasure is by foreign trade wherein we must observe this rule; to sell more to strangers yearly than we consume of theirs in value." What distinguished English mercantilism was the unusual idea that governmental economic regulations could and should serve the private interest of individuals and groups as well as the public

needs of the state. As Josiah Child, a very wealthy brewer and director of the East India Company, put it, in the ideal economy "Profit and Power ought jointly to be considered."[8]

In France and other continental countries, by contrast, seventeenth-century mercantilists generally put the needs of the state far above those of businessmen and workers. And they seldom saw a possible union of public and private interests for a common good.

The result of the English desire to increase both its military power and private wealth was the mercantile system of the Navigation Acts. Oliver Cromwell established the first of these laws in 1651, and the restored monarchy of Charles II extended them further in 1660 and 1663; the Navigation Acts of the seventeenth century were not seriously modified until 1786. The acts required that most goods imported from Europe into England and Scotland be carried on British-owned ships with British crews or on ships of the country producing the article. Moreover, these laws gave British merchants and shipowners a virtual monopoly on trade with the colonies. The colonists were required to ship their products—sugar, tobacco, and cotton—on British ships and to buy almost all of their European goods from the mother country. It was believed that these economic regulations would provide British merchants and workers with profits and employment, and colonial plantation owners and farmers with a guaranteed market for their products. And the state would develop a shipping industry with a large number of tough, experienced deepwater seamen, who could be drafted when necessary into the Royal Navy to protect the island nation.

The Navigation Acts were a form of economic warfare. Their initial target was the Dutch, who were far ahead of the English in shipping and foreign trade in the mid-seventeenth century. The Navigation Acts, in conjunction with three Anglo-Dutch wars between 1652 and 1674, did seriously damage Dutch shipping and commerce. The thriving Dutch colony of New Amsterdam was seized in 1664 and rechristened "New York." By the later seventeenth century, when the Dutch and the English became allies to stop the expansion of France's Louis XIV, the Netherlands was falling behind England in shipping, trade, and colonies.

As the Netherlands followed Spain into relative decline, France stood clearly as England's most serious

COLONIAL COMPETITION AND WAR, 1651–1763

1651–1663	British Navigation Acts create the mercantile system, which is not seriously modified until 1786
1652–1674	Three Anglo-Dutch wars damage Dutch shipping and commerce
1664	New Amsterdam is seized and renamed New York
1701–1714	War of the Spanish Succession
1713	Peace of Utrecht: Britain wins parts of Canada from France and control of the western African slave trade from Spain
1740–1748	War of the Austrian Succession, resulting in no change in territorial holdings in North America
1756–1763	Seven Years' War (known in North America as the French and Indian War), a decisive victory for Britain
1763	Treaty of Paris: Britain receives all French territory on the North American mainland and achieves dominance in India

rival in the competition for overseas empire. Rich in natural resources and endowed with a population three or four times that of England, continental Europe's leading military power was already building a powerful fleet and a worldwide system of rigidly monopolized colonial trade. And France, aware that Great Britain coveted large parts of Spain's American empire, was determined to revitalize its Spanish ally. Thus from 1701 to 1763, Britain and France were locked in a series of wars to decide, in part, which nation would become the leading maritime power and claim a lion's share of the profits of Europe's overseas expansion (see Map 19.1).

The first round was the War of the Spanish Succession (page 520), which started when Louis XIV declared his willingness to accept the Spanish crown willed to his grandson. Besides upsetting the continental balance of power, a union of France and Spain threatened to destroy the British colonies in North America. The thin ribbon of British settlements along the Atlantic seaboard from Massachusetts to the Carolinas would be surrounded by a great arc of Franco-Spanish power stretching south and west from French Canada to Florida and the Gulf of Mexico (see Map 19.1). Defeated by a great coalition of states after twelve years of fighting, Louis XIV was forced in the Peace of Utrecht (1713) to cede Newfoundland, Nova Scotia, and the Hudson Bay territory to Britain. Spain was compelled to give Britain

control of the lucrative West African slave trade—the so-called *asiento*—and to let Britain send one ship of merchandise into the Spanish colonies annually, through Porto Bello on the Isthmus of Panama.

France was still a mighty competitor. In 1740 the War of the Austrian Succession (1740–1748), which started when Frederick the Great of Prussia seized Silesia from Austria's Maria Theresa (page 594), became a world war, including Anglo-French conflicts in India and North America. Indeed, it was the seizure of French territory in Canada by New England colonists that led France to sue for peace in 1748 and to accept a return to the territorial situation existing in North America at the beginning of the war. France's Bourbon ally, Spain, defended itself surprisingly well, and Spain's empire remained intact.

This inclusive stand-off helped set the stage for the Seven Years' War (1756–1763). In central Europe, Austria's Maria Theresa sought to win back Silesia and crush Prussia, thereby re-establishing the Habsburgs' traditional leadership in German affairs. She almost succeeded (see page 595), skillfully winning both France—the Habsburgs' long-standing enemy —and Russia to her cause. Yet the Prussian state survived, saved by its army and the sudden decision of Russia to withdraw from the war in 1762.

Outside of Europe, the Seven Years' War was the decisive round in the Franco-British competition for colonial empire (see Map 19.2). Led by William Pitt,

The East India Dock, London This painting by Samuel Scott captures the spirit and excitement of British maritime expansion. Great sailing ships line the quay, bringing profit and romance from far-off India. London grew in population from 350,000 in 1650 to 900,000 in 1800, when it was twice as big as Paris, its nearest rival. (*Victoria & Albert Museum, London*)

MAP 19.1 The Economy of the Atlantic Basin in 1701 The growth of trade encouraged both economic development and military conflict in the Atlantic Basin.

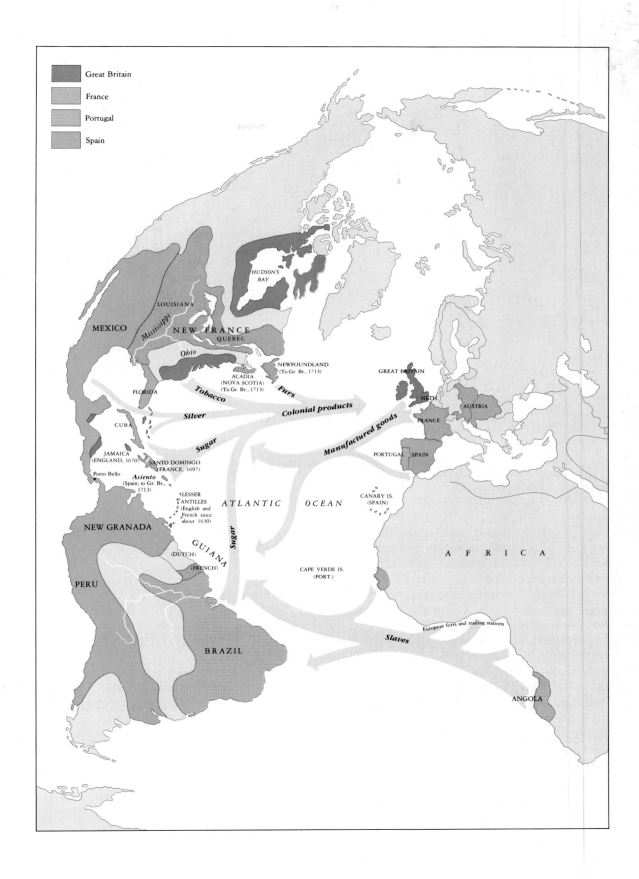

Great Britain
France
Portugal
Spain

HUDSON'S BAY

LOUISIANA

MEXICO

NEW FRANCE

QUEBEC

Ohio

NEWFOUNDLAND
(To Gr. Br., 1713)

GREAT BRITAIN

ACADIA
(NOVA SCOTIA)
(To Gr. Br., 1713)

Furs

NETH.

FLORIDA

Tobacco

Colonial products

AUSTRIA

Silver

FRANCE

Manufactured goods

CUBA

Sugar

PORTUGAL   SPAIN

JAMAICA
(ENGLAND, 1670)

SANTO DOMINGO
(FRANCE, 1697)

Porto Bello

Asiento
(Spain; to Gr. Br.,
1713)

CANARY IS.
(SPAIN)

LESSER
ANTILLES
(English and
French since
about 1630)

ATLANTIC   OCEAN

AFRICA

NEW GRANADA

Sugar

GUIANA
(DUTCH)
(FRENCH)

CAPE VERDE IS.
(PORT.)

PERU

European forts and trading stations

BRAZIL

Slaves

ANGOLA

MAP 19.2 European Claims in North America Before and After the Seven Years' War (1756–1763) France lost its vast claims in North America, though the British government then prohibited colonists from settling west of a line drawn in 1763. The British wanted to avoid costly wars with Indians living in the newly conquered territory.

whose grandfather had made a fortune as a trader in India, the British concentrated on using superior sea power to destroy the French fleet and choke off French commerce around the world. Capturing Quebec in 1759 and winning a great naval victory at Quiberon Bay, the British also strangled France's valuable sugar trade with its Caribbean islands and smashed French forts in India. After Spain entered the war on France's side in 1761, the surging British temporarily occupied Havana in Cuba and Manila in the Philippines. With the Treaty of Paris (1763), France lost all its possessions on the mainland of North America. French Canada as well as French territory east of the Mississippi River passed to Britain, and France ceded Louisiana to Spain as compensation for Spain's loss of Florida to Britain. France also gave up most of its holdings in India, opening the way to British dominance on the subcontinent. By 1763 British naval power, built in large part on the rapid growth of the British shipping industry after the pas-

sage of the Navigation Acts, had triumphed decisively. Britain had realized its goal of monopolizing a vast trading and colonial empire for its exclusive benefit.

LAND AND WEALTH IN NORTH AMERICA

Of all Britain's colonies, those on the North American mainland proved most valuable in the long run. The settlements along the Atlantic coast provided an important outlet for surplus population, so that migration abroad limited poverty in England, Scotland, and northern Ireland. The settlers also benefited. In the mainland colonies, they had privileged access to virtually free and unlimited land. The availability of farms was a precious asset in preindustrial Europe, where agriculture was the main source of income and prestige.

The possibility of having one's own farm was particularly attractive to ordinary men and women from the British Isles. Land in England was already highly concentrated in the hands of the nobility and gentry in 1700 and became more so with agricultural improvement in the eighteenth century. White settlers who came to the colonies as free men and women, or as indentured servants pledged to work seven years for their passage, or as prisoners and convicts, could obtain their own farms on easy terms as soon as they had their personal freedom. Many poor white farmers also came to the mainland from the British West Indies, crowded out of those islands by the growth of big sugar plantations using black slave labor. To be sure, life in the mainland colonies was hard, especially on the frontier. Yet the settlers succeeded in paying little or no rent to grasping landlords, and taxes were very low. Unlike the great majority of European peasants, who had to accept high rents and taxes as part of the order of things, American farmers could keep most of what they managed to produce.

The availability of land made labor expensive in the colonies. This basic fact, rather than any repressive aspects of the Navigation Acts, limited the growth of industry in the colonies. As the Governor of New York put it in 1767:

The price of labor is so great in this part of the world that it will always prove the greatest obstacle to any manufacturers attempting to set up here, and the genius of the people in a country where everyone can have land to work upon leads them so naturally into agriculture that it prevails over every other occupation.[9]

The advantage for colonists was in farming, and farm they did.

Cheap land and scarce labor were also critical factors in the growth of slavery in the southern colonies. By 1700 British indentured servants were carefully avoiding the Virginia lowlands, where black slavery was spreading, and by 1730 the large plantations there had gone over completely to black slaves. Slave labor permitted an astonishing tenfold increase in tobacco production between 1700 and 1774 and created a wealthy aristocratic planter class in Maryland and Virginia.

In the course of the eighteenth century, the farmers of New England and, particularly, the middle colonies of Pennsylvania and New Jersey began to produce more food than they needed. They exported ever more foodstuffs, primarily to the West Indies. There the owners of the sugar plantations came to depend on the mainland colonies for grain and dried fish to feed their slaves. The plantation owners, whether they grew tobacco in Virginia and Maryland or sugar in the West Indies, had the exclusive privilege of supplying the British Isles with their products. Englishmen could not buy cheaper sugar from Brazil, nor were they allowed to grow tobacco in the home islands. Thus the colonists, too, had their place in the protective mercantile system of the Navigation Acts. The American shipping industry grew rapidly in the eighteenth century, for example, because colonial shippers enjoyed the same advantages as their fellow British citizens in the mother country.

The abundance of almost-free land resulted in a rapid increase in the colonial population in the eighteenth century. In a mere three-quarters of a century after 1700, the white population of the mainland colonies multiplied a staggering ten times, as immigrants arrived and colonial couples raised large families. In 1774, 2.2 million whites and 330,000 blacks inhabited what would soon become the independent United States.

Rapid population growth did not reduce the settlers to poverty. On the contrary, agricultural development resulted in fairly high standards of living, in eighteenth-century terms, for mainland colonists. There was also an unusual degree of economic equality, by European standards. Few people were extremely rich and few were extremely poor. Most remarkable of all, on eve of the American Revolution, the *average* white man or woman in the mainland British colonies probably had the highest income and standard of living in the world. It has been estimated that between 1715 and 1775 the real income of the average American was increasing about 1 percent per year per person, almost two-thirds as fast as it increased with massive industrialization between 1840 and 1959. When one considers that between 1775 and 1840 Americans experienced no improvement in their standard of living, it is clear just how much the colonists benefited from hard work and the mercantile system created by the Navigation Acts.[10]

THE GROWTH OF FOREIGN TRADE

England also profited greatly from the mercantile system. Above all, the rapidly growing and increasingly wealthy agricultural populations of the main-

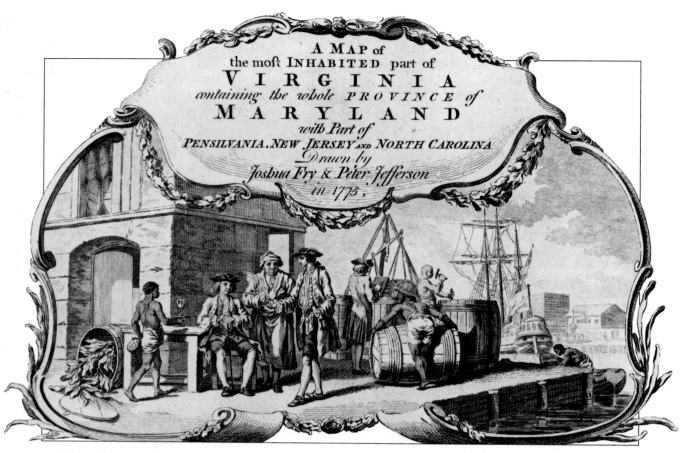

Tobacco was a key commodity in the Atlantic trade. This engraving from 1775 shows a merchant and his slaves preparing a cargo for sail. *(The British Library)*

land colonies provided an expanding market for English manufactured goods. This situation was extremely fortunate, for England in the eighteenth century was gradually losing, or only slowly expanding, its sales to many of its traditional European markets. However, rising demand for manufactured goods from North America, as well as from the West Indies, Africa, and Latin America, allowed English cottage industry to continue to grow and diversify. Merchant-capitalists and manufacturers found new and exciting opportunities for profit and wealth.

Since the late Middle Ages, England had relied very heavily on the sale of woolen cloth in foreign markets. Indeed, as late as 1700, woolen cloth was the only important manufactured good exported from England, and fully 90 percent of it was sold to Europeans. In the course of the eighteenth century, the states of continental Europe were trying to develop their own cottage textile industries in an effort to deal with rural poverty and overpopulation. Like England earlier, these states adopted protectionist, mercantilist policies. They tried by means of tariffs and other measures to exclude competing goods from abroad, whether English woolens or the cheap but beautiful cotton calicos the English East India Company brought from India and sold in Europe.

France had already closed its markets to the English in the seventeenth century. In the eighteenth century, German states purchased much less woolen cloth from England and encouraged cottage production of coarse, cheap linens, which became a feared competitor in all of central and southern Europe. By 1773 England was selling only about two-thirds as much woolen cloth to northern and western Europe as it had in 1700. The decline of sales to the Continent meant that the English economy badly needed new markets and new products in order to develop and prosper.

Protected colonial markets came to the rescue. More than offsetting stagnating trade with Europe, they provided a great stimulus for many branches of English manufacturing. The markets of the Atlantic economy led the way, as may be seen in Figure 19.3. English exports of manufactured goods to continental Europe increased very modestly, from roughly £2.9 million in 1700 to only £3.3 million in 1773. Meanwhile, sales of manufactured products to the Atlantic economy—primarily the mainland colonies of North America and the West Indian sugar islands, with an important assist from West Africa and Latin America—soared from £500,000 to £3.9 million. Sales to other "colonies"—Ireland and India—also rose substantially in the eighteenth century.

English exports became much more balanced and diversified. To America and Africa went large quantities of metal items—axes to frontiersmen, firearms, chains for slaveowners. There were also clocks and coaches, buttons and saddles, china and furniture, musical instruments and scientific equipment, and a host of other things. By 1750 half the nails made in England were going to the colonies. Foreign trade became the bread and butter of some industries.

Thus the mercantile system formed in the seventeenth century to attack the Dutch and to win power and profit for England continued to shape trade in the eighteenth century. The English concentrated in their hands much of the demand for manufactured goods from the growing Atlantic economy. The pressure of demand from three continents on the cottage industry of one medium-sized country heightened the efforts of English merchant-capitalists to find new and improved ways to produce more goods. By the 1770s England stood on the threshold of the radical industrial change to be described in Chapter 22.

REVIVAL IN
COLONIAL LATIN AMERICA

When the last Spanish Habsburg, the feeble-minded Charles II, died in 1700 (page 520), Spain was "little less cadaverous than its defunct master."[11] Its vast empire lay before Europe awaiting dismemberment. Yet, in one of those striking reversals with which history is replete, Spain revived. The empire held together and even prospered, while a European-oriented landowning aristocracy enhanced its position in colonial society.

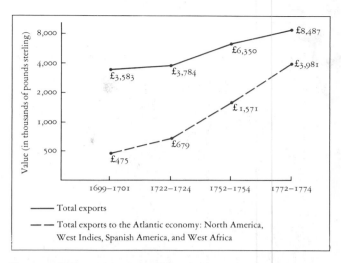

FIGURE 19.3 **Exports of English Manufactured Goods 1700–1774** While trade between England and Europe stagnated after 1700, English exports to Africa and the Americas boomed and greatly stimulated English economic development. *(Source: R. Davis, "English Foreign Trade, 1700–1774,"* Economic History Review, *2d series, 15 [1962]; 302–303)*

Spain recovered in part because of better leadership. Louis XIV's grandson, who took the throne as Philip V (1700–1746), brought new men and fresh ideas with him from France and rallied the Spanish people to his Bourbon dynasty in the long War of the Spanish Succession. When peace was restored, a series of reforming ministers reasserted royal authority, overhauling state finances and strengthening defense. To protect the colonies, they restored Spain's navy to a respectable third place in Europe behind Great Britain and France. Philip's ministers also promoted the economy with vigorous measures that included a gradual relaxation of the state monopoly on colonial trade. The able Charles III (1759–1788), a truly enlightened monarch, further extended economic and administrative reform.

Revitalization in Madrid had positive results in the colonies. The colonies succeeded in defending themselves from numerous British attacks and even increased in size. Spain received Louisiana from France in 1763, and missionaries and ranchers extended Spanish influence all the way to northern California.

Political success was matched by economic improvement. After declining markedly in the seven-

Porto Bello Located on the isthmus of Panama, little Porto Bello was a major port in Spanish America. When ships arrived for 40-day trade fairs, it bustled with the energy of merchants, slaves, and soldiers. *(Pierpont Morgan Library)*

teenth century, silver mining recovered in Mexico and Peru. Output quadrupled between 1700 and 1800, when Spanish America accounted for half of world silver production. Ever a risky long shot at sudden riches, silver mining encouraged a gambler's attitude toward wealth and work. The big profits of the lucky usually went into land. Silver mining also encouraged food production for large mining camps and gave the *creoles*—people of Spanish blood born in America—the means to purchase more and more European luxuries and manufactured goods. A class of wealthy merchants arose to handle this flourishing trade, which often relied on smuggled goods from Great Britain. As in British North America, industry remained weak, although workshops employing forced Indian labor were occupied with fashioning Mexican and Peruvian wool into coarse fabrics for purchase by the Latin American masses. Spain's col-

onies were an important element of the Atlantic economy.

Economic development strengthened the creole elite, which came to rival the top government officials dispatched from Spain. As in most preindustrial societies, land was the main source of wealth. In contrast to their British American counterparts but like Spanish and eastern European aristocracy, creole estate owners controlled much of the land. Small independent farmers were rare.

The Spanish crown had given large holdings to the conquering pioneers and their followers, and beginning in the late sixteenth century many large tracts of state land were sold to favored settlers. Thus, though the crown decreed that Indian communities were to retain the use of their tribal lands, a class of large landholders grew up in sparsely settled regions and in the midst of the defeated Indian populations.

The Spanish settlers strove to become a genuine European aristocracy, and they largely succeeded. As good aristocrats, they believed that work in the fields was the proper occupation of a depressed, impoverished peasantry. The defenseless Indians suited their needs. As the Indian population recovered in numbers, slavery and periodic forced labor gave way to widespread debt peonage from 1600 on. Under this system, a planter or rancher would keep his christianized, increasingly hispanicized Indians in perpetual debt bondage by periodically advancing food, shelter, and a little money. Debt peonage subjugated the Indians and was a form of agricultural serfdom.

The landowning class practiced *primogeniture,* passing everything from eldest son to eldest son to prevent fragmentation of land and influence. Also like European nobles, wealthy creoles built ornate townhouses, contributing to the development of a lavish colonial baroque style that may still be seen in Lima, Peru, and Mexico City. The creole elite followed European cultural and intellectual trends. Enlightenment ideas spread to colonial salons and universities, encouraging a questioning attitude and preparing the way for the creoles' rise to political power with the independence movements of the early nineteenth century.

There were also creoles of modest means, especially in the cities, since estate agriculture discouraged small white farmers. (Chile was an exception: since it had few docile Indians to exploit, white settlers had to work their small farms to survive.) The large middle group in Spanish colonies consisted of racially mixed *mestizos,* the offspring of Spanish men and Indian women. The most talented mestizos realistically aspired to join the creoles, for enough wealth and power could make one white. This ambition siphoned off the most energetic mestizos and lessened the build-up of any lower-class discontent. Thus, by the end of the colonial era roughly 20 percent of the population was classified as white and about 30 percent as mestizo. Pure-blooded Indians accounted for most of the remainder, for only on the sugar plantations of Cuba and Puerto Rico did black slavery ever take firm root in Spanish America.

The situation was quite the opposite in Portuguese Brazil. As in the West Indies, enormous numbers of blacks were brought in chains to work the sugar plantations. About half the population of Brazil was of African origin in the early nineteenth century. Even more than in the Spanish territories, the people of Brazil intermingled sexually and culturally. In contrast to North America, where racial lines were hard and fast, at least in theory, colonial Brazil made a virtue of miscegenation, and the population grew to include every color in the racial rainbow.

While some European intellectual elites were developing a new view of the world in the eighteenth century, Europe as a whole was experiencing a gradual but far-reaching expansion. As agriculture showed signs of modest improvement across the continent, first the Low Countries and then England succeeded in launching the epoch-making Agricultural Revolution. Plague disappeared, and the populations of all countries grew significantly, encouraging the progress of cottage industry and merchant capitalism.

Europeans also continued their overseas expansion, fighting for empire and profit and consolidating their hold on the Americas in particular. A revived Spain and its Latin American colonies participated fully in this expansion. As in agriculture and cottage industry, however, England and its empire proved most successful. The English concentrated much of the growing Atlantic trade in their hands, which challenged and enriched English industry and intensified the search for new methods of production. Thus, by the 1770s, England was on the verge of an economic breakthrough fully as significant as the great political upheaval destined to develop shortly in neighboring France.

NOTES

1. M. Bloch, *Les caractères originaux de l'histoire rurale française,* Librarie Armand Colin, Paris, 1960, 1.244–245.
2. B.H. Slicher van Bath, *The Agrarian History of Western Europe, A.D. 500–1850,* St. Martin's Press, New York, 1963, p. 240.

3. Quoted in E. E. Rich and C. H. Wilson, eds., *Cambridge Economic History of Europe,* Cambridge University Press, Cambridge, Eng., 4.74.

4. Ibid., p. 85.

5. Quoted by I. Pinchbeck, *Women Workers and the Industrial Revolution, 1750–1850,* F. S. Crofts, New York, 1930, p. 113.

6. Quoted by S. Chapman, *The Lancashire Cotton Industry,* Manchester University Press, Manchester, Eng., 1903, p. 13.

7. Quoted by P. Mantoux, *The Industrial Revolution in the Eighteenth Century,* Harper & Row, New York, 1961, p. 75.

8. Quoted by C. Wilson, *England's Apprenticeship, 1603–1763,* Longmans, Green, London, 1965, p. 169.

9. Quoted by D. Dillard, *Economic Development of the North Atlantic Community,* Prentice-Hall, Englewood Cliffs, N.J., 1967, p. 192.

10. G. Taylor, "America's Growth Before 1840," *Journal of Economic History* 24 (December 1970):427–444.

11. J. Rippy, *Latin America: A Modern History,* rev. ed., University of Michigan Press, Ann Arbor, 1968, p. 97.

SUGGESTED READING

B. H. Slicher van Bath, *The Agrarian History of Western Europe, A.D. 500–1850* (1963), is a wide-ranging general introduction to the gradual transformation of European agriculture, as is M. Bloch's great classic, cited in the Notes, which has been translated as *French Rural History* (1966). J. Blum, *The End of the Old Order in Rural Europe* (1978), is an impressive comparative study. J. de Vries, *The Dutch Rural Economy in the Golden Age, 1500–1700* (1974), skillfully examines the causes of early Dutch leadership in farming, and E. L. Jones, *Agriculture and Economic Growth in England, 1650–1815* (1967), shows the importance of the agricultural revolution for England. Two recommended and complementary studies on landowning nobilities are R. Forster, *The Nobility of Toulouse in the Eighteenth Century* (1960), and G. E. Mingay, *English Landed Society in the Eighteenth Century* (1963). A. Goodwin, ed., *The European Nobility in the Eighteenth Century* (1967), is an exciting group of essays on aristocrats in different countries. R. and E. Forster, eds., *European Society in the Eighteenth Century* (1969), assembles a rich collection of contemporary writing on a variety of economic and social topics. E. Le Roy Ladurie, *The Peasants of Languedoc* (1976), a brilliant and challenging study of rural life in southern France for several centuries, complements J. Goody et al., eds., *Family and Inheritance: Rural Society in Western Europe, 1200–1800* (1976). Life in small-town preindustrial France comes alive in P. Higonnet, *Pont-de-Montvert: Social Structure and Politics in a French Village, 1700–1914* (1971), while O. Hufton deals vividly and sympathetically with rural migration, work, women, and much more in *The Poor in Eighteenth-Century France* (1974). P. Mantoux, *The Industrial Revolution in the Eighteenth Century* (1928), and D. Landes, *The Unbound Prometheus* (1969), provide excellent discussions of the development of cottage industry.

Two excellent multivolume series, *The Cambridge Economic History of Europe,* and C. Cipolla, ed., *The Fontana Economic History of Europe,* cover the sweep of economic developments from the Middle Ages to the present and have extensive bibliographies. F. Braudel, *Civilization and Capitalism, 15th–18th Century* (1981–1984), is a monumental and highly recommended three-volume synthesis. In the area of trade and colonial competition, V. Barbour, *Capitalism in Amsterdam* (1963), and C. R. Boxer, *The Dutch Seaborne Empire* (1970), are very interesting on Holland. C. Wilson, *Profit and Power: A Study of England and the Dutch Wars* (1957), is exciting scholarship, as are W. Dorn, *The Competition for Empire, 1740–1763* (1963), D. K. Fieldhouse, *The Colonial Empires* (1971), and R. Davies, *The Rise of Atlantic Economies* (1973). R. Pares, *Yankees and Creoles* (1956), is a short, lively work on trade between the mainland colonies and the West Indies. E. Williams, *Capitalism and Slavery* (1966), provocatively argues that slavery provided the wealth necessary for England's industrial development. Another exciting work is J. Nef, *War and Human Progress* (1968), which examines the impact of war on economic and industrial development in European history between about 1500 and 1800 and may be compared with M. Gutmann, *War and Rural Life in the Early Modern Low Countries* (1980). J. Fagg's *Latin America* (1969) provides a good introduction to the colonial period and has a useful bibliography, while C. Haring, *The Spanish in America* (1947), is a fundamental modern study.

Three very fine books on the growth of population are C. Cipolla's short and lively *The Economic History of World Population* (1962); E. A. Wrigley's more demanding *Population and History* (1969); and T. McKeown's scholarly *The Modern Rise of Population* (1977). W. McNeill, *Plagues and Peoples* (1976), is also noteworthy. In addition to works on England cited in the Suggested Reading for Chapter 22, D. George, *England in Transition* (1953), and C. Wilson, *England's Apprenticeship, 1603–1763* (1965), are highly recommended. The greatest novel of eighteenth-century English society is Henry Fielding's unforgettable *Tom Jones,* although Jane Austen's novels about country society, *Emma* and *Pride and Prejudice,* are not far behind.

20

THE LIFE OF THE PEOPLE

*T*HE DISCUSSION of agriculture and industry in the last chapter showed the ordinary man and woman at work, straining to make ends meet and earn a living. Yet work is only part of human experience. What about the rest? What about such basic things as marriage and childhood, food and diet, health and religion? How, in short, did the peasant masses and urban poor really live in western Europe before the age of revolution at the end of the eighteenth century? This is the simple but profound question that the economic and social developments naturally raise.

MARRIAGE AND THE FAMILY

The basic unit of social organization is the family. It is within the structure of the family that human beings love, mate, and reproduce themselves. It is primarily the family that teaches the child, imparting values and customs that condition an individual's behavior for a lifetime. The family is also an institution woven into the web of history. It evolves and changes, assuming different forms in different times and places.

EXTENDED AND NUCLEAR FAMILIES

In many traditional Asian and African societies, the typical family has often been an extended family. A newly married couple, instead of establishing their own home, will go to live with either the bride's or the groom's family. The couple raises their children while living under the same roof with their own brothers and sisters, who may also be married. The family is a big, three- or four-generation clan, headed by a patriarch or perhaps a matriarch, and encompassing everyone from the youngest infant to the oldest grandparent.

Extended families, it is often said, provide security for adults and children in traditional agrarian peasant economies. Everyone has a place within the extended family, from cradle to grave. Sociologists frequently assume that the extended family gives way to the conjugal, or nuclear, family with the advent of in-dustrialization and urbanization. Couples establish their own households and their own family identities when they marry. They live with the children they raise, apart from their parents. Something like this is indeed happening in much of Asia and Africa today. And since Europe was once agrarian and preindustrial, it has often been believed that the extended family must also have prevailed in Europe before being destroyed by the Industrial Revolution.

In fact, the situation was quite different in western and central Europe. By 1700 the extended three-generational family was a great rarity. Indeed, the extended family may never have been common in Europe, although it is hard to know about the Middle Ages because fewer records survive. When young European couples married, they normally established their own households and lived apart from their parents. When a three-generation household came into existence, it was usually a parent who moved in with a married child, rather than a newly married couple moving in with either set of parents. The married couple, and the children that were sure to follow, were on their own from the beginning.

Perhaps because European couples set up separate households when they married, people did not marry young in the seventeenth and early eighteenth centuries. Indeed, the average person, who was neither rich nor aristocratic, married surprisingly late, many years after reaching adulthood and many more after beginning to work. In one well-studied, typical English village, both men and women married for the first time at an average age of twenty-seven or older in the seventeenth and eighteenth centuries. A similar pattern existed in early eighteenth-century France. Moreover, a substantial portion of men and women never married at all.

Between two-fifths and three-fifths of European women capable of bearing children—that is, women between fifteen and forty-four—were unmarried at any given time. The contrast with traditional non-Western societies is once again striking. In those societies, the pattern has very often been almost universal and very early marriage. The union of a teenage bride and her teenage groom has been the general rule.

The custom of late marriage and nuclear family was a distinctive characteristic of European society. The consequences have been tremendous, though still only partially explored. It seems likely that the dynamism and creativity that have characterized European society were due in large part to the pattern of marriage and family. This pattern fostered and required self-reliance and independence. In preindustrial western Europe in the sixteenth through eighteenth centuries, marriage normally joined a mature man and a mature woman—two adults who had already experienced a great deal of life and could transmit self-reliance and real skills to the next generation.

Why was marriage delayed? The main reason was that couples normally could not marry until they could support themselves economically. The land was the main source of income. The peasant son often needed to wait until his father's death to inherit the family farm and marry his sweetheart. Similarly, the peasant daughter and her family needed to accumulate a small dowry to help her boyfriend buy land or build a house.

There were also laws and regulations to temper impetuous love and physical attraction. In some areas, couples needed the legal permission or tacit approval of the local lord or landowner in order to marry. In Austria and Germany, there were legal restrictions on marriage, and well into the nineteenth century poor couples had particular difficulty securing the approval of local officials. These officials believed that freedom to marry for the lower classes would mean more paupers, more abandoned children, and more money for welfare. Thus prudence, custom, and law combined to postpone the march to the altar. This pattern helped society maintain some kind of balance between the number of people and the available economic resources.

Work Away from Home

Many young people worked within their families until they could start their own households. Boys plowed and wove; girls spun and tended the cows. Many others left home to work elsewhere. In the towns, a lad might be apprenticed to a craftsman for seven or fourteen years to learn a trade. During that time he would not be permitted to marry. In most trades he earned little and worked hard, but if he were lucky he might eventually be admitted to a guild and establish his economic independence. More often, the young man would drift from one tough job to another: hired hand for a small farmer, laborer on a new road, carrier of water in a nearby town. He was always subject to economic fluctuations, and unemployment was a constant threat.

The Chimney Sweep Some boys and girls found work as chimney sweeps, especially if they were small. Climbing up into chimneys was dirty, dangerous work. Hot stones could set the sweep's clothing on fire. Such work for youngsters eventually died out in the nineteenth century, the period of this drawing. *(Photo: Caroline Buckler)*

Girls also left their families to work, at an early age and in large numbers. The range of opportunities open to them was more limited, however. Service in another family's household was by far the most common job. Even middle-class families often sent their daughters into service and hired others as servants in return. Thus, a few years away from home as a servant was a normal part of growing up. If all went well, the girl (or boy) would work hard and save some money for parents and marriage. At the least, there would be one less mouth to feed at home.

The legions of young servant girls worked hard but had little real independence. Sometimes the employer paid the girl's wages directly to her parents. Constantly under the eye of her mistress, her tasks were many—cleaning, shopping, cooking, caring for the baby—and often endless, for there were no laws to limit her exploitation. Few girls were so brutalized that they snapped under the strain, like the Russian servant girl Varka in Chekhov's chilling story, "Sleepy," who, driven beyond exhaustion, finally quieted her mistress's screaming child by strangling it in its cradle. But court records are full of complaints by servant girls of physical mistreatment by their mistresses. There were many others like the fifteen-year-old English girl in the early eighteenth century who told the judge that her mistress had not only called her "very opprobrious names, as Bitch, Whore and the like," but also "beat her without provocation and beyond measure."[1]

There was also the pressure of seducers and sexual attack. In theory, domestic service offered protection and security for a young girl leaving home. The girl had food, lodging, and a new family. She did not drift in a strange and often dangerous environment. But in practice, she was often the easy prey of a lecherous master, or his sons, or his friends. Indeed, "the evidence suggests that in all European countries, from Britain to Russia, the upper classes felt perfectly free to exploit sexually girls who were at their mercy."[2] If the girl became pregnant, she was quickly fired and thrown out in disgrace to make her own way. Prostitution and petty thievery were often the harsh alternatives that lay ahead. "What are we?" exclaimed a bitter Parisian prostitute. "Most of us are unfortunate women, without origins, without education, servants and maids for the most part."[3]

PREMARITAL SEX AND BIRTH-CONTROL PRACTICES

Did the plight of some ex-servant girls mean that late marriage in preindustrial Europe went hand in hand with premarital sex and many illegitimate children? For most of western and central Europe, until at least 1750, the answer seems to be no. English parish registers, in which the clergy recorded the births and deaths of the population, seldom list more than one bastard out of every twenty children baptized. Some French parishes in the seventeenth century had extraordinarily low rates of illegitimacy, with less than 1 percent of the babies born out of wedlock. Illegitimate babies were apparently a rarity, at least as far as the official church records are concerned.

At the same time, premarital sex was clearly commonplace. In one well-studied English village, one-third of all first children were conceived before the couple was married, and many were born within three months of the marriage ceremony. No doubt many of these couples were already betrothed, or at least "going steady," before they entered into an intimate relationship. But the very low rates of illegitimate birth also reflect the powerful social controls of the traditional village, particularly the open-field village with its pattern of cooperation and common action. Irate parents and village elders, indignant priests and authoritative landlords, all combined to pressure any young people who wavered about marriage in the face of unexpected pregnancy. These controls meant that premarital sex was not entered into lightly. In the countryside it was generally limited to those contemplating marriage.

Once a woman was married, she generally had several children. This does not mean that birth control within marriage was unknown in western and central Europe before the nineteenth century. But it was primitive and quite undependable. The most common method was *coitus interruptus*—withdrawal by the male before ejaculation. The French, who were apparently early leaders in contraception, were using this method extensively to limit family size by the end of the eighteenth century. Withdrawal as a method of birth control was in keeping with the European pattern of nuclear family, in which the father bore the direct responsibility of supporting his children. Withdrawal—a male technique—was one way to meet that responsibility.

Mechanical and other means of contraception were not unknown in the eighteenth century, but they appear to have been used mainly by certain sectors of the urban population. The "fast set" of London used the "sheath" regularly, although primarily to protect against venereal disease, not pregnancy. Prostitutes used various contraceptive techniques to prevent pregnancy, and such information was probably available to anyone who really sought it. The second part of an indictment for adultery against a late-sixteenth-century English vicar charged that the wayward minister was "also an instructor of young folks [in] how to commit the sin of adultery or fornication and not to beget or bring forth children."[4]

New Patterns of Marriage and Illegitimacy

In the second half of the eighteenth century, the pattern of late marriage and few illegitimate children began to break down. It is hard to say why. Certainly, changes in the economy had a gradual but profound impact. The growth of cottage industry created new opportunities for earning a living, opportunities not tied to limited and hard-to-get land. Because a scrap of ground for a garden and a cottage for the loom and spinning wheel could be quite enough for a modest living, young people had greater independence and did not need to wait for a good-sized farm. A contemporary observer of an area of rapidly growing cottage industry in Switzerland at the end of the eighteenth century described these changes: "The increased and sure income offered by the combination of cottage manufacture with farming hastened and multiplied marriages and encouraged the division of landholdings, while enhancing their value; it also promoted the expansion and embellishment of houses and villages."[5]

As a result, cottage workers married not only earlier but for different reasons. Nothing could be so businesslike, so calculating, as a peasant marriage which was often dictated by the needs of the couple's families. After 1750, however, courtship became more extensive and freer as cottage industry grew. It was easier to yield to the attraction of the opposite sex and fall in love. The older generation was often shocked by the lack of responsibility they saw in the early marriages of the poor, the union of "people with only two spinning wheels and not even a bed." But the laws and regulations they imposed, especially in Germany, were often disregarded. Unions based on love rather than on economic considerations were increasingly the pattern for cottage workers. Factory workers, numbers of whom first began to appear in England after about 1780, followed the path blazed by cottage workers.

Changes in the timing and motivation of marriage went hand in hand with a rapid increase in illegitimate births between about 1750 and 1850. Some historians even speak of an "illegitimacy explosion." In Frankfurt, Germany, for example, only about 2 percent of all births were illegitimate in the early 1700s. This figure rose to 5 percent in about 1760, to about 10 percent in 1800, and peaked at about 25 percent around 1850. In Bordeaux, France, illegitimate births rose steadily until by 1840 one out of every three babies was born out of wedlock. Small towns and villages less frequently experienced such startlingly high illegitimacy rates, but increases from a range of 1 to 3 percent initially to 10 to 20 percent between 1750 and 1850 were commonplace. A profound sexual and cultural transformation was taking place. Fewer girls were abstaining from premarital intercourse, and fewer boys were marrying the girls they got pregnant.

It is hard to know exactly why this change occurred and what it meant. The old idea of a safe, late, economically secure marriage did not reflect economic and social realities. The growing freedom of thought in the turbulent years beginning with the French Revolution in 1789 influenced sexual and marital behavior. And illegitimate births, particularly in Germany, were also the result of open rebellion against class laws limiting the right of the poor to marry. Unable to show a solid financial position and thereby obtain a marriage license, couples asserted their independence and lived together anyway. Children were the natural and desired result of "true love" and greater freedom. Eventually, when the stuffy, old-fashioned propertied classes gave in and repealed their laws against "imprudent marriage," poor couples once again went to the altar, often accompanied by their children, and the number of illegitimate children declined.

More fundamentally, the need to seek work outside farming and the village made young people more mobile. Mobility in turn encouraged new sexual and marital relationships, which were less subject to parental pressure and village tradition. As in the case of young servant girls who became pregnant and were then forced to fend for themselves, some of these relationships promoted loose living or prostitution. This resulted in more illegitimate births and strengthened an urban subculture of habitual illegitimacy.

Early Sexual Emancipation?

It has been suggested that the increase in illegitimate births represented a stage in the emancipation of women. According to this view, new economic opportunities outside the home, in the city and later in the factory, revolutionized women's attitudes about themselves. Young working women became indivi-

The Face of Poverty This woman and her children live by begging. Families of beggars roamed all over eighteenth-century Europe, and many observers feared they were increasing in numbers. *(John Freeman/Fotomas Index)*

dualistic and rebelled against old restrictions like late marriage. They sought fulfillment in the pleasure of sexuality. Since there was little birth control, freer sex for single women meant more illegitimate babies.

No doubt single working women in towns and cities were of necessity more independent and self-reliant. Yet, until at least the late nineteenth century, it seems unlikely that such young women were motivated primarily by visions of emancipation and sexual liberation. Most women were servants or textile workers. These jobs paid poorly, and the possibility of a truly independent "liberated" life was correspondingly limited. Most women in the city probably looked to marriage and family life as an escape from hard, poorly paid work and as the foundation of a satisfying life.

Hopes and promises of marriage from men of the working girl's own class led naturally enough to sex.[6]

In one medium-sized French city in 1787 to 1788, the great majority of unwed mothers stated that sexual intimacy had followed promises of marriage. Many soldiers, day laborers, and male servants were no doubt sincere in their proposals. But their lives were insecure, and many hesitated to take on the heavy economic burdens of wife and child. Nor were their backbones any longer stiffened by the traditional pressures of the village.

In a growing number of cases, therefore, the intended marriage did not take place. The romantic yet practical dreams and aspirations of many young working women and men were frustrated by low wages, inequality, and changing economic and social conditions. Old patterns of marriage and family were breaking down among the common people. Only in the late nineteenth century would more stable patterns reappear.

WOMEN AND CHILDREN

In the traditional framework of preindustrial Europe, women married late but then began bearing children rapidly. If a woman married before she was thirty, and if both she and her husband lived to forty-five, the chances were roughly one in two that she would give birth to six or more children. The newborn child entered a dangerous world. Infant mortality was high. One in five was sure to die and one in three was quite likely to, in the poorer areas. Newborn children were very likely to catch infectious diseases of the stomach and chest, which were not understood. Thus little could be done for an ailing child, even in rich families. Childhood itself was dangerous. Parents in preindustrial Europe could count themselves fortunate if half their children lived to adulthood.

CHILD CARE AND NURSING

Women of the lower classes generally breast-fed their infants, and for much longer periods than is customary today. Breast-feeding decreases the likelihood of pregnancy for the average woman by delaying the resumption of ovulation. Although women may have been only vaguely aware of the link between nursing and not getting pregnant, they were spacing their children—from two to three years apart—and limiting their fertility by nursing their babies. If a newborn baby died, nursing stopped and a new life could be created. Nursing also saved lives: the breast-fed infant was more likely to survive on its mother's milk than on any artificial foods. In many areas of Russia, where common practice was to give a new child a sweetened (and germ-laden) rag to suck on for its subsistence, half the babies did not survive the first year.

In contrast to the laboring poor, the women of the aristocracy and upper-middle class seldom nursed their own children. The upper-class woman felt that breast-feeding was crude, common, and well beneath her dignity. Instead she hired a wet nurse to suckle her child. The urban mother of more modest means —the wife of a shopkeeper or artisan—also commonly used a wet nurse, sending her baby to some poor woman in the country as soon as possible.

Wet-nursing was a very widespread and flourishing business in the eighteenth century, a dismal business within the framework of the putting-out system. The traffic was in babies rather than in wool and cloth, and two or three years often passed before the wet-nurse worker finished her task. The great French historian Jules Michelet described with compassion the plight of the wet nurse, who was still going to the homes of the rich in early nineteenth-century France:

People do not know how much these poor women are exploited and abused, first by the vehicles which transport them (often barely out of their confinement), and afterward by the employment offices which place them. Taken as nurses on the spot, they must send their own child away, and consequently it often dies. They have no contact with the family that hires them, and they may be dismissed at the first caprice of the mother or doctor. If the change of air and place should dry up their milk, they are discharged without any compensation. If they stay here [in the city] they pick up the habits of the easy life, and they suffer enormously when they are forced to return to their life of [rural] poverty. A good number become servants in order to stay in the town. They never rejoin their husbands, and the family is broken.[7]

Other observers noted the flaws of wet nursing. It was a common belief that a nurse passed her bad traits to the baby with her milk. When a child turned out poorly, it was assumed that "the nurse changed it." Many observers charged that nurses were often negligent and greedy. They claimed that there were large numbers of "killing nurses" with whom no child every survived. The nurse let the child die quickly, so that she could take another child and another fee. No matter how the adults fared in the wet-nurse business, the child was a certain loser.

FOUNDLINGS AND INFANTICIDE

In the ancient world and in Asian societies it was not uncommon to allow or force newborn babies, particularly girl babies, to die when there were too many mouths to feed. To its great and eternal credit, the early medieval church, strongly influenced by Jewish law, denounced infanticide as a pagan practice and insisted that every human life was sacred. The willful destruction of newborn children became a crime punishable by death. And yet, as the reference to "killing nurses" suggests, direct and indirect methods of eliminating unwanted babies did not disap-

Abandoned Children At this Italian foundlings' home a frightened, secretive mother could discreetly deposit her baby. *(The Bettmann Archive)*

The young girl—very likely a servant—who could not provide for her child had few choices. If she would not stoop to abortion or the services of a killing nurse, she could bundle up her baby and leave it on the doorstep of a church. In the late seventeenth century, Saint Vincent de Paul was so distressed by the number of babies brought to the steps of Notre Dame in Paris that he established a home for foundlings. Others followed his example. In England the government acted on a petition calling for a foundling hospital "to prevent the frequent murders of poor, miserable infants at birth" and "to suppress the inhuman custom of exposing newborn children to perish in the streets."

In much of Europe in the eighteenth century, foundling homes became a favorite charity of the rich and powerful. Great sums were spent on them. The foundling home in St. Petersburg, perhaps the most elaborate and lavish of its kind, occupied the former palaces of two members of the high nobility. In the early nineteenth century it had 25,000 children in its care and was receiving 5,000 new babies a year. At their best, the foundling homes of the eighteenth century were a good example of Christian charity and social concern in an age of great poverty and inequality.

Yet the foundling home was no panacea. By the 1770s one-third of all babies born in Paris were immediately abandoned to the foundling home by their mothers. Fully a third of all those foundlings were abandoned by married couples, a powerful commentary on the standard of living among the working poor, for whom an additional mouth to feed often meant tragedy. In London competition for space in the foundling home soon became so great that it led "to the disgraceful scene of women scrambling and fighting to get to the door, that they might be of the fortunate few to reap the benefit of the Asylum."[8]

Furthermore, great numbers of babies entered, but few left. Even in the best of these homes half the babies normally died within a year. In the worst, fully 90 percent did not survive. They succumbed to long journeys over rough roads, the intentional and unintentional neglect of their wet nurses, and the customary childhood illnesses. So great was the carnage that some contemporaries called the foundling hospitals "legalized infanticide."

Certainly some parents and officials looked on the hospitals as a dump for unwanted babies. In the early 1760s, when the London Foundling Hospital was

pear. There were, for example, many cases of "overlaying"—parents rolling over and suffocating the child placed between them in their bed. Such parents claimed they were drunk and had acted unintentionally. In Austria in 1784, suspicious authorities made it illegal for parents to take children under five into bed with them. Severe poverty on the one hand and increasing illegitimacy on the other conspired to force the very poor to thin their own ranks.

obliged to accept all babies offered, it was deluged with babies from the countryside. Many parish officers placed with the foundling home the abandoned children in their care, just as others apprenticed five-year-old children to work in factories. Both practices reduced the cost of welfare at the local level. Throughout the eighteenth century, millions of children of the poor continued to exit after the briefest of appearances on the earthly stage. True, they died after being properly baptized, an important consideration in still-Christian Europe. Yet those who dream of an idyllic past would do well to ponder the foundling's fate.

ATTITUDES TOWARD CHILDREN

What were the more typical circumstances of children's lives? Did the treatment of foundlings reflect the attitudes of normal parents? Harsh as it may sound, the young child was very often of little concern to its parents and to society in the eighteenth century. This indifference toward children was found in all classes; rich children were by no means exempt. The practice of using wet nurses, who were casually selected and often negligent, is one example of how even the rich and the prosperous put the child out of sight and out of mind. One French moralist, writing in 1756 about how to improve humanity, observed that "one blushes to think of loving one's children." It has been said that the English gentleman of the period "had more interest in the diseases of his horses than of his children."[9]

Parents believed that the world of the child was an uninteresting one. When parents did stop to notice their offspring, they often treated them as dolls or playthings—little puppies to fondle and cuddle in a moment of relaxation. The psychological distance between parent and child remained vast.

Much of the indifference was due to the terrible frequency, the terrible banality, of death among children of all classes. Parents simply could not afford to become too emotionally involved with their children, who were so unlikely to survive. The great eighteenth-century English historian Edward Gibbon (1737–1794) wrote that "the death of a new born child before that of its parents may seem unnatural but it is a strictly probable event, since of any given number the greater part are extinguished before the ninth year, before they possess the faculties of the mind and the body." Gibbon's father named all his boys Edward, hoping that at least one of them would survive to carry his name. His prudence was not misplaced. Edward the future historian and eldest survived. Five brothers and sisters who followed him all died in infancy.

Doctors were seldom interested in the care of children. One contemporary observer quoted a famous doctor as saying that "he never wished to be called to a young child because he was really at a loss to know what to offer for it." There were "physicians of note who make no scruple to assert that there is nothing to be done for children when they are ill." Children were caught in a vicious circle: they were neglected because they were very likely to die and they were likely to die because they were neglected.

Indifference toward children often shaded off into brutality. When parents and other adults did turn toward children, it was normally to discipline and control them. The novelist Daniel Defoe (1660?–1731), always delighted when he saw very young children working hard in cottage industry, coined the axiom "Spare the rod and spoil the child." He meant it. So did Susannah Wesley, mother of John Wesley (1703–1791), the founder of Methodism. According to her, the first task of a parent toward her children was "to conquer the will, and bring them to an obedient temper." She reported that her babies were "taught to fear the rod, and to cry softly; by which means they escaped the abundance of correction they might otherwise have had, and that most odious noise of the crying of children was rarely heard in the house."[10]

It was hardly surprising that, when English parish officials dumped their paupers into the first factories late in the eighteenth century, the children were beaten and brutalized (see page 703). That was part of the childrearing pattern—widespread indifference on the one hand and strict physical discipline on the other—that prevailed through most of the eighteenth century.

Late in the century, this pattern came under attack. Critics like Jean-Jacques Rousseau called for greater love, tenderness, and understanding toward children. In addition to supporting foundling homes to discourage infanticide and urging wealthy women to nurse their own babies, these new voices ridiculed the practice of swaddling. Wrapping youngsters in tight-fitting clothes and blankets was generally believed to form babies properly by "straightening them out."

The Five Senses Published in 1774, J. B. Basedow's *Elementary Reader* helped spread new attitudes toward child development and education. Drawing heavily upon the theories of Locke and Rousseau, the German educator advocated nature study and contact with everyday life. In this illustration for Basedow's reader, gentle teachers allow uncorrupted children to learn about the five senses through direct experience. *(Photo: Caroline Buckler)*

By the end of the century, small children were often dressed in simpler, more comfortable clothing, allowing much greater freedom of movement. More parents expressed a delight in the love and intimacy of the child and found real pleasure in raising their offspring. These changes were part of the general growth of humanitarianism and optimism about human potential that characterized the eighteenth-century Enlightenment.

SCHOOLS AND EDUCATION

The role of formal education outside the home, in those special institutions called schools, was growing more important. The aristocracy and the rich had led the way in the sixteenth century with special colleges, often run by the Jesuits. But "little schools," charged with elementary education of the children of the masses, did not appear until the seventeenth century.

Unlike medieval schools, which mingled all age groups, the little schools specialized in boys and girls from seven to twelve, who were instructed in basic literacy and religion.

Although large numbers of common people got no education at all in the eighteenth century, the beginnings of popular education were recognizable. France made a start in 1682 with the establishment of Christian schools, which taught the catechism and prayers as well as reading and writing. The Church of England and the dissenting congregations established "charity schools" to instruct the children of the poor. As early as 1717, Prussia made attendance at elementary schools compulsory. Inspired by the old Protestant idea that every believer should be able to read and study the Bible in the quest for personal salvation and by the new idea of a population capable of effectively serving the state, Prussia led the way in the development of universal education. Religious motives were also extremely important elsewhere. From the middle of the seventeenth century, Presbyterian Scotland was convinced that the path to salvation lay in careful study of the Scriptures, and this belief led to an effective network of parish schools for rich and poor alike. The Enlightenment commitment to greater knowledge through critical thinking reinforced interest in education in the eighteenth century.

The result of these efforts was a remarkable growth of basic literacy between 1600 and 1800, especially after 1700. Whereas in 1600 only one male in six was barely literate in France and Scotland, and one in four in England, by 1800 almost 90 percent of the Scottish male population was literate. At the same time, two out of three males were literate in France, and in advanced areas such as Normandy, literacy approached 90 percent (see Map 20.1). More than half of English males were literate by 1800. In all three countries the bulk of the jump occurred in the eighteenth century. Women were also increasingly literate, although they probably lagged behind men somewhat in most countries. Some elementary education was becoming a reality for European peoples, and schools were of growing significance in everyday life.

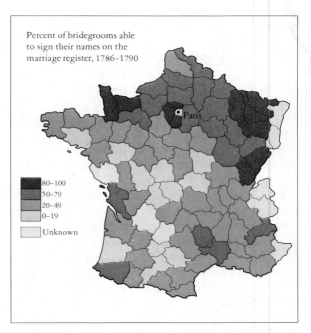

Percent of bridegrooms able to sign their names on the marriage register, 1786–1790

80–100
50–79
20–49
0–19
Unknown

MAP 20.1 Literacy in France on the Eve of the French Revolution Literacy rates varied widely between and within states in eighteenth-century Europe. Northern France was clearly ahead of southern France.

THE EUROPEAN'S FOOD

Plague and starvation, which recurred often in the seventeenth century, gradually disappeared in the eighteenth century. This phenomenon probably accounts in large part for the rapid growth in the total number of Europeans and for their longer lives. The increase in the average life span, allowing for regional variations, was remarkable. In 1700 the average European could expect at birth to live only twenty-five years. A century later, a newborn European could expect to live fully ten years longer, to age thirty-five. The doubling of the adult life span meant that there was more time to produce and create, and more reason for parents to stress learning and preparation for adulthood.

People also lived longer because ordinary years were progressively less deadly. People ate better and somewhat more wisely. Doctors and hospitals probably saved a few more lives than they had in the past. How and why did health and life expectancy im-

prove, and how much did they improve? And what were the differences between rich and poor? To answer these questions, it is necessary first to follow the eighteenth-century family to the table and then to see what contribution doctors made.

DIETS AND NUTRITION

Although the accomplishments of doctors and hospitals are constantly in the limelight today, the greater, if less spectacular, part of medicine is preventive medicine. The great breakthrough of the second half of the nineteenth century was the development of public health techniques—proper sanitation and mass vaccinations—to prevent outbreaks of communicable diseases. Even before the nineteenth century, when medical knowledge was slight and doctors were of limited value, prevention was the key to longer life. Good clothing, warm dry housing, and plentiful food make for healthier populations, much more capable of battling off disease. Clothing and housing for the masses probably improved only modestly in the eighteenth century, but the new agricultural methods and increased agricultural output had a beneficial effect. The average European ate more and better food and was healthier as a result in 1800 than in 1700. This pattern is apparent if we look at the fare of the laboring poor.

At the beginning of the eighteenth century, ordinary men and women depended on grain as fully as they had in the past. Bread was quite literally the staff of life. Peasants in the Beauvais region of France ate two pounds of bread a day, washing it down with water, green wine, beer, or a little skimmed milk. Their dark bread was made from a mixture of rough-ground wheat and rye—the standard flour of the poor. The poor also ate grains in soup and gruel. In rocky northern Scotland, for example, people depended on oatmeal, which they often ate half-cooked so it would swell in their stomachs and make them feel full. No wonder, then, that the supply of grain and the price of bread were always critical questions for most of the population.

The poor, rural and urban, also ate a fair quantity of vegetables. Indeed, vegetables were considered "poor people's food." Peas and beans were probably the most common; grown as field crops in much of Europe since the Middle Ages, they were eaten fresh in late spring and summer. Dried, they became the basic ingredients in the soups and stews of the long winter months. In most regions, other vegetables appeared in season on the tables of the poor, primarily cabbages, carrots, and wild greens. Fruit was uncommon and limited to the summer months.

The European poor loved meat and eggs, but even in England—the wealthiest country in Europe in 1700—they seldom ate their fill. Meat was too expensive. When the poor did eat meat—on a religious holiday or at a wedding or other special occasion—it was most likely lamb or mutton. Sheep could survive on rocky soils and did not compete directly with humans for the slender resources of grain.

Milk was rarely drunk. It was widely believed that milk caused sore eyes, headaches, and a variety of ills, except among the very young and very old. Milk was used primarily to make cheese and butter, which the poor liked but could afford only occasionally. Medical and popular opinion considered whey, the watery liquid left after milk was churned, "an excellent temperate drink."

The diet of the rich—aristocrats, officials, and the comfortable bourgeoisie—was traditionally quite different from that of the poor. The men and women of the upper classes were rapacious carnivores, and a person's standard of living and economic well-being were often judged by the amount of meat eaten. A truly elegant dinner among the great and powerful consisted of one rich meat after another—a chicken pie, a leg of lamb, a grilled steak, for example. Three separate meat courses might be followed by three fish courses, laced with piquant sauces and complemented with sweets, cheeses, and nuts of all kinds. Fruits and vegetables were not often found on the tables of the rich. The long-standing dominance of meat and fish in the diet of the upper classes continued throughout the eighteenth century. There was extravagant living, and undoubtedly great overeating and gluttony, not only among the aristocracy but also among the prosperous professional classes.

There was also an enormous amount of overdrinking among the rich. The English squire, for example, who loved to ride with his hounds, loved drink with a similar passion. He became famous as the "four-bottle man." With his dinner he drank red wine from France or white wine from the Rhineland, and with his desert he took sweet but strong port or Maderia from Portugal. Sometimes he ended the evening under the table in a drunken stupor, but very often he did not. The wine and the meat were consumed together in long hours of sustained excess, permitting the gentleman and his guests to drink enormous quantities.

The diet of small traders, master craftsmen, minor bureaucrats—the people of the towns and cities—was probably less monotonous than that of the peasantry. The markets, stocked by market gardens in the outskirts, provided a substantial variety of meats, vegetables, and fruits, although bread and beans still formed the bulk of the poor family's diet.

There were also regional dietary differences in 1700. Generally speaking, northern, Atlantic Europe ate better than southern, Mediterranean Europe. The poor of England probably ate best of all. Contemporaries on both sides of the Channel often contrasted the Englishman's consumption of meat with the French peasant's greater dependence on bread and vegetables. The Dutch were also considerably better fed than the average European, in large part because of their advanced agriculture and diversified gardens.

Le Nain: Peasant Family A little wine and a great deal of dark bread: the traditional food of the poor French peasantry accentuates the poetic dignity of this masterpiece, painted about 1640 by Louis Le Nain. *(Cliché des Musées Nationaux, Paris)*

The Impact of Diet on Health

How were the poor and the rich served by their quite different diets? Good nutrition depends on a balanced supply of food as well as on an adequate number of calories. Modern research has shown that the chief determinant of nutritional balance is the relationship between carbohydrates (sugar and starch) and proteins. A diet consisting primarily of carbohydrates is seriously incomplete.

At first glance, the diet of the laboring poor, relying as it did on carbohydrates, seems unsatisfactory. Even when a peasant got his daily two or three pounds of bread, his supply of protein and essential vitamins would seem too low. A closer look reveals a brighter picture. Most bread was "brown" or "black," made from wheat or rye. The flour of the eighteenth century was a whole-meal flour, produced by stone grinding. It contained most of the bran—the ground-up husk—and the all-important wheat germ. The bran and germ contain higher proportions of some minerals, vitamins, and good-quality proteins than does the rest of the grain. Only when they are removed does bread become a foodstuff providing relatively more starch and less of the essential nutrients.

In addition, the field peas and beans eaten by poor people since Carolingian days contained protein that complemented the proteins in whole-meal bread.

The proteins in whey, cheese, and eggs, which the poor ate at least occasionally, also supplemented the value of the protein in the bread and vegetables. Indeed, a leading authority concludes that if a pint of milk and some cheese and whey were eaten each day, the balance of the poor people's diet "was excellent, far better indeed than in many of our modern diets."[11]

The basic bread-and-vegetables diet of the poor *in normal times* was satisfactory. It protected effectively against most of the disorders associated with a deficiency of the vitamin B complex, for example. The lack of sugar meant that teeth were not so plagued by cavities. Constipation was almost unknown to peasants and laborers living on coarse cereal breads, which provided the roughage modern diets lack. The common diet of the poor also generally warded off anemia, although anemia among infants was not uncommon.

The key dietary problem was probably getting enough green vegetables (or milk), particularly in the late winter and early spring, to ensure adequate supplies of vitamins A and C. A severe deficiency of vitamin C produces scurvy, a disease that leads to rotting gums, swelling of the limbs, and great weakness. Before the season's first vegetables, many people had used up their bodily reserves of vitamin C and were suffering from mild cases of scurvy. Sailors on long voyages suffered most. By the end of the sixteenth century the exceptional antiscurvy properties of lemons and limes led to the practice of supplying some crews with a daily ration of lemon juice, which had highly beneficial effects. "Scurvy grass"—a kind of watercress—also guarded against scurvy, and this disease was increasingly controlled on even the longest voyages.

The practice of gorging on meat, sweets, and spirits caused the rich their own nutritional problems. They, too, were very often deficient in vitamins A and C because of their great disdain for fresh vegetables. Gout was a common affliction of the overfed and underexercised rich. No wonder they were often caricatured dragging their flabby limbs and bulging bellies to the table, to stuff their swollen cheeks and poison their livers. People of moderate means, who could afford some meat and dairy products with fair regularity but who had not abandoned the bread and vegetables of the poor, were probably best off from a nutritional standpoint.

NEW FOODS AND NEW KNOWLEDGE

In nutrition and food consumption, Europe in the early eighteenth century had not gone beyond its medieval accomplishments. This situation began to change markedly as the century progressed. Although the introduction of new methods of farming was confined largely to the Low Countries and England, a new food—the potato—came to the aid of the poor everywhere.

Introduced into Europe from the Americas, along with corn, squash, tomatoes, chocolate, and many other useful plants, the humble potato is an excellent food. It contains a good supply of carbohydrates and calories, and is rich in vitamins A and C, especially if the skin is eaten and it is not overcooked. The lack of green vegetables that could lead to scurvy was one of the biggest deficiencies in the poor person's winter and early spring diet. The potato, which gave a much higher caloric yield than grain for a given piece of land, provided the needed vitamins and supplemented the bread-based diet. Doctors, increasingly aware of the dietary benefits of potatoes, prescribed them for the general public and in institutions such as schools and prisons.

For some poor people, especially desperately poor peasants who needed to get every possible calorie from a tiny plot of land, the potato replaced grain as the primary food in the eighteenth century. This happened first in Ireland, where in the seventeenth century Irish rebellion had led to English repression and the perfection of a system of exploitation worthy of the most savage Eastern tyrant. The foreign (and Protestant) English landlords took the best land, forcing large numbers of poor (and Catholic) peasants to live off tiny scraps of rented ground. By 1700 the poor in Ireland lived almost exclusively on the bountiful fruits of the potato plot.

Elsewhere in Europe, the potato took hold more slowly. Potatoes were first fed to pigs and livestock, and there was considerable debate over whether they were fit for humans. In Germany the severe famines caused by the Seven Years' War (page 595) settled the matter: potatoes were edible and not "famine food." By the end of the century, the potato was an important dietary supplement in much of Europe.

There was also a general growth of market gardening and a greater variety of vegetables in towns and cities. Potatoes, cabbages, peas, beans, radishes, spinach, asparagus, lettuce, parsnips, carrots, and other vegetables were sold in central markets and streets. In the course of the eighteenth century, the large towns and cities of maritime Europe began to receive semi-tropical fruit, such as oranges, lemons, and limes, from Portugal and the West Indies, although they were not cheap.

The growing variety of food was matched by some improvement in knowledge about diet and nutrition. For the poor, such improvement was limited primarily to the insight that the potato and other root crops improved health in the winter and helped to prevent scurvy. The rich began to be aware of the harmful effects of their meat-laden, wine-drowned meals.

The waning influence of Galen's medical teachings was another aspect of progress. Galen's Roman synthesis of ancient medical doctrines held that the four basic elements—air, fire, water, and earth—combine to produce in each person a complexion and a corresponding temperament. Foods were grouped into four categories appropriate for each complexion. Galen's notions dominated the dietary thinking of the seventeenth-century medical profession: "Galen said that the flesh of a hare preventeth fatness, causeth sleep and cleanseth the blood," and so on for a thousand things. For instance, vegetables were seen as "windy" and tending to cause fevers, and fruits as dangerous except in very small amounts.

The growth of scientific experimentation in the seventeenth century led to a generally beneficial questioning of the old views. Haphazardly, by trial and error, and influenced by advances in chemistry, saner ideas developed. Experiments with salts led to the belief that foods were by nature either acid (all fruits and most vegetables) or alkaline (all meats). Doctors and early nutritionists came to believe that one key to good health was a *balance* of the two types.

Not all changes in the eighteenth century were for the better, however. Bread began to change, most noticeably in England. Rising incomes and new tastes led to a shift from whole-meal black or brown bread to white bread made from finely ground and sifted flour. On the Continent, such white bread was generally limited to the well-to-do. To the extent that the preferred wheaten flour was stone-ground and sifted for coarse particles only, white bread remained satisfactory. But the desire for "bread as white as snow" was already leading to a decline in nutritional value.

The coarser bran, which is necessary for roughage, and at least some of the germ, which darkened the bread but contained the grain's nutrients, were already being sifted out to some extent. Bakers in English cities added the chemical alum to their white loaves to make them smoother, whiter, and larger. In the nineteenth century, "improvements" in milling were to lead to the removal of almost all the bran and germ from the flour, leaving it perfectly white and greatly reduced in nutritional value. The only saving grace in the sad deterioration of bread was that people began to eat and therefore to depend on it less.

Another sign of nutritional decline was the growing consumption of sweets in general and sugar in particular. Initially a luxury, sugar dropped rapidly in price, as slave-based production increased in the Americas, and it was much more widely used in the eighteenth century. This development probably led to an increase in cavities and to other ailments as well. Overconsumption of refined sugar can produce, paradoxically, low blood sugar (hypoglycemia) and, for some individuals at least, a variety of physical and mental ailments. Of course the greater or lesser poverty of the laboring poor saved most of them from the problems of the rich and well-to-do.

MEDICAL SCIENCE AND THE SICK

Advances in medical science played a very small part in improving the health and lengthening the lives of people in the eighteenth century. Such seventeenth-century advances as William Harvey's discovery of the circulation of blood were not soon translated into better treatment. The sick had to await the medical revolution of the later nineteenth century for much help from doctors.

Yet developments in medicine reflected the general thrust of the Enlightenment. The prevailing focus on discovering the laws of nature and on human problems, rather than on God and the heavens, gave rise to a great deal of research and experimentation. The century saw a remarkable rise in the number of doctors, and a high value was placed on their services. Thus when the great breakthroughs in knowledge came in the nineteenth century, they could be rapidly diffused and applied. Eighteenth-century medicine, in short, gave promise of a better human existence, but most of the realization lay far in the future.

Knives for Bloodletting In the eighteenth century doctors continued to use these diabolical instruments to treat almost every illness, with disastrous results. *(Courtesy, World Heritage Museum. Photo: Caroline Buckler)*

THE MEDICAL PROFESSIONALS

Care of the sick was the domain of several competing groups—faith healers, apothecaries, surgeons, and physicians. Since the great majority of common ailments have a tendency to cure themselves, each group could point to successes and win adherents. When the doctor's treatment made the patient worse, as it often did, the original medical problem could always be blamed.

Faith healers, who had been one of the most important kinds of physicians in medieval Europe, remained active. They and their patients believed that demons and evil spirits caused disease by lodging in people and that the proper treatment was to exorcise or drive out the offending devil. This demonic view of disease was strongest in the countryside, as was faith in the healing power of religious relics, prayer, and the laying on of hands. Faith healing was particularly effective in the treatment of mental disorders like hysteria and depression, where the link between attitude and illness is most direct.

Apothecaries, or pharmacists, sold a vast number of herbs, drugs, and patent medicines for every conceivable "temperament and distemper." Early pharmacists were seldom regulated, and they frequently diagnosed as freely as the doctors whose prescriptions they filled. Their prescriptions were incredibly complex—a hundred or more drugs might be included in a single prescription—and often very expensive. Some of the drugs undoubtedly worked: strong laxatives were given to the rich for their constipated bowels. Indeed the medical profession continued to believe that regular "purging" of the bowels was essential for good health and the treatment of illness. Much purging was harmful, however, and only bloodletting for the treatment of disease was more effective in speeding patients to their graves.

Drugs were prescribed and concocted in a helter-skelter way. With so many different drugs being combined, it was impossible to isolate cause and effect. Nor was there any standardization. A complicated prescription filled by ten different pharmacists would result in ten different preparations with different medical properties.

Surgeons competed vigorously with barbers and "bone benders," the forerunners of chiropractors. The eighteenth-century surgeon (and patient) labored in the face of incredible difficulties. Almost all operations were performed without any painkiller, for anesthesia was believed too dangerous. The terrible screams of people whose limbs were being sawed off shattered hospitals and battlefields. Such operations were common, because a surgeon faced with an extensive wound sought to obtain a plain surface that he could cauterize with fire. Thus, if a person broke an arm or a leg and the bone stuck out, off came the limb. Many patients died from the agony and shock of such operations.

Surgery was also performed in the midst of filth and dirt. There simply was no knowledge of bacteriology and the nature of infection. The simplest wound treated by a surgeon festered, often fatally. In fact, surgeons encouraged wounds to fester in the belief—a remnant of Galen's theory—that the pus was beneficially removing the base portions of the body.

Physicians, the fourth major group, were trained like surgeons. They were apprenticed in their teens to a practicing physician for several years of on-the-job training. This training was then rounded out with hospital work or some university courses. To their credit, physicians in the eighteenth century were increasingly willing to experiment with new methods, but the hand of Galen lay heavily on them. Bloodletting was still considered a medical cure-all. It was the way "bad blood," the cause of illness, was removed and the balance of humors necessary for good health restored.

According to a physician practicing medicine in Philadelphia in 1799, "No operation of surgery is so frequently necessary as bleeding. . . . But though practiced by midwives, gardeners, blacksmiths, etc., very few know when it is proper." The good doctor went on to explain that bleeding was proper at the onset of all inflammatory fevers, in all inflammations, and for "asthma, sciatic pains, coughs, headaches, rheumatisms, the apoplexy, epilepsy, and bloody fluxes."[12] It was also necessary after all falls, blows, and bruises.

Physicians, like apothecaries, laid great stress on purging. They also generally believed that disease was caused by bad odors, and for this reason they carried canes whose heads contained ammonia salts. As they made their rounds in the filthy, stinking hospitals, physicians held their canes to their noses to protect themselves from illness.

While ordinary physicians were bleeding, apothecaries purging, surgeons sawing, and faith healers praying, the leading medical thinkers were attempting to pull together and assimilate all the information and misinformation they had been accumulating. The attempt was ambitious: to systematize medicine around simple, basic principles, as Newton had done in physics. But the schools of thought resulting from such speculation and theorizing did little to improve medical care. Proponents of *animism* explained life and disease in terms of *anima,* the "sensitive soul," which they believed was present throughout the body and prevented its decay and self-destruction. Another school, *vitalism,* stressed "the vital principle," which inhabited all parts of the body. Vitalists tried to classify diseases systematically.

More interesting was the *homeopathic* system of Samuel Hahnemann of Leipzig. Hahnemann believed that very small doses of drugs that produce certain symptoms in a healthy person will cure a sick person with those symptoms. This theory was probably preferable to most eighteenth-century treatments, in that it was a harmless alternative to the extravagant and often fatal practices of bleeding, purging, drug taking, and induced vomiting. The patient gained confidence, and the body had at least a fighting chance of recovering.

HOSPITALS

Hospitals were terrible throughout most of the eighteenth century. There was no isolation of patients. Operations were performed in the patient's bed. The nurses were old, ignorant, greedy, and often drunk women. Fresh air was considered harmful, and infections of every kind were rampant. Diderot's article in the *Encyclopedia* on the Hôtel-Dieu in Paris, the "richest and most terrifying of all French hospitals," vividly describes normal conditions of the 1770s:

Imagine a long series of communicating wards filled with sufferers of every kind of disease who are sometimes packed three, four, five or even six into a bed, the living alongside the dead and dying, the air polluted by this mass of unhealthy bodies, passing pestilential germs of their afflictions from one to the other, and the spectacle of suffering and agony on every hand. That is the Hôtel-Dieu.

The result is that many of these poor wretches come out with diseases they did not have when they went in, and often pass them on to the people they go back to live

Hospital Life Patients crowded into hospitals like this one in Hamburg in 1746 had little chance of recovery. A priest by the window administers last rites, while in the center a surgeon coolly saws off the leg of a man who has received no anesthesia. *(Germanisches Nationalmuseum, Nuremberg)*

with. Others are half-cured and spend the rest of their days in an invalidism as hard to bear as the illness itself; and the rest perish, except for the fortunate few whose strong constitutions enable them to survive.[13]

No wonder the poor of Paris hated hospitals and often saw confinement there as a plot to kill paupers.

In the last years of the century, the humanitarian concern already reflected in Diderot's description of the Hôtel-Dieu led to a movement for hospital reform through western Europe. Efforts were made to improve ventilation and eliminate filth, on the grounds that bad air caused disease. The theory was wrong, but the results were beneficial, since the spread of infection was somewhat reduced.

MENTAL ILLNESS

Mental hospitals, too, were incredibly savage institutions. The customary treatment for mental illness was bleeding and cold water, administered more to maintain discipline than to effect a cure. Violent persons were chained to the wall and forgotten. A breakthrough of sorts occurred in the 1790s, when William Tuke founded the first humane sanatorium in England. In Paris an innovative warden, Philippe Pinel, took the chains off the mentally disturbed in 1793 and tried to treat them as patients rather than as prisoners.

In the eighteenth century, there were all sorts of wildly erroneous ideas about mental illness. One was that moonlight caused madness, a belief reflected in the word *lunatic*—someone harmed by lunar light. Another mid-eighteenth-century theory, which lasted until at least 1914, was that masturbation caused madness, not to mention acne, epilepsy, and premature ejaculation. Thus parents, religious institutions, and schools waged relentless war on masturbation by males, although they were curiously uninterested in female masturbation. In the nineteenth century, this misguided idea was to reach its greatest height, resulting in increasingly drastic medical treatment. Doctors ordered their "patients" to wear mittens, fitted them with wooden braces between the knees, or simply tied them up in straitjackets.

MEDICAL EXPERIMENTS AND RESEARCH

In the second half of the eighteenth century, medicine in general turned in a more practical and experimental direction. Some of the experimentation was creative quackery involving the recently discovered phenomenon of electricity. One magnificent quack, James Graham of London, opened a great hall filled with the walking sticks, crutches, eyeglasses, and ear trumpets of supposedly cured patients, which he kept as symbols of his victory over disease. Great glass globes and the rich perfumes of burning incense awaited all who entered. Graham's principal treatment involved his Celestial Bed, which was lavishly decorated with magnets and electrical devices. Graham claimed that by sleeping in it youths would keep their good looks, their elders would be rejuvenated, and couples would have beautiful, healthy children. The fee for a single night in the Medico-Magnetico-Musico-Electrical Bed was £100—a great sum of money.

The rich could buy expensive treatments, but the prevalence of quacks and the general lack of knowledge meant they often got little for their money. Because so many treatments were harmful, the poor were probably much less deprived by their almost total lack of access to medical care than one might think.

Renewed experimentation and the intensified search for solutions to human problems also led to some real, if still modest, advances in medicine after 1750. The eighteenth century's greatest medical triumph was the conquest of smallpox.

With the progressive decline of bubonic plague, smallpox became the most terrible of the infectious diseases. In the words of the historian Thomas Macaulay, "smallpox was always present, filling the churchyard with corpses, tormenting with constant fears all whom it had not stricken." In the seventeenth century, one in every four deaths in the British Isles was due to smallpox, and it is estimated that 60 million Europeans died of it in the eighteenth century. Fully 80 percent of the population was stricken at some point in life, and 25 percent of the total population was left permanently scarred. If ever a human problem cried out for solution, it was smallpox.

The first step in the conquest of this killer came in the early eighteenth century. An English aristocrat whose great beauty had been marred by the pox, Lady Mary Wortley Montague, learned about the practice of inoculation in the Ottoman Empire while her husband was serving as British ambassador there. She had her own son successfully inoculated in Constantinople and was instrumental in spreading the practice in England after her return in 1722.

Inoculation against smallpox had long been practiced in the Middle East. The skin was deliberately broken, and a small amount of matter taken from the pustule of a smallpox victim was applied. The person thus contracted a mild case of smallpox that gave lasting protection against further attack. Inoculation was risky, however, and about one person in fifty died from it. In addition, people who had been inoculated were just as infectious as those who had caught the disease by chance. Inoculated people thus spread the disease, and the practice of inoculation against smallpox was widely condemned in the 1730s.

Success in overcoming this problem in British colonies led the British College of Physicians in 1754 to strongly advocate inoculation. Moreover, a successful search for cheaper methods led to something approaching mass inoculation in England in the 1760s. One specialist treated seventeen thousand patients and only five died. Both the danger and the cost had been reduced, and deadly smallpox struck all classes less frequently. On the Continent, the well-to-do were also inoculated, beginning with royal families like those of Maria Theresa and Catherine the Great. The practice then spread to the middle classes. Smallpox inoculation played some part in the decline of the death rate at the end of the century and the increase in population.

The Fight Against Smallpox This Russian illustration dramatically urges parents to inoculate their children against smallpox. The good father's healthy youngsters flee from their ugly and infected playmates, who hold their callous father responsible for their shameful fate. *(Yale Medical Library)*

The final breakthrough against smallpox came at the end of the century. Edward Jenner (1749–1823), a talented country doctor, noted that in the English countryside there was a long-standing belief that dairy maids who had contracted cowpox did not get smallpox. Cowpox produces sores on the cow's udder and on the hands of the milker. The sores resemble those of smallpox, but the disease is mild and not contagious.

For eighteen years Jenner practiced a kind of Baconian science, carefully collecting data on protection against smallpox by cowpox. Finally, in 1796 he performed his first vaccination on a young boy, using matter taken from a milkmaid with cowpox. Two months later he inoculated the boy with smallpox pus, but the disease did not take. In the next two years, twenty-three successful vaccinations were performed, and in 1798 Jenner published his findings. There was some skepticism and hostility, but after Austrian medical authorities replicated Jenner's re-sults, the new method of treatment spread rapidly. Smallpox soon declined to the point of disappearance in Europe and then throughout the world. Jenner eventually received prizes of £30,000 from the British government for his great discovery, a fitting recompense for a man who gave an enormous gift to humanity and helped lay the foundation for the science of immunology in the nineteenth century.

RELIGION AND CHRISTIAN CHURCHES

Though the critical spirit of the Enlightenment spread among the educated elite in the eighteenth century, the great mass of ordinary men and women remained firmly committed to the Christian religion, especially in rural areas. Religion offered answers to life's mysteries and gave comfort and courage in the face of sorrow and fear. Religion also remained strong because it was usually embedded in local traditions and everyday social experience.

Yet the popular religion of village Europe was everywhere enmeshed in a larger world of church hierarchies and state power. These powerful outside forces sought to regulate religious life at the local level. These efforts created tensions that helped set the scene for a vigorous religious revival in Germany and England.

THE INSTITUTIONAL CHURCH

As in the Middle Ages (Chapters 9–12), the local parish church remained the basic religious unit all across Europe. Still largely coinciding with the agricultural village, the parish fulfilled many needs. The parish church was the focal point of religious devotion, which went far beyond sermons and Holy Communion. The parish church organized colorful processions and pilgrimages to local shrines. Even in Protestant countries, where such activities were severely restricted, congregations gossiped and swapped stories after services, and neighbors came together in church for baptisms, marriages, funerals, and special events. Thus the parish church was woven into the very fabric of community life.

Moreover, the local church had important administrative tasks. Priests and parsons were truly the bookkeepers of agrarian Europe, and it is because parish registers were so complete that historians have learned so much about population and family life. Parishes also normally distributed charity to the destitute, looked after orphans, and provided whatever primary education was available.

The many tasks of the local church were usually the responsibility of a resident priest or pastor, a full-time professional working with assistants and lay volunteers. Moreover, all clerics—whether Catholic, Protestant, or Orthodox—shared the fate of middlemen in a complicated institutional system. Charged most often with ministering to poor peasants, the priest or parson was the last link in a powerful church-state hierarchy that was everywhere determined to control religion down to the grassroots. However, the regulatory framework of belief, which went back at least to the fourth century, when Christianity became the official religion of the Roman Empire, had undergone important changes since 1500.

The Protestant Reformation had begun as a culmination of medieval religiosity and a desire to purify Christian belief. Martin Luther, the greatest of the reformers (pages 431–438), preached that all men and women were saved from their sins and God's damnation only by personal faith in Jesus Christ. The individual could reach God directly, without need of priestly intermediaries. This was the revolutionary meaning of Luther's "priesthood of all believers," which broke forever the monopoly of the priestly class over medieval Europe's most priceless treasury—eternal salvation.

As the Reformation gathered force, with peasant upheaval and doctrinal competition, Luther turned more conservative. The monkish professor called on willing German princes to put themselves at the head of official churches in their territories. Other monarchs in northern Europe followed suit. Protestant authorities, with generous assistance from state-certified theologians like Luther, then proceeded to regulate their "territorial churches" strictly, selecting personnel and imposing detailed rules. They joined with Catholics to crush the Anabaptists (pages 445–447), who with their belief in freedom of conscience and separation of church and state had become the real revolutionaries. Thus the Reformation, initially so radical in its rejection of Rome and its stress on individual religious experience, eventually resulted in a bureaucratization of the church and local religious life in Protestant Europe.

The Reformation era also increased the practical power of Catholic rulers over "their" churches, but it was only in the eighteenth century that some Catholic monarchs began to impose striking reforms. These reforms, which had their counterparts in Orthodox Russia, had a very "Protestant" aspect. They increased state control over the Catholic church, making it less subject to papal influence.

Spain provides a graphic illustration of changing church-state relations in Catholic lands. A deeply Catholic country with devout rulers, Spain nevertheless took firm control of ecclesiastical appointments. Papal proclamations could not even be read in Spanish churches without prior approval from the government. Spain also asserted state control over the Spanish Inquisition (pages 420–421), which had been ruthlessly pursuing heresy as an independent agency under Rome's direction for two hundred years. In sum, Spain went far toward creating a "national" Catholic church, as France had done earlier.

A more striking indication of state power and papal weakness was the fate of the Society of Jesus. As the most successful of the Catholic Reformation's new religious orders (see page 457), the well-educated Jesuits were extraordinary teachers, missionaries, and agents of the papacy. In many Catholic countries, the Jesuits exercised tremendous political influence, since individual members held high government positions, and Jesuit colleges formed the minds of Europe's Catholic nobility. Yet, by playing politics so effectively, the Jesuits eventually raised a broad coalition of enemies, which destroyed their order. Especially bitter controversies over the Jesuits rocked the entire Catholic hierarchy in France. Following the earlier example of Portugal, the French king ordered the Jesuits out of France in 1763 and confiscated their property. France and Spain then pressured Rome to dissolve the Jesuits completely. In 1773 a reluctant pope caved in, although the order was revived after the French Revolution.

Some Catholic rulers also turned their reforming efforts on monasteries and convents, believing that the large monastic clergy should make a more practical contribution to social and religious life. Austria, a leader in controlling the church (see page 601), showed how far the process could go. Whereas Maria Theresa sharply restricted entry into "unproductive" orders, Joseph II recalled the radical initiatives of the Protestant Reformation. In his *Edict on Idle Institutions,* Joseph abolished contemplative orders, henceforth permitting only orders engaged in teaching, nursing, or other practical work. The number of monks plunged from 65,000 to 27,000. The state also expropriated the dissolved monasteries and used their great wealth for charitable purposes and higher salaries for ordinary priests.

CATHOLIC PIETY

Catholic territorial churches also sought to purify religious practice somewhat. As might be expected, Joseph II went the furthest. Above all, he and his agents sought to root out what they considered to be idolatry and superstition. Yet pious peasants saw only an incomprehensible attack on the true faith and drew back in anger. Joseph's sledgehammer approach and the resulting reaction dramatized an underlying tension between Christian reform and popular piety after the Reformation.

Protestant reformers had taken very seriously the commandment that "Thou shalt not make any graven image" (Exodus 20:4), and their radical reforms had reordered church interiors. Relics and crucifixes had been permanently removed from crypt and altar, while stained-glass windows had been smashed and walls and murals covered with whitewash. Processions and pilgrimages, saints and shrines—all such nonessentials had been rigorously suppressed in the attempt to recapture the vital core of the Christian religion. Such revolutionary changes had often troubled ordinary churchgoers, but by the late seventeenth century, these reforms had been thoroughly routinized by official Protestant churches.

The situation was quite different in Catholic Europe around 1700. First of all, the visual contrast was striking; baroque art (pages 561–562) had lavished rich and emotionally exhilarating figures and images on Catholic churches, just as Protestants had removed theirs. From almost every indication, people in Catholic Europe remained intensely religious. More than 95 percent of the population probably attended church for Easter Communion, the climax of the Catholic church year.

Much of the tremendous popular strength of religion in Catholic countries reflected that its practice went far beyond Sunday churchgoing and was an important part of community life. Thus, although Catholics reluctantly confessed their sins to the priest, they enthusiastically joined together in public processions to celebrate the passage of the liturgical year. In addition to the great processional days—such as Palm Sunday, the joyful re-enactment of Jesus' triumphal entry into Jerusalem, or Rogations, with its chanted supplications and penances three days before the bodily ascent of Jesus into heaven on Ascension Day—each parish had its own local processions. Led by its priest, a congregation might march around the village, or across the countryside to a local shrine or chapel. There were endless variations. In the southern French Alps, the people looked forward especially to "high-mountain" processions in late spring. Parishes came together from miles around on some high mountain. There the assembled priests asked God to bless the people with healthy flocks and pure waters, and then all joined together in an enormous picnic. Before each procession, the priest explained its religious significance to kindle group piety. But processions were also folklore

Planting Crosses After their small wooden crosses were blessed at church as part of the Rogation Days' ceremonies in early May, French peasants traditionally placed them in their fields and pastures to protect the seed and help the crops grow. This illustration shows the custom being performed in the French Alps in the mid-nineteenth century, when it was still widely practiced. *(L' Illustration/Library of Congress)*

and tradition, an escape from work and a form of recreation. A holiday atmosphere sometimes reigned on longer processions, with drinking and dancing and couples disappearing into the woods.

Devout Catholics held many religious beliefs that were marginal to the Christian faith, often of obscure or even pagan origin. On the feast of Saint Anthony, priests were expected to bless salt and bread for farm animals to protect them from disease. One saint's relics could help cure a child of fear, and there were healing springs for many ailments. The ordinary person combined a strong Christian faith with a wealth of time-honored superstitions.

Parish priests and Catholic hierarchies were frequently troubled by the limitations of their parishioners' Christian understanding. One parish priest in France, who kept an invaluable daily diary, lamented that his parishioners were "more superstitious than devout . . . and sometimes appear as baptized idolators."[14]

Many parish priests in France, often acting on instructions from their bishops, made an effort to purify popular religious culture. For example, one priest tried to abolish pilgrimages to a local sacred spring of Our Lady, reputed to revive dead babies long enough for a proper baptism. French priests denounced par-

"Clipping the Church" The ancient English ceremony of dancing around the church once each year on the night before Lent undoubtedly had pre-Christian origins, for its purpose was to create a magical protective chain against evil spirits and the devil. The Protestant reformers did their best to stamp them out, but such "pagan practices" sometimes lingered on. *(Somerset Archaeological and Natural History Society)*

ticularly the "various remnants of paganism" found in popular bonfire ceremonies during Lent, in which young men, "yelling and screaming like madmen," tried to jump over the bonfires in order to help the crops grow and protect themselves from illness. One priest saw rational Christians turning back into pagan animals—"the triumph of Hell and the shame of Christianity."[15]

Yet, whereas Protestant reformers had already used the power of the territorial state to crush such practices, Catholic church leaders generally pro-

ceeded cautiously in the eighteenth century. They knew that old beliefs—such as the belief common throughout Europe that the priest's energetic ringing of churchbells and his recitation of ritual prayers would protect the village from hail and thunderstorms—were an integral part of the people's religion. Thus Catholic priests and hierarchies generally preferred a compromise between theological purity and the people's piety, realizing perhaps that the line between divine truth and mere superstition is not easily drawn.

PROTESTANT REVIVAL

By the late seventeenth century, official Protestant churches had completed their vast reforms and had generally settled into a smug complacency. In the Reformation heartland, one concerned German minister wrote that the Lutheran church "had become paralyzed in forms of dead doctrinal conformity" and badly needed a return to its original inspiration.[16] This voice was one of many that would prepare and then guide a powerful Protestant revival, a revival largely successful because it answered the intense but increasingly unsatisfied needs of common people.

The Protestant revival began in Germany. It was known as "Pietism," and three aspects helped explain its powerful appeal. First, Pietism called for warm emotional religion that everyone could experience. Enthusiasm—in prayer, in worship, in preaching, in life itself—was the key concept. "Just as a drunkard becomes full of wine, so must the congregation become filled with spirit," declared one exuberant writer. Another said simply, "The heart must burn."[17]

Second, Pietism reasserted the earlier radical stress on the "priesthood of all believers," thereby reducing the large gulf between the official clergy and the Lutheran laity, which had continued to exist after the Reformation. Bible reading and study were enthusiastically extended to all classes, which provided a powerful spur for popular education as well as individual religious development. Finally, Pietists believed in the practical power of Christian rebirth in everyday affairs. Reborn Christians were expected to lead good, moral lives and come from all walks of life.

Pietism had a major impact on John Wesley (1703–1791), who served as the catalyst for popular religious revival in England. Wesley came from a long line of ministers, and when he went to Oxford University to prepare for the clergy, he mapped a fanatically earnest "scheme of religion." Like some students during final exam period, he organized every waking moment. After becoming a teaching fellow at Oxford, he organized a Holy Club for similarly minded students, who were soon known contemptuously as "Methodists" because they were so methodical in their devotion. Yet, like the young Luther, Wesley remained intensely troubled about his own salvation, even after his ordination as an Anglican priest in 1728.

Wesley's anxieties related to grave problems of the faith in England. The Church of England was shamelessly used by the government to provide favorites with high-paying jobs and sinecures. Building of churches practically stopped while the population grew, and in many parishes there was a grave shortage of pews. Services and sermons had settled into an uninspiring routine. That the properly purified religion had been separated from local customs and social life was symbolized by church doors that were customarily locked on weekdays. Moreover, the skepticism of the Enlightenment was making inroads among the educated classes, and deism was becoming popular. Some bishops and church leaders acted as if they believed that doctrines like the Virgin Birth or the Ascension were little more than particularly elegant superstitions.

Living in an atmosphere of religious decline and uncertainty, Wesley became profoundly troubled by his lack of faith in his own salvation. Yet spiritual counseling from a sympathetic Pietist minister from Germany prepared Wesley for a mystical, emotional "conversion" in 1738. He described this critical turning point in his *Journal*:

In the evening I went to a [Christian] society in Aldersgate Street where one was reading Luther's preface to the Epistle to the Romans. *About a quarter before nine, while he was describing the change which God works in the heart through faith in Christ, I felt my heart strangely warmed. I felt I did trust in Christ, Christ alone for salvation; and an assurance was given me that he had taken away my sins, even mine, and saved me from the law of sin and death.*[18]

Wesley's emotional experience resolved his intellectual doubts. Moreover, he was convinced that any person, no matter how poor or simple, might have a similar heartfelt conversion and gain the same blessed assurance.

Wesley took the good news to the people. Since existing churches were often overcrowded and the church-state establishment was hostile, Wesley preached in open fields. People came in large numbers. Of critical importance, Wesley expanded on earlier Dutch theologians' views and emphatically rejected Calvinist predestination—the doctrine of salvation granted only to a select few (see page 444). Rather, *all* men and women who earnestly sought salvation might be saved. It was a message of hope and joy, of free will and universal salvation.

Open-Air Preaching In an age when the established Church of England lacked religious fervor and smugly reinforced the social status quo, John Wesley carried the good news of salvation to common people across the land. Wesley sparked a powerful religious revival, symbolized by the joyful bell-ringing of the town crier in this illustration. *(Historical Pictures Service)*

Traveling some 225,000 miles by horseback and preaching more than 40,000 sermons in fifty years, Wesley's ministry won converts, formed Methodist cells, and eventually resulted in a new denomination. Evangelicals in the Church of England and the old dissenting groups also followed Wesley's example, giving impetus to an even broader awakening among the lower classes. That result showed that in England, as throughout Europe despite different churches and different practices, religion remained a vital force in the lives of the people.

In recent years, imaginative research has greatly increased the specialist's understanding of ordinary life and social patterns in the past. The human experience, as recounted by historians, has become richer and more meaningful, and many mistaken ideas have fallen. This has been particularly true of eighteenth-century, preindustrial Europe. The intimacies of family life, the contours of women's history and of childhood, and vital problems of medicine and religion are emerging from obscurity. Nor is this all. A deeper, truer understanding of the life of common people can shed light on the great economic and political developments of long-standing concern, to be seen in the next chapter.

NOTES

1. Quoted by J. M. Beattie, "The Criminality of Women in Eighteenth-Century England," *Journal of Social History* 8 (Summer 1975): 86.
2. W. L. Langer, "Infanticide: A Historical Survey," *History of Childhood Quarterly* 1 (Winter 1974): 357.

3. Quoted in R. Cobb, *The Police and the People: French Popular Protest, 1789–1820,* Clarendon Press, Oxford, Eng., 1970, p. 238.

4. Quoted by E. A. Wrigley, *Population and History,* McGraw-Hill, New York, 1969, p. 127.

5. Quoted in D. S. Landes, ed., *The Rise of Capitalism,* Macmillan, New York, 1966, pp. 56–57.

6. See L. A. Tilly, J. W. Scott, and M. Cohen, "Women's Work and European Fertility Patterns," *Journal of Interdisciplinary History* 6 (Winter 1976): 447–476.

7. J. Michelet, *The People,* trans. with an introduction by J. P. McKay, University of Illinois Press, Urbana, 1973 (original publication, 1846), pp. 38–39.

8. J. Brownlow, *The History and Design of the Foundling Hospital,* London, 1868, p. 7.

9. Quoted by B. W. Lorence, "Parents and Children in Eighteenth-Century Europe," *History of Childhood Quarterly* 2 (Summer 1974): 1–2.

10. Ibid., pp. 13, 16.

11. J. C. Drummond and A. Wilbraham, *The Englishman's Food: A History of Five Centuries of English Diet,* 2nd ed., Jonathan Cape, London, 1958, p. 75.

12. Quoted by L. S. King, *The Medical World of the Eighteenth Century,* University of Chicago Press, Chicago, 1958, p. 320.

13. Quoted by R. Sand, *The Advance to Social Medicine,* Staples Press, London, 1952, pp. 86–87.

14. Quoted by I. Woloch, *Eighteenth-Century Europe: Tradition and Progress, 1715–1789,* W. W. Norton, New York, 1982, p. 292.

15. Quoted by T. Tackett, *Priest and Parish in Eighteenth-Century France,* Princeton University Press, Princeton, N. J., 1977, p. 214.

16. Quoted by K. Pinson, *Pietism as a Factor in the Rise of German Nationalism,* Columbia University Press, New York, 1934, p. 13.

17. Ibid., pp. 43–44.

18. Quoted by S. Andrews, *Methodism and Society,* Longmans, Green, London, 1970, p. 327.

SUGGESTED READING

Though often ignored in many general histories of the Western world, social topics of the kind considered in this chapter flourish in specialized journals today. The articles cited in the Notes are typical of the exciting work being done, and the reader is strongly advised to take time to look through recent volumes of some leading journals: *Journal of Social History, Past and Present, History of Childhood Quarterly,* and *Journal of Interdisciplinary History.* In addition, the number of book-length studies has begun to expand rapidly.

Among general introductions to the history of the family, women, and children, E. A. Wrigley, *Population and History* (1969), is excellent. P. Laslett, *The World We Have Lost* (1965), is an exciting, pioneering investigation of England before the Industrial Revolution, though some of his conclusions have been weakened by further research. L. Stone, *The Family, Sex and Marriage in England, 1500–1800* (1977), is a brilliant general interpretation, and L. Tilly and J. Scott, *Women, Work and Family* (1978), is excellent. P. Ariès, *Centuries of Childhood: A Social History of Family Life* (1962), is another stimulating study. E. Shorter, *The Making of the Modern Family* (1975), is an all-too-lively and rather controversial interpretation. All four works are highly recommended. T. Rabb and R. I. Rothberg, eds., *The Family in History* (1973), is a good collection of articles dealing with both Europe and the United States. A. MacFarlane, *The Family Life of Ralph Josselin* (1970), is a brilliant re-creation of the intimate family circle of a seventeenth-century English clergyman who kept a detailed diary; MacFarlane's *Origins of English Individualism: The Family, Property and Social Transition* (1978) is a major work. I. Pinchbeck and M. Hewitt, *Children in English Society* (1973), is a good introduction. E. Flexner has written a fine biography on the early feminist Mary Wollstonecraft (1972). Various aspects of sexual relationships are treated imaginatively by M. Foucault, *The History of Sexuality* (1981), and R. Wheaton and T. Hareven, eds., *Family and Sexuality in French History* (1980).

J. Burnett, *A History of the Cost of Living* (1969), has a great deal of interesting information about what people spent their money on in the past and complements the fascinating work of J. C. Drummond and A. Wilbraham, *The Englishman's Food: A History of Five Centuries of English Diet* (1958). J. Knyveton, *Diary of a Surgeon in the Year 1751–1752* (1937), gives a contemporary's unforgettable picture of both eighteenth-century medicine and social customs. Good introductions to the evolution of medical practices are B. Ingles, *History of Medicine* (1965); O. Bettmann, *A Pictorial History of Medicine* (1956); and H. Haggard's old but interesting *Devils, Drugs, and Doctors* (1929). W. Boyd, *History of Western Education* (1966), is a standard survey, which may be usefully supplemented by an important article by L. Stone, "Literacy and Education in England, 1640–1900," *Past and Present* 42 (February 1969): 69–139. M. D. George, *London Life in the Eighteenth Century* (1965), is a delightfully written book, while L. Chevalier, *Labouring Classes and Dangerous Classes* (1973), is a keen analysis of the poor people of Paris in a slightly later period. G. Rudé, *The Crowd in History, 1730–1848* (1964), is an innovative effort to see politics and popular protest from below. An important series edited by R. Forster and O. Ranuum considers neglected social questions such as diet, abandoned children, and deviants, as does P. Burke's excellent study, *Popular Culture in Early Modern Europe* (1978).

Good works on religious life include J. Delumeau, *Catholicism Between Luther and Voltaire: A New View of the Counter-Reformation* (1977); T. Tackett, *Priest and Parish in Eighteenth-Century France* (1977); B. Semmel, *The Methodist Revolution* (1973); and J. Bettey, *Church and Community: The Parish Church in English Life* (1979).

21

THE REVOLUTION IN POLITICS, 1775–1815

*T*HE LAST YEARS of the eighteenth century were a time of great upheaval. A series of revolutions and revolutionary wars challenged the old order of kings and aristocrats. The ideas of freedom and equality, ideas that have not stopped shaping the world since that era, flourished and spread. The revolution began in North America in 1775. Then in 1789 France, the most influential country in Europe, became the leading revolutionary nation. It established first a constitutional monarchy, then a radical republic, and finally a new empire under Napoleon. The armies of France also joined forces with patriots and radicals abroad in an effort to establish new governments based on new principles throughout much of Europe. The world of modern domestic and international politics was born.

What caused this era of revolution? What were the ideas and objectives of the men and women who rose up violently to undo the established system? What were the gains and losses for privileged groups and for ordinary people in a generation of war and upheaval? These are the questions on which this chapter's examination of the French and American revolutions will be based.

LIBERTY AND EQUALITY

Two ideas fueled the revolutionary period in both America and Europe: liberty and equality. What did eighteenth-century politicians and other people mean by liberty and equality, and why were those ideas so radical and revolutionary in their day?

The call for liberty was first of all a call for individual human rights. Even the most enlightened monarchs customarily claimed that it was their duty to regulate what people wrote and believed. Liberals of the revolutionary era protested such controls from on high. They demanded freedom to worship according to the dictates of their consciences instead of according to the politics of their prince. They demanded the end of censorship and the right to express their beliefs freely in print and at public meetings. They demanded freedom from arbitrary laws and from judges who simply obeyed orders from the government.

These demands for basic personal freedoms, which were incorporated into the American Bill of Rights and other liberal constitutions, were very far-reaching. Indeed, eighteenth-century revolutionaries demanded more freedom than most governments today believe it is desirable to grant. The Declaration of the Rights of Man, issued at the beginning of the French Revolution, proclaimed, "Liberty consists in being able to do anything that does not harm another person." A citizen's rights had, therefore, "no limits except those which assure to the other members of society the enjoyment of these same rights." Liberals called for the freedom of the individual to develop and to create to the fullest possible extent. In the context of the aristocratic and monarchial forms of government that then dominated Europe, this was a truly radical idea.

The call for liberty was also a call for a new kind of government. The revolutionary liberals believed that the people were sovereign—that is, that the people alone had the authority to make laws limiting the individual's freedom of action. In practice, this system of government meant choosing legislators who represented the people and who were accountable to them. Moreover, liberals of the revolutionary era believed that every people—every ethnic group—had this right of self-determination and thus the right to form a free nation.

By equality, eighteenth-century liberals meant that all citizens were to have identical rights and civil liberties. Above all, the nobility had no right to special privileges based on the accident of birth.

Liberals did not define equality as meaning that everyone should be equal economically. Quite the contrary. As Thomas Jefferson wrote in an early draft of the American Declaration of Independence, before changing "property" to the more noble-sounding "happiness," everyone was equal in "the pursuit of property." Jefferson and other liberals certainly did not expect equal success in that pursuit. Great differences in wealth and income between rich and poor were perfectly acceptable to liberals. The essential point was that everyone should legally have an equal chance. French liberals and revolutionaries said they wanted "careers opened to talent." They wanted employment in government, in business, and in the professions to be based on ability, not on family background or legal status.

Equality of opportunity was a very revolutionary idea in eighteenth-century Europe. Legal inequality between classes and groups was the rule, not the exception. Society was still legally divided into groups with special privileges, such as the nobility and the clergy, and groups with special burdens, like the peasantry. In many countries, various middle-class groups—professionals, businessmen, townspeople, and craftsmen—enjoyed privileges that allowed them to monopolize all sorts of economic activity. It was this kind of economic inequality, an inequality based on artificial legal distinctions, against which liberals protested.

THE ROOTS OF LIBERALISM

The ideas of liberty and equality—the central ideas of classical liberalism—have deep roots in Western history. The ancient Greeks and the Judeo-Christian tradition had affirmed for hundreds of years the sanctity and value of the individual human being. The Judeo-Christian tradition, reinforced by the Reformation, had long stressed personal responsibility on the part of both common folk and exalted rulers, thereby promoting the self-discipline without which liberty becomes anarchy. The hounded and persecuted Protestant radicals of the later sixteenth century had died for the revolutionary idea that individuals were entitled to their own religious beliefs.

Although the liberal creed had roots deep in the Western tradition, classical liberalism first crystallized at the end of the seventeenth century and during the Enlightenment of the eighteenth century.

Liberal ideas reflected the Enlightenment's stress on human dignity and human happiness on earth. Liberals shared the Enlightenment's general faith in science, rationality, and progress: the adoption of liberal principles meant better government and a better society for all. Almost all the writers of the Enlightenment were passionately committed to greater personal liberty. They preached religious toleration, freedom of press and speech, and fair and equal treatment before the law.

Certain English and French thinkers were mainly responsible for joining the Enlightenment's concern for personal freedom and legal equality to a theoretical justification of liberal self-government. The two most important were John Locke and the baron de Montesquieu, considered earlier. Locke (page 530) maintained that England's long political tradition rested on "the rights of Englishmen" and on representative government through Parliament. Locke ad-

The Marquis de Lafayette was the most famous great noble to embrace the liberal revolution. Shown here directing a battle in the American Revolution, he returned to champion liberty and equality in France. For admirers he was the "hero of two worlds." *(Anne S. K. Brown Military)*

mired especially the great Whig noblemen who had made the bloodless revolution of 1688, and he argued that a government that oversteps its proper functions —protecting the natural rights of life, liberty, and private property—becomes a tyranny. Montesquieu (page 585) was also inspired by English constitutional history. He, too, believed that powerful "intermediary groups"—such as the judicial nobility of which he was a proud member—offered the best defense of liberty against despotism.

THE ATTRACTION OF LIBERALISM

The belief that representative institutions could defend their liberty and interests appealed powerfully to ambitious and educated bourgeois. Yet it is important to realize that liberal ideas about individual rights and political freedom also appealed to much of the aristocracy, at least in western Europe and as formulated by Montesquieu. Representative government did not mean democracy, which liberal thinkers tended to equate with mob rule. Rather, they envisioned voting for representatives as being restricted to those who owned property, those with "a stake in society." England had shown the way. After 1688 it had combined a parliamentary system and considerable individual liberty with a restricted franchise and unquestionable aristocratic pre-eminence. In the course of the eighteenth century, many leading French nobles, led by a judicial nobility inspired by Montesquieu, as shown in Chapter 18, were increasingly eager to follow the English example.

Eighteenth-century liberalism, then, appealed not only to the middle class, but also to some aristocrats. It found broad support among the educated elite and the substantial classes in western Europe. What it lacked from the beginning was strong mass support. For comfortable liberals, the really important questions were theoretical and political. They had no need to worry about their stomachs and the price of bread. For the much more numerous laboring poor, the great questions were immediate and economic. Getting enough to eat was the crucial challenge. These differences in outlook and well-being were to lead to many misunderstandings and disappointments for both groups in the revolutionary era.

THE AMERICAN REVOLUTION, 1775–1789

The era of liberal revolution began in the New World. The thirteen mainland colonies of British North America revolted against their mother country and then succeeded in establishing a new unified government.

Americans have long debated the meaning of their revolution. Some have even questioned whether or not it was a real revolution, as opposed to a war for independence. According to some scholars, the Revolution was conservative and defensive in that its demands were for the traditional liberties of Englishmen; Americans were united against the British, but otherwise they were a satisfied people, not torn by internal conflict. Other scholars have argued that, on the contrary, the American Revolution was quite radical. It split families between patriots and Loyalists and divided the country. It achieved goals that were fully as advanced as those obtained by the French in their great revolution a few years later.

How does one reconcile these positions? Both contain large elements of truth. The American revolutionaries did believe they were demanding only the traditional rights of English men and women. But those traditional rights were liberal rights, and in the American context they had very strong democratic and popular overtones. Thus the American Revolution was fought in the name of established ideals that were still quite radical in the context of the times. And in founding a government firmly based on liberal principles, the Americans set an example that had a forceful impact on Europe and speeded up political development there.

THE ORIGINS OF THE REVOLUTION

The American Revolution had its immediate origins in a squabble over increased taxes. The British government had fought and decisively won the Seven Years' War (page 625) on the strength of its professional army and navy. The American colonists had furnished little real aid. The high cost of the war to the British, however, had led to a doubling of the British national debt. Anticipating further expense defending its recently conquered western lands from Indian uprisings like that of Pontiac, the British government in London set about reorganizing the empire with a series of bold, largely unprecedented measures. Breaking with tradition, the British decided to maintain a large army in North America after peace was restored in 1763. Moreover, they sought to exercise strict control over their newly conquered western lands and to tax the colonies directly. In 1765 the government pushed through Parliament the Stamp Act, which levied taxes on a long list of commercial and legal documents, diplomas, pamphlets, newspapers, almanacs, dice, and playing cards. A stamp glued to each article indicated the tax had been paid.

The effort to increase taxes as part of tightening up the empire seemed perfectly reasonable to the British. Heavier stamp taxes had been collected in Great Britain for two generations, and Americans were being asked only to pay a share of their own defense.

The Boston Tea Party This contemporary illustration shows men disguised as Indians dumping East India Company tea into Boston's harbor. The enthusiastic crowd cheering from the wharf indicates widespread popular support. *(Library of Congress)*

Moreover, Americans had been paying only very low local taxes. The Stamp Act would have doubled taxes to about two shillings per person. No other people in the world (except the Poles) paid so little. The British, meanwhile, paid the world's highest taxes in about 1765—twenty-six shillings per person. It is not surprising that taxes per person in the newly independent American nation were much higher in 1785 than in 1765, when the British no longer subsidized American defense. The colonists protested the Stamp Act vigorously and violently, however, and after rioting and boycotts against British goods, Parliament reluctantly repealed the new tax.

As the fury of the Stamp Act controversy revealed, much more was involved than taxes. The key question was political. To what extent could the home government refashion the empire and reassert its power while limiting the authority of colonial legislatures and their elected representatives? Accordingly, who should represent the colonies, and who had the right to make laws for Americans? While a troubled majority of Americans searched hard for a compromise, some radicals began to proclaim that "taxation without representation is tyranny." The British government replied that Americans were represented in Parliament, albeit indirectly (like most Englishmen themselves), and that the absolute supremacy of Parliament throughout the empire could not be questioned. Many Americans felt otherwise. As John Adams put it, "A Parliament of Great Britain can have no more rights to tax the colonies than a Parliament of Paris." Thus imperial reorganization and Parliamentary supremacy came to appear as grave threats to Americans' existing liberties and time-honored institutions.

Americans had long exercised a great deal of independence and gone their own way. In British North America, unlike England and Europe, no powerful established church existed, and personal freedom in questions of religion was taken for granted. The colonial assemblies made the important laws, which were seldom overturned by the home government. The right to vote was much more widespread than in England. In many parts of colonial Massachusetts, for example, as many as 95 percent of the adult males could vote.

Moreover, greater political equality was matched by greater social and economic equality. Neither a hereditary nobility nor a hereditary serf population existed, although the slavery of the Americas consigned blacks to a legally oppressed caste. Independent farmers were the largest group in the country and set much of its tone. In short, the colonial experience had slowly formed a people who felt themselves separate and distinct from the home country. The controversies over taxation intensified those feelings of distinctiveness and separation and brought them to the fore.

In 1773 the dispute over taxes and representation flared up again. The British government had permitted the financially hard-pressed East India Company to ship its tea from China directly to its agents in the colonies, rather than through London middlemen, who then sold to independent merchants in the colonies. Thus the company secured a vital monopoly on the tea trade, and colonial merchants were suddenly excluded from a highly profitable business. The colonists were quick to protest.

In Boston, men disguised as Indians had a rowdy "tea party" and threw the company's tea into the harbor. This led to extreme measures. The so-called Coercive Acts closed the port of Boston, curtailed local elections and town meetings, and greatly expanded the royal governor's power. County conventions in Massachusetts protested vehemently and urged that the acts be "rejected as the attempts of a wicked administration to enslave America." Other colonial assemblies joined in the denunciations. In September 1774, the First Continental Congress met in Philadelphia, where the more radical members argued successfully against concessions to the crown. Compromise was also rejected by the British parliament, and in April 1775 fighting began at Lexington and Concord.

INDEPENDENCE

The fighting spread, and the colonists moved slowly but inevitably toward open rebellion and a declaration of independence. The uncompromising attitude of the British government and its use of German mercenaries went a long way toward dissolving long-standing loyalties to the home country and rivalries among the separate colonies. *Common Sense* (1775), a brilliant attack by the recently arrived English radical Thomas Paine (1737–1809), also mobilized public opinion in favor of independence. A runaway best seller with sales of 120,000 copies in a few months,

Paine's tract ridiculed the idea of a small island ruling a great continent. In his call for freedom and republican government, Paine expressed Americans' growing sense of separateness and moral superiority.

On July 4, 1776, the Second Continental Congress adopted the Declaration of Independence. Written by Thomas Jefferson, the Declaration of Independence boldly listed the tyrannical acts committed by George III (1760–1820) and confidently proclaimed the natural rights of man and the sovereignty of the American states. Sometimes called the world's greatest political editorial, the Declaration of Independence in effect universalized the traditional rights of Englishmen and made them the rights of all mankind. It stated that "all men are created equal . . . they are endowed by their Creator with certain unalienable rights . . . among these are life, liberty, and the pursuit of happiness." No other American political document has ever caused such excitement, both at home and abroad.

Many American families remained loyal to Britain; many others divided bitterly. After the Declaration of Independence, the conflict often took the form of a civil war pitting patriot against Loyalist. The Loyalists tended to be wealthy and politically moderate. Many patriots, too, were wealthy—individuals such as John Hancock and George Washington—but willingly allied themselves with farmers and artisans in a broad coalition. This coalition harassed the Loyalists and confiscated their property to help pay for the American war effort. The broad social base of the revolutionaries tended to make the liberal revolution democratic. State governments extended the right to vote to many more people in the course of the war and re-established themselves as republics.

On the international scene, the French sympathized with the rebels from the beginning. They wanted revenge for the humiliating defeats of the Seven Years' War. Officially neutral until 1776, they supplied the great bulk of guns and gunpowder used by the American revolutionaries, very much as neutral great powers supply weapons for "wars of national liberation" today. By 1777 French volunteers were arriving in Virginia, and a dashing young nobleman, the marquis de Lafayette (1757–1834), quickly became one of Washington's most trusted generals. In 1778 the French government offered the Americans a formal alliance, and in 1779 and 1780 the Spanish and Dutch declared war on Britain. Catherine the

The Signing of the Declaration, July 4, 1776 John Trumbull's famous painting shows the dignity and determination of America's revolutionary leaders. An extraordinarily talented group, they succeeded in rallying popular support without losing power to more radical forces in the process. *(Yale University Art Gallery)*

Great of Russia helped organize a League of Armed Neutrality in order to protect neutral shipping rights, which Britain refused to recognize.

Thus, by 1780 Great Britain was engaged in an imperial war against most of Europe as well as the thirteen colonies. In these circumstances, and in the face of severe reverses in India, the West Indies, and at Yorktown in Virginia, a new British government decided to cut its losses. American negotiators in Paris were receptive. They feared that France wanted a treaty that would bottle up the new United States east of the Alleghenies and give British holdings west of the Alleghenies to France's ally, Spain. Thus the American negotiators ditched the French and accepted the extraordinarily favorable terms Britain offered.

By the Treaty of Paris of 1783, Britain recognized the independence of the thirteen colonies and ceded all its territory between the Appalachians and the Mississippi River to the Americans. Out of the bitter rivalries of the Old World, the Americans snatched dominion over half a continent.

Framing the Constitution

The liberal program of the American Revolution was consolidated by the federal Constitution, the Bill of Rights, and the creation of a national republic. Assembling in Philadelphia in the summer of 1787, the delegates to the Constitutional Convention were determined to end the period of economic depression, social uncertainty, and very weak central government that had followed independence. The delegates decided, therefore, to grant the federal, or central, government important powers: regulation of domestic and foreign trade, the right to levy taxes, and the means to enforce its laws.

Strong rule was placed squarely in the context of representative self-government. Senators and congressmen would be the lawmaking delegates of the voters, and the president of the republic would be an elected official. The central government was to operate in Montesquieu's framework of checks and balances. The executive, legislative, and judicial branches would systematically balance each other.

Benjamin Franklin in France Franklin served with distinction as American ambassador to France during the War for Independence. Shown signing the crucial Treaties of Commerce and Alliance in 1778, Franklin was lionized by the French as scientist and sage. *(Brown Brothers)*

The power of the federal government would in turn be checked by the powers of the individual states.

When the results of the secret deliberation of the Constitutional Convention were presented to the states for ratification, a great public debate began. The opponents of the proposed constitution—the Anti-Federalists—charged that the framers of the new document had taken too much power from the individual states and made the federal government too strong. Moreover, many Anti-Federalists feared for the personal liberties and individual freedoms for which they had just fought. In order to overcome these objections, the Federalists solemnly promised to spell out these basic freedoms as soon as the new constitution was adopted. The result was the first ten amendments to the Constitution, which the first Congress passed shortly after it met in New York in March 1789. These amendments formed an effective bill of rights to safeguard the individual. Most of them—trial by jury, due process of law, right to assemble, freedom from unreasonable search—had their origins in English law and the English Bill of Rights of 1689. Others—the freedoms of speech, the press, and religion—reflected natural-law theory and the American experience.

The American Constitution and the Bill of Rights exemplified the great strengths and the limits of what came to be called "classical liberalism." Liberty meant individual freedoms and political safeguards. Liberty also meant representative government but did not necessarily mean democracy with its principle of one man, one vote.

Equality—slaves excepted—meant equality before the law, not equality of political participation or economic well-being. Indeed, economic inequality was resolutely defended by the elite who framed the Constitution. The right to own property was guaranteed by the Fifth Amendment, and if the government took private property, the owner was to receive "just compensation." The radicalism of liberal revolution in America was primarily legal and political, not economic or social.

THE REVOLUTION'S IMPACT ON EUROPE

Hundreds of books, pamphlets, and articles analyzed and romanticized the American upheaval. Thoughtful Europeans noted, first of all, its enormous long-term implications for international politics. A secret report by the Venetian ambassador to Paris in 1783 stated what many felt: "If only the union of the Provinces is preserved, it is reasonable to expect that, with the favorable effects of time, and of European arts and sciences, it will become the most formidable power in the world."[1] More generally, American independence fired the imaginations of those few aristocrats who were uneasy with their privileges and of those commoners who yearned for greater equality. Many Europeans believed that the world was advancing now and that America was leading the way. As one French writer put it in 1789: "This vast continent which the seas surround will soon change Europe and the universe."

Europeans who dreamed of a new era were fascinated by the political lessons of the American Revolution. The Americans had begun with a revolutionary defense against tyrannical oppression, and they had been victorious. They had then shown how rational beings could assemble together to exercise sovereignty and write a permanent constitution—a new social contract. All this gave greater reality to the concepts of individual liberty and representative government. It reinforced one of the primary ideas of the Enlightenment, the idea that a better world was possible.

THE FRENCH REVOLUTION, 1789–1791

No country felt the consequences of the American Revolution more directly than France. Hundreds of French officers served in America and were inspired by the experience. The most famous of these, the young and impressionable marquis de Lafayette left home as a great aristocrat determined only to fight France's traditional foe, England. He returned with a love of liberty and firm republican convictions. French intellectuals and publicists engaged in passionate analysis of the federal Constitution, as well as the constitutions of the various states of the new United States. The American Revolution undeniably hastened upheaval in France.

Yet the French Revolution did not mirror the American example. It was more violent and more complex, more influential and more controversial, more loved and more hated. For Europeans and most of the rest of the world, it was *the* great revolution of the eighteenth century, the revolution that opened the modern era in politics.

THE BREAKDOWN OF THE OLD ORDER

Like the American Revolution, the French Revolution had its immediate origins in the financial difficulties of the government. As we noted in Chapter 18, the efforts of Louis XV's ministers to raise taxes had been thwarted by the Parlement of Paris, strengthened in its opposition by widespread popular support. When renewed efforts to reform the tax system met a similar fate in 1776, the government was

Louis XVI Idealized in this stunning portrait by Duplessis as a majestic, self-confident ruler and worthy heir of Louis XIV, Louis XVI was actually shy, indecisive, and somewhat stupid. *(Château de Versailles/Giraudon/Art Resource)*

forced to finance all of its enormous expenditures during the American war with borrowed money. The national debt and the annual budget deficit soared. By the 1780s fully half of France's annual budget went for ever-increasing interest payments on the ever-increasing debt. Another quarter went to maintain the military, while 6 percent was absorbed by the costly and extravagant king and his court at Versailles. Less than one-fifth of the entire national budget was available for the productive functions of the state, such as transportation and general administration. It was an impossible financial situation.

One way out would have been for the government to declare partial bankruptcy, forcing its creditors to accept greatly reduced payments on the debt. The powerful Spanish monarchy had regularly repudiated large portions of its debt in earlier times, and France had done likewise, after an attempt to establish a French national bank ended in financial disaster in 1720. Yet by the 1780s the French debt was held by an army of aristocratic and bourgeois creditors, and the French monarchy, though absolute in theory, had become far too weak for such a drastic and unpopular action.

Nor could the king and his ministers, unlike modern governments, print money and create inflation to cover their deficits. Unlike England and Holland, which had far larger national debts relative to their populations, France had no central bank, no paper currency, and no means of creating credit. French money was good gold coin. Therefore, when a depressed economy and a lack of public confidence made it increasingly difficult for the government to obtain new gold loans in 1786, it had no alternative but to try to increase taxes. And since France's tax system was unfair and out of date, increased revenues were possible only through fundamental reforms. Such reforms would affect all groups in France's complex and fragmented society and opened a Pandora's box of social and political demands.

LEGAL ORDERS AND SOCIAL REALITIES

As in the Middle Ages, France's 25 million inhabitants were still legally divided into three orders or "estates"—the clergy, the nobility, and everyone else. As the nation's first estate, the clergy numbered about 100,000 and had important privileges. It owned about 10 percent of the land and paid only a "voluntary gift" to the government every five years. Moreoever, the church levied a tax (the tithe) on landowners, which averaged somewhat less than 10 percent. Much of the church's income was actually drained away from local parishes by political appointees and worldly aristocrats at the top of the church hierarchy, to the intense dissatisfaction of the poor parish priests.

The second legally defined estate consisted of some 400,000 noblemen and noblewomen—the descendants of "those who fought" in the Middle Ages. The nobles owned outright about 25 percent of the land in France, and they, too, were taxed very lightly. Moreoever, nobles continued to enjoy certain manorial rights, or privileges of lordship, that dated back to medieval times and allowed them to tax the peasantry for their own profit. This was done by means of exclusive rights to hunt and fish, village monopolies on baking bread and pressing grapes for wine, fees for justice, and a host of other "useful privileges." In addition, nobles had "honorific privileges," such as the right to precedence on public occasions and the right to wear a sword. These rights conspicuously proclaimed the nobility's legal superiority and exalted social position.

Everyone else was a commoner, a member of the third estate. A few commoners were rich merchants or highly successful doctors and lawyers. Many more were urban artisans and unskilled day laborers. The vast majority of the third estate consisted of the peasants and agricultural workers in the countryside. Thus the third estate was a conglomeration of vastly different social groups, united only by their shared legal status as distinct from the privileged nobility and clergy.

In discussing the long-term origins of the French Revolution, historians have long focused on growing tensions between the nobility and the comfortable members of the third estate, usually known as the bourgeoisie, or middle class. A dominant historical interpretation has held sway for at least two generations. According to this interpretation, the bourgeoisie was basically united by economic position and class interest. Aided by the general economic expansion discussed in Chapter 19, the middle class grew rapidly in the eighteenth century, tripling to about 2.3 million persons, or about 8 percent of France's population. Increasing in size, wealth, culture, and self-confidence, this rising bourgeoisie became progressively exasperated by archaic "feudal" laws restraining the economy and by the growing pretensions of a reactionary nobility, which was closing ranks against middle-class needs and aspirations. As a result, the French bourgeoisie eventually rose up to lead the entire third estate in a great social revolution, a revolution that destroyed feudal privileges and established a capitalist order based on individualism and a market economy.

In recent years, a flood of new research has challenged these accepted views, and once again the French Revolution is a subject of heated scholarly debate. Above all, revisionist historians have questioned the existence of a growing social conflict between a progressive capitalistic bourgeoisie and a reactionary feudal nobility in eighteenth-century France. Instead, these historians see both bourgeoisie and nobility as being riddled with internal rivalries and highly fragmented. The great nobility, for example, was profoundly separated from the lesser nobility by differences in wealth, education, and worldview. Differences within the bourgeoisie—between wealthy financiers and local lawyers, for example— were no less profound. Rather than standing as unified blocs against each other, nobility and bourgeoisie formed two parallel social ladders, increasingly linked together at the top by wealth, marriage, and Enlightenment culture.

Revolutionist historians stress in particular three developments in their reinterpretation. First, the nobility remained a fluid and relatively open order. Throughout the eighteenth century, substantial numbers of successful commoners continued to seek and obtain noble status through government service and purchase of expensive positions conferring nobility. Thus the nobility of the robe continued to attract the wealthiest members of the middle class and to permit social mobility. Second, key sections of the nobility were no less liberal than the middle class, which until revolution actually began, generally supported the judicial opposition led by the Parlement of Paris. Finally, the nobility and the bourgeoisie were not really at odds in the economic sphere. Both looked to investment in land and government service as their preferred activities, and the ideal of the merchant capitalist was to gain enough wealth to retire from trade, purchase estates, and live nobly as a large landowner. At the same time, wealthy nobles often acted as aggressive capitalists, investing especially in mining, metallurgy, and foreign trade.

The revisionists have clearly shaken the belief that the bourgeoisie and the nobility were inevitably locked in growing conflict before the revolution. But in stressing the similarities between the two groups, especially at the top, they have also reinforced the view, long maintained by historians, that the Old Regime had ceased to correspond with social reality by the 1780s. Legally, society was still based on rigid orders inherited from the Middle Ages. In reality, France had already moved far toward being a society based on wealth and economic achievement, where an emerging elite that included both aristocratic and bourgeois notables was frustrated by a bureaucratic monarchy that had long claimed the right to absolute power.

The Formation of the National Assembly

The Revolution was under way by 1787, though no one could have realized what was to follow. Spurred by a depressed economy and falling tax receipts, Louis XVI's minister of finance revived old proposals to impose a general tax on all landed property, as well as provincial assemblies to help administer the tax, and he convinced the king to call an Assembly of Notables to gain support for the idea. The assembled notables, who were mainly important noblemen and high-ranking clergy, were not in favor of it. In return for their support, they demanded that control over all government spending be given to the provincial assemblies, which they expected to control. When the government refused, the nobles responded that such sweeping tax changes required the approval of the Estates General, the representative body of all three estates, which had not met since 1614.

Facing imminent bankruptcy, the king tried to reassert his authority. He dismissed the nobles and established new taxes by decree. In stirring language, the Parlement of Paris promptly declared the royal initiative null and void. The Parlement went so far as to specify some of the "fundamental laws" against which no king could transgress, such as national consent to taxation and freedom from arbitrary arrest and imprisonment. When the king tried to exile the judges, a tremendous wave of protest swept the country. Frightened investors also refused to advance more loans to the state. Finally, in July 1788, a beaten Louis XVI called for a spring session of the Estates General. Absolute monarchy was collapsing.

What would replace it? Throughout the unprecedented election campaign of 1788 and 1789, that question excited France. All across the country, clergy, nobles, and commoners came together in their respective orders to draft petitions for change and to elect their respective delegates to the Estates General. The local assemblies of the clergy showed considerable dissatisfaction with the church hierarchy, and two-thirds of the delegates were chosen from the poorer parish priests, who were commoners by birth. The nobles, already badly split by wealth and education, remained politically divided. A conservative majority was drawn from the poorer and more numerous provincial nobility, but fully a third of the nobility's representatives were liberals committed to major changes.

As for the third estate, there was great popular participation in the elections. Almost all male commoners twenty-five years or older had the right to vote. However, voting required two stages, which meant that most of the representatives finally selected by the third estate were well-educated, prosperous members of the middle class. Most of them were not businessmen, but lawyers and government officials. Social status and prestige were matters of particular concern to this economic elite. There were no delegates from the great mass of laboring poor—the peasants and the artisans.

The petitions for change from the three estates showed a surprising degree of agreement on most issues, as recent research has clearly revealed. There was general agreement that royal absolutism should give way to constitutional monarchy, in which laws and taxes would require the consent of an Estates General meeting regularly. All agreed that, in the future, individual liberties must be guaranteed by law and that the position of the parish clergy had to be improved. It was generally acknowledged that economic development required reforms, such as the abolition of internal trade barriers. The striking similarities in the grievance petitions of the clergy, nobility, and third estate reflected the broad commitment of France's elite to liberalism.

Yet an increasingly bitter quarrel undermined this consensus during the intense election campaign: *how* would the Estates General vote, and precisely *who* would lead in the political reorganization that was generally desired? The Estates General of 1614 had sat as three separate houses. Any action had required the agreement of at least two branches, a requirement that had guaranteed control by the privileged orders —the nobility and the clergy. Immediately after its victory over the king, the aristocratic Parlement of Paris ruled that the Estates General should once again sit separately, mainly out of respect for tradition but partly to enhance the nobility's political position. The ruling was quickly denounced by certain middle-class intellectuals and some liberal nobles. They demanded instead a single assembly dominated by representatives of the third estate, to ensure fundamental reforms. Reflecting a growing hostility toward aristocratic aspirations, the abbé Sieyès argued in 1789 in his famous pamphlet, *What Is the Third Estate?,* that the nobility was a tiny, overprivileged minority and that the neglected third estate constituted the true strength of the French nation. When the government agreed that the third estate should have as many delegates as the clergy and the nobility combined, but then rendered its act meaningless by upholding voting by separate order, middle-class leaders saw fresh evidence of an aristocratic conspiracy.

In May 1789, the twelve hundred delegates of the three estates paraded in medieval pageantry through the streets of Versailles to an opening session resplendent with feudal magnificence. The estates were almost immediately deadlocked. Delegates of the third estate refused to transact any business until the king ordered the clergy and nobility to sit with them in a single body. Finally, after a six-week war of nerves, a few parish priests began to go over to the third estate, which on June 17 voted to call itself the National Assembly. On June 20, excluded from their hall because of "repairs," the delegates of the third estate moved to a large indoor tennis court. There they swore the famous Oath of the Tennis Court, pledging never to disband until they had written a new constitution.

The king's actions were then somewhat contradictory. On June 23, he made a conciliatory speech to a joint session, urging reforms, and then ordered the three estates to meet together. At the same time, he apparently followed the advice of relatives and court nobles, who urged the king to dissolve the Estates General by force. The king called an army of eighteen thousand troops toward Versailles, and on July 11 he dismissed his finance minister and his other more liberal ministers. Faced with growing opposition since 1787, Louis XVI had resigned himself to bankruptcy. Now he sought to reassert his divine and historic right to rule. The middle-class delegates had done their best, but they were resigned to being disbanded at bayonet point. One third-estate delegate reassured a worried colleague: "You won't hang—you'll only have to go back home."[2]

THE REVOLT OF THE POOR AND THE OPPRESSED

While the third estate pressed for symbolic equality with the nobility and clergy in a single legislative body at Versailles, economic hardship gripped the masses of France in a tightening vise. Grain was the basis of the diet of ordinary people, and in 1788 the harvest had been extremely poor. The price of bread, which had been rising gradually since 1785, began to soar. By July 1789, the price of bread in the provinces climbed as high as eight sous per pound. In Paris, where bread was subsidized by the government in an attempt to prevent popular unrest, the price rose to four sous. The poor could scarcely afford to pay two sous per pound, for even at that price a laborer with a wife and three children had to spend half of his wages to buy the family's bread.

Harvest failure and high bread prices unleashed a classic economic depression of the preindustrial age.

Storming the Bastille This contemporary drawing conveys the fury and determination of the revolutionary crowd on July 14, 1789. This successful popular action had enormous symbolic significance, and July 14 has long been France's most important national holiday. *(Photo: Flammarion)*

With food so expensive and with so much uncertainty, the demand for manufactured goods collapsed. Thousands of artisans and small traders were thrown out of work. By the end of 1789, almost half of the French people would be in need of relief. One person in eight was a pauper, living in extreme want. In Paris the situation was desperate in July 1789: perhaps 150,000 of the city's 600,000 people were without work.

Against this background of dire poverty and excited by the political crisis, the people of Paris entered decisively onto the revolutionary stage. They believed in a general, though ill-defined, way that the economic distress had human causes. They believed that they should have steady work and enough bread to survive. Specifically, they feared that the dismissal

of the king's moderate finance minister would throw them at the mercy of aristocratic landowners and grain speculators. Stories like that quoting the wealthy financier Joseph François Foulon as saying that the poor "should eat grass, like my horses," and rumors that the king's troops would sack the city began to fill the air. Angry crowds formed and passionate voices urged action. On July 13, the people began to seize arms for the defense of the city, and on July 14, several hundred of the most determined people marched to the Bastille to search for gunpowder.

An old medieval fortress with walls ten feet thick and eight great towers each a hundred feet high, the Bastille had long been used as a prison. It was guarded by eighty retired soldiers and thirty Swiss guards. The governor of the fortress-prison refused to hand over the powder, panicked, and ordered his men to fire, killing ninety-eight people attempting to enter. Cannon were brought to batter the main gate, and fighting continued until the governor of the prison surrendered. While he was being taken under guard to city hall, a band of men broke through and hacked him to death. His head and that of the mayor of Paris, who had been slow to give the crowd arms, were stuck on pikes and paraded through the streets. The next day, a committee of citizens appointed the marquis de Lafayette commander of the city's armed forces. Paris was lost to the king, who was forced to recall the finance minister and to disperse his troops. The uprising had saved the National Assembly.

As the delegates resumed their long-winded and inconclusive debates at Versailles, the people in the countryside sent them a radical and unmistakable message. All across France, peasants began to rise in spontaneous, violent, and effective insurrection against their lords, ransacking manor houses and burning feudal documents that recorded the peasants' obligations. Neither middle-class landowners, who often owned manors and village monopolies, nor the larger, more prosperous farmers were spared. In some areas, the nobles and bourgeoisie combined forces and organized patrols to protect their property. Yet the peasant insurrection went on. Recent enclosures were undone, old common lands were reoccupied, and the forests were seized. Taxes went unpaid. Fear of vagabonds and outlaws—the so-called Great Fear—seized the countryside and fanned the flames of rebellion. The long-suffering peasants were doing their best to free themselves from aristocratic privilege and exploitation.

Faced with chaos, yet fearful of calling on the king to restore order, some liberal nobles and middle-class delegates at Versailles responded to peasant demands with a surprise maneuver on the night of August 4, 1789. The duke of Aiguillon, one of France's greatest noble landowners, declared that

in several provinces the whole people forms a kind of league for the destruction of the manor houses, the ravaging of the lands, and especially for the seizure of the archives where the title deeds to feudal properties are kept. It seeks to throw off at last a yoke that has for many centuries weighted it down.[3]

He urged equality in taxation and the elimination of feudal dues. In the end, all the old exactions were abolished, generally without compensation: serfdom where it still existed, exclusive hunting rights for nobles, fees for justice, village monopolies, the right to make peasants work on the roads, and a host of other dues. Though a clarifying law passed a week later was less generous, the peasants ignored the "fine print." They never paid feudal dues again. Thus the French peasantry, which already owned about 30 percent of all the land, quickly achieved a great and unprecedented victory. Henceforth, the French peasants would seek mainly to consolidate their triumph. As the Great Fear subsided, they became a force for order and stability.

A LIMITED MONARCHY

The National Assembly moved forward. On August 27, 1789, it issued the Declaration of the Rights of Man. This great liberal document had a very American flavor, and Lafayette even discussed his draft in detail with the American ambassador in Paris, Thomas Jefferson, the author of the American Declaration of Independence. According to the French declaration, "men are born and remain free and equal in rights." Mankind's natural rights are "liberty, property, security, and resistance to oppression." Also, "every man is presumed innocent until he is proven guilty." As for law, "it is an expression of the general will; all citizens have the right to concur personally or through their representatives in its formation. . . . Free expression of thoughts and opinions is one of the most precious rights of mankind: every citizen may therefore speak, write, and publish freely." In short, this clarion call of the liberal revolutionary ideal guaranteed equality before the law, representative government for a sovereign people, and individual freedom. This revolutionary credo, only two pages long, was propagandized throughout France and Europe and around the world.

Moving beyond general principles to draft a constitution proved difficult. The questions of how much power the king should retain and whether he could permanently veto legislation led to another deadlock. Once again the decisive answer came from the poor, in this instance the poor women of Paris.

To understand what happened, one must remember that the work and wages of women and children were essential in the family economy of the laboring poor. In Paris great numbers of women worked, particularly within the putting-out system in the garment industry—making lace, fancy dresses, embroidery, ribbons, bonnets, corsets, and so on. Many of these goods were beautiful luxury items, destined for an aristocratic and international clientele.[4] Immediately after the fall of the Bastille, many of France's great court nobles began to leave Versailles for foreign lands, so that a plummeting demand for luxuries intensified the general economic crisis. International markets also declined, and the church was no longer able to give its traditional grants of food and money to the poor. Unemployment and hunger increased further, and the result was another popular explosion.

On October 5, some seven thousand desperate women marched the twelve miles from Paris to Versailles to demand action. A middle-class deputy looking out from the assembly saw "multitudes arriving from Paris including fishwives and bullies from the market, and these people wanted nothing but bread." This great crowd invaded the assembly, "armed with scythes, sticks and pikes." One coarse, tough old woman directing a large group of younger women defiantly shouted into the debate: "Who's that talking down there? Make the chatterbox shut up. That's not the point: the point is that we want bread."[5] Hers was the genuine voice of the people, essential to any understanding of the French Revolution.

The women invaded the royal apartments, slaughtered some of the royal bodyguards, and furiously searched for the despised queen, Marie Antoinette. "We are going to cut off her head, tear out her heart, fry her liver, and that won't be the end of it," they shouted, surging through the palace in a frenzy. It seems likely that only the intervention of Lafayette and the National Guard saved the royal family. But the only way to calm the disorder was for the king to go and live in Paris, as the crowd demanded.

The next day, the king, the queen, and their son left for Paris in the midst of a strange procession. The heads of two aristocrats, stuck on pikes, led the way. They were followed by the remaining members of the royal bodyguard, unarmed and surrounded and mocked by fierce men holding sabers and pikes. A mixed and victorious multitude surrounded the king's carriage, hurling crude insults at the queen. There was drinking and eating among the women. "We are bringing the baker, the baker's wife, and the baker's boy," they joyfully sang. The National Assembly followed the king to Paris. Reflecting the more radical environment, it adopted a constitution that gave the virtually imprisoned "baker" only a temporary veto in the lawmaking process. And, for a time, he and the government made sure that the masses of Paris did not lack bread.

"To Versailles" This print is one of many commemorating the women's march on Versailles. Notice on the left that the fashionable lady from the well-to-do is a most reluctant revolutionary. *(Photo: Flammarion)*

The next two years until September 1791 saw the consolidation of the liberal Revolution. Under middle-class leadership, the National Assembly abolished the French nobility as a legal order and pushed forward with the creation of a constitutional monarchy, which Louis XVI reluctantly agreed to accept in July 1790. In the final constitution, the king remained the head of state, but all lawmaking power was placed in the hands of the National Assembly, elected by the economic upper half of French males. Eighty-three departments of approximately equal size replaced the complicated old patchwork of provinces with their many historic differences. The jumble of weights and measures that varied from province to province was reformed, leading to the introduction of the simple, rational metric system in 1793. The National Assembly promoted economic freedom. Monopolies, guilds, and workers' combinations were prohibited, and barriers to trade within France were abolished in the name of economic liberty. Thus the National Assembly applied the critical spirit of the Enlightenment to reform France's laws and institutions completely.

The assembly also threatened nobles who had emigrated from France with the loss of their lands. It nationalized the property of the church and abolished the monasteries as useless relics of a distant past. The government used all former church property as collateral to guarantee a new paper currency, the *assignats,* and then sold these properties in an attempt to put the state's finances on a solid footing. Although the church's land was sold in large blocks, a procedure that favored nimble speculators and the rich, peasants eventually purchased much of it as it was subdivided. These purchases strengthened their attachment to the revolutionary state.

The most unfortunate aspect of the reorganization of France was that it brought the new government into conflict with the Catholic church. Many middle-class delegates to the National Assembly, imbued with the rationalism and skepticism of the eighteenth-century philosophes, harbored a deep distrust of popular piety and "superstitious religion." They were interested in the church only to the extent that they could seize its land and use the church to strengthen the new state. Thus they established a national church, with priests chosen by voters. In the face of resistance, the National Assembly required the clergy to take a loyalty oath to the new government. The clergy became just so many more employees of the state. The pope formally condemned this attempt to subjugate the church. Against such a backdrop, it is not surprising that only half the priests of France took the oath of allegiance. The result was a deep division within both the country and the clergy itself on the religious question, and confusion and hostility among French Catholics were pervasive. The attempted reorganization of the Catholic church was the revolutionary government's first important failure.

WORLD WAR AND REPUBLICAN FRANCE, 1791–1799

When Louis XVI accepted the final version of the completed constitution in September 1791, a young and still obscure provincial lawyer and member of the National Assembly named Maximilien Robespierre (1758–1794) evaluated the work of two years and concluded, "The Revolution is over." Robespierre was both right and wrong. He was right in the sense that the most constructive and lasting reforms were in place. Nothing substantial in the way of liberty and equality would be gained in the next generation, though much would be lost. He was wrong in the sense that a much more radical stage lay ahead. New heroes and new ideologies were to emerge in revolutionary wars and international conflict.

THE BEGINNING OF WAR

The outbreak and progress of revolution in France produced great excitement and a sharp division of opinion in Europe and the United States. Liberals and radicals such as the English scientist Joseph Priestly (1733–1804) and the American patriot Thomas Paine saw a mighty triumph of liberty over despotism. Conservative spirits like Edmund Burke (1729–1797) were deeply troubled. In 1790 Burke published *Reflections on the Revolution in France,* one of the great intellectual defenses of European conservatism. He defended inherited privileges in general and those of the English monarchy and aristocracy in particular. He predicted that unlimited reform would lead only to chaos and renewed tyranny. By 1791 fear was growing outside France that the great hopes raised by the Revolution might be tragically dashed. The moderate German writer Friedrich von Gentz was apprehensive that, if moderate and intelligent revolution failed in France, all the old evils would be ten times worse: "It would be felt that men could be happy only as slaves, and every tyrant, great or small, would use this confession to seek revenge for the fright that the awakening of the French nation had given him."[6]

The kings and nobles of Europe, who had at first welcomed the revolution in France as weakening a competing power, began to feel threatened themselves. At their courts they listened to the diatribes of great court nobles who had fled France and were urging intervention in France's affairs. When Louis XVI and Marie Antoinette were arrested and returned to Paris after trying unsuccessfully to slip out of France in June 1791, the monarchs of Austria and Prussia issued the Declaration of Pillnitz. This carefully worded statement declared their willingness to intervene in France, but only with the unanimous agreement of all the Great Powers, which they did not expect to receive. Austria and Prussia expected their threat to have a sobering effect on revolutionary France without causing war.

The crowned heads of Europe misjudged the revolutionary spirit in France. When the National Assembly had disbanded, it had sought popular support by decreeing that none of its members would be eligible for election to the new Legislative Assembly. This meant that, when the new representative body was duly elected and convened in October 1791, it had a different character. The great majority were still prosperous, well-educated, and middle class, but they were younger and less cautious than their predecessors. Loosely allied as "Jacobins," so named after their political club, the new representatives to the Assembly were passionately committed to liberal revolution.

The Jacobins increasingly lumped "useless aristocrats" and "despotic monarchs" together, and they easily whipped themselves into a patriotic fury with bombastic oratory. So the courts of Europe were attempting to incite a war of kings against France; well then, "we will incite a war of people against kings. . . . Ten million Frenchmen, kindled by the fire of liberty, armed with the sword, with reason, with eloquence would be able to change the face of the world and make the tyrants tremble on their thrones."[7] Only Robespierre and a very few others argued that people do not welcome liberation at the point of a gun. Such warnings were brushed aside. France would "rise to the full height of her mission," as one deputy urged. In April 1792, France declared war on Francis II, archduke of Austria and king of Hungary and Bohemia.

France's crusade against tyranny went poorly at first. Prussia joined Austria in the Austrian Netherlands (present-day Belgium), and French forces broke and fled at their first encounter with armies of this First Coalition. The road to Paris lay open, and it is possible that only conflict between the eastern monarchs over the division of Poland saved France from defeat.

Military reversals and Austro-Prussian threats caused a wave of patriotic fervor to sweep France. The Legislative Assembly declared the country in danger. Volunteer armies from the provinces streamed through Paris, fraternizing with the people and singing patriotic songs like the stirring *Marseillaise,* later the French national anthem.

In this supercharged wartime atmosphere, rumors of treason by the king and queen spread in Paris. Once again, as in the storming of the Bastille, the common people of Paris acted decisively. On August 10, 1792, a revolutionary crowd attacked the royal palace at the Tuileries, capturing it after heavy fighting with the Swiss Guards. The king and his family fled for their lives to the nearby Legislative Assembly, which suspended the king from all his functions, imprisoned him, and called for a new National Convention to be elected by universal male suffrage. Monarchy in France was on its deathbed, mortally wounded by war and popular revolt.

THE SECOND REVOLUTION

The fall of the monarchy marked a rapid radicalization of the Revolution, which historians often call the "second revolution." Louis's imprisonment was followed by the September Massacres, which sullied the Revolution in the eyes of most of its remaining foreign supporters. Wild stories seized the city that imprisoned counter-revolutionary aristocrats and priests were plotting with the allied invaders. As a result, angry crowds invaded the prisons of Paris and summarily slaughtered half the men and women they found. In late September 1792, the new, popularly elected National Convention proclaimed France a republic. The republic adopted a new revolutionary calendar, and citizens were expected to address each other with the friendly "thou" of the people, rather than with the formal "you" of the rich and powerful.

All of the members of the National Convention were Jacobins and republicans, and the great majority continued to come from the well-educated middle class. But the convention was increasingly divided into two well-defined, bitterly competitive groups—the Girondists and the Mountain, so called because its members, led by Danton and Robespierre, sat on the uppermost left-hand benches of the assembly hall. Many indecisive members seated in the "Plain" below floated back and forth between the rival factions.

The division was clearly apparent after the National Convention overwhelmingly convicted Louis XVI of treason. By a single vote, 361 of the 720 members of the convention then unconditionally sentenced him to death in January 1793. Louis died with tranquil dignity on the newly invented guillotine. One of his last sentences was, "I am innocent and shall die without fear. I would that my death might bring happiness to the French, and ward off the dangers which I foresee."[8]

Both the Girondists and the Mountain were determined to continue the "war against tyranny." The Prussians had been stopped at the indecisive battle of Valmy on September 20, 1792, one day before the republic was proclaimed. Republican armies then successfully invaded Savoy and captured Nice. A second army corps invaded the German Rhineland and took the city of Frankfurt. To the north, the revolutionary armies won their first major battle at Jemappes and occupied the entire Austrian Netherlands by November 1792. Everywhere they went, French armies of occupation chased the princes, "abolished feudalism," and found support among some peasants and middle-class people.

But the French armies also lived off the land, requisitioning food and supplies and plundering local treasures. The liberators looked increasingly like foreign invaders. International tensions mounted. In February 1793, the National Convention, at war with Austria and Prussia, declared war on Britain, Holland, and Spain as well. Republican France was now at war with almost all of Europe, a great war that would last almost without interruption until 1815.

As the forces of the First Coalition drove the French from the Austrian Netherlands, peasants in western France revolted against being drafted into the army. They were supported and encouraged in their resistance by devout Catholics, royalists, and foreign agents.

In Paris, the quarrelsome National Convention found itself locked in a life-and-death political struggle between the Girondists and the Mountain. The two groups were in general agreement on questions of policy. Sincere republicans, they hated privilege and wanted to temper economic liberalism with social concern. Yet personal hatreds ran deep. The Girondists feared a bloody dictatorship by the Mountain, and the Mountain was no less convinced that the more moderate Girondists would turn to conservatives and even royalists in order to retain power. With the middle-class delegates so bitterly divided, the laboring poor of Paris emerged as the decisive political factor.

The great mass of the Parisian laboring poor always constituted—along with the peasantry in the summer of 1789—the elemental force that drove the Revolution forward. It was the artisans, shopkeepers, and day laborers who had stormed the Bastille, marched on Versailles, driven the king from the Tuileries, and carried out the September Massacres. The petty traders and laboring poor were often known as the *sans-culottes,* "without breeches," because they wore trousers instead of the knee breeches of the aristocracy and the solid middle class. The immediate interests of the sans-culottes were mainly economic, and in the spring of 1793, the economic situation was as bad as the military situation. Rapid inflation, unemployment, and food shortages were again weighing heavily on the poor.

Moreover, by the spring of 1793, the sans-culottes were keenly interested in politics. Encouraged by the so-called angry men, such as the passionate young ex-priest and journalist Jacques Roux, the sans-culottes were demanding radical political action to guarantee them their daily bread. At first the Mountain joined the Girondists in violently rejecting these demands. But in the face of military defeat, peasant revolt, and hatred of the Girondists, the Mountain and especially Robespierre became more sympathetic. The Mountain joined with sans-culottes activists in the city government to engineer a popular uprising, which forced the convention to arrest thirty-one Girondist deputies for treason on June 2. All power passed to the Mountain.

Robespierre and others from the Mountain joined the recently formed Committee of Public Safety, to which the convention had given dictatorial power to

The Reign of Terror A man, woman, and child accused of political crimes are brought before a special revolutionary committee for trial. The Terror's iron dictatorship crushed individual rights as well as treason and opposition. *(Photo: Flammarion)*

deal with the national emergency. These developments in Paris triggered revolt in leading provincial cities, such as Lyons and Marseilles, where moderates denounced Paris and demanded a decentralized government. The peasant revolt spread and the republic's armies were driven back on all fronts. By July 1793, only the areas around Paris and on the eastern frontier were firmly controlled by the central government. Defeat appeared imminent.

TOTAL WAR AND THE TERROR

A year later, in July 1794, the Austrian Netherlands and the Rhineland were once again in the hands of conquering French armies, and the First Coalition was falling apart. This remarkable change of fortune was due to the revolutionary government's success in harnessing, for perhaps the first time in history, the explosive forces of a planned economy, revolutionary terror, and modern nationalism in a total war effort.

Robespierre and the Committee of Public Safety advanced with implacable resolution on several fronts in 1793 and 1794. In an effort to save revolutionary France, they collaborated with the fiercely patriotic and democratic sans-culottes. They established, as best they could, a planned economy with egalitarian social overtones. Rather than let supply and demand determine prices, the government decreed the maximum allowable prices, fixed in paper assignats, for a host of key products. Though the state was too weak to enforce all its price regulations, it did fix the price of bread in Paris at levels the poor could afford. Rationing and ration cards were introduced to make sure that the limited supplies of bread were shared fairly. Quality was also controlled. Bakers were permitted to make only the "bread of equality" —a brown bread made of a mixture of all available flours. White bread and pastries were outlawed as frivolous luxuries. The poor of Paris may not have eaten well, but they ate.

They also worked, mainly to produce arms and munitions for the war effort. Craftsmen and small manufacturers were told what to produce and when to deliver. The government nationalized many small

THE FRENCH REVOLUTION

May 5, 1789	Estates General convene at Versailles
June 17, 1789	Third Estate declares itself the National Assembly
June 20, 1789	Oath of the Tennis Court
July 14, 1789	Storming of the Bastille
July–August 1789	The Great Fear in the countryside
August 4, 1789	National Assembly abolishes feudal privileges
August 27, 1789	National Assembly issues Declaration of the Rights of Man
October 5, 1789	Parisian women march on Versailles and force royal family to return to Paris
November 1789	National Assembly confiscates church lands
July 1790	Civil Constitution of the Clergy establishes a national church
	Louis XVI reluctantly agrees to accept a constitutional monarchy
June 1791	Arrest of the royal family while attempting to flee France
August 1791	Declaration of Pillnitz by Austria and Prussia
April 1792	France declares war on Austria
August 1792	Parisian mob attacks palace and takes Louis XVI prisoner
September 1792	September Massacres
	National Convention declares France a republic and abolishes monarchy
January 1793	Execution of Louis XVI
February 1793	France declares war on Britain, Holland, and Spain
	Revolts in provincial cities
March 1793	Bitter struggle in the National Convention between Girondists and the Mountain
April–June 1793	Robespierre and the Mountain organize the Committee of Public Safety and arrest Girondist leaders
September 1793	Price controls to aid the sans-culottes and mobilize war effort
1793–1794	Reign of Terror in Paris and the provinces
Spring 1794	French armies victorious on all fronts
July 1794	Execution of Robespierre
	Thermidorean Reaction begins
1795–1799	The Directory
1795	End of economic controls and suppression of the sans-culottes
1797	Napolean defeats Austrian armies in Italy and returns triumphant to Paris
1798	Austria, Great Britain, and Russia form the Second Coalition against France
1799	Napoleon overthrows the Directory and seizes power

workshops and requisitioned raw materials and grain from the peasants. Sometimes planning and control did not go beyond orders to meet the latest emergency: "Ten thousand soldiers lack shoes. You will take the shoes of all the aristocrats in Strasbourg and deliver them ready for transport to headquarters at 10 A.M. tomorrow." Failures to control and coordinate were failures of means and not of desire: seldom if ever before had a government attempted to manage an economy so thoroughly. The second revolution and the ascendancy of the sans-culottes had produced an embryonic emergency socialism, which was to have great influence on the subsequent development of socialist ideology.

While radical economic measures supplied the poor with bread and the armies with weapons, a Reign of Terror (1793–1794) was solidifying the home front. Special revolutionary courts, responsible only to Robespierre's Committee of Public Safety, tried rebels and "enemies of the nation" for political crimes. Drawing on popular, sans-culottes support centered in the local Jacobin clubs, these local courts ignored normal legal procedures and judged severely. Some 40,000 French men and women were executed or died in prison. Another 300,000 suspects crowded the prisons and often brushed close to death in a revolutionary court.

Robespierre's Reign of Terror was one of the most controversial phases of the French Revolution. Most historians now believe that the Terror was not directed against any single class. Rather, it was a political weapon directed impartially against all who might oppose the revolutionary government. For many Europeans of the time, however, the Reign of Terror represented a terrifying perversion of the generous ideals of 1789. It strengthened the belief that France had foolishly replaced a weak king with a bloody dictatorship.

The third and perhaps most decisive element in the French republic's victory over the First Coalition was its ability to continue drawing on the explosive power of patriotic dedication to a national state and a national mission. This is the essence of modern nationalism. With a common language and a common tradition, newly reinforced by the ideas of popular sovereignty and democracy, the French people were stirred by a common loyalty. The shared danger of foreign foes and internal rebels unified all classes in a heroic defense of the nation.

In such circumstances, war was no longer the gentlemanly game of the eighteenth century, but a life-and-death struggle between good and evil. Everyone had to participate in the national effort. According to a famous decree of August 23, 1793:

The young men shall go to battle and the married men shall forge arms. The women shall make tents and clothes, and shall serve in the hospitals; children shall tear rags into lint. The old men will be guided to the public places of the cities to kindle the courage of the young warriors and to preach the unity of the Republic and the hatred of kings.

Like the wars of religion, war in 1793 was a crusade; this war, though, was fought for a secular rather than a religious ideology.

As all unmarried young men were subject to the draft, the French armed forces swelled to 1 million men in fourteen armies. A force of this size was unprecedented in the history of European warfare. The soldiers were led by young, impetuous generals, who had often risen rapidly from the ranks and personified the opportunities the Revolution seemed to offer gifted sons of the people. These generals used mass attacks at bayonet point by their highly motivated forces to overwhelm the enemy. By the spring of 1794, French armies were victorious on all fronts. The republic was saved.

THE THERMIDORIAN REACTION AND THE DIRECTORY, 1794–1799

The success of the French armies led Robespierre and the Committee of Public Safety to relax the emergency economic controls, but they extended the political Reign of Terror. Their lofty goal was increasingly an ideal democratic republic, where justice would reign and there would be neither rich nor poor. Their lowly means were unrestrained despotism and the guillotine, which struck down any who might seriously question the new order. In March 1794, to the horror of many sans-culottes, Robespierre's Terror wiped out many of the "angry men," led by the radical social democrat Jacques Hébert. Two weeks later, several of Robespierre's long-standing collaborators, led by the famous orator Danton, marched up the steps to the guillotine. Knowing that they might be next, a strange assortment of radicals and moderates in the convention organized a conspiracy. They howled down Robespierre when he tried to speak to the National Convention on 9 Thermidor (July 27, 1794). On the following day, it was Robespierre's turn to be shaved by the revolutionary razor.

As Robespierre's closest supporters followed their leader, France unexpectedly experienced a thorough reaction to the despotism of the Reign of Terror. In a general way, this "Thermidorian reaction" recalled the early days of the Revolution. The respectable middle-class lawyers and professionals who had led the liberal Revolution of 1789 reasserted their authority. Drawing support from their own class, the provincial cities, and the better-off peasants, the National Convention abolished many economic controls, printed more paper currency, and let prices rise sharply. It severely restricted the local political organizations where the sans-culottes had their strength. And all the while, the wealthy bankers and newly rich speculators celebrated the sudden end of the Terror with an orgy of self-indulgence and ostentatious luxury.

The collapse of economic controls, coupled with runaway inflation, hit the working poor very hard. The gaudy extravagance of the rich wounded their pride. The sans-culottes accepted private property, but they believed passionately in small business and the right of all to earn a decent living. Increasingly disorganized after Robespierre purged their radical spokesmen, the common people of Paris finally revolted against the emerging new order in early 1795. The Convention quickly used the army to suppress these insurrections. For the first time since the fall of the Bastille, bread riots and uprisings by Parisians living on the edge of starvation were effectively put down by a government that made no concessions to the poor.

In the face of all these catastrophes, the revolutionary fervor of the laboring poor finally subsided. As far as politics was concerned, their interest and influence would remain very limited until 1830. There arose, especially from the women, a great cry for peace and a turning toward religion. As the government looked the other way, the women brought back the Catholic church and the worship of God. In one French town, women fought with each other over which of their children should be baptized first. After six tumultuous years, the women of the poor concluded that the Revolution was a failure.

As for the middle-class members of the National Convention, they wrote yet another constitution, which they believed would guarantee their economic position and political supremacy. The mass of the population could vote only for electors, who would be men of means. Electors then elected the members of a reorganized legislative assembly, as well as key officials throughout France. The assembly also chose the five-man executive—the Directory.

The men of the Directory continued to support French military expansion abroad. War was no longer so much a crusade as a means to meet the ever-present, ever-unsolved economic problem. Large, victorious French armies reduced unemployment at home, and they were able to live off the territories they conquered and plundered.

The unprincipled action of the Directory reinforced widespread disgust with war and starvation. This general dissatisfaction revealed itself clearly in the national elections of 1797, which returned a large number of conservative and even monarchist deputies who favored peace at almost any price. Fearing for their skins, the members of the Directory used the army to nullify the elections and began to govern dictatorially. Two years later, Napoleon Bonaparte ended the Directory in a coup d'état and substituted a strong dictatorship for a weak one. Truly, the Revolution was over.

THE NAPOLEONIC ERA, 1799–1815

For almost fifteen years, from 1799 to 1814, France was in the hands of a keen-minded military dictator of exceptional ability. One of history's most fascinating leaders, Napoleon Bonaparte realized the need to put an end to civil strife in France, in order to create unity and consolidate his rule. And he did. But Napoleon saw himself as a man of destiny, and the glory of war and the dream of universal empire proved irresistible. For years he spiraled from victory to victory; but in the end he was destroyed by a mighty coalition united in fear of his restless ambition.

NAPOLEON'S RULE OF FRANCE

In 1799, when he seized power, young General Napoleon Bonaparte was a national hero. Born in Corsica into an impoverished noble family in 1769, Napoleon left home to become a lieutenant in the French artillery in 1785. After a brief and unsuccessful adventure fighting for Corsican independence in 1789, he returned to France as a French patriot and a dedicated revolutionary. Rising rapidly in the new army, Napoleon was placed in command of French forces in Italy and won brilliant victories there in 1796 and 1797. His next campaign, in Egypt, was a failure, but Napoleon made his way back to France before the fiasco was generally known. His reputation remained intact.

Napoleon soon learned that some prominent members of the legislative assembly were plotting against the Directory. The dissatisfaction of these plotters stemmed not so much from the fact that the Directory was a dictatorship, as from the fact that it was a weak dictatorship. Ten years of upheaval and uncertainty had made firm rule much more appealing than liberty and popular politics to these disillusioned revolutionaries. The abbé Sieyès personified this evolution in thinking. In 1789 he had written in his famous pamphlet, *What Is the Third Estate?,* that the nobility was grossly overprivileged and that the entire people should rule the French nation. Now Sieyès's motto was "confidence from below, authority from above."

Like the other members of his group, Sieyès wanted a strong military ruler. The flamboyant thirty-year-old Napoleon was ideal. Thus the conspirators and Napoleon organized a takeover. On November 9, 1799, they ousted the Directors, and the following day soldiers disbanded the assembly at bayonet point. Napoleon was named first consul of the republic, and a new constitution consolidating his position was overwhelmingly approved in a plebiscite in December 1799. Republican appearances were maintained, but Napoleon was already the real ruler of France.

The essence of Napoleon's domestic policy was to use his great and highly personal powers to maintain order and put an end to civil strife. He did so by working out unwritten agreements with powerful groups in France, whereby these groups received favors in return for loyal service. Napoleon's bargain with the solid middle class was codified in the famous Civil Code of 1804, which reasserted two of the fundamental principles of the liberal and essentially moderate revolution of 1789: equality of all citizens before the law and absolute security of wealth and private property. Napoleon and the leading bankers of Paris established a privately owned Bank of France, which loyally served the interests of both the state and the financial oligarchy. Napoleon's defense of the economic status quo also appealed to the peasants, who had bought some of the lands confiscated from the church and nobility. Thus Napoleon reconfirmed the gains of the peasantry and reassured the middle class, which had already lost a large number of its revolutionary illusions in the face of social upheaval.

Napoleon Crossing the Alps: David Bold and commanding, with flowing cape and surging stallion, the daring young Napoleon Bonaparte leads his army across the Alps from Italy to battle the Austrians in 1797. This painting by the great Jacques-Louis David (1748–1825) is a stirring glorification of Napoleon, a brilliant exercise in mythmaking. *(The Granger Collection)*

At the same time, Napoleon accepted and strengthened the position of the French bureaucracy. Building on the solid foundations that revolutionary governments had inherited from the Old Regime, he perfected a thoroughly centralized state. A network of prefects, subprefects, and centrally appointed mayors depended on Napoleon and served him well. Nor were members of the old nobility slighted. In 1800 and again in 1802 Napoleon granted amnesty to a hundred thousand émigrés on the condition that they return to France and take a loyalty oath. Members of this returning elite soon ably occupied many high posts in the expanding centralized state. Only a thousand diehard monarchists were exempted and remained abroad. Napoleon also created a new imperial nobility in order to reward his most talented generals and officials.

THE NAPOLEONIC ERA

November 1799	Napoleon overthrows the Directory
December 1799	French voters overwhelmingly approve Napoleon's new constitution
1800	Napoleon founds the Bank of France
1801	France defeats Austria and acquires Italian and German territories in the Treaty of Lunéville
	Napoleon signs a concordat with the pope
1802	Treaty of Amiens with Britain
March 1804	Execution of the Duke of Engheim
December 1804	Napoleon crowns himself emperor
October 1805	Battle of Trafalgar: Britain defeats the French and Spanish fleets
December 1805	Battle of Austerlitz: Napoleon defeats Austria and Prussia
1807	Treaties of Tilsit: Napoleon redraws the map of Europe
1810	Height of the Grand Empire
June 1812	Napoleon invades Russia with 600,000 men
Winter 1812	Disastrous retreat from Russia
March 1814	Russia, Prussia, Austria, and Britain form the Quadruple Alliance to defeat France
April 1814	Napoleon abdicates and is exiled to Elba
February–June 1815	Napoleon escapes from Elba and rules France until suffering defeat at Battle of Waterloo

Napoleon's great skill in gaining support from important and potentially hostile groups is illustrated by his treatment of the Catholic church in France. In 1800 the French clergy was still divided into two groups: those who had taken an oath of allegiance to the revolutionary government and those in exile or hiding who had refused to do so. Personally uninterested in religion, Napoleon wanted to heal the religious division so that a united Catholic church in France could serve as a bulwark of order and social peace. After long and arduous negotiations, Napoleon and Pope Pius VII (1800–1823) signed the Concordat of 1801. The pope gained for French Catholics the precious right to practice their religion freely, but Napoleon gained the most politically. His government now nominated bishops, paid the clergy, and exerted great influence over the church in France.

The domestic reforms of Napoleon's early years were his greatest achievement. Much of his legal and administrative reorganization has survived in France to this day. More generally, Napoleon's domestic initiatives gave the great majority of French people a welcome sense of order and stability. And when Napoleon added the glory of military victory, he rekindled a spirit of national unity that would elude France throughout most of the nineteenth century.

Order and unity had their price: Napoleon's authoritarian rule. Free speech and freedom of the press —fundamental rights of the liberal revolution, enshrined in the Declaration of the Rights of Man— were continually violated. Napoleon constantly reduced the number of newspapers in Paris. By 1811 only four were left, and they were little more than organs of government propaganda. The occasional elections were a farce. Later laws prescribed harsh penalties for political offenses.

These changes in the law were part of the creation of a police state in France. Since Napoleon was usually busy making war, this task was largely left to Joseph Fouché, an unscrupulous opportunist who had earned a reputation for brutality during the Reign of Terror. As minister of police, Fouché organized a ruthlessly efficient spy system, which kept thousands of citizens under continuous police surveillance. People suspected of subversive activities were arbitrarily detained, placed under house arrest, or even consigned to insane asylums. After 1810 political suspects were held in state prisons, as they had been during the Terror. There were about 2,500 such political prisoners in 1814.

Napoleon on Campaign This picture of the bloody Battle of Bordino in Russia in 1812 captures important features of Napoleonic warfare. While cannon boomed, infantry fired, and cavalry charged, commanders watching from on high directed their forces like pieces on a chessboard. *(Brown Brothers)*

NAPOLEON'S WARS AND FOREIGN POLICY

Napoleon was above all a military man, and a great one. After coming to power in 1799, he sent peace feelers to Austria and Great Britain, the two remaining members of the Second Coalition, which had been formed against France in 1798. When these overtures were rejected, French armies led by Napoleon decisively defeated the Austrians. In the Treaty of Lunéville (1801) Austria accepted the loss of its Italian possessions, and German territory on the west bank of the Rhine was incorporated into France. Once more, as in 1797, the British were alone, and war-weary, like the French.

Still seeking to consolidate his regime domestically, Napoleon concluded the Treaty of Amiens with Great Britain in 1802. Britain agreed to return Trinidad and the Caribbean islands, which it had seized from France in 1793. The treaty said very little about Europe, though. France remained in control of Holland, the Austrian Netherlands, the west bank of the Rhine, and most of the Italian peninsula. Napoleon was free to reshape the German states as he wished. To the dismay of British businessmen, the Treaty of Amiens did not provide for expansion of the commerce between Britain and the Continent. It was clearly a diplomatic triumph for Napoleon, and peace with honor and profit increased his popularity at home.

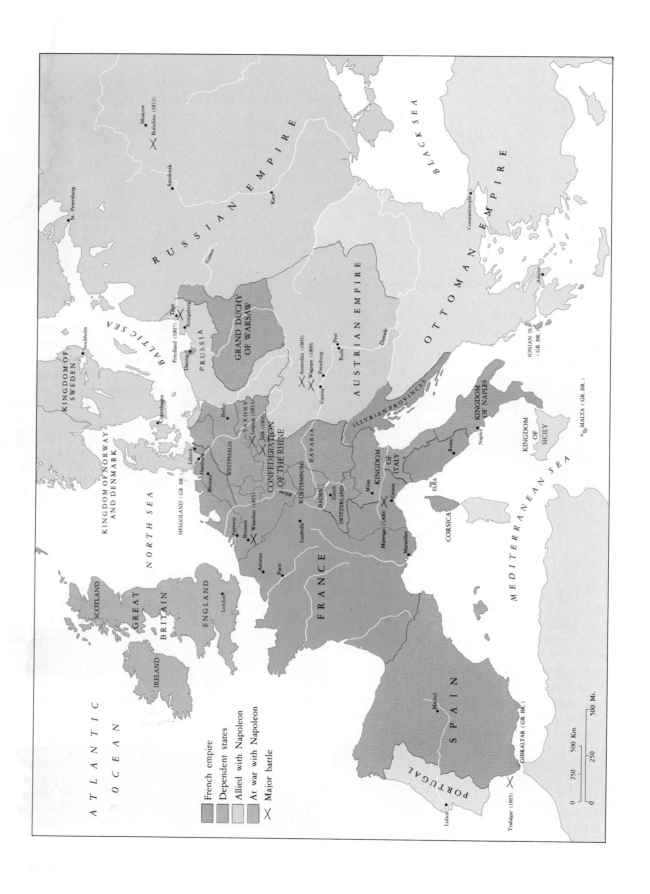

ATLANTIC
OCEAN

GREAT BRITAIN

SCOTLAND

IRELAND

ENGLAND

London

NORTH SEA

KINGDOM OF SWEDEN

Stockholm

KINGDOM OF NORWAY AND DENMARK

Copenhagen

HELGOLAND (GR. BR.)

BALTIC SEA

St. Petersburg

RUSSIAN EMPIRE

Moscow
Borodino (1812)

Smolensk

Kiev

Niemen

Königsberg
Thorn
Friedland (1807)
Danzig

PRUSSIA

Berlin

GRAND DUCHY OF WARSAW

Lübeck
Hamburg
Bremen

WESTPHALIA

SAXONY
Leipzig (1813)
Jena (1806)

CONFEDERATION OF THE RHINE

Rhine

Antwerp
Brussels
Waterloo (1815)

Amiens
Paris

Lunéville

FRANCE

WÜRTTEMBERG
BADEN
Zürich
SWITZERLAND

BAVARIA

Austerlitz (1805)
Wagram (1809)
Pressburg
Buda Pest
Vienna

AUSTRIAN EMPIRE

Danube

ILLYRIAN PROVINCES

OTTOMAN EMPIRE

BLACK SEA

Constantinople

Athens

IONIAN IS. (GR. BR.)

KINGDOM OF ITALY

Milan
Genoa
Marengo (1800)
Marseilles

Rome

KINGDOM OF NAPLES

Naples

ELBA

CORSICA

KINGDOM OF SICILY

MEDITERRANEAN SEA

MALTA (GR. BR.)

SPAIN

Madrid

PORTUGAL

Lisbon

Trafalgar (1805)

GIBRALTAR (GR. BR.)

French empire
Dependent states
Allied with Napoleon
At war with Napoleon
Major battle

0   250   500 Km.
0   250   500 Mi.

In 1802 Napoleon was secure but unsatisfied. Ever a romantic gambler as well as a brilliant administrator, he could not contain his power drive. Aggressively redrawing the map of Germany so as to weaken Austria and attract the secondary states of southwestern Germany toward France, Napoleon was also mainly responsible for renewed war with Great Britain. Regarding war with Britain as inevitable, he threatened British interests in the eastern Mediterranean and tried to restrict British trade with all of Europe. Britain had technically violated the Treaty of Amiens by failing to evacuate the island of Malta, but it was Napoleon's decision to renew war in May 1803. He concentrated his armies in the French ports on the Channel in the fall of 1803 and began making preparations to invade England. Yet Great Britain remained mistress of the seas. When Napoleon tried to bring his Mediterranean fleet around Gibraltar to northern France, a combined French and Spanish fleet was, after a series of mishaps, virtually annihilated by Lord Nelson at the Battle of Trafalgar on 21 October 1805. Invasion of England was henceforth impossible. Renewed fighting had its advantages, however, for the first consul used the wartime atmosphere to have himself proclaimed emperor in late 1804.

Austria, Russia, and Sweden joined with Britain to form the Third Coalition against France shortly before the Battle of Trafalgar. Actions like Napoleon's assumption of the Italian crown had convinced both Alexander I of Russia and Francis II of Austria that Napoleon was a threat to their interests and to the European balance of power. Yet the Austrians and the Russians were no match for Napoleon, who scored a brilliant victory over them at the Battle of Austerlitz in December 1805. Alexander I decided to pull back, and Austria accepted large territorial losses in return for peace as the Third Coalition collapsed.

Victorious at Austerlitz, Napoleon proceeded to reorganize the German states to his liking. In 1806 he abolished many of the tiny German states, as well as the ancient Holy Roman Empire, whose emperor had traditionally been the ruler of Austria. Napoleon established by decree a German Confederation of the Rhine, a union of fifteen German states minus Austria, Prussia, and Saxony. Naming himself "protector" of the confederation, Napoleon firmly controlled western Germany.

Napoleon's intervention in German affairs alarmed the Prussians, who had been at peace with France for more than a decade. Expecting help from his ally Russia, Frederick William III of Prussia mobilized his armies. Napoleon attacked and won two more brilliant victories in October 1806 at Jena and Auerstädt, where the Prussians were outnumbered two to one. The war with Prussia and Russia continued into the following spring, and after Napoleon's larger armies won another victory, Alexander decided to seek peace.

For several days in June 1807, the young tsar and the French emperor negotiated face to face on a raft anchored in the middle of the Niemen River. All the while, the helpless Frederick William rode back and forth on the shore, anxiously awaiting the results. As the German poet Heinrich Heine said later, Napoleon had but to whistle and Prussia would have ceased to exist. In the subsequent treaties of Tilsit, Prussia lost half of its population, while Russia accepted Napoleon's reorganization of western and central Europe. Alexander also promised to enforce Napoleon's recently decreed economic blockade against British goods and to declare war on Britain if Napoleon could not make peace on favorable terms with his island enemy.

After the victory of Austerlitz and even more after the treaties of Tilsit, Napoleon saw himself as the emperor of Europe and not just of France. The so-called Grand Empire he built had three parts. The core was an ever-expanding France, which by 1810 included Belgium, Holland, parts of northern Italy, and much German territory on the east bank of the Rhine. Beyond French borders Napoleon established a number of dependent satellite kingdoms, on the thrones of which he placed (and replaced) the members of his large family. Third, there were the independent but allied states of Austria, Prussia, and Russia. Both satellites and allies were expected after 1806 to support Napoleon's continental system and thus to cease all trade with Britain.

The impact of the Grand Empire on the peoples of Europe was considerable. In the areas incorporated into France and in the satellites (see Map 21.1), Napoleon introduced many French laws, abolishing

MAP 21.1 Napoleonic Europe in 1810

feudal dues and serfdom where French revolutionary armies had not already done so. Some of the peasants and middle class benefited from these reforms. Yet while he extended progressive measures to his cosmopolitan empire, Napoleon had to put the prosperity and special interests of France first in order to safeguard his power base. Levying heavy taxes in money and men for his armies, Napoleon came to be regarded more as a conquering tyrant than as an enlightened liberator.

The first great revolt occurred in Spain. In 1808 a coalition of Catholics, monarchists, and patriots rebelled against Napoleon's attempts to make Spain a French satellite with a Bonaparte as its king. French armies occupied Madrid, but the foes of Napoleon fled to the hills and waged uncompromising guerrilla warfare. Spain was a clear warning. Resistance to French imperialism was growing.

Yet Napoleon pushed on, determined to hold his complex and far-flung empire together. In 1810, when the Grand Empire was at its height, Britain still remained at war with France, helping the guerrillas in Spain and Portugal (see Map 21.1). The continental system, organized to exclude British goods from the Continent and force that "nation of shopkeepers" to its knees, was a failure. Instead, it was France that suffered from Britain's counter-blockade, which created hard times for French artisans and the middle class. Perhaps looking for a scapegoat, Napoleon turned on Alexander I of Russia, who had been fully supporting Napoleon's war of prohibitions against British goods.

Napoleon's invasion of Russia began in June 1812 with a force that eventually numbered 600,000, probably the largest force yet assembled in a single army. Only one-third of this force was French, however; nationals of all the satellites and allies were drafted into the operation. Originally planning to winter in the Russian city of Smolensk if Alexander did not sue for peace, Napoleon reached Smolensk and recklessly pressed on. The great battle of Borodino that followed was a draw, and the Russians retreated in good order. Alexander ordered the evacuation of Moscow, which then burned, and refused to negotiate. Finally, after five weeks in the burned-out city, Napoleon ordered a retreat. That retreat was one of the great military disasters in history. The Russian army and the Russian winter cut Napoleon's army to pieces. Only 30,000 men returned to their homelands.

Leaving his troops to their fate, Napoleon raced to Paris to raise yet another army. Possibly he might still have saved his throne if he had been willing to accept a France reduced to its historical size—the proposal offered by Austria's foreign minister Metternich. But Napoleon refused. Austria and Prussia deserted Napoleon and joined Russia and Great Britain in the Fourth Coalition. All across Europe, patriots called for a "war of liberation" against Napoleon's oppression, and the well-disciplined regular armies of Napoleon's enemies closed in for the kill. This time the coalition held together, cemented by the Treaty of Chaumont, which created a Quadruple Alliance to last for twenty years. Less than a month later, on April 4, 1814, a defeated, abandoned Napoleon abdicated his throne. After this unconditional abdication, the victorious allies granted Napoleon the island of Elba off the coast of Italy as his own tiny state. Napoleon was even allowed to keep his imperial title, and France was required to pay him a large yearly income of 2 million francs.

The allies also agreed to the restoration of the Bourbon dynasty, in part because demonstrations led by a few dedicated French monarchists indicated some support among the French people for that course of action. The new monarch, Louis XVIII (1814–1824), tried to consolidate that support by issuing the Constitutional Charter, which accepted many of France's revolutionary changes and guaranteed civil liberties. Indeed, the Charter gave France a constitutional monarchy roughly similar to that established in 1791, although far fewer people had the right to vote for representatives to the resurrected Chamber of Deputies. Moreover, after Louis XVIII stated firmly that his government would not pay any war reparations, France was treated leniently by the allies, who agreed to meet in Vienna to work out a general peace settlement.

Yet Louis XVIII—old, ugly, and crippled by gout —totally lacked the glory and magic of Napoleon. Hearing of political unrest in France and diplomatic tensions in Vienna, Napoleon staged a daring escape from Elba in February 1815. Landing in France, he issued appeals for support and marched on Paris with a small band. French officers and soldiers who had fought so long for their emperor responded to the call. Louis XVIII fled, and once more Napoleon took command. But Napoleon's gamble was a desperate long shot, for the allies were united against him. At the end of a frantic period known as the Hundred

Days, they crushed his forces at Waterloo on June 18, 1815, and imprisoned him on the rocky island of St. Helena, far off the western coast of Africa. Old Louis XVIII returned again—this time "in the baggage of the allies," as his detractors scornfully put it—and recommenced his reign. The allies now dealt rather harshly with the apparently incorrigible French (see Chapter 23). And Napoleon, doomed to suffer crude insults at the hands of sadistic English jailers on distant St. Helena, could take revenge only by writing his memoirs, skillfully nurturing the myth that he had been Europe's revolutionary liberator, a romantic hero whose lofty work had been undone by oppressive reactionaries. An era had ended.

The revolution that began in America and spread to France was a liberal revolution. Inspired by English history and some of the teachings of the Enlightenment, revolutionaries on both sides of the Atlantic sought to establish civil liberties and equality before the law within the framework of representative government. Success in America was subsequently matched by success in France. There liberal nobles and an increasingly class-conscious middle class overwhelmed declining monarchial absolutism and feudal privilege, thanks to the common people—the sans-culottes and the peasants. The government and society established by the Declaration of the Rights of Man and the French constitution of 1791 were remarkably similar to those created in America by the federal Constitution and the Bill of Rights. Thus the new political system, based on electoral competition and civil equality, came into approximate harmony with France's evolving social structure, which had become increasingly based on wealth and achievement rather than on tradition and legal privileges.

Yet the Revolution in France did not end with the liberal victory of 1789 to 1791. As Robespierre led the determined country in a total war effort against foreign foes, French revolutionaries became more democratic, radical, and violent. Their effort succeeded, but at the price of dictatorship—first by Robespierre himself and then by the Directory and Napoleon. Some historians blame the excesses of the French revolutionaries for the emergence of dictatorship, while others hold the conservative monarchs of Europe responsible. In any case, historians have often concluded that the French Revolution ended in failure.

This conclusion is highly debatable, though. After the fall of Robespierre, the solid middle class, with its liberal philosophy and Enlightenment world-view, reasserted itself. Under the Directory, it salvaged a good portion of the social and political gains that it and the peasantry had made between 1789 and 1791. In so doing, the middle-class leaders repudiated the radical social and economic measures associated with Robespierre, but they never re-established the old pattern of separate legal orders and absolute monarchy. Napoleon built on the policies of the Directory. With considerable success he sought to add the support of the old nobility and the church to that of the middle class and the peasantry. And though Napoleon sharply curtailed thought and speech, he effectively promoted the reconciliation of old and new, of centralized government and careers open to talent, of noble and bourgeois in a restructured property-owning elite. Little wonder, then, that Louis XVIII had no choice but to accept a French society solidly based on wealth and achievement. In granting representative government and civil liberties to facilitate his restoration to the throne in 1814, Louis XVIII submitted to the rest of the liberal triumph of 1789 to 1791. The core of the French Revolution had survived a generation of war and dictatorship. Old Europe would never be the same.

NOTES

1. Quoted by R. R. Palmer, *The Age of the Democratic Revolution,* Princeton University Press, Princeton, N.J., 1959, 1.239.
2. G. Lefebvre, *The Coming of the French Revolution,* Vintage Books, New York, 1947, p. 81.
3. P. H. Beik, ed., *The French Revolution,* Walker, New York, 1970, p. 89.
4. O. Hufton, "Women in Revolution," *Past and Present* 53 (November 1971): 91–95.
5. G. Pernoud and S. Flaisser, eds., *The French Revolution,* Fawcett Publications, Greenwich, Conn., 1960, p. 61.
6. L. Gershoy, *The Era of the French Revolution, 1789–1799,* Van Nostrand, New York, 1957, p. 135.
7. Ibid., p. 150.
8. Pernoud and Flaisser, pp. 193–194.

SUGGESTED READING

In addition to the fascinating eyewitness reports on the French Revolution in P. Beik, *The French Revolution,* and G. Pernoud and S. Flaisser, eds., *The French Revolution* (1960), A. Young's *Travels in France During the Years 1787, 1788 and 1789* (1969) offers an engrossing contemporary description of France and Paris on the eve of revolution. Edmund Burke, *Reflections on the Revolution in France,* first published in 1790, is the classic conservative indictment. The intense passions the French Revolution has generated may be seen in the nineteenth-century French historians, notably the enthusiastic Jules Michelet, *History of the French Revolution;* the hostile Hippolyte Taine; and the judicious Alexis de Tocqueville, whose masterpiece, *The Old Regime and the French Revolution,* was first published in 1856. Important recent general studies on the entire period are R. R. Palmer, *The Age of the Democratic Revolution* (1959, 1964), which paints a comparative international picture; E. J. Hobsbawm, *The Age of Revolution, 1789–1848* (1962); C. Breunig, *The Age of Revolution and Reaction, 1789–1850* (1970); O. Connelly, *French Revolution—Napoleonic Era* (1979); and L. Dehio, *The Precarious Balance: Four Centuries of the European Power Struggle* (1962). C. Brinton's older but delightfully written *A Decade of Revolution, 1789–1799* (1934) complements his stimulating *Anatomy of Revolution* (1938, 1965), an ambitious comparative approach to revolution in England, America, France, and Russia. A Cobban, *The Social Interpretation of the French Revolution* (1964), and F. Furet, *Interpreting the French Revolution* (1981), are exciting reassessments of many well-worn ideas, to be compared with W. Doyle, *Origins of the French Revolution* (1981); G. Lefebvre, *The Coming of the French Revolution* (1947); and N. Hampson, *A Social History of the French Revolution* (1963). G. Rudé makes the men and women of the great days of upheaval come alive in his *The Crowd in the French Revolution* (1959). R. R. Palmer studies sympathetically the leaders of the Terror in *Twelve Who Ruled* (1941). Two other particularly interesting, detailed works are C. L. R. James, *The Black Jacobins* (1938, 1980), on black slave revolt in Haiti, and J. C. Herold, *Mistress to an Age* (1955), on the remarkable Madame de Staël. On revolution in America, E. Morgan, *The Birth of the Republic, 1763–89* (1956), and B. Bailyn, *The Ideological Origins of the American Revolution* (1967), are noteworthy. Three important recent studies on aspects of revolutionary France are D. Jordan's vivid *The King's Trial: Louis XVI vs. the French Revolution* (1979); W. Sewell, Jr.'s imaginative *Work and Revolution in France: The Language of Labor from the Old Regime to 1848* (1980); and P. Higonnet, *Class, Ideology and the Rights of Nobles During the French Revolution* (1981).

P. Geyl, *Napoleon, For and Against* (1949), is a delightful discussion of changing historical interpretations of Napoleon, which may be compared with a more recent treatment by R. Jones, *Napoleon: Man and Myth* (1977). Good biographies are J. M. Thompson, *Napoleon Bonaparte: His Rise and Fall* (1952); F. H. M. Markham, *Napoleon* (1964); and V. Cronin, *Napoleon Bonaparte* (1972). L. Bergeron, *France Under Napoleon* (1981), is an important synthesis. Wonderful novels inspired by this period include Raphael Sabatini's *Scaramouche,* a swashbuckler of revolutionary intrigue with accurate historical details; Charles Dickens's classic *Tale of Two Cities;* and Leo Tolstoy's monumental saga of Napoleon's invasion of Russia (and much more), *War and Peace.*

22

THE REVOLUTION IN ENERGY AND INDUSTRY

HILE THE REVOLUTION in France was opening a new political era, another revolution was transforming economic and social life. This was the Industrial Revolution, which began in England in the 1780s and spread after 1815 to continental Europe and then around the world. Because the Industrial Revolution was less dramatic than the French Revolution, some historians see industrial development as basically moderate and evolutionary. In the long perspective, however, it was rapid and brought about radical changes. Perhaps only the development of agriculture during Neolithic times had a similar impact and significance.

The Industrial Revolution profoundly modified much of human experience. It changed patterns of work, transformed the social class structure, and eventually even altered the international balance of political power. It may quite possibly have saved Europe from the poverty of severe overpopulation and even from famine. How did this happen? How and why did drastic changes occur in industry, and how did these changes affect people and society? These are the questions this chapter will seek to answer. Chapter 24 will examine in detail the emergence of accompanying changes in urban civilization.

THE INDUSTRIAL REVOLUTION IN ENGLAND

The Industrial Revolution began in England. It was something new in history, and it was quite unplanned. With no models to copy and no idea of what to expect, England had to pioneer not only in industrial technology but also in social relations and urban living. Between 1793 and 1815, these formidable tasks were complicated by almost constant war with France. As the trailblazer in economic development, as France was in political change, England must command special attention.

EIGHTEENTH-CENTURY ORIGINS

The Industrial Revolution grew out of the expanding Atlantic economy of the eighteenth century, which served mercantilist England remarkably well. England's colonial empire, augmented by a strong position in Latin America and in the African slave trade, provided a growing market for English manufactured goods. So did England itself. In an age when it was much cheaper to ship goods by water than by land, no part of England was more than twenty miles from navigable water. Beginning in the 1770s, a canal-building boom greatly enhanced this natural advantage (see Map 22.1). Nor were there any tariffs within the country to hinder trade, as there were in France before 1789 and in politically fragmented Germany.

Agriculture played a central role in bringing about the Industrial Revolution in England. English farmers were second only to the Dutch in productivity in 1700, and they were continuously adopting new methods of farming as the century went on. The result, especially before 1760, was a period of bountiful crops and low food prices. The ordinary English family did not have to spend almost everything it earned just to buy bread. It could spend more on other items, on manufactured goods—leather shoes or a razor for the man, a bonnet or a shawl for the woman, toy soldiers for the son, and a doll for the daughter. Thus demand for goods within the country complemented the demand from the colonies.

England had other assets that helped give rise to the Industrial Revolution. Unlike eighteenth-century France, England had an effective central bank and well-developed credit markets. The monarchy and the aristocratic oligarchy, which had jointly ruled the country since 1688. provided stable and predictable government. At the same time, the government let the domestic economy operate fairly freely and with few controls, encouraging personal initiative, technical change, and a free market. Finally, England had long had a large class of hired agricultural laborers, whose numbers were further increased by the enclosure movement of the late eighteenth century. These rural wage earners were relatively mobile—compared to village-bound peasants in France and western Germany, for example—and along with cottage workers they formed a potential industrial labor force for capitalist entrepreneurs.

All these factors combined to initiate the Industrial Revolution, which began in the 1780s—after the American war for independence and just before the French Revolution. Thus the great economic and political revolutions that have shaped the modern world occurred almost simultaneously, though they began in different countries. The Industrial Revolution was, however, a longer process. It was not complete in England until 1830 at the earliest, and it had no real impact on continental countries until after the Congress of Vienna ended the era of revolutionary wars in 1815.

THE FIRST FACTORIES

The pressure to produce more goods for a growing market was directly related to the first decisive break-through of the Industrial Revolution—the creation of the world's first large factories in the English cotton textile industry. Technological innovations in the manufacture of cloth led to a whole new system of production and social relationships. Since no other industry experienced such a rapid or complete trans-formation before 1830, these trail-blazing develop-ments deserve special consideration.

Although the putting-out system of merchant capi-talism (page 621) was expanding all across Europe in the eighteenth century, this pattern of rural industry was most fully developed in England. Thus it was in England, under the pressure of growing demand, that the system's shortcomings first began to outweigh its advantages. This was especially true in the textile in-dustry after about 1760.

The constant shortage of thread in the textile in-dustry focused attention on ways of improving spin-ning. Many a tinkering worker knew that a better spinning wheel promised rich rewards. Spinning of the traditional raw materials—wool and flax—proved hard to change, but cotton was different. Cot-ton textiles had first been imported into England from India by the East India Company, and by 1760 there was a tiny domestic industry in northern Eng-land. After many experiments over a generation, a gifted carpenter and jack-of-all-trades, James Har-greaves, invented his cotton spinning jenny about 1765. At almost the same moment a barber-turned-manufacturer named Richard Arkwright invented (or possibly pirated) another kind of spinning ma-chine, the water frame. These breakthroughs pro-duced an explosion in the infant industry. By 1790 the new machines produced ten times as much cot-ton yarn as had been made in 1770. By 1800 the pro-duction of cotton thread was England's most impor-tant industry.

Hargreaves's jenny was simple and inexpensive. It was also hand operated. In early models, from six to twenty-four spindles were mounted on a sliding car-

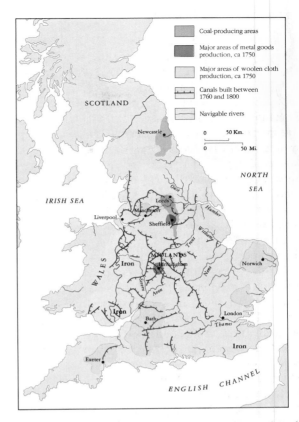

MAP 22.1 Cottage Industry and Transportation in Eighteenth-Century England England had an unusually good system of navigable waterways even before river-linking canals made it better.

riage, and each spindle spun a fine, slender thread. The woman moved the carriage back and forth with one hand and turned a wheel to supply power with the other. Now it was the weaver who could not keep up with his vastly more efficient wife.

Arkwright's water frame employed a different principle. It quickly acquired a capacity of several hundred spindles and demanded much more power —water power. The water frame thus required large specialized mills, factories that employed as many as a thousand workers from the very beginning. The water frame could spin only coarse, strong thread, which was then put out for respinning on hand-powered cottage jennies. Around 1790 Samuel Crompton's innovation, the "mule," began to re-quire more power than the human arm could supply. (Crompton's invention was so named because it

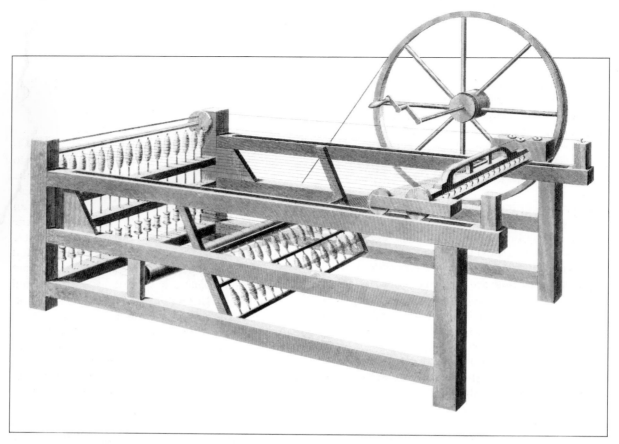

Hargreaves's Spinning Jenny The loose cotton strands on the slanted bobbins passed up to the sliding carriage and then on to the spindles in back for fine spinning. By 1783 one woman could spin by hand a hundred threads at a time on an improved model. *(Photo: Caroline Buckler)*

united the best aspects of the jenny and the water frame, just as a mule combines the traits of its dam the horse and its sire the donkey.) After that time, all cotton spinning was gradually concentrated in factories.

The first consequences of these revolutionary developments were much more beneficial than is generally believed. Cotton goods became much cheaper, and they were bought and treasured by all classes. In the past, only the wealthy could afford the comfort and cleanliness of underwear, which was called "body linen" because it was made from expensive linen cloth. Now millions of poor people, who had earlier worn nothing underneath their coarse, filthy outergarments, could afford to wear cotton slips and underpants.

The family was freed from its constant search for adequate yarn from scattered, part-time spinners, since all the thread needed could be spun in the cot-

tage on the jenny or obtained from a nearby factory. The wages of weavers, now hard pressed to keep up with the spinners, rose markedly until about 1792. Weavers were among the best-paid workers in England. They were known to walk proudly through the streets with £5 notes stuck in their hatbands, and they dressed like the middle class.

One result of this unprecedented prosperity was that large numbers of agricultural laborers became weavers. Meanwhile, however, mechanics and capitalists were seeking to invent a power loom to save on labor costs. This Edmund Cartwright achieved in 1785. But the power looms of the factories worked poorly at first, and handloom weavers continued to receive good wages until at least 1800.

Working conditions in the early factories were less satisfactory than those of cottage weavers and spinners. But until the late 1780s, most English factories were in rural areas, where they had access to water power. These factories employed a relatively small percentage of all cotton textile workers. People were reluctant to work in them, partly because they resembled the poorhouses where destitute inmates had to labor for very little pay. Therefore, factory owners turned to young children as a source of labor. More precisely, they turned to children who had been abandoned by their parents and put in the care of local parishes. The parish officers often "apprenticed" such unfortunate orphans to factory owners. The parish thus saved money and the factory owners gained workers over whom they exercised almost the authority of slaveowners. The hours were terrible, the conditions appalling. But only the nakedness of this exploitation was new. These children and the women who came to work beside them in the next generation were simply doing in the factory, under different conditions, the same kind of work they had long done in their cottages. It is some consolation that such exploitation of small children was at this point more nearly ending than beginning.

The creation of the world's first modern factories in the English cotton textile industry in the 1770s and 1780s, which grew out of the putting-out system of cottage production, was a momentous development. Both symbolically and in substance, the big new cotton mills marked the beginning of the Industrial Revolution in England.

THE PROBLEM OF ENERGY

The growth of the cotton textile industry might have been stunted or cut short, however, if water from rivers and streams had remained the primary source of power for the new factories. But this did not occur. Instead, an epoch-making solution was found to the age-old problem of energy and power. It was this solution to the energy problem—a problem that has reappeared in recent times—that permitted continued rapid development in cotton textiles, the gradual generalization of the factory system, and the triumph of the Industrial Revolution.

Human beings, like all living organisms, require energy. Adult men and women need 2,000 to 4,000 calories (units of energy) daily, simply to fuel their bodies, work, and survive. Energy comes from a variety of sources; energy also takes different forms, and one form may be converted into another. Plants have been converting solar energy into caloric matter for

eons. And human beings have used their toolmaking abilities to construct machines that convert one form of energy into another for their own benefit.

Prehistoric people relied on plants and plant-eating animals as their sources of energy. With the development of agriculture, early civilizations were able to increase the number of useful plants and thus the supply of energy. Some plants could be fed to domesticated animals, like the horse. Stronger than human beings, these animals converted the energy in the plants into work. In the medieval period, people began to develop water mills to grind their grain and windmills to pump water and drain swamps. More efficient use of water and wind in the sixteenth and seventeenth centuries enabled human beings to accomplish more; intercontinental sailing ships are a prime example. Nevertheless, even into the eighteenth century, society continued to rely for energy mainly on plants, and human beings and animals continued to perform most work. This dependence meant that Western civilization remained poor in energy and power.

Lack of power lay at the heart of the poverty that afflicted the large majority of people. The man behind the plow and the woman at the spinning wheel could employ only horsepower and human muscle in their labor. No matter how hard they worked, they could not produce very much. What people needed were new sources of energy and more power at their disposal. Then they would be able to work more efficiently, produce more, and live better.

Where was more energy to be found? Almost all energy came directly or indirectly from plants and therefore from the land: grain for people, hay for animals, and wood for heat. The land was also the principal source of raw materials needed for industrial production: wool and flax for clothing; leather for shoes; wood for housing, tools, and ironmaking. And though swamps could be drained and marshes reclaimed from the sea, it was difficult to expand greatly the amount of land available. True, its yield could be increased, such as by the elimination of fallow; nonetheless there were definite limits to such improvements.

The shortage of energy was becoming particularly severe in England by the eighteenth century. Because of the growth of population, most of the great forests of medieval England had long ago been replaced by fields of grain and hay. Wood was in ever shorter sup-

Making Charcoal After wood was carefully cut and stacked, iron masters slowly burned it to produce charcoal. Before the Industrial Revolution, a country's iron industry depended largely on the size of its forests. *(Photo: Caroline Buckler)*

ply; yet it remained tremendously important. It was the primary source of heat for all homes and industries. It was also the key to transportation, since ships and wagons were made of wood. Moreover, wood was, along with iron ore, the basic raw material of the iron industry. Processed wood (charcoal) was the fuel mixed with iron ore in the blast furnace to produce pig iron. The iron industry's appetite for wood was enormous, and even very modest and constant levels of iron production had gone far toward laying bare the forests of England, as well as parts of Europe. By 1740 the English iron industry was stagnating. Vast forests enabled Russia in the eighteenth century to become the world's leading producer of iron, much of which was exported to England. But Russia's potential for growth was limited, too, and in a few decades Russia would reach the barrier of inadequate energy that was already holding England back.

"STEAM IS AN ENGLISHMAN"

As this early energy crisis grew worse, England looked toward its abundant and widely scattered reserves of coal as an alternative to its vanishing wood. Coal was first used in England in the late Middle Ages as a source of heat. By 1640 most homes in London were heated with it, and it also provided heat for making beer, glass, soap, and other products. Coal was not used, however, to produce mechanical energy or to power machinery. It was there that coal's potential was enormous, as a simple example shows.

One pound of good bituminous coal contains about 3,500 calories of heat energy. A miner who eats 3,500 calories of food can dig out 500 pounds of coal a day, using hand tools. Even an extremely efficient converter, which transforms only 1 percent of the heat energy in coal into mechanical energy, will pro-

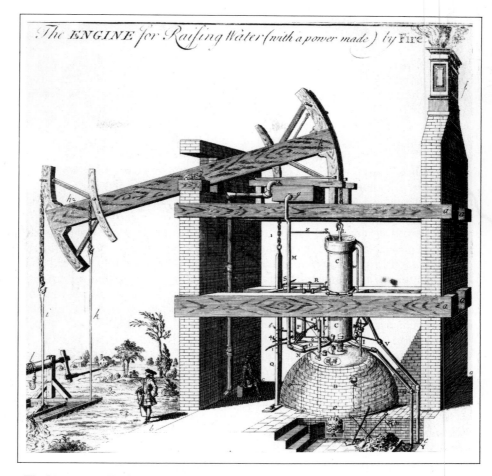

The ENGINE for Raising Water (with a power made) by Fire

The Newcomen Engine The huge steam-filled cylinder (C) was cooled by injecting water from the tank above (G) through a pipe (M). Atmospheric pressure then pushed down the piston, raised the beam, and pumped water from the mine. *(Science Museum, London)*

duce 27 horsepower-hours of work from the 500 pounds of coal the miner cut out of the earth. (The miner, by contrast, produces only about 1 horsepower-hour in the course of a day.) Much more energy is consumed by the converter, but much more work can be done.

Early steam engines were just such inefficient converters. As more coal was produced, mines were dug deeper and deeper and were constantly filling with water. Mechanical pumps, usually powered by animals walking in circles at the surface, had to be installed. At one mine, fully five hundred horses were used in pumping. Such power was expensive and bothersome. In an attempt to overcome these disadvantages, Thomas Savery in 1698 and Thomas Newcomen in 1705 invented the first primitive steam engines.

Both engines were extremely inefficient. Both burned coal to produce steam, which was then injected into a cylinder or reservoir. In Newcomen's engine, the steam in the cylinder was cooled, creating a partial vacuum in the cylinder. This vacuum allowed the pressure of the earth's atmosphere to push the piston in the cylinder down and operate a pump. By the early 1770s, many of the Savery engines and hundreds of the Newcomen engines were operating successfully, though inefficiently, in English mines.

In the early 1760s, a gifted young Scot named James Watt (1736–1819) was drawn to a critical study of the steam engine. Watt was employed at the time by the University of Glasgow as a skilled craftsman making scientific instruments. The Scottish universities were pioneers in practical technical education, and in 1763 Watt was called on to repair a Newcomen engine being used in a physics course. After a series of observations, Watt saw why the Newcomen engine wasted so much energy: the cylinder was being heated and cooled for every single stroke of the piston. To remedy this problem, Watt added a separate condenser, where the steam could be condensed without cooling the cylinder. This splendid invention greatly increased the efficiency of the steam engine.

To invent something in a laboratory is one thing; to make it a practical success is quite another. Watt needed skilled workers, precision parts, and capital, and the relatively advanced nature of the English economy proved essential. A partnership with a wealthy, progressive toymaker provided risk capital and a manufacturing plant. In the craft tradition of locksmiths, tinsmiths, and millwrights, Watt found skilled mechanics who could install, regulate, and repair his sophisticated engines. From ingenious manufacturers like the cannonmaker John Wilkinson, who learned to bore cylinders with a fair degree of accuracy, Watt was gradually able to purchase precision parts. This support allowed him to create an effective vacuum and regulate a complex engine. In more than twenty years of constant effort, Watt made many further improvements. By the late 1780s, the steam engine was a practical and commercial success in England. As a nineteenth-century saying put it, "Steam is an Englishman."

The steam engine of Watt and his followers was the Industrial Revolution's most fundamental advance in technology. For the first time in history, humanity had, at least for a few generations, almost unlimited power at its disposal. For the first time, inventors and engineers could devise and implement all kinds of power equipment to aid people in their work. For the first time, abundance was at least a possibility for ordinary men and women.

The steam engine was quickly put to use in many industries in England. It made possible the production of ever more coal to feed steam engines elsewhere. The steam-power plant began to replace water power in the cotton-spinning mills during the 1780s, contributing greatly to that industry's phenomenal rise. Steam also took the place of water power in flour mills, in the malt mills used in breweries, in the flint mills supplying the china industry, and in the mills exported by England to the West Indies to crush sugar cane.

Steam power promoted important breakthroughs in other industries. The English iron industry was radically transformed. The use of powerful, steam-driven bellows in blast furnaces helped ironmakers switch over rapidly from limited charcoal to unlimited coke (which is made from coal) in the smelting of pig iron after 1770. In the 1780s Henry Cort developed the puddling furnace, which allowed pig iron to be refined in turn with coke. Strong, skilled ironworkers—the puddlers—"cooked" molten pig iron in a great vat, raking off globs of refined iron for further processing. Cort also developed heavy-duty steam-powered rolling mills, which were capable of spewing out finished iron in every shape and form.

The economic consequences of these technical innovations was a great boom in the English iron industry. In 1740 annual British iron production was only 17,000 tons. With the spread of coke smelting and the first impact of Cort's inventions, production reached 68,000 tons in 1788, 125,000 tons in 1796, and 260,000 tons in 1806. In 1844 Britain produced 3 million tons of iron. This was truly phenomenal expansion. Once scarce and expensive, iron became the cheap, basic building block of the economy.

THE COMING OF THE RAILROADS

Sailing ships had improved noticeably since the Age of Discovery, and the second half of the eighteenth century saw extensive construction of hard and relatively smooth roads, particularly in France before the Revolution. Yet it was passenger traffic that benefited most from this construction. Overland shipment of freight, relying solely on horsepower, was still quite limited and frightfully expensive; shippers used rivers and canals for heavy freight whenever possible. It was logical therefore that inventors would try to use steam power to improve inland transportation.

As early as 1800, an American ran a "steamer on wheels" through city streets. Other experiments followed. In the 1820s, English engineers perfected steam cars capable of carrying fourteen passengers at ten miles an hour—as fast as the mail coach. But the noisy, heavy steam automobiles frightened passing horses and damaged themselves as well as the roads with their vibrations. For the rest of the century, horses continued to reign on highways and city streets.

Early Railroad Construction presented innumerable challenges, like the building of bridges to span broad rivers and deep gorges. Civil engineers responded with impressive feats and their profession bounded ahead. *(The Bettmann Archive)*

The coal industry had long been using plank roads and rails to move coal wagons within mines and at the surface. Rails reduced friction and allowed a horse or a human being to pull a heavier load. Thus, once a rail capable of supporting a heavy locomotive was developed in 1816, all sorts of experiments with steam engines on rails went forward. In 1825, after ten years of work, George Stephenson built an effective locomotive. In 1830 his *Rocket* sped down the track of the just-completed Liverpool and Manchester Railway at sixteen miles per hour. This was the world's first important railroad, fittingly steaming in the heart of industrial England.

The line from Liverpool to Manchester was a financial as well as a technical success, and many private companies were quickly organized to build more rail lines. These companies had to get permission for their projects from Parliament and pay for the rights of way they needed; otherwise, their freedom was great. Within twenty years, they had completed the main trunk lines of Great Britain. Other countries followed quickly with similar railway construction.

The significance of the railroad was tremendous. The railroad dramatically reduced the cost and uncertainty of shipping freight overland. This advance had many economic consequences. Previously, mar-

The Third-Class Carriage The French artist Honoré Daumier was fascinated by the railroad and its human significance. This great painting focuses on the peasant grandmother, absorbed in memories. The nursing mother represents love and creativity; the sleeping boy, innocence. *(The Metropolitan Museum of Art. Bequest of Mrs. H. O. Havemeyer, 1929. The H. O. Havemeyer Collection)*

kets had tended to be small and local; as the barrier of high transportation costs was lowered, they became larger and even nationwide. Larger markets encouraged larger factories with more sophisticated machinery. Such factories could make goods cheaper, enabling people to pay less for them. They also tended to drive most cottage workers, many urban artisans, and other manufacturers out of business.

In all countries, the construction of railroads contributed to the growth of a class of urban workers. Cottage workers, farm laborers, and small peasants did not generally leave their jobs and homes to go directly to work in factories. However, the building of railroads created a strong demand for labor, especially unskilled labor, throughout a country. Like farm work, hard work on construction gangs was done in the open air with animals and hand tools. Many farm laborers and poor peasants, long accustomed to leaving their villages for temporary employment, went to build railroads. By the time the work was finished, life back home in the village often seemed dull and unappealing, and many men drifted to towns in search of work—with the railroad companies, in construction, in factories. By the time they sent for their wives and sweethearts to join them, they had become urban workers.

The railroad changed the outlook and values of the entire society. The last and culminating invention of the Industrial Revolution, the railroad dramatically revealed the power and increased the speed of the new age. Racing down a track at sixteen miles per hour or, by 1850, at a phenomenal fifty miles per hour was a new and awesome experience. As a noted French economist put it after a ride on the Liverpool and Manchester in 1833, "There are certain impressions that one cannot put into words!"

Some great painters, notably J. M. W. Turner (1775–1851) and Claude Monet (1840–1926), succeeded in expressing this sense of power and awe. So did the massive new train stations, the cathedrals of the industrial age. Leading railway engineers like Isambard Kingdom Brunel and Thomas Brassey, whose tunnels pierced mountains and whose bridges spanned valleys, became public idols—the astronauts of their day. Everyday speech absorbed the images of railroading. After you got up a "full head of steam," you "highballed" along. And if you didn't "go off the track," you might "toot your own whistle." The railroad fired the imagination.

BRITAIN AT MIDCENTURY

In 1851 London was the site of a famous industrial fair. This exposition was held in the newly built Crystal Palace, an architectural masterpiece made entirely of glass and iron, both of which were now cheap and abundant. For the hundreds of thousands who visited, one fact stood out. The little island of Britain—England, Wales, and Scotland—was the "workshop of the world." It alone produced two-thirds of the world's coal and more than half of its iron and cotton cloth. Britain was the first industrial nation (see Map 22.2).

Britain had unlocked and developed a new source of energy. With practically unlimited power, the British economy had significantly increased its production of manufactured goods. Between 1780 and 1800, Britain doubled its production of industrial goods. Between 1801 and 1851, the gross national product (GNP) rose three and a half times at constant prices. In other words, the British increased their wealth and their national income dramatically. At the same time, the population of Great Britain boomed, growing from about 9 million in 1780 to almost 21 million in 1851.

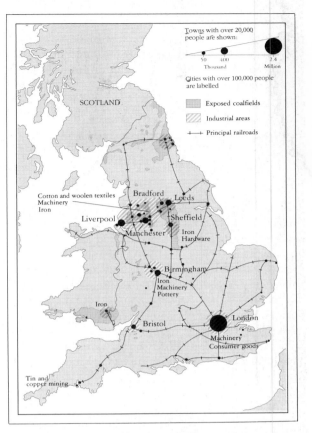

MAP 22.2 The Industrial Revolution in England, ca 1850 Industry concentrated in the rapidly growing cities of the north and the midlands, where rich coal and iron deposits were in close proximity.

Since the economy grew much faster than the number of people, average real income per person increased markedly. (*Real income* is the actual monetary value of people's wages after adjusting for the effects of inflation or deflation.) In fact, average real income per person in Britain just about *doubled* between 1801 and 1851, from £13 per person to £24 per person. Put very simply, and all other things being equal, the woman or man of 1851 could buy twice as much as the woman or man of 1801. Considering the poverty of the eighteenth century, poverty that all the drama and excitement of the French Revolution did little or nothing to reduce, this would appear to be a monumental achievement.

But perhaps all other things were not equal. Perhaps workers, farmers, and ordinary people did not share in the new wealth. Perhaps only the rich got richer, while the poor got poorer or made no progress. We will turn to this great issue after looking at the spread of the Industrial Revolution from Britain to the Continent.

THE SPREAD OF THE INDUSTRIAL REVOLUTION

The new methods of the Industrial Revolution spread slowly at first. Whereas Britain's economy began to speed up about 1780 and had created an industrial urban society by 1850, the economies of continental Europe began to follow only after 1815 and particularly after about 1830. First Belgium took up the challenge; then between about 1840 and 1860, France and the various states of Germany began developing rapidly, as did the United States. After 1870, Sweden, Russia, and Japan started to industrialize, and during the twentieth century many more countries did so.

THE CHALLENGE OF INDUSTRIALIZATION

If poverty was so widespread in Europe and if industrial development created so much more wealth per person in Great Britain, why did continental countries wait years and even decades before they followed the British example? The eighteenth century was certainly an era of agricultural improvement, population increase, expanding foreign trade, and growing cottage industry. England led in these developments, but other countries participated in the general trend. Thus, when the pace of English industry began to accelerate in the 1780s, countries like France began to copy the new methods. English industry enjoyed clear superiority, but the Continent was not very far behind.

By 1815, however, the situation was quite different. In spite of wartime difficulties, English industry maintained the momentum of the 1780s and continued to grow and improve rapidly between 1789 and 1815. On the Continent, the unending political and economic upheavals that began with the French Revolution had another effect. They disrupted trade, created runaway inflation, and fostered social anxiety.

War severed normal communications between England and the Continent, severely handicapping continental efforts to use new British machinery and technology. Moreover, the years from 1789 to 1815 were, even for the privileged French economy, a time of "national catastrophe"—in the graphic words of a recent French scholar.[1] Thus, whatever the French Revolution and the Napoleonic era meant politically, economically and industrially they meant that France and the rest of Europe were much further behind Britain in 1815 than in 1789.

This widening gap made it more difficult for other countries to follow the British example in energy and industry after 1815. British goods were being produced very economically, and they had come to dominate world markets completely while the continental states were absorbed in war between 1792 and 1815. In addition, British technology had become so advanced and complicated that very few engineers or skilled technicians outside England understood it. Moreover, the technology of steam power had grown much more expensive. It involved large investments in the iron and coal industries and, after 1830, required the existence of railroads, which were very costly. Continental businessmen had great difficulty finding the large sums of money the new methods demanded, and there was a shortage of laborers accustomed to working in factories. Landowners and government officials were often so suspicious of the new form of industry and the changes it brought that they did little at first to encourage it. All these disadvantages slowed the spread of modern industry (see Map 22.3).

After 1815, however, when continental countries began to industrialize seriously, they had at least two important advantages. First, they did not need to develop, ever so slowly and expensively, their own advanced technology. Instead, they could simply "borrow" the new methods developed in Great Britain, as well as engineers and some of the financial resources they lacked. European countries like France and Russia had a second asset that many non-Western areas lacked in the nineteenth century. They had strong independent governments, which did not fall under foreign political control. These governments could fashion economic policies to serve their own interests, as they proceeded to do. They would eventually use the power of the state to promote the growth of industry.

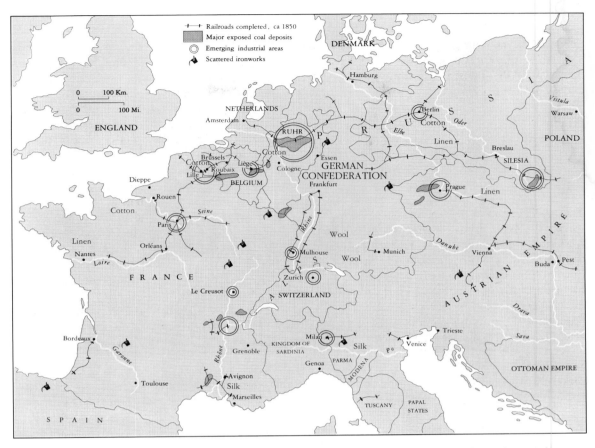

MAP 22.3 Continental Industrialization, ca 1850 Though continental countries were beginning to make progress by 1850, they still lagged far behind England. For example, continental railroad building was still in an early stage, whereas the English rail system was essentially complete.

AGENTS OF INDUSTRIALIZATION

To understand better the spread of modern industry, one should look at the fascinating careers of a few of the businessmen, workers, and apostles of industrialization who were involved. For economic life is as much the product of particular human efforts as of vast impersonal forces.

The British realized the great value of their technical discoveries and tried to keep their secrets to themselves. Until 1825 it was illegal for artisans and skilled mechanics to leave Britain; until 1843 the export of textile machinery and other equipment was forbidden. Many talented, ambitious workers, however, slipped out of the country illegally and introduced the new methods abroad.

One such man was William Cockerill, a Lancashire carpenter. He and his sons began building cotton-spinning equipment in French-occupied Belgium in 1799. In 1817 the most famous son, John Cockerill, purchased the old summer palace of the deposed bishops of Liège at Seraing, around five miles from Liège in southern Belgium. Cockerill converted the palace into a large industrial enterprise, which produced machinery, steam engines, and then railway locomotives. He also established modern ironworks and coal mines at Liège, as well as other operations throughout western Europe.

Cockerill's plants at Liège and Seraing became an industrial nerve center, continually gathering new information and transmitting it across Europe. Many skilled British workmen came, illegally, to work for

Cockerill's Works light up the night and display the awesome power of the new industrial technology in this lithograph of 1852. *(The British Museum)*

Cockerill, and some went on to found their own companies throughout Europe. Newcomers brought the latest plans and secrets, so that Cockerill could boast that, ten days after an industrial advance occurred in Britain, he knew all about it in Belgium. Thus, British technicians and skilled workers were a powerful force in the spread of early industrialization.

Another instructive career is that of Fritz Harkort, a pioneer in the German machinery industry. Harkort came from an old commercial family in Westphalia. He studied engineering developments in England while serving there as a Prussian army officer during the Napoleonic wars. Impressed and enchanted with what he saw, Harkort concluded that Germany had to match all these English achievements as quickly as possible. Setting up shop in an abandoned castle in the still-tranquil Ruhr valley, Harkort felt an almost religious calling to build steam engines and become the "Watt of Germany."

Harkort's basic idea was simple, but it was enormously difficult to carry out. Steam engines had been greatly improved in the course of thirty years, and the new models Harkort was trying to copy required much accuracy and know-how. Lacking skilled laborers to do the job, Harkort turned to England for experienced, though expensive, mechanics. He could not be choosy. As he later reminisced, "I had to cut several of my English workers down from the gallows, so to speak, if only in order to get some of them."[2] Harkort longed for the day he could afford to replace the haughty foreigners with his fellow countrymen.

Getting materials posed a great problem as well. German ironsmiths could not supply the thick iron boilers Harkort needed, and he had to import them from England at great cost and with frequent damage. There was a modest market for Harkort's engines, for the German coal industry was beginning to expand. But German roads were so bad—Harkort denounced them as deathtraps for man and beast—that steam engines had to be built at the works, completely dismantled and shipped piece by piece to the buyer, and then reassembled by Harkort's technicians. No wonder Harkort was a very early promoter

Heavy Industry required skilled workers and large capital investments. In this illustration English dignitaries visit a plant with a new technology for making steel wheels. *(The Bettmann Archive)*

of railroads, which, he predicted in 1829, "will bring countless revolutions to the world."

In spite of all these problems, Harkort built engines, sold them throughout Germany and the rest of Europe, and won fame and praise. His ambitious efforts also resulted in large financial losses for himself and his partners. These proved fatal, for Harkort's enterprise, like almost all the others of the day, was a private, capitalistic undertaking. It could not lose money indefinitely. In 1832, after sixteen years of activity and accomplishment, Harkort was forced out of his company by his financial backers, who cut back operations to reduce losses. In one sense, then, his career was a failure; yet Harkort was a pioneering visionary, the most creative German businessman of his era. His career illustrates both the great efforts of a few important business leaders to duplicate the British achievement and the extreme difficulty of the task.

Support from the government often helped businessmen in continental countries to overcome some of their difficulties. Tariff protection was one such support. For example, after Napoleon's wars ended in 1815, France was suddenly flooded with cheaper and better English goods. The French government responded by laying high tariffs on many English imports, in order to protect the French economy. After 1815 continental governments bore the cost of building roads and canals to improve transportation, and they also bore to a significant extent the cost of building railroads.

The career of the German journalist and thinker Friedrich List (1789–1846) reflects government's greater role in the Industrial Revolution on the Continent than in England. List considered the growth of modern industry of the utmost importance because manufacturing was a primary means of increasing people's well-being and relieving their poverty. Moreover, List was a dedicated nationalist. He wrote that the "wider the gap between the backward and advanced nations becomes, the more dangerous it is to remain behind." For an agricultural nation was not only poor but weak, increasingly unable to defend itself and maintain its political independence. To promote industry was to defend the nation.

The practical policy List focused on in articles and in his *National System of Political Economy* (1841) was the tariff. He supported the formation of a customs union, or *Zollverein,* among the separate German states. Such a tariff union came into being in 1834. It allowed goods to move between the German member states without tariffs, and a single uniform tariff was erected against all other nations. List wanted a high protective tariff, which would encourage infant industries, allowing them to develop and eventually to hold their own against their more advanced British counterparts. List denounced the English doctrine of free trade as little more than England's attempt "to make the rest of the world, like the Hindus, its serfs in all industrial and commercial relations." By the 1840s List's ideas were increasingly popular in Germany and elsewhere.

Banks, like governments, also played a larger and more creative role on the Continent than in England. Previously, almost all banks in Europe had been private, organized as secretive partnerships. Such banks were content to deal with a few rich clients and a few big merchants. They avoided industry. In the 1830s, two important Belgian banks pioneered in a new direction. They operated as big corporations with many stockholders, large and small. Thus their financial resources were large. The banks were able to use that money to develop industrial companies. They became, in short, industrial banks.

Similar banks became important in France and Germany in the 1850s. They established and developed many railroads and many companies working in heavy industry. The most famous such bank was the Crédit Mobilier of Paris, founded by Isaac and Emile Pereire, two young Jewish journalists from Bordeaux. The Crédit Mobilier advertised extensively. It used the savings of thousands of small investors, as well as the resources of big ones. The activities of the bank were far-reaching; it built railroads all over France and Europe. As Emile Pereire had said in 1835, "It is not enough to outline gigantic programs on paper. I must write my ideas on the earth."

Industrial banks like the Crédit Mobilier mobilized the savings of thousands of small investors and invested those savings in industry and transportation, particularly in the 1850s. In doing so, the directors of these banks helped their countries find the capital needed for industrialization. They also often made themselves very wealthy.

CAPITAL AND LABOR

Industrial development brought new social relations and problems between capital and labor. A new group of factory owners and industrial capitalists arose. These men strengthened the wealth and size of the middle class, which had previously been made up mainly of merchants and professional people. The nineteenth century became the golden age of the middle class. Modern industry also created a much larger group—the factory workers. For the first time, large numbers of men and women came together under one roof to work with complicated machinery for major capitalists and large companies. What was the nature of relations between these two new groups —capital and labor? Did the new industrial middle class ruthlessly exploit the workers, as Karl Marx and others have charged?

The New Class of Factory Owners

Early industrialists operated in a highly competitive economic system. As the careers of Watt and Harkort illustrate, there were countless production problems, and success and large profits were by no means certain. Manufacturers, therefore, waged a constant battle to cut their production costs and stay afloat. Most profit had to go back into the business for new and better machinery. "Dragged on by the frenzy of this terrible life," according to one of his dismayed critics, the struggling manufacturer had "no time for niceties. He must conquer or die, make a fortune or drown himself."[3]

The early industrialists came from a variety of backgrounds. Many, like Harkort, were from well-established merchant families, who provided capital and contacts. Others, like Watt and Cockerill, were of modest means, especially in the early days. Artisans and skilled workmen of exceptional ability had unparalleled opportunities. The ethnic and religious groups that had been discriminated against in the traditional occupations controlled by the landed aristocracy jumped at the new chances. Quakers and Scots were tremendously important in England; Protestants and Jews dominated banking in Catholic France. Many of the industrialists were newly rich, and, not surprisingly, they were very proud and self-satisfied.

Cotton Mill Workers Family members often worked side by side in industry. Here women and children are combing raw cotton and drawing it into loose strands called rovings, which will then be spun into fine thread. *(The Mansell Collection)*

As factories grew larger, opportunities declined, at least in well-developed industries. It became considerably harder for a gifted but poor young mechanic to end up as a wealthy manufacturer. Formal education became more important as a means of advancement, and formal education at the advanced level was expensive. In England by 1830 and in France and Germany by 1860, leading industrialists were more likely to have inherited their well-established enterprises, and they were financially much more secure than their fathers and grandfathers. They were also aware of a greater gap between themselves and their workers.

THE NEW FACTORY WORKERS

The social consequences of the Industrial Revolution have long been hotly debated. Since any honest observer will see that some conditions got better and

others got worse, vigorous debate is likely to continue. (Also, industry promoted rapid urbanization with its own great problems, as will be shown in Chapter 24.) Nevertheless, for workers and ordinary families, the Industrial Revolution brought a great transformation, which was, on balance, desirable. It marked a great step forward from the pattern of preindustrial life for the common people and the poor.

The condition of English workers in the Industrial Revolution has always generated the most controversy among historians, because England was the first country to industrialize and because the social consequences seem harshest there. Before 1850, other countries had not proceeded very far with industrialization, and almost everyone agrees that the economic conditions of European workers improved after 1850. The countries that followed England were able to benefit from English experience in social as well as technical matters. Thus the early English Industrial Revolution provides the strongest case for the harmful social consequences of modern industrial development, at least prior to 1914, and it is fitting to focus on it.

From the beginning, the Industrial Revolution in England had its critics. Among the first were the romantic poets. William Blake (1757–1827) called the early factories "satanic mills" and protested against the hard life of the London poor. William Wordsworth (1770–1850) lamented the destruction of the rural way of life and the pollution of the land and water. Doctors and reformers wrote eloquently of problems in the factories and new towns. Some handicraft workers—notably the Luddites, who attacked whole factories in northern England in 1812 and after—smashed the new machines, which they believed were putting them out of work.

Another early critic was Friedrich Engels (1820–1895), the future revolutionary and colleague of Karl Marx. After studying conditions in northern England, this young middle-class German published *The Condition of the Working Class in England* in 1844. Engels cast the problem of industrial life in class terms. "At the bar of world opinion," he wrote, "I charge the English middle classes with mass murder, wholesale robbery, and all the other crimes in the calendar."[4] Engels's charge of middle-class exploitation and increasing worker poverty was embellished by Marx and later socialists. It was extremely influential.

Meanwhile, other observers believed that conditions were improving for the working class. Andrew Ure wrote in 1835 in his study of the cotton industry that conditions in most factories were not harsh and were even quite good. Edwin Chadwick, a great and conscientious government official, well acquainted with the problems of the working class, concluded that the "whole mass of the laboring community" was increasingly able "to buy more of the necessities and minor luxuries of life."[5]

If all the contemporary indictments of observers like Engels and all the defenses of those like Ure were counted up, those who thought conditions were getting worse for working people would probably be the majority. Yet it is clear that opinions differed greatly. In an attempt to go deeper into the problem, historians must look at different kinds of sources.

Statistical evidence is one such source. It should help resolve the conflicting opinions of contemporary and often biased observers. If working people

suffered a great decline, as Engels and later socialists asserted, then they must have bought less and less food, clothing, and other necessities as time went on. The purchasing power of the working person's wages must have declined drastically.

At the end of the nineteenth century, dispassionate British statisticians tried to pull together all the evidence on wages and prices and thereby measure what working-class people could or could not have bought. Such an approach was only partially successful. England was not in a prestatistical age during its Industrial Revolution, but there were many gaps and shortcomings in the available numbers. Nevertheless, this approach does offer important insights.

During the period from about 1750 to 1790, when cottage industry was still dominant, the purchasing power of the average British laborer's wages seems to have risen somewhat. The workers—primarily cottage workers, artisans, and farm hands—could buy more goods, like food and clothing, over the years. Wages in industry were substantially higher than in agriculture, and all kinds of wages rose faster in the industrializing areas of the north than in the purely agricultural counties of the south. The cautious conclusion must be that from 1750 to 1790 the growth of industry made for a more abundant life for working people, in terms of material goods.

The years from 1792 to 1815, a period of constant war against revolutionary and Napoleonic France, brought very different circumstances. Wages rose, but they did not keep up with inflation. Food prices rose most, as the price of wheat approximately doubled from 1790 to 1810. The condition of the working poor declined.

Between 1815 and 1850, the purchasing power of workers' wages increased again. Money wages remained steady or fell somewhat, but prices fell more. The fullest studies show that the real wages of the average worker—agricultural and industrial—increased 25 percent between 1800 and 1825 and another 40 percent between 1825 and 1850.[6] The trend was definitely upward, but the course was erratic. Between 1820 and 1840, real wages increased by only 5 to 10 percent. However, the wages of unskilled workers in British industry were again, as before 1790, about twice as high as those of unskilled workers in British agriculture. In short, throughout the Industrial Revolution, with the exception of the wartime period, there was apparently substantial economic improvement for British workers.

This important conclusion must be qualified, though. Increased purchasing power meant more goods, but it did not necessarily mean greater happiness. Also, these figures do not say anything about how the level of unemployment may have risen, for the simple reason that there are no good unemployment statistics from this period. Furthermore, the hours in the average workweek increased; to an unknown extent, workers earned more simply because they worked more. Finally, the wartime decline was of great importance. The war years were formative years for the new factory labor force. They were also some of the hardest yet experienced. They colored the early experience of modern industrial life in somber tones.

Another way to consider workers' standard of living is to look at the goods they purchased. Again the evidence is somewhat contradictory. Speaking generally, workers ate somewhat more food of higher nutritional quality as the Industrial Revolution progressed, except during wartime. Diets became more varied; people ate more potatoes, dairy products, fruits, and vegetables.

Clothing improved, but housing for working people did not. In short, per capita use of specific goods supports the position that the standard of living of the working classes rose, at least moderately, during the Industrial Revolution. The rich did get richer. So did the poor to some extent, especially if they worked in industry.

Conditions of Work

What about working conditions? Did workers earn more only at the cost of working longer and harder? Were workers exploited harshly by the new factory owners?

The first factories were cotton mills, which began functioning along rivers and streams in the 1770s. Cottage workers, accustomed to the putting-out system, were reluctant to work in factories even when they received relatively good wages, because factory work was different from what they were used to and unappealing. In the factory, workers had to keep up with the machine and follow its tempo. They had to show up every day and work long, monotonous hours. Factory workers had to adjust their daily lives to the shrill call of the factory whistle.

Cottage workers were not used to that kind of life

and discipline. All members of the family worked hard and long, but in spurts, setting their own pace. They could interrupt their work when they wanted to. Women and children could break up their long hours of spinning with other tasks. On Saturday afternoon the head of the family delivered the week's work to the merchant-manufacturer and got paid. Saturday night was a time of relaxation and drinking, especially for the men. Recovering from his hangover on Tuesday, the weaver bent to his task on Wednesday and then worked frantically to meet his deadline on Saturday. Like some students today, he might "pull an all-nighter" on Thursday or Friday in order to get his work in.

Also, early factories resembled English poorhouses, where totally destitute people went to live on welfare. Some poorhouses were industrial prisons, where the inmates had to work in order to receive their food and lodging. The similarity between large brick factories and large stone poorhouses increased the cottage workers' fear of factories and their hatred of factory discipline.

It was cottage workers' reluctance to work in factories that prompted the early cottonmill owners to turn to abandoned and pauper children for their labor. As we have seen, they contracted with local officials to employ large numbers of these children, who had no say in the matter. Pauper children were often badly treated and terribly overworked in the mills, as they were when they were apprenticed as chimney sweeps, market girls, shoemakers, and so forth. In the eighteenth century, semiforced child labor seemed necessary and was socially accepted. From our modern point of view, it was cruel exploitation and a blot on the record of the new industrial system.

By 1790 the early pattern was rapidly changing. The use of pauper apprentices was in decline, and in 1802 it was forbidden by Parliament. Many more factories were being built, mainly in urban areas, where they could use steam rather than water power and attract a work force more easily than in the countryside. The need for workers was great. Indeed, people came from near and far to work in the cities, both as factory workers and as laborers, builders, and domestic servants. Yet, as they took these new jobs, working people did not simply give in to a system of labor that had formerly repelled them. Rather, they helped modify the system by carrying over old, familiar working traditions.

Cotton Mill near Manchester The simple rural scene in the foreground of this 1834 engraving contrasts vividly with the massive brick factory building dominating the landscape. *(BBC Hulton/The Bettmann Archive)*

For one thing, they came to the mills and the mines as family units. This was how they had worked on farms and in the putting-out system. The mill or mine owner bargained with the head of the family and paid him or her for the work of the whole family. In the cotton mills, children worked for their mothers or fathers, collecting wastes and "piecing" broken threads together. In the mines, children sorted coal and worked the ventilation equipment. Their mothers hauled coal in the narrow tunnels below the surface, while their fathers hewed with pick and shovel at the face of the seam.

The preservation of the family as an economic unit in the factories from the 1790s on made the new surroundings more tolerable, both in Great Britain and in other countries during the early stages of industrialization. Parents disciplined their children, making firm measures socially acceptable, and directed their upbringing. The presence of the whole family meant that children and adults worked the same long hours

(twelve-hour shifts were normal in cotton mills in 1800). In the early years, some very young children were employed solely to keep the family together. Jedediah Strutt, for example, believed children should be at least ten years old to work in his mills, but he reluctantly employed seven-year-olds to satisfy their parents. Adult workers were not particularly interested in limiting the minimum working age or hours of their children, as long as they worked side by side. Only when technical changes threatened to place control and discipline in the hands of impersonal managers and foremen did they protest against inhuman conditions in the name of their children.

But some enlightened employers and social reformers in Parliament definitely felt otherwise. "In an age of rising standards of humanitarianism the few were determined to impose higher standards on the many; and were able to exploit developing means of mass communication to do it."[7] These reformers had important successes.

Girl Dragging Coal Tubs Published by reformers in Parliament in 1842, this picture shocked public opinion and contributed to the Mines Act of 1842. *(The British Library)*

Their first major accomplishment was the Factory Act of 1833. It limited the workday for children between nine and thirteen to eight hours and that of adolescents between fourteen to eighteen to twelve hours. The law also prohibited the employment of children under nine; they were to be enrolled in the elementary schools factory owners were required to establish. Since efficiency required standardized shifts for all workers, the Factory Act shattered the pattern of whole families working together in the factory. The employment of children declined rapidly. Similarly, the Mines Act of 1842 prohibited all women and boys under ten from working underground.

Ties of blood and kinship remained important in other ways in England in the formative years between about 1790 and 1840. Many manufacturers and builders hired workers not directly but through subcontractors. They paid the subcontractors on the basis of what the subcontractors and their crews produced—for smelting so many tons of pig iron or moving so much dirt or gravel for a canal or roadbed. Subcontractors in turn hired and fired their own workers, many of whom were friends and relations.

The subcontractor might be as harsh as the greediest capitalist, but the relationship between subcontractor and work crew was close and personal. This kind of traditional relationship was more acceptable to workers than impersonal factory discipline. This system also provided people an easy way to find a job. Even today, a friend or relative who is a foreman is frequently worth a hundred formal application forms.

Ties of kinship were particularly important for newcomers, who often traveled considerable distances to find work. Many urban workers in Great Britain were from Ireland. Forced out of rural Ireland by population growth and deteriorating economic conditions from 1817 on, Irish in search of jobs could not be choosy; they took what they could get. As early as 1824, most of the workers in the Glasgow cotton mills were Irish; in 1851 one-sixth of the population of the great port of Liverpool was Irish. Even when Irish workers were not related directly by blood, they were held together by ethnic and religious ties. Like other immigrant groups elsewhere, they worked together, formed their own neighborhoods, and not only survived but thrived.

A MATURE WORKING CLASS

By about 1850, the working people of urban Britain had, like British industry, gone a long way toward attaining maturity. Family employment in the factory had given way to the employment of adults, for whom the discipline of the clock and the regularity of the machine were familiar taskmasters. Gone were violent demonstrations against industrialization. In their place were increasing acceptance of the emerging industrial system and an ongoing effort to make that system serve workers better.

In Great Britain and in other countries later on, workers slowly created a labor movement to serve their needs. In 1799, partly in panicked reaction to the French Revolution, Parliament had passed the Combination Acts outlawing unions and strikes. These acts were widely disregarded by workers. Societies of skilled factory workers organized unions, as printers, papermakers, carpenters, and other such craftsmen had long since done. The unions sought to control the number of skilled workers, limit apprenticeship to members' own children, and bargain with owners over wages. They were not afraid to strike; there was, for example, a general strike of adult cotton spinners in Manchester in 1810. In the face of widespread union activity, Parliament repealed the Combination Acts in 1824, and unions were tolerated though not fully accepted after 1825.

The next stage in the development of the British trade-union movement was the attempt to create a single large national union. This effort was led not so much by working people as by social reformers like Robert Owen (1771–1858). Owen, a self-made cotton manufacturer, had pioneered in industrial relations by combining firm discipline with concern for the health, safety, and hours of his workers. After 1815 he experimented with cooperative and socialist communities, including one at New Harmony, Indiana. Then, in 1834, Owen organized one of the largest and most visionary of the early national unions, the Grand National Consolidated Trades Union. When this and other grandiose schemes collapsed, the British labor movement moved once again after 1851 in the direction of bread-and-butter craft unions. The most famous of these "new model" unions was the Amalgamated Society of Engineers. These craft unions won real benefits for their members by fairly conservative means and thus became an accepted part of the industrial scene.

The maturity of British workers was also expressed in direct political activity in defense of their own interests. After the collapse of Owen's national trade union, a great deal of the energy of working people went into the Chartist movement, whose goal was political democracy. The key Chartist demand—that all men be given the right to vote—became the great hope of millions of aroused people. Workers were also active in campaigns to limit the workday in the factories to ten hours and to permit duty-free importation of wheat into Great Britain to secure cheap bread. Thus working people played an active role in shaping the new industrial system. Clearly, they were neither helpless victims nor passive beneficiaries.

THE ALTERNATIVE TO INDUSTRIALIZATION

What was the alternative to the Industrial Revolution and the new urban society? What would have been the likely course of events—the likely alternative for Europe—if industrialization had not occurred? It is impossible to know exactly, yet a look at general developments and at the case of Ireland, which did not industrialize, may shed some light on this question.

THE GROWTH OF POPULATION

The drama of industrialization must be viewed alongside the drama of rapid population growth. Europe's population began growing after 1720 (pages 618–620), leading to severe pressures on available resources and overpopulation in many areas. Large numbers of people had serious difficulty growing or buying the food they needed. There was widespread underemployment, acute poverty, and constant migration in search of work.

All these forces operated during and after the era of the French Revolution. Europe had roughly 140 million people in 1750, 188 million in 1800, and 266 million in 1850—an increase of almost 40 percent in each half-century. Overpopulation worsened between 1800 and 1850 on much of the Continent, most noticeably in Flanders, parts of Scandinavia, and southwestern Germany. One result was migration from the countryside to nearby cities and towns, where unskilled laborers were already irregularly em-

"Be United and Industrious" This handsome membership certificate of the "new model" Amalgamated Society of Engineers exalts the nobility of skilled labor and the labor movement. Union members are shown rejecting the call of Mars, the God of War, and accepting well-deserved honors from the Goddess of Peace. Other figures represent the strength of union solidarity, famous English inventors, and the trades of the members. *(Bridgeman Art Library)*

Evicting Irish Peasants, 1848 Unable to pay their rent, famine-stricken peasants are ordered from their home, which is already being torn down. Soldiers with fixed bayonets stand ready to quell any disturbance. *(Illustrated London News/Library of Congress)*

ployed and poorly paid. Another result was that growing numbers of peasants liquidated their small and inadequate landholdings and went abroad. Thus, in the early nineteenth century, particularly in the hungry 1840s, many German and Swedish settlers tried their luck and skill on prairie lands of the American Midwest.

The pressure of increasing numbers and rural poverty was most severe in Ireland. Although Ireland supplied many workers for factories in Britain, Ireland itself did not industrialize in the nineteenth century. Therefore, although Ireland was a particularly oppressed and exploited nation, its fate could have been that of much of Europe if not for the Industrial Revolution.

THE POTATO FAMINE IN IRELAND

Late eighteenth-century Ireland was a conquered country. The great mass of the population (outside the northern counties of Ulster, which were partly Presbyterian) were Irish Catholic peasants, who rented their land from a tiny minority of Church of England Protestants, many of whom lived in England (page 650). These Protestant landlords lacked the improving zeal of their English counterparts. They knew they were perched on top of a volcano that erupted periodically, but they were quite content to use their powers to grab as much as possible, as quickly as possible.

The result was that the condition of the Irish peasantry around 1800 was abominable. The typical peasant family lived in a wretched cottage made of mud and could afford neither shoes nor stockings. Hundreds of shocking accounts describe hopeless poverty. Sir Walter Scott wrote:

The poverty of the Irish peasantry is on the extreme verge of human misery; their cottages would scarce serve for pig styes even in Scotland; and their rags seem the very refuse of a sheep, and are spread over their bodies with such an ingenious variety of wretchedness that you would think nothing but some sort of perverted taste could have assembled so many shreds together.

For a French traveler, Ireland was "pure misery, naked and hungry. . . . I saw the American Indian in his forests and the black slave in his chains, and I believed that I was seeing in their pitiful condition the most extreme form of human misery; but that was before I knew the lot of poor Ireland."[8] Yet in spite of these terrible conditions, population growth sped onward. The 3 million of 1725 reached 4 million in 1780 and doubled to 8 million in 1840. Between 1780 and 1840, 1.75 million men and women left Ireland for Britain and America.

The population of Ireland grew so quickly for three reasons: extensive cultivation of the potato, early marriage, and ruthless exploitation of peasants by landlords. The potato, first introduced into Ireland in the late sixteenth century, was the principal food of the Irish peasantry by the last years of the eighteenth century. The reason for dependence on the potato was originally the pressure of numbers, which forced the peasants to wring as many calories as they could out of a given piece of land. But once peasants began to live almost exclusively on potatoes, many more people could exist. A single acre of land spaded and planted with potatoes could feed a family of six for a year, whereas it would take at least two and probably four acres of grain and pasture to feed the same number. Moreover, the potato was not choosy and could thrive on boggy wastelands.

Needing only a potato patch of an acre or two for survival, Irish boys and girls married much earlier than did their counterparts in rural England and France by the end of the eighteenth century. Setting up housekeeping was easy, for a cabin of mud and stone could be slapped together in a few days with the willing assistance of the young couple's neighbors and relatives. A mat for a bed, a chair or two, a table, and an iron pot to boil potatoes were easily acquired. To be sure, the young couple was accepting the life of extreme poverty that travelers and people of good conscience lamented. They would literally live on potatoes—ten pounds a day every day all year long for the average male—moistened with a cup of milk if they were lucky.

Nonetheless, the decision to marry early and have large families was quite reasonable, given Irish conditions. The landlords, not the peasants, owned and controlled the land. Because land was leased only for short periods on uncertain terms, peasants had no in-

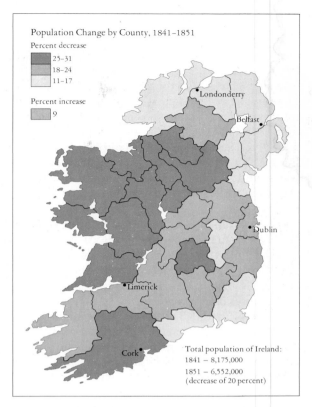

MAP 22.4 **The Irish Potato Famine** Though all Ireland suffered, population losses were highest in the west where dependency on the potato was greatest.

centive to make permanent improvements. Any increase in profits went to the landlord, and anything beyond what preserved the peasants from absolute starvation was extorted from them. Poverty thus being inescapable in rural Ireland, it was better shared with a wife or husband. Children were a precious asset, as in many poor countries today, for there was no welfare or social security system, and an infirm or aged person's best hope of escaping starvation was a dutiful son or a loving daughter.

As the population continued to grow, conditions became increasingly precarious. The peasantry depended on a single crop, the size of which varied substantially from year to year. Potato failures cannot be detected in time to plant other crops, nor can potatoes be stored for more than a year. Furthermore, a potato economy is a subsistence economy. It lacks a well-developed network of roads and trade capable of distributing other foods in time of disaster. From

1820 on, deficiencies in the potato crop became increasingly serious. Disease in the potato crop was becoming more common, and the accompanying fever epidemics that struck the population were growing more frequent. Some great catastrophe in the near future was almost completely inevitable.

In 1845 and 1846 and again in 1848 and 1851, the potato crop failed in Ireland and throughout much of Europe. The general result was high food prices, widespread suffering, and social unrest. In Ireland, which was furthest down the road to rural overpopulation and dependence on a disease-prone plant, the result was unmitigated disaster—the Great Famine. Blight attacked the young plants, the leaves withered, and the tubers rotted. Widespread starvation and mass fever epidemics followed. Cannibalism occurred, although starving people generally lived on the carcasses of diseased cattle, dogs, and horses and on herbs of the field. In some places, dead people were found with grass in their mouths.

Total losses were staggering. The population of Ireland was roughly 8 million in 1845, and without the famine it would have reached 9 million in 1851 (see Map 22.4). But that year, Ireland's population was only 6.5 million. Fully 1 million emigrants fled the famine between 1845 and 1851 (2 million left between 1840 and 1855), going primarily to the United States and Great Britain. Thus at least 1.5 million people died or went unborn because of the disaster. The British government's efforts at famine relief were too little and too late. Moreover, the government continued to collect its taxes, and the landlords continued to demand their rents. Tenants who could not pay were evicted and their homes broken up or burned. Famine or no, Ireland was still the conquered jewel of foreign landowners.

The Great Famine shattered and reversed the pattern of Irish population growth. Alone among the nations of Europe, Ireland's numbers declined in the nineteenth century, to 4.4 million in 1911. Ireland remained a land of continuous out-migration. It also became a land of late marriage and widespread celibacy, as the landowning classes discouraged potato farming and converted much of the country into pasture for cattle and sheep. After great population decline and untold suffering, Ireland found a new demographic equilibrium within the framework of a poor pastoral economy.

The fate of Ireland has real relevance for an understanding of the Industrial Revolution. The rapid population growth without industrialization that occurred in Ireland between 1780 and 1845 occurred elsewhere, too—in central Russia, in western Germany, and in southern Italy, to name only three crucial regions. In these areas, there were indications of acute poverty and overpopulation, and the potato played a crucial role as it had done in Ireland. In Prussia, for example, annual potato production grew from 1 to 11 million tons from 1815 to 1860. By 1850 in some parts of Europe, bread was a luxury; workers and peasants were subsisting almost entirely on potatoes. In 1500 the average German had eaten about 200 pounds of meat a year; in 1850 his counterpart ate about 40 pounds.[9] The standard of living was declining. Other Irelands were in the making.

Population growth threatened to produce a morass of rural poverty, a demographic catastrophe, or both. In this connection, the historian T. S. Ashton once argued that the Industrial Revolution was the salvation rather than the curse of England and of the parts of Europe fortunate enough to follow England's lead. He may have overstated the case, but Ashton was surely closer to the truth than those who persist in arguing the contrary. The alternative to the revolution in energy and industry would probably have been, sooner or later, disaster.

NOTES

1. M. Lévy-Leboyer, *Les banques européennes et l'industrialisation dans la première moitié du XIXe siècle,* Presses Universitaires de France, Paris, 1964, p. 29.

2. Quoted by D. S. Landes, *The Unbound Prometheus: Technological Change and Industrial Development in Western Europe from 1750 to the Present,* Cambridge University Press, Cambridge, Eng., 1969, p. 150.

3. J. Michelet, *The People,* University of Illinois Press, Urbana, 1973 (originally published, 1846), p. 64.

4. F. Engels, *The Condition of the Working Class in England,* trans. and ed. W. O. Henderson and W. H. Chaloner, Stanford University Press, Stanford, Calif., 1968, p. xxiii.

5. Quoted in W. A. Hayek, ed., *Capitalism and the Historians,* University of Chicago Press, Chicago, 1954, p. 126.

6. P. Deane and W. A. Cole, *British Economic Growth, 1688–1959,* Cambridge University Press, Cambridge, Eng., 1964, p. 25.

7. P. Mathias, *The First Industrial Nation: An Economic History of Britain, 1700–1914,* Charles Scribner's Sons, New York, 1969, p. 205.

8. Quoted by G. O'Brien, *The Economic History of Ireland from the Union to the Famine,* Longmans, Green, London, 1921, pp. 21–24.

9. W. L. Langer, *Political and Social Upheaval, 1832–1852,* Harper & Row, New York, 1969, p. 188.

SUGGESTED READING

There is a vast and exciting literature on the Industrial Revolution. D. S. Landes's *The Unbound Prometheus* (1969), cited in the Notes, and S. Pollard, *Peaceful Conquest: The Industrialization of Europe* (1981), are the best general treatments of European industrial growth since 1750. P. Mathias, *The First Industrial Nation: An Economic History of Britain, 1700–1914* (1969); P. Deane, *The First Industrial Revolution* (1966); and P. Mantoux, *The Industrial Revolution in the Eighteenth Century* (1961), admirably discuss the various aspects of the English breakthrough and offer good bibliographies. (See also the Suggested Reading for Chapter 23.) W. Rostow, *The Stages of Economic Growth: A Non-Communist Manifesto* (1960), is a popular, provocative study. R. Cameron brilliantly traces the spread of railroads and industry across Europe in *France and the Economic Development of Europe, 1800–1914* (1961). The recent works of A. S. Milward and S. B. Saul, *The Economic Development of Continental Europe, (1780–1870* (1973) and *The Development of the Economies of Continental Europe, 1850–1914* (1977), may be compared with J. Clapham's old-fashioned classic, *Economic Development of France and Germany* (1963). C. Kindleberger, *Economic Growth in France and Britain, 1851–1950* (1964), is a stimulating study, especially for those with some background in economics. Other important works in recent years on industrial developments are C. Tilly and E. Shorter, *Strikes in France, 1830–1848* (1974); D. Ringrose, *Transportation and Economic Stagnation in Spain, 1750–1850* (1970); L. Schofer, *The Formation of a Modern Labor Force* (1975), which focuses on the Silesian part of Germany; and W. Blackwell, *The Industrialization of Russia,* 2nd ed. (1982).

The debate between "optimists" and "pessimists" about the consequences of industrialization in England goes on. P. Taylor, ed., *The Industrial Revolution: Triumph or Disaster?* (1970), is a useful introduction to different viewpoints, while W. A. Hayek, ed., *Capitalism and the Historians* (1954), is a good collection of essays stressing positive aspects. It is also fascinating to compare Friedrich Engels's classic condemnation, *The Condition of the Working Class in England,* with Andrew Ure's optimistic defense, *The Philosophy of Manufactures,* first published in 1835 and reprinted recently. E. P. Thompson continues and enriches the Engels tradition in *The Making of the English Working Class* (1963), an exciting book rich in detail and early working-class lore. An unorthodox but moving account of a doomed group is D. Bythell, *The Handloom Weavers* (1969). F. Klingender, *Art and the Industrial Revolution,* rev. ed. (1968), is justly famous, and M. Ignatieff, *A Just Measure of Pain* (1980), is an engrossing study of prisons during English industrialization. D. S. Landes, *Revolution in Time: Clocks and the Making of the Modern World* (1983), is a brilliant integration of industrial and cultural history.

Among general studies, many of which are cited in the Suggested Reading for Chapter 23, G. S. R. Kitson Clark, *The Making of Victorian England* (1967), is particularly imaginative. A. Briggs, *Victorian People* (1955), provides an engrossing series of brief biographies. H. Ausubel discusses a major reformer in his work, *John Bright* (1966), and B. Harrison skillfully illuminates the problem of heavy drinking in *Drink and the Victorians* (1971). On poverty and politics in Ireland, K. H. Connell, *The Population of Ireland, 1750–1850* (1950), and S. Cronin, *Irish Nationalism: A History of Its Roots and Ideology* (1981), are excellent points of departure, while C. Smith, *The Great Hunger* (1962), is a moving account of the famine. The most famous contemporary novel dealing with the new industrial society is Charles Dickens's *Hard Times,* an entertaining but exaggerated story. *Mary Barton* and *North and South* by Elizabeth Gaskill are more realistic portrayals, and both are highly recommended, as is Emile Zola's *Germinal,* a grim, powerful story of love and hate during a violent strike by French coal miners.

23

IDEOLOGIES AND UPHEAVALS, 1815–1850

*T*HE MOMENTOUS economic and political transformation of modern times began in the late eighteenth century with the Industrial Revolution in England and then the French Revolution. Until about 1815, these economic and political revolutions were separate, involving different countries and activities and proceeding at very different paces. The Industrial Revolution created the factory system and new groups of capitalists and industrial workers in northern England, but almost continuous warfare with France checked its spread to continental Europe. Meanwhile, England's ruling aristocracy suppressed all forms of political radicalism at home and joined with crowned heads abroad to oppose and eventually defeat revolutionary and Napoleonic France. The economic and political revolutions worked at cross-purposes and even neutralized each other.

After peace returned in 1815, the situation changed. Economic and political changes tended to fuse, reinforcing each other and bringing about what the historian Eric Hobsbawm has incisively called the "dual revolution." For instance, the growth of the industrial middle class encouraged the drive for representative government, while the demands of the French sans-culottes in 1793 and 1794 inspired many socialist thinkers. Gathering strength and threatening almost every aspect of the existing political and social framework, the dual revolution rushed on to alter completely first Europe and then the world. Much of world history in the last two centuries can be seen as the progressive unfolding of the dual revolution.

Yet three qualifications must be kept firmly in mind. In Europe in the nineteenth century, as in Asia and Africa in more recent times, the dual revolution was not some inexorable mechanical monster grinding peoples and cultures into a homogenized mass. The economic and political transformation it wrought was built on complicated histories, strong traditions, and highly diverse cultures. Radical change was eventually a constant, but the particular results varied enormously.

Nor should the strength of the old forces be underestimated. In Europe especially, the traditional elites —the monarchs, noble landowners, and bureaucrats —long proved capable of defending their privileges and even of rerouting the dual revolution to serve their interests.

Finally, the dual revolution posed a tremendous intellectual challenge. The meanings of the economic, political, and social changes that were occurring, as well as the ways they could be shaped by human action, were anything but clear. These questions fascinated observers and stimulated new ideas and ideologies.

How, then, did the political revolution, derailed by class antagonisms in France and resisted by European monarchs, break out again in the era of early industrialization? And what ideas did thinkers develop to describe and shape the transformation going on before their eyes? These are the questions this chapter will explore.

THE PEACE SETTLEMENT

The eventual triumph of revolutionary economic and political forces was by no means certain in 1814. Quite the contrary. The conservative, aristocratic monarchies with their preindustrial armies and economies (Great Britain excepted) appeared firmly in control once again. France had been decisively defeated by the off-again, on-again alliance of Russia, Prussia, Austria, and Great Britain. That alliance had been strengthened and reaffirmed in March 1814, when the allies pledged not only to defeat France but to hold it in line for twenty years thereafter. The Quadruple Alliance had then forced Napoleon to abdicate in April 1814 and restored the Bourbon dynasty to the French throne (page 694). But there were many other international questions outstanding, and the allies agreed to meet in Vienna to fashion a general peace settlement. Interrupted by Napoleon's desperate gamble during the Hundred Days, the allies concluded their negotiations at the Congress of Vienna after Napoleon's defeat at Waterloo.

Most people felt profound longing for peace. The great challenge for statesmen in 1814 was to construct a peace settlement that would last and not sow the seeds of another war. Their efforts were largely successful and contributed to a century unmarred by destructive, generalized war (see Map 23.1).

MAP 23.1 Europe in 1815 Europe's leaders re-established a balance of political power after the defeat of Napoleon.

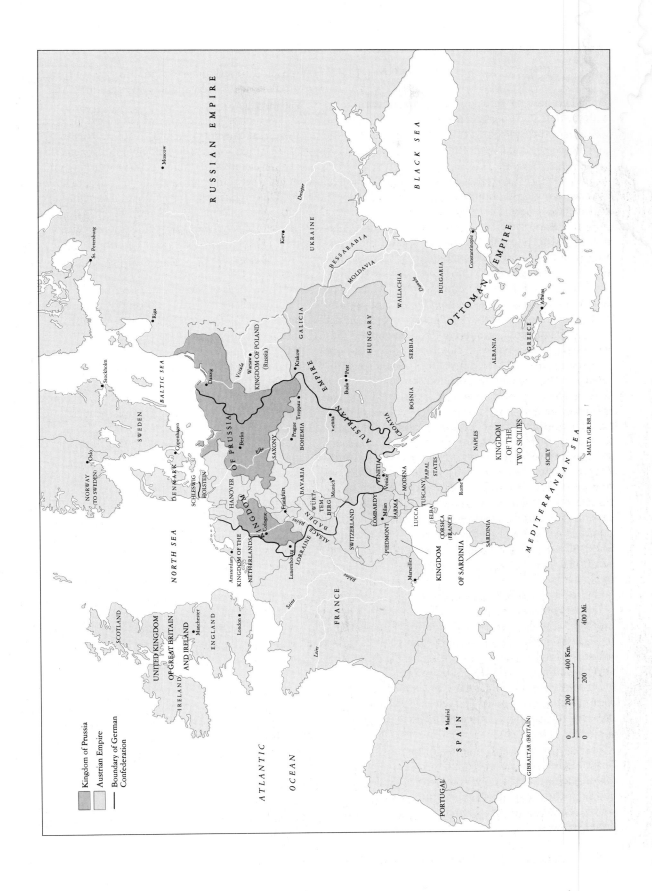

RUSSIAN EMPIRE

BLACK SEA

• Moscow

• St. Petersburg

• Riga

BALTIC SEA

Stockholm •

SWEDEN

NORWAY
(TO SWEDEN)

Oslo •

DENMARK

Copenhagen •

NORTH SEA

ATLANTIC
OCEAN

SCOTLAND

IRELAND

UNITED KINGDOM
OF GREAT BRITAIN
AND IRELAND

ENGLAND

Manchester •

London •

Kiev •

UKRAINE

Dnieper

BESSARABIA

MOLDAVIA

Danube

WALLACHIA

BULGARIA

Constantinople •

OTTOMAN EMPIRE

GREECE

Athens •

ALBANIA

BOSNIA

SERBIA

CROATIA

HUNGARY

GALICIA

KINGDOM OF POLAND
(Russia)

Warsaw •

Vistula

Krakow •

KINGDOM OF PRUSSIA

Danzig •

Berlin •

Elbe

SAXONY

Prague •

BOHEMIA

Troppau •

Vienna •

AUSTRIAN EMPIRE

VENETIA

Venice •

Pest •

Buda •

Munich •

BAVARIA

BERG

WÜRT-
TEM-
BERG

Frankfurt •

HANOVER

KINGDOM OF THE
NETHERLANDS

Amsterdam •

Cologne •

Rhine

BADEN

ALSACE

LORRAINE

Luxembourg •

SWITZERLAND

FRANCE

Seine

Loire

Rhone

Marseilles •

LOMBARDY

Milan •

PIEDMONT

KINGDOM
OF SARDINIA

CORSICA
(FRANCE)

SARDINIA

MODENA

PARMA

LUCCA

TUSCANY

PAPAL
STATES

Rome •

ELBA

NAPLES

KINGDOM
OF THE
TWO SICILIES

SICILY

MEDITERRANEAN SEA

MALTA (GR. BR.)

SPAIN

Madrid •

PORTUGAL

GIBRALTAR (BRITAIN)

SCHLESWIG
HOLSTEIN

Kingdom of Prussia

Austrian Empire

Boundary of German
Confederation

400 Km.

400 Mi.

200

200

0

0

THE CONGRESS OF VIENNA

The allied powers were concerned first and foremost with the defeated enemy, France. Agreeing to the restoration of the Bourbon dynasty, the allies signed the first Peace of Paris with Louis XVIII on May 30, 1814.

The allies were quite lenient toward France. France was given the boundaries it possessed in 1792, which were larger than those of 1789. France lost only the territories it had conquered in Italy, Germany, and the Low Countries, in addition to a few colonial possessions. Although there was some sentiment for levying a fine on France to pay for the war, the allies did not press the matter when Louis XVIII stated firmly that his government would not pay any reparations. France was even allowed to keep the art treasures Napoleon's agents had looted from the museums of Europe. Thus the victorious powers did not punish harshly, and they did not foment a spirit of injustice and revenge in the defeated country.

When the four allies met together at the Congress of Vienna, assisted in a minor way by a host of delegates from the smaller European states, they also agreed to raise a number of formidable barriers against renewed French aggression. The Low Countries—Belgium and Holland—were united under an enlarged Dutch monarchy capable of opposing France more effectively. Moreover, Prussia received considerably more territory on France's eastern border, so as to stand as the "sentinel on the Rhine" against France. In these ways the Quadruple Alliance combined leniency toward France with strong defensive measures. They held out a carrot with one hand and picked up a bigger stick with the other.

In their moderation toward France the allies were motivated by self-interest and traditional ideas about the balance of power. To Metternich and Castlereagh, the foreign ministers of Austria and Great Britain, as well as their French counterpart Talleyrand, the balance of power meant an international equilibrium of political and military forces, which would preserve the freedom and independence of each of the Great Powers. Such a balance would discourage aggression by any combination of states or, worse, the domination of Europe by any single state. As they saw it, the task of the powers was thus twofold. They had to make sure that France would not dominate Europe again, and they also had to arrange international relations so that none of the victors would be tempted to strive for domination in its turn. Such a balance involved many considerations and all of Europe.

The balance of power was the mechanism used by the Great Powers—Austria, Britain, Prussia, Russia, and France—to settle their own dangerous disputes at the Congress of Vienna. There was general agreement among the victors that each of them should receive compensation in the form of territory for their successful struggle against the French. Great Britain had already won colonies and strategic outposts during the long wars, and these it retained. Metternich's Austria gave up territories in Belgium and southern Germany but expanded greatly elsewhere, taking the rich provinces of Venetia and Lombardy in northern Italy as well as its former Polish possessions and new lands on the eastern coast of the Adriatic (see Map 23.1). There was also agreement that Prussia and Russia should be compensated. But where, and to what extent? That was the ticklish question that almost led to renewed war in January 1815.

The vaguely progressive, impetuous Alexander I of Russia had already taken Finland and Bessarabia on his northern and southern borders. Yet he burned with ambition to restore the ancient kingdom of Poland, on which he expected to bestow the benefits of his rule. The Prussians were willing to go along and give up their Polish territories, provided they could swallow up the large and wealthy kingdom of Saxony, their German neighbor to the south.

These demands were too much for Castlereagh and Metternich, who feared an unbalancing of forces in central Europe. In an astonishing about-face, they turned for diplomatic support to the wily Talleyrand and the defeated France he represented. On January 3, 1815, Great Britain, Austria, and France signed a secret alliance directed against Russia and Prussia. As Castlereagh concluded somberly, it appeared that the "peace we have so dearly purchased will be of short duration."

The outcome, however, was compromise rather than war. When rumors of the alliance were intentionally leaked, the threat of war caused the rulers of Russia and Prussia to moderate their demands. They accepted Metternich's proposal: Russia established a small Polish kingdom, and Prussia received two-fifths rather than all of Saxony (see Map 23.1). This compromise was very much within the framework of balance-of-power ideology and eighteenth-century diplomacy: Great Powers became greater, but not too

The Congress of Vienna While the Great Powers hammered out a peace settlement, a host of delegates from all over Europe celebrated with endless balls, receptions, and romantic intrigues. Here the "dancing congress" enjoys a glittering evening-dress ball given by the Austrian emperor and empress. *(The Bettmann Archive)*

much greater. In addition, France had been able to intervene and tip the scales in favor of the side seeking to prevent undue expansion of Russia and Prussia. In so doing France regained its Great Power status and was no longer isolated, as Talleyrand gleefully reported to Louis XVIII.

Unfortunately for France, as the final touches were being put on the peace settlement at Vienna, Napoleon suddenly reappeared on the scene. Escaping from his "comic kingdom" on the island of Elba in February 1815 and rallying his supporters for one last campaign during the Hundred Days, Napoleon was defeated at Waterloo and exiled to St. Helena. Yet the resulting peace—the second Peace of Paris—was still

relatively moderate toward France. Fat old Louis XVIII was restored to his throne for a second time. France lost some territory, had to pay an indemnity of 700 million francs, and had to support a large army of occupation for five years.

The rest of the settlement already concluded at the Congress of Vienna was left intact. The members of the Quadruple Alliance did, however, agree to meet periodically to discuss their common interests and to consider appropriate measures for the maintenance of peace in Europe. This agreement marked the beginning of the European "congress system," which lasted long into the nineteenth century and settled international crises through diplomatic conferences.

INTERVENTION AND REPRESSION

There was also a domestic political side to the re-establishment of peace. Within their own countries, the leaders of the victorious states were much less flexible. In 1815, under Metternich's leadership, Austria, Prussia, and Russia embarked on a crusade against the ideas and politics of the dual revolution. The crusade lasted until 1848.

The first step was the Holy Alliance, formed by Austria, Prussia, and Russia in September 1815. First proposed by Russia's Alexander I, the alliance proclaimed the intention of the three eastern monarchs to rule exclusively on the basis of Christian principles and to work together to maintain peace and justice on all occasions. Castlereagh refused to sign, characterizing the vague statement of principle as "a piece of sublime mysticism and nonsense." Yet it soon became a symbol of the repression of liberal and revolutionary movements all over Europe.

In 1820 revolutionaries succeeded in forcing the monarchs of Spain and the southern Italian kingdom of the Two Sicilies to grant liberal constitutions against their wills. Metternich was horrified: revolution was rising once again. Calling a conference at Troppau in Austria, under the provisions of the Quadruple Alliance, he and Alexander I proclaimed the principle of active intervention to maintain all autocratic regimes whenever they were threatened. Austrian forces then marched into Naples and restored Ferdinand I to the throne of the Two Sicilies. The French armies of Louis XVIII likewise restored the Spanish regime—after the Congress of Troppau had rejected Alexander's offer to send his Cossacks across Europe to teach the Spanish an unforgettable lesson.

Great Britain remained aloof, arguing that intervention in the domestic politics of foreign states was not an object of British diplomacy. In particular, Great Britain opposed any attempts by the restored Spanish monarchy to reconquer its former Latin American possessions, which had gained their independence during and after the Napoleonic wars. Encouraged by the British position, the young United States proclaimed its celebrated Monroe Doctrine in 1823. This bold document declared that European powers were to keep their hands off the New World and in no way attempt to re-establish their political system there. In the United States, constitutional liberalism, an ongoing challenge to the conservatism of continental Europe, retained its cutting edge.

In the years following the crushing of liberal revolution in southern Italy in 1821 and in Spain in 1823, Metternich continued to battle against liberal political change. Sometimes he could do little, as in the case of the new Latin American republics. Nor could he undo the dynastic changes of 1830 in western Europe. Nonetheless, until 1848 Metternich's system proved quite effective in central Europe, where his power was greatest.

Metternich's policies dominated not only Austria and the Italian peninsula but the entire German Confederation, which the peace settlement of Vienna had called into being. The confederation was composed of thirty-eight independent German states, including Prussia and Austria. (The Hungarian half of the Austrian Empire was not a member.) These states met in complicated assemblies dominated by Austria, with Prussia a willing junior partner in the planning and execution of repressive measures.

It was through the German Confederation that Metternich had the infamous Carlsbad Decrees issued in 1819. The decrees required the thirty-eight German member states to root out subversive ideas in their universities and newspapers. They also established a permanent committee with spies and informers to investigate and punish any liberal or radical organizations. Metternich's ruthless imposition of repressive internal policies on the governments of central Europe contrasted with the intelligent moderation he had displayed in the general peace settlement of 1815.

METTERNICH AND CONSERVATISM

Metternich's determined defense of the status quo made him a villain in the eyes of most progressive, optimistic historians of the nineteenth century. Yet rather than denounce the man, it is more useful to try to understand him and the general conservatism he represented.

Born into the middle ranks of the landed nobility of the Rhineland, Prince Klemens von Metternich (1773–1859) was an internationally oriented aristocrat. In 1795 his splendid marriage to Eleonora von Kaunitz, granddaughter of Austria's famous statesman and heiress to vast estates, opened the door to the highest court circles and a brilliant diplomatic career. Austrian ambassador to Napoleon's court in 1806 and Austrian foreign minister from 1809 to

1848, the cosmopolitan Metternich always remained loyal to his class and jealously defended its rights and privileges to the day he died. Like most other conservatives of his time, he did so with a clear conscience. The nobility was one of Europe's most ancient institutions, and conservatives regarded tradition as the basic source of human institutions. In their view, the proper state and society remained that of pre-1789 Europe, which rested on a judicious blend of monarchy, bureaucracy, and aristocracy.

Metternich's commitment to conservatism was coupled with a passionate hatred of liberalism. He firmly believed that liberalism, as embodied in revolutionary America and France, had been responsible for a generation of war with untold bloodshed and suffering. Liberal demands for representative government and civil liberties had unfortunately captured the imaginations of some middle-class lawyers, businessmen, and intellectuals. Metternich thought that these groups had been and still were engaged in a vast conspiracy to impose their beliefs on society and destroy the existing order. Like many conservatives then and since, Metternich blamed liberal revolutionaries for stirring up the lower classes, whom he believed to be indifferent or hostile to liberal ideas, desiring nothing more than peace and quiet.

The threat of liberalism appeared doubly dangerous to Metternich because it generally went with national aspirations. Liberals, especially liberals in central Europe, believed that each people, each national group, had a right to establish its own independent government and seek to fulfill its own destiny. The idea of national self-determination was repellent to Metternich. It not only threatened the existence of the aristocracy, it also threatened to destroy the Austrian Empire and revolutionize central Europe.

The vast Austrian Empire of the Habsburgs was a great dynastic state. Formed over centuries by war, marriage, and luck, it was made up of many peoples speaking many languages (see Map 23.2). The Germans, long the dominant element, had supported and profited by the long-term territorial expansion of Austria; yet they accounted for only a quarter of the population. The Magyars (Hungarians), a substantially smaller group, dominated the kingdom of Hungary—which was part of the Austrian Empire—though they did not account for a majority of the population even there.

The Czechs, the third major group, were concentrated in Bohemia and Moravia. There were also

Metternich This portrait by Sir Thomas Lawrence reveals much of Metternich the man. Handsome, refined, and intelligent, Metternich was a great aristocrat passionately devoted to the defense of his class and its interests. *(The Bettmann Archive)*

large numbers of Italians, Poles, and Ukrainians, as well as smaller groups of Slovenes, Croats, Serbs, Ruthenians, and Rumanians. The various Slavic peoples, together with the Italians and the Rumanians, represented a widely scattered and completely divided majority in an empire dominated by Germans and Hungarians. Different ethnic groups often lived in the same provinces and even the same villages. Thus the different parts and provinces of the empire differed in languages, customs, and institutions. They were held together primarily by their ties to the Habsburg emperor.

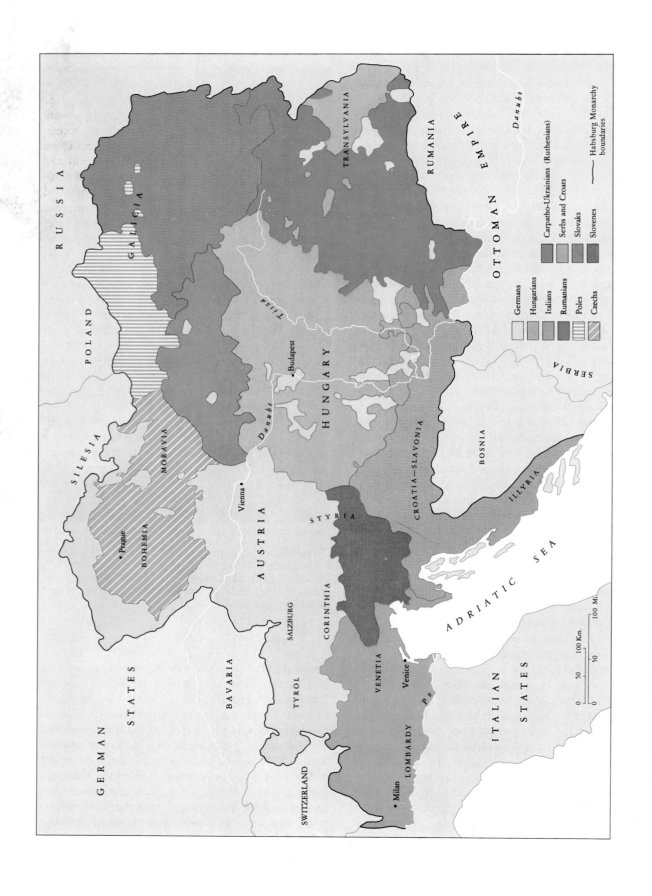

RUSSIA

GALICIA

POLAND

SILESIA

MORAVIA

BOHEMIA

Prague •

GERMAN

STATES

BAVARIA

SWITZERLAND

TYROL

SALZBURG

Vienna •

AUSTRIA

STYRIA

CORINTHIA

VENETIA

Venice •

LOMBARDY

Milan •

Po

ITALIAN

STATES

ADRIATIC   SEA

ILLYRIA

BOSNIA

CROATIA-SLAVONIA

SERBIA

HUNGARY

Budapest •

Danube

Tisza

TRANSYLVANIA

RUMANIA

OTTOMAN   EMPIRE

Danube

Germans
Hungarians
Italians
Rumanians
Poles
Czechs

Carpatho-Ukrainians (Ruthenians)
Serbs and Croats
Slovaks
Slovenes

Habsburg Monarchy
boundaries

100 Mi.

100 Km.

50

50

0

0

MAP 23.2 Peoples of the Habsburg Monarchy, 1815
The old dynastic state was a patchwork of nationalities. Note the widely scattered pockets of Germans and Hungarians.

The multinational state Metternich served was both strong and weak. It was strong because of its large population and vast territories; it was weak because of its many and potentially dissatisfied nationalities. In these circumstances, Metternich virtually had to oppose liberalism and nationalism, for Austria was simply unable to accommodate those ideologies of the dual revolution. Other conservatives supported Austria because they could imagine no better fate for the jumble of small nationalities wedged precariously between masses of Germans and hordes of Russians in east central Europe. Castlereagh even went so far as to say that Austria was the "great hinge upon which the fate of Europe must ultimately depend." Metternich's repressive conservatism may not hold appeal for many people today, but it had understandable roots in the dilemma of a multinational state in an age of rising nationalism.

RADICAL IDEAS AND EARLY SOCIALISM

The years following the peace settlement of 1815 were years of profound intellectual activity. Intellectuals and social observers were seeking to understand the revolutionary changes that had occurred and were still taking place. These efforts led to ideas that still motivate the world.

Almost all of these basic ideas were radical. In one way or another they opposed the old, deeply felt conservatism that Metternich exemplified so well. The revived conservatism, with its stress on tradition, a hereditary monarchy, a strong and privileged landowning aristrocracy, and an official church, was rejected by radicals. Instead, radicals developed and refined alternative visions—alternative ideologies—and tried to convince society to act on them. With time, they were very successful.

LIBERALISM

The ideas of liberalism—liberty and equality—were by no means defeated in 1815. First realized successfully in the American Revolution and then achieved in part in the French Revolution, this political and social philosophy continued to pose a radical challenge to revived conservatism. Liberalism demanded representative government as opposed to autocratic monarchy, equality before the law as opposed to legally separate classes. Liberty also continued to mean specific individual freedoms: freedom of the press, freedom of speech, freedom of assembly, and freedom from arbitrary arrest. In Europe, only France with Louis XVIII's Constitutional Charter and Great Britain with its Parliament and historic rights of Englishmen and women had realized much but by no means all of the liberal program in 1815. Elsewhere, liberal demands were still a call for revolutionary change.

Yet although "classical" liberalism still had its cutting edge, it was not as sharp a tool as it had been. This was especially true of liberal economic principles, which called for unrestricted private enterprise and no government interference in the economy. This philosophy was popularly known as the doctrine of *laissez faire.*

The idea of a free economy had first been persuasively formulated by a Scottish professor of philosophy, Adam Smith (1723–1790). Smith, whose *Inquiry into the Nature and Causes of the Wealth of Nations* (1776) founded modern economics, was highly critical of eighteenth-century mercantilism. Mercantilism, he said, meant stifling government regulations as well as unjust privileges for private monopolies and government favorites. Far preferable was free competition, which would give all citizens a fair and equal opportunity to do what they did best. Smith argued effectively that freely competitive private enterprise would result in greater income for everyone, not just the rich.

Unlike some of his contemporaries, Smith applauded the modest rise in real wages of British workers in the eighteenth century and went so far as to say, "No society can surely be flourishing and happy, of which the far greater part of the members are poor and miserable." Smith also believed that greater competition meant higher wages for workers, since manufacturers and "masters are always and everywhere in a sort of tacit, but constant and uniform, combination, not to raise the wages of laborers above their actual rate." In short, Adam Smith was a spokesman for general economic development, not narrow business interests.

In the early nineteenth century, the British economy was progressively liberalized, as old restrictions on trade and industry were relaxed or eliminated. This liberalization promoted continued rapid economic growth in the Industrial Revolution. At the same time, however, economic liberalism and laissez-faire economic thought were tending to become a doctrine serving business interests. Businessmen used the doctrine to defend their right to do exactly as they wished in their factories. Labor unions were outlawed because they supposedly restricted free competition and the individual's "right to work."

The teachings of a kindly parson, Thomas Malthus (1776–1834), helped make economic liberalism an ideology of business interests in many people's minds. In his "Essay on the Principle of Population" (1798), Malthus argued that population would always tend to grow faster than the supply of food. In Malthus's opinion, the only hope of warding off such "positive checks" to population growth as war, famine, and disease was "prudential restraint." That is , young men and women had to limit the growth of population by the old tried-and-true means of marrying late in life. But Malthus was not optimistic about this possibility. The powerful attraction of the sexes would cause most people to marry early and have many children.

The wealthy English stockbroker and economist David Ricardo (1772–1823) was even less optimistic. His depressing "iron law of wages" posited that, because of the pressure of population growth, wages would always sink to the subsistence level. That is, wages would be just high enough to keep the workers from starving. Malthus and Ricardo thought of themselves as objective social scientists. Yet their teachings were often used by industrial and middle-class interests in England, the Continent, and the United States to justify opposing any kind of government intervention to protect or improve the lot of workers: if workers were poor, it was their own fault, the result of their breeding like rabbits.

In the early nineteenth century, liberal political ideals also became more closely associated with narrow class interests. Early nineteenth-century liberals favored representative government, but they generally wanted property qualifications attached to the right to vote. In practice, this meant limiting the vote to well-to-do aristocratic landowners, substantial businessmen, and successful members of the professions. Workers and peasants as well as the lower middle class of shopkeepers, clerks, and artisans did not own the necessary property and thus could not vote.

As liberalism became increasingly middle class after 1815, some intellectuals and foes of conservatism felt that it did not go nearly far enough. Inspired by memories of the French Revolution and the contemporary example of exuberant Jacksonian democracy in the young American republic, they called for universal voting rights, at least for males. Giving all men the vote, they felt, would allow the masses to join in government and would lead to democracy.

Many people who believed in democracy also believed in the republican form of government. They detested the power of the monarchy, the privileges of the aristocracy, and the great wealth of the upper middle class. These democrats and republicans were more radical than the liberals. Taking for granted much of the liberal program, they sought to go beyond it. Democrats and republicans were also more willing than most liberals to endorse violent upheaval to achieve goals. All of which meant that liberals and radical, democratic republicans could join forces against conservatives only up to a point.

NATIONALISM

Nationalism was a second radical idea in the years after 1815, an idea destined to have an enormous influence in the modern world. In a summation of this complex ideology, three points stand out. First, nationalism has normally evolved from a real or imagined *cultural* unity, manifesting itself especially in a common language, history, and territory. Second, nationalists have usually sought to turn this cultural unity into *political* reality, so that the territory of each people coincides with its state boundaries. It was this goal that made nationalism so potentially explosive in central and eastern Europe after 1815, when there were either too few states (Austria, Russia, and the Ottoman Empire) or too many (the Italian peninsula and the German Confederation) and when different peoples overlapped and intermingled. Third, modern nationalism had its immediate origins in the French Revolution and the Napoleonic wars. Nationalism was effectively harnessed by the French republic during the Reign of Terror to help repel foreign foes, and all across Europe patriots tried to kindle nationalist flames in the war against Napoleon. Thus by 1815 there were already hints of nationalism's remarkable ability to spread and develop.

Between 1815 and 1850, most people who believed in nationalism also believed in either liberalism or radical, democratic republicanism. In more recent times, however, many governments have been very nationalistic without favoring liberty and democracy. Why, then, was love of liberty almost synonymous with love of nation in the early nineteenth century?

A common faith in the creativity and nobility of the people was perhaps the single most important reason for people's linking these two concepts. Liberals and especially democrats saw the people as the ultimate source of all government. The people (or some of them) elected their officials and governed themselves within a framework of personal liberty. Yet such self-government would be possible only if the people were united by common traditions and common loyalties. In practice, common loyalties rested above all on a common language. Thus liberals and nationalists agreed that a shared language forged the basic unity of a people, a unity that transcended local or provincial interests and even class differences.

Early nationalists usually believed that every nation, like every citizen, has the right to exist in freedom and to develop its character and spirit. They were confident that the independence and freedom of other nations, as in the case of other citizens within a nation, would not lessen the freedom of their own country. Rather, the symphony of nations would promote the harmony and ultimate unity of all peoples. As the French historian Jules Michelet put it in *The People* in 1846, each citizen "learns to recognize his country . . . as a note in the grand concert; through it he himself participates and loves the world." Similarly, the Italian patriot Giuseppe Mazzini believed that "in laboring according to the true principles of our country we are laboring for Humanity." Thus the liberty of the individual and the love of a free nation overlapped greatly in the early nineteenth century.

Nationalism also had a negative side. Even as they talked of serving the cause of humanity, early nationalists stressed the differences between peoples. The German pastor and philosopher Johann Herder (1744–1803) had argued that every people has its own particular spirit and genius, which it expresses through its culture and language. Yet Herder (and others after him) could not define the uniqueness of the French, German, and Slavic peoples without comparing and contrasting one people with another. Thus, even early nationalism developed a strong sense of "we" and "they."

"They" were often the enemy. The leader of the Czech cultural revival, the passionate democrat and nationalist historian Francis Palacký, is a good example of this tendency. In his histories he lauded the achievements of the Czech people, which he characterized as a long struggle against brutal German domination. To this "we—they" outlook, it was all too easy for nationalists to add two other highly volatile ingredients: a sense of national mission and a sense of national superiority. As Mazzini characteristically wrote, "Peoples never stop before they have achieved the ultimate aim of their existence, before having fulfilled their mission." Even Michelet, so alive to the aspirations of other peoples, could not help speaking in 1846 of the "superiority of France"; the principles espoused in the French Revolution had made France the "salvation of mankind."

German and Spanish nationalists had a very different opinion of France. To them the French often seemed as oppressive as the Germans seemed to the Czechs, as hateful as the Russians seemed to the Poles. The despised enemy's mission might seem as oppressive as the American national mission—as the American journalist and strident nationalist John Louis O'Sullivan sketched it in 1845 after the annexation of Texas—seemed to the Mexicans. O'Sullivan wrote that taking land from an "imbecile and distracted Mexico" was a laudable step in the "fulfillment of our manifest destiny to overspread the continent allotted by Providence for the free development of our yearly multiplying millions."[2]

Early nationalism was thus ambiguous. Its main thrust was liberal and democratic. But below the surface lurked ideas of national superiority and national mission, which could lead to aggressive crusades and counter-crusades, as had happened in the French Revolution and in the "wars of liberation" against Napoleon.

Fourier's Utopia The vision of a harmonious planned community freed from capitalism and selfish individualism radiates from this 1847 illustration of Fourier's principles. *(Mary Evans Picture Library)*

French Utopian Socialism

To understand the rise of socialism, one must begin with France. Despite the fact that France lagged far behind Great Britain in developing modern industry, almost all the early socialists were French. Although they differed on many specific points, these French thinkers were acutely aware that the political revolution in France and the rise of modern industry in England had begun a transformation of society. Yet they were disturbed by what they saw. Liberal practices in politics and economics appeared to be fomenting selfish individualism and splitting the com-

munity into isolated fragments. There was, they believed, an urgent need for a further reorganization of society to establish cooperation and a new sense of community. Starting from this shared outlook, individual French thinkers went in many different directions. They searched the past, analyzed existing conditions, and fashioned luxurious utopias. Yet certain ideas tied their critiques and visions together.

Early French socialists believed in economic planning. Inspired by the emergency measures of 1793 and 1794 in France, they argued that the government should rationally organize the economy and not depend on destructive competition to do the job. Early socialists also shared an intense desire to help the poor and to protect them from the rich. With passionate moral fervor they preached that the rich and the poor should be more nearly equal economically. Finally, socialists believed that most private property should be abolished and replaced by state or community ownership. Planning, greater economic equality, and state ownership of property: these were the key ideas of early French socialism and of all socialism since.

One of the most influential of these thinkers was a nobleman, Count Henri de Saint-Simon (1760–1825). A curious combination of radical thinker and successful land speculator, Saint-Simon optimistically proclaimed the tremendous possibilities of industrial development: "The age of gold is before us!" The key to progress was proper social organization. Such an arrangement of society required the "parasites"—the court, the aristocracy, lawyers, churchmen—to give way, once and for all, to the "doers"—the leading scientists, engineers, and industrialists. The doers would carefully plan the economy and guide it forward by undertaking vast public works projects and investment banks. Saint-Simon also stressed in highly moralistic terms that every social institution ought to have as its main goal improved conditions for the poor. Saint-Simon's stress on industry and science inspired middle-class industrialists and bankers, like the Pereire brothers, founders of the Crédit Mobilier (Chapter 22).

After 1830, the socialist critique of capitalism became sharper. Charles Fourier (1772–1837), a lonely, saintly man with a tenuous hold on reality, described a socialist utopia in lavish mathematical detail. Hating the urban wage system, Fourier envisaged self-sufficient communities of 1,620 people living communally on five thousand acres devoted to a combination of agriculture and industry. Fourier was also an early proponent of the total emancipation of women, abolition of marriage, and complete sexual freedom. Although Fourier waited in vain each day at noon in his apartment for a wealthy philanthropist to endow his visionary schemes, he was very influential. Several utopian communities were founded along the lines he prescribed, mainly in the United States.

Louis Blanc (1811–1882), a sharp-eyed, intelligent journalist, was much more practical. In his *Organization of Work* (1839), he urged workers to agitate for universal voting rights and to take control of the state peacefully. Blanc believed that the full power of the state should be directed at setting up government-backed workshops and factories to guarantee full employment. The right to work had to become as sacred as any other right. Finally, there was Pierre Joseph Proudhon (1809–1865), a self-educated printer, who wrote a pamphlet in 1840 entitled *What Is Property?* His answer was that it was nothing but theft. Property was profit that was stolen from the worker, who was the source of all wealth. Unlike most socialists, Proudhon feared the power of the state and thus was often considered an anarchist.

Thus a variety of French thinkers blazed the way with utopian socialism in the 1830s and 1840s. Their ideas were very influential, particularly in Paris, where poverty-stricken workers with a revolutionary tradition were attentive students. Yet the economic arguments of the French utopians were weak, and their specific programs usually seemed too fanciful to be taken seriously. To Karl Marx was left the task of establishing firm foundations for modern socialism.

THE BIRTH OF MARXIAN SOCIALISM

In 1848 the thirty-year-old Karl Marx (1818–1883) and the twenty-eight-year-old Friedrich Engels (1820–1895) published the *Communist Manifesto,* the Bible of socialism. The son of a Jewish lawyer who had converted to Christianity, the atheistic young Marx had studied philosophy at the University of Berlin before turning to journalism and economics. He read widely in French socialist thought and was developing his own socialist ideas by the time he was twenty-five.

Early French socialists often appealed to the middle class and the state to help the poor. Marx argued that the interests of the middle class and those of the industrial working class are inevitably opposed to each other. Indeed, according to the *Manifesto,* the "history of all previously existing society is the history of class struggles." In Marx's view, one class had always exploited the other, and with the advent of modern industry, society was split more clearly than ever before: between the middle class—the bourgeoisie—and the modern working class—the proletariat. Moreover, the bourgeoisie had reduced everything to a matter of money and "naked self-interest." "In a

The Marx Family In 1849 the exiled Marx settled in London. There he wrote *Capital,* the weighty exposition of his socialist theories, and worked to organize the working class. With his coauthor and financial supporter Friedrich Engels (left), Marx is shown here with his daughters, ironically a picture of middle-class respectability. *(Culver Pictures)*

word, for exploitation, veiled by religious and political illusions, the bourgeoisie had substituted naked, shameless, direct brutal exploitation."

Just as the bourgeoisie had triumphed over the feudal aristocracy, Marx predicted, the proletariat was destined to conquer the bourgeoisie in a violent revolution. While a tiny minority owned the means of production and grew richer, the ever-poorer proletariat was constantly growing in size and in class consciousness. In this process, the proletariat was aided, according to Marx, by a portion of the bourgeoisie

who had gone over to the proletariat and who (like Marx and Engels) "had raised themselves to the level of comprehending theoretically the historical moment." And the critical moment was very near. "Let the ruling classes tremble at a Communist revolution. The proletarians have nothing to lose but their chains. They have a world to win. WORKING MEN OF ALL COUNTRIES, UNITE!" So ends the *Communist Manifesto.*

In brief outline, Marx's ideas may seem to differ only slightly from the wild and improbable ideas of the utopians of his day. Yet whatever one may think of the validity of Marx's analysis, he must be taken seriously. He united sociology, economics, and all human history in a vast and imposing edifice. He synthesized in his socialism not only French utopian schemes but English classical economics and German philosophy—the major intellectual currents of his day. Moreover, after the young Marx fled to England as a penniless political refugee following the revolutions of 1848, he continued to show a rare flair for combining complex theorization with both lively popular writing and practical organizational ability. This combination of theoretical and practical skills contributed greatly to the subsequent diffusion of Marx's socialist synthesis after 1860, as will be shown in Chapter 25.

Marx's debt to England was great. He was the last of the classical economists. Following David Ricardo, who had taught that labor was the source of all value, Marx went on to argue that profits were really wages stolen from the workers. Moreover, Marx incorporated Engels's charges of terrible oppression of the new class of factory workers in England; thus his doctrines seemed to be based on hard facts.

Marx's theory of historical evolution was built on the philosophy of the German Georg Hegel (1770–1831). Hegel believed that history is "ideas in motion": each age is characterized by a dominant set of ideas, which produces opposing ideas and eventually a new synthesis. The idea of being had been dominant initially, for example, and it had produced its antithesis, the idea of nonbeing. This idea in turn had resulted in the synthesis of becoming. History has, therefore, pattern and purpose.

Marx retained Hegel's view of history as a dialectic process of change but made economic relationships between classes the driving force. This dialectic explained the decline of agrarian feudalism and the rise of industrial capitalism. And Marx stressed again and again that the "bourgeoisie, historically, has played a most revolutionary part. . . . During its rule of scarcely one hundred years the bourgeoisie has created more massive and more colossal productive forces than have all preceding generations together." Here was a convincing explanation for people trying to make sense of the dual revolution. Marx's next idea, that it was now the bourgeoisie's turn to give way to the socialism of revolutionary workers, appeared to many the irrefutable capstone of a brilliant interpretation of humanity's long development. Thus Marx pulled together powerful ideas and insights to create one of the great secular religions out of the intellectual ferment of the early nineteenth century.

THE ROMANTIC MOVEMENT

Developing radical concepts of politics and society were accompanied by comparable changes in literature and other arts during the dual revolution. The early nineteenth century marked the acme of the romantic movement, which profoundly influenced the arts and enriched European culture immeasurably.

The romantic movement was in part a revolt against classicism and the Enlightenment. Classicism was essentially a set of artistic rules and standards that went hand in glove with the Enlightenment's belief in rationality, order, and restraint. The classicists believed that the ancient Greeks and Romans had discovered eternally valid aesthetic rules long ago and that playwrights and painters should continue to follow them. Classicists could enforce these rules in the eighteenth century because they dominated the courts and academies for which artists worked.

Forerunners of the romantic movement appeared from about 1750 on. Of these, Rousseau (pages 590–591)—the passionate advocate of feeling, freedom, and natural goodness—was the most influential. Romanticism then crystallized fully in the 1790s, primarily in England and Germany. The French Revolution kindled the belief that radical reconstruction was also possible in cultural and artistic life (even though many early English and German romantics became disillusioned with events in France and turned from liberalism to conservatism in politics). Romanticism gained strength until the 1840s, when realism began to challenge it seriously.

Romanticism was characterized by a belief in emotional exuberance, unrestrained imagination, and spontaneity in both art and personal life. In Germany early romantics of the 1770s and 1780s called themselves the "Storm and Stress" (*Sturm und Drang*) group, and many romantic artists of the early nineteenth century lived lives of tremendous emotional intensity. Suicide, duels to the death, madness, and strange illnesses were not uncommon among leading romantics. Romantic artists typically led bohemian lives, wearing their hair long and uncombed in preference to powdered wigs and living in cold garrets rather than frequenting stiff drawing rooms. They rejected materialism and sought to escape to lofty spiritual heights through their art. Great individualists, the romantics believed the full development of one's unique human potential to be the supreme purpose in life. The romantics were driven by a sense of an unlimited universe and by a yearning for the unattained, the unknown, the unknowable.

Nowhere was the break with classicism more apparent than in romanticism's general conception of nature. Classicism was not particularly interested in nature. In the words of the eighteenth-century English author Samuel Johnson, "A blade of grass is always a blade of grass; men and women are my subjects of inquiry." Nature was portrayed by classicists as beautiful and chaste, like an eighteenth-century formal garden. The romantics, on the other hand, were enchanted by nature. Sometimes they found it awesome and tempestuous, as in Théodore Géricault's painting *The Raft of the Medusa,* which shows the survivors of a shipwreck adrift in a turbulent sea. Others saw nature as a source of spiritual inspiration. As the great English landscape artist John Constable (1776–1837) declared, "Nature is Spirit visible."

Most romantics saw the growth of modern industry as an ugly, brutal attack on their beloved nature and on the human personality. They sought escape—in the unspoiled Lake District of northern England, in exotic North Africa, in an idealized Middle Ages. Yet some romantics found a vast, awesome, terribly moving power in the new industrial landscape. In ironworks and cotton mills they saw the flames of Hell and the evil genius of Satan himself. One of John Martin's last and greatest paintings, *The Great Day of His Wrath* (1850), vividly depicts the last judgment foretold in Revelation VI, "when the

Delacroix: Liberty Leading the People This great romantic painting glorifies the July Revolution in Paris in 1830. Raising high the revolutionary tricolor, Liberty unites the worker, bourgeois, and street child in a righteous crusade against privilege and oppression. *(Louvre, Paris/Giraudon/Art Resource)*

sun became black as sackcloth of hair, and the moon became as blood; and the stars of heaven fell unto the earth." Martin's romantic masterpiece was inspired directly by a journey through the "Black country" of the industrial Midlands in the dead of night. According to Martin's son:

The glow of the furnaces, the red blaze of light, together with the liquid fire, seemed to him truly sublime and

awful. He could not imagine anything more terrible even in the regions of everlasting punishment. All he had done or attempted in ideal painting fell far short, very far short, of the fearful sublimity.[3]

Fascinated by color and diversity, the romantic imagination turned toward the study and writing of history with a passion. For romantics, history was not a minor branch of philosophy from which philosophers picked suitable examples to illustrate their teachings. History was beautiful, exciting, and important in its own right. It was the art of change over time—the key to a universe that was now perceived to be organic and dynamic, no longer mechanical and static as it had appeared to the philosophes of the eighteenth-century Enlightenment.

Historical studies supported the development of national aspirations and encouraged entire peoples to seek in the past their special destinies. This trend was especially strong in Germany and eastern Europe. As the famous English historian Lord Acton put it, the growth of historical thinking associated with the romantic movement was a most fateful step in the story of European thought.

LITERATURE

Britain was the first country where romanticism flowered fully in poetry and prose, and the British romantic writers were among the most prominent in Europe. Wordsworth, Coleridge, and Scott were all active by 1800, to be followed shortly by Byron, Shelley, and Keats. All were poets: romanticism found its distinctive voice in poetry, as the Enlightenment had in prose.

A towering leader of English romanticism, William Wordsworth (1770–1850) traveled in France after his graduation from Cambridge. There he fell passionately in love with a French woman, who bore him a daughter. He was deeply influenced by the philosophy of Rousseau and the spirit of the early French Revolution. Back in England, prevented by war and the Terror from returning to France, Wordsworth settled in the countryside with his sister Dorothy and Samuel Taylor Coleridge (1772–1834).

In 1798 the two poets published their *Lyrical Ballads,* one of the most influential literary works in the history of the English language. In defiance of classical rules, Wordsworth and Coleridge abandoned flowery poetic conventions for the language of ordinary speech, simultaneously endowing simple subjects with the loftiest majesty. This twofold rejection of classical practice was at first ignored and then harshly criticized, but by 1830 Wordsworth had triumphed.

One of the best examples of Wordsworth's romantic credo and genius is "Daffodils":

I wandered lonely as a cloud
That floats on high o'er vales and hills,
When all at once I saw a crowd,
A host, of golden daffodils;
Beside the lake, beneath the trees,
Fluttering and dancing in the breeze.

Continuous as the stars that shine
And twinkle on the Milky Way,
They stretched in never-ending line
Along the margin of a bay:
Ten thousand saw I at a glance,
Tossing their heads in sprightly dance.

The waves beside them danced, but they
Out-did the sparkling waves in glee:
A poet could not but be gay,
In such a jocund company:
I gazed—and gazed—but little thought
What wealth the show to me had brought:

For oft, when on my couch I lie
In vacant or in pensive mood,
They flash upon that inward eye
Which is the bliss of solitude;
And then my heart with pleasure fills,
And dances with the daffodils.

Here indeed is simplicity and love of nature in commonplace forms. Here, too, is Wordsworth's romantic conviction that nature has the power to elevate and instruct, especially when interpreted by a high-minded poetic genius. Wordsworth's conception of poetry as the "spontaneous overflow of powerful feeling recollected in tranquility" is well illustrated by the last stanza.

Born in Edinburgh, Walter Scott (1771–1832) personified the romantic movement's fascination with history. Raised on his grandfather's farm, Scott fell under the spell of the old ballads and tales of the Scottish border. He was also deeply influenced by German romanticism, particularly by the immortal poet and dramatist Johann Wolfgang von Goethe (1749–1832). Scott translated Goethe's famous *Götz von Berlichingen,* a play about a sixteenth-century knight who revolted against centralized authority and championed individual freedom—at least in Goethe's romantic drama. A natural storyteller, Scott then composed long narrative poems and a series of historical novels. Scott excelled in faithfully recreating the spirit of bygone ages and great historical events, especially those of Scotland.

At first, the strength of classicism in France inhibited the growth of romanticism there. Then, between 1820 and 1850, the romantic impulse broke through in the poetry and prose of Lamartine, Alfred de Vigny, Victor Hugo, Alexander Dumas, and George Sand. Of these, Victor Hugo (1802–1885) was the greatest in both poetry and prose.

Son of a Napoleonic general, Hugo achieved an amazing range of rhythm, language, and image in his lyric poetry. His powerful novels exemplified the romantic fascination with fantastic characters, strange settings, and human emotions. The hero of Hugo's famous *Hunchback of Notre Dame* (1831) is the great cathedral's deformed bellringer, a "human gargoyle" overlooking the teeming life of fifteenth-century Paris. A great admirer of Shakespeare, whom classical critics had derided as undisciplined and excessive, Hugo also championed romanticism in drama. His play *Hernani* (1830) consciously broke all the old rules, as Hugo renounced his early conservatism and equated freedom in literature with liberty in politics and society. Hugo's political evolution was thus exactly the opposite of Wordsworth's, in whom youthful radicalism gave way to middle-aged caution. As the contrast between the two artists suggests, romanticism was a cultural movement compatible with many political beliefs.

George Sand (1804–1876), a strong-willed and gifted woman, defied the narrow conventions of her time in an unending search for self-fulfillment. After eight years of unhappy marriage in the provinces, she abandoned her dullard of a husband and took her two children to Paris to pursue a career as a writer. There she soon achieved fame and wealth, eventually writing over eighty novels on a variety of romantic and social themes. All were shot through with a typically romantic love of nature and moral idealism. George Sand's striking individualism went far beyond her flamboyant preference for men's clothing and cigars and her notorious affairs with the poet Alfred Musset and the composer Frédéric Chopin, among others. Her semi-autobiographical novel *Lélia* was shockingly modern, delving deeply into her tortuous quest for sexual and personal freedom.

In central and eastern Europe, literary romanticism and early nationalism often reinforced each other. Seeking a unique greatness in every people, well-educated romantics plumbed their own histories and cultures. Like modern anthropologists, they turned their attention to peasant life and transcribed the folk songs, tales, and proverbs that the cosmopolitan Enlightenment had disdained. The brothers Jacob and Wilhelm Grimm were particularly successful at rescuing German fairy tales from oblivion. In the Slavic lands, romantics played a decisive role in converting spoken peasant languages into modern written languages. The greatest of all Russian poets, Alexander Pushkin (1799–1837), rejecting eighteenth-century attempts to force Russian poetry into a classical straitjacket, used his lyric genius to mold the modern literary language.

Art and Music

The greatest and most moving romantic painter in France was Eugène Delacroix (1798–1863), probably the illegitimate son of the French foreign minister Talleyrand. Delacroix was a master of dramatic, colorful scenes that stir the emotions. He was fascinated with remote and exotic subjects, whether lion hunts in Morocco or the languishing, sensuous women of a sultan's harem. Yet he was also a passionate spokesman for freedom. His masterpiece, *Liberty Leading the People,* celebrated the nobility of popular revolution in general and revolution in France in particular.

In England, the most outstanding romantic painters were J. M. W. Turner (1775–1851) and John Constable (1776–1837). Both were fascinated by nature, but their interpretations of it contrasted sharply, aptly symbolizing the tremendous emotional range of the romantic movement. Turner depicted nature's power and terror; wild storms and sinking ships were favorite subjects. Constable painted gentle Wordsworthian landscapes in which human beings are at one with their environment, the comforting countryside of unspoiled rural England (see Color Insert V).

It was in music that romanticism realized most fully and permanently its goals of free expression and emotional intensity. Whereas the composers of the eighteenth century had remained true to well-defined structures, like the classical symphony, the great romantics used a great range of forms to paint a thousand landscapes and evoke a host of powerful emotions. Romantic composers also transformed the small classical orchestra, tripling its size by adding wind instruments, percussion, and more brass and strings. The crashing chords evoking the surge of the masses in Chopin's "Revolutionary" etude, the bottomless despair of the funeral march in Beethoven's Third Symphony, the solemn majesty of a great relig-

Heroes of Romanticism Observed by a portrait of Byron and bust of Beethoven, Liszt plays for friends. From left to right sit Alexander Dumas, George Sand (characteristically wearing men's garb), and Marie d'Agoult, Liszt's mistress. Standing are Victor Hugo, Paganini, and Rossini. *(Bildarchiv Preussischer Kulturbesitz)*

ious event in Schumann's Rhenish Symphony— such were the modern orchestra's musical paintings that plumbed the depths of human feeling.

This range and intensity gave music and musicians much greater prestige than in the past. Music no longer simply complemented a church service or helped a nobleman digest his dinner. Music became a sublime end in itself. It became for many the greatest of the arts, precisely because it achieved the most ecstatic effect and most perfectly realized the endless yearning of the soul. It was worthy of great concert

halls and the most dedicated sacrifice. The unbelievable one-in-a-million performer—the great virtuoso who could transport the listener to ecstasy and hysteria—became a cultural hero. The composer Franz Liszt (1811–1886) vowed to do for the piano what Paganini had done for the violin, and he was lionized as the greatest pianist of his age. People swooned for Liszt as they scream for rock stars today.

Though romanticism dominated music until late in the nineteenth century, no composer ever surpassed its first great master, Ludwig van Beethoven

(1770–1827). Extending and breaking open classical forms, Beethoven used contrasting themes and tones to produce dramatic conflict and inspiring resolutions. As the contemporary German novelist Ernst Hoffmann (1776–1822) wrote, "Beethoven's music sets in motion the lever of fear, of awe, of horror, of suffering, and awakens just that infinite longing which is the essence of Romanticism." Beethoven's range was tremendous; his output included symphonies, chamber music, sonatas for violin and piano, masses, an opera, and a great many songs.

At the peak of his fame, in constant demand as a composer and recognized as the leading concert pianist of his day, Beethoven began to lose his hearing. He considered suicide but eventually overcame despair: "I will take fate by the throat; it will not bend me completely to its will."[4] Beethoven continued to pour out immortal music. Among other achievements, he fully exploited for the first time the richness and beauty of the piano. Beethoven never heard much of his later work, including the unforgettable choral finale to the Ninth Symphony, for his last years were silent, spent in total deafness.

REFORMS AND REVOLUTIONS

While the romantic movement was developing, liberal, national, and socialist forces battered against the conservatism of 1815. In some countries, change occurred gradually and peacefully. Elsewhere, pressure built up like steam in a pressure cooker without a safety valve and eventually caused an explosion in 1848. Three important countries—Greece, Great Britain, and France—experienced variations on this basic theme.

NATIONAL LIBERATION IN GREECE

National, liberal revolution, frustrated in Italy and Spain by conservative statesmen, succeeded first after 1815 in Greece. Since the fifteenth century, the Greeks had been living under the domination of the Ottoman Turks. In spite of centuries of foreign rule, the Greeks had survived as a people, united by their language and the Greek orthodox religion. It was perfectly natural that the general growth of national aspirations and a desire for independence would inspire some Greeks in the early nineteenth century.

This rising national movement led to the formation of secret societies and then to revolt in 1821, led by Alexander Ypsilanti, a Greek patriot and a general in the Russian army.

The Great Powers, particularly Metternich, were opposed to all revolution, even revolution against the Islamic Turks. They refused to back Ypsilanti and supported the Ottoman Empire. Yet for many Europeans the Greek cause became a holy one. Educated Americans and Europeans were in love with the culture of classical Greece; Russians were stirred by the piety of their Orthodox brethren. Writers and artists, moved by the romantic impulse, responded enthusiastically to the Greek struggle. The flamboyant, radical poet Lord Byron went to Greece and died there in the struggle "that Greece might still be free." Turkish atrocities toward the rebels fanned the fires of European outrage and Greek determination. One of Delacroix's romantic masterpieces memorialized the massacre at Chios, where the Turks slaughtered nearly 100,000 Greeks.

The Greeks, though often quarreling among themselves, battled on against the Turks and hoped for the eventual support of European governments. In 1827 Great Britain, France, and Russia responded to popular demands at home and directed Turkey to accept an armistice. When the Turks refused, the navies of these three powers trapped the Turkish fleet at Navarino and destroyed it. Russia then declared another of its periodic wars of expansion against the Turks. This led to the establishment of a Russian protectorate over much of present-day Rumania, which had also been under Turkish rule. Great Britain, France, and Russia finally declared Greece independent in 1830 and installed a German prince as king of the new country in 1832. In the end the Greeks had won: a small nation had gained its independence in a heroic war against a foreign empire.

LIBERAL REFORM IN GREAT BRITAIN

Eighteenth-century British society had been both flexible and remarkably stable. It was dominated by the landowning aristocracy, but that class was neither closed nor rigidly defined. Successful business and professional people could buy land and become gentlemen, while the common people had more than the usual opportunities of the preindustrial world. Basic civil rights for all were balanced by a tradition of def-

Delacroix: Massacre at Chios The Greek struggle for freedom and independence won the enthusiastic support of liberals, nationalists, and romantics. The Ottoman Turks were seen as cruel oppressors holding back the course of history, as in this powerful masterpiece by Delacroix. *(Louvre/Cliché des Musées Nationaux)*

erence to one's social superiors. Parliament was manipulated by the king and was thoroughly undemocratic. Only about 6 percent of the population could vote for representatives to Parliament, and by the 1780s there was growing interest in some kind of political reform.

But the French Revolution threw the aristocracy into a panic for a generation, making it extremely hostile to any attempts to change the status quo. The Tory party, completely controlled by the landed aristocracy, was particularly fearful of radical movements at home and abroad. Castlereagh initially worked closely with Metternich to restrain France and restore a conservative balance in central Europe. This same intense conservatism motivated the Tory government at home. After 1815, the aristocracy defended its ruling position by repressing every kind of popular protest.

THE PRELUDE TO 1848

March 1814	Russia, Prussia, Austria, and Britain form the Quadruple Alliance to defeat France
April 1814	Napoleon abdicates
May–June 1814	Restoration of the Bourbon monarchy; Louis XVIII issues Constitutional Charter providing for civil liberties and representative government
	First Peace of Paris: allies combine leniency with defensive posture toward France
October 1814– June 1815	Congress of Vienna peace settlement: establishes balance-of-power principle and creates the German Confederation
February 1815	Napoleon escapes from Elba and marches on Paris
June 1815	Battle of Waterloo
September 1815	Austria, Prussia, and Russia form the Holy Alliance to repress liberal and revolutionary movements
November 1815	Second Peace of Paris and renewal of Quadruple Alliance: punishes France and establishes the European "congress system"
1819	Carlsbad Decrees: Metternich imposes harsh measures throughout the German Confederation
1820	Revolution in Spain and the Kingdom of the Two Sicilies
	Congress of Troppau: Metternich and Alexander I of Russia proclaim principle of intervention to maintain autocratic regimes
1821	Austria crushes liberal revolution in Naples and restores the Sicilian autocracy
	Greek revolt against the Ottoman Turks
1823	French armies restore the Spanish regime
	United States proclaims the Monroe Doctrine
1824	Reactionary Charles X succeeds Louis XVIII in France
1830	Charles X repudiates the Constitutional Charter; insurrection and collapse of government; Louis Philippe succeeds to the throne and maintains a narrowly liberal regime until 1848
	Greece wins independence from the Ottoman Empire
1832	Reform Bill expands British electorate and encourages the middle class
1839	Louis Blanc, *Organization of Work*
1840	Pierre Joseph Proudhon, *What Is Property?*
1846	Jules Michelet, *The People*
1848	Karl Marx and Friedrich Engels, *The Communist Manifesto*

The first step in this direction was the Corn Law of 1815. During a generation of war with France, the British had been unable to import food. As shortages occurred and agricultural prices skyrocketed, a great deal of marginal land had been brought under cultivation. This development had been a bonanza for the landed aristocracy, whose fat rent rolls became even fatter. Peace meant that grain could be imported again and that the price of wheat and bread would go down. To almost everyone except the aristocracy, lower prices seemed highly desirable. The aristocracy, however, rammed the Corn Law through Parliament. This law prohibited the importation of foreign grain unless the price at home rose above eighty shillings per quarter-ton—a level reached only in time of harvest disaster before 1790. Seldom has a class legislated more selfishly for its own narrow economic advantage.

The Corn Law, coming at a time of widespread unemployment and postwar adjustment, led to protests and demonstrations by urban laborers. They were supported by radical intellectuals, who campaigned for a reformed House of Commons that would serve the nation and not just the aristocracy. In 1817 the Tory government responded by temporarily suspending the traditional rights of peaceable assembly and habeas corpus. Two years later, Parliament passed the infamous Six Acts, which among other things controlled a heavily taxed press and practically eliminated all mass meetings. These acts followed an enormous but orderly protest at Saint Peter's Fields in Manchester, which had been savagely broken up by armed cavalry. Nicknamed the "Battle of Peterloo," in scornful reference to the British victory at Waterloo, this incident expressed the government's determination to repress and stand fast.

Ongoing industrial development was not only creating urban and social problems but also strengthening the upper-middle classes. The new manufacturing and commercial groups insisted on a place for their new wealth alongside the landed wealth of the aristocracy in the framework of political power and social prestige. They called for certain kinds of liberal reform: reform of town government, organization of a new police force, and more rights for Catholics and dissenters. In the 1820s, a less frightened Tory government moved in the direction of better urban administration, greater economic liberalism, and civil equality for Catholics. The prohibition on imports of foreign grain was replaced by a heavy tariff. These actions encouraged the middle classes to press on for reform of Parliament, so they could have a larger say in government and perhaps repeal the revised Corn Law, that symbol of aristocratic domination.

The Whig party, though led like the Tories by great aristocrats, had by tradition been more responsive to commercial and manufacturing interests. In 1830 a Whig ministry introduced "an act to amend the representation of the people of England and Wales." Defeated, then passed by the House of Commons, this reform bill was rejected by the House of Lords. But when in 1832 the Whigs got the king to promise to create enough new peers to pass the law, the House of Lords reluctantly gave in rather than see its snug little club ruined by upstart manufacturers and plutocrats. A mighty surge of popular protest had helped the king and lords make up their minds.

THE BRITISH LION IN 1850;

OR, THE EFFECTS OF FREE TRADE.

Free-Trade Optimism Appearing in *Punch* in 1846 as the Corn Law was being repealed, this cartoon looked to the future and reflected British self-confidence. Socially and economically advanced Great Britain had no need for protective tariffs. The British economy actually did boom after 1850. *(The British Library)*

The Reform Bill of 1832 had profound significance. The House of Commons had emerged as the all-important legislative body. In the future, an obstructionist House of Lords could always be brought into line by the threat of creating new peers. The new industrial areas of the country gained representation in the Commons, and many old "rotten boroughs"—electoral districts with very few voters that the landed aristocracy had bought and sold—were eliminated.

The redistribution of seats reflected the shift in population to the northern manufacturing counties and the gradual emergence of an urban society. As a result of the Reform Bill of 1832, the number of voters increased about 50 percent. Comfortable middle-class groups in the urban population, as well as some substantial farmers who leased their land, received the vote. Thus the pressures building in Great Britain were successfully—though only temporarily—released. A major reform had been achieved peacefully, without revolution or civil war. More radical reforms within the system appeared difficult but not impossible.

The principal radical program was embodied in the "People's Charter" of 1838 and the Chartist movement (page 720). Partly inspired by the economic distress of the working class, the Chartists' core demand was universal male (not female) suffrage. They saw complete political democracy and rule by the common people as the means to a good and just society. Hundreds of thousands of people signed gigantic petitions calling on Parliament to grant all men the right to vote, first and most seriously in 1839, again in 1842, and yet again in 1848. Parliament rejected all three petitions. In the short run, the working poor failed with their Chartist demands, but they learned a valuable lesson in mass politics.

While calling for universal suffrage, many working-class people joined with middle-class manufacturers in the Anti-Corn Law League, founded in Manchester in 1839. Mass participation made possible a popular crusade against the tariff on imported grain and against the landed aristocracy. People were fired up by dramatic popular orators such as John Bright and Richard Cobden. These fighting liberals argued that lower food prices and more jobs in industry depended on repeal of the Corn Law. Much of the working class agreed. The climax of the movement came in 1845, when Ireland's potato crop failed and famine seemed likely in England. In 1846 the Tory prime minister Robert Peel joined with the Whigs and a minority of his own party to repeal the Corn Law. Thereafter, free trade became almost sacred doctrine in Great Britain.

The following year, the Tories passed a bill designed to help the working classes, but in a different way. This was the Ten Hours Act of 1847, which limited the workday for women and young people in factories to ten hours. Tory aristocrats continued to champion legislation regulating factory conditions.

They were competing vigorously with the middle class for the support of the working class. This healthy competition between a still-vigorous aristocracy and a strong middle class was a crucial factor in Great Britain's peaceful evolution. The working classes could make temporary alliances with either competitor to better their own conditions.

THE REVOLUTION OF 1830 IN FRANCE

Louis XVIII's Constitutional Charter of 1814—theoretically a gift from the king but actually a response to political pressures—was basically a liberal constitution (page 748). The economic gains of the middle class and the prosperous peasantry were fully protected; great intellectual and artistic freedom was permitted; and a real parliament with upper and lower houses was created. Immediately after Napoleon's abortive Hundred Days, the moderate, worldly-wise king refused to bow to the wishes of die-hard aristocrats like his brother Charles, who wished to sweep away all the revolutionary changes and return to a bygone age of royal absolutism and aristocratic pretension. Instead, Louis appointed as his ministers moderate royalists, who sought and obtained the support of a majority of the representatives elected to the lower Chamber of Deputies between 1816 and Louis's death in 1824.

Louis XVIII's charter was anything but democratic. Only about 100,000 of the wealthiest people out of a total population of 30 million had the right to vote for the deputies who, with the king and his ministers, made the laws of the nation. Nonetheless, the "notable people" who did vote came from very different backgrounds. There were wealthy businessmen, war profiteers, successful professionals, ex-revolutionaries, large landowners from the middle class, Bourbons, and Bonapartists.

The old aristocracy with its pre-1789 mentality was a minority within the voting population. It was this situation that Louis's successor, Charles X (1824–1830), could not abide. Crowned in a lavish, utterly medieval, five-hour ceremony in the cathedral of Rheims in 1824, Charles was a true reactionary. He wanted to re-establish the old order in France. Increasingly blocked by the opposition of the deputies, Charles finally repudiated the Constitutional Charter in an attempted coup in July 1830. He issued decrees stripping much of the wealthy middle class of its voting rights, and he censored the press.

The reaction was an immediate insurrection. In "three glorious days" the government collapsed. Paris boiled with revolutionary excitement, and Charles fled. Then the upper-middle class, which had fomented the revolt, skillfully seated Charles's cousin, Louis Philippe, duke of Orléans, on the vacant throne.

Louis Philippe (1830–1848) accepted the Constitutional Charter of 1814, adopted the red, white, and blue flag of the French Revolution, and admitted that he was merely the "king of the French people." In spite of such symbolic actions, the situation in France remained fundamentally unchanged. As Casimir Périer, a wealthy banker and Louis Philippe's new chief minister, bluntly told a deputy who complained when the vote was extended only from 100,000 to 170,000 citizens: "The trouble with this country is that there are too many people like you who imagine that there has been a revolution in France."[5] The wealthy "notable" elite actually tightened its control as the old aristocracy retreated to the provinces to sulk harmlessly. For the upper-middle class there had been a change in dynasty, in order to protect the status quo and the narrowly liberal institutions of 1815. Republicans, democrats, social reformers, and the poor of Paris were bitterly disappointed. They had made a revolution, but it seemed for naught.

THE REVOLUTIONS OF 1848

In 1848 revolutionary political and social ideologies combined with economic crisis and the romantic impulse to produce a vast upheaval. Only the most advanced and the most backward major countries —reforming Great Britain and immobile Russia— escaped untouched. Governments toppled; monarchs and ministers bowed or fled. National independence, liberal-democratic constitutions, and social reform: the lofty aspirations of a generation seemed at hand. Yet, in the end, the revolutions failed. Why was this so?

A DEMOCRATIC REPUBLIC IN FRANCE

The late 1840s in Europe were hard economically and tense politically. The potato famine in Ireland in 1845 had echoes on the Continent. Bad harvests jacked up food prices and caused misery and unemployment in the cities. "Prerevolutionary" outbreaks occurred all across Europe: an abortive Polish revolution in the northern part of Austria in 1846, a civil war between radicals and conservatives in Switzerland in 1847, and an armed uprising in Naples, Italy, in January 1848. Revolution was almost universally expected, but it took revolution in Paris—once again —to turn expectations into realities.

From its beginning in 1830, Louis Philippe's "bourgeois monarchy" was characterized by stubborn inaction. There was a glaring lack of social legislation, and politics was dominated by corruption and selfish special interests. The king's chief minister in the 1840s, François Guizot, was complacency personified. Guizot was especially satisfied with the electoral system. Only the rich could vote for deputies, and many of the deputies were docile government bureaucrats. It was the government's stubborn refusal to consider electoral reform that touched off popular revolt in Paris. Barricades went up on the night of February 22, 1848, and by February 24, Louis Philippe had abdicated in favor of his grandson. But the common people in arms would tolerate no more monarchy. This refusal led to the proclamation of a provisional republic, headed by a ten-man executive committee and certified by cries of approval from the revolutionary crowd.

In the flush of victory, there was much about which Parisian revolutionaries could agree. A generation of historians and journalists had praised the First French Republic, and their work had borne fruit: the revolutionaries were firmly committed to a republic as opposed to any form of constitutional monarchy, and they immediately set about drafting a constitution for France's Second Republic. Moreover, they wanted a truly popular and democratic republic, so that the healthy, life-giving forces of the common people—the peasants and the workers—could reform society with wise legislation. In practice, building such a republic meant giving the right to vote to every adult male, and this was quickly done. Revolutionary compassion and sympathy for freedom were expressed in the freeing of all slaves in French colonies, abolition of the death penalty, and the establishment of a ten-hour workday for Paris.

Yet there were profound differences within the revolutionary coalition in Paris. On the one hand there were the moderate, liberal republicans of the middle class. They viewed universal manhood suffrage as the ultimate concession to be made to popular forces and

Daumier: The Legislative Belly Protected by freedom of the press after 1830, French radicals bitterly attacked the do-nothing government of Louis Philippe. Here Daumier savagely ridicules the corruption of the Chamber of Deputies. *(Charles Deering Collection. Courtesy of the Art Institute of Chicago)*

strongly opposed any further radical social measures. On the other hand were the radical republicans. Influenced by the critique of capitalism and unbridled individualism elaborated by a generation of utopian socialists, and appalled by the poverty and misery of the urban poor, the radical republicans were committed to socialism. To be sure, socialism came in many utopian shapes and sizes for the Parisian working poor and their leaders, but that did not make their commitment to it any less real. Finally, wedged in between were individuals like the poet Lamartine and the democrat Ledru-Rollin, who were neither doctrinaire socialists nor stand-pat liberals and who sought to escape an impending tragedy.

Worsening depression and rising unemployment brought these conflicting goals to the fore. Louis Blanc (page 739), who along with a worker named Albert represented the republican socialists in the provisional government, pressed for recognition of a socialist right to work. Blanc asserted that perma-

nent government-sponsored cooperative workshops should be established for workers. Such workshops would be an alternative to capitalist employment and a decisive step toward a new social order.

The moderate republicans wanted no such thing. They were willing to provide only temporary relief. The resulting compromise set up national workshops —soon to become a vast program of pick-and-shovel public works—and established a special commission under Louis Blanc to "study the question." This satisfied no one. As bad as the national workshops were, though, they were better than nothing. An army of desperate poor from the French provinces and even from foreign countries streamed into Paris to sign up. The number enrolled in the workshops soared from 10,000 in March to 120,000 by June, and another 80,000 were trying unsuccessfully to join.

While the workshops in Paris grew, the French masses went to the polls in late April. Voting in most cases for the first time, the people elected to the new

February	Revolt in Paris against Louis Philippe's "bourgeois monarchy"; Louis Philippe abdicates; proclamation of a provisional republic
February–June	Establishment and rapid growth of government-sponsored workshops in France
March 3	Hungarians under Kossuth demand autonomy from Austrian Empire
March 13	Uprising of students and workers in Vienna; Metternich flees to London
March 19–21	Frederick William IV of Prussia is forced to salute the bodies of slain revolutionaries in Berlin and agrees to a liberal constitution and merger into a new German state
March 20	Ferdinand I of Austria abolishes serfdom and promises reforms
March 26	Workers in Berlin issue a series of socialist demands
April 22	French voters favor moderate republicans over radicals 5:1
May 15	Parisian socialist workers invade the Constitutional Assembly and unsuccessfully proclaim a new revolutionary state
May 18	Frankfurt Assembly begins writing a new German constitution
June 17	Austrian army crushes working-class revolt in Prague
June 22–26	French government abolishes the national workshops, provoking an uprising
	June Days: republican army defeats rebellious Parisian working class
October	Austrian army besieges and retakes Vienna from students and working-class radicals
December	Conservatives force Ferdinand I of Austria to abdicate in favor of young Francis Joseph
	Frederick William IV disbands Prussian Constituent Assembly and grants Prussia a conservative constitution
	Louis Napoleon wins a landslide victory in French presidential elections
March 1849	Frankfurt Assembly elects Frederick William IV of Prussia emperor of the new German state; Frederick William refuses and reasserts royal authority in Prussia
June–August 1849	Habsburg and Russian forces defeat the Hungarian independence movement

Constituent Assembly about five hundred moderate republicans, three hundred monarchists, and one hundred radicals who professed various brands of socialism. One of the moderate republicans was the author of *Democracy in America,* Alexis de Tocqueville (1805–1859), who had predicted the overthrow of Louis Philippe's government. To this brilliant observer, socialism was the most characteristic aspect of the revolution in Paris.

This socialist revolution had evoked a violent reaction not only among the frightened middle and upper classes but also among the bulk of the population—the peasants. The French peasants owned land, and according to Tocqueville, "private property had become with all those who owned it a sort of bond of fraternity."[6] The countryside, Tocqueville wrote, had been seized with a universal hatred of radical Paris. Returning from Normandy to take his seat in the new Constituent Assembly, Tocqueville saw that a majority of the members were firmly committed to the republic and strongly opposed to the socialists, and he shared their sentiments.

The clash of ideologies—of liberal capitalism and socialism—became a clash of classes and arms after the elections. The new government's executive committee dropped Louis Blanc and thereafter included no representative of the Parisian working class. Fearing that their socialist hopes were about to be dashed, the workers invaded the assembly on May 15 and tried to proclaim a new revolutionary state. But the government was ready and used the middle-class National Guard to squelch this uprising. As the workshops continued to fill and grow more radical, the fearful but powerful propertied classes in the assembly took the offensive. On June 22 the government dissolved the national workshops in Paris, giving the workers the choice of joining the army or going to workshops in the provinces.

The result was a spontaneous and violent uprising. Frustrated in their attempts to create a socialist society, masses of desperate people were now losing even their life-sustaining relief. As a voice from the crowd cried out when the famous astronomer François Arago counseled patience: "Ah, Monsieur Arago, you have never been hungry!"[7] Barricades sprang up in the narrow streets of Paris, and a terrible class war began. Working people fought with the courage of utter desperation, but the government had the army and the support of peasant France. After three terrible "June Days" and the death or injury of more than ten thousand people, the republican army under General Louis Cavaignac stood triumphant in a sea of working-class blood and hatred.

The revolution in France thus ended in spectacular failure. The February coalition of the middle and working classes had in four short months become locked in mortal combat. In place of a generous democratic republic, the Constituent Assembly completed a constitution featuring a strong executive. This allowed Louis Napoleon, nephew of Napoleon Bonaparte, to win a landslide victory in the election of December 1848. The appeal of his great name, as well as the desire of the propertied classes for order at any cost, had produced a semi-authoritarian regime.

THE AUSTRIAN EMPIRE IN 1848

Throughout central Europe, news of the upheaval in France evoked feverish excitement and eventually revolution. Liberals demanded written constitutions, representative government, and greater civil liberties. When governments hesitated, popular revolts followed. Urban workers and students served as the shock troops, but they were allied with middle-class liberals and peasants. In the face of this united front, monarchs collapsed and granted almost everything. The popular revolutionary coalition, having secured great and easy victories, then broke down as it had in France. The traditional forces—the monarchy, the aristocracy, and the regular army—recovered their nerve, reasserted their authority, and took back many

though not all of the concessions. Reaction was everywhere victorious.

The revolution in the Austrian Empire began in Hungary. Nationalism had been growing among Hungarians since about 1790, and in 1848 under the leadership of Louis Kossuth, the Hungarians demanded national autonomy, full civil liberties, and universal suffrage. When the monarchy in Vienna hesitated, Viennese students and workers took to the streets on March 13 and added their own demands. Peasant disorders broke out in parts of the empire. The Habsburg emperor Ferdinand I (1835–1848) capitulated and promised reforms and a liberal constitution. Metternich fled in disguise toward London. The old order seemed to be collapsing with unbelievable rapidity.

The coalition of revolutionaries was not completely stable, though. The Austrian Empire was overwhelmingly agricultural, and serfdom still existed. On March 20, as part of its capitulation before upheaval, the monarchy abolished serfdom with its degrading forced labor and feudal services. Peasants throughout the empire felt they had won a victory reminiscent of that in France in 1789. Newly free, men and women of the land lost interest in the political and social questions agitating the cities. The government had in the peasants a potential ally of great importance, especially since, in central Europe as in France, the army was largely composed of peasants.

The coalition of March was also weakened—and ultimately destroyed—by conflicting national aspirations. In March the Hungarian revolutionary leaders pushed through an extremely liberal, almost democratic, constitution granting widespread voting rights and civil liberties and ending feudal obligations. So far, well and good. Yet the Hungarian revolutionaries were also nationalists with a mission. They wanted the ancient Crown of Saint Stephen, with its mosaic of provinces and nationalities, transformed into a unified centralized Hungarian nation. To the minority groups that formed half the population of the kingdom of Hungary—the Croats, the Serbs, and the Rumanians—such unification was completely unacceptable. Each felt entitled to political autonomy and cultural independence. The Habsburg monarchy in Vienna exploited the fears of the minority groups, and they were soon locked in armed combat with the new Hungarian government.

In a somewhat different way, Czech nationalists

Revolutionary Justice in Vienna As part of the conservative resurgence, in October 1848 the Austrian minister of war ordered up reinforcements for an army marching on Hungary. In a last defiant gesture the outraged revolutionaries in Vienna seized the minister and lynched him from a lamppost for treason. The army then reconquered the city in a week of bitter fighting. *(Mary Evans Picture Library)*

based in Bohemia and the city of Prague, led by the Czech historian Palacký, came into conflict with German nationalists. Like the minorities in Hungary, the Czechs saw their struggle for autonomy as a struggle against a dominant group—the Germans. Thus the national aspirations of different peoples in the Austrian Empire came into sharp conflict, and the monarchy was able to play off one group against the other.

Nor was this all. The urban working classes of poor artisans and day laborers were not as radical in the Austrian Empire as they were in France, but then neither were the middle class and lower-middle class. Throughout Austria and the German states, where Metternich's brand of absolutism had so recently ruled supreme, the middle class wanted liberal reform, complete with constitutional monarchy, limited voting rights, and modest social measures. They wanted a central European equivalent of the English Reform Bill of 1832 and the Corn Law repeal of 1846. When the urban poor rose in arms, as they did in the Austrian cities of Vienna, Prague, and Milan and throughout the German Confederation as well, and presented their own demands for universal voting rights and socialist workshops, the prosperous middle classes recoiled in alarm. As in Paris, the union of the urban poor and the middle class was soon a mere memory, and a bad memory at that.

Finally, the conservative aristocratic forces gathered around Emperor Ferdinand I regained their nerve and reasserted their great strength. The archduchess Sophia, a conservative but intelligent and courageous Bavarian princess married to the emperor's brother, provided a rallying point. Deeply ashamed of the emperor's collapse before a "mess of students,"[8] she insisted that Ferdinand, who had no heir, abdicate in favor of her eighteen-year-old son, Francis Joseph. Powerful nobles who held high positions in the government, the army, and the church agreed completely. They organized around Sophia in a secret conspiracy to reverse and crush the revolution.

Their first breakthrough came when one of the most dedicated members of the group, Prince Alfred Windischgrätz, bombarded Prague and savagely crushed a working-class revolt there on June 17. Other Austrian officials and nobles began to lead the minority nationalities of Hungary against the revolutionary government proclaimed by the Hungarian patriots. Another Austrian army reconquered Austria's possessions in northern Italy in late July 1848. Revolution failed as miserably in Italy as everywhere else. At the end of October, the well-equipped, predominantly peasant troops of the regular Austrian army attacked the student and working-class radicals in Vienna and retook the city at the cost of more than four thousand casualties. Thus, the determination of the Austrian aristocracy and the loyalty of its army were the final ingredients in the triumph of reaction and the defeat of revolution.

Only in Hungary were the forces represented by Sophia's son Francis Joseph (1848–1916), crowned emperor of Austria immediately after his eighteenth birthday in December 1848, at first unsuccessful. Yet another determined conservative, Nicholas I of Russia (1825–1855), obligingly lent his iron hand. On June 6, 1849, 130,000 Russian troops poured into Hungary. After bitter fighting—in which the Hungarian army supported the revolutionary Hungarian government—they subdued the country. For a number of years the Habsburgs ruled Hungary as a conquered territory.

PRUSSIA AND THE FRANKFURT ASSEMBLY

The rest of the states in the German Confederation generally recapitulated the ebb and flow of developments in France and Austria. The key difference was the additional goal of unifying the thirty-eight states of the German Confederation, with the possible exception of Austria, into a single sovereign nation. Therefore events in Germany were extraordinarily complex, since they were occurring not only in the individual principalities but at the all-German level as well.

After Austria, Prussia was the largest and most influential German kingdom. Prior to 1848, the goal of middle-class Prussian liberals had been to transform absolutist Prussia into a liberal constitutional monarchy. Such a monarchy would then take the lead in merging itself and all the other German states into a liberal unified nation. The agitation following the fall of Louis Philippe encouraged Prussian liberals to press their demands. When they were not granted, the artisans and factory workers in Berlin exploded, joining temporarily with the middle-class liberals in the struggle against the monarchy. The autocratic yet paternalistic Frederick William IV (1840–1861), already displaying the instability that later became insanity, vacillated. Humiliated by the revolutionary

Revolution in Berlin Barricades were erected on March 18 and fierce fighting lasted until dawn. The fury of midnight battle burns with a romantic glow in this contemporary illustration. *(The Bettman Archive)*

crowd, which forced him to salute from his balcony the blood-spattered corpses of workers who had fallen in an uprising on March 18, the nearly hysterical king finally caved in. On March 21 he promised to grant Prussia a liberal constitution and to merge it into a new national German state that was to be created. He appointed two wealthy businessmen from the Rhineland—perfect representatives of moderate liberalism—to form a new government.

The situation might have stabilized at this point if the workers had not wanted much more and the Prussian aristocracy much less. On March 26, the workers issued a series of radical and vaguely socialist demands, which troubled their middle-class allies: universal voting rights, a ministry of labor, a minimum wage, and a ten-hour day. At the same time, a wild-tempered Prussian landowner and aristocrat,

Otto von Bismarck, joined the conservative clique gathered around the king to urge counter-revolution. While these tensions in Prussia were growing, an elected assembly arrived in Berlin to write a constitution for the Prussian state.

To add to the complexity of the situation, a self-appointed committee of liberals from various German states successfully called for the formation of a national constituent assembly to begin writing a federal constitution for a unified German state. That body met for the first time on May 18 in Saint Paul's Church in Frankfurt. The Frankfurt National Assembly was a most curious revolutionary body. It was really a serious middle-class body whose 820 members included some 200 lawyers; 100 professors; many doctors, judges, and officials; and 140 businessmen for good measure.

Called together to write a constitution, the learned body was soon absorbed in a battle with Denmark over the provinces of Schleswig and Holstein. Jurisdiction over them was a hopelessly complicated issue from a legal point of view. Britain's Foreign Minister Lord Palmerston once said that only three people had ever understood the Schleswig-Holstein question, and of those one had died, another had gone mad, and he himself had forgotten the answer. The provinces were inhabited primarily by Germans but were ruled by the king of Denmark, although Holstein was a member of the German Confederation. When Frederick VII, the new nationalistic king of Denmark, tried to integrate both provinces into the rest of his state, the Germans there revolted.

Hypnotized by this conflict, the National Assembly at Frankfurt debated ponderously and finally called on the Prussian army to oppose Denmark in the name of the German nation. Prussia responded and began war with Denmark. As the Schleswig-Holstein issue demonstrated, the national ideal was a crucial factor motivating the German middle classes in 1848.

Almost obsessed with the fate of Germans under Danish rule, many members of the Frankfurt assembly also wanted to bring the German-speaking provinces of Austria into the new German state. Yet resurgent Austria resolutely opposed any division of its territory. Once this Austrian action made a "big German state" impossible, the Frankfurt assembly completed drafting a liberal constitution. Finally, in March 1849, the assembly elected King Frederick William of Prussia emperor of the new German national state (minus Austria and Schleswig-Holstein).

By early 1849, however, reaction had been successful almost everywhere. Frederick William reasserted his royal authority, disbanded the Prussian Constituent Assembly, and granted his subjects a limited, essentially conservative, constitution. Reasserting that he ruled by divine right, Frederick William contemptuously refused to accept the "crown from the gutter." The reluctant revolutionaries in Frankfurt had waited too long and acted too timidly.

When Frederick William, who really wanted to be emperor but only on his own authoritarian terms, tried to get the small monarchs of Germany to elect him emperor, Austria balked. Supported by Russia, Austria forced Prussia to renounce all its schemes of unification in late 1850. The German Confederation was re-established. After two turbulent years, the political map of the German states remained unchanged. Attempts to unite the Germans—first in a liberal national state and then in a conservative Prussian empire—had failed completely.

The liberal and nationalistic revolutions of 1848 were abortive. Political, economic, and social pressures that had been building since 1815 exploded dramatically, but very few revolutionary goals were realized. The moderate, nationalistic middle classes were unable to consolidate their initial victories in France or elsewhere in Europe. Instead, they drew back when artisans, factory workers, and radical socialists rose up to present their own much more revolutionary demands. This retreat facilitated the efforts of dedicated aristocrats in central Europe and made possible the crushing of Parisian workers by a coalition of solid bourgeoisie and landowning peasantry in France. A host of fears, a sea of blood, and a torrent of disillusion had drowned the lofty ideals and utopian visions of a generation. The age of romantic revolution was over.

NOTES

1. A. J. May, *The Age of Metternich, 1814–1848,* rev. ed., Holt, Rinehart & Winston, New York, 1963, p. 11.
2. H. Kohn, *Nationalism,* Van Nostrand, New York, 1955, pp. 141–142.
3. Quoted by F. D. Klingender, *Art and the Industrial Revolution,* Paladin, St. Albans, England, 1972, p. 117.
4. Quoted by F. B. Artz, *From the Renaissance to Romanticism: Trends in Style in Art, Literature, and Music, 1300–1830,* University of Chicago Press, Chicago, 1962, pp. 276, 278.
5. Quoted by G. Wright, *France in Modern Times,* Rand McNally, Chicago, 1960, p. 145.
6. A. de Tocqueville, *Recollections,* Columbia University Press, New York, 1949, p. 94.
7. M. Agulhon, *1848,* Editions du Seuil, Paris, 1973, pp. 68–69.

8. Quoted by W. L. Langer, *Political and Social Upheaval, 1832–1852,* Harper & Row, New York, 1969, p. 361.

SUGGESTED READING

All of the works cited in the Notes are highly recommended. May's is a good brief survey, while Kohn has written perceptively on nationalism in many books. Wright's *France in Modern Times* is a lively introduction to French history with stimulating biographical discussions; Langer's is a balanced synthesis with an excellent bibliography. Among general studies, C. Morazé, *The Triumph of the Middle Classes* (1968), a wide-ranging procapitalist interpretation, may be compared with E. J. Hobsbawm's flexible Marxism in *The Age of Revolution, 1789–1848* (1962). For English history, A. Brigg's socially oriented *The Making of Modern England, 1784–1867* (1967) and D. Thomson's *England in the Nineteenth Century, 1815–1914* (1951) are excellent. Restoration France is sympathetically portrayed by G. de Bertier de Sauvigny in *The Bourbon Restoration* (1967). T. Hamerow studies the social implications of the dual revolution in Germany in *Restoration, Revolution, Reaction 1815–1871* (1966), which may be compared to H. Treitschke's bombastic, pro-Prussian *History of Germany in the Nineteenth Century* (1915–1919), a classic of nationalistic history, and L. Snyder, *Roots of German Nationalism* (1978). E. Kedourie, *Nationalism* (1960), is a stimulating critique of the new faith. H. Kissinger, *A World Restored* (1957), offers not only a provocative interpretation of the Congress of Vienna but also insights into the mind of Richard Nixon's famous secretary of state. Compare with H. Nicolson's entertaining *The Congress of Vienna* (1946). On 1848, L. B. Namier's highly critical *1848: The Revolution of the Intellectuals* (1964) and P. Robertson's *Revolutions of 1848: A Social History* (1960) are outstanding. I. Deak, *The Lawful Revolution: Louis Kossuth and the Hungarians, 1848–49* (1979), is a noteworthy study of an interesting figure.

On early socialism and Marxism, there are W. Sewell, Jr.'s *Work and Revolution in France* (1980) and E. Wilson's engrossing survey of nineteenth-century developments, *To the Finland Station* (1953), as well as G. Lichtheim's high-powered *Marxism* (1961) and his *Short History of Socialism* (1970). J. Schumpeter, *Capitalism, Socialism and Democracy* (1947), is magnificent but difficult, a real mind-stretcher. On liberalism, there is R. Heilbroner's entertaining *The Worldly Philosophers* (1967) and G. de Ruggiero's classic *History of European Liberalism* (1959). J. Barzun, *Classic, Romantic and Modern* (1961), skillfully discusses the emergence of romanticism. R. Stromberg, *An Intellectual History of Modern Europe,* 3rd ed. (1981), and F. Baumer, *Modern European Thought: Continuity and Change in Ideas, 1600–1950* (1970), are valuable surveys. The important place of religion in nineteenth-century thought is considered from different perspectives in H. McLeod, *Religion and the People of Western Europe* (1981), and O. Chadwick, *The Secularization of the European Mind in the Nineteenth Century* (1976). Two good church histories with useful bibliographies are J. Altholz, *The Churches in the Nineteenth Century* (1967), and A. Vidler, *The Church in an Age of Revolution: 1789 to the Present Day* (1961).

The thoughtful reader is strongly advised to delve into the incredibly rich writing of contemporaries. J. Bowditch and C. Ramsland, eds., *Voices of the Industrial Revolution* (1961), is an excellent starting point, with well-chosen selections from leading economic thinkers and early socialists. H. Hugo, ed., *The Romantic Reader,* is another fine anthology. Jules Michelet's compassionate masterpiece *The People,* a famous historian's anguished examination of French social divisions on the eve of 1848, draws one into the heart of the period and is highly recommended. Alexis de Tocqueville covers some of the same ground less romantically in his *Recollections,* which may be compared with Karl Marx's white-hot "instant history," *Class Struggles in France, 1848–1850* (1850). Great novels that accurately portray aspects of the times are Victor Hugo, *Les Misérables,* an exciting story of crime and passion among France's poor; Honoré de Balzac, *Cousin Bette* and *Père Goriot;* and Thomas Mann, *Buddenbrooks,* a wonderful historical novel that traces the rise and fall of a prosperous German family over three generations during the nineteenth century.

24

**LIFE IN URBAN
SOCIETY**

*T*HE ERA of intellectual and political upheaval that culminated in the revolutions of 1848 was also an era of rapid urbanization. After 1848 Western political development veered off in a novel and uncharted direction, but the growth of towns and cities rushed forward with undiminished force. Thus Western society was urban and industrial in 1900, as surely as it had been rural and agrarian in 1800. The urbanization of society was both a result of the Industrial Revolution and a reflection of its enormous impact. What was life like in the cities, and how did it change? What did the emergence of urban industrial society mean for rich and poor and in between? How did families cope with the challenges and respond to the opportunities of the developing urban civilization? Finally, what changes in science and thought inspired and gave expression to this new civilization? These are the questions this chapter will investigate.

TAMING THE CITY

The consequences of economic transformation were, from the beginning, more positive than historians have often recognized. Indeed, given the poverty and uncertainty of preindustrial life, the history of industrialization is probably better written in terms of increasing opportunities than of greater hardships. But does not this relatively optimistic view of the consequences of industrialization neglect the quality of life in urban areas? Were not the new industrial towns and cities awful places where people, especially the poor, suffered from bad housing, lack of sanitation, and a sense of hopelessness? Did not these drawbacks more than cancel out higher wages and greater opportunity?

INDUSTRY AND THE GROWTH OF CITIES

Since the Middle Ages, European cities had been centers of government, culture, and large-scale commerce. They had also been congested, dirty, and unhealthy. People were packed together almost as tightly as possible within the city limits. The typical city was a "walking city": for all but the wealthiest classes, walking was the only available form of transportation.

Infectious disease spread with deadly speed in cities, and people were always more likely to die in the city than in the countryside. In the larger towns, more people died each year than were born, on the average, and urban populations were able to maintain their numbers only because newcomers were continuously arriving from rural areas. Little could be done to improve these conditions. Given the pervasive poverty, absence of urban transportation, and lack of medical knowledge, the deadly and overcrowded conditions could only be accepted fatalistically. They were the urban equivalents of bad weather and poor crops, the price of urban excitement and opportunity.

Clearly, deplorable urban conditions did not originate with the Industrial Revolution. What the Industrial Revolution did was to reveal those conditions more nakedly than ever before. The steam engine freed industrialists from dependence on the energy of fast-flowing streams and rivers, which meant that by 1800 there was every incentive to build new factories in urban areas. Cities had better shipping facilities and thus better supplies of coal and raw materials. There were also many hands wanting work in the cities, for cities drew people like a magnet. And it was a great advantage for a manufacturer to have other factories nearby to supply his needs and buy his products. Therefore, as industry grew, there was also a rapid expansion of already overcrowded and unhealthy cities.

The challenge of the urban environment was felt first and most acutely in Great Britain. The number of people living in cities of 20,000 or more in England and Wales jumped from 1.5 million in 1801 to 6.3 million in 1851 and reached 15.6 million by 1891. Such cities accounted for 17 percent of the total English population in 1801, 35 percent as early as 1851, and fully 54 percent in 1891. Other countries duplicated the English pattern as they industrialized. An American observer was hardly exaggerating when he wrote in 1899 that "the most remarkable social phenomenon of the present century is the concentration of population in cities"[1] (see Map 24.1).

In the 1820s and 1830s, people in Britain and France began to worry about the condition of their cities. In those years, the populations of a number of

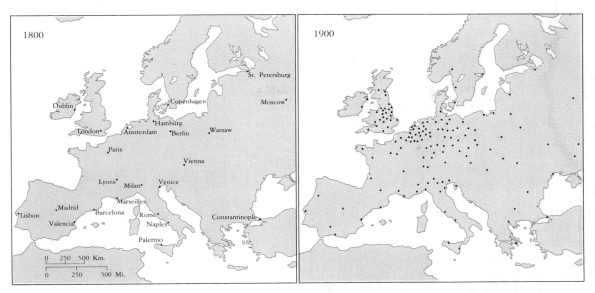

MAP 24.1 European Cities of 100,000 or More, 1800 and 1900 There were more large cities in Great Britain in 1900 than in all Europe in 1800.

British cities were increasing by 40 to 70 percent each decade. Manchester, the cotton city, grew by 40 percent between 1811 and 1821, and by 47 percent between 1821 and 1831. The population of the principal Scottish manufacturing city, Glasgow, grew by 30 percent or more each decade between 1801 and 1841. With urban areas expanding at such previously undreamed-of rates, people's traditional fatalistic indifference to overcrowded, unsanitary urban living conditions began to give way to active concern. Something had to be done.

On one point everyone could agree: except on the outskirts, each town and city was using every scrap of land to the fullest extent. Parks and open areas were almost nonexistent. A British parliamentary committee reported in 1833 that "with a rapidly increasing population, lodged for the most part in narrow courts and confined streets, the means of occasional exercise and recreation in fresh air are every day lessened, as inclosures [of vacant areas] take place and buildings spread themselves on every side."[2] Buildings were erected on the smallest possible lots, in order to pack the maximum number of people into a given space. Narrow houses were built wall to wall, in long rows. These row houses had neither front nor back yards, and only a narrow alley in back separated one row from the next. Or buildings were built around tiny courtyards completely enclosed on all four sides. Many people lived in cellars and attics. The tiny rooms within such buildings were often overcrowded. "Six, eight, and even ten occupying one room is anything but uncommon," wrote a doctor from Aberdeen in Scotland for a government investigation in 1842.

These highly concentrated urban populations lived in extremely unsanitary and unhealthy conditions. Open drains and sewers flowed alongside or down the middle of unpaved streets. Due to poor construction and an absence of running water, the sewers often filled with garbage and excrement. Toilet facilities were primitive in the extreme. In parts of Manchester, as many as two hundred people shared a single outhouse. Such privies filled up rapidly, and since they were infrequently emptied, sewage often overflowed and seeped into cellar dwellings.

The extent to which filth lay underfoot and the smell of excrement filled the air is hard to believe; yet it was abundantly documented between 1830 and 1850. One London construction engineer found, for example, that the cellars of two large houses on a major road were "full of night-soil [human excrement], to the depth of three feet, which had been permitted for years to accumulate from the overflow of the cesspools." Moreover, some courtyards in poorer

Filth and Disease This 1852 drawing from *Punch* tells volumes about the unhealthy living conditions of the urban poor. In the foreground children play with a dead rat and a woman scavenges a dungheap. Cheap rooming houses provide shelter for the frightfully overcrowded population. *(The British Library)*

neighborhoods became dunghills, collecting excrement that was sometimes sold as fertilizer. By the 1840s there was among the better-off classes a growing, shocking "realization that, to put it as mildly as possible, millions of English men, women, and children were living in shit."[3]

Who or what was responsible for these awful conditions? The crucial factors were the tremendous pressure of more people coupled with the *total* absence of public transportation. People simply had to jam themselves together if they were to be able to walk to shops and factories. Another factor was that government in Great Britain, both local and national, was slow to provide sanitary facilities and establish adequate building codes. This slow pace was probably attributable more to a need to explore and

identify what precisely should be done than to rigid middle-class opposition to government action. Certainly Great Britain had no monopoly on overcrowded and unhealthy urban conditions; may continental cities were every bit as bad.

Most responsible of all was the sad legacy of rural housing conditions in preindustrial society, combined with appalling ignorance. As the author of a recent study concludes, there "were rural slums of a horror not surpassed by the rookeries of London. . . . The evidence shows that the decent cottage was the exception, the hovel the rule."[4] Thus housing was far down on the newcomer's list of priorities, and it is not surprising that many people carried the filth of the mud floor and the dung of the barnyard with them to the city.

Indeed, ordinary people generally took dirt and filth for granted, and some even prized it. As one English miner told an investigator, "I do not think it usual for the lasses [in the coal mines] to wash their bodies; my sisters never wash themselves." As for the men, "their legs and bodies are as black as your hat." When poor people were admitted to English workhouses, they often resisted the required bath. One man protested that it was "equal to robbing him of a great coat which he had had for some years."[5]

THE PUBLIC HEALTH MOVEMENT

Although cleanliness was not next to godliness in most people's eyes, it was becoming so for some reformers. The most famous of these was Edwin Chadwick, one of the commissioners charged with the administration of relief to paupers under the revised Poor Law of 1834. Chadwick was a good *Benthamite* —that is, a follower of the radical philosopher Jeremy Bentham (1748–1832). Bentham had taught that public problems ought to be dealt with on a rational, scientific basis and according to the "greatest good for the greatest number." Applying these principles, Chadwick soon saw that much more than economics was involved in the problems of poverty and the welfare budget. Indeed, he soon became convinced that disease and death actually caused poverty, simply because a sick worker was an unemployed worker and orphaned children were poor children. Most important, Chadwick believed that disease could be prevented by quite literally cleaning up the urban environment. That was his "sanitary idea."

Building on a growing number of medical and sociological studies, Chadwick collected detailed reports from local Poor Law officials on the "sanitary conditions of the laboring population." After three years of investigation, these reports and Chadwick's hard-hitting commentary were published in 1842 to wide publicity. This mass of evidence proved that disease was related to filthy environmental conditions, which were in turn caused largely by lack of drainage, sewers, and garbage collection. Putrefying, smelly excrement was no longer simply disgusting. For reformers like Chadwick, it was a threat to the entire community. It polluted the atmosphere and caused disease.

The key to the energetic action Chadwick proposed was an adequate supply of clean piped water. Such water was essential for personal hygiene, public bathhouses, street cleaning, firefighting, and industry. Chadwick correctly believed that the stinking excrement of communal outhouses could be dependably carried off by water through sewers at less than one-twentieth the cost of removing it by hand. The cheap iron pipes and tile drains of the industrial age would provide running water and sewerage for all sections of town, not just the wealthy ones. In 1848, spurred on by the cholera epidemic of 1846, Chadwick's report became the basis of Great Britain's first public health law, which created a national health board and gave cities broad authority to build modern sanitary systems.

The public health movement won dedicated supporters in the United States, France, and Germany from the 1840s on. As in Great Britain, governments accepted at least limited responsibility for the health of all citizens. Moreover, they adopted increasingly concrete programs of action, programs that broke decisively with the age-old fatalism of urban populations in the face of shockingly high mortality. Thus, despite many people's skepticism about sanitation, European cities were making real progress toward adequate water supplies and sewage systems by the 1860s and 1870s. And city dwellers were beginning to reap the reward of better health.

THE BACTERIAL REVOLUTION

Effective control of communicable disease required more than a clean water supply and good sewers. Victory over disease also required a great leap forward in medical knowledge and biological theory. Reformers like Chadwick were seriously handicapped by the prevailing *miasmatic theory* of disease—the belief that people contract disease when they breathe the bad odors of decay and putrefying excrement; in short, the theory that smells cause disease. The miasmatic theory was a reasonable deduction from empirical observations: cleaning up filth did produce laudable results. Yet the theory was very incomplete.

Keen observation by doctors and public health officials in the 1840s and 1850s pinpointed the role of bad drinking water in the transmission of disease and suggested that contagion was *spread through* filth and not caused by it. Examples of particularly horrid

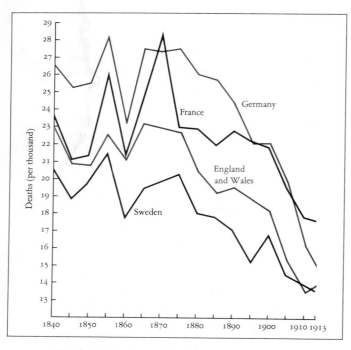

FIGURE 24.1 The Decline of Death Rates in England and Wales, Germany, France, and Sweden, 1840–1913
A rising standard of living, improvements in public health, and better medical knowledge all contributed to the dramatic decline of death rates in the nineteenth century.

stenches, such as that of the sewage-glutted Thames River at London in 1858, that did not lead to widely feared epidemics also weakened the miasmatic idea. Another factor was the successful merging of anatomical and clinical approaches to medicine between 1800 and 1850, particularly at the University of Paris school of medicine. Doctors there recognized a definite connection between the symptoms of certain illnesses observed at the bedside and the diseased organs seen when the body was dissected at autopsy. Medical research began zeroing in on specific diseases in an attempt to find specific treatments. When an improved theory was developed, progress could be rapid.

The breakthrough was the development of the germ theory of disease by Louis Pasteur (1822–1895). Pasteur was a French chemist by profession, not a physician. After important discoveries about the structure of crystals, he turned in 1854 to the study of fermentation. For ages people had used fermentation to make bread and wine, beer and cheese, but with-

out really understanding what was going on. And from time to time, beer and wine would mysteriously spoil for no apparent reason. As rapidly growing cities provided a vast concentrated demand, large brewers and winemakers were seeking ways to prevent spoilage and financial loss. Responding to their calls for help, Pasteur used his microscope to develop a simple test brewers could use to monitor the fermentation process and avoid spoilage. He then investigated various kinds of fermentation.

Pasteur found that fermentation depended on the growth of living organisms. Moreover, he demonstrated that the activity of these organisms could be suppressed by heating the wine or milk—by *pasteurizing* it. The breathtaking implication was that specific diseases were caused by specific living organisms —germs—and that those organisms could be controlled in people as well as in milk and wine. This theory was confirmed in 1868. After three years of intensive research, Pasteur isolated and controlled parasitic microorganisms that were killing off the silkworms used in France's large silk industry. Once again, scientific research had been stimulated by and had responded to the needs of the emerging industrial society.

By 1870 the work of Pasteur and others had demonstrated the general connection between germs and disease. When, in the middle of the 1870s, the German country doctor Robert Koch and his coworkers developed pure cultures of harmful bacteria and described their life cycles, the dam broke. Over the next twenty years, researchers—mainly Germans—identified the organisms responsible for disease after disease, often identifying several in a single year. At the same time, Pasteur and his colleagues concentrated on modifying and controlling the virulence of disease-producing germs. Building on the example of Edward Jenner's pioneering conquest of smallpox, Pasteur and his team developed a number of effective vaccines. The most famous was his vaccination for rabies in 1885, a crucial step in the development of modern immunology.

Acceptance of the germ theory brought about dramatic improvements in the deadly environment of hospitals and surgery. The English surgeon Joseph Lister (1827–1912) had noticed that patients with simple fractures were much less likely to die than those with compound fractures, in which the skin was broken and internal tissues were exposed to the air. In 1865, when Pasteur showed that the air was full of bacteria, Lister immediately grasped the connection between aerial bacteria and the problem of wound infection. He reasoned that a chemical disinfectant applied to a wound dressing would "destroy the life of the floating particles." Lister's "antiseptic principle" worked wonders. In the 1880s, German surgeons developed the more sophisticated practice of sterilizing not only the wound but everything—hands, instruments, clothing—that entered the operating room.

The achievements of the bacterial revolution coupled with the ever-more-sophisticated public health movement saved millions of lives, particularly after about 1890. Mortality rates began to decline dramatically in European countries (see Figure 24.1), as the awful death sentences of the past—diphtheria, typhoid and typhus, cholera, yellow fever—became vanishing diseases. City dwellers benefited especially from these developments. By 1910 the likelihood of death for people of all ages in urban areas was generally no greater than in rural areas, and sometimes it was less. Particularly striking was the decline in infant mortality in the cities after 1890. In many countries, an urban mother was less likely than a rural mother to see her child die before its first birthday by 1910. A great silent revolution had occurred: the terrible ferocity of death from disease-carrying bacteria in the cities had almost been tamed.

URBAN PLANNING AND PUBLIC TRANSPORTATION

Public health was only part of the urban challenge. Overcrowding, bad housing, and lack of transportation could not be solved by sewers and better medicine; yet in these areas, too, important transformations significantly improved the quality of urban life after midcentury.

More effective urban planning was one of the keys to improvement. Earlier urban planning had declined by the early nineteenth century; after 1850 it was revived and extended. France took the lead during the rule of Napoleon III (1848–1870), who sought to stand above class conflict and promote the welfare of all his subjects through government action. He believed that rebuilding much of Paris would provide employment, improve living conditions, and testify to the power and glory of his empire. In the baron

Georges Haussmann, an aggressive, impatient Alsatian whom he placed in charge of Paris, Napoleon III found an authoritarian planner capable of bulldozing both buildings and opposition. In twenty years Paris was quite literally transformed (see Map 24.2).

The Paris of 1850 was a labyrinth of narrow, dark streets, the results of desperate overcrowding. In an area of a central city not twice the size of New York's Central Park lived more than one-third of the city's 1 million inhabitants. Terrible slum conditions and extremely high death rates were facts of life. There were few open spaces and only two public parks for the entire metropolis. Public transportation played a very small role in this enormous walking city.

Haussmann and his fellow planners proceeded on many interrelated fronts. With a bold energy that often shocked their contemporaries, they razed old buildings in order to cut broad, straight, tree-lined boulevards through the center of the city as well as in new quarters on the outskirts. These boulevards, designed in part to prevent the easy construction and defense of barricades by revolutionary crowds, also permitted traffic to flow freely. Their construction also demolished some of the worst slums. New streets stimulated the construction of better housing, especially for the middle classes. Small neighborhood parks and open spaces were created throughout the city, and two very large peaks suitable for all kinds of holiday activities were developed on either side of the city. The city also improved its sewers, and a system of aqueducts more than doubled the city's supply of good fresh water.

Haussmann and Napoleon III tried to make Paris a more beautiful city, and to a large extent they succeeded. The broad, straight boulevards, such as those radiating out like the spokes of a wheel from the Arch of Triumph and those centering on the new Opera House, afforded impressive vistas. If for most people Paris remains one of the world's most beautiful and enchanting cities, it is in part because of the transformations of the Second Empire.

The rebuilding of Paris provided a new model for urban planning and stimulated modern urbanism throughout Europe, particularly after 1870. In city after city, public authorities mounted a coordinated attack on many of the interrelated problems of the urban environment. As in Paris, improvements in public health through better water supply and waste disposal often went hand in hand with new boulevard

Apartment Living in Paris This contemporary drawing shows how different social classes lived close together in European cities about 1850. Passing the middle-class family on the first (American second) floor, the economic condition of the tenants declined until one reached abject poverty in the garret. *(Bibliothèque Nationale, Paris)*

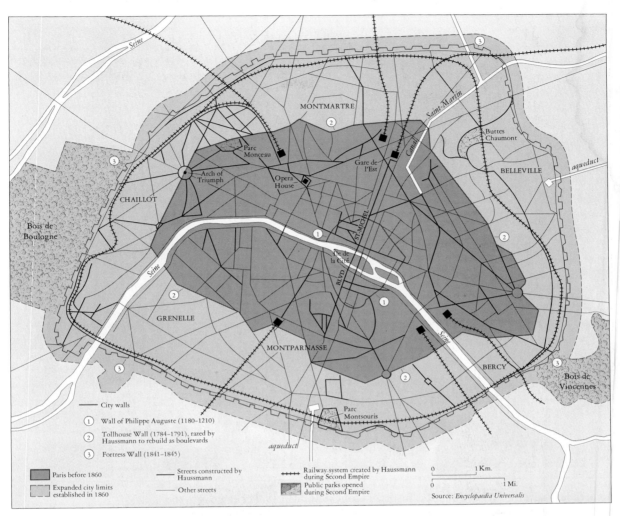

Map legend:

— City walls

① Wall of Philippe Auguste (1180–1210)

② Tollhouse Wall (1784–1791), razed by Haussmann to rebuild as boulevards

③ Fortress Wall (1841–1845)

Paris before 1860

Expanded city limits established in 1860

Streets constructed by Haussmann

Other streets

Railway system created by Haussmann during Second Empire

Public parks opened during Second Empire

0   1 Km.

0   1 Mi.

Source: *Encyclopaedia Universalis*

MAP 24.2 The Modernization of Paris, ca 1850–1870 Broad boulevards, large parks, and grandiose train stations transformed Paris. The cutting of the new north-south axis—known as the Central Boulevard—was one of Haussmann's most controversial projects. It razed much of Paris's medieval core and filled the Île de la Cité with massive government buildings.

construction. Cities like Vienna and Cologne followed the Parisian example of tearing down old walled fortifications and replacing them with broad, circular boulevards on which office buildings, town halls, theaters, opera houses, and museums were erected. These ring roads and the new boulevards that radiated out from them toward the outskirts eased movement and encouraged urban expansion (see Map 24.2). *Zoning expropriation laws,* which allowed a majority of the owners of land in a given quarter of the city to impose major street or sanitation improvements on a reluctant minority, were an important mechanism of the new urbanism.

The development of mass public transportation was also of great importance in the improvement of urban living conditions. Such transportation came late, but in a powerful rush. In the 1870s, many European cities authorized private companies to operate horse-drawn streetcars, which had been developed in the United States, to carry riders along the growing number of major thoroughfares. Then, in the 1890s, occurred the real revolution: European countries adopted another American transit innovation, the electric streetcar.

Electric streetcars were cheaper, faster, more dependable, and more comfortable than their horse-

Experimenting with Steam Countless inventors sought to adapt steam engines to the demands of urban transit. Yet even the most ingenious steam locomotives, like the one above being introduced in Paris in 1876, remained dirty, noisy, and undependable. And they frightened horses, which toiled on until relieved by electric motors. *(Photo: Caroline Buckler)*

drawn counterparts. Service improved dramatically. Millions of Europeans—workers, shoppers, schoolchildren—hopped on board during the workweek. And on weekends and holidays, streetcars carried millions on happy outings to parks and countryside, racetracks and music halls. In 1886 the horse-drawn streetcars of Austria-Hungary, France, Germany, and Great Britain were carrying about 900 million riders. By 1910 electric streetcar systems in the four countries were carrying 6.7 billion riders.[6] Each man, woman, and child was using public transportation four times as often in 1910 as in 1886.

Good mass transit helped greatly in the struggle for decent housing. Just as the new boulevards and horse-drawn streetcars had facilitated the middle-class move to better housing in the 1860s and 1870s, so electric streetcars gave people of modest means access to new, improved housing after 1890. The still-crowded city was able to expand and become less congested. In England in 1901, only 9 percent of the urban population was "overcrowded" in terms of the official definition of more than two persons per room. On the Continent, many city governments in the early twentieth century were building electric streetcar systems that provided transportation to new public and private housing developments in outlying areas of the city for the working classes. Poor, over-crowded housing, long one of the blackest blots on the urban landscape, was in retreat—another graphic example of the gradual taming of the urban environment.

RICH AND POOR AND IN BETWEEN

General improvements in health and in the urban environment had beneficial consequences for all kinds of people. Yet differences in living conditions between social classes remained gigantic.

SOCIAL STRUCTURE

How much had the almost-completed journey to an urban, industrialized world changed the social framework of rich and poor? The first great change was a substantial and undeniable increase in the standard of living for the average person. The real wages of British workers, for example, which had already risen substantially by 1850, almost doubled between 1850 and 1906. Similar unmistakable increases occurred in continental countries as industrial development quickened after 1850. Ordinary people took a great step forward in the centuries-old battle against poverty, reinforcing efforts to improve many aspects of human existence.

There is another side to the income coin, however, and it must be stressed as well. Greater economic rewards for the average person did *not* eliminate poverty, nor did they make the wealth and income of the rich and the poor significantly more equal. In almost every advanced country around 1900, the richest 5 percent of all households in the population received fully one-third of all national income. The richest one-fifth of households received anywhere from 50 to 60 percent of all national income, while the entire bottom four-fifths received only 40 to 50 percent. Moreover, the bottom 30 percent of households received 10 percent or less of all income. These enormous differences are illustrated in Figure 24.2.

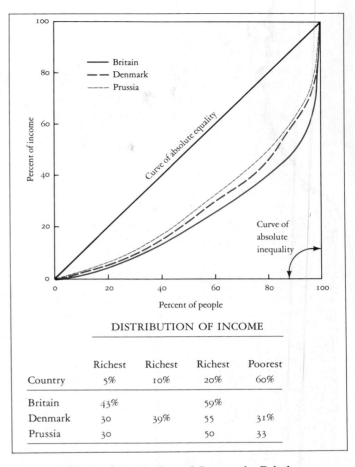

DISTRIBUTION OF INCOME

Country	Richest 5%	Richest 10%	Richest 20%	Poorest 60%
Britain	43%		59%	
Denmark	30	39%	55	31%
Prussia	30		50	33

FIGURE 24.2 The Distribution of Income in Britain, Denmark, and Prussia in 1913 The so-called Lorenz curve is useful for showing the degree of economic inequality in a given society. The closer the actual distribution of income lies to the (theoretical) curve of absolute equality, where each 20 percent of the population receives 20 percent of all income, the more incomes are nearly equal. European society was very far from any such equality before World War One. Notice that incomes in Prussia were somewhat more equal than those in Britain. *(Source: S. Kuznets,* Modern Economic Growth, *Yale University Press, New Haven, 1966, pp. 208–209)*

The middle classes were smaller than they are today and accounted for only about 20 percent of the population; thus, statistics show that the upper and middle classes alone received more than one-half of all income. The poorest four-fifths—the working classes, including peasants and agricultural laborers—received less altogether than the two richest classes.

And since many wives and teenagers in poor families worked, these figures actually understate the enduring gap between rich and poor. Moreover, income taxes on the wealthy were light or nonexistent. Thus the gap between rich and poor remained enormous at the beginning of the twentieth century. It was probably almost as great as it had been in the age of agriculture and aristocracy, before the Industrial Revolution.

The great gap between rich and poor endured, in part, because industrial and urban development made society more diverse and less unified. By no means did society split into two sharply defined opposing classes, as Marx had predicted. Instead, economic specialization enabled society to produce more effectively and in the process created more new social groups than it destroyed. There developed an almost unlimited range of jobs, skills, and earnings; one group or subclass shaded off into another in a complex, confusing hierarchy. Thus the tiny elite of the very rich and the sizable mass of the dreadfully poor were separated from each other by many subclasses, each filled with individuals struggling to rise or at least to hold their own in the social order. In this atmosphere of competition and hierarchy, neither the middle classes nor the working classes acted as a unified force. The age-old pattern of great economic inequality remained firmly intact.

THE MIDDLE CLASSES

By the beginning of the twentieth century, the diversity and range within the urban middle class were striking. Indeed, it is more meaningful to think of a confederation of middle classes, loosely united by occupations requiring mental rather than physical skill. At the top stood the upper-middle class, composed mainly of the most successful business families from banking, industry, and large-scale commerce. These families were the prime beneficiaries of modern industry and scientific progress. As the incomes of people in the upper-middle class rose and as they progressively lost all traces of radicalism after the trauma of 1848, they were almost irresistibly drawn toward the aristocratic lifestyle.

As the aristocracy had long divided the year between palatial country estates and lavish townhouses during "the season," so the upper-middle class purchased country places or built beach houses for week-

end and summer use. (Little wonder that a favorite scenario in late nineteenth-century middle-class novels was a mother and children summering gloriously in the country home, with only sporadic weekend intrusions by a distant, shadowy father.) The number of servants was an important indicator of wealth and standing for the middle class, as it had always been for the aristocracy. Private coaches and carriages, ever an expensive item in the city, were also signs of rising social status. More generally, the rich businessman and certainly his son devoted less time to business and more to "culture" and easy living than was the case in less wealthy or well-established commercial families.

The topmost reaches of the upper-middle class tended to shade off into the old aristocracy to form a new upper class. This was the 5 percent of the population that, as we have seen, received roughly one-third of the national income in European countries before 1914. Much of the aristocracy welcomed this development. Having experienced a sharp decline in its relative income in the course of industrialization, the landed aristocracy had met big business coming up the staircase and was often delighted to trade titles, country homes, and snobbish elegance for good hard cash. Some of the best bargains were made through marriages to American heiresses. Correspondingly, wealthy aristocrats tended increasingly to exploit their agricultural and mineral resources as if they were businessmen. Bismarck was not the only proud nobleman to make a fortune distilling brandy on his estates.

Below the wealthy upper-middle class were much larger, much less wealthy, and increasingly diversified middle-class groups. Here one found the moderately successful industrialists and merchants, as well as professionals in law and medicine. This was the middle-middle class, solid and quite comfortable but lacking great wealth. Below them were independent shopkeepers, small traders, and tiny manufacturers—the lower-middle class. Both of these traditional elements of the middle class expanded modestly in size with economic development.

Meanwhile, the traditional middle class was gaining two particularly important additions. The expansion of industry and technology created a growing demand for experts with specialized knowledge. The most valuable of the specialties became solid middle-class professions. Engineering, for example, emerged from the world of skilled labor as a full-fledged profession of great importance, considerable prestige, and many branches. Architects, chemists, accountants, and surveyors—to name only a few—first achieved professional standing in this period. They established criteria for advanced training and certification and banded together in organizations to promote and defend their interests.

Management of large public and private institutions also emerged as a kind of profession, as governments provided more services and as very large corporations like railroads came into being. Government officials and many private executives were not capitalists in the sense that they owned business enterprises. But public and private managers did have specialized knowledge and the capacity to earn a good living. And they shared most of the values of the business-owning entrepreneurs and the older professionals.

Industrialization also expanded and diversified the lower-middle class. The number of independent, property-owning shopkeepers and small businessmen grew and so did the number of white-collar employees—a mixed group of traveling salesmen, bookkeepers, store managers, and clerks who staffed the offices and branch stores of large corporations. White-collar employees were propertyless and often earned no more than the better-paid skilled or semiskilled workers did. Yet white-collar workers were fiercely committed to the middle class and to the ideal of moving up in society. In the Balkans, for example, clerks let their fingernails grow very long to distinguish themselves from people who worked with their hands. The tie, the suit, and soft clean hands were no-less-subtle marks of class distinction than wages.

Relatively well educated but without complex technical skills, many white-collar groups aimed at achieving professional standing and the accompanying middle-class status. Elementary school teachers largely succeeded in this effort. From being miserably paid part-time workers in the early nineteenth century, teachers rode the wave of mass education to respectable middle-class status and income. Nurses also rose from the lower ranks of unskilled labor to precarious middle-class standing. Dentistry was taken out of the hands of the working-class barbers and placed in the hands of highly trained (and middle-class) professionals.

In spite of their growing occupational diversity and conflicting interests, the middle classes were loosely united by a certain style of life. Food was the largest item in the household budget, for middle-class people liked to eat very well. In France and Italy, the middle classes' love of good eating meant that, even in large cities, activity ground almost to a halt between half past twelve and half past two on weekdays, as husbands and schoolchildren returned home for the midday meal. Around eight in the evening, the serious business of eating was taken up once again.

The English were equally attached to substantial meals, which they ate three times a day if income allowed. The typical English breakfast of bacon and eggs, toast and marmalade, and stewed fruits—not to mention sardines, kidneys, or fresh fish—always astonished French and German travelers, though large-breakfast enthusiasts like the Dutch and Scandinavians were less awed. The European middle classes consumed meat in abundance, and a well-off family might spend fully 10 percent of its substantial earnings on meat alone. In the 1890s, even a very prosperous English family—with an income of, say, $10,000 a year while the average working-class family earned perhaps $400 a year—spent fully a quarter of its income on food and drink.

Spending on food was also great because the dinner party was this class's favored social occasion. A wealthy family might give a lavish party for eight to twelve almost every week, while more modest households would settle for once a month. Throughout middle-class Europe, such dinners were served in the "French manner" (which the French had borrowed from the Russian aristocracy): eight or nine separate courses, from appetizers at the beginning to coffee and liqueurs at the end. In summer, a picnic was in order. But what a picnic! For a party of ten, one English cookbook suggested five pounds of cold salmon, a quarter of lamb, eight pounds of pickled brisket, a beef tongue, a chicken pie, salads, cakes, and six pounds of strawberries. An ordinary family meal normally consisted of only four courses—soup, fish, meat, and dessert.

The middle-class wife could cope with this endless procession of meals, courses, and dishes because she had both servants and money at her disposal. The middle classes were solid members of what some contemporary observers called the "servant-keeping classes." Indeed, the employment of at least one

"A Corner of the Table" With photographic precision this 1904 oil painting by the French academic artist Paul-Emile Chabas (1867–1937) skillfully idealizes the elegance and intimacy of a sumptuous dinner party. *(The Granger Collection)*

enormously helpful full-time maid to cook and clean was the best single sign that a family had crossed the vague line separating the working classes from the middle classes. The greater its income, the greater the number of servants a family employed. The all-purpose servant gave way to a cook and a maid, then to a cook, a maid, and a boy, and so on. A prosperous English family, far up the line with $10,000 a year, in 1900 spent fully one-fourth of its income on a hierarchy of ten servants: a manservant, a cook, a kitchen maid, two housemaids, a serving maid, a governess, a gardner, a coachman, and a stable boy. Domestic servants were the second largest item in the budget of the middle classes. Thus food and servants absorbed about one-half of income at all levels of the middle classes.

Well fed and well served, the middle classes were also well housed by 1900. Many quite prosperous families rented rather than owned their homes. Apartment living, complete with tiny rooms for servants under the eaves of the top floor, was commonplace (outside Great Britain), and wealthy investors and speculative builders found good profits in middle-class housing. By 1900 the middle classes were also quite clothes-conscious. The factory, the sewing machine, and the department store had all helped to reduce the cost and expand the variety of clothing. Middle-class women were particularly attentive to the fickle dictates of fashion.

Education was another growing expense, as middle-class parents tried to provide their children with ever-more-crucial advanced education. The keystones of culture and leisure were books, music, and travel. The long realistic novel, the heroics of Wagner and Verdi, the diligent striving of the dutiful daughter on a piano, and the packaged tour to a foreign country were all sources of middle-class pleasure.

Finally, the middle classes were loosely united by a shared code of expected behavior and morality. This code was strict and demanding. It laid great stress on hard work, self-discipline, and personal achievement. Men and women who fell into crime or poverty were generally assumed to be responsible for their own circumstances. Traditional Christian morality was reaffirmed by this code and preached tirelessly by middle-class people who took pride in their own good conduct and regular church attendance. Drinking and gambling were denounced as vices, sexual purity and fidelity were celebrated as virtues. In short, the middle-class person was supposed to know right from wrong and was expected to act accordingly.

The Working Classes

About four out of five people belonged to the working classes at the turn of the century. Many members of the working classes—that is, people whose livelihoods depended on physical labor and who did not employ domestic servants—were still small landowning peasants and hired farm hands. This was especially true in eastern Europe. In western and central Europe, however, the typical worker had left the land. In Great Britain, less than 8 percent of the people worked in agriculture, while in rapidly industrializing Germany only one person in four was employed in agriculture and forestry. Even in less-industrialized France, less than half the people depended on the land in 1900.

The urban working classes were even less unified and homogeneous than the middle classes. In the first place, economic development and increased specialization expanded the traditional range of working-class skills, earnings, and experiences. Meanwhile, the old sharp distinction between highly skilled artisans and unskilled manual workers was gradually breaking down. To be sure, highly skilled printers and masons, as well as unskilled dock workers and common laborers, continued to exist. But between these extremes there were ever-more semiskilled groups,

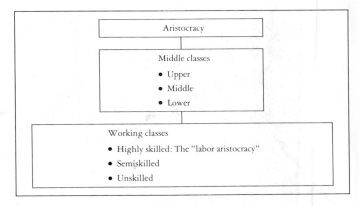

Figure 24.3 The Urban Social Hierarchy

many of which were composed of factory workers and machine tenders (see Figure 24.3).

In the second place, skilled, semiskilled, and unskilled workers had widely divergent lifestyles and cultural values, and their differences contributed to a keen sense of social status and hierarchy within the working classes. The result was great variety and limited class unity.

Highly skilled workers, who comprised about 15 percent of the working classes, were a real "labor aristocracy." By 1900 they were earning about £2 a week in Great Britain, or roughly $10 a week and $500 per year. This was only about two-thirds the income of the bottom ranks of the servant-keeping classes. But it was fully twice as much as the earnings of unskilled workers, who averaged about $5 per week, and substantially more than the earnings of semiskilled workers, who averaged perhaps $7 per week. Other European countries had a similar range of earnings.

The most "aristocratic" of the highly skilled workers were construction bosses and factory foremen, men who had risen from the ranks and were fiercely proud of their achievement. The labor aristocracy also included members of the traditional highly skilled handicraft trades that had not been mechanized or placed in factories. These included makers of scientific and musical instruments, cabinetmakers, potters, jewelers, bookbinders, engravers, and printers. This group as a whole was under constant long-term pressure. Irregularly but inexorably, factory methods were being extended to more crafts, and many skilled artisans were being replaced by lower-paid semiskilled factory workers. Traditional woodcarvers and watchmakers virtually disappeared, for example, as the making of furniture and time-pieces was taken out of the shop and put into the factory.

At the same time, a contrary movement was occurring. The labor aristocracy was consistently being enlarged by the growing need for highly skilled workers, such as shipbuilders, machine-tool makers, railway locomotive engineers, fine cotton textile spinners, and some metalworkers. Thus, the labor elite was in a state of flux as individuals and whole crafts moved in and out of it.

To maintain their precarious standing, the upper working class adopted distinctive values and strait-laced, almost puritanical, behavior. Like the middle classes, the labor aristocracy was strongly committed to the family and to economic improvement. Families in the upper working class saved money regularly, worried about their children's education, and valued good housing. Despite these similarities, which superficial observers were quick to exaggerate, skilled workers viewed themselves not as aspirants to the middle class but as the pacesetters and natural leaders of all the working classes. Well aware of the poverty and degradation not so far below them, they practiced self-discipline and stern morality.

The upper working class in general frowned on heavy drinking and sexual permissiveness. The organized temperance movement was strong in the countries of northern Europe, such as Great Britain, where a generation advocated tea as the "cup that cheers but does not inebriate." As one German labor aristocrat somberly warned, "the path to the brothel leads through the tavern" and from there quite possibly to drastic decline or total ruin for person and family.[7]

Men and women of the labor aristocracy were quick to find fault with those below them who failed to meet their standards. In 1868 William Lovett, an English labor aristocrat if ever there was one, denounced "this ignorant recklessness and improvidence that produce the swarms of half-starved, neglected, and ignorant children we see in all directions; who mostly grow up to become the burdens and often the pests of society, which the industrious and frugal have to support."[8] Finally, many members of the labor aristocracy had definite political and philosophical beliefs, whether Christian or socialist, or both. Such beliefs further strengthened the stern moral code of the upper working class.

Below the labor aristocracy stood semiskilled and unskilled urban workers. The enormous complexity of this sector of the world of labor is not easily summarized. Workers in the established crafts—carpenters, bricklayers, pipefitters—stood near the top of the semiskilled hierarchy, often flirting with (or having backslid from) the labor elite. A large number of the semiskilled were factory workers, who earned highly variable but relatively good wages and whose relative importance in the labor force was increasing.

The unskilled was the larger group, made up of day laborers such as longshoremen, wagon-driving teamsters, teenagers, and every kind of "helper." Many of these people had real skills and performed valuable services, but they were unorganized and divided, united only by the common fate of meager earnings. The same lack of unity characterized street vendors and market people—self-employed workers who competed savagely with each other and with the established shopkeepers of the lower-middle class.

One of the largest components of the unskilled group was domestic servants, whose numbers grew steadily in the nineteenth century. In advanced Great Britain, for example, one out of every seven employed persons was a domestic servant in 1911. The majority were women; indeed, one out of every three girls in Britain between the ages of fifteen and twenty was a domestic servant. Throughout Europe and America, a great many female domestics in the cities were recent migrants from rural areas. As in earlier times, domestic service was still hard work at low pay with limited personal independence. For the full-time general maid in a lower-middle-class family, there was an unending routine of babysitting, shopping, cooking, and cleaning. In the great households, the girl was at the bottom of a rigid hierarchy; status-conscious butlers and housekeepers were determined to stand almost as far above her as the wealthy master and mistress.

Nonetheless, domestic service had real attractions for "rough country girls" with strong hands and few specialized skills. Marriage prospects were better, or at least more varied, in the city. And though wages were low, they were higher and more regular than in hard agricultural work. Finally, as one London observer noted, young girls and other migrants were drawn to the city by "the contagion of numbers, the sense of something going on, the theaters and the music halls, the brightly lighted streets and busy

Cotton Textile Workers in Germany Factories became larger, faster, and more efficient in the nineteenth century. Compare this cotton mill with that of the early Industrial Revolution on page 715, where women and children are working together. *(Süddeutscher Verlag)*

crowds—all, in short, that makes the difference between the Mile End fair on a Saturday night, and a dark and muddy country lane, with no glimmer of gas and with nothing to do."[9]

Many young domestics from the countryside made a successful transition to working-class wife and mother. Yet, with an unskilled or unemployed husband and a growing family, such a woman often had to join the broad ranks of working women in the "sweated industries." These industries resembled the old putting-out and cottage industries of the eighteenth and early nineteenth centuries. The women normally worked at home, though sometimes together in some loft or garret, for tiny merchant-manufacturers. Paid by the piece and not by the hour, these women (and their young daughters), for whom organization was impossible, earned pitiful wages and lacked any job security.

Some women did hand-decorating of every conceivable kind of object; the majority, however, made clothing, especially after the advent of the sewing machine. Foot-powered sewing machines allowed the poorest wife or widow in the foulest dwelling to rival and eventually supplant the most highly skilled male tailor. By 1900 only a few such tailors lingered on in high-priced "tailor-made" shops. An army of poor women accounted for the bulk of the inexpensive "ready-made" clothes displayed on department store racks and in tiny shops. All of these considerations graphically illustrate the rise and fall of groups and individuals within the working classes.

The urban working classes sought fun and recreation, and they found it. Across the face of Europe, drinking was unquestionably the favorite leisure-time activity of working people. For many middle-class moralists, as well as moralizing historians since,

Servants Seeking Work in Moscow bargained with prospective employers (or their agents) in this special hiring yard just outside the ancient city walls. Moscow's bustling "market for servants" was open every day of the year and was busiest on Sundays. *(Photo: Caroline Buckler)*

love of drink has been a curse of the modern age—a sign of social dislocation and popular suffering. Certainly, drinking was deadly serious business. One English slum dweller recalled that "drunkenness was by far the commonest cause of dispute and misery in working class homes. On account of it one saw many a decent family drift down through poverty into total want."[10]

Generally, however, heavy "problem" drinking declined by the late nineteenth century, as it became less and less socially acceptable. This decline reflected in part the firm moral leadership of the upper working class. At the same time, drinking became more public and social, especially as on-the-job drinking, an ancient custom of field laborers and urban artisans, declined. Cafés and pubs became increasingly bright, friendly places. Working-class political activities, both moderate and radical, were also concentrated in taverns and pubs. Moreover, social drinking by married couples and sweethearts became an accepted and widespread practice for the first time. This greater participation by women undoubtedly helped to civilize the world of drink and hard liquor.

The two other leisure-time passions of the working classes were sports and music halls. By the late nine-teenth century there had been a great decline in "cruel sports," such as bullbaiting and cockfighting, throughout Europe. Their place was filled by modern spectator sports, of which racing and soccer were the most popular. There was a great deal of gambling on sports events, and for many a workingman the desire to decipher the racing forms was a powerful incentive toward literacy. Music halls and vaudeville theaters, the working-class counterparts of middle-class opera and classical theater, were enormously popular throughout Europe. In the words of one English printer, "It is to the music halls that the vast body of working people look for recreation and entertainment."[11] In 1900 there were more than fifty in London alone. Music-hall audiences were thoroughly mixed, which may account for the fact that drunkenness, sexual intercourse and pregnancy before marriage, marital difficulties, and problems with mothers-in-law were favorite themes of broad jokes and bittersweet songs.

In more serious moments, religion and the Christian churches continued to provide working people with solace and meaning. The eighteenth-century vitality of popular religion in Catholic countries and the Protestant rejuvenation exemplified by German Pietism and English Methodism (pages 661–662)

Sweated Industry About 1900 This moving photograph shows an English family making cheap toys at home for low wages. Women and children were the backbone of sweated industry, and this husband may be filling in while unemployed. *(University of Reading, Museum of English Rural Life)*

carried over into the nineteenth century. Indeed, many historians see the early nineteenth century as an age of religious revival. Yet historians also recognize that, by the last two or three decades of the nineteenth century, a considerable decline in both church attendance and church donations was occurring in most European countries. And it seems clear that this decline was greater for the urban working classes than for their rural counterparts or for the middle classes.

What did the decline in working-class church attendance really mean? Some have argued that it accurately reflected a general decline in faith and religious belief. Others disagree, noting correctly that most working-class families still baptized their children and considered themselves Christians. Admitting that more research is necessary, it appears that the urban working classes in Europe did become more secular and less religious in the late nineteenth and early twentieth centuries. They rarely repudiated the Christian religion, but it tended to play a diminishing role in their daily lives.

Part of the reason was that the construction of churches failed to keep up with the rapid growth of urban population, especially in new working-class neighborhoods. Thus the vibrant, materialistic urban environment undermined popular religious impulses, which were poorly served in the cities. Equally important, however, was the fact that throughout the nineteenth century both Catholic and Protestant churches were normally seen as they saw themselves —as conservative institutions defending social order and custom. Therefore, as the European working classes became more politically conscious, as the next chapter will show, they tended to see the established (or quasi-established) "territorial church" as defending what they wished to change and allied with their political opponents. Especially the men of the urban working classes developed vaguely antichurch attitudes, even though they remained neutral or positive toward religion. They tended to regard regular church attendance as "not our kind of thing"—not part of urban working-class culture.

The pattern was different in the United States. There, most churches also preached social conservatism in the nineteenth century. But because church and state had always been separated and because there was always a host of competing denominations and even different religions, working people identified churches much less with the political and social status quo. Instead, individual churches in the United States were often closely identified with an ethnic group rather than with a social class; and churches thrived, in part, as a means of asserting ethnic identity.

THE FAMILY

Urban life wrought many fundamental changes in the family. Although much is still unknown, it seems clear that by the late nineteenth century, the family had stabilized considerably after the disruption of the late eighteenth and early nineteenth centuries. The home became more important for both men and women. The role of women and attitudes toward children underwent substantial change, and adolescence emerged as a distinct stage of life. These are but a few of the transformations that affected all social classes in varying degrees.

PREMARITAL SEX AND MARRIAGE

By 1850 the preindustrial pattern of lengthy courtship and mercenary marriage was pretty well dead among the working classes. In its place, the ideal of romantic love had triumphed. As one French observer in a small seaport remarked about 1850: "The young men are constantly letting partners with handsome dowries go begging. When they marry, it's ordinarily for inclination and not for advantage."[12] Couples were ever more likely to come from different, even distant, towns and to be more nearly the same age, further indicating that romantic sentiment was replacing tradition and financial considerations. The calculating practice whereby wealthy old craftsmen took pretty young brides, who as comfortable middle-aged widows later married poor apprentices, was increasingly heard of only in old tales and folk songs.

Economic considerations in marriage long remained much more important to the middle classes than to the working classes. In France, dowries and elaborate legal marriage contracts were standard practice, and marriage was for many families life's most crucial financial transaction. A popular author advised young Frenchmen that "marriage is in general a means of increasing one's credit and one's fortune and of insuring one's success in the world."[13] This preoccupation with money led many middle-class men, in France and elsewhere, to marry late and

to choose women considerably younger and less sexually experienced than themselves. These differences between husband and wife became a source of tension in many middle-class marriages.

A young woman of the middle class found her romantic life carefully supervised by her well-meaning mother, who schemed for a proper marriage and guarded her daughter's virginity like the family's credit. After marriage, middle-class morality sternly demanded fidelity.

Middle-class boys were watched, too, but not as vigilantly. By the time they reached late adolescence, they had usually attained considerable sexual experience with maids or prostitutes. With marriage a distant, uncertain possibility, it was all too easy for the young man of the middle classes to turn to the urban underworld of whoredom and sexual exploitation to satisfy his desires.

Sexual experimentation before marriage had also triumphed, as had illegitimacy. There was an "illegitimacy explosion" between 1750 and 1850 (page 641). By the 1840s, as many as one birth in three was occurring outside of wedlock in many large cities. Although poverty and economic uncertainty undoubtedly prevented many lovers from marrying, there were also many among the poor and propertyless who saw little wrong with having illegitimate offspring. As one young Bavarian woman answered happily when asked why she kept having illegitimate children: "It's O.K. to make babies. . . . The king has o.k.'d it!"[14] Thus the pattern of romantic ideals, premarital sexual activity, and widespread illegitimacy was firmly established by midcentury among the urban working classes.

It is hard to know how European couples managed sex, pregnancy, and marriage in the second half of the nineteenth century, because such questions were considered improper both in polite conversation and in public opinion polls. Yet there are many telltale clues. The rising rate of illegitimacy was reversed: more babies were born to married mothers. Some observers have argued that this shift reflected the growth of puritanism and a lessening of sexual permissiveness among the unmarried. This explanation, however, is unconvincing.

The percentage of brides who were pregnant continued to be high and showed little or no tendency to decline. In many parts of urban Europe around 1900, as many as one woman in three was going to the altar an expectant mother. Moreover, unmarried people

Prostitution was commonly known as the "great social evil" because it was so widespread. This young woman probably sold more than flowers. *(Mary Evans Picture Library)*

almost certainly used the cheap condoms and diaphragms the industrial age had made available to prevent pregnancy, at least in predominantly Protestant countries.

Unmarried young people were probably engaging in just as much sexual activity as their parents and grandparents who had created the illegitimacy explosion of 1750 to 1850. But toward the end of the nineteenth century, pregnancy usually meant marriage and the establishment of a two-parent household. This important development reflected the growing respectability of the working classes, as well as their gradual economic improvement. Skipping out was less acceptable, and marriage was less of an economic disaster. Thus the urban working-class couple became more stable, and their stability strengthened the family as an institution.

PROSTITUTION

In Paris alone, 155,000 women were registered as prostitutes between 1871 and 1903, and 750,000 others were suspected of prostitution in the same years. Men of all classes visited prostitutes, but the middle and upper classes supplied much of the motivating cash. Thus, though many middle-class men abided by the publicly professed code of stern puritanical morality, many others indulged their appetites for prostitutes and sexual promiscuity.

My Secret Life, the anonymous eleven-volume autobiography of an English sexual adventurer from the servant-keeping classes, provides a remarkable picture of such a man. Beginning at an early age with a maid, the author becomes progressively obsessed with sex and devotes his life to living his sexual fantasies. In almost every one of his innumerable encounters all across Europe, this man of wealth simply buys his pleasure. Usually meetings are arranged in a businesslike manner: regular and part-time prostitutes quote their prices; working-class girls are corrupted by hot meals and warm baths.

At one point, however, he offers a young girl a sixpence for a kiss and gets it. Learning that the pretty, unskilled working girl earns nine pence a day, he offers her the equivalent of a week's salary for a few moments of fondling. When she finally agrees, he savagely exults that *"her* want was my opportunity."[15] Later he offers more money for more gratification, and when she refuses, he tries unsuccessfully to rape her in a hackney cab. On another occasion he takes a farm worker by force: "Her tears ran down. If I had not committed a rape, it looked uncommonly like one." He then forces his victim to take money to prevent a threatened lawsuit, while the foreman advises the girl to keep quiet and realize that "you be in luck if he likes you."

Obviously atypical in its excesses, the encyclopedic thoroughness of *My Secret Life* does mirror accurately the dark side of sex and class in urban society. Thinking of their wives largely in terms of money and social position, the men of the comfortable classes often purchased sex and even affection from poor girls both before and after marriage. Moreover, the great continuing differences between rich and poor made for every kind of debauchery and sexual exploitation, including the brisk trade in poor virgins that the author of *My Secret Life* particularly relished. Brutal sexist behavior was part of life—a part the sternly moral women (and men) of the upper working class detested and tried to shield their daughters from. For many poor young women, prostitution, like domestic service, was a stage of life. Having passed through it, they went on to marry men of their own class and establish homes and families.

KINSHIP TIES

Within working-class homes, ties to relatives after marriage—kinship ties—were in general much stronger than superficial social observers have recognized. Most newlyweds tried to live near their parents, though not in the same house. Indeed, for many married couples in the cities, ties to mothers and fa-thers, uncles and aunts, became more important, and ties to nonrelated acquaintances became weaker.

People turned to their families to help in coping with sickness, unemployment, death, and old age. Although governments were generally providing more welfare services by 1900, the average couple and their children inevitably faced crises. Funerals, for example, were an economic catastrophe, requiring a sudden large outlay for special clothes, carriages, and burial services. Unexpected death or desertion could leave widows and orphans in need of financial aid or perhaps a foster home. Relatives responded to such cries, knowing full well that their time of need and repayment would undoubtedly come.

Relatives were also valuable at less tragic moments. If a couple was very poor, an aged relation often moved in to cook and mind the children so the wife could earn badly needed income outside the home. Sunday dinners and holiday visits were often shared, as was outgrown clothing and useful information. Often the members of a large family group all lived in the same neighborhood.

WOMEN AND FAMILY LIFE

Industrialization and the growth of modern cities brought great changes to the lives of European women. These changes were particularly consequential for married women, and most women did marry in the nineteenth century.

The work of most wives became quite distinct and separate from that of their husbands. Husbands became wage earners in factories and offices, while wives tended to stay home and manage the household and care for the children. The preindustrial pattern among both peasants and cottage workers, in which husbands and wives worked together and divided up household duties and child rearing, declined. Only in a few occupations, such as retail trade, did married couples live where they worked and struggle together to make their mom-and-pop operations a success. Factory employment for married women also declined as the early practice of hiring entire families in the factory disappeared.

As economic conditions improved late in the nineteenth century, married women tended to work outside the home only in poor families. One old English worker recalled that "the boy wanted to get into a position that would enable him to keep a wife and fam-

A Working-Class Home, 1875 Emotional ties within ordinary families grew stronger in the nineteenth century. *(Illustrated London News, LXVI, 1875. Photo courtesy of Boston Public Library)*

ily, as it was considered a thoroughly unsatisfactory state of affairs if the wife had to work to help maintain the home."[16] The ideal was a strict division of labor by sex: the wife as mother and homemaker, the husband as wage earner.

This rigid division of labor meant that married women faced great injustice if they tried to move into the man's world, the world of employment outside the home. Husbands were unsympathetic or hostile. Well-paying jobs were off limits to women, and a woman's wage was almost always less than a man's, even for the same work. No wonder some women rebelled by the second half of the nineteenth century and began the long-continuing fight for equality of the sexes and the rights of women. More generally, rigidly separate roles narrowed women's horizons and fenced in their world.

There was a brighter side to the same coin. As home and children became the wife's main concerns, her control and influence there apparently became increasingly absolute throughout Europe. Among the

English working classes, it was the wife who generally determined how the family's money was spent. In many families the husband gave all his earnings to his wife to tend. She returned to him only a small allowance for carfare, beer, tobacco, and union dues. All the major domestic decisions, from the children's schooling and religious instruction to the selection of new furniture or a new apartment, were hers. In France women had even greater power in their assigned domain. One English feminist noted in 1908 that "though legally women occupy a much inferior status than men [in France], in practice they constitute the superior sex. They are the power behind the throne." Another Englishwoman believed that "in most French households, women reign with unchallenged sway."[17]

Women ruled at home partly because running the urban household was a complicated and extremely demanding task. Twice-a-day food shopping, penny pinching, economizing, and the growing crusade against dirt—not to mention child raising—were a full-time occupation. Nor were there any laborsaving appliances to help. The wife also ruled at home because a good deal of her effort was directed toward pampering her husband as he expected. In countless humble households, she saw that he had meat while she ate bread, that he relaxed by the fire while she did the dishes.

The woman's guidance of the household went hand in hand with the increased emotional importance of home and family. The home she ran was idealized as a warm shelter in a hard and impersonal urban world. By the 1820s, one observer of the comfortable middle classes in Marseilles had noted, for example, that "the family father, obliged to occupy himself with difficult business problems during the day, can relax only when he goes home. . . . Family evenings together are for him a time of the purest and most complete happiness."[18]

In time the central place of the family spread down the social scale. For a child of the English slums in the early 1900s,

home, however, poor, was the focus of all love and interests, a sure fortress against a hostile world. Songs about its beauties were ever on people's lips. "Home, sweet home," first heard in the 1870s, had become "almost a second national anthem." Few walls in lower-working-class houses lacked "mottoes"—colored strips of paper, about nine inches wide and eighteen inches in length, attesting to domestic joys: EAST, WEST, HOME'S BEST; BLESS OUR HOME; GOD IS MASTER OF THIS HOUSE; HOME IS THE NEST WHERE ALL IS BEST.[19]

By 1900 home and family were what life was all about for millions of people of all classes.

Women also developed stronger emotional ties to their husbands. Even in the comfortable classes, marriages were increasingly founded on sentiment and sexual attraction rather than on money and calculation. Affection and eroticism became more central to the couple after marriage. Gustave Droz, whose bestseller *Mr., Mrs., and Baby* went through 121 editions between 1866 and 1884, saw love within marriage as the key to human happiness. He condemned men who made marriage sound dull and practical, men who were exhausted by prostitutes and rheumatism and who wanted their young wives to be little angels. He urged women to follow their hearts and marry a man more nearly their own age:

A husband who is stately and a little bald is all right, but a young husband who loves you and who drinks out of your glass without ceremony, is better. Let him, if he ruffles your dress a little and places a kiss on your neck as he passes. Let him, if he undresses you after the ball, laughing like a fool. You have fine spiritual qualities, it is true, but your little body is not bad either and when one loves, one loves completely. Behind these follies lies happiness.[20]

Many French marriage manuals of the late 1800s stressed that women had legitimate sexual needs, such as the "right to orgasm." Perhaps the French were a bit more enlightened in these matters than other nationalities. But the rise of public socializing by couples in cafés and music halls, as well as franker affection within the family, suggest a more erotic, pleasurable intimate life for women throughout Western society. This, too, helped make the woman's role as mother and homemaker acceptable and even satisfying.

CHILD RAISING

One of the most striking signs of deepening emotional ties within the family was the mother's love and concern for her tiny infants. This was a sharp break with the past. It may seem scarcely believable today that the typical mother in preindustrial Western society was very often indifferent toward her baby. This indifference—unwillingness to make real sacrifices for the welfare of the infant—was giving way among the comfortable classes by the later part of the eighteenth century, but the ordinary mother adopted new attitudes only as the nineteenth century progressed. The baby became more important, and women became better mothers.

Mothers increasingly breast-fed their infants, for example, rather than paying wet nurses to do so. Breast-feeding involved sacrifice—a temporary loss of freedom, if nothing else. Yet in an age when there was no good alternative to mother's milk, it saved lives. The surge of maternal feeling also gave rise to a wave of specialized books on child rearing and infant hygiene, such as Droz's phenomenally successful book. Droz urged fathers to get into the act and pitied those "who do not know how to roll around on the carpet, play at being a horse and a great wolf, and undress their baby."[21] Another sign, from France, of increased affection is that fewer illegitimate babies were abandoned as foundlings, especially after about 1850. Moreover, the practice of swaddling disappeared completely. Instead, ordinary mothers allowed their babies freedom of movement and delighted in their spontaneity.

The loving care lavished on infants was matched by greater concern for older children and adolescents. They, too, were wrapped in the strong emotional ties of a more intimate and protective family. For one thing, European women began to limit the number of children they bore, in order to care adequately for those they had. It was evident by the end of the century that the birthrate was declining across Europe, as Figure 24.4 shows, and it continued to do so until after World War Two. The Englishwoman who married in the 1860s, for example, had an average of about six children; her daughter marrying in the 1890s had only four; and her granddaughter marrying in the 1920s had only two or possibly three.

The most important reason for this revolutionary reduction in family size, in which the comfortable and well-educated classes took the lead, was parents' desire to improve their economic and social position and that of their children. Children were no longer an economic asset. By having fewer youngsters, parents could give those they had valuable advantages, from music lessons and summer vacations to long, expensive university educations and suitable dowries. A young German skilled worker with only one child spoke for many in his class when he said, "We want to get ahead, and our daughter should have things better than my wife and sisters did."[22] Thus, the growing tendency of couples in the late nineteenth century to use a variety of contraceptive methods—rhythm, withdrawal, and mechanical devices—certainly reflected increased concern for children.

Indeed, many parents were probably *too* concerned about their children, unwittingly subjecting them to an emotional pressure cooker of almost unbearable intensity. The result was that many children and especially adolescents came to feel trapped and in desperate need of greater independence.

Biological and medical theories led parents to believe that their own emotional characteristics were passed on to their offspring and that they were thus directly responsible for any abnormality in a child. The moment the child was conceived was thought to be of enormous importance. "Never run the risk of conception when you are sick or over-tired or unhappy," wrote one influential American woman.

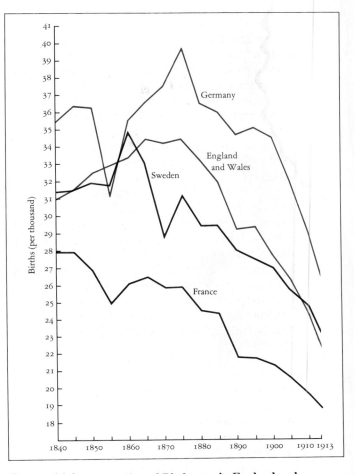

FIGURE 24.4 The Decline of Birthrates in England and Wales, France, Germany, and Sweden, 1840–1913 Women had fewer babies for a variety of reasons, including the fact that their children were increasingly less likely to die before reaching adulthood. Compare with Figure 24.2 on page 771.

"For the bodily condition of the child, its vigor and magnetic qualities, are much affected by conditions ruling this great moment."[23] So might the youthful "sexual excess" of the father curse future generations. Although this was true in the case of syphilis, which could be transmitted to unborn children, the rigid determinism of such views left little scope for the child's individual development.

Another area of excessive parental concern was the sexual behavior of the child. Masturbation was viewed with horror, for it represented an act of independence and even defiance. Diet, clothing, games, and sleeping were carefully regulated. Girls were dis-

The Drawing Room The middle-class ideal of raising cultured, educated, and properly protected young women is captured in this illustration. A serious mother lovingly teaches her youngest child while the older daughters practice their genteel skills. A drawing room was a kind of nineteenth-century family room, mercifully spared the tyranny of television. *(The Bettmann Archive)*

couraged from riding horses and bicycling because rhythmic friction simulated masturbation. Boys were dressed in trousers with shallow and widely separated pockets. Between 1850 and 1880, there were surgical operations for children who persisted in masturbating. Thereafter until about 1905, various restraining apparatuses were more often used.

These and less blatant attempts to repress the child's sexuality were a source of unhealthy tension, often made worse by the rigid division of sexual roles within the family. It was widely believed that mother and child love each other easily, but that relations between father and child are necessarily difficult and often tragic. The father was a stranger; his world of business was far removed from the maternal world of spontaneous affection. Moreover, the father was demanding, often expecting the child to succeed where he himself had failed and making his love conditional on achievement. Little wonder that the imaginative

literature of the late nineteenth century came to deal with the emotional and destructive elements of father-son relationships. In the Russian Feodor Dostoevsky's great novel *The Brothers Karamazov* (1880–1881), for example, four sons work knowingly or unknowingly to destroy their father. Later, at the murder trial, one of the brothers claims to speak for all mankind and screams out: "Who doesn't wish his father dead?"

Sigmund Freud (1856–1939), the Viennese founder of psychoanalysis, formulated the most striking analysis of the explosive dynamics of the family, particularly the middle-class family in the late nineteenth century. A physician by training, Freud began his career treating mental illness. He noted that the hysteria of his patients appeared to originate in bitter early childhood experiences, wherein the child had been obliged to repress strong feelings. When these painful experiences were recalled and reproduced under hypnosis or through the patient's free association of ideas, the patient could be brought to understand his or her unhappiness and eventually to deal with it.

One of Freud's most influential ideas concerned the Oedipal tensions resulting from the son's instinctive competition with the father for the mother's love and affection. More generally, Freud postulated that much of human behavior is motivated by unconscious emotional needs, whose nature and origins are kept from conscious awareness by various mental devices he called "defense mechanisms." Freud concluded that much unconscious psychological energy is sexual energy, which is in turn repressed and precariously controlled by rational thinking and moral rules. If Freud exaggerated the sexual and familial roots of adult behavior, that exaggeration was itself a reflection of the tremendous emotional intensity of family life in the late nineteenth century.

The working classes probably had more avenues of escape from such tensions than did the middle classes. Unlike the middle-class counterparts, who remained economically dependent on their families until a long education was finished or a proper marriage secured, working-class boys and girls went to work when they reached adolescence. Earning wages on their own, they could bargain with their parents for greater independence within the household by the time they were sixteen or seventeen. If they were unsuccessful, they could and did leave home, to live cheaply as paying lodgers in other working-class homes. Thus, the young person from the working classes broke away from the family more easily when emotional ties became oppressive. In the twentieth century, middle-class youth would follow this lead.

SCIENCE AND THOUGHT

Major changes in Western thought accompanied the emergence of urban society. Two aspects of these complex intellectual developments stand out as especially significant. Scientific knowledge expanded rapidly and came to influence the Western world-view even more profoundly than it had since the Scientific Revolution and the early Enlightenment. And, between about the 1840s and the 1890s, European literature underwent a shift from soaring romanticism to tough-minded realism.

As the pace of scientific advance quickened and as theoretical advances resulted in great practical benefits, science exercised growing influence on human thought. The intellectual achievements of the Scientific Revolution had resulted in few such benefits, and theoretical knowledge had also played a relatively small role in the Industrial Revolution in England. But breakthroughs in industrial technology enormously stimulated basic scientific inquiry, as researchers sought to explain theoretically how such things as steam engines and blast furnaces actually worked. The result was an explosive growth of fundamental scientific discoveries from the 1830s onward. And unlike earlier periods, these theoretical discoveries were increasingly transformed into material improvements for the general population.

A perfect example of the translation of better scientific knowledge into practical human benefits was the work of Pasteur and his followers in biology and the medical sciences. Another was the development of the branch of physics known as *thermodynamics*. Building on Newton's laws of mechanics and on studies of steam engines, thermodynamics investigated the relationship between heat and mechanical energy. By midcentury, physicists had formulated the fundamental laws of thermodynamics, which were then applied to mechanical engineering, chemical processes, and many other fields. The *law of conservation of energy* held that different forms of energy—such as heat, electricity, and magnetism—could be converted but neither created nor destroyed. Nineteenth-century thermodynamics demonstrated that the physical world is governed by firm, unchanging laws.

Chemistry and electricity were two other fields characterized by extremely rapid progress. Chemists devised ways of measuring the atomic weight of different elements, and in 1869 the Russian chemist Dmitri Mendeleev (1834–1907) codified the rules of chemistry in the periodic law and the periodic table. Chemistry was subdivided into many specialized branches, such as *organic chemistry*—the study of the compounds of carbon. Applying theoretical insights gleaned from this new field, researchers in large German chemical companies discovered ways of transforming the dirty, useless coal tar that accumulated in coke ovens into beautiful, expensive synthetic dyes for the world of fashion. The basic discoveries of Michael Faraday (1791–1867) on electromagnetism in the 1830s and 1840s resulted in the first dynamo (generator) and opened the way for the subsequent development of electric motors, electric lights, and electric streetcars.

The triumph of science and technology had at least three significant consequences. First, though ordinary citizens continued to lack detailed scientific knowledge, everyday experience and innumerable popularizers impressed the importance of science on the popular mind.

As science became more prominent in popular thinking, the philosophical implications of science formulated in the Enlightenment spread to broad sections of the population. Natural processes appeared to be determined by rigid laws, leaving little room for either divine intervention or human will. Yet scientific and technical advances had also fed the Enlightenment's optimistic faith in human progress, which now appeared endless and automatic to many middle-class minds.

Finally, the methods of science acquired unrivaled prestige after 1850. For many, the union of careful experiment and abstract theory was the only reliable route to truth and objective reality. The "unscientific" intuitions of poets and the revelations of saints seemed hopelessly inferior.

SOCIAL SCIENCE AND EVOLUTION

From the 1830s onward, many thinkers tried to apply the objective methods of science to the study of society. In some ways these efforts simply perpetuated the critical thinking of the philosophes. Yet there were important differences. The new "social scientists" had access to the massive sets of numerical data that governments had begun to collect, on everything from children to crime, from population to prostitution. In response, they developed new statistical methods to analyze these facts "scientifically" and supposedly to test their theories. And the systems of the leading nineteenth-century social scientists were more unified, all-encompassing, and dogmatic than those of the philosophes. Marx was a prime example (see pages 739–741).

Another extremely influential system builder was the French philosopher Auguste Comte (1798–1857). Initially a disciple of the utopian socialist Saint-Simon (page 739), Comte wrote a six-volume *System of Positive Philosophy* (1830–1842), which

was largely overlooked during the romantic era. But when the political failures of 1848 completed the swing to realism, Comte's philosophy came into its own. Its influence has remained great to this day.

Comte postulated that all intellectual activity progresses through predictable stages:

The great fundamental law . . . is this:—that each of our leading conceptions—each branch of our knowledge—passes successively through three different theoretical conditions: the Theological, or fictitious; the Metaphysical, or abstract; and the Scientific, or positive . . . The first is the necessary point of departure of human understanding, and the third is the fixed and definitive state. The second is merely a transition.[24]

By way of example, Comte noted that the prevailing explanation of cosmic patterns had shifted, as knowledge of astronomy developed, from the will of God (the theological) to the will of an orderly Nature (the metaphysical) to the rule of its own unchanging laws (the scientific). Later, this same intellectual progression took place in increasingly complex fields—physics, chemistry, and finally, the study of society. By applying the scientific, positivist method, Comte believed, his new discipline of sociology would soon discover the eternal laws of human relations. This colossal achievement would in turn enable expert social scientists to impose a disciplined harmony and well-being on less-enlightened citizens. Dismissing the "fictions" of traditional religions, Comte became the chief priest of the religion of science and rule by experts.

Comte's stages of knowledge exemplify the nineteenth-century fascination with the idea of evolution and dynamic development. Thinkers in many fields, like the romantic historians and "scientific" Marxists, shared and applied this basic concept. In geology, Charles Lyell (1797–1875) effectively discredited the long-standing view that the earth's surface had been formed by short-lived cataclysms, such as biblical floods and earthquakes. Instead, according to Lyell's principle of uniformitarianism, the same geological processes that are at work today slowly formed the earth's surface over an immensely long time. The evolutionary view of biological development, first proposed by the Greek Anaximander in the sixth century B.C., reemerged in a more modern form in the work of Jean Baptiste Lamarck (1744–1829). Lamarck asserted that all forms of life had

Attracting Females was an integral part of the struggle for survival, according to Darwin. He theorized that those males who were most attractive to females would have the most offspring, like this type of monkey that had developed ornamental hair with devastating sex appeal. Darwin used this illustration in *The Descent of Man* (1871). *(Library of Congress)*

arisen through a long process of continuous adjustment to the demands of the environment.

Lamarck's work was flawed—he believed that characteristics parents acquired in the course of their lives could be inherited by their children—and was not accepted, but it helped prepare the way for Charles Darwin (1809–1882), the most influential of all nineteenth-century evolutionary thinkers. As the official naturalist on a five-year scientific cruise to Latin America and the South Pacific in 1831, Darwin carefully collected specimens of the different animal species he encountered on the voyage. Back in England and convinced by fossil evidence and by his friend Lyell that the earth and life on it were immensely ancient, Darwin came to doubt the general belief in a special divine creation of each species of animals. Instead, he concluded, all life had gradually evolved from a common ancestral origin in an unending "struggle for survival." After long hesitation, Darwin published his research, which immediately attracted wide attention.

Darwin's great originality lay in suggesting precisely *how* biological evolution might have occurred. His theory is summarized in his title—*On the Origin of Species by the Means of Natural Selection* (1859). Decisively influenced by Malthus's gloomy theory that populations naturally grow faster than their food supplies, Darwin argued that chance differences among the members of a given species help some to survive while others died. Thus the variations that prove useful in the struggle for survival are selected naturally and gradually spread to the entire species through reproduction. Darwin did not explain why such variations occurred in the first place, and not until the early twentieth century did the study of genetics and the concept of mutation provide some answers.

As the capstone of already-widespread evolutionary thinking, Darwin's theory had a powerful and many-sided influence on European thought and the European middle classes. Darwin was hailed as the great scientist par excellence, the "Newton of biology," who had revealed once again the powers of objective science. Darwin's findings also reinforced the teachings of secularists like Comte and Marx, who scornfully dismissed religous belief in favor of agnostic or atheistic materialism. In the great cities especially, religion was on the defensive. Finally, many writers applied the theory of biological evolution to human affairs. Herbert Spencer (1820–1903), an English disciple of Auguste Comte, saw the human race as driven forward to ever-greater specialization and progress by the brutal econon ic struggle that efficiently determined the "survival of the fittest." The poor were the ill-fated weak, the prosperous the chosen strong. Understandably, Spencer and other Social Darwinists were especially popular with the upper-middle class.

REALISM IN LITERATURE

In 1868 Emile Zola (1840–1902), the giant of the realist movement in literature, defended his violently criticized first novel against charges of pornography and corruption of morals. Such accusations were meaningless, Zola claimed: he was only a purely objective scientist using "the modern method, the universal instrument of inquiry of which this age makes such ardent use to open up the future."

I chose characters completely dominated by their nerves and their blood, deprived of free-will, pushed to each action of their lives by the fatality of their flesh. . . . I have simply done on living bodies the work of analysis which surgeons perform on corpses.[25]

Zola's literary manifesto articulated the key themes of realism, which had emerged in the 1840s and continued to dominate Western culture and style until the 1890s. Realist writers believed that literature should depict life exactly as it was. Forsaking poetry for prose and the personal, emotional viewpoint of the romantics for strict, scientific objectivity, the realists simply observed and recorded—content to let the facts speak for themselves.

The major realist writers focused their extraordinary powers of observation on contemporary everyday life. Emphatically rejecting the romantic search for the exotic and the sublime, they energetically pursued the typical and the commonplace. Beginning with a dissection of the middle classes, from which

most of them sprang, many realists eventually focused on the working classes, especially the urban working classes, who had been neglected in imaginative literature before this time. They put a microscope to many unexplored and taboo subjects—sex, strikes, violence, alcoholism—and hastened to report that slums and factories teemed with savage behavior. Many shocked middle-class critics denounced realism as ugly sensationalism, wrapped provocatively in pseudoscientific declarations and crude language.

The realists' claims of objectivity did not prevent the elaboration of a definite world-view. Unlike the romantics, who had gloried in individual freedom and an unlimited universe, realists such as Zola were strict determinists. Human beings, like atoms, were components of the physical world, and all human actions were caused by unalterable natural laws. Heredity and environment determined human behavior; good and evil were merely social conventions.

The realist movement began in France, where romanticism had never been completely duminant, and three of its greatest practitioners—Balzac, Flaubert, and Zola—were French. Honoré de Balzac (1799–1850) spent thirty years writing a vastly ambitious panorama of postrevolutionary French life. Known collectively as *The Human Comedy,* this series of nearly one hundred books vividly portrays more than two thousand characters from virtually all sectors of French society. Balzac pictures urban society as grasping, amoral, and brutal, characterized by a Darwinian struggle for wealth and power. In *Père Goriot* (1835), the hero, a poor student from the provinces, eventually surrenders his idealistic integrity to feverish ambition and society's all-pervasive greed.

Madame Bovary (1857), the masterpiece of Gustave Flaubert (1821–1880), is far narrower in scope than Balzac's work but unparalleled in its depth and accuracy of psychological insight. Unsuccessfully prosecuted as an outrage against public morality and religion, Flaubert's carefully crafted novel tells the ordinary, even banal, story of a frustrated middle-class housewife who has an adulterous love affair and is betrayed by her lover. Without moralizing, Flaubert portrays the provincial middle class as petty, smug, and hypocritical.

Zola was most famous for his seamy, animalistic view of working-class life. But he also wrote gripping, carefully researched stories featuring the stock exchange, the big department store, and the army, as well as urban slums and bloody coal strikes. Like many later realists, Zola sympathized with socialism, a sympathy evident in his overpowering *Germinal* (1885).

Realism quickly spread beyond France. In England, Mary Ann Evans (1819–1880), who wrote under the pen name George Eliot, brilliantly achieved a more deeply felt, less sensational kind of realism. "It is the habit of my imagination," George Eliot wrote, "to strive after as full a vision of the medium in which a character moves as one of the character itself." Her great novel *Middlemarch: A Study of Provincial Life* examines masterfully the ways in which people are shaped by their social medium as well as their own inner strivings, conflicts, and moral choices. Thomas Hardy (1840–1928) was more in the Zola tradition. His novels, such as *Tess of the D'Urbervilles* and *Return of the Native,* depicted men and women frustrated and crushed by fate and bad luck.

The greatest Russian realist, Count Leo Tolstoy (1828–1910), combined realism in description and character development with an atypical moralizing, which came to dominate his later work. Tolstoy's greatest work was *War and Peace,* a monumental novel set against the historical background of Napoleon's invasion of Russia in 1812. Tolstoy probes deeply into the lives of a multitude of unforgettable characters, such as the ill-fated Prince Andrei; the shy, fumbling Pierre; and the enchanting, level-headed Natasha. Tolstoy goes to great pains to develop his fatalistic theory of history, which regards free will as an illusion and the achievements of even the greatest leaders as only the channeling of historical necessity. Yet Tolstoy's central message is one that most of the people discussed in this chapter would readily accept: human love, trust, and everyday family ties are life's enduring values.

Thoroughgoing realism (or "naturalism," as it was often called) arrived late in the United States, most arrestingly in the work of Theodore Dreiser (1871–1945). Dreiser's first novel, *Sister Carrie* (1900), the story of an ordinary farm girl who does well going wrong in Chicago, so outraged conventional morality that the publisher withdrew the book. The United States subsequently became a bastion of literary realism in the twentieth century after the movement had faded away in Europe.

The Industrial Revolution had a decisive influence on the urban environment. The populations of towns

George Eliot Reared in a strict religious atmosphere against which she later rebelled, Mary Ann Evans accepted scientific attitudes but never lost a strong moral sense of personal responsibility. Her first novels appeared when she was in her early forties. *(National Portrait Gallery, London)*

and cities grew rapidly because it was economically advantageous to locate factories and offices in urban areas. This rapid growth worsened long-standing overcrowding and unhealthy living conditions and posed a frightening challenge for society. Eventually government leaders, city planners, reformers, scientists, and ordinary citizens responded. They took effective action in public health and provided themselves with other badly needed urban services. Gradually they tamed the ferocious savagery of the traditional city.

As urban civilization came to prevail, there were major changes in family life. Especially among the lower classes, family life became more stable, more loving, and less mercenary. These improvements had a price, though. Sex roles for men and women became sharply defined and rigidly separate. Women especially tended to be locked into a subordinate and stereotypic role. Nonetheless, on balance, the quality of family life improved for all family members. Better, more stable family relations reinforced the benefits for the masses of higher real wages, increased social security, political participation, and education.

While the quality of urban and family life improved, the class structure became more complex and diversified than before. Urban society featured many distinct social groups, which existed in a state of constant flux and competition. Thus, the gap between rich and poor remained enormous and really quite traditional in mature urban society, although there were countless gradations between the extremes. Large numbers of poor women in particular continued to labor as workers in sweated industries, as domestic servants, and as prostitutes in order to satisfy the demands of their masters in the servant-keeping classes. Urban society in the late nineteenth century represented a great step forward for humanity, but it remained very unequal.

Inequality was a favorite theme of realist novelists like Balzac and Zola. More generally, literary realism reflected Western society's growing faith in science, progress, and evolutionary thinking. The emergence of urban, industrial civilization accelerated the secularization of the Western world-view.

NOTES

1. A Weber, *The Growth of Cities in the Nineteenth Century,* Columbia University Press, New York, 1899, p. 1.
2. Quoted by W. Ashworth, *The Genesis of Modern British Town Planning,* Routledge & Kegan Paul, London, 1954, p. 17.
3. S. Marcus, "Reading the Illegible," in *The Victorian City: Images and Realities,* ed. H. J. Dyos and Michael Wolff, Routledge & Kegan Paul, London, 1973, 1.266.
4. E. Gauldie, *Cruel Habitations: A History of Working-Class Housing, 1780–1918,* George Allen & Unwin, London, 1974, p. 21.
5. Quoted in E. Chadwick, *Report on the Sanitary Condition of the Labouring Population of Great Britain,* ed. M. W. Flinn, University Press, Edinburgh, 1965 (originally published, 1842). pp. 315–316.
6. J. P. McKay, *Tramways and Trolleys: The Rise of Urban Mass Transport in Europe,* Princeton University Press, Princeton, N.J., 1976, p. 81.
7. Quoted by R. P. Neuman, "The Sexual Question and Social Democracy in Imperial Germany," *Journal of Social History* 7 (Winter 1974):276.
8. Quoted by B. Harrison, "Underneath the Victorians," *Victorian Studies* 10 (March 1967):260.
9. Quoted by J. A. Banks, "The Contagion of Numbers," in Dyos and Wolff, 1.112.
10. R. Roberts, *The Classic Slum: Salford Life in the First Quarter of the Century,* University Press, Manchester, Eng., 1971, p. 95.
11. Quoted by B. Harrison, "Pubs," in Dyos and Wolff, 1.175.
12. Quoted by E. Shorter, *The Making of the Modern Family,* Basic Books, New York, 1975, p. 150.
13. Quoted by T. Zeldin, *France, 1848–1945,* Clarendon Press, Oxford, Eng., 1973, 1.288.
14. Quoted by J. M. Phayer, "Lower-Class Morality: The Case of Bavaria," *Journal of Social History* 8 (Fall 1974):89.
15. Quoted by S. Marcus, *The Other Victorians: A Study of Sexuality and Pornography in Mid-Nineteenth-Century England,* Basic Books, New York, 1966, p. 142,
16. Quoted by G. S. Jones, "Working-Class Culture and Working-Class Politics in London, 1870–1900: Notes on the Remaking of a Working Class," *Journal of Social History* 7 (Summer 1974): 486.
17. Quoted by Zeldin, 1.346.
18. Quoted by Shorter, pp. 230–231.
19. Roberts, p. 35.
20. Quoted by Zeldin, 1.295.
21. Ibid., 1.328
22. Quoted by Neuman, p. 281.
23. Quoted by S. Kern, "Explosive Intimacy: Psychodynamics of the Victorian Family," *History of Childhood Quarterly* 1 (Winter 1974):439.
24. A. Comte, *The Positive Philosophy of Auguste Comte,* trans. H. Martineau, J. Chapman, London, 1853, 1. 1–2.
25. Quoted by G. J. Becker, ed., *Documents of Modern Literary Realism,* Princeton University Press, Princeton, N.J., 1963, p. 159.

ART: A MIRROR OF SOCIETY

Art reveals the interests and values of society and frequently gives intimate and unique glimpses of how people actually lived. In portraits and statues, whether of saints, generals, philosophers, popes, poets, or merchants, it preserves the memory and fame of men and women who shaped society. In paintings, drawings, and carvings, it also shows how people worked, played, relaxed, suffered, and triumphed. Art, therefore, is extremely useful to the historian, especially for periods when written records are scarce. Every work of art and every part of it has meaning and has something of its own to say.

Art also manifests the changes and continuity of European life; as values changed in Europe, so did major artistic themes. In the eighteenth century some artists recalled the Renaissance by choosing to focus on aristocratic lifestyles and interests. Painters like Fragonard (overleaf) developed the rococo style, whose elements reflected the elegant refinement of Enlightenment culture. The romantic artists of the eighteenth and nineteenth centuries, however, rejected materialism and, driven by a sense of an unlimited universe, sought to reach new levels of spiritual understanding through their art. The romantic movement testified to a turbulent Europe caught up in revolutionary change. For these painters, nature replaced rationalism as the proper source of inspiration. Whereas the English landscape artist John Constable saw nature as the manifestation of a beneficent spirit, the nature portrayed by Joseph Turner, England's other great romantic painter, seethed with awesome uncontrollable power. The fury of the sea, a favorite subject, is evident in *Calais Pier* (1806), below. In this early painting the waves roll in higher and higher while black clouds weigh ominously on fishermen setting out to sea. Half sailor and vagabond, Turner lent seascapes unprecedented passion. (Tate Gallery, London.)

Realism, the next great artistic movement, reflected in part the concern for the working class aroused by the revolutionary failures of 1848. After 1850 social concerns found full expression in the art of realists like Courbet and Degas. Later in the nineteenth century, the impressionists, seeking to capture a given moment as the eye perceives it, gloried in the vibrant diversity of urban society. Though the twentieth century witnessed the disintegration of their faith in science and democracy, the impressionists, by valuing color and abstract design for their own sake, proved the crucial bridge between traditional representational and modern art.

The Swing *(left)* Jean-Honoré Fragonard (1732–1806). The sophistication and frivolity of the eighteenth-century French salon radiate from this delicately naughty work by Fragonard, a brilliant colorist in perfect harmony with the elitist taste of his age. An aging bishop swings a coy beauty, who "accidentally" loses her shoe, allowing her lover an enraptured peek under her petticoat. *(The Wallace Collection)*

The Haywain *(above)* John Constable (1776–1837). Even as the Industrial Revolution was transforming the land, the beauties of the English countryside found their loftiest celebration in the landscapes of John Constable, England's other great romantic painter. In sharp contrast to that of Turner, his nature was peculiarly harmonious, well maintained, and rich in spiritual values. The first artist of importance to paint outdoors, the bright pure colors of this 1821 masterpiece had a powerful impact on young French painters like Delacroix. *(Reproduced by courtesy of the Trustees, The National Gallery, London)*

The Threshing Floor *(below)* Francisco Goya (1746–1828). Until the late nineteenth century, agriculture remained the biggest single employer in most European countries. Most work was still done by hand and often in a community framework. This scene by the independent Spanish master Goya captures the joy of relaxation in the middle of a long day's work. *(Museo del Prado, Spain)*

Woman Ironing *(right, above)* Edgar Degas (1834–1917). After the failure of the revolutions of 1848, European society turned from soaring romanticism to tough-minded realism. The French realist Degas managed to portray the whole range of urban classes and individuals with extraordinary sensitivity and accuracy. In this sympathetic painting a weary woman succumbs to the fatigue and boredom of unskilled labor. *(Cliché des Musées Nationaux-Paris)*

The Stone Breakers *(right, below)* Gustave Courbet (1819–1877). Another famous French painter who rejected "noble ideals" and romantic flights of fancy was Courbet. Socialist and passionate advocate for plain working people, like the stone breakers portrayed here, Courbet believed that art must be firmly rooted in concrete objects and everyday experience. "Show me an angel," he said, "and I will paint it." *(Staatlichen Kunstsammlungen, Dresden)*

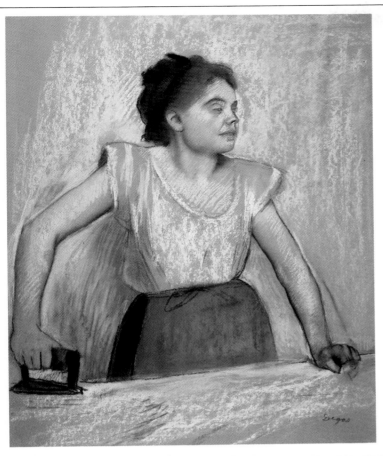

Le Moulin de la Galette à Montmartre *(above)* Auguste Renoir (1841–1919). The painters of the French impressionist school generally affirmed the beauty and value of modern life, reflecting western Europe's nineteenth-century faith in science, progress, and democracy. In this 1876 masterpiece, the joyous Renoir has transformed a popular outdoor dance hall of the urban masses into an enchanted fairyland. Impressionist painters applied colors directly to the canvas without first mixing them, a revolutionary technique that let the eye participate (by itself "mixing" the colors) in this ultimate form of optical realism. *(Cliché des Musées Nationaux-Paris)*

The Boating Party *(above)* Mary Cassatt (1844–1926). Born into a wealthy business family in the United States, Mary Cassatt moved to Paris, where she painted mothers and their children with a sensitivity unequaled in recent times. Here she captures with tender realism an attentive mother and her squirming child on a hot afternoon outing. Cassatt helped many French impressionists by successfully encouraging American collectors to buy their paintings. *(National Gallery of Art, Washington; Chester Dale Collection)*

Square of the Théâtre Français, Afternoon Winter Sun, 1900 *(above)* Camille Pissarro (1830–1803). This painting by the pure impressionist Pissarro captures the excitement and vitality of busy Paris boulevards, which brought all classes together, at least temporarily. The grandiose opera house stands in the distance, connected with France's most distinguished classical theater by the recently completed Avenue of the Opera. *(Courtesy of the Lefevre Gallery, London)*

SUGGESTED READING

All of the books and articles cited in the Notes are highly recommended; each in its own way is an important contribution to social history and life in the urban society. Note that the *Journal of Social History,* which has a strong European orientation, is excellent both for its articles and for its reviews of new books. T. Zeldin, *France, 1848–1945,* 2 vols. (1973, 1977), is a pioneering social history that opens many doors, as is the ambitious synthesis by T. Hamerow, *The Birth of a New Europe: State and Society in the Nineteenth Century* (1983).

On the European city, D. Pickney, *Napoleon III and the Rebuilding of Paris* (1972), is fascinating, as are G. Masur, *Imperial Berlin* (1970), and M. Hamm, ed., *The City in Russian History* (1976). So also are N. Evenson's beautifully illustrated *Paris: A Century of Change, 1878–1978* (1979); D. Grew's authoritative *Town in the Ruhr: A Social History of Bochum, 1860–1914* (1979); and the essays in J. Merriman, ed., *French Cities in the 19th Century: Class, Power, and Urbanization* (1982). D. Olsen's scholarly *Growth of Victorian London* (1978) complements H. Mayhew's wonderful contemporary study, *London Labour and the Labouring Poor* (1861), reprinted recently. M. Crichton's realistic historical novel on organized crime, *The Great Train Robbery* (1976), is excellent. J. J. Tobias, *Urban Crime in Victorian England* (1972), is a lively, scholarly approach to declining criminal activity in the nineteenth century, with a wealth of detail. G. Rosen, *History of Public Health* (1958), is an excellent introduction to medical developments. For society as a whole, J. Burnett, *History of the Cost of Living* (1969), cleverly shows how different classes spent their money, and B. Tuchman, *The Proud Tower* (1966), draws an unforgettable portrait of people and classes before 1914. J. Laver's handsomely illustrated *Manners and Morals in the Age of Optimism, 1848–1914* (1966), investigates the urban underworld and relations between the sexes. Sexual attitudes are also examined by E. Trudgill, *Madonnas and Magdalenas: The Origin and Development of Victorian Sexual Attitudes* (1976); A. McLaren, *Sexuality and Social Order: Birth Control in Nineteenth-Century France* (1982); and J. Phayer, *Sexual Liberation and Religion in Nineteenth Century Europe* (1977).

Women are coming into their own in historical studies. In addition to the general works by Shorter, Wrigley, Stone, and Tilly and Scott cited in Chapter 20, there are a growing number of eye-opening specialized investigations. These include L. Davidoff, *The Best Circles* (1973), on upper-class society types; O. Banks, *Feminism and Family Planning in Victorian England* (1964); and P. Branca, *Women in Europe Since 1750* (1978). L. Holcombe, *Victorian Ladies at Work* (1973), pioneers in examining middle-class women at work. M. Vicinus, ed., *Suffer and Be Still* (1972) and *A Widening Sphere* (1981), are far-ranging collections of essays on women's history, as is R. Bridenthal and C. Koonz, eds., *Becoming Visible: Women in European History* (1976). Feminism is treated perceptively in R. Evans, *The Feminists: Women's Emancipation in Europe, America, and Australia* (1979), and K. Blair, *The Clubwoman as Feminist: True Womanhood Redefined, 1868–1914* (1980). J. Gillis, *Youth and History* (1974), is a good introduction. D. Ransel, ed., *The Family in Imperial Russia* (1978), is an important work on the subject, as is J. Donzelot, *The Policing of Families* (1979), which stresses the loss of family control of all aspects of life to government agencies.

Among studies of special groups, J. Scott, *The Glass-Workers of Carmaux* (1974), is outstanding on skilled French craftsmen, and D. Lockwood, *The Blackcoated Worker* (1958), carefully examines class consciousness in the English lower-middle class. Two fine studies on universities and their professors are S. Rothblatt, *Revolution of the Dons: Cambridge and Society in Victorian England* (1968), and F. Ringer, *The Decline of the German Mandarins* (1969). Servants and their employers receive excellent treatment in T. McBride, *The Domestic Revolution: The Modernization of Household Service in England and France, 1820–1920* (1976), and B. Smith, *Ladies of the Leisure Class: The Bourgeoises of Northern France in the Nineteenth Century* (1981), which may be compared with the innovative study by M. Miller, *The Bon Marché: Bourgeois Culture and the Department Store, 1869–1920* (1981).

On Darwin, M. Ruse, *The Darwinian Revolution* (1979), is a good starting point, as is G. Himmelfarb, *Darwin and the Darwinian Revolution* (1968). O. Chadwick, *The Secularization of the European Mind in the Nineteenth Century* (1976), analyzes the impact of science (and other factors) on religious belief. The masterpieces of the great realist social novelists remain one of the best and most memorable introductions to nineteenth-century culture and thought. In addition to the novels discussed in this chapter, and those cited in the Suggested Reading for Chapters 22 and 23, I. Turgenev's *Fathers and Sons* and Zola's *The Dram-Shop (L'Assommoir)* are especially recommended.

25

THE AGE OF NATIONALISM, 1850–1914

*T*HE REVOLUTIONS OF 1848 closed one era and opened another. Urban industrial society began to take strong hold on the Continent, as it already had in Great Britain. Internationally, the repressive peace and diplomatic stability of Metternich's time was replaced by a period of war and rapid change. In thought and culture, soaring romanticism gave way to tough-minded realism. In the European economy, the hard years of the 1840s were followed by good times and prosperity throughout most of the 1850s and 1860s. Perhaps most important of all, European society progressively found, for better or worse, a new and effective organizing principle, capable of coping with the many-sided challenge of the dual revolution and the emerging urban civilization. That principle was nationalism—dedication to and identification with the nation-state.

The triumph of nationalism in Europe after 1850 is a development of enormous historical significance. It was by no means completely predictable. After all, nationalism had been a powerful force since at least 1789. Yet it had repeatedly failed to realize its goals, most spectacularly so in 1848. Why, then, did nationalism become in one way or another an almost universal faith in Europe between 1850 and 1914? More specifically, how did nationalism evolve so that it appealed not only to predominantly middle-class liberals but to the broad masses of society as well? These are the weighty questions this chapter will seek to answer.

NAPOLEON III IN FRANCE

Early nationalism was at least liberal and idealistic and often democratic and radical as well. The ideas of nationhood and popular sovereignty posed an awesome revolutionary threat to conservatives like Metternich. Yet, from the vantage point of the twentieth century, it is clear that nationalism wears many masks; it may be democratic and radical, as it was for Mazzini and Michelet; but it can also flourish in dictatorial states, which may be conservative, fascist, or communist. Napoleon I's France had already combined national devotion with authoritarian rule. Significantly, it was Napoleon's nephew, Louis Napoleon, who revived and extended this merger. It was he who showed how governments could reconcile popular and conservative forces in an authoritarian nationalism. In doing so, he provided a model for political leaders elsewhere.

THE SECOND REPUBLIC AND LOUIS NAPOLEON

The overwhelming victory of Louis Napoleon Bonaparte in the French presidential elections of December 1848 has long puzzled historians. The nephew of Napoleon I, Louis Napoleon had lived most of his life outside of France and played no part in French politics before 1848. Why did universal manhood suffrage give such an unproven nobody 5.5 million votes, while the runner-up, General Cavaignac of June Days fame, polled only 1.5 million and the other three candidates (including the poet Lamartine) received insignificant support?

The usual explanation is that, though Louis Napoleon had only his great name in common with his uncle, that was enough. According to some historians, the Napoleonic legend—a monument to the power of romanticism between 1820 and 1848—had transformed a dictator into a demigod in the minds of the unsophisticated French masses. Another explanation, popularized by Karl Marx, has stressed the fears of middle-class and peasant property owners in the face of the socialist challenge of urban workers. These classes wanted protection. They wanted a tough cop with a big stick on the beat. They found him in Louis Napoleon, who had indeed served briefly as a special constable in London at the height of the Chartist agitation.

These explanations are not wrong, but there was more to Louis Napoleon's popularity than stupidity and fear. In late 1848, Louis Napoleon had a positive "program" for France, which was to guide him throughout most of his long reign. This program had been elaborated earlier in two pamphlets, *Napoleonic Ideas* and *The Elimination of Poverty,* which Louis Napoleon had written while imprisoned for a farcical attempt to overthrow Louis Philippe's government. The pamphlets had been widely circulated prior to the presidential election.

Louis Napoleon believed that the government should represent the people and that it should also try hard to help them economically. How was this to be done? Parliaments and political parties were not the answer, according to Louis Napoleon. Politicians represented special-interest groups, particularly middle-class ones. When they ran a parliamentary government, they stirred up class hatred because they were not interested in helping the poor. This had occurred under Louis Philippe, and it was occurring again under the Second Republic. The answer was a strong, even authoritarian, national leader, like the first Napoleon, who would serve all the people, rich and poor. This leader would be linked to the people by direct democracy and universal male suffrage. Sovereignty would flow from the entire population to the leader and would not be diluted or corrupted by politicians and legislative bodies.

These political ideas went hand in hand with Louis Napoleon's vision of national unity and social progress. Unlike his uncle, who had reduced unemployment and social tensions by means of foreign wars, Louis Napoleon favored peaceful measures to relieve the awful poverty of the poor. Rather than doing nothing or providing only temporary relief, the state and its leader had a sacred duty to provide jobs and stimulate the economy. All classes would benefit by such action.

Louis Napoleon's political and social ideas were at least vaguely understood by large numbers of French peasants and workers in December 1848. To many common people he appeared to be both a strong man *and* a forward-looking champion of their interests, and that is why they voted for him.

Elected to a four-year term, President Louis Napoleon had to share power with a conservative National Assembly. With some misgivings he signed a bill to increase greatly the role of the Catholic church in primary and secondary education. In France as elsewhere in Europe after 1848, the anxious well-to-do saw religion as a bulwark against radicalism. As one leader of the church in France put it, "There is only one recipe for making those who own nothing believe in property-rights: that is to make them believe in God, who dictated the Ten Commandments and who promises eternal punishment to those who steal."[1] Very reluctantly, Louis Napoleon also signed another conservative law depriving many poor people of the right to vote. He took these conservative measures for two main reasons: he wanted the assembly to vote funds to pay his personal debts, and he wanted it to change the constitution so he could run for a second term.

The assembly did neither. Thus in 1851, Louis Napoleon began to organize a conspiracy with key army officers. On December 2, 1851, he illegally dismissed the assembly and seized power in a coup d'état. There was some armed resistance in Paris and other cities, but the actions of the assembly had left the Second Republic with few defenders. Restoring universal male suffrage, Louis Napoleon called on the French people to legalize his actions as his uncle had done. They did: 92 percent voted to make him a strong president for ten years. A year later, 97 percent agreed in a national plebiscite to make him hereditary emperor. For the third time, and by the greatest margin yet, the authoritarian Louis Napoleon was overwhelmingly elected to lead the French nation.

NAPOLEON III'S SECOND EMPIRE

Louis Napoleon—now Emperor Napoleon III—experienced both success and failure between 1852 and 1870. His greatest success was with the economy, particularly in the 1850s. His government encouraged the new investment banks and massive railroad construction that were at the heart of the industrial revolution on the Continent. General economic expansion was also fostered by the government's ambitious program of public works, which included the rebuilding of Paris to improve the urban environment. The profits of businessmen soared with prosperity, and the working classes did not fare poorly either. Their wages more than kept up with inflation, and jobs were much easier to find. France's economy benefited from a worldwide economic boom and other external events, such as gold discoveries in California and Australia. Yet the contribution of Napoleon III's economic policies was real all the same.

Louis Napoleon always hoped that economic progress would reduce social and political tensions. This hope was at least partially realized. Until the mid-1860s, there was little active opposition and even considerable support for his government from France's most dissatisfied group, the urban workers. Napoleon III's regulation of pawnshops and his support of credit unions and better housing for the working class were evidence of positive concern in the 1850s. In the 1860s, he granted workers the right to form unions and the right to strike—important economic rights denied by earlier governments.

Rebuilding Paris Expensive and time consuming, boulevard construction in Paris brought massive demolition, considerable slum clearance, and protests of ruin to the old city. In addition to expecting economic benefits, Napoleon III rightly believed that broad boulevards would be harder for revolutionaries to barricade than narrow twisting streets. *(The Mansell Collection)*

At first, political power remained in the hands of the emperor. He alone chose his ministers, and they had great freedom of action. At the same time, Napoleon III restricted but did not abolish the assembly. To be sure, the French parliament in the 1850s had little power. It could not initiate legislation, and it did not control the budget. Parliamentary sessions were not open to the public, and the government permitted only a dry summary of its debates to be published. Yet the members of the assembly were elected by universal male suffrage every six years. In each district the government put up its candidate and permitted opposition candidates, although it restricted speeches and discussions during the electoral campaigns.

Louis Napoleon and his government took the parliamentary elections very seriously. They tried to entice notable people, even those who had opposed the regime, to stand as government candidates in order to expand is base of support. Moreover the government rewarded districts that elected government candidates. It used its officials and appointed mayors to spread the word that the election of the government's candidate was the key to roads, schools, tax rebates, and a thousand other local concerns.

In 1857 and again in 1863, Louis Napoleon's system worked well and produced overwhelming electoral victories. The poet-politician Alphonse de Lamartine was convinced that Louis Napoleon was

France's greatest politician since Talleyrand, and possibly even greater than he. Yet in the course of the 1860s Napoleon III's electoral system gradually disintegrated, for several reasons. France's problems in Italy and the rising power of Prussia led to increasing criticism at home from his Catholic and nationalist supporters. With increasing effectiveness, the middle-class liberals who had always detested his dictatorship continued to denounce his rule as a disgrace to France's republican tradition.

Napoleon was always sensitive to the public mood. Public opinion, he once said, always wins the last victory. Thus in the 1860s, he progressively "liberalized" his empire. He gave the assembly greater powers and the opposition candidates greater freedom, which they used to good advantage. In 1869 the opposition, consisting of republicans, monarchists, and liberals, polled almost 45 percent of the vote.

The following year, a sick and weary Louis Napoleon once again granted France a new constitution, which combined a basically parliamentary regime with a hereditary emperor as chief of state. In a final great plebiscite on the eve of a disastrous war with Prussia, 7.5 million Frenchmen voted in favor of the new constitution, and only 1.5 million opposed it. Napoleon III's attempt to reconcile a strong national state with universal manhood suffrage was still evolving, in a democratic direction.

NATION BUILDING IN ITALY AND GERMANY

Louis Napoleon's triumph in 1848 and his authoritarian rule in the 1850s provided the old ruling classes of Europe with a new model in politics. As the great Swiss historian Jacob Burckhardt later noted,

Louis Napoleon had risked universal suffrage for the elections, and others followed his lead. The conservative streak in the rural populations had been recognized, though no attempt had been made to assess precisely how far it might be extended from the elections to everything and everybody."[2]

To what extent was it possible that the expanding urban middle classes and even the growing working classes might, like people in rural areas, rally to a strong and essentially conservative national state? This was one of the great political questions in the 1850s and 1860s. In central Europe, a resounding and definitive answer came with the national unification of Italy and Germany.

ITALY TO 1850

Italy had never been a united nation prior to 1860. Part of Rome's great empire in ancient times, the Italian peninsula was divided in the Middle Ages into competing city-states, which led the commercial and cultural revival of the West with amazing creativity. A battleground for great powers after 1494, Italy had been reorganized in 1815 at the Congress of Vienna. The rich northern provinces of Lombardy and Venetia were taken by Metternich's Austria. Sardinia and Piedmont were under the rule of an Italian monarch, and Tuscany with its famous capital of Florence shared north central Italy with several smaller states. Central Italy and Rome were ruled by the papacy, which had always considered an independent political existence necessary to fulfill its spiritual mission. Naples and Sicily were ruled, as they had been for almost a hundred years, by a branch of the Bourbons. Metternich was not wrong in dismissing Italy as "a geographical expression" (see Map 25.1).

Between 1815 and 1848, the goal of a unified Italian nation captured the imaginations of increasing numbers of Italians. There were three basic approaches. The first was the radical program of the idealistic patriot Mazzini, who preached a centralized democratic republic based on universal suffrage and the will of the people. The second was that of Gioberti, a Catholic priest, who called for a federation of existing states under the presidency of a progressive pope. Finally, there were those who looked for leadership toward the autocratic kingdom of Sardinia-Piedmont, much as many Germans looked toward Prussia.

The third alternative was strengthened by the failures of 1848, when Austria smashed and discredited Mazzini's republicanism. Almost by accident, Sardinia's monarch Victor Emmanuel retained the liberal constitution granted under duress in March 1848. This constitution provided for a fair degree of civil liberties and real parliamentary government, complete with elections and parliamentary control of taxes. To the Italian middle classes, Sardinia ap-

MAP 25.1 The Unification of Italy, 1859–1870 The leadership of Sardinia-Piedmont and nationalist fervor were decisive factors in the dramatic political unification of the Italian peninsula.

peared to be a liberal, progressive state, ideally suited to achieve the goal of national unification. By contrast, Mazzini's brand of democratic republicanism seemed quixotic and too radical. As for the papacy, the initial cautious support by Pius IX (1846–1878) for unification had given way to fear and hostility after he was temporarily driven from Rome during the upheavals of 1848. For a long generation, the pa-

pacy would stand resolutely opposed not only to national unification but to most modern trends. In 1864, in the *Syllabus of Errors,* Pius IX strongly denounced rationalism, socialism, separation of church and state, and religious liberty, denying that "the Roman pontiff can and ought to reconcile and align himself with progress, liberalism, and modern civilization."

CAVOUR AND GARIBALDI

Sardinia had the good fortune of being led by a brilliant statesman, Count Camillo Benso di Cavour, the dominant figure in the Sardinian government from 1850 until his death in 1861. Cavour's development was an early sign of the coming tacit alliance between the aristocracy and the solid middle class throughout much of Europe. Beginning as a successful manager of his father's large landed estates in Piedmont, Cavour was also an economic liberal. He turned toward industry and made a substantial fortune in sugar mills, steamships, banks, and railroads. Economically secure, he then entered the world of politics and became chief minister in the liberalized Sardinian monarchy. Cavour's national goals were limited and realistic. Until 1859 he sought unity only for the states of northern and perhaps central Italy in a greatly expanded kingdom of Sardinia. It was not one of his goals to incorporate the papal states or the kingdom of the Two Sicilies, with their very different cultures and governments, into an Italy of all the Italians. Cavour was a moderate nationalist.

In the 1850s Cavour worked to consolidate Sardinia as a liberal state capable of leading northern Italy. His program of highways and railroads, of civil liberties and opposition to clerical privilege, increased support for Sardinia throughout northern Italy. Yet Cavour realized that Sardinia could not drive Austria out of Lombardy and Venetia and unify northern Italy under Victor Emmanuel without the help of a powerful ally. He sought that ally in the person of Napoleon III, who sincerely believed in the general principle of nationality, as well as modest expansion for France.

In a complicated series of diplomatic maneuvers, Cavour in 1854 entered the Crimean War against Russia, on the side of Great Britain and France, and tenaciously worked for a diplomatic alliance with Napoleon III against Austria. Finally he succeeded. In July 1858, Cavour and Napoleon III agreed orally in the utmost secrecy that if Cavour could goad Austria into attacking Sardinia, France would come to Sardinia's "defense."

For a time, Cavour feared that an international congress and a diplomatic compromise would thwart his plans. But in the end, Austria obligingly issued an ultimatum and declared war. Napoleon III came to Sardinia's defense. Then, after the victory of the combined Franco-Sardinian forces, he did a complete about-face. Nauseated by the gore of war and criticized by French Catholics for supporting the pope's declared enemy, Napoleon III abandoned Cavour. He made a compromise peace with the Austrians at Villafranca in July 1859. Sardinia would receive only Lombardy, the area around Milan. The rest of the map of Italy would remain essentially unchanged. Cavour resigned in a rage.

Yet Cavour's plans were salvaged by popular revolts and Italian nationalism. While the war against Austria had raged in the north, dedicated nationalists in central Italy had risen and driven out their rulers. Nationalist fervor seized the urban masses. Large crowds demonstrated, chanting, "Italy and Victor Emmanuel!" and singing passionately, "Foreigners, get out of Italy!" Buoyed up by this enthusiasm, the leaders of the nationalist movement in central Italy ignored the compromise peace of Villafranca and called for fusion with Sardinia. This was not at all what France and the other Great Powers wanted, but the nationalists held firm and eventually had their way. Cavour returned to power in early 1860 and worked out a diplomatic deal with Napoleon III. The people of central Italy voted overwhelmingly to join a greatly enlarged kingdom of Sardinia. Cavour had achieved his original goal of a north Italian state (see Map 25.1).

For superpatriots like Giuseppe Garibaldi (1801–1882), the job of unification was still only half done. The son of a poor sailor, Garibaldi personified the romantic, revolutionary nationalism of Mazzini and 1848. As a lad of seventeen, he had traveled to Rome and been converted to the "New Italy, the Italy of all the Italians." As he later wrote in his *Autobiography,* "The Rome that I beheld with the eyes of youthful imagination was the Rome of the future—the dominant thought of my whole life." Sentenced to death in 1834 for his part in an uprising in Genoa, Garibaldi escaped to South America. For twelve years he led a guerilla band in Uruguay's struggle for independence. "Shipwrecked, ambushed, shot through the neck," he found in a tough young woman, Anna da Silva, a mate and companion in arms. Their first children nearly starved in the jungle while Garibaldi, clad in his long red shirt, fashioned a legend not unlike like that of the Cuban Ché Guevara in recent times. He returned to Italy to fight in 1848 and led a corps of volunteers against Austria in 1859. By the spring of 1860, Garibaldi had emerged as a powerful independent force in Italian politics.

Garibaldi Landing in Sicily With a thousand volunteers the flamboyant Garibaldi conquered the kingdom of the Two Sicilies in 1860 and paved the way for Italian unification. *(Historical Pictures Service, Chicago)*

Partly to use him and partly to get rid of him, Cavour secretly supported Garibaldi's bold plan to "liberate" Sicily. Landing in Sicily in May 1860, Garibaldi's guerrilla band of a thousand "Red Shirts" captured the imagination of the Sicilian peasantry. Outwitting the twenty-thousand-man royal army, the guerrilla leader took Palermo. Then he and his men crossed to the mainland, marched triumphantly toward Naples, and prepared to attack Rome and the pope. But the wily Cavour quickly sent Sardinian forces to occupy most of the Papal States (but not Rome) and to intercept Garibaldi.

Cavour realized that an attack on Rome would bring about war with France, and he also feared Garibaldi's popular appeal. Therefore, he immediately organized a plebiscite in the conquered territories. Despite the urging of some of his more radical supporters, the patriotic Garibaldi did not oppose Cavour, and the people of the south voted to join Sardinia. When Garibaldi and Victor Emmanuel rode through Naples to cheering crowds, they symbolically sealed the union of north and south, of monarch and people.

Cavour had succeeded. He had controlled Garibaldi and had turned popular nationalism in a conservative direction. The new kingdom of Italy, which did not include Venice until 1866 or Rome until 1870, was neither radical nor democratic. Italy was a parliamentary monarchy under Victor Emmanuel, but in accordance with the Sardinian constitution only a small minority of Italians had the right to vote. There was a definite division between the propertied classes and the common people. There was also a great social and cultural gap between the progressive, industrializing north and the stagnant, agrarian south. This gap would increase, since peasant industries in the south would not be able to survive. Italy was united politically. Other divisions remained.

GERMANY BEFORE BISMARCK

In the aftermath of 1848, while Louis Napoleon consolidated his rule and Cavour schemed, the German states were locked in a political stalemate. With Russian diplomatic support, Austria had blocked the halfhearted attempt of Frederick William IV of Prussia (1840–1861) to unify Germany "from above." This action contributed to a growing tension between Austria and Prussia, as each power sought to block the other within the reorganized German Confederation (pages 732 and 756). Stalemate also prevailed in the domestic politics of the individual states, as Austria, Prussia, and the smaller German kingdoms entered a period of reaction and immobility.

At the same time, powerful economic forces were undermining the political status quo. As we have seen, modern industry grew rapidly in Europe throughout the 1850s. Nowhere was this growth more rapid than within the German customs union (Zollverein). Developing gradually under Prussian leadership after 1818 and founded officially in 1834 to stimulate trade and increase the revenues of member states, the customs union had not included Austria. After 1848 it became a crucial factor in the Austro-Prussian rivalry.

Tariff duties were substantially reduced so that Austria's highly protected industry could not bear to join. In retaliation, Austria tried to destroy the Zollverein by inducing the south German states to leave it, but without success. Indeed, by the end of 1853 all the German states except Austria had joined the customs union. A new Germany excluding Austria was becoming an economic reality, and the middle class and business groups were finding solid economic reasons to bolster their idealistic support of national unification. Thus economic developments helped Prussia greatly in its struggle against Austria's traditional supremacy in German affairs.

The national uprising in Italy in 1859 made a profound impression in the German states. In Prussia, great political change and war—perhaps with Austria, perhaps with France—seemed quite possible. The tough-minded William I of Prussia (1858–1888), who had replaced the unstable Frederick William IV as regent in 1858 and became king in 1861, and his top military advisers were convinced of the need for major army reforms. William I wanted to double the size of the regular army. He also wanted to reduce the importance of the reserve militia, a semipopular force created during the Napoleonic wars. William had contempt for the "dirty reservists," those "civilians in uniform," who lacked efficiency and complete obedience. By drafting every young man into the army for three years, the king and his conservative supporters hoped to promote military attitudes in daily life. Of course, reform of the army meant a bigger defense budget and higher taxes.

Prussia had emerged from 1848 with a parliament of sorts, and by 1859 the Prussian parliament was in the hands of the liberal middle class. The middle class, like the landed aristocracy, was overrepresented by the Prussian electoral system, and it wanted society to be less, not more, militaristic. Above all, middle-class representatives wanted to establish once and for all that parliament, not the king, had the ultimate political power. They also wanted to ensure that the army was responsible to the people and not a "state within a state." These demands were popular. The parliament rejected the military budget in 1862, and the liberals triumphed so completely in new elections that the conservatives "could ride to the parliament

Otto von Bismarck A fierce political fighter with a commanding personality and a brilliant mind, Bismarck was devoted to Prussia and its king and aristocracy. Uniforms were worn by civilian officials as well as by soldiers in Prussia. *(Brown Brothers)*

building in a single coach." King William considered abdicating in favor of his more liberal son. In the end, he called on Count Otto von Bismarck to head a ministry and defy the parliament. It was a momentous choice.

BISMARCK TAKES COMMAND

The most important figure in German history between Luther and Hitler, Otto von Bismarck (1815–1898), has been the object of enormous interest and debate. Like his contemporary Abraham Lincoln, who successfully led the North against the South in a great civil war between 1861 and 1865, Bismarck used military victory to forge a strong, unified national state.

A great hero to some, a great villain to others, Bismarck was above all a master of politics. Born into the Prussian landowning aristocracy, the young Bismark was a wild and tempestuous student, given to duels and drinking. Proud of his Junker heritage— "my fathers have been born and have lived and died in the same rooms for centuries"—and always devoted to his Prussian sovereign, Bismarck had a strong personality and an unbounded desire for power.

Bismarck entered the civil service, which was the only socially acceptable career except the army for a Prussian aristocrat. But he soon found bureaucratic life unbearable and fled to his ancestral estate. The civil servant was like a musician in an orchestra, he said, and "I want to play the tune the way it sounds to me or not at all. . . . My pride bids me command rather than obey."[3] Yet in his drive for power, power for himself and for Prussia, Bismarck was extraordinarily flexible and pragmatic. "One must always have two irons in the fire," he once said. He kept his options open, pursuing one policy and then another as he moved with skill and cunning toward his goal.

Bismarck first honed his political skills as a diplomat. Acquiring a reputation as an ultraconservative in the Prussian assembly in 1848, he fought against Austria as the Prussian ambassador to the German Confederation from 1851 to 1859. Transferred next to St. Petersburg and then to Paris, Bismarck had an excellent opportunity to evaluate Alexander II and Napoleon III at close range. A blunt, expansive talker, especially after a few drinks, Bismarck's basic goal was well known in 1862—to build up Prussia's strength and consolidate Prussia's precarious Great Power status.

To achieve this goal, Bismarck was convinced that Prussia had to control completely the northern, predominantly Protestant part of the German Confederation. He saw three possible paths open before him. He might work with Austria to divide up the smaller German states lying between them. Or he might combine with foreign powers—France and Italy, or even Russia—against Austria. Or he might ally with the forces of German nationalism to defeat and expel Austria from German affairs. Each possibility was explored in many complicated diplomatic maneuvers, but in the end the last path was the one Bismarck took.

That Bismarck would join with the forces of German nationalism to increase Prussia's power seemed unlikely when he took office in 1862. Bismarck's appointment made a strong but unfavorable impression. One of the liberal middle-class members of the Prussian parliament expressed enlightened public opinion throughout Prussia and the other German states: "Bismarck, that is to say: government without budget, rule by the sword in home affairs, and war in foreign affairs. I consider him the most dangerous Minister for Prussia's liberty and happiness."[4]

Bismarck's speeches were a sensation and a scandal. Declaring that the government would rule without parliamentary consent, Bismarck lashed out at the middle-class opposition: "The great questions of the day will not be decided by speeches and resolutions—that was the blunder of 1848 and 1849—but by blood and iron." In 1863 he told the Prussian parliament, "If a compromise cannot be arrived at and a conflict arises, then the conflict becomes a question of power. Whoever has the power then acts according to his opinion." Denounced for this view that "might makes right," Bismarck and the bureaucracy went right on collecting taxes, even though the parliament refused to approve the budget, and reorganized the army. And for four years, from 1862 to 1866, the voters of Prussia continued to express their opposition by sending large liberal majorities to the parliament.

THE AUSTRO-PRUSSIAN WAR OF 1866

Opposition at home spurred the search for success abroad. The every-knotty question of Schleswig-Holstein provided a welcome opportunity. When the Danish king tried again, as in 1848, to bring the provinces into a centralized Danish state against the will of the German Confederation, Prussia joined Austria in a short and successful war against Denmark in 1864. Then, rather than following nationalist sentiment and allowing the conquered provinces to become another medium-sized independent state within the German Confederation, Bismarck maneuvered Austria into a tricky position. Prussia and Austria agreed to joint administration of the conquered provinces, thereby giving Bismarck a weapon he could use either to force Austria into peacefully accepting Prussian domination in northern Germany or to start a war against Austria.

Bismarck knew that a war with Austria would have to be localized war. He had to be certain that Prussian expansion did not provoke a mighty armed coalition, such as the coalition that had almost crushed Frederick the Great in the eighteenth century. Russia, the great bear to the east, was no problem. Bismarck had already gained Alexander II's gratitude by supporting Russia's repression of a Polish uprising in 1863. Napoleon III—the "sphinx without a riddle," according to Bismarck—was another matter. But Bismarck charmed him into neutrality with vague promises of more territory along the Rhine. Thus, when Austria proved unwilling to give up its historic role in German affairs, Bismarck was in a position to engage in a war of his own making.

The Austro-Prussian War of 1866 lasted only seven weeks. Utilizing railroads to mass troops and the new breechloading needle gun for maximum firepower, the reorganized Prussian army overran northern

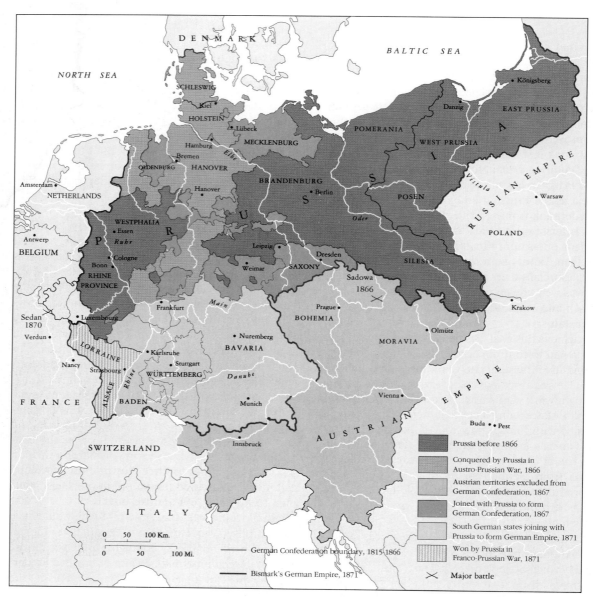

MAP 25.2 The Unification of Germany, 1866–1871 This map deserves careful study. Note how Prussian expansion, Austrian expulsion from the old German Confederation, and the creation of a new German Empire went hand in hand. Austria lost no territory but Prussia's neighbors in the north suffered grievously or simply disappeared.

Germany and defeated Austria decisively at the battle of Königgrätz in Bohemia. Anticipating Prussia's future needs, Bismarck offered Austria realistic, even generous, peace terms. Austria paid no reparations and lost no territory to Prussia, although Venice was ceded to Italy. But the German Confederation was dissolved, and Austria agreed to withdraw from German affairs. The states north of the Main River were grouped in a new North German Confederation led by an expanded Prussia. The mainly Catholic states of the south were permitted to remain independent, while forming military alliances with Prussia. Bismarck's fundamental goal of Prussian expansion was being realized (see Map 25.2).

The Taming of Parliament

Bismarck had long been convinced that the old order he so ardently defended should make peace—on its own terms—with the liberal middle class and the nationalist movement. Inspired somewhat by Louis Napoleon, he realized that nationalism was not necessarily hostile to conservative, authoritarian government. Moreover, Bismarck believed that, because of the events of 1848, the German middle class could be led to prefer the reality of national unity to a long, uncertain battle for truly liberal institutions. During the constitutional struggle over army reform and parliamentary authority, he had delayed but not abandoned this goal. Thus, during the attack on Austria in 1866, he increasingly identified Prussia's fate with the "national development of Germany."

In the aftermath of victory, Bismarck fashioned a federal constitution for the new North German Confederation. Each state retained its own local government, but the king of Prussia was to be president of the confederation and the chancellor—Bismarck—was to be responsible only to the president. The federal government—William I and Bismarck—controlled the army and foreign affairs. There was also a legislature, consisting of an upper house whose delegates were appointed by the different states and a lower house. Both houses shared equally in the making of laws. Members of the lower house were elected by universal, equal manhood suffrage. With this radical innovation, Bismarck opened the door to popular participation and went over the head of the middle class directly to the people. All the while, however, ultimate power rested as securely as ever in the hands of Prussia and its king and army.

Events within Prussia itself were even more significant than those at the federal level. In the flush of victory, the ultraconservatives expected Bismarck to suspend the Prussian constitution or perhaps abolish the Prussian parliament altogether. Yet he did nothing of the sort. Instead, he held out an olive branch to the parliamentary opposition. Marshaling all his diplomatic skill, Bismarck asked the parliament to pass a special indemnity bill to approve after the fact all of the government's spending between 1862 and 1866. Most of the liberals snatched at the chance to cooperate. For four long years, they had opposed and criticized Bismarck's "illegal" measures. And what had happened? Bismarck, the king, and the army had persevered, and in the end these conservative forces

"His First Thought" This 1896 cartoon provides a brilliant commentary on German middle-class attitudes. Suddenly crippled, the man's first thought is "Disaster! Now I can no longer be an army reserve officer." Being a part-time junior officer, below the dominant aristocratic career officers, became a great middle-class status symbol. *(Photo: Caroline Buckler)*

had succeeded beyond the wildest dreams of the liberal middle class. In 1866 German unity was in sight, and the people were going to be allowed to participate actively in the new state. Many liberals repented their "sins" and were overjoyed that Bismarck would forgive them.

None repented more ardently or more typically than Hermann Baumgarten, a mild-mannered, thoroughly decent history professor and member of the liberal opposition. In an essay entitled "A Self Criticism of German Liberalism," he confessed in 1866:

We thought by agitation we could transform Germany. But . . . almost all the elements of our political system have been shown erroneous by the facts themselves. . . . Yet we have experienced a miracle almost without parallel. The victory of our principles would have brought us misery, whereas the defeat of our principles has brought boundless salvation.[5]

The constitutional struggle was over. The German middle class was bowing respectfully before Bismarck and the monarchial authority and aristocratic superiority he represented. They did not stand upright again in the years before 1914.

THE FRANCO-PRUSSIAN WAR OF 1870–1871

The rest of the story of German unification is anticlimactic. In 1867 Bismarck brought the four south German states into the customs union and established a customs parliament. But the south Germans were reluctant to go further because of their different religious and political traditions. Bismarck realized that a patriotic war with France would drive the south German states into his arms. The French obligingly played their part. The apparent issue—whether a distant relative of Prussia's William I (and France's Napoleon III) might become king of Spain—was only a diplomatic pretext. By 1870 the French leaders of the Second Empire, alarmed by their powerful new neighbor on the Rhine, had decided on a war to teach Prussia a lesson.

As soon as war against France began in 1870, Bismarck had the wholehearted support of the south German states. With other governments standing still—Bismarck's generosity to Austria in 1866 was paying big dividends—German forces under Prussian leadership decisively defeated Louis Napoleon's armies at Sedan on September 1, 1870. Three days later, French patriots in Paris proclaimed yet another French republic and vowed to continue fighting. But after five months, in January 1871, a starving Paris surrendered, and France went on to accept Bismarck's harsh peace terms. By this time, the south German states had agreed to join a new German Empire. The victorious William I was proclaimed emperor of Germany in the Hall of Mirrors in the palace of Versailles. Europe had a nineteenth-century German "sun king." As in the 1866 constitution, the king of Prussia and his ministers had ultimate power in the new empire, and the lower house of the legislature was elected popularly by universal male suffrage.

The Franco-Prussian War of 1870 to 1871, which Europeans generally saw as a test of nations in a pitiless Darwinian struggle for existence, released an enormous surge of patriotic feeling in Germany. Bismarck's genius, the invincible Prussian army, the solidarity of king and people in a unified nation—these and similar themes were trumpeted endlessly during and after the war. The weakest of the Great Powers in 1862—after Austria, Britain, France, and Russia—Prussia fortified by the other Germans states had become the most powerful state in Europe in less than a decade. Most Germans were enormously proud, enormously relieved. And they were somewhat drunk with success, blissfully imagining themselves the fittest and best of the European species. Semi-authoritarian nationalism had triumphed. Only a few critics remained dedicated to the liberal ideal of truly responsible parliamentary government.

THE MODERNIZATION OF RUSSIA

In Russia, unlike Italy and Germany, there was no need to build a single state out of a jumble of principalities. The vast Russian Empire was a great multinational state. In the early nineteenth century, nationalism there was a subversive ideology, identified with revolution. After 1853, however, old autocratic Russia was in serious trouble. It became clear to Russia's leaders that the country had to embrace the process of modernization.

A vague and often overworked term, *modernization* is a great umbrella under which some writers place most of the major developments of the last two hundred or even five hundred years. Yet defined narrowly—as changes that enable a country to compete effectively with the leading countries at a given time—modernization can be a useful concept. It fits Russia after the Crimean War particularly well.

THE "GREAT REFORMS"

In the 1850s Russia was a poor agrarian society. Industry was little developed, and almost 90 percent of the population lived on the land. Agricultural techniques were backward: the ancient open-field system reigned supreme. Serfdom was still the basic social institution. Bound to the lord on a hereditary basis, the peasant serf was little more than a slave. Individual serfs and serf families were regularly sold, with and without land, in the early nineteenth century. Serfs were obliged to furnish labor services or money payments as the lord saw fit. Moreover, the lord could choose freely among them for army recruits, who had to serve for twenty-five years, and he could punish a serf with deportation to Siberia whenever he wished. Sexual exploitation of female serfs by their lords was common.

Serfdom had become the great moral and political issue for the government by the 1840s, but it might still have lasted many more years had it not been for the Crimean War of 1853 to 1856. The war began as a dispute with France over who should protect certain Christian shrines in the Ottoman Empire. Because the fighting was concentrated in the Crimean peninsula in the Black Sea, Russia's transportation network of rivers and wagons failed to supply the distant Russian armies adequately. France and Great Britain, aided by Sardinia, inflicted a humiliating defeat on Russia.

The military defeat marked a turning point in Russian history. The Russian state had been built on the military, and Russia had not lost a major war for a century and a half. This defeat demonstrated that Russia had fallen behind the rapidly industrializing nations of western Europe in many areas. At the very least, Russia needed railroads, better armaments, and reorganization of the army if it was to maintain its international position. Moreover, the disastrous war had caused hardship and raised the specter of massive peasant rebellion. Reform of serfdom was imperative. And, as the new tsar, Alexander II (1855–1881), told the serf owners, it would be better if reform came from above rather than from below. Military disaster thus forced Alexander II and his ministers along the path of rapid social change and general modernization.

The first and greatest of the reforms was the freeing of the serfs in 1861. Human bondage was abolished forever, and the emancipated peasants received, on the average, about half of the land. Yet they had to pay fairly high prices for their land, and because the land was owned collectively, each peasant village was jointly responsible for the payments of all the fami-

"Farewell," says the triumphant German soldier on the left in this French cartoon. "No, till we meet again," replies the French soldier. "Visits must be returned." German victory and Bismarck's seizure of French territory poisoned Franco-German relations after 1871. *(Photo: Caroline Buckler)*

lies in the village. The government hoped that collective responsibility would strengthen the peasant village as a social unit and prevent the development of a class of landless peasants. In practice, collective ownership and responsibility made it very difficult for individual peasants to improve agricultural methods or leave their villages. Thus the effects of the reform were limited, for it did not encourage peasants to change their old habits and attitudes.

Most of the later reforms were also halfway measures. In 1864 the government established a new institution of local government, the *zemstvo*. Members of

Novgorod Merchants Drinking Tea This late nineteenth-century photograph suggests how Russian businessmen were slow to abandon traditional dress and attitudes in the face of change. Stern authoritarians in the family circle and staunchly devoted to church and tsar, they were often suspicious of foreigners as well as the lawyers and journalists who claimed to speak for the nation's middle class. *(BBC Hulton/The Bettmann Archive)*

this local assembly were elected by a three-class system of towns, peasant villages, and noble landowners. A zemstvo executive council dealt with local problems. The establishment of the zemstvos marked a significant step toward popular participation, and Russian liberals hoped it would lead to a national parliament. They were soon disappointed. The local zemstvo remained subordinate to the traditional bureaucracy and the local nobility, who were heavily favored by the property-based voting system. More successful was reform of the legal system, which established independent courts and equality before the law. Education was also liberalized somewhat, and censorship was relaxed but not removed.

THE INDUSTRIALIZATION OF RUSSIA

Until the twentieth century, Russia's greatest strides toward modernization were economic rather than political. Industry and transport, both so vital to the military, were transformed in two industrial surges. The first of these came after 1860. The government encouraged and subsidized private railway companies, and construction boomed. In 1860 the empire had only about 1,250 miles of railroads; by 1880 it had about 15,500 miles. The railroads enabled agricultural Russia to export grain and thus earn money for further industrialization. Domestic manufacturing was stimulated, and by the end of the 1870s Russia had a sophisticated and well-developed railway-equipment industry. Industrial suburbs grew up around Moscow and St. Petersburg, and a class of modern factory workers began to take shape.

Industrial development strengthened Russia's military forces and gave rise to territorial expansion to the south and east. Imperial expansion greatly excited many ardent Russian nationalists and superpatriots, who became some of the government's most enthusiastic supporters. Industrial development also contributed mightily to the spread of Marxian thought and the transformation of the Russian revolutionary movement after 1890.

In 1881 Alexander II was assassinated by a small group of terrorists. The era of reform came to an abrupt end, for the new tsar, Alexander III (1881–1894), was a determined reactionary. Russia, and indeed all of Europe, experienced hard times economically in the 1880s. Political modernization remained frozen until 1905, but economic modernization sped forward in the massive industrial surge of the 1890s. As it had after the Crimean War, nationalism played

a decisive role. The key leader was Sergei Witte, the tough, competent minister of finance from 1892 to 1903. Early in his career, Witte found in the writings of Friedrich List (page 713) an analysis and a program for action. List had stressed the peril for Germany of remaining behind England in the 1830s and 1840s. Witte saw the same threat of industrial backwardness threatening Russia's power and greatness.

Witte moved forward on several fronts. A railroad manager by training, he believed that railroads were "a very powerful weapon . . . for the direction of the economic development of the country."[6] Therefore, the government built railroads rapidly, doubling the network to 35,000 miles by the end of the century. The gigantic trans-Siberian line connecting Moscow with Vladivostok on the Pacific Ocean 5,000 miles away was Witte's pride, and it was largely completed during his term of office. Following List's advice, Witte raised high protective tariffs to build Russian industry, and he put the country on the gold standard of the "civilized world" in order to strengthen Russian finances.

Building the Trans-Siberian Railroad Constructed largely in the 1890s as part of Witte's industrialization drive, the world's longest railroad facilitated Russian penetration of northern China and Korea. That penetration then led to war with Japan. *(BBC Hulton/ The Bettmann Archive)*

Witte's greatest innovation, however, was to use the West to catch up with the West. He aggressively encouraged foreigners to use their abundant capital and advanced technology to build great factories in backward Russia. As he told the tsar, "The inflow of foreign capital is . . . the only way by which our industry will be able to supply our country quickly with abundant and cheap products."[7] This policy was brilliantly successful, especially in southern Russia. There, in the eastern Ukraine, foreign capitalists and their engineers built an enormous and very modern steel and coal industry almost from scratch in little more than a decade. By 1900 only the United States, Germany, and Great Britain were producing more steel than Russia. The Russian petroleum industry had even pulled up alongside that of the United States and was producing and refining half the world's output of oil.

Witte knew how to keep foreigners in line. Once a leading foreign businessman came to him and angrily demanded that the Russian government fulfill a contract it had signed and pay certain debts immediately. Witte asked to see the contract. He read it and then carefully tore it to pieces and threw it in the wastepaper basket without a word of explanation. It was just such a fiercely independent Russia that was catching up with the advanced nations of the West.

The Revolution of 1905

Catching up partly meant vigorous territorial expansion, for this was the age of Western imperialism. By 1903 Russia had established a sphere of influence in Chinese Manchuria and was casting greedy eyes on northern Korea. When the protests of equally imperialistic Japan were ignored, the Japanese launched a surprise attack in February 1904. To the world's amazement, Russia suffered repeated losses, forced in August 1905 to accept a humiliating defeat.

As is often the case, military disaster abroad brought political upheaval at home. The business and professional classes had long wanted to match economic with political modernization. Their minimal goal was to turn the last of Europe's absolutist monarchies into a liberal, representative regime. Factory workers, strategically concentrated in the large cities, had all the grievances of early industrialization and were organized in a radical labor movement. Peasants had gained little from the era of reforms and

were suffering from poverty and overpopulation. Finally, nationalist sentiment was emerging among the empire's minorities. The politically and culturally dominant ethnic Russians were only about 45 percent of the population, and by 1900 some intellectuals among the subject nationalities were calling for self-rule and autonomy. Separatist nationalism was strongest among the Polish and Ukrainians. With the army pinned down in Manchuria, all these currents of discontent converged in the revolution of 1905.

The beginning of the revolution pointed up the incompetence of the government. On a Sunday in January 1905, a massive demonstration of workers and their families converged peacefully on the Winter Palace in St. Petersburg to present a petition to the tsar. The workers were led by a trade unionist priest named Father Gapon, who had been secretly supported by the police as a preferable alternative to more radical unions. Carrying icons and respectfully singing "God Save the Tsar," the workers did not know Nicholas II had fled the city. Suddenly troops opened fire, killing and wounding hundreds. The "Bloody Sunday" massacre turned ordinary workers against the tsar and produced a wave of general indignation.

Outlawed political parties came out into the open, and by the summer of 1905 strikes, peasant uprisings, revolts among minority nationalities, and troop mutinies were sweeping the country. The revolutionary surge culminated in October 1905 in a great paralyzing general strike, which forced the government to capitulate. The tsar issued the October Manifesto, which granted full civil rights and promised a popularly elected Duma (parliament) with real legislative power. The Manifesto split the opposition. It satisfied most moderate and liberal demands, but the Social Democrats rejected it and led a bloody workers' uprising in Moscow in December 1905. Frightened middle-class moderates helped the government repress the uprising and survive as a constitutional monarchy.

On the eve of the opening of the first Duma in May 1906, the government issued the new constitution, the Fundamental Laws. The tsar retained great powers. The Duma, elected indirectly by universal male suffrage, and a largely appointive upper house could debate and pass laws, but the tsar had an absolute veto. As in Bismarck's Germany, the emperor appointed his ministers, who did not need to command a majority in the Duma.

The disappointed, predominantly middle-class liberals, the largest group in the newly elected Duma, saw the Fundamental Laws as a great step backwards. Efforts to cooperate with the tsar's ministers soon broke down. The government then dismissed the Duma, only to find that a more hostile and radical opposition was elected in 1907. After three months of deadlock, the second Duma was also dismissed. Thereupon the tsar and his reactionary advisors unilaterally rewrote the electoral law so as to increase greatly the weight of the propertied classes at the expense of workers, peasants, and national minorities.

The new law had the intended effect. With landowners assured half the seats in the Duma, the government finally secured a loyal majority in 1907 and again in 1912. Thus armed, the tough, energetic chief minister, Peter Stolypin, pushed through important agrarian reforms designed to break down collective village ownership of land and to encourage the more enterprising peasants—the so-called wager on the strong. On the eve of the First World War, Russia was partially modernized, a conservative constitutional monarchy with a peasant-based but industrializing economy.

THE RESPONSIVE NATIONAL STATE, 1871–1914

For central and western Europe, the unification of Italy and Germany by "blood and iron" marked the end of a dramatic period of nation building. After 1871 the heartland of Europe was organized in strong national states. Only on the borders of Europe—in Ireland and Russia, in Austria-Hungary and the Balkans—did subject peoples still strive for political unity and independence. Despite national differences, European domestic politics after 1871 had a common framework—the firmly established national state. The common themes within that framework were the emergence of mass politics and growing mass loyalty toward the national state.

For good reason, ordinary people—the masses of an industrializing, urbanizing society—felt increasing loyalty to their governments. More and more people could vote. By 1914 universal manhood suffrage was the rule rather than the exception. This development had as much psychological as political significance. Ordinary men were no longer denied the right to vote because they lacked wealth or education. They counted; they could influence the government to some extent. They could feel that they were becoming "part of the system."

Women began to demand the right to vote. The women's suffrage movement achieved its first success in the western United States, and by 1913 women could vote in twelve states. Europe, too, moved slowly in this direction. In 1914 Norway gave the vote to most women. Elsewhere, women like the English Emmeline Pankhurst were very militant in their demands. They heckled politicians and held public demonstrations. These efforts generally failed before 1914, but they prepared the way for the triumph of the women's suffrage movement immediately after World War One.

As the right to vote spread, politicians and parties in national parliaments represented the people more responsively. Most countries soon had many political parties. The multiparty system meant that parliamentary majorities were built on shifting coalitions, which were unstable but did give parties leverage. They could obtain benefits for their supporters. Governments increasingly passed laws to alleviate general problems and to help specific groups. Governments seemed to care, and they seemed more worthy of support.

THE GERMAN EMPIRE

Politics in Germany after 1871 reflected many of these developments. The new German Empire was a federal union of Prussia and twenty-four smaller states. Much of the everyday business of government was conducted by the separate states, but there was a strong national government with a chancellor—until 1890, Bismarck—and a popularly elected parliament, called the *Reichstag*. Although Bismarck refused to be bound by a parliamentary majority, he tried nonetheless to maintain such a majority. This situation gave the political parties opportunities. Until 1878 Bismarck relied mainly on the National Liberals, who had rallied to him after 1866. They supported legislation useful for further economic and legal unification of the country.

Less wisely, they backed Bismarck's attack on the Catholic church, the so-called *Kulturkampf,* or "struggle for civilization." Like Bismarck, the middle-class National Liberals were particularly alarmed by Pius IX's declaration of papal infallibility in 1870. That dogma seemed to ask German Catholics to put loyalty to their church above loyalty to their nation. Only in Protestant Prussia did the *Kulturkampf* have even limited success. Catholics throughout the country generally voted for the Catholic Center party, which blocked passage of national laws hostile to the church. Finally in 1878, Bismarck abandoned his attack. Indeed, he and the Catholic Center Party entered into an uneasy but mutually advantageous alliance. The reasons were largely economic.

After a worldwide financial bust in 1873, European agriculture was in an increasingly difficult position. Wheat prices plummeted as cheap grain poured in from the United States, Canada, and Russia. New lands were opening up in North America and Russia, and the combination of railroads and technical improvements in shipping cut freight rates for grain drastically. European peasants with their smaller, less efficient farms could not compete in cereal production, especially in western and southern Germany. The peasantry there was largely Catholic, and the Catholic Center party was thus converted to the cause of higher tariffs to protect the economic interests of its supporters.

The same competitive pressures caused the Protestant Junkers, who owned large estates in eastern Germany, to embrace the cause of higher tariffs. They were joined by some of the iron and steel magnates of the Prussian Rhineland and Westphalia, who had previously been for free trade. With three such influential groups lobbying energetically, Bismarck was happy to go along with a new protective tariff in 1879. In doing so, he won new supporters in parliament—the Center party of the Catholics and the Conservative party of the Prussian landowners—and he held on to most of the National Liberals.

Bismarck had been looking for a way to increase taxes and raise more money for the government. The solution was higher tariffs. Many other governments acted similarly. The 1880s and 1890s saw a widespread return to protectionism. France in particular established very high tariffs to protect agriculture and industry, peasants and manufacturers. Thus the German government and other governments responded to a major economic problem and simultaneously won greater loyalty.

At the same time, Bismarck tried to stop the growth of German socialism because he genuinely feared its revolutionary language and allegiance to a movement transcending the nation state. In 1878, after two attempts on the life of William I by radicals (though not socialists), Bismarck succeeded in ramming through the Reichstag a law repressing socialists. Socialist meetings and publications were strictly controlled. The Social Democratic party was outlawed and driven underground. However, German socialists displayed a discipline and organization worthy of the Prussian army itself. Bismarck had to try another tack.

Thus Bismarck's state pioneered with social measures designed to win the support of working-class people. In 1883 he pushed through the parliament the first of several modern social security laws to help wage earners. The laws of 1883 and 1884 established national sickness and accident insurance; the law of 1889 established old-age pensions and retirement benefits. Henceforth sick, injured, and retired workers could look forward to regular weekly benefits from the state. This national social security system, paid for through compulsory contributions by wage earners and employers as well as grants from the state, was the first of its kind anywhere. It was to be fifty years before similar measures would be taken in the United States. Bismarck's social security system did not wean workers from socialism, but it did protect them from some of the uncertainties of the complex urban industrial world. This enormously significant development was a product of political competition and governmental efforts to win popular support.

Increasingly, the great issues in German domestic politics were socialism and the Marxian Social Democratic party. In 1890 the new emperor, the young, idealistic, and unstable William II (1888–1918), opposed Bismarck's attempt to renew the law outlawing the Social Democratic party. Eager to rule in his own right, as well as to earn the support of the workers, William II forced Bismarck to resign. After the "dropping of the pilot," German foreign policy changed profoundly and mostly for the worse, but the government did pass new laws to aid workers and to legalize socialist political activity.

Yet William II was no more successful than Bismarck in getting workers to renounce socialism. In-

Bismarck and William II Shown here visiting Bismarck's country estate in 1888, shortly after he became emperor of Germany (and king of Prussia), the young and impetuous William II soon quarrelled with his chief minister. Determined to rule, not merely to reign, his dismissal of Bismarck in 1890 was a fatal decision. *(Bildarchiv Preussicher Kulturbesitz)*

deed, socialist ideas spread rapidly, and more and more Social Democrats were elected to the parliament in the 1890s. After opposing a colonial war in German Southwest Africa in 1906 and thus suffering important losses in the general elections of 1907, the German Social Democratic party broadened its base in the years before World War One. In the elections of 1912, the party scored a great victory, becoming the largest single party in the Reichstag. The "revolutionary" socialists were, however, becoming less and less revolutionary in Germany. In the years before World War One, the strength of socialist opposition to greater military spending and imperialist expansion declined greatly. German socialists marched under the national banner.

REPUBLICAN FRANCE

In 1871 France seemed hopelessly divided once again. The patriotic republicans who proclaimed the Third Republic in Paris after the military disaster at Sedan refused to admit defeat. They defended Paris with great heroism for weeks, living off rats and zoo animals, until they were quite literally starved into submission by German armies in January 1871. When national elections then sent a large majority of conservatives and monarchists to the National Assembly, the traumatized Parisians exploded and proclaimed the Paris Commune in March 1871. Vaguely radical, the leaders of the Commune wanted to govern Paris without interference by the conservative

Civil War in France When the French army invaded Paris, the Communards retaliated by placing hostages before firing squads, as this photograph reveals. The conquering army replied by summarily executing many prisoners and deporting others. Atrocities on both sides nurtured a tradition of class conflict that has often plagued modern France. *(The Bettmann Archive)*

French countryside. The National Assembly, led by the aging politician Adolphe Thiers, would hear none of it. The Assembly ordered the French army into Paris and brutally crushed the Commune. Twenty thousand people died in the fighting. As in June 1848, it was Paris against the provinces, French against French.

Out of this tragedy France slowly formed a new national unity, achieving considerable stability before 1914. How is one to account for this? Luck played a part. Until 1875 the monarchists in the "republican"

National Assembly had a majority but could not agree who should be king. The compromise Bourbon candidate refused to rule except under the white flag of his ancestors—a completely unacceptable condition. In the meantime, Thiers' slaying of the radical Commune and his other firm measures showed the fearful provinces and the middle class that the Third Republic might be moderate and socially conservative. France therefore retained the republic, though reluctantly. As President Thiers cautiously said, it was "the government which divides us least."

Another stabilizing factor was the skill and determination of the moderate republican leaders in the early years. The most famous of these was Léon Gambetta, the son of an Italian grocer, a warm, easygoing, unsuccessful lawyer turned professional politician. A master of emerging mass politics, Gambetta combined eloquence with the personal touch as he preached a republic of truly equal opportunity. Gambetta was also instrumental in establishing absolute parliamentary supremacy between 1877 and 1879, when the somewhat autocratic president Marie Edmé MacMahon was forced to resign. By 1879 the great majority of members of both the upper and the lower houses of parliament were republicans. Although these republicans were split among many parliamentary groups and later among several parties— a situation that led to constant coalition politics and the rapid turnover of ministers—the Third Republic had firm foundations after almost a decade.

The moderate republicans sought to preserve their creation by winning the hearts and minds of the next generation. Trade unions were fully legalized, and France acquired a colonial empire. More important, under the leadership of Jules Ferry, the moderate republicans of small towns and villages passed a series of laws between 1879 and 1886 establishing free compulsory elementary education for both girls and boys. At the same time, they greatly expanded the state system of public tax-supported schools. Thus France shared fully in the general expansion of public education, which served as a critical nation-building tool throughout the Western world in the late nineteenth century.

In France most elementary and much secondary education had traditionally been in the parochial schools of the Catholic church, which had long been hostile to republics and to much of secular life. Free compulsory elementary education in France became secular republican education. The pledge of allegiance and the national anthem replaced the catechism and the "Ave Maria." Militant young elementary teachers carried the ideology of patriotic republicanism into every corner of France. In their classes, they sought to win the loyalty of the young citizens to the republic, so that France would never again vote en masse for dictators like the two Napoleons.

Although these educational reforms disturbed French Catholics, many of them rallied to the republic in the 1890s. The limited acceptance of the modern world by the more liberal Pope Leo XIII (1878–1903) eased tensions between church and state. Unfortunately, the Dreyfus affair changed all that.

Alfred Dreyfus, a Jewish captain in the French army, was falsely accused and convicted of treason. His family never doubted his innocence and fought unceasingly to reopen the case, enlisting the support of prominent republicans and intellectuals such as the novelist Emile Zola. In 1898 and 1899, the case split France apart. On one side was the army, which had manufactured evidence against Dreyfus, joined by anti-Semites and most of the Catholic establishment. On the other side stood the civil libertarians and most of the more radical republicans.

This battle, which eventually led to Dreyfus's being declared innocent, revived republican feeling against the church. Between 1901 and 1905, the government severed all ties between the state and the Catholic church, after centuries of close relations. The salaries of priests and bishops were no longer paid by the government, and all churches were given to local committees of lay Catholics. Catholic schools were put completely on their own financially, and in a short time they lost a third of their students. The state school system's power of indoctrination was greatly strengthened. In France, only the growing socialist movement, with its very different and thoroughly secular ideology, stood in opposition to patriotic, republican nationalism.

GREAT BRITAIN AND IRELAND

Britain in the late nineteenth century has often been seen as a shining example of peaceful and successful political evolution. Germany was stuck with a manipulated parliament that gave an irresponsible emperor too much power; France had a quarrelsome parliament that gave its presidents too little power. Great Britain, in contrast, seemed to enjoy an effective two-party parliament that skillfully guided the country from classical liberalism to full-fledged democracy with hardly a misstep.

This view of Great Britain is not so much wrong as incomplete. After the right to vote was granted to males of the solid middle class in 1832, opinion leaders and politicians wrestled long and hard with the uncertainties of a further extension of the franchise. In his famous "Essay on Liberty," published in

The Spread of Nationalism in Europe, 1850–1914

1851	Louis Napoleon dismisses French National Assembly in coup d'état
1852–1870	Second Empire in France
1853–1856	Crimean War
1859	Mill, *Essay on Liberty*
1859–1870	Unification of Italy
1861	Abolition of serfdom in Russia
1862–1890	Bismarck's reign of power in German affairs
1864–1871	First Socialist International
1866	Prussia wins decisive victory in Austro-Prussian War
1866–1871	Unification of the German Empire
1867	Magyar nobility increases its power by restoring the constitution of 1848 in Hungary, thereby further dividing the Austro-Hungarian Empire
	Marx, *Das Capital*
	Second Reform Act passed by British parliament
1870–1871	Prussia wins decisive victory in Franco-Prussian War; William I proclaimed emperor of a united Germany
1871	Paris Commune
1871–1914	Third Republic in France
1878	Suppression of Social Democrats in Germany
1881	Assassination of Tsar Alexander II
1883–1889	Enactment of social security laws in Germany
1884	Third Reform Act passed by British parliament
1889–1914	Second Socialist International
1890	Repeal of anti–Social Democrat law in Germany
1892–1903	Witte directs modernization of Russian economy
1904–1905	Japan wins decisive victory in Russo-Japanese War
1905	Revolution in Russia: Tsar Nicholas II forced to issue the October Manifesto promising a popularly elected Duma
1906–1914	Liberal reform in Great Britain
1907–1912	Stolypin's agrarian reforms in Russia
1912	German Social Democratic party becomes largest party in the German Reichstag
1914	Irish Home Rule bill passed by British parliament but immediately suspended with outbreak of First World War

1859, the philosopher John Stuart Mill (1806–1873), the leading heir to the Benthamite tradition (page 765), probed the problem of how to protect the rights of individuals and minorities in the emerging age of mass electoral participation. Mill pleaded eloquently for the practical and moral value inherent in safeguarding individual differences and unpopular opinions. In 1867 Benjamin Disraeli and the Conservatives extended the vote to all middle-class males and the best-paid workers. The son of a Jewish stockbroker, himself a novelist and urban dandy, the ever-fascinating Disraeli (1804–1881) was willing to risk this "leap in the dark" in order to gain new supporters. The Conservative party, he believed, needed to broaden its traditional base of aristocratic and landed support if it was to survive. After 1867 English political parties and electoral campaigns became more modern, and the "lower orders" appeared to vote as responsibly as their "betters." Hence the Third Reform Bill of 1884 gave the vote to almost every adult male.

While the House of Commons was drifting toward democracy, the House of Lords was content to slumber nobly. Between 1901 and 1910, however, that bastion of aristocratic conservatism tried to reassert itself. Acting as supreme court of the land, it ruled against labor unions in two important decisions. And after the Liberal party came to power in 1906, the Lords vetoed several measures passed by the Commons, including the so-called People's Budget. The Lords finally capitulated, as they had done in 1832, when the king threatened to create enough new peers to pass the bill.

Aristocratic conservatism yielded to popular democracy, once and for all. The result was that extensive social welfare measures, slow to come to Great Britain, were passed in a spectacular rush between 1906 and 1914. During those years, the Liberal party, inspired by the fiery Welshman David Lloyd George (1863–1945), substantially raised taxes on the rich as part of the People's Budget. This income helped the government pay for national health insurance, unemployment benefits, old-age pensions, and a host of other social measures. The state was integrating the urban masses socially as well as politically.

This record of accomplishment was only part of the story, though. On the eve of World War One, the ever-emotional, ever-unanswered question of Ireland brought Great Britain to the brink of civil war. In the 1840s, Ireland had been decimated by famine, which fueled an Irish revolutionary movement. Thereafter, the English slowly granted concessions, such as the abolition of the privileges of the Anglican church and rights for Irish peasants. The Liberal prime minister William Gladstone (1809–1898), who had proclaimed twenty years earlier that "my mission is to pacify Ireland," introduced bills to give Ireland self-government in 1886 and in 1893. They failed to pass. After two decades of relative quiet, Irish nationalists in the British Parliament saw their chance. They supported the Liberals in their battle for the People's Budget and received passage of a home-rule bill for Ireland in return.

Thus Ireland, the emerald isle, achieved self-government—but not quite, for Ireland is composed of two peoples. As much as the Irish Catholic majority in the southern counties wanted home rule, precisely that much did the Irish Protestants of the northern countries of Ulster come to oppose it. Motivated by the accumulated fears and hostilities of generations, the Protestants of Ulster refused to submerge themselves in a Catholic Ireland, just as Irish Catholics had refused to submit to a Protestant Britain.

The Ulsterites vowed to resist home rule in northern Ireland. By December 1913, they had raised 100,000 armed volunteers, and they were supported by much of English public opinion. Thus in 1914, the Liberals in the House of Lords introduced a compromise home-rule law that did not apply to the northern counties. This bill, which openly betrayed promises made to Irish nationalists, was rejected and in September the original home-rule plan was passed but simultaneously suspended for the duration of the hostilities. The momentous Irish question had been overtaken by earth-shattering world war in August 1914.

Irish developments illustrated once again the power of national feeling and national movements in the nineteenth century. Moreover, they were proof that governments could not elicit greater loyalty unless they could capture and control that elemental current of national feeling. Though Great Britain had much going for it—power, Parliament, prosperity—none of these availed in the face of the conflicting nationalisms espoused by Catholics and Protestants in northern Ireland. Similarly, progressive Sweden was

Magyar Nationalism flourished in Buda and Pest, built on opposite sides of the Danube and merged together in 1872. A whole series of splendid new buildings rose up, reflecting the desire of Hungarians to make Budapest a truly great capital city. *(Historical Pictures Service, Chicago)*

powerless to stop the growth of the Norwegian national movement, which culminated in Norway's breaking away from Sweden and becoming a fully independent nation in 1905. In this light, one can also see how hopeless was the case of the Ottoman Empire in Europe in the later nineteenth century. It was only a matter of time before the Serbs, Bulgarians, and Rumanians would break away, and they did.

THE AUSTRO-HUNGARIAN EMPIRE

The dilemma of conflicting nationalisms in Ireland also helps one appreciate how desperate the situation in the Austro-Hungarian Empire had become by the early twentieth century. In 1849 Magyar nationalism had driven Hungarian patriots to declare an independent Hungarian republic, which was savagely crushed by Russian and Austrian armies (pages 754–756). Throughout the 1850s, Hungary was ruled as a conquered territory, and Emperor Francis Joseph and his bureaucracy tried hard to centralize the state and germanize the language and culture of the different nationalities.

Then, in the wake of defeat by Prussia in 1866, a weakened Austria was forced to strike a compromise and establish the so-called dual monarchy. The empire was divided in two and the nationalistic Magyars gained virtual independence for Hungary. Henceforth each half of the empire agreed to deal with its own "barbarians"—its own minorities—as it saw fit. The two states were joined only by a shared monarch and common ministries for finance, defense, and foreign affairs. After 1867 the disintegrating force of competing nationalisms continued unabated, for both Austria and Hungary had several "Irelands" within their borders.

In Austria, ethnic Germans were only one-third of the population, and by the late 1890s many Germans saw their traditional dominance threatened by Czechs, Poles, and other Slavs. A particularly emotional and divisive issue in the Austrian parliament was the language used in government and elementary education at the local level. From 1900 to 1914, the parliament was so divided that ministries generally could not obtain a majority and ruled instead by decree. Efforts by both conservatives and socialists to defuse national antagonisms by stressing economic issues cutting across ethnic lines—which led to the introduction of universal male suffrage in 1907—proved largely unsuccessful.

One aspect of such national antagonisms was anti-Semitism, which was particlarly virulent in Austria. The Jewish populations of Austrian cities grew very rapidly after Jews obtained full legal equality in 1867, reaching 10 percent of the population of Vienna by 1900. Many Jewish businessmen were quite successful in banking and retail trade, while Jewish artists, intellectuals, and scientists, like the world-famous Sigmund Freud, played a major role in making Vienna a leading center of European culture and modern thought. When extremists charged the Jews with controlling the economy and corrupting German culture with alien ideas and ultramodern art, anxious Germans of all classes tended to listen. The popular mayor of Vienna from 1897 to 1910, Dr. Karl Lueger, combined anti-Semitic rhetoric with calls for "Christian socialism" and municipal ownership of basic services. Lueger appealed especially to the German lower-middle class—and to an unsuccessful young artist named Adolf Hitler.

In Hungary, the Magyar nobility in 1867 restored the constitution of 1848 and used it to dominate both the Magyar peasantry and the minority populations until 1914. Only the wealthiest one-fourth of adult males had the right to vote, making the parliament the creature of the Magyar elite. Laws promoting use of the Magyar (Hungarian) language in schools and government were rammed through and bitterly resented, especially by the Croatians and Rumanians. While Magyar extremists campaigned loudly for total separation from Austria, the radical leaders of the subject nationalities dreamed in turn of independence from Hungary. Unlike most major countries, which harnessed nationalism to strengthen the state after 1871, the Austro-Hungarian Empire was progressively weakened and destroyed by it.

MARXISM AND THE SOCIALIST MOVEMENT

Nationalism served, for better or worse, as a new unifying principle. But what about socialism? Did the rapid growth of socialist parties, which were generally Marxian parties, dedicated to an international proletarian revolution, mean that national states had failed to gain the support of workers? Certainly, many prosperous and conservative citizens were greatly troubled by the socialist movement. And many historians have portrayed the years before 1914 as a time of increasing conflict between revolutionary socialism on the one hand and a nationalist alliance between conservative aristocracy and the prosperous middle class on the other. This question requires close examination.

THE SOCIALIST INTERNATIONAL

The growth of socialist parties after 1871 was phenomenal. Neither Bismarck's antisocialist laws nor his extensive social security system checked the growth of the German Social Democratic party, which espoused the Marxian ideology. By 1912 it had attracted millions of followers and was the largest party in the parliament. Socialist parties also grew in other countries, though nowhere else with quite such success. In 1883 Russian exiles in Switzerland founded a Russian Social Democratic party, which grew rapidly in the 1890s and thereafter, despite internal disputes. In France, various socialist parties reemerged in the 1880s after the carnage of the Commune. Most of them were finally unified in a single, increasingly powerful Marxian party, called the French Section of the Workers International, in 1905. Belgium and Austria-Hungary also had strong socialist parties of the Marxian persuasion.

As the name of the French party suggests, Marxian socialist parties were eventually linked together in an international organization. As early as 1848, Marx had laid out his intellectual system in the *Communist Manifesto* (pages 739–740). He had declared that "the working men have no country," and he had urged proletarians of all nations to unite against their governments. Joining the flood of radicals and republicans who fled continental Europe for England and America after the revolutions of 1848, Marx settled in London. Poor and depressed, he lived on his meager earnings as a journalist and on the gifts of his friend Engels. Marx never stopped thinking of revolution. Digging deeply into economics and history, he concluded that revolution follows economic crisis and tried to prove it in *Critique of Political Economy* (1859) and his greatest theoretical work, *Capital* (1867).

The bookish Marx also excelled as a practical organizer. In 1864 he played an important role in founding the First International of socialists—the International Working Men's Association. In the following years, he battled successfully to control the organization and used its annual meetings as a means of spreading his realistic, "scientific" doctrines of inevitable socialist revolution. Then Marx enthusiastically embraced the passionate, vaguely radical patriotism of the Paris Commune and its terrible conflict with the French National Assembly as a giant step toward socialist revolution. This impetuous action frightened many of his early supporters, especially the more moderate British labor leaders. The First International collapsed.

Yet international proletarian solidarity remained an important objective for Marxists. In 1889, as the individual parties in different countries grew stronger, socialist leaders came together to form the Second International, which lasted until 1914. Although the International was only a federation of various national socialist parties, it had great psychological impact. Every three years, delegates from the different parties met to interpret Marxian doctrines and plan coordinated action. May 1—May Day—was declared an annual international one-day strike, a day of marches and demonstrations. A permanent executive for the International was established. Many feared and many others rejoiced in the growing power of socialism and the Second International.

UNIONS AND REVISIONISM

Was socialism really radical and revolutionary in these years? On the whole, it was not. Indeed, as socialist parties grew and attracted large numbers of members, they looked more and more toward gradual change and steady improvement for the working class, less and less toward revolution. The mainstream of European socialism became militantly moderate; that is, they increasingly combined radical rhetoric with sober action.

Workers themselves were progressively less inclined to follow radical programs. There were several reasons for this. As workers gained the right to vote and to participate politically in the nation-state, their attention focused more on elections than on revolutions. And as workers won real, tangible benefits, this furthered the process. Workers were not immune to patriotic education and indoctrination during military service, however ardently socialist intellectuals might wish the contrary. Nor were workers a unified social group, as demonstrated in Chapter 24.

Perhaps most important of all, workers' standard of living rose substantially after 1850 as the promise of the Industrial Revolution was at least partially realized. In Great Britain, for example, workers could buy almost twice as much with their wages in 1906 as in 1850, and most of the increase came after 1870. Workers experienced similar increases in most continental countries after 1850, though much less strikingly in late-developing Russia. Improvement in the standard of living was much more than merely a matter of higher wages. The quality of life improved dramatically in urban areas. For all these reasons, workers tended more and more to become militantly moderate: they demanded gains, but they were less likely to take to the barricades in pursuit of them.

The growth of labor unions reinforced this trend toward moderation. In the early stages of industrialization, modern unions were generally prohibited by law. A famous law of the French Revolution had declared all guilds and unions illegal in the name of "liberty" in 1791. In Great Britain, attempts by workers to unite were considered criminal conspiracies after 1799. Other countries had similar laws, and these obviously hampered union development. In France, for example, about two hundred workers were imprisoned each year between 1825 and 1847 for taking part in illegal combinations. Unions were considered subversive bodies, only to be hounded and crushed.

From this sad position workers struggled to escape. Great Britain led the way in 1824 and 1825, when unions won the right to exist but (generally) not the right to strike. After the collapse of Robert Owen's attempt to form one big union in the 1830s (page 720), new and more practical kinds of unions appeared. Limited primarily to highly skilled workers such as machinists and carpenters, the "new model unions" avoided both radical politics and costly strikes. Instead, their sober, respectable leaders concentrated

Socialist Clubs helped spread Marxian doctrines among the working classes. There workers (and intellectuals) from different backgrounds debated the fine points and developed a sense of solidarity. *(Historical Pictures Service, Chicago)*

on winning better wages and hours for their members through collective bargaining and compromise. This approach helped pave the way to full acceptance in Britain in the 1870s, when unions won the right to strike without being held legally liable for the financial damage inflicted on employers. After 1890 unions for unskilled workers developed, and between 1901 and 1906, the legal position of British unions was further strengthened.

Germany was the most industrialized, socialized, and unionized continental country by 1914. German unions were not granted important rights until 1869, and until the antisocialist law was repealed in 1890, they were frequently harassed by the government as socialist fronts. Nor were socialist leaders particularly interested in union activity, believing as they did in the iron law of low wages and the need for political

revolution. The result was that, as late as 1895, there were only about 270,000 union members in a male industrial work force of nearly 8 million. Then, with German industrialization still storming ahead and almost all legal harassment eliminated, union membership skyrocketed to roughly 3 million in 1912.

This great expansion both reflected and influenced the changing character of German unions. Increasingly, unions in Germany focused on concrete bread-and-butter issues—wages, hours, working conditions—rather than on instilling pure socialist doctrine. Genuine collective bargaining, long opposed by socialist intellectuals as a "sellout," was officially recognized as desirable by the German Trade Union Congress in 1899. When employers proved unwilling to bargain, a series of strikes forced them to change their minds.

Between 1906 and 1913, successful collective bargaining was gaining a prominent place in German industrial relations. In 1913 alone, over ten thousand collective bargaining agreements affecting 1.25 million workers were signed. Further gradual improvement, not revolution, was becoming the primary objective of the German trade union movement.

The German trade unions and their leaders were —in fact, if not in name—thoroughgoing revisionists. *Revisionism*—that most awful of sins in the eyes of militant Marxists in the twentieth century—was an effort by various socialists to update Marxian doctrines to reflect the realities of the time. Thus the socialist Edward Bernstein argued in 1899 in his *Evolutionary Socialism* that Marx's predictions of ever-greater poverty for workers and ever-greater concentration of wealth in ever-fewer hands had been proven false. Therefore, Bernstein suggested, socialists should reform their doctrines and tactics. They should combine with other progressive forces to win gradual evolutionary gains for workers through legislation, unions, and further economic development. These views were formally denounced as heresy by the German Social Democratic party and later by the entire Second International. Nevertheless, the revisionist, gradualist approach continued to gain the tacit acceptance of many German socialists, particularly in the trade unions.

Moderation found followers elsewhere. In France, the great humanist and socialist leader Jean Jaurès formally repudiated revisionist doctrines in order to establish a unified socialist party, but he remained at heart a gradualist. Questions of revolutionary versus gradualist policies split Russian Marxists.

Socialist parties before 1914 had clear-cut national characteristics. Russians and socialists in the Austro-Hungarian Empire tended to be the most radical. The German party talked revolution and practiced reformism, greatly influenced by its enormous trade union movement. The French party talked revolution and tried to practice it, unrestrained by a trade union movement that was both very weak and very radical. In England, the socialist but non-Marxian Labour party, reflecting the well-established union movement, was formally committed to gradual reform. In Spain and Italy, Marxian socialism was very weak. There anarchism, seeking to smash the state rather than the bourgeoisie, dominated radical thought and action.

In short, socialist policies and doctrines varied from country to country. Socialism itself was to a large extent "nationalized" behind the imposing façade of international unity. This helps explain why, when war came in 1914, socialist leaders almost without exception supported their governments.

From the mid-nineteenth century on, Western society became nationalistic as well as urban and industrial. Nation-states and strong-minded national leaders gradually enlisted widespread support and gave men and women a sense of belonging. Even socialism became increasingly national in orientation, gathering strength as a champion of working-class interests in domestic politics. Yet, while nationalism served to unite peoples, it also drove them apart. Though most obvious in Austria-Hungary and Ireland, this was in a real sense true for all of Western civilization. For the universal national faith, which reduced social tensions within states, promoted a bitter, almost Darwinian competition between states and thus ominously threatened the progress and unity it had helped to build.

NOTES

1. Quoted by G. Wright, *France in Modern Times,* Rand McNally, Chicago, 1960, p. 179.
2. J. Burckhardt, *Reflections on History,* G. Allen & Unwin, London, 1943, p. 165.
3. Quoted by O. Pflanze, *Bismarck and the Development of Germany: The Period of Unification, 1815–1871,* Princeton University Press, Princeton, N.J., 1963, p. 60.
4. Quoted by E. Eyck, *Bismarck and the German Empire,* W. W. Norton, New York, 1964, p. 59.
5. Quoted by H. Kohn, *The Mind of Germany: The Education of a Nation,* Charles Scribner's Sons & Macmillan, New York, 1960, pp. 156–161.
6. Quoted by T. von Laue, *Sergei Witte and the Industrialization of Russia,* Columbia University Press, New York, 1963, p. 78.
7. Quoted by J. P. McKay, *Pioneers for Profit: Foreign Entrepreneurship and Russian Industrialization, 1885–1913,* Chicago University Press, Chicago, 1970, p. 11.

SUGGESTED READING

In addition to the general works mentioned in the Suggested Reading for Chapter 23, which treat the entire nineteenth century, G. Craig, *Germany, 1866–1945* (1980), and B. Moore, *Social Origins of Dictatorship and Democracy* (1966), are outstanding.

Among specialized works of high quality, R. Williams, *Gaslight and Shadows* (1957), brings the world of Napoleon III vibrantly alive, while Karl Marx's *The Eighteenth Brumaire of Louis Napoleon* is a famous denunciation of the coup d'état. The engaging collective biography by R. Shattuck, *The Banquet Years* (1968), captures the spirit of artistic and intellectual Paris at the end of the century. E. Weber, *Peasants into Frenchmen* (1976), stresses the role of education and modern communications in the transformation of rural France after 1870. E. Thomas, *The Women Incendiaries* (1966), examines radical women in the Paris Commune. G. Chapman, *The Dreyfus Case: A Reassessment* (1955), and D. Johnson, *France and the Dreyfus Affair* (1967), are careful examinations of the famous case. In *Jean Barois*, Nobel Prize winner R. M. Du Gard accurately recreates in novel form the Dreyfus affair, and Emile Zola's novel *The Debacle* treats the Franco-Prussian War realistically.

D. M. Smith has written widely on Italy, and his *Garibaldi* (1956) and *Italy: A Modern History*, rev. ed. (1969) are recommended. P. Schroeder, *Austria, Great Britain and the Crimean War* (1972), is an outstanding and highly original diplomatic study. In addition to the important studies on Bismarck and Germany by Pflanze, Eyck, and Kohn cited in the Notes, F. Stern, *Gold and Iron* (1977), is a fascinating examination of relations between Bismarck and his financial adviser, the Jewish banker Bleichröder. G. Iggers, *The German Conception of History* (1968); K. D. Barkin, *The Controversy Over German Industrialization, 1890–1902* (1970); and E. Spencer, *Management and Labor in Imperial Germany: Ruhr Industrialists as Employers* (1984), are valuable in-depth investigations. H. Glasser, ed., *The German Mind in the Nineteenth Century* (1981), is an outstanding anthology, as is P. Mendes-Flohr, *The Jew in the Modern World: A Documentary History* (1980). C. Schorske, *Fin de Siècle Vienna: Politics and Culture* (1980), and P. Gay, *Freud, Jews, and Other Germans* (1978), are brilliant on aspects of modern culture. R.

Kann, *The Multinational Empire*, 2 vols. (1950, 1964), probes the intricacies of the nationality problem in Austria-Hungary, while S. Stavrianos has written extensively on southeastern Europe, including *The Balkans, 1815–1914* (1963).

In addition to the studies on Russian industrial development by von Laue and McKay cited in the Notes, W. Blackwell, *The Industrialization of Russia*, 2nd. ed. (1982), and A. Rieber, *Merchants and Entrepreneurs in Imperial Russia* (1982), are recommended. Among fine studies on Russian social development and modernization, T. Emmons, *The Russian Landed Gentry and the Peasant Emancipation of 1861* (1968); R. Zelnik, *Labor and Society in Tsarist Russia, 1855–1870* (1971); R. Johnson, *Peasant and Proletarian: The Working Class of Moscow at the End of the Nineteenth Century* (1979); and H. Troyat, *Daily Life in Russia Under the Last Tsar* (1962), are particularly noteworthy. W. E. Mosse, *Alexander II and the Modernization of Russia* (1958), provides a good discussion of midcentury reforms, while C. Black, ed., *The Transformation of Russian Society* (1960), offers a collection of essays on Russian modernization. I. Turgenev's great novel *Fathers and Sons* probes the age-old conflict of generations as well as nineteenth-century Russian revolutionary thought.

G. Dangerfield, *The Strange Death of Liberal England* (1961), brilliantly examines social tensions in Ireland as well as Englishwomen's struggle for the vote before 1914. W. Arnstein convincingly shows how the Victorian aristocracy survived and even flourished in nineteenth-century Britain in F. Jaher, ed., *The Rich, the Well-Born, and the Powerful* (1973), an interesting collection of essays on social elites in history. The theme of aristocratic strength and survival is expanded in A. Mayer's provocative *Persistence of the Old Regime: Europe to the Great War* (1981).

On late-nineteenth-century socialism, C. Schorske, *German Social Democracy, 1905–1917* (1955), is a modern classic. V. Lidtke, *The Outlawed Party* (1966), ably treats the German socialists between 1878 and 1890. H. Goldberg, *The Life of Jean Jaurès* (1962), is a sympathetic account of the great French socialist leader. P. Stearns, who has written several books on European labor history, considers radical labor leaders in *Revolutionary Syndicalism and French Labor* (1971). M. Hanagan, *The Logic of Solidarity* (1980), examines the working class in three French towns between 1870 and 1914.

26

THE WEST AND THE WORLD

HILE BOTH NATIONALISM and urban life were transforming Western society, Western society itself was reshaping the world. At the peak of its power and pride, the West entered the third and most dynamic phase of the aggressive expansion that began with the Crusades and continued with the great discoveries and the rise of seaborne colonial empires. An ever-growing stream of products, people, and ideas flowed out of Europe in the nineteenth century. Hardly any corner of the globe was left untouched. The most spectacular manifestations of Western expansion came in the late nineteenth century, when the leading European nations established or enlarged their far-flung political empires. The political annexation of territory in the 1880s—the "new imperialism," as it is often called by historians—was the capstone of a profound underlying economic and technological process. How and why did this many-sided, epoch-making expansion occur, and what were some of its consequences for the West and the rest of the world? This chapter will focus on these questions.

BUILDING A WORLD ECONOMY

The Industrial Revolution created, first in Great Britain and then in continental Europe and North America, a growing and tremendously dynamic economic system. In the course of the nineteenth century, that system was extended across the face of the earth. Much of this extension into non-Western areas was peaceful and beneficial for all concerned, for the West had many products and techniques the rest of the world desired. If peaceful methods failed, however, Europeans did not stand on ceremony. They used their superior military power to force non-Western nations to open their doors to trade and investment.

TRADE AND COMMUNICATIONS

Commerce between nations has always been a powerful stimulus to economic development. Never was this more true than in the nineteenth century, when world trade grew prodigiously. As Figure 26.1 shows, world trade grew modestly until about 1840, and

then it took off. After a slowdown in the last years of the century, another surge lasted until World War One. The value of world trade in 1913 was roughly *twenty-five* times what it had been in 1800. This figure actually understates growth, since average prices of both manufactured goods and raw materials were substantially *lower* in 1913 than in 1800. In a general way, the enormous increase in international commerce summed up the growth of an interlocking world economy, centered in and directed by Europe.

Great Britain played a key role in using trade to tie all corners of the world together economically. In 1815 Britain already had a colonial empire, for India, Canada, Australia, and other scattered areas remained British possessions after American independence. The technological breakthroughs of the Industrial Revolution allowed Britain to manufacture cotton textiles, iron, and other goods more cheaply and to far outstrip domestic demand for such products. By 1820 Britain was exporting half of its cotton textiles, for example. As European nations and the United States erected protective tariff barriers and began to industrialize, British cotton-textile manufacturers aggressively sought and found other foreign markets. In 1820 Europe bought half of Britain's cotton-textile exports and India bought only 6 percent. By 1850 India bought 25 percent and Europe only 16 percent of a much larger total.

Moreover, after the repeal of the Corn Laws in 1846, Britain's commitment to free trade was unswerving. The decisive argument in the battle against tariffs on imported grain had been, "We must give, if we mean honestly to receive, and buy as well as sell." Until 1914 Britain thus remained the world's emporium, where not only agricultural products and raw materials but also manufactured goods entered freely. Free access to the enormous market of Britain and its empire stimulated business activities around the world.

The growth of trade was facilitated by the conquest of distance. The earliest railroad construction occurred in Europe (including Russia) and in America north of the Rio Grande; other parts of the globe saw the building of rail lines after 1860. By 1920 more than one-quarter of the world's railroads were in Latin America, Asia, Africa, and Australia. Wherever railroads were built, they drastically reduced transportation costs, opened new economic opportunities, and called forth new skills and attitudes. Moreover, in the areas of massive European settlement—North America and Australia—they were built in advance of the population and provided a means of settling the land.

The power of steam revolutionized transportation by sea as well as by land. In 1807 inhabitants of the Hudson Valley in New York saw the "Devil on the way to Albany in a saw-mill," as Robert Fulton's steamship *Clermont* traveled 150 miles upstream in thirty-two hours. Steam power, long used to drive paddle-wheelers on rivers, particularly in Russia and North America, finally began to supplant sails on the oceans of the world in the late 1860s. Lighter, stronger, cheap steel replaced iron, which had replaced wood. Screw propellers superseded paddle wheels, while mighty compound steam engines cut fuel consumption by half. Passenger and freight rates tumbled, and the intercontinental shipment of low-priced raw materials became feasible. In addition to the large passenger liners and freighters of the great shipping companies, there were innumerable independent tramp steamers searching endlessly for cargo around the world.

An account of an actual voyage by a typical tramp freighter will highlight nineteenth-century developments in global trade. The ship left England in 1910, carrying rails and general freight to western Australia. From there, it carried lumber to Melbourne in southeastern Australia, where it took on harvester combines for Argentina. In Buenos Aires it loaded wheat for Calcutta, and in Calcutta it took on jute for New York. From New York it carried a variety of industrial products to Australia, before returning to England with lead, wool, and wheat after a voyage of approximately 72,000 miles to six continents in seventeen months.

The revolution in land and sea transportation helped European pioneers to open up vast new territories and to produce agricultural products and raw materials there for sale in Europe. Moreover, the development of refrigerated railway cars and, from the 1880s, refrigerator ships enabled first Argentina and then the United States, Australia, and New Zealand to ship mountains of chilled or frozen beef and mutton to European (mainly British) consumers. From Asia, Africa, and Latin America came not only the traditional tropical products—spices, tea, sugar, coffee—but new raw materials for industry, such as jute, rubber, cotton, and coconut oil.

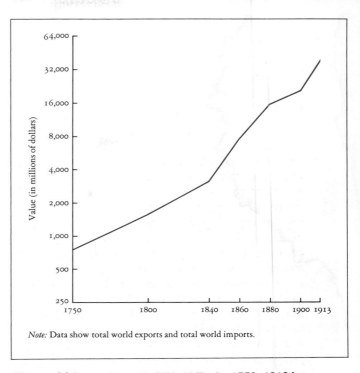

Note: Data show total world exports and total world imports.

FIGURE 26.1 The Growth of World Trade, 1750–1913 in 1913 Dollars The expansion of international commerce encouraged and reflected Western economic development in the nineteenth century. *(Source: W. Woodruff, Impact of Western Man: A Study of Europe's Role in the World Economy. St. Martin's Press, New York, 1967, p. 313 and references cited therein.)*

Intercontinental trade was enormously facilitated by the Suez and Panama canals. Of great importance, too, was large and continuous investment in modern port facilities, which made loading and unloading cheaper, faster, and more dependable. Finally, transoceanic telegraph cables inaugurated rapid communications among the financial centers of the world. While a British tramp freighter steamed from Calcutta to New York, a broker in London was arranging, by telegram, for it to carry an American cargo to Australia. World commodity prices were also instantaneously conveyed by the same network of communications.

In surveying these dramatic and impressive developments, one must remember that, in terms of value, most *trade* (as opposed to most *shipping*) was among European nations, the United States, and Canada. It was not between Europe and the colonial-tropical lands of Africa, Asia, and Latin America. For example, Britain and Germany, both great world traders, carried on a very large and profitable trade with each

The Opening of the Suez Canal in 1869 revolutionized communications between Europe and Asia. This drawing shows opening-day ceremonies. *(BBC Hulton/The Bettmann Archive)*

other before World War One. Between 1900 and 1913, Britain's second-best customer in the entire world (after India) was Germany, and Britain was Germany's largest single customer. Germany sold twice as much to Britain alone as to all of Africa and Asia combined. Before 1914 world trade was centered in the prosperous, tightly integrated European economy.

FOREIGN INVESTMENT

The growth of trade and the conquest of distance encouraged the expanding European economy to make massive foreign investments. Beginning about 1840, European capitalists started to invest large sums in foreign lands. They did not stop until the outbreak of World War One in 1914. By that year, Europeans had invested more than $40 billion abroad. Great Britain, France, and Germany were the principal investing countries, although by 1913 the United States was emerging as a substantial foreign investor. The sums involved were enormous (see Map 26.1). In the decade before 1914, Great Britain was investing 7 percent of its annual national income abroad, or slightly more than it was investing in its entire domestic economy. The great gap between rich and poor meant that the wealthy and moderately well-to-do could and did send great sums abroad in search of interest and dividends.

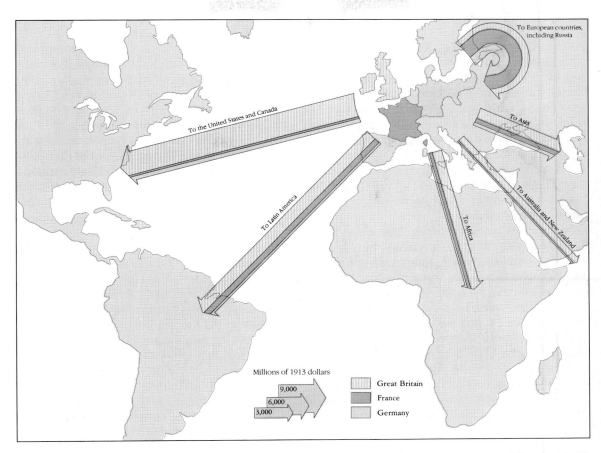

MAP 26.1 European Investment to 1914 Foreign investment grew rapidly after 1850, and Britain, France, and Germany were the major investing nations. As shown, most European investment was not directed to the area seized by the "new imperialism."

Contrary to what many people assume, most of the capital exported did *not* go to European colonies or protectorates in Asia and Africa. About three-quarters of total European investment went to other European countries, the United States and Canada, Australia and New Zealand, and Latin America. The reason was simple: Europe found its most profitable opportunities for investment in construction of the railroads, ports, and utilities that were necessary to settle and develop those almost-vacant lands. By loaning money for a railroad in Argentina or in Canada's prairie provinces, for example, Europeans not only collected interest but also enabled white settlers to buy European rails and locomotives, developed sources of cheap wheat, and opened still more territory for European settlement. Much of this invest-

ment—such as in American railroads, fully a third of whose capital in 1890 was European, or in Russian railroads, which drew heavily on loans from France —was peaceful and mutually beneficial. The victims were native American Indians and Australian aborigines, who were decimated by the diseases, liquor, and guns of an aggressively expanding Western society.

THE OPENING OF CHINA AND JAPAN

Europe's relatively peaceful developuent of robust offshoots in sparsely populated North America, Australia, and much of Latin America absorbed huge quantities of goods, investments, and migrants. From a Western point of view, that was the most important aspect of Europe's global thrust. Yet Europe's economic and cultural penetration of old, densely populated civilizations was also profoundly significant, especially for the non-European peoples affected by it. With such civilizations Europeans also increased their trade and profit. Moreover, as had been the case ever since Vasco da Gama and Christopher Columbus, the expanding Western society was prepared to use force to attain its desires, if necessary. This was what happened in China and Japan, two crucial examples of the general pattern of intrusion into non-Western lands.

Traditional Chinese civilization was self-sufficient. For centuries China had sent more to Europe in the way of goods and inventions than it received, and this was still the case in the eighteenth century. Europeans and the English in particular had developed a taste for Chinese tea, but they had to pay for it with hard silver since China was supremely uninterested in European wares. Trade with Europe was carefully regulated by the Chinese imperial government—the Manchu dynasty—which was more interested in isolating and controlling the strange "sea barbarians" than in pursuing commercial exchange. The imperial government refused to establish diplomatic relations with the "inferior" European states, and it required all foreign merchants to live in the southern city of Canton and to buy and sell only from the local merchant monopoly. Practices considered harmful to Chinese interests, such as the sale of opium and the export of silver from China, were strictly forbidden.

For years the little community of foreign merchants in Canton had to accept the Chinese system. By the 1820s, however, the dominant group, the British, was flexing its muscles. Moreover, in the smoking of opium—that "destructive and ensnaring vice" denounced by Chinese decrees—they had found something the Chinese really wanted. Grown legally in British-occupied India, opium was smuggled into China by means of fast ships and bribed officials. The more this rich trade developed, the greedier British merchants became and the more they resented the patriotic attempts of the Chinese government to stem the tide of drug addiction. By 1836 the aggressive goal of the British merchants in Canton was an independent British colony in China and "safe and unrestricted liberty" in trade. They pressured the British government to take decisive action and enlisted the support of British manufacturers with visions of vast Chinese markets to be opened.

At the same time, the Manchu government decided that the opium trade had to be stamped out. It was ruining the people and stripping the empire of its silver, which was going to British merchants to pay for the opium. The government began to prosecute Chinese drug dealers vigorously and in 1839 sent special envoy Lin Tse-hsü to Canton. Lin Tse-hsü ordered the foreign merchants to obey China's laws, "for our great unified Manchu Empire regards itself as responsible for the habits and morals of its subjects and cannot rest content to see any of them become victims of a deadly poison."[1] The British merchants refused and were expelled, whereupon war soon broke out.

Using troops from India and in control of the seas, the British occupied several coastal cities and forced China to surrender. In the Treaty of Nanking in 1842, the imperial government was forced to cede the island of Hong Kong to Britain forever, pay an indemnity of $100 million, and open up four large cities to foreign trade with low tariffs.

Thereafter the opium trade flourished, and Hong Kong developed rapidly as an Anglo-Chinese enclave. China continued to nurture illusions of superiority and isolation, however, and refused to accept foreign diplomats to Peking, the imperial capital. Finally, there was a second round of foreign attack between 1856 and 1860, culminating in the occupation of Peking by seventeen thousand British and French troops and the intentional burning of the emperor's summer palace. Another round of harsh treaties gave European merchants and missionaries greater privileges and protection. Thus did Europeans use military aggression to blow a hole in the wall of Chinese seclusion and open the country to foreign trade and foreign ideas.

China's neighbor, Japan, had its own highly distinctive civilization and even less use for Westerners. European traders and missionaries first arrived in Japan in the sixteenth century. By 1640 Japan had reacted quite negatively to their presence. The government decided to seal off the country from all European influences, in order to preserve its traditional culture and society. It ruthlessly persecuted Japanese Christians and expelled all but a few Dutch merchants, who were virtually imprisoned in a single port and rigidly controlled. When American and British whaling ships began to appear off Japanese coasts almost two hundred years later, the policy of exclusion was still in effect. An order of 1825 com-

East Meets West This painting gives a Japanese view of the first audience of the American Consul and his staff with the shogun, Japan's hereditary military governor, in 1859. The Americans appear strange and ill at ease. *(Bradley Smith)*

manded Japanese officials to "drive away foreign vessels without second thought."[2]

Japan's unbending isolation seemed hostile and barbaric to the West, particularly to the United States. It complicated the practical problems of shipwrecked American sailors and provisioning of whaling ships and China traders sailing in the eastern Pacific. It also thwarted the hope of trade and profit. Also, Americans shared the self-confidence and dynamism of expanding Western society. They had taken California from Mexico in 1848, and Americans felt destined to play a great role in the Pacific. It seemed, therefore, the United States' duty to force the Japanese to share their ports and behave like a "civilized" nation.

After several unsuccessful American attempts to establish commercial relations with Japan, Commodore Matthew Perry steamed into Edo (now Tokyo) Bay in 1853 and demanded diplomatic negotiations with the emperor. Japan entered a grave crisis. Some Japanese warriors urged resistance, but senior officials realized how defenseless their cities were against naval bombardment. Shocked and humiliated, they reluctantly signed a treaty with the United States that opened two ports and permitted trade. Over the next five years, more treaties spelled out the rights and privileges of the Western nations and their merchants in Japan. Japan was "opened." What the British had done in China with war, the Americans had done in Japan with the threat of war.

WESTERN PENETRATION OF EGYPT

Egypt's experience illustrates not only the explosive power of the expanding European economy and society but also their seductive appeal in non-Western lands. Of great importance in African and Middle Eastern history, the ancient land of the pharaohs had since 525 B.C. been ruled by a succession of foreigners, most recently by the Ottoman Turks. In 1798 French armies under young General Napoleon Bonaparte invaded the Egyptian part of the Ottoman Empire and occupied the territory for three years. Into the power vacuum left by the French withdrawal stepped an extraordinary Albanian-born Turkish general, Mohammed Ali (1769–1849).

First appointed governor of Egypt by the Turkish sultan, Mohammed Ali soon disposed of his political rivals and set out to build his own state on the strength of a large, powerful army organized along European lines. He drafted for the first time the illiterate, despised peasant masses of Egypt, and he hired French and Italian army officers to train these raw recruits and their Turkish officers. The government was also reformed, new lands were cultivated, and communications were improved. By the time of his death in 1849, Mohammed Ali had established a strong and virtually independent Egyptian state, to be ruled by his family on an hereditary basis within the Turkish empire.

Mohammed Ali's policies of modernization attracted large numbers of Europeans to the banks of the Nile. As one Arab sheik of the Ottoman Empire remarked in the 1830s, "Englishmen are like ants; if one finds a bit of meat, hundreds follow."[3] The port city of Alexandria had more than fifty thousand Europeans by 1864, most of them Italians, Greeks, French, and English. Europeans served not only as army officers but also as engineers, doctors, high government officials, and policemen. Others found their "meat" in trade, finance, and shipping. This was particularly true after 1863, when Mohammed Ali's grandson Ismail began his sixteen-year rule as Egypt's *khedive*, or "prince."

Educated at France's leading military academy, Ismail was a westernizing autocrat. He dreamed of using European technology and capital to modernize Egypt quickly and build a vast empire in northwest Africa. The large irrigation networks he promoted caused cotton production and exports to Europe to boom. Ismail also borrowed large sums to install modern communications, and with his support the Suez Canal was completed by a French company in 1869. The Arabic of the masses rather than the Turkish of the conquerors became the official language, and young Egyptians educated in Europe helped spread new skills and new ideas in the bureaucracy. Cairo acquired modern boulevards, Western hotels, and an opera house. As Ismail proudly declared: "My country is no longer in Africa, we now form part of Europe."[4]

Yet Ismail was too impatient and too reckless. His projects were enormously expensive, and the sale of his stock in the Suez Canal to the British government did not relieve the situation. By 1876 Egypt owed foreign bondholders a colossal $450 million and could not pay the interest on its debt. Rather than let Egypt go bankrupt and repudiate its loans, as had some Latin American countries and U.S. state governments in the early nineteenth century, the governments of France and Great Britain intervened politically in support of the European bankers who held the Egyptian bonds. They forced Ismail to appoint French and British commissioners to oversee Egyptian finances, in order that the Egyptian debt would be paid in full. This was a momentous decision. It implied direct European political control and was a sharp break with the previous pattern of trade investment, and relatively peaceful economic and cultural penetration. Some English critics denounced this action as naked aggression, cloaked in hypocrisy about guarding the Suez Canal, the "life line to India."

Foreign financial control evoked a violent nationalistic reaction among Egyptian religious leaders, young intellectuals, and army officers. In 1879, under the leadership of Colonel Ahmed Arabi, they formed the Egyptian Nationalist party. Continuing diplomatic pressure, which forced Ismail to abdicate in favor of his weak son Tewfiq (1879–1892), resulted in bloody anti-European riots in Alexandria in 1882. A number of Europeans were killed, and Tewfiq and his court had to flee to British ships for safety. When the British fleet bombarded Alexandria, more riots swept the country, and Colonel Arabi declared that "an irreconcilable war existed between the Egyptians and the English." But a British expeditionary force decimated Arabi's forces and occupied all of Egypt.

The British said their occupation was temporary, but British armies remained in Egypt until 1956. They maintained the façade of the khedive's government as an autonomous province of the Ottoman

British Influence in Egypt was pervasive after 1882. In this unusual photograph from 1890, Scottish soldiers swarm over the ancient and mysterious Great Sphinx like school children on an outing. *(BBC Hulton/The Bettmann Archive)*

Empire, but the khedive was a mere puppet. The able British consul general Evelyn Baring, later Lord Cromer, ruled the country after 1883. Once a vocal opponent of involvement in Egypt, Baring was a paternalistic reformer who had come to believe that "without European interference and initiative reform is impossible here." Baring's rule did result in better conditions for peasants and tax reforms, while foreign bondholders tranquilly clipped their coupons and Egyptian nationalists nursed their injured pride.

In Egypt, Baring and the British reluctantly but spectacularly provided a new model for European expansion in densely populated lands. Such expansion was based on military force, political domination, and a self-justifying ideology of beneficial reform. This model was to predominate until 1914.

THE GREAT MIGRATION

A poignant human drama was interwoven with economic expansion: literally millions of people picked up stakes and left their ancestral lands in the course of history's greatest migration. To millions of ordinary people, for whom the opening of China and the interest on the Egyptian debt had not the slightest significance, this great movement was the central experience in the saga of Western expansion. It was, in part, because of this great migration that the West's impact on the world in the nineteenth century was so many-sided, affecting far more than just economic matters.

Ellis Island in New York's harbor was the main entry point into the United States after 1892. For millions of migrants the first frightening experience in the new land was being inspected and processed through its crowded "pens." *(Culver Pictures)*

In the early eighteenth century, the growth of European population entered its third and decisive stage, which continued unabated until the twentieth century (page 618). Birthrates eventually declined in the nineteenth century, but so did death rates, mainly because of the rising standard of living and secondarily because of the medical revolution. Thus the population of Europe (including Asiatic Russia) more than doubled, from approximately 188 million in 1800 to roughly 432 million in 1900.

These figures actually understate Europe's population explosion, for between 1815 and 1932 more than 60 million people left Europe. These migrants went primarily to the "areas of European settlement"—North and South America, Australia, New Zealand, and Siberia—where they contributed to a rapid growth of numbers. The population of North America (the United States and Canada) alone grew from 6 million to 81 million between 1800 and 1900 because of continuous immigration and the high fertility rates of North American women. Since population grew more slowly in Africa and Asia than in Europe, as Figure 26.2 shows, Europeans and people of European origin jumped from about 22 percent of the world's total to about 38 percent on the eve of World War One.

The growing number of Europeans provided further impetus for Western expansion. It was a driving force behind emigration. As in the eighteenth century, the rapid increase in numbers put pressure on the land and led to land hunger and relative overpopulation in area after area. In most countries, migration increased twenty years after a rapid growth in population, as many children of the baby boom grew up, saw little available land and few opportunities, and migrated. This pattern was especially prevalent when rapid population increase predated extensive industrial development, which offered the best long-term hope of creating jobs within the country and reducing poverty. Thus millions of country folk went abroad, as well as to nearby cities, in search of work and economic opportunity. The case of the Irish, who left en masse for Britain during the Industrial Revolution and for the United States after the potato famine, was extreme but not unique.

Before looking at the people who migrated, let us consider three facts. First, the number of men and women who left Europe increased steadily until

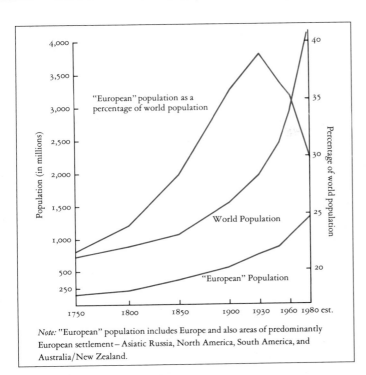

FIGURE 26.2 The Increase of European and World Populations, 1750–1980 *(Sources: W. Woodruff,* Impact of Western Man: A Study of Europe's Role in the World Economy. *St. Martin's Press, New York, 1967, p. 103; United Nations,* Statistical Yearbook, 1982, 1985, pp. 2–3.)

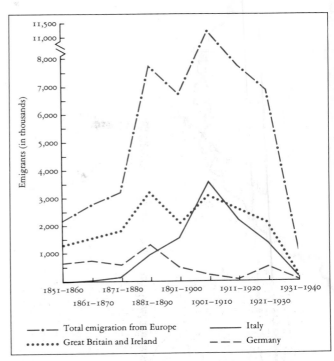

FIGURE 26.3 Emigration from Europe by Decades, 1851–1940 *(Source: W. Woodruff,* Impact of Western Man: A Study of Europe's Role in the World Economy. *St. Martin's Press, New York, 1967, pp. 106–107 and references cited therein.)*

World War One. As Figure 26.3 shows, more than 11 million left in the first decade of the twentieth century, over five times the number departing in the 1850s. The outflow of migrants was clearly an enduring characteristic of European society for the entire period.

Second, different countries had very different patterns of movement. As Figure 26.3 also shows, people left Britain and Ireland (which are not distinguished in the British figures) in large numbers from the 1840s on. This emigration reflected not only rural poverty but also the movement of skilled, industrial technicians and the preferences shown to British migrants in the British Empire. Ultimately, about one-third of all European migrants between 1840 and 1920 came from the British Isles. German migration was quite different. It grew irregularly after about 1830, reaching a first peak in the early 1850s and another in the early 1880s. Thereafter it declined rapidly, for Germany's rapid industrialization was providing adequate jobs at home. This pattern contrasted sharply with that of Italy. More and more Italians left the country right up to 1914, reflecting severe problems in Italian villages and relatively slow

industrial growth. In sum, migration patterns mirrored social and economic conditions in the various European countries and provinces.

Third, although the United States absorbed the largest number of European migrants, only slightly more than half went to the United States. Asiatic Russia, Canada, Argentina, Brazil, and Australia also attracted large numbers, as Figure 26.4 shows. Moreover, migrants accounted for a larger proportion of the total population in Argentina, Brazil, and Canada than in the United States. Between 1900 and 1910, for example, new arrivals represented 3 percent of Argentina's population each year, as opposed to only 1 percent for the United States. The common American assumption that European migration meant migration to the United States is quite inaccurate.

EUROPEAN MIGRANTS

What kind of people left Europe, and what were their reasons for doing so? Most were poor people from rural areas, though seldom from the poorest classes. Indeed, the European migrant was most often a small

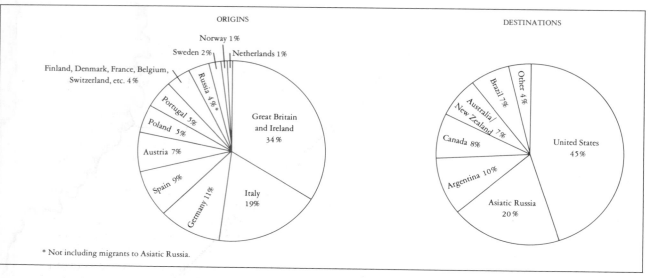

ORIGINS

DESTINATIONS

Norway 1%

Sweden 2% | Netherlands 1%

Finland, Denmark, France, Belgium, Switzerland, etc. 4%

Russia 4%*

Portugal 5%

Poland 5%

Austria 7%

Spain 9%

Germany 11%

Great Britain and Ireland 34%

Italy 19%

Other 4%

Brazil 7%

Australia/ New Zealand 7%

Canada 8%

Argentina 10%

United States 45%

Asiatic Russia 20%

* Not including migrants to Asiatic Russia.

FIGURE 26.4 Origin and Destination of European Emigrants, 1851–1960 *(Source: W. Woodruff,* Impact of Western Man: A Study of Europe's Role in the World Economy. *St. Martin's Press, New York, 1967, pp. 108–109 and references cited therein.)*

peasant landowner or a village craftsman, whose traditional way of life was threatened by too little land, estate agriculture, and cheap, factory-made goods. German peasants who left the Rhineland and southwestern Germany between 1830 and 1854, for example, felt trapped by what Friedrich List called the "dwarf economy," with its tiny landholdings and declining craft industries. Selling out and moving to buy much cheaper land in the American Midwest became a common response. Contrary to what is often said, the European migrant was generally not a desperately impoverished landless peasant or urban proletarian, but an energetic small farmer or skilled artisan trying hard to stay ahead of poverty.

Determined to maintain or improve their status, migrants were a great asset to the countries that received them. This was doubly so because the vast majority were young and very often unmarried. Fully two-thirds of those admitted to the United States were under thirty-one years of age, and 90 percent were under forty. They came in the prime of life and were ready to work hard in the new land, at least for a time.

Many Europeans, especially by the end of the nineteenth century, were truly migrants as opposed to immigrants—that is, they returned home after some time abroad. One in two migrants to Argentina, and

probably one in three to the United States, eventually returned to their native land. The likelihood of repatriation varied greatly by nationality. Seven out of eight people who migrated from the Balkans to the United States in the late nineteenth century returned to their countries. At the other extreme, only one person in ten from Ireland and only one in twenty among eastern European Jews returned to the country of origin.

Once again, the possibility of buying land in the old country was of central importance. Land in Ireland (as well as in England and Scotland) was tightly held by large, often-absentee landowners, and little land was available for purchase. In Russia, Jews were left in relative peace until the assassination of Alexander II by non-Jewish terrorists in 1881 brought a new tsar and an official policy of pogroms and savage discrimination. Russia's 5 million Jews were already confined to the market towns and small cities of the so-called Pale of Settlement, where they worked as artisans and petty traders. Most land was held by non-Jews. When, therefore, Russian Jewish artisans began in the 1880s to escape both factory competition and oppression by migrating—a migration that eventually totaled 2 million people—it was basically a once-and-for-all departure. Non-Jewish migrants from Russia, who constituted a majority of those leaving the tsar's empire after 1905, had access to land and thus returned much more frequently to their peasant villages in central Russia, Poland, and the Ukraine.

The mass movement of Italians illustrates many of the characteristics of European migration. As late as the 1880s, which was for Italians as for Russian Jews the first decade of substantial exodus, three in every four Italians depended on agriculture. With the influx of cheap North American wheat, the long-standing problems of the Italian village became more acute. And since industry was not advancing fast enough to provide jobs for the rapidly growing population, many Italians began to leave their country for economic reasons. Most Italian migrants were not landless laborers from areas dominated by large estates; such people tended to stay in Italy and turned increasingly toward radical politics. Instead, most

were small landowning peasants, whose standard of living was falling because of rural overpopulation and agricultural depression. Migration provided them both an escape valve and a possible source of income to buy more land.

Many Italians went to the United States, but before 1900 more went to Argentina and Brazil. Indeed, two out of three migrants to those two developing countries came from Italy. In Brazil, the large coffee planters, faced with the collapse of black slavery, attracted Italians to their plantations with subsidized travel and promises of relatively high wages.

Many Italians had no intention of settling abroad permanently. Some called themselves "swallows": after harvesting their own wheat and flax in Italy, they "flew" to Argentina to harvest wheat between December and April. Returning to Italy for the spring planting, they repeated the exhausting process.

Cheap Land in distant North America was an irresistible magnet for millions of Europeans. *The Modern Ship of the Plains* by Rufus Zogbaum portrays with sympathy the long journey by rail to the farming frontier in the 1880s. *(Library of Congress)*

This was a very hard life, but a frugal worker could save $250 to $300 in the course of a season. A one-way passage from Latin America to Italy usually cost only $25 to $30, and sometimes as little as $8. Italian migrants also dominated the building trades and the architectural profession in Latin America and succeeded in giving a thoroughly Italian character to many Latin American cities.

Other Italians migrated to other European countries. France was a favorite destination. In 1911 the Italian-born population of France was roughly a third as large as that in the United States.

Ties of family and friendship played a crucial role in the movement of peoples. There are many examples of people from a given province or village settling together in rural enclaves or tight-knit urban neighborhoods thousands of miles away. Very often a strong individual—a businessman, a religious leader—would blaze the way and others would follow.

Many landless young European men and women were spurred to leave by a spirit of revolt and independence. In Sweden and in Norway, in Jewish Russia and in Italy, these young people felt frustrated by the small privileged classes, who often controlled both church and government and resisted demands for change and greater opportunity. Many a young Norwegian seconded the passionate cry of their national poet, Bjørnson: "Forth will I! Forth! I will be crushed and consumed if I stay."[5]

Many young Jews wholeheartedly agreed with a spokesman of Kiev's Jewish community in 1882, who declared, "Our human dignity is being trampled upon, our wives and daughters are being dishonored, we are looted and pillaged: either we get decent human rights or else let us go wherever our eyes may lead us."[6] Thus, for many, migration was a radical way to "get out from under." Migration slowed down when the people won basic political and social reforms, such as the right to vote and social security.

ASIAN MIGRANTS

Not all migration was from Europe. A substantial number of Chinese, Japanese, Indians, and Filipinos —to name only four key groups—responded to rural hardship with temporary or permanent migration. At least 3 million Asians (as opposed to more than 60 million Europeans) moved abroad before 1920. Most went as indentured laborers to work under incredibly difficult conditions on the plantations or in the gold-fields of Latin America, southern Asia, Africa, California, Hawaii, and Australia. White estate owners very often used Asians to replace or supplement blacks after the suppression of the slave trade.

In the 1840s, for example, there was a strong demand for field hands in Cuba, and the Spanish government actively recruited Chinese laborers. They came under eight-year contracts, were paid about twenty-five cents a day, and were fed potatoes and salted beef. Between 1853 and 1873, when such migration was stopped, more than 130,000 Chinese laborers went to Cuba. The majority spent their lives as virtual slaves. The great landlords of Peru also brought in more than 100,000 workers from China in the nineteenth century, and there were similar movements of Asians elsewhere.

Such migration from Asia would undoubtedly have grown to much greater proportions if planters and mine owners in search of cheap labor had had their way. But they did not. Asians fled the plantations and goldfields as soon as possible, seeking greater opportunities in trade and towns. There they came into conflict with other brown-skinned peoples —such as in Malaya and East Africa—and with white settlers in areas of European settlement.

These settlers demanded a halt to Asian migration. One Australian brutally summed up the typical view: "The Chinaman knows nothing about Caucasian civilization. . . . In fact, a Chinaman is a mere dumb animal . . . and could never be anything else. It would be less objectionable to drive a flock of sheep to the poll than to allow Chinamen to vote. The sheep at all events would be harmless."[7] By the 1880s Americans and Australians were building "great white walls"— discriminatory laws designed to keep Asians out. Thus a final, crucial factor in the migrations before 1914 was the general policy of "whites only" in the open lands of possible permanent settlement. Racism meant that Asian migration was always of secondary importance in the world of expanding European society.

WESTERN IMPERIALISM

The expansion of Western society reached its apex between about 1880 and 1914. In those years, the leading European nations not only continued to send massive streams of migrants, money, and manufac-

The Chinese Exclusion Act This vicious cartoon from a San Francisco newspaper celebrates American anti-migration laws. Americans and Europeans generally shared the same attitudes regarding the non-Western world. *(Photo: Caroline Buckler)*

tured goods around the world, but also rushed to create or enlarge vast *political* empires abroad. This political empire building contrasted sharply with the economic penetration of non-Western territories between 1816 and 1880, which had left a China or a Japan "opened" but politically independent. By contrast, the empires of the late nineteenth century recalled the old European colonial empires of the seventeenth and eighteenth centuries and led contemporaries to speak of the new imperialism.

Characterized by a frantic rush to plant the flag over as many people and as much territory as possible, the new imperialism had momentous consequences. It resulted in new tensions among competing European states, and it led to wars and rumors of war with non-European powers. The new imperialism was aimed primarily at Africa and Asia. It put millions of black, brown, and tan peoples directly under the rule of whites. How and why did whites come to rule these peoples?

THE SCRAMBLE FOR AFRICA

The most spectacular manifestation of the new imperialism was the seizure of Africa, which broke sharply with previous patterns and fascinated contemporary Europeans and Americans.

As late as 1880, European nations controlled only 10 percent of the African continent, and their possessions were hardly increasing. The French had begun conquering Algeria in 1830, and within fifty years substantial numbers of French, Italian, and Spanish colonists had settled among the overwhelming Arab majority.

At the other end of the continent, in South Africa, the British had taken possession of the Dutch settlements at Capetown during the wars with Napoleon I. This takeover had led disgruntled Dutch cattlemen and farmers in 1835 to make their so-called Great Trek into the interior, where they fought the Zulu and Kaffir peoples for land. After 1853, while British colonies like Canada and Australia were beginning to evolve toward self-government, the Boers (as the Dutch in South Africa were called) proclaimed their political independence and defended it against British armies. By 1880 Dutch and British settlers, who detested each other, had wrested control of much of South Africa from the Zulus and Kaffirs.

European trading posts and forts dating back to the Age of Discovery and the slave trade dotted the coast of West Africa. The Portuguese proudly but ineffectively held their old possessions in Angola and Mozambique. Elsewhere, over the great mass of the continent, Europeans did not rule.

Between 1880 and 1900, the situation changed drastically. Britain, France, Germany, and Italy scrambled for African possessions as if their lives depended on it. By 1900 nearly the whole continent had been carved up and placed under European rule: only Ethiopia in northeast Africa and Liberia on the west African coast remained independent. Even the Dutch settler republics of southern Africa were conquered by the British in the bloody Boer War (1899–1902). In the years before 1914, the European powers tightened their control and established colonial governments to rule their gigantic empires (see Map 26.2).

In the complexity of the European seizure of Africa, certain events and individuals stand out. Of enormous importance was the British occupation of Egypt, which established the new model of formal political control. There was also the role of Leopold II of Belgium (1865–1909), an energetic, strong-willed monarch with a lust for distant territory. "The sea bathes our coast, the world lies before us," he had exclaimed in 1861. "Steam and electricity have annihilated distance, and all the non-appropriated lands on the surface of the globe can become the field of our operations and of our success."[8] By 1876 Leopold was focusing on central Africa. Subsequently he formed a financial syndicate under his personal control to send H. M. Stanley, a sensation-seeking journalist and part-time explorer, to the Congo basin.

MAP 26.2 **The Partition of Africa** European nations carved up Africa after 1880 and built vast political empires.

Stanley established trading stations, signed "treaties" with African chiefs, and planted Leopold's flag. Leopold's actions alarmed the French, who quickly sent out an expedition under Pierre de Brazza. In 1880 de Brazza signed a treaty of protection with the chief of the large Teke tribe and began to establish a French protectorate on the north bank of the Congo River.

Leopold's buccaneering intrusion into the Congo area raised the question of the political fate of black Africa—Africa south of the Sahara. By the time the British successfully invaded and occupied Egypt, the richest and most developed land in Africa in 1882, Europe had caught "African fever." There was a gold-rush mentality, and the race for territory was on.

To lay down some basic rules for this new and dangerous game of imperialist competition, Jules Ferry of France and Bismarck of Germany arranged an international conference on Africa in Berlin in 1884 and 1885. The conference established the principle that European claims to African territory had to rest on "effective occupation" in order to be recognized by other states. This principle was very important. It meant that Europeans would push relentlessly into interior regions from all sides and that no single European power would be able to claim the entire continent. The conference recognized Leopold's personal rule over a neutral Congo Free State and declared all of the Congo basin a free-trade zone. The conference also agreed to work to stop slavery and the slave trade in Africa.

The Berlin conference coincided with Germany's sudden emergence as an imperial power. Prior to about 1880, Bismarck, like many European leaders at the time, had seen little value in colonies. Colonies reminded him, he said, of a poor but proud nobleman who wore a fur coat when he could not afford a shirt underneath. Then, in 1884 and 1885, as political agitation for expansion increased, Bismarck did an abrupt about-face, and Germany established protectorates over a number of small African kingdoms and tribes in Togo, Cameroon, South West Africa, and later in East Africa.

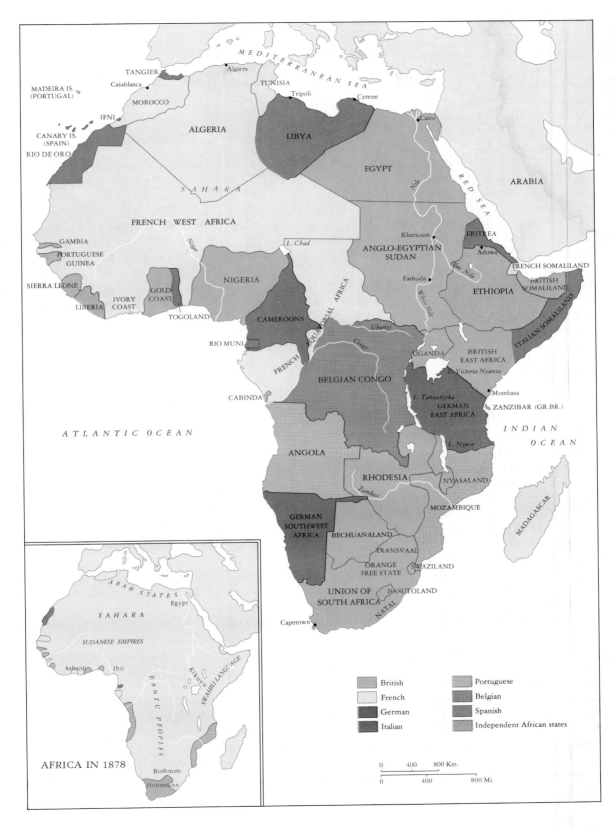

MEDITERRANEAN SEA

TANGIER
MADEIRA IS.
(PORTUGAL)
Casablanca · Algiers
TUNISIA
MOROCCO
Tripoli
Cyrene ·
IFNI
CANARY IS.
(SPAIN)
RIO DE ORO
ALGERIA
LIBYA
EGYPT
Cairo
RED SEA
ARABIA

SAHARA
Nile

FRENCH WEST AFRICA
L. Chad
Khartoum
ERITREA
Adowa
ANGLO-EGYPTIAN
SUDAN
FRENCH SOMALILAND
BRITISH
SOMALILAND
GAMBIA
PORTUGUESE
GUINEA
Niger
SIERRA LEONE
IVORY
COAST
LIBERIA
GOLD
COAST
NIGERIA
Blue Nile
Fashoda ·
White Nile
ETHIOPIA
ITALIAN SOMALILAND

TOGOLAND
CAMEROONS
EQUATORIAL AFRICA
Ubangi
Congo
UGANDA
BRITISH
EAST AFRICA
RIO MUNI
FRENCH
BELGIAN CONGO
L. Victoria Nyanza
CABINDA
L. Tanganyika
GERMAN
EAST AFRICA
Mombasa ·
ZANZIBAR (GR.BR.)

ATLANTIC OCEAN
INDIAN
OCEAN
ANGOLA
L. Nyasa
RHODESIA
NYASALAND
Zambezi
MOZAMBIQUE
MADAGASCAR
GERMAN
SOUTHWEST
AFRICA
BECHUANALAND
TRANSVAAL
ORANGE
FREE STATE
SWAZILAND
UNION OF
SOUTH AFRICA
BASUTOLAND
NATAL
Capetown ·

ARAB STATES
SAHARA
Egypt
SUDANESE EMPIRES
Ashanti
Ibo
KIKUYU
SWAHILI LANGUAGE
BANTU PEOPLES

AFRICA IN 1878
Bushmen
Hottentots

British
French
German
Italian
Portuguese
Belgian
Spanish
Independent African states

0   400   800 Km.
0   400   800 Mi.

843

Omdurman, 1898 The military superiority of the Europeans made it impossible for these brave tribesmen to defend their homeland. Thus the Sudan was conquered and one million square miles were added to the British empire. *(The Mansell Collection)*

In acquiring colonies, Bismarck cooperated against the British with France's Jules Ferry, who was as ardent for empire as he was for education. With Bismarck's tacit approval, the French pressed vigorously southward from Algeria, eastward from their old forts on the Senegal coast, and northward from de Brazza's newly formed protectorate on the Congo River. The object of these three thrusts was Lake Chad, a malaria-infested swamp on the edge of the Sahara Desert.

Meanwhile, the British began enlarging their west African enclaves and impatiently pushing northward from the Cape Colony and westward from Zanzibar. Their thrust southward from Egypt was blocked in the Sudan by fiercely independent Muslims, who massacred a British force at Khartoum in 1885.

A decade later, another British force under General Horatio H. Kitchener moved cautiously and more successfully up the Nile River, building a railroad to supply arms and reinforcements as it

went. Finally, in 1898, these British troops met their foe at Omdurman, where Muslim tribesmen charged time and time again only to be cut down by the recently invented machine gun. For one smug participant, the young British officer Winston Churchill, it was "like a pantomime scene" in a play. "These extraordinary foreign figures . . . march up one by one from the darkness of Barbarism to the footlights of civilization . . . and their conquerors, taking their possessions, forget even their names. Nor will history record such trash." For another more somber English observer, "It was not a battle but an execution. The bodies were not in heaps . . . but they spread evenly over acres and acres."[9] In the end, eleven thousand fanatical Muslim tribesmen lay dead, while only twenty-eight Britons had been killed.

Continuing up the Nile after the battle of Omdurman, Kitchener's armies found that a small French force had already occupied the village Fashoda. Locked in imperial competition ever since Britain had occupied Egypt, France had tried to beat the British to one of Africa's last unclaimed areas—the upper reaches of the Nile. The result was a serious diplomatic crisis, and even the threat of war. Eventually, wracked by the Dreyfus affair (see page 817) and unwilling to fight, France backed down and withdrew its forces.

The reconquest of the Sudan exemplifies the general process of empire building in Africa. The fate of the Muslim force at Omdurman was eventually inflicted on all native peoples who resisted European rule: they were blown away by vastly superior military force. But however much the European powers squabbled for territory and privilege around the world, they always had the sense to stop short of actually fighting each other for it. Imperial ambitions were not worth a great European war.

IMPERIALISM IN ASIA

Although the sudden division of Africa was more spectacular, Europeans also extended their political control in Asia. In 1815 the Dutch ruled little more than the island of Java in the East Indies. Thereafter they gradually brought almost all of the three-thousand-mile archipelago under their political authority, though—in good imperialist fashion—they had to share some of the spoils with Britain and Germany. In the critical decade of the 1880s, the French under the leadership of Jules Ferry took Indochina. India, Japan, and China also experienced a profound imperialist impact (see Map 26.3).

Two other great imperialist powers, Russia and the United States, also acquired rich territories in Asia. Russia, whose history since the later Middle Ages has been marked by almost continuous expansion, moved steadily forward on two fronts throughout the nineteenth century. Russians conquered Muslim areas to the south in the Caucasus and in central Asia and also proceeded to nibble greedily on China's outlying provinces in the Far East, especially in the 1890s.

The United States' great conquest was the Philippines, taken from Spain in 1898 after the Spanish-American War. When it quickly became clear that the United States had no intention of granting independence, Philippine patriots rose in revolt and were suppressed only after long, bitter fighting. (Not until 1933 was a timetable for independence established.)

Some Americans protested the taking of the Philippines, but to no avail. Thus another great Western power joined the imperialist ranks in Asia.

CAUSES OF THE NEW IMPERIALISM

Many factors contributed to the late nineteenth-century rush for territory and empire, which was in turn one aspect of Western society's generalized expansion in the age of industry and nationalism. Little wonder that controversies have raged over interpretation of the new imperialism, especially since authors of every persuasion have often exaggerated particular aspects in an attempt to prove their own theories. Yet despite complexity and controversy, basic causes are clearly identifiable.

Economic motives played an important role in the extension of political empires, especially the British Empire. By the late 1870s, France, Germany, and the United States were industrializing rapidly behind rising tariff barriers. Great Britain was losing its early lead and facing increasingly tough competition in foreign markets. In this new economic situation, Britain came to value old possessions, such as India and Canada, more highly. The days when a leading free-trader like Richard Cobden could denounce the "bloodstained fetish of Empire" and statesman Benjamin Disraeli could call colonies a "millstone round our necks" came to an abrupt end. When continental powers began to grab any and all unclaimed territory in the 1880s, the British followed suit immediately. They feared that France and Germany would seal off their empires with high tariffs and restrictions and that future economic opportunities would be lost forever.

Actually, the overall economic gains of the new imperialism proved quite limited before 1914. The new colonies were simply too poor to buy much, and they offered few immediately profitable investments. Nonetheless, even the poorest, most barren desert was jealously prized, and no territory was ever abandoned. Colonies became important for political and diplomatic reasons. Each leading country saw colonies as crucial to national security, military power, and international prestige. For instance, safeguarding the Suez Canal played a key role in the British occupation of Egypt, and protecting Egypt in turn led to the bloody reconquest of the Sudan. National security was a major factor in the United States' decision

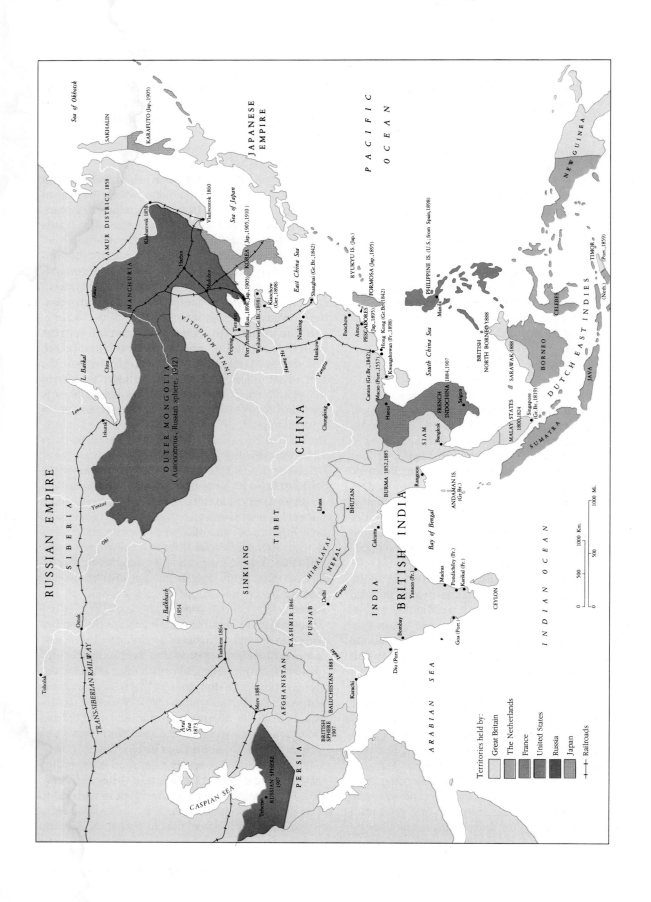

Sea of Okhotsk

SAKHALIN

KARAFUTO (Jap.,1905)

RUSSIAN EMPIRE

SIBERIA

AMUR DISTRICT 1858

Khabarovsk 1858

Amur

MANCHURIA

Harbin

Mukden

Vladivostok 1860

Sea of Japan

KOREA Jap.,1905,1910)

JAPANESE EMPIRE

PACIFIC OCEAN

NEW GUINEA

L. Baikal

Lena

Irkutsk

OUTER MONGOLIA
(Autonomous, Russian sphere, 1912)

INNER MONGOLIA

Chita

Yenisei

Ob

TRANS-SIBERIAN RAILWAY

Tobolsk

Omsk

L. Balkhash
1854

Tashkent 1864

Merv 1884

SINKIANG

TIBET

Lhasa

CHINA

Pepine

Port Arthur Rus.,1898,Jap.,1905)

Tientsin

Weihaiwei (Gr.Br.1898)

Kiaochow (Ger.,1898)

Shanghai (Gr.Br.1842)

Nanking

Huang Ho

Hankow

Yangtze

Foochow

Amoy

Canton (Gr.Br.,1842)

Macao (Port.,1557)

Chungking

East China Sea

RYUKYU IS. (Jap.)

FORMOSA (Jap.,1895)

PESCADORES (Jap.,1895)

Hong Kong (Gr.Br.1842)

Kwangchowan (Fr.,1898)

South China Sea

PHILIPPINE IS. (U.S. from Spain,1898)

Manila

BORNEO

BRITISH NORTH BORNEO 1888

SARAWAK 1888

CELEBES

TIMOR
(Port.,1859)

(Neth.)

DUTCH EAST INDIES

JAVA

SUMATRA

FRENCH INDOCHINA 1884,1907

Hanoi

Saigon

SIAM

Bangkok

MALAY STATES
1800,1824

Singapore (Gr.Br.,1819)

BURMA 1852,1885

Rangoon

HIMALAYAS

NEPAL

BHUTAN

KASHMIR 1846

PUNJAB

Delhi

Ganges

INDIA

BRITISH INDIA

Calcutta

Bay of Bengal

ANDAMAN IS.
(Gr.Br.)

AFGHANISTAN

BALUCHISTAN 1883

BRITISH SPHERE 1907

Indus

Karachi

Bombay

Madras

Yanaon (Fr.)

Pondichéry (Fr.)

Karikal (Fr.)

CEYLON

Goa (Port.)

Diu (Port.)

ARABIAN SEA

INDIAN OCEAN

Aral Sea
1873

CASPIAN SEA

Teheran

PERSIA

RUSSIAN SPHERE 1907

Territories held by:
  Great Britain
  The Netherlands
  France
  United States
  Russia
  Japan
+—+— Railroads

1000 Mi.

1000 Km.

500

500

0

0

MAP 26.3 **Asia in 1914** India remained under British rule while China precariously preserved its political independence.

to establish firm control over the Panama Canal Zone in 1903. Far-flung possessions guaranteed ever-growing navies the safe havens and the dependable coaling stations they needed in time of crisis or war.

Many people were convinced that colonies were essential to great nations. "There has never been a great power without great colonies," wrote one French publicist in 1877. "Every virile people has established colonial power," echoed the famous nationalist historian of Germany, Heinrich von Treitschke. "All great nations in the fullness of their strength have desired to set their mark upon barbarian lands and those who fail to participate in this great rivalry will play a pitiable role in time to come."[10]

Treitschke's harsh statement reflects not only the increasing aggressiveness of European nationalism after Bismarck's wars of German unification but also social Darwinian theories of brutal competition between races. As one prominent English economist argued, the "strongest nation has always been conquering the weaker . . . and the strongest tend to be best." Thus European nations, which were seen as racially distinct parts of the dominant white race, had to seize colonies to show they were strong and virile. Moreover, since racial struggle was nature's inescapable law, the conquest of inferior peoples was just. "The path of progress is strewn with the wreck . . . of inferior races," wrote one professor in 1900. "Yet these dead peoples are, in very truth, the stepping stones on which mankind has risen to the higher intellectual and deeper emotional life of to-day."[11] Social Darwinism and racial doctrines fostered imperial expansion.

Finally, certain special-interest groups in each country were powerful agents of expansion. Shipping companies wanted lucrative subsidies. White settlers on dangerous, turbulent frontiers constantly demanded more land and greater protection. Missionaries and humanitarians wanted to spread religion and stop the slave trade. Explorers and adventurers sought knowledge and excitement. Military men and colonial officials, whose role has often been overlooked by writers on imperialism, foresaw rapid advancement and high-paid positions in growing empires. The actions of such groups and the determined individuals who led them thrust the course of empire forward.

Western society did not rest the case for empire solely on naked conquest and a Darwinian racial struggle, or on power politics and the need for naval bases on every ocean. In order to satisfy their consciences and answer their critics, imperialists developed additional arguments.

A favorite idea was that Europeans could and should "civilize" more primitive nonwhites. According to this view, nonwhites would eventually receive the benefits of modern economies, cities, advanced medicine, and higher standards of living. In time, they might be ready for self-government and Western democracy. Thus the French spoke of their sacred "civilizing mission." Rudyard Kipling (1865–1936), who wrote masterfully of Anglo-Indian life and was perhaps the most influential writer of the 1890s, exhorted Europeans to unselfish service in distant lands:

Take up the White Man's Burden—
  Send forth the best ye breed—
Go bind your sons to exile
  To serve your captives' need,
To wait in heavy harness,
  On fluttered folk and wild—
Your new-caught, sullen peoples
  Half-devil and half-child.[12]

Many Americans accepted the ideology of the white man's burden. It was an important factor in the decision to rule rather than liberate the Philippines after the Spanish-American War. Like their European counterparts, these Americans sincerely believed that their civilization had reached unprecedented height and that they had unique benefits to bestow on all "less-advanced" peoples. Another argument was that imperial government protected natives from tribal warfare as well as cruder forms of exploitation by white settlers and businessmen.

Peace and stability under European control also permitted the spread of Christianity—the "true" religion. In Africa, Catholic and Protestant missionaries competed with Islam south of the Sahara, seeking converts and building schools to spread the Gospel.

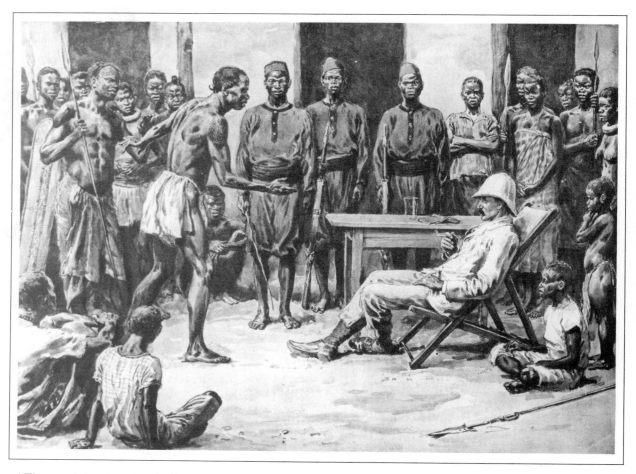

"The Administration of Justice" In this 1895 illustration from a popular magazine, a Belgian official, flanked by native soldiers, settles a tribal dispute in the Congo State. This flattering view of Europe's "civilizing mission" suggests how imperial rule rested on more than just brute force. *(BBC Hulton/The Bettmann Archive)*

Many Africans' first real contact with whites was in mission schools. As late as 1942, for example, 97 percent of Nigeria's student population was in mission schools. Some peoples, like the Ibos in Nigeria, became highly christianized.

Such occasional successes in black Africa contrasted with the general failure of missionary efforts in India, China, and the Islamic world. There, Christians often preached in vain to peoples with ancient, complex religious beliefs. Yet the number of Christian believers around the world did increase substantially in the nineteenth century, and missionary groups kept trying. Unfortunately, "many missionaries had drunk at the well of European racism," and this probably prevented them from doing better.[13]

CRITICS OF IMPERIALISM

The expansion of empire aroused sharp, even bitter, critics. A forceful attack was delivered in 1902, after the unpopular Boer War, by the radical English economist J. A. Hobson (1858–1940) in his *Imperialism,* a work that influenced Lenin and others. Hobson contended that the rush to acquire colonies was due to the economic needs of unregulated capitalism, particularly the need of the rich to find outlets for their surplus capital. Yet, Hobson argued, imperial possessions do not pay off economically for the country as a whole. Only unscrupulous special-interest groups profit from them, at the expense of both the European taxpayer and the natives. Moreover, the quest for empire diverts attention from domestic reform and closing the gap between rich and poor. These and similar arguments were not very persuasive. Most people then (and now) believed that imperialism was economically profitable for the homeland, and a broad and genuine enthusiasm for empire developed among the masses.

Hobson and many other critics struck home, however, with their moral condemnation of whites imperiously ruling nonwhites. They rebelled against crude Social Darwinian thought. "O Evolution, what crimes are committed in thy name!" cried one foe. Another sardonically coined a new beatitude: "Blessed are the strong, for they shall prey on the weak."[14] Kipling and his kind were lampooned as racist bullies, whose rule rested on brutality, racial contempt, and the Maxim machine gun. Henry Labouchère, a member of Parliament and prominent spokesman for this position, mocked Kipling's famous poem:

Pile on the Brown Man's burden!
And if ye rouse his hate,
Meet his old-fashioned reasons
With Maxims up to date,
With shells and Dum-Dum bullets
A hundred times plain
The Brown Man's loss must never
Imply the White Man's gain.[15]

In *Heart of Darkness,* the Polish-born novelist Joseph Conrad (1857–1924) castigated the "pure selfishness" of Europeans in "civilizing" Africa; the main character, once a liberal scholar, turns into a savage brute.

Critics charged Europeans with applying a degrading double standard and failing to live up to their own noble ideals. At home, Europeans had won or were winning representative government, individual liberties, and a certain equality of opportunity. In their empires, Europeans imposed military dictatorships on Africans and Asians, forced them to work involuntarily, almost like slaves, and discriminated against them shamelessly. Only by renouncing imperialism, its critics insisted, and giving captive peoples the freedoms Western society had struggled for since the French Revolution, would Europeans be worthy of their traditions. Europeans who denounced the imperialist tide provided colonial peoples with a Western ideology of liberation.

RESPONSES TO WESTERN IMPERIALISM

To consider the great surge of European expansion from the Western point of view is to see only half the story. It is time to try to examine what foreign domination and imperialism meant to those who were ruled.

To peoples in Africa and Asia, Western expansion represented a profoundly disruptive assault. Everywhere it threatened traditional ruling classes, traditional economies, and traditional ways of life. Christian missionaries and European secular ideologies challenged established beliefs and values. Non-Western peoples experienced a crisis of identity, a crisis made all the more painful by the power and arrogance of the white intruders.

The initial response of African and Asian rulers was to try to drive the unwelcome foreigners away. This was the case in China, Japan, and the upper Sudan, as we have seen. Violent antiforeign reactions exploded elsewhere again and again, but the superior military technology of the industrialized West almost invariably prevailed. Beaten in battle, many Africans and Asians concentrated on preserving their cultural traditions at all costs. Others found themselves forced to reconsider their initial hostility. Some (like Ismail of Egypt) concluded that the West was indeed superior in some ways and that it was therefore necessary to reform their societies and copy European achievements. Thus it is possible to think of responses to the Western impact as a spectrum, with "traditionalists" at one end, "westernizers" or "modernizers" at the other, and many shades of opinion in between. Both before and after European domination, the struggle among these groups was often intense. With time, however, the modernizers tended to gain the upper hand.

When the power of both the traditionalists and the modernizers was thoroughly shattered by superior force, the great majority of Asians and Africans accepted imperial rule. Political participation in non-Western lands was historically limited to small elites, and the masses were used to doing what their rulers told them. In these circumstances Europeans, clothed in power and convinced of their righteousness, governed smoothly and effectively. They received considerable support from both traditionalists —local chiefs, landowners, religious leaders—and

THE SPREAD OF WESTERN IMPERIALISM

1800–1913	World trade increases 25-fold
1816–1880	European economic penetration of non-Western countries
1835	Great Trek: Boers proclaim independence from Great Britain in the South African hinterland
1840s	European capitalists begin large-scale foreign investment
1842	Treaty of Nanking: Manchu government of China cedes Hong Kong to Great Britain
1846	Repeal of Corn Laws: Great Britain declares its strong support of free trade
1848	British defeat of last independent native state in India
1853	Perry's arrival in Tokyo: Japan opened to European influence
1857–1858	Great Rebellion in India
1858–1863	Anti-foreign reaction in Japan
1867	Meiji Restoration in Japan: adoption of Western reforms
1869	Completion of Suez Canal
1871	Abolition of feudal domains in Japan
1876	Ismail, khedive of Egypt, appoints British and French commissioners to oversee government finances
1880	Establishment of French protectorate on the northern bank of the Congo
1880–1900	European powers intensify their "scramble for Africa"
1882	British occupation of Egypt
1883	Formation of the Indian National Congress
1884–1885	International conference on Africa in Berlin: European powers require "effective occupation"; Germany acquires protectorates in Togo, Cameroon, South West Africa, and East Africa; Belgium acquires the Congo Free State
1890	Establishment of an authoritarian constitution in Japan
1893	France completes its acquisition of Indochina
1894	Sino-Japanese War: Japan acquires Formosa
1898	Battle of Omdurman: under Kitchener, British forces reconquer the Sudan Spanish-American War: United States acquires the Philippines "Hundred Days of Reform" in China
1899–1902	Boer War: British defeat Dutch settlers in South Africa
1900–1903	The Boxer Rebellion in China
1903	American occupation of the Panama Canal zone
1904–1905	Russo-Japanese War: Japan wins protectorate over Port Arthur in China
1910	Japanese annexation of Korea
1912	Fall of Manchu dynasty in China

Senegalese Scouts, 1913 Europeans recruited large numbers of native soldiers to expand and enforce their rule in Africa and Asia. Senegalese scouts were the pride of the French army in black Africa. *(Roger-Viollet)*

modernizers—the Western-educated professional classes and civil servants.

Nevertheless, imperial rule was in many ways a hollow shell built on sand. Support for European rule among the conforming and accepting millions was shallow and weak. Thus the conforming masses followed with greater or lesser enthusiasm a few determined personalities who came to oppose the Europeans. Such leaders always arose, both when Europeans ruled directly and when they manipulated native governments, for at least two basic reasons.

First, the nonconformists—the eventual anti-imperialist leaders—developed a burning desire for human dignity. They came to feel that such dignity was incompatible with foreign rule with its smirks and smiles, its paternalism and condescension. Second, potential leaders found in the Western world the ideologies and justification for their protest. They discovered liberalism with its credo of civil liberty and political self-determination. They echoed the demands of anti-imperialists in Europe and America that the West live up to its own ideals.

More important, they found themselves attracted to modern nationalism, which asserted that every people had the right to control its own destiny. After 1917 anti-imperialist revolt would find another weapon in Lenin's version of Marxian socialism. Thus the anti-imperialist search for dignity drew strength from Western culture, as is apparent in the development of three major Asian countries—India, Japan, and China.

EMPIRE IN INDIA

India was the jewel of the British Empire, and no colonial area experienced a more profound British impact. Unlike Japan and China, which maintained a real or precarious independence, and unlike African territories, which were annexed by Europeans only at the end of the nineteenth century, India was ruled more or less absolutely by Britain for a very long time.

The British in India This photo suggests not only the incredible power and luxury of the British ruling class in India but its confidence and self-satisfaction as well. As one British viceroy said: "We are all British gentlemen engaged in the magnificent work of governing an inferior race." *(BBC Hulton/The Bettmann Archive)*

Arriving in India on the heels of the Portuguese in the seventeenth century, the British East India Company had conquered the last independent native state by 1848. The last "traditional" response to European rule—the attempt by the established ruling classes to drive the white man out by military force—was broken in India in 1857 and 1858. Those were the years of the Great Rebellion (which the British called a "mutiny"), when an insurrection by Muslim and Hindu mercenaries in the British army spread throughout northern and central India before it was finally crushed, primarily by loyal native troops from southern India. Thereafter Britain ruled India directly. India illustrates, therefore, for better and for worse, what generations of European domination might produce.

After 1858 India was ruled by the British Parliament in London and administered by a tiny, all-white civil service in India. In 1900 this elite consisted of fewer than 3,500 top officials, for a population of 300 million. The white elite, backed by white officers and native troops, was competent and generally well disposed toward the welfare of the Indian peasant masses. Yet it practiced strict job discrimination and social segregation, and most of its members quite frankly considered the jumble of Indian peoples and castes to be racially inferior. As Lord Kitchener, one of the most distinguished top military commanders of India, stated:

It is this consciousness of the inherent superiority of the European which has won for us India. However well educated and clever a native may be, and however brave he may prove himself, I believe that no rank we can bestow on him would cause him to be considered an equal of the British officer.[16]

When, for example, the British Parliament in 1883 was considering a major bill to allow Indian judges to try white Europeans in India, the British community rose in protest and defeated the measure. The idea that they might be judged by Indians was inconceivable to Europeans, for it was clear to the Europeans that the empire in India rested squarely on racial inequality.

In spite of (perhaps even because of) their strong feelings of racial and cultural superiority, the British acted energetically and introduced many desirable changes to India. Realizing that they needed well-educated Indians to serve as skilled subordinates in the government and army, the British established a modern system of progressive secondary education, in which all instruction was in English. Thus, through education and government service the British offered some Indians excellent opportunities for both economic and social advancement. High-caste Hindus were particularly quick to respond and emerged as skillful intermediaries between the British rulers and the Indian people—a new elite profoundly influenced by Western thought and culture.

This new bureaucratic elite played a crucial role in modern economic development, which was a second result of British rule. Irrigation projects for agriculture, the world's third largest railroad network for good communications, and large tea and jute plantations geared to the world economy were all developed. Unfortunately, the lot of the Indian masses improved little, for the increase in production was quite literally eaten up by population increase.

Finally, with a well-educated, English-speaking Indian bureaucracy and modern communications, the British created a unified, powerful state. They placed under the same general system of law and administration the different Hindu and Muslim peoples and the vanquished kingdoms of the entire subcontinent —groups that had fought each other for centuries during the Middle Ages and had been repeatedly conquered by Muslim and Mongol invaders. It was as if Europe, with its many states and varieties of Christianity, had been conquered and united in a single great empire.

In spite of these achievements, the decisive reaction to European rule was the rise of nationalism among the Indian elite. No matter how anglicized and necessary a member of the educated classes became, he or she could never become the white ruler's equal. The top jobs, the best clubs, the modern hotels, and even certain railroad compartments were sealed off to brown-skinned men and women. The peasant masses might accept such inequality as the latest version of age-old oppression, but the well-educated, English-speaking elite eventually could not. For the elite, racial discrimination meant not only injured pride but bitter injustice. It flagrantly contradicted those cherished Western concepts of human rights and equality. Moreover, it was based on dictatorship, no matter how benign.

By 1883, when educated Indians came together to found the predominantly Hindu Indian National Congress, demands were increasing for the equality and self-government Britain enjoyed and had already granted white-settler colonies, such as Canada and Australia. By 1907, emboldened in part by Japan's success (see the next section), the radicals in the Indian National Congress were calling for complete independence. Even the moderates were demanding home rule for India through an elected parliament. Although there were sharp divisions between Hindus and Muslims, Indians were finding an answer to the foreign challenge. The common heritage of British rule and Western ideals, along with the reform and revitalization of the Hindu religion, had created a genuine movement for national independence.

THE EXAMPLES OF JAPAN

When Commodore Perry arrived in Japan in 1853 with his crude but effective gunboat diplomacy, Japan was a complex feudal society. At the top stood a figurehead emperor, but for more than two hundred years, real power had been in the hands of a hereditary military governor, the *shogun*. With the help of a warrior nobility known as *samurai*, the sho-

gun governed a country of hardworking, productive peasants and city dwellers. Often poor and restless, the intensely proud samurai were deeply humiliated by the sudden American intrusion and the unequal treaties with Western countries. When foreign diplomats and merchants began to settle in Yokohama, radical samurai reacted with a wave of antiforeign terrorism and antigovernment assassinations between 1858 and 1863. The imperialist response was swift and unambiguous. An allied fleet of American, British, Dutch, and French warships demolished key forts, which further weakened the power and prestige of the shogun's government. Then, in 1867, a coalition led by patriotic samurai seized control of the government with hardly any bloodshed and restored the political power of the emperor. This was the Meiji Restoration, a great turning point in Japanese development.

The immediate, all-important goal of the new government was to meet the foreign threat. The battle cry of the Meiji reformers was "enrich the state and strengthen the armed forces." Yet how was this to be done? In an about-face that was one of history's most remarkable chapters, the young but well-trained, idealistic but flexible, leaders of Meiji Japan dropped their antiforeign attacks. Convinced that Western civilization was indeed superior in its military and industrial aspects, they initiated from above a series of measures to reform Japan along modern lines. They were convinced that "Japan must be reborn with America its mother and France its father."[17] In the broadest sense, the Meiji leaders tried to harness the power inherent in Europe's dual revolution, in order to protect their country and catch up with the West.

In 1871 the new leaders abolished the old feudal structure of aristocratic, decentralized government and formed a strong unified state. Following the example of the French Revolution, they dismantled the four-class legal system and declared social equality. They decreed freedom of movement in a country where traveling abroad had been a most serious crime. They created a free, competitive, government-stimulated economy. Japan began to build railroads and modern factories. Thus the new generation adopted many principles of a free, liberal society; and, as in Europe, such freedom resulted in a tremendously creative release of human energy.

Yet the overriding concern of Japan's political leadership was always a powerful state, and to achieve this, more than liberalism was borrowed

横濱名所之内
野毛の眺望

永林筆

The Modernization of Japan Soon after it reluctantly opened its doors to foreigners, Japan built its first railroad, sketched here by a native artist. *(Historical Pictures Service, Chicago)*

from the West. A powerful modern navy was created, and the army was completely reorganized along French and German lines, with three-year military service for all males and a professional officer corps. This army of draftees effectively put down disturbances in the countryside, and in 1877 it was used to crush a major rebellion by feudal elements protesting the loss of their privileges. Japan also borrowed rapidly and adopted skillfully the West's science and modern technology, particularly in industry, medicine, and education. Many Japanese were encouraged to study abroad, and the government paid large salaries to attract foreign experts. These experts were

always carefully controlled, though, and replaced by trained Japanese as soon as possible.

By 1890, when the new state was firmly established, the wholesale borrowing of the early restoration had given way to more selective emphasis on those things foreign that were in keeping with Japanese tradition. Following the model of the German Empire, Japan established an authoritarian constitution and rejected democracy. The power of the emperor and his ministers was vast, that of the legislature limited.

Japan successfully copied the imperialism of Western society. Expansion not only proved that Japan was strong; it also cemented the nation together in a great mission. Having "opened" Korea with the gunboat diplomacy of imperialism in 1876, Japan decisively defeated China in a war over Korea in 1894 and took Formosa. In the next years, Japan competed aggressively with the leading European powers for influence and territory in China, particularly Manchuria. There Japanese and Russian imperialism met and collided. In 1904 Japan attacked Russia without warning, and after a bloody war, Japan emerged with a valuable foothold in China, Russia's former protectorate over Port Arthur (see Map 26.3). By 1910, when it annexed Korea, Japan was a major imperial power, continuously expanding its influence in China in spite of sharp protests from its distant Pacific neighbor, the United States.

Japan became the first non-Western country to use an ancient love of country to transform itself and thereby meet the many-sided challenge of Western expansion. Moreover, Japan demonstrated convincingly that a modern Asian nation could defeat and humble a great Western power. Many Chinese nationalists were fascinated by Japan's achievement. A group of patriots in French-ruled southern Vietnam sent Vietnamese students to Japan to learn the island empire's secret of success. Japan provided patriots in Asia and Africa with an inspiring example of national recovery and liberation.

TOWARD REVOLUTION IN CHINA

In 1860 the two-hundred-year-old Manchu dynasty in China appeared on the verge of collapse. Efforts to repel the foreigner had failed, and rebellion and chaos wracked the country. Yet the government drew on its traditional strengths and made a surprising comeback that lasted more than thirty years.

The Hatred of Foreigners burns in the eyes of this Chinese prisoner condemned to death for murdering foreign missionaries in the aftermath of the Sino-Japanese war. Both his face and crime foretell the fury of the Boxer Rebellion. *(BBC Hulton/The Bettmann Archive)*

Two factors were crucial in this reversal. First, the traditional ruling groups temporarily produced new and effective leadership. Loyal scholar-statesmen and generals quelled disturbances like the great Tai Ping rebellion. A truly remarkable woman, the empress dowager Tzu Hsi, governed in the name of her young son and combined shrewd insight with vigorous action to revitalize the bureaucracy.

Second, destructive foreign aggression lessened, for the Europeans had obtained their primary goal of commercial and diplomatic relations. Indeed, some Europeans contributed to the dynasty's recovery. A talented Irishman effectively reorganized China's customs office and increased the government tax receipts, while a sympathetic American diplomat represented China in foreign lands and helped strengthen the central government. Such efforts dovetailed with the dynasty's efforts to adopt some

aspects of Western government and technology while maintaining traditional Chinese values and beliefs.

The parallel movement toward domestic reform and limited cooperation with the West collapsed under the blows of Japanese imperialism. The Sino-Japanese war of 1894–1895 and the subsequent harsh peace treaty revealed China's helplessness in the face of aggression, triggering a rush for foreign concessions and protectorates in China. At its high point in 1898, it appeared that the European powers might actually divide China among themselves, as they had recently divided Africa. Probably only the jealousy each nation felt toward its imperial competitors saved China from partition, although the United States' Open Door policy, which opposed formal annexation of Chinese territory, may have helped tip the balance. In any event, the tempo and impact of foreign penetration greatly accelerated after 1894.

So, too, did the intensity and radicalism of the Chinese reaction. Like the men of the Meiji Restoration, some modernizers saw salvation in Western institutions. In 1898 the government launched a desperate "hundred days of reform" in an attempt to meet the foreign challenge. More radical reformers like the revolutionary Sun Yat-sen (1866–1925), who came from the peasantry and was educated in Hawaii by Christian missionaries, sought to overthrow the dynasty altogether, and establish a republic.

On the other side, some traditionalists turned back toward ancient practices, political conservatism, and fanatical hatred of the "foreign devils." "Protect the country, destroy the foreigner" was their simple motto. Such conservative, antiforeign patriots had often clashed with foreign missionaries, whom they charged with undermining reverence for ancestors and thereby threatening the Chinese family and the entire society. In the agony of defeat and unwanted reforms, secret societies like the Boxers rebelled. In northeastern China, more than two hundred foreign missionaries and several thousand Chinese Christians were killed. Once again, the imperialist response was swift and harsh. Peking was occupied and plundered by foreign armies. A heavy indemnity was imposed.

The years after the Boxer Rebellion (1900–1903) were ever more troubled. Anarchy and foreign influence spread, as the power and prestige of the Manchu dynasty declined still further. Antiforeign, antigovernment revolutionary groups agitated and plotted. Finally, in 1912, a spontaneous uprising topped the Manchu dynasty. After thousands of years of emperors and empires, a loose coalition of revolutionaries proclaimed a Western-style republic and called for an elected parliament. The transformation of China under the impact of expanding Western society entered a new phase, and the end was not in sight.

In the nineteenth century the West entered the third and most dynamic phase of is centuries-old expansion into non-Western lands. In so doing, Western nations forged an integrated world economy, sent forth millions of emigrants, and established political influence in Asia and vast political empires in Africa. The reasons for this culminating surge were many, but the economic thrust of robust industrial capitalism, an ever-growing lead in technology, and the competitive pressures of European nationalism were particularly important.

Western expansion had far-reaching consequences. For the first time in human history, the world became in many ways a single unit. Moreover, European expansion diffused the ideas and techniques of a highly developed civilization. Yet the West relied on force to conquer and rule, and it treated non-Western peoples as racial inferiors. Thus non-Western elites, often armed with Western doctrines, gradually responded to the Western challenge. They launched a national, anti-imperialist struggle for dignity, genuine independence, and modernization. This struggle would emerge as a central drama of world history after the great European civil war of 1914 to 1918, which reduced the West's technological advantage and shattered its self-confidence and complacent moral superiority.

NOTES

1. Quoted by A. Waley, *The Opium War Through Chinese Eyes,* Macmillan, New York, 1958, p. 29.
2. Quoted by J. W. Hall, *Japan, from Prehistory to Modern Times,* Delacorte Press, New York, 1970, p. 250.
3. Quoted by R. Hallett, *Africa to 1875,* University of Michigan Press, Ann Arbor, 1970, p. 109.
4. Quoted by Earl of Cromer, *Modern Egypt,* London, 1911, p. 48.
5. Quoted by T. Blegen, *Norwegian Migration to America,* Norwegian-American Historical Association, Northfield, Minn., 1940, 2.468.
6. Quoted by I. Howe, *World of Our Fathers,* Harcourt Brace Jovanovich, New York, 1976, p. 25.
7. Quoted by C. A. Price, *The Great White Walls Are Built: Restrictive Immigration to North America and Australia, 1836–1888,* Australian National University Press, Canberra, 1974, p. 175.
8. Quoted by W. L. Langer, *European Alliances and Alignments, 1871–1890,* Vintage Books, New York, 1931, p. 290.
9. Quoted by J. Ellis, *The Social History of the Machine Gun,* Pantheon Books, New York, 1975, pp. 86, 101.
10. Quoted by G. H. Nadel and P. Curtis, eds., *Imperialism and Colonialism,* Macmillan, New York, 1964, p. 94.

11. Quoted by W. L. Langer, *The Diplomacy of Imperialism,* 2nd ed., Knopf, New York, 1951, pp. 86, 88.
12. Rudyard Kipling, *The Five Nations,* London, 1903, quoted by the permission of Mrs. George Bambridge, Methuen & Company, and Doubleday & Company, Inc.
13. E. H. Berman, "African Responses to Christian Mission Education," *African Studies Review* 17:3 (1974):530.
14. Quoted in Langer, *Diplomacy of Imperialism,* p. 88.
15. Quoted by Ellis, pp. 99–100.
16. Quoted by K. M. Panikkar, *Asia and Western Dominance,* George Allen & Unwin, London, 1959, p. 116.
17. Quoted by Hall, p. 289.

SUGGESTED READING

Hall and Hallett, cited in the Notes, are excellent introductions to the histories of Japan and Africa. A. Waley, also cited in the Notes, has written extensively and well on China. K. Latourette, *The Chinese: Their History and Culture,* rev. ed. (1964), is a fine survey with many suggestions for further reading. Howe and Blegen, cited in the Notes, provide dramatic accounts of Jewish and Norwegian migration to the United States. Most other migrant groups have also found their historians: M. Walker, *Germany and the Emigration, 1816–1885* (1964), and W. Adams, *Ireland and Irish Emigration to the New World* (reissued 1967), are outstanding. Langer's volumes consider the diplomatic aspects of imperialism in exhaustive detail. Ellis's well-illustrated study of the machine gun is fascinating, as is Price on the restriction of Asian migration to Australia. All these works are cited in the Notes.

General surveys of European expansion in a broad perspective include R. Betts, *Europe Overseas* (1968); A. Thornton, *Imperialism in the 20th Century* (1977); T. Smith, *The Patterns of Imperialism* (1981); and W. Woodruff, *Impact of Western Man* (1967), which has an extensive bibliography. D. K. Fieldhouse has also written two fine surveys, *Economics and Empire, 1830–1914* (1970) and *Colonialism, 1870–1945* (1981). G. Barraclough, *An Introduction to Contemporary History* (1964), argues powerfully that Western imperialism and the non-Western reaction to it have been crucial in world history since about 1890. J. A. Hobson's classic *Imperialism* (1902) is readily available, and the Marxist-Leninist case is effectively presented in V. G. Kieran, *Marxism and Imperialism* (1975). Two excellent anthologies on the problem of European expansion are G. Nadel and P. Curtis, eds., *Imperialism and Colonialism* (1964), and H. Wright, ed., *The "New Imperialism,"* rev. ed. (1975).

Britain's leading position in European imperialism is examined in a lively way by B. Porter, *The Lion's Share* (1976); J. Morris, *Pax Britannica* (1968); and D. Judd, *The Victorian Empire* (1970), a stunning pictorial history. B. Semmel has written widely on the intellectual foundations of English expansion, as in *The Rise of Free Trade Imperialism* (1970). J. Gallegher and R. Robinson, *Africa and the Victorians: The Climax of Imperialism* (1961), is an influential reassessment. H. Brunschwig, *French Colonialism, 1871–1914* (1966), and W. Baumgart, *Imperialism: The Idea and Reality of British and French Colonial Expansion* (1982), are well-balanced studies. A. Moorehead, *The White Nile* (1971), tells the fascinating story of the European exploration of the mysterious upper Nile. Volumes 5 and 6 of K. Latourette, *History of the Expansion of Christianity,* 7 vols. (1937–1945), examines the powerful impulse for missionary work in non-European areas. D. Headrick stresses Western technological superiority in *Tools of Empire* (1981).

Two unusual and provocative studies on personal relations between European rulers and non-European subjects are D. Mannoni, *Prospero and Caliban: The Psychology of Colonialization* (1964), and F. Fanon, *Wretched of the Earth* (1965), a bitter attack on white racism by a black psychologist active in the Algerian revolution. Novels also bring the psychological and human dimensions of imperialism alive. H. Rider Haggard, *King Solomon's Mines,* portrays the powerful appeal of adventure in exotic lands, while Rudyard Kipling, the greatest writer of European expansion, is at his stirring best in *Kim* and *Soldiers Three.* Joseph Conrad unforgettably probes European motives in *Heart of Darkness,* while André Gide, *The Immoralist,* closely examines European moral corruption in North Africa.

27

THE GREAT BREAK:
WAR AND REVOLUTION

*I*N THE SUMMER OF 1914 the nations of Europe went willingly to war. They believed they had no other choice. Moreover, both peoples and governments confidently expected a short war leading to a decisive victory. Such a war, they believed, would "clear the air," and European society would go on as before.

These expectations were almost totally mistaken. The First World War was long, indecisive, and tremendously destructive. To the shell-shocked generation of survivors, it was known simply as the Great War: the war of unprecedented scope and intensity. From today's perspective it is clear that the First World War marked a great break in the course of Western historical development since the French and Industrial Revolutions. A noted British political scientist has gone so far as to say that even in victorious and relatively fortunate Great Britain, the First World War was *the* great turning point in government and society, "as in everything else in modern British history. . . . There's a much greater difference between the Britain of 1914 and, say, 1920, than between the Britain of 1920 and today."[1]

This is a strong statement, but it contains much truth, for all of Europe as well as for Britain. It suggests three questions this chapter will try to answer. What caused the Great War? How and why did war and revolution have such enormous and destructive consequences? And where in the trauma and bloodshed were formed elements of today's world, many of which people now accept and even cherish?

THE FIRST WORLD WAR

The First World War was so long and destructive because it involved all the Great Powers and because it quickly degenerated into a senseless military stalemate. Like two evenly matched boxers in a championship bout, each side tried to wear down its opponent. There was no referee to call a draw, only the blind hammering of a life-or-death struggle.

THE BISMARCKIAN SYSTEM OF ALLIANCES

The Franco-Prussian War and the foundation of the German Empire opened a new era in international relations. France was decisively defeated in 1871 and forced to pay a large war indemnity and give up Alsace-Lorraine. In ten short years, from 1862 to 1871, Bismarck had made Prussia-Germany—traditionally the weakest of the Great Powers—the most powerful nation in Europe (pages 804–808). Had Bismarck been a Napoleon I or a Hitler, for whom no gain was ever sufficient, continued expansion would no doubt sooner or later have raised a powerful coalition against the new German Empire. Yet he was not. As Bismarck never tired of repeating after 1871, Germany was a "satisfied" power. Germany had no territorial ambitions and only wanted peace in Europe.

But how was peace to be preserved? The most serious threat to peace came from the east, from Austria-Hungary and from Russia. Those two enormous multinational empires had many conflicting interests, particularly in the Balkans, where the Ottoman Empire—the "sick man of Europe"—was ebbing fast. There was a real threat that Germany might be dragged into a great war between the two rival empires. Bismarck's solution was a system of alliances (Figure 27.1) to restrain both Russia and Austria-Hungary, to prevent conflict between them, and to isolate a hostile France.

A first step was the creation in 1873 of the conservative Three Emperors' League, which linked the monarchs of Austria-Hungary, Germany, and Russia in an alliance against radical movements. In 1877 and 1878, when Russia's victories over the Ottoman Empire threatened the balance of Austrian and Russian interests in the Balkans and the balance of British and Russian interests in the Middle East, Bismarck played the role of sincere peacemaker. At the Congress of Berlin in 1878, he saw that Austria obtained the right to "occupy and administer" the Ottoman provinces of Bosnia and Herzegovnia to counterbalance Russian gains, while independent Balkan states were also carved from the disintegrating Ottoman Empire.

Bismarck's balancing efforts at the Congress of Berlin infuriated Russian nationalists, which led Bismarck to conclude a defensive military alliance with Austria against Russia in 1879. Motivated by tensions with France, Italy joined Germany and Austria in 1882, thereby forming the Triple Alliance.

Bismarck continued to work for peace in eastern Europe, seeking to neutralize tensions between Austria-Hungary and Russia. In 1881 he capitalized on their mutual fears and cajoled them both into a secret

The Congress of Berlin, 1878 With the Austrian representative on his right and with other participants looking on, Bismarck the mediator symbolically seals the hard-won agreement by shaking hands with the chief Russian negotiator. The Great Powers often relied on such special conferences to settle their international disputes. *(The Bettmann Archive)*

alliance with Germany. This Alliance of the Three Emperors lasted until 1887. It established the principle of cooperation among all three powers in any further division of the Ottoman Empire, while each state pledged friendly neutrality in case one of the three found itself at war with a fourth power (except the Ottoman Empire).

Bismarck also maintained good relations with Britain and Italy, while cooperating with France in Africa but keeping France isolated in Europe. In 1887 Russia declined to renew the Alliance of the Three Emperors because of new tensions in the Balkans. Bismarck craftily substituted a Russian-German Reinsurance Treaty, by which both states promised neutrality if the other were attacked.

Bismarck's accomplishments in foreign policy after 1871 were great. For almost a generation, he maintained German leadership in international affairs, and he worked successfully for peace by managing conflicts and by restraining Austria-Hungary and Russia with defensive alliances.

THE RIVAL BLOCS

In 1890 the young, impetuous emperor William II dismissed Bismarck, in part because of the chancellor's friendly policy toward Russia since the 1870s. William then adamantly refused to renew the Russian-German Reinsurance Treaty, in spite of Russian willingness to do so. This fateful departure in foreign affairs prompted long-isolated republican France to court absolutist Russia, offering loans, arms, and friendship. In both countries there were enthusiastic public demonstrations, and in St. Petersburg the autocratic Alexander III stood bareheaded on a French battleship while a band played the "Marseillaise," the hymn of the Revolution. A preliminary agreement between the two countries was reached in 1891, and in early 1894 France and Russia became military allies. This alliance (Figure 27.1) was to remain in effect as long as the Triple Alliance of Austria, Germany, and Italy: continental Europe was dangerously divided into two rival blocs.

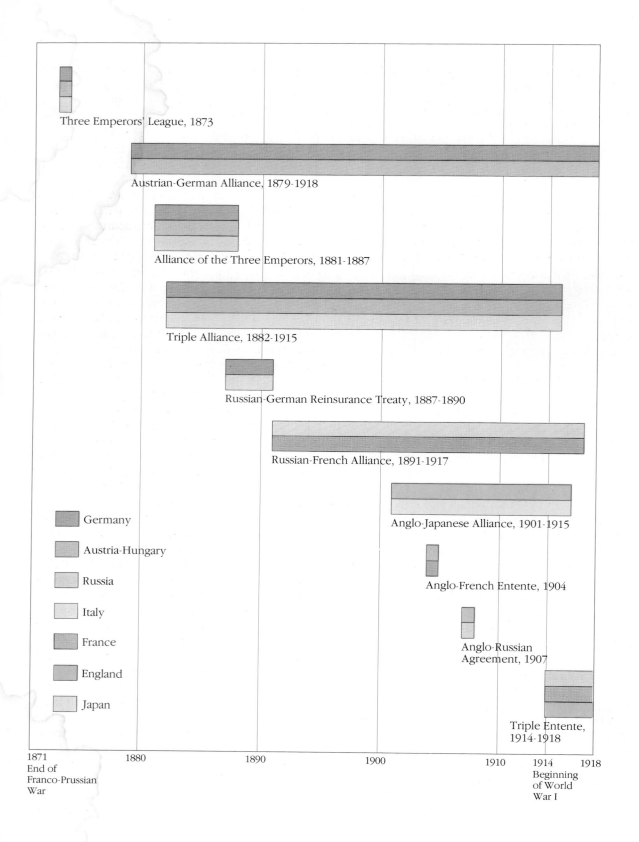

Three Emperors' League, 1873

Austrian-German Alliance, 1879-1918

Alliance of the Three Emperors, 1881-1887

Triple Alliance, 1882-1915

Russian-German Reinsurance Treaty, 1887-1890

Russian-French Alliance, 1891-1917

Anglo-Japanese Alliance, 1901-1915

Anglo-French Entente, 1904

Anglo-Russian Agreement, 1907

Triple Entente, 1914-1918

Germany
Austria-Hungary
Russia
Italy
France
England
Japan

1871
End of
Franco-Prussian
War

1880

1890

1900

1910

1914
Beginning
of World
War I

1918

FIGURE 27.1 The Alliance System After 1871 Bismarck's subtle diplomacy maintained reasonably good relations among the eastern monarchies—Germany, Russia, and Austria-Hungary—and kept France isolated. The situation changed dramatically in 1891, when the Russian-French Alliance divided the Great Powers into two fairly equal military blocs.

The policy of Great Britain became increasingly crucial. Long content with "splendid isolation" and no permanent alliances, Britain after 1891 was the only uncommitted Great Power. Could Britain afford to remain isolated, or would it feel compelled to take sides? Alliance with France or Russia certainly seemed highly unlikely. With its vast and rapidly expanding empire, Britain was often in serious conflict with these countries around the world in the heyday of imperialism.

Britain also squabbled with Germany, for Emperor William II was a master of tactless public statements, and Britain found Germany's pursuit of greater world power after about 1897 vaguely disquieting. Nevertheless, many Germans and some Britons believed that their statesmen would eventually formalize the "natural alliance" they felt already united the advanced, racially related Germanic and Anglo-Saxon peoples. Alas, such an understanding never materialized. Instead, the generally good relations that has prevailed between Prussia and Great Britain ever since the mid-eighteenth century, and certainly under Bismarck, gave way to a bitter Anglo-German rivalry.

There were several reasons for this tragic development. The hard-fought Boer War (1899–1902) between the British and the tiny Dutch republics of South Africa had a major impact on British policy. British statesmen saw that Britain was overextended around the world. The Boer War also brought into the open widespread anti-British feeling, as editorial writers in many nations denounced the latest manifestation of British imperialism. There was even talk of Germany, Austria, France, and Russia forming a grand alliance against the bloated but insatiable British Empire. Therefore British statesmen prudently set about shoring up their exposed position with alliance and agreements.

Britain improved its often-strained relations with the United States and in 1902 concluded a formal alliance with Japan (Figure 27.1). Britain then responded favorably to the advances of France's skillful foreign minister, Théophile Delcassé, who wanted better relations with Britain and was willing to accept British rule in Egypt in return for British support of French plans to dominate Morocco. The resulting Anglo-French Entente of 1904 (Figure 27.1) settled all outstanding colonial disputes between Britain and France.

Frustrated by Britain's turn toward France in 1904, Germany decided to test the strength of the entente and drive Britain and France apart. First Germany threatened and bullied France into dismissing Delcassé. However, rather than accept the typical territorial payoff of imperial competition—a slice of French jungle in Africa or a port in Morocco—in return for French primacy in Morocco, the Germans foolishly rattled their swords in 1905. They insisted on an international conference on the whole Moroccan question without presenting precise or reasonable demands. Germany's crude bullying forced France and Britain closer together, and Germany left the Algeciras Conference of 1906 empty-handed and isolated (except for Austria-Hungary).

The result of the Moroccan crisis and the Algeciras Conference was something of a diplomatic revolution. Britain, France, Russia, and even the United States began to see Germany as a potential threat, which might seek to dominate all Europe. At the same time, German leaders began to see sinister plots to "encircle" Germany and block its development as a world power. In 1907 Russia, battered by the disastrous war with Japan and the revolution of 1905, agreed to settle its quarrels with Great Britain in Persia and central Asia with a special Anglo-Russian Agreement (Figure 27.1). As a result of that agreement, Germany's blustering paranoia increased and so did Britain's thinly disguised hostility.

Germany's decision to add a large, enormously expensive fleet of big-gun battleships to its already expanding navy also heightened tensions after 1907. German nationalists, led by the all-too-persuasive Admiral Tirpitz, saw a large navy as the legitimate mark of a great world power. But British leaders like Lloyd George saw it as a detestable military challenge, which forced them to spend the "People's Budget" on battleships rather than on social welfare. As Germany's rapid industrial growth allowed it to overcome Britain's early lead, economic rivalry also contributed to distrust and hostility between the two

German Warships Under Full Steam As this impressive row of ships on maneuvers in 1911 suggests, Germany did succeed in building a large modern navy. But Britain was equally determined to maintain its naval superiority, and the spiraling arms race helped poison relations between the two countries. *(Süddeutscher Verlag)*

nations. Unscrupulous journalists and special-interest groups in both countries portrayed healthy competition in foreign trade and investment as a form of economic welfare.

Many educated shapers of public opinion and ordinary people in Britain and Germany were increasingly locked in a fateful "love-hate" relationship between the two countries. Proud nationalists in both countries simultaneously admired and feared the power and accomplishments of their nearly equal rival. In 1909 the mass-circulation London *Daily Mail* hysterically informed its readers in a series of reports that "Germany is deliberately preparing to destroy the British Empire."[2] By then, Britain was psychologically, if not officially, in the Franco-Russian camp. The leading nations of Europe were divided into two hostile blocs, both ill prepared to deal with upheaval on Europe's southeastern frontier.

THE OUTBREAK OF WAR

In the early years of this century, war in the Balkans was as inevitable as anything can be in human history. The reason was simple: nationalism was destroying the Ottoman Empire and threatening to break up the Austro-Hungarian Empire. The only questions were what kinds of wars would occur and where they would lead.

Greece had long before led the struggle for national liberation, winning its independence in 1832. In 1875 widespread nationalist rebellion in the Ottoman Empire had resulted in Turkish repression, Russian intervention, and Great Power tensions. Bismarck had helped resolve this crisis at the 1878 Congress of Berlin, which worked out the partial division of Turkish possessions in Europe. Austria-Hungary obtained the right to "occupy and adminis-

MAP 27.1 The Balkans After the Congress of Berlin, 1878 The Ottoman Empire suffered large territorial losses but remained a power in the Balkans.

MAP 27.2 The Balkans in 1914 Ethnic boundaries did not follow political boundaries, and Serbian national aspirations threatened Austria-Hungary.

ter" Bosnia and Herzegovina. Serbia and Rumania won independence, and a part of Bulgaria won local autonomy. The Ottoman Empire retained important Balkan holdings, for Austria-Hungary and Russia each feared the other's domination of totally independent states in the area (see Map 27.1).

After 1878 the siren call of imperialism lured European energies, particularly Russian energies, away from the Balkans. This division helped preserve the fragile balance of interests in southeastern Europe. By 1903, however, Balkan nationalism was on the rise once again. Serbia led the way, becoming openly hostile toward both Austria-Hungary and the Ottoman Empire. The Serbs, a Slavic people, looked to Slavic Russia for support of their national aspirations. To block Serbian expansion and to take advantage of Russia's weakness after the revolution of 1905, Austria in 1908 formally annexed Bosnia and

Herzegovina with their predominantly Serbian populations. The kingdom of Serbia erupted in rage but could do nothing without Russian support.

Then in 1912, in the First Balkan War, Serbia turned southward. With Greece and Bulgaria it took Macedonia from the Ottoman Empire and then quarreled with its ally Bulgaria over the spoils of victory—a dispute that led in 1913 to the Second Balkan War. Austria intervened in 1913 and forced Serbia to give up Albania. After centuries, nationalism had finally destroyed the Ottoman Empire in Europe. This sudden but long-awaited event elated the Balkan nationalists and dismayed the leaders of multinational Austria-Hungary. The former hoped and the latter feared that Austria might be next to be broken apart.

Within this tense context, Archduke Francis Ferdinand, heir to the Austrian and Hungarian thrones, and his wife Sophie were assassinated by Bosnian revolutionaries on June 28, 1914, during a state visit to the Bosnian capital of Sarajevo. The assassins were closely connected to the ultranationalist Serbian society The Black Hand. This revolutionary group was secretly supported by members of the Serbian government and was dedicated to uniting all Serbians in a single state. Although the leaders of Austria-Hungary did not and could not know all the details of Serbia's involvement in the assassination plot, they concluded after some hesitation that Serbia had to be severely punished once and for all. After a month of maneuvering, Austria-Hungary presented Serbia with an unconditional ultimatum, on July 23.

The Serbian government had just forty-eight hours in which to agree to cease all subversion in Austria and all anti-Austrian propaganda in Serbia. Moreover, a thorough investigation of all aspects of the assassination at Sarajevo was to be undertaken in Serbia by a joint commission of Serbian and Austrian officials. These demands amounted to control of the Serbian state. When Serbia replied moderately but evasively, Austria began to mobilize and then declared war on Serbia on July 28. Thus a desperate multinational Austria-Hungary deliberately chose war in a last-ditch attempt to stem the rising tide of hostile nationalism. The "Third Balkan War" had begun (see Map 27.2).

Of prime importance in Austria-Hungary's fateful decision was Germany's unconditional support. Emperor William II and his chancellor Theobald von Bethmann-Hollweg gave Austria-Hungary a "blank check" and urged aggressive measures in early July, even though they realized that war between Austria and Russia was the most probable result. They knew Russian pan-Slavs saw Russia not only as the protector, but also as the eventual liberator, of southern Slavs. As one pan-Slav had said much earlier, "Austria can hold her part of the Slavonian mass as long as Turkey holds hers and vice versa."[3] At the very least a resurgent Russia could not stand by, as in the Bosnian crisis, and simply watch the Serbs be crushed. Yet Bethmann-Hollweg apparently hoped that while Russia (and therefore France) would go to war, Great Britain would remain neutral, unwilling to fight for "Russian aggression" in the distant Balkans. After all, Britain had reached only "friendly understandings" with France and Russia on colonial questions and had no alliance with either power.

In fact, the diplomatic situation was already out of control. Military plans and timetables began to dictate policy. Russia, a vast country, would require much longer to mobilize its armies than Germany and Austria-Hungary. On July 28, as Austrian armies bombarded Belgrade, Tsar Nicholas II ordered a partial mobilization against Austria-Hungary. Almost immediately he found that this was impossible. All the complicated mobilization plans of the Russian general staff had assumed a war with both Austria *and* Germany: Russia could not mobilize against one without mobilizing against the other. On July 29, therefore, Russia ordered full mobilization and in effect declared general war. For, as the French general Goisdeffre had said to the agreeing Russian tsar when the Franco-Russian military convention was being negotiated in 1892, "mobilization is a declaration of war."[4]

The same tragic subordination of political considerations to military strategy descended on Germany. The German general staff had also thought only in terms of a two-front war. Their plan for war—the Schlieffen plan, the work of Count Alfred von Schlieffen, chief of the German general staff from 1891 to 1906 and a professional military man—called for knocking out France first with a lightning attack through neutral Belgium before turning on Russia.

Thus, on August 2, 1914, General Helmuth von Moltke, "acting under a dictate of self-preservation," demanded that Belgium permit German armies to pass through its territory. Belgium, whose neutrality was solemnly guaranteed by all the great states including Prussia, refused. Germany attacked. Thus Germany's terrible, politically disastrous response to a war in the Balkans was an all-out invasion of France by way of the plains of neutral Belgium on August 3. In the face of this act of aggression, Great Britain declared war on Germany the following day. The First World War had begun.

REFLECTIONS ON THE ORIGINS OF THE WAR

Although few events in history have aroused such interest and controversy as the coming of the First World War, the question of immediate causes and responsibilities can be answered with considerable certainty. Austria-Hungary deliberately started the "Third Balkan War." A war for the right to survive was Austria-Hungary's desperate, if understandable, response to the aggressive, yet understandable, revolutionary drive of Serbian nationalists to unify their people in a single state. In spite of Russian intervention in the quarrel, it is clear from the beginning of the crisis that Germany not only pushed and goaded Austria-Hungary but was also responsible for turning a little war into the Great War by means of its sledgehammer attack on Belgium and France.

After Bismarck's resignation in 1890, German leaders lost control of the international system. They felt increasingly that Germany's status as a world power was declining while that of Britain, France, Russia, and the United States was growing. Indeed, the powers of what officially became in August 1914 the Triple Entente—Great Britain, France, and Russia—were checking Germany's vague but real aspirations, as well as working to strangle Austria-Hungary, Germany's only real ally. Germany's aggression in 1914 reflected the failure of all European statesmen, not just German leaders, to incorporate Bismarck's mighty empire permanently and peacefully into the international system.

There were other underlying causes. The new overseas expansion—imperialism—did not play a direct role, since the European powers always settled their colonial conflicts peacefully. Yet the easy imperialist victories did contribute to a general European overconfidence and reinforced national rivalries. In this respect it was influential.

The triumph of nationalism was a crucial underlying precondition of the Great War. Nationalism was at the heart of the Balkan wars, in the form of Serbian aspirations and the grandiose pan-German versus pan-Slavic racism of some fanatics. Nationalism drove the spiraling arms race. More generally, as shown in Chapter 25, the aristocracy and middle classes arrived at nationalistic compromises, while ordinary people looked toward increasingly responsive states for psychological and material well-being.

Broad popular commitment to "my country right or wrong" weakened groups that thought in terms of international communities and consequences. Thus the big international bankers, who were frightened by the prospect of war in July 1914, and the extreme-left socialists, who believed that the enemy was at home and not abroad, were equally out of step with national feeling.

Finally, the wealthy governing classes underesti-

mated the risk of war in 1914. They had forgotten that great wars and great social revolutions very often go together in history. Metternich's alliance of conservative forces in support of international peace and the domestic status quo had become only a distant memory.

THE FIRST BATTLE OF THE MARNE

When the Germans invaded Belgium in August 1914, they and everyone else believed that the war would be short, for urban society rested on the food and raw materials of the world economy: "The boys will be home by Christmas." The Belgian army heroically defended its homeland, however, and fell back in good order to join a rapidly landed British army corps near the Franco-Belgian border. This action complicated the original Schlieffen plan of concentrating German armies on the right wing and boldly capturing Paris in a vast encircling movement. Moreover, the German left wing in Lorraine failed to retreat, thwarting the plan to suck French armies into Germany and then annihilate them. Instead, by the end of August dead-tired German soldiers were advancing along an enormous front in the scorching summer heat. The neatly designed prewar plan to surround Paris from the north and west had been thrown into confusion.

French armies totaling 1 million, reinforced by more than 100,000 British troops, had retreated in orderly fashion before Germany's 1.5 million men in the field. Under the leadership of the steel-nerved General Joseph Joffre, the French attacked a gap in the German line at the Battle of the Marne on September 6. For three days, France threw everything into the attack. At one point, the French government desperately requisitioned all the taxis of Paris to rush reserves to the troops at the front. Finally, the Germans fell back. Paris and France had been miraculously saved.

STALEMATE AND SLAUGHTER

The attempts of French and British armies to turn the German retreat into a rout were unsuccessful, and so were moves by both sides to outflank each other in northern France. As a result, both sides began to dig trenches to protect themselves from machine gun fire. By November 1914, an unbroken line of trenches extended from the Belgian ports through

Preparing the Attack The great offenses of the First World War required the mobilization of men and material on an unprecedented scale. This photo shows American troops moving up. *(U.S. Army Signal Corps)*

northern France past the fortress of Verdun and on to the Swiss frontier.

In the face of this unexpected stalemate, slaughter on the western front began in earnest. The defenders on both sides dug in behind rows of trenches, mines, and barbed wire. For days and even weeks ceaseless shelling by heavy artillery supposedly "softened up" the enemy in a given area (and also signaled the coming attack). Then young draftees and their junior officers went "over the top" of the trenches in frontal attacks on the enemy's line.

The cost in lives was staggering, the gains in territory minuscule. The massive French and British offensives during 1915 never gained more than three miles of blood-soaked earth from the enemy. In the

Battle of the Somme in the summer of 1916, the British and French gained an insignificant 125 square miles at the cost of 600,000 dead or wounded, while the Germans lost half a million men. That same year, the unsuccessful German campaign against Verdun cost 700,000 lives on both sides. The British poet Siegfried Sassoon (1886–1967) wrote of the Somme offensive: "I am staring at a sunlit picture of Hell."

Terrible 1917 saw General Robert Nievelle's French army almost destroyed in a grand spring attack at Champagne, while at Passchendaele in the fall, the British traded 400,000 casualties for fifty square miles of Belgian Flanders. The hero of Erich Remarque's great novel *All Quiet on the Western Front* (1929) describes one such attack:

The Fruits of War The extent of carnage, the emotional damage, and the physical destruction were equally unprecedented. Once great cathedrals standing in ruin symbolized the disaster. *(UPI/Bettmann Newsphotos)*

We see men living with their skulls blown open; we see soldiers run with their two feet cut off. . . . Still the little piece of convulsed earth in which we lie is held. We have yielded no more than a few hundred yards of it as a prize to the enemy. But on every yard there lies a dead man.

Such was war on the western front.

The war of the trenches shattered an entire generation of young men. Millions who could have provided political creativity and leadership after the war were forever missing. Moreover, those who lived through the holocaust were maimed, shell-shocked, embittered, and profoundly disillusioned. The young soldiers went to war believing in the world of their leaders and elders, the pre-1914 world of order, progress, and patriotism. Then, in Remarque's words, the "first bombardment showed us our mistake, and under it the world as they had taught it to us broke in pieces." For many, the sacrifice and comradeship of the battlefield became life's crucial experience, an experience that "soft" civilians could never understand. A chasm opened up between veterans and civilians, making the difficult postwar reconstruction all the more difficult.

THE WIDENING WAR

On the eastern front, slaughter did not degenerate into suicidal trench warfare. With the outbreak of the war, the "Russian steamroller" immediately moved

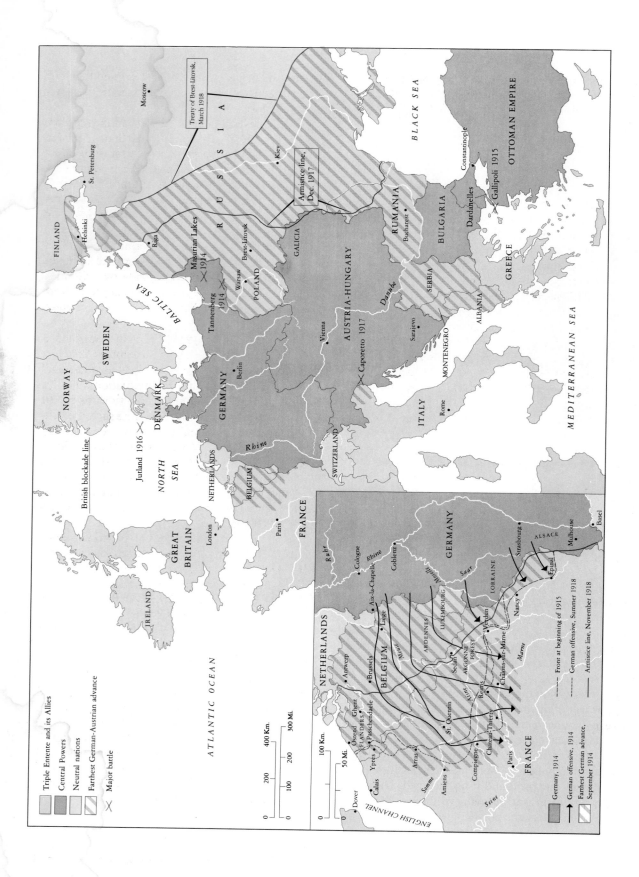

Triple Entente and its Allies
Central Powers
Neutral nations
Farthest German-Austrian advance
✕ **Major battle**

ATLANTIC OCEAN

0   200   400 Km.
0   100   200   300 Mi.

IRELAND

GREAT BRITAIN

London •

NORTH SEA

Jutland 1916 ✕

British blockade line

NORWAY

SWEDEN

BALTIC SEA

FINLAND

Helsinki •

St. Petersburg •

Moscow •

Treaty of Brest-Litovsk, March 1918

R U S S I A

Kiev •

Armistice line, Dec. 1917

Riga •

Masurian Lakes ✕ 1914

Tannenberg ✕ 1914

Warsaw •

Brest-Litovsk •

POLAND

GALICIA

Berlin •

GERMANY

Rhine

DENMARK

NETHERLANDS

BELGIUM

Paris •

FRANCE

SWITZERLAND

Vienna •

AUSTRIA-HUNGARY

Danube

Caporetto 1917 ✕

Sarajevo •

SERBIA

MONTENEGRO

ALBANIA

ITALY

Rome •

RUMANIA

Bucharest •

BULGARIA

Dardanelles

Constantinople •

Gallipoli 1915 ✕

OTTOMAN EMPIRE

BLACK SEA

GREECE

MEDITERRANEAN SEA

Germany, 1914
→ German offensive, 1914
Farthest German advance, September 1914
–––– Front at beginning of 1915
------ German offensive, Summer 1918
––– Armistice line, November 1918

0   50 Mi.
0   100   Km.

ENGLISH CHANNEL

Dover •

Calais •

Ostend •

FLANDERS

Ghent •

Ypres •

Passchendaele •

Arras •

Somme

Amiens •

Compiègne •

Seine

Paris •

NETHERLANDS

Antwerp •

Brussels •

BELGIUM

Meuse

Liège •

Aix-la-Chapelle •

ARDENNES

Sedan •

St. Quentin •

Aisne

Reims •

Marne

Château-Thierry •

Châlons-sur-Marne •

LUXEMBOURG

ARGONNE FOREST

Verdun •

Nancy •

LORRAINE

Saar

Moselle

Coblenz •

Rhine

Cologne •

Ruhr

GERMANY

Strasbourg •

ALSACE

Épinal •

Mulhouse •

Basel •

FRANCE

MAP 27.3 The First World War in Europe The trench war on the western front was concentrated in Belgium and northern France, while the war in the east encompassed an enormous territory.

into eastern Germany. Very badly damaged by the Germans under Generals Paul von Hindenburg and Erich Ludendorff at the battles of Tannenberg and the Masurian Lakes in August and September 1914, Russia never threatened Germany again. On the Austrian front, enormous armies seesawed back and forth, suffering enormous losses. Austro-Hungarian armies were repulsed twice by little Serbia in bitter fighting. But with the help of German forces, they reversed the Russian advances of 1914 and forced the Russians to retreat deep into their own territory in the eastern campaign of 1915. A staggering 2.5 million Russians were killed, wounded, or taken prisoner that year.

These changing tides of victory and defeat brought neutral countries into the war (see Map 27.3). Italy, a member of the Triple Alliance since 1882, had declared its neutrality in 1914 on the grounds that Austria had launched a war of aggression. Then, in May 1915, Italy joined the Triple Entente of Great Britain, France, and Russia in return for promises of Austrian territory. Bulgaria allied with Austria and Germany, now known as the Central Powers, in September 1915 in order to settle old scores with Serbia.

The entry of Italy and Bulgaria in 1915 was part of a general widening of the war. The Balkans, with the exception of Greece, came to be occupied by the Central Powers, and British forces were badly defeated in 1915 trying to take the Dardanelles from Turkey, Germany's ally. More successful was the entente's attempt to incite Arab nationalists against their Turkish overlords. An enigmatic British colonel, soon known to millions as Lawrence of Arabia, aroused the Arab princes to revolt in early 1917. In 1918 British armies from Egypt smashed the Ottoman Empire once and for all. In their Middle East campaign, the British drew on forces from Australia, New Zealand, and India. Contrary to German hopes, the colonial subjects of the British (and French) did not revolt but loyally supported their foreign masters.

Instead, the European war extended around the globe as Great Britain, France, and Japan seized Germany's colonies.

A crucial development in the expanding conflict came in April 1917, when the United States declared war on Germany. American intervention grew out of the war at sea, sympathy for the entente, and the increasing desperation of total war. At the beginning of the war, Britain and France had established a total naval blockade to strangle the Central Powers and prevent deliveries of food and raw materials from overseas. No neutral ship was permitted to sail to Germany with any cargo. The blockade annoyed Americans, but effective propaganda over German atrocities in occupied Belgium and lush profits from selling war supplies to Britain and France blunted American indignation.

Moreover, in early 1915 Germany launched a counter-blockade using the murderously effective submarine, a new weapon that violated traditional niceties of fair warning under international law. In May 1915, after sinking about ninety ships in the British war zone, a German submarine sank the British passenger liner *Lusitania,* which was also carrying arms and munitions. More than a thousand lives, among them 139 Americans, were lost. President Woodrow Wilson protested vigorously. Germany was forced to relax its submarine warfare for almost two years; the alternative was almost certain war with the United States.

Early in 1917, the German military command—confident that improved submarines could starve their island enemy, Britain, into submission before the United States could come to its rescue—resumed unrestricted submarine warfare. Like the invasion of Belgium, this was a reckless gamble. British shipping losses reached staggering proportions, though by late 1917 naval strategists came up with the inevitable effective response: the convoy system for safe transatlantic shipping. In the meantime, the embattled President Wilson had told a sympathetic Congress and people that the "German submarine warfare against commerce is a warfare against mankind." Thus the last uncommitted great nation, as fresh and enthusiastic as Europe had been in 1914, entered the world war in April 1917, almost three years after it began. Eventually the United States was to tip the balance in favor of Great Britain and France.

THE HOME FRONT

Before looking at the last year of the Great War, let us turn our attention to the people on the home front. The people behind the lines were tremendously involved in the titanic struggle. War's impact on them was no less massive than on the men crouched in the trenches.

MOBILIZING FOR TOTAL WAR

In August 1914 most people had greeted the outbreak of hostilities enthusiastically. In every country, the masses believed that their nation was in the right and defending itself from aggression. With the exception of a few extreme left-wingers, even socialists supported the war. Tough standby plans to imprison socialist leaders and break general strikes protesting the war proved quite unnecessary in 1914. In Germany, for example, the trade unions voted not to strike, and socialists in the parliament voted money for war credits in order to counter the threat of Russian despotism. A German socialist volunteered for the front, explaining to fellow members of the Reichstag that "to shed one's blood for the fatherland is not difficult: it is enveloped in romantic heroism."[5] Everywhere the patriotic support of the masses and the working class contributed to national unity and an energetic war effort.

By mid-October generals and politicians began to realize that more than patriotism would be needed to win the war, whose end was not in sight. Each country experienced a relentless, desperate demand for men and weapons. In France, for example, the generals found themselves needing 100,000 heavy artillery shells a day, as opposed to the 12,000 they had anticipated using. This enormous quantity had to come from a French steel industry that had lost three-fourths of its iron resources in the first days of the war, when Germany seized the mines of French Lorraine. Each belligerent quickly faced countless shortages, for prewar Europe had depended on foreign trade and a great international division of labor. In each country economic life and organization had to change and change fast to keep the war machine from sputtering to a stop. And change they did.

In each country a government of national unity began to plan and control economic and social life in order to wage "total war." Free-market capitalism was abandoned, at least "for the duration." Instead, government planning boards established priorities and decided what was to be produced and consumed. Rationing, price and wage controls, and even restrictions on workers' freedom of movement were imposed by government. Only through such regimentation could a country make the greatest possible military effort. Thus, though there were national variations, the great nations all moved toward planned economies commanded by the established political leadership.

This revolutionary development would burn deeply into the twentieth-century consciousness. The planned economy of total war released the tremendous energies first harnessed by the French under Robespierre during the French Revolution. Total war, however, was based on tremendously productive industrial economies not confined to a single nation. The result was an effective—and therefore destructive—war effort on all sides.

Moreover, the economy of total war blurred the old distinction between soldiers on the battlefield and civilians at home. As President Wilson told Americans shortly after the United States entered the war, there were no armies in the struggle in the traditional sense. Rather, "there are entire nations armed. Thus the men [and women] who remain to till the soil and man the factories are not less a part of the army than the men beneath the battle flags."[6] The war was a war of whole peoples and entire populations, and the loser would be the society that cracked first.

Finally, however awful the war was, the ability of governments to manage and control highly complicated economies strengthened the cause of socialism. With the First World War, socialism became for the first time a realistic economic blueprint rather than a utopian program.

Germany illustrates the general trend. It also went furthest in developing a planned economy to wage total war. As soon as war began, Walter Rathenau, the talented, foresighted Jewish industrialist in charge of Germany's largest electrical company, convinced the government to set up a War Raw Materials Board to ration and distribute raw materials. Under Rathenau's direction, every useful material from foreign oil to barnyard manure was inventoried and rationed. Moreover, the board launched successful attempts to produce substitutes, such as synthetic rubber and synthetic nitrates. Without the spectacular double achievement of discovering a way to "fix" nitrogen present in the air and then of producing synthetic nitrates in enormous quantity, the blockaded German war machine would have stalled in a matter of months.

Food was also rationed in accordance with physical need. Men and women doing hard manual work were given extra rations. During the last two years of the war, only children and expectant mothers received milk rations. Sometimes mistakes were made that would have been funny if they had not been tragic. In early 1915, German authorities calculated that greedy pigs were eating food that hungry people needed, and ordered a "hog massacre" only to find that there were too few pigs left to eat an abundant potato crop. Germany also failed to tax the war profits of private firms heavily enough. This contributed to massive deficit financing, inflation, the growth of a black market, and the eventual re-emergence of class conflict.

Following the terrible battles of Verdun and the Somme in 1916, the military leaders Hindenburg and Ludendorff became the real rulers of Germany, and they decreed the ultimate mobilization for total war. Germany, said Hindenburg, could win only "if all the treasures of our soil that agriculture and industry can produce are used exclusively for the conduct of War. . . . All other considerations must come second."[7] This goal, they believed, required that every German man, woman, and child be drafted into the service of the war. Thus, in December 1916, the military leaders rammed through the parliament the Auxiliary Service Law, which required all males between seventeen and sixty to work only at jobs considered critical to the war effort.

Waging Total War A British war plant strains to meet the insatiable demand for trench-smashing heavy artillery shells. Quite typically, many of these defense workers are women. *(By courtesy of the Trustees of the Imperial War Museum)*

Although women and children were not specifically mentioned, this forced-labor law was also aimed at them. Many women already worked in war factories, mines, and steel mills, where they labored like men at the heaviest and most dangerous jobs. With the passage of the Auxiliary Service Law, many more women followed. Children were organized by their teachers into garbage brigades to collect every scrap of useful materials: grease strained from dishwater, coffee grounds, waste paper, tin cans, metal door knockers, bottles, rags, hair, bones, and so forth, as well as acorns, chestnuts, pinecones, and rotting leaves. Potatoes gave way to turnips, and people averaged little more than a thousand calories a day. Thus in Germany total war led to the establishment of history's first "totalitarian" society, and war production increased while some people literally starved to death.

Great Britain mobilized for total war less rapidly and less completely than Germany, for it could import materials from its empire and from the United States. By 1915, however, a serious shortage of shells led to the establishment of a Ministry of Munitions under David Lloyd George. The ministry organized private industry to produce for the war, controlled profits, allocated labor, fixed wage rates, and settled labor disputes. By December 1916, when Lloyd George became prime minister, the British economy was largely planned and regulated. More than two hundred factories and 90 percent of all imports were bought and allocated directly by the state. Subsequently, even food was strictly rationed, while war production continued to soar. Great Britain had followed successfully in Germany's footsteps.

THE SOCIAL IMPACT

The social impact of total war was no less profound than the economic, though again there were important national variations. The millions of men at the front and the insatiable needs of the military created a tremendous demand for workers. Jobs were available for everyone. This situation had seldom if ever been seen before 1914, when unemployment and poverty had been facts of urban life. The exceptional demand for labor brought about momentous changes.

One such change was greater power and prestige for labor unions. Having proved their loyalty in Au-

gust 1914, labor unions became an indispensable partner of government and private industry in the planned war economy. Unions cooperated with war governments on work rules, wages, and production schedules in return for real participation in important decisions. This entry of labor leaders and unions into policy-making councils paralleled the entry of socialist leaders into the war governments.

The role of women changed dramatically. In every country, large numbers of women left home and domestic service to work in industry, transportation, and offices. By 1917 women formed fully 43 percent of the labor force in Russia. The number of women driving buses and streetcars increased tenfold in Great Britain. Moreover, women became highly visible—not only as munitions workers but as bank tellers, mail carriers, even policewomen.

At first, the male-dominated unions were hostile to women moving into new occupations, believing that their presence would lower wages and change work rules. But government pressure and the principle of equal pay for equal work (at least until the end of the war) overcame these objections. Women also served as nurses and doctors at the front. In general, the war greatly expanded the range of women's activities and changed attitudes toward them. As a direct result of their many-sided war effort, Britain, Germany, and Austria granted women the right to vote immediately after the war. Women also showed a growing spirit of independence during the war, as they started to bob their hair, shorten their skirts, and smoke in public.

War also promoted great social equality, blurring class distinctions and lessening the gap between rich and poor. This blurring was most apparent in Great Britain, where wartime hardship was never extreme. In fact, the bottom third of the population generally lived *better* than ever before, for the poorest gained most from the severe shortage of labor. The English writer Robert Roberts recalled how his parents' tiny grocery store in the slums of Manchester thrived as never before during the war, when people who had scrimped to buy bread and soup bones were able to afford fancy cakes and thick steaks. In 1924 a British government study revealed that the distribution of income had indeed shifted in favor of the poorest; only half as many families lived in severe poverty as in 1911, even though total production of goods had not increased. In continental countries greater equality was reflected in full employment, rationing according to physical needs, and a sharing of hardships.

Wartime Propaganda was skillful and effective. The poster on the left spurred men to volunteer bravely for military service before the draft was introduced in Britain in 1916. The grim warrior on the right calls on French men and women at home to unite as firmly as the soldiers at the front against defeatist plots in 1918. *(The Trustees of the Imperial War Museum)*

There, too, society became more uniform and more egalitarian, in spite of some war profiteering.

Finally, death itself had no respect for traditional social distinctions. It savagely decimated the young aristocratic officers who led the charge, and it fell heavily on the mass of drafted peasants and unskilled workers who followed. Yet death often spared the aristocrats of labor, the skilled workers and foremen. Their lives were too valuable to squander at the front, for they were needed to train and direct the newly recruited women and older unskilled men laboring valiantly in war plants at home.

GROWING POLITICAL TENSIONS

During the first two years of war, most soldiers and civilians supported their governments. Even in Austria-Hungary—the most vulnerable of the belligerents, with its competing nationalities—loyalty to the state and monarchy remained astonishingly strong through 1916. Belief in a just cause, patriotic nationalism, the planned economy, and a sharing of burdens united peoples behind their various national leaders. Furthermore, each government did its best to control public opinion to bolster morale. Newspa-

The Easter Rebellion, 1916 Irish nationalists rose but were suppressed by overwhelming military force. Shelling by British gunboats devastated central Dublin, shown here. *(BBC Hulton/The Bettmann Archive)*

pers, letters, and public addresses were rigorously censored. Good news was overstated; bad news was repressed or distorted.

Each government used both crude and subtle propaganda to maintain popular support. German propaganda hysterically pictured black soldiers from France's African empire raping German women, while German atrocities in Belgium and elsewhere were ceaselessly recounted and exaggerated by the French and British. Patriotic posters and slogans, slanted news and biased editorials inflamed national hatreds and helped sustain superhuman efforts.

By the spring of 1916, however, people were beginning to crack under the strain of total war. In April 1916, Irish nationalists in Dublin tried to take advantage of this situation and rose up against British rule in their great Easter Rebellion. A week of bitter fighting passed before the rebels were crushed and their leaders executed. Strikes and protest marches over inadequate food began to flare up on every home front. Soldiers' morale began to decline. Italian troops mutinied. Numerous French units refused to fight after General Nivelle's disastrous offensive of May 1917. Only tough military justice and a tacit agreement with his troops that there would be no

more grand offensives enabled the new general in chief, Henri-Philippe Pétain, to restore order. A rising tide of war-weariness and defeatism also swept France's civilian population before Georges Clemenceau emerged as a ruthless and effective wartime leader in November 1917. Clemenceau established a virtual dictatorship, pouncing on strikers and jailing without trial journalists and politicians who dared to suggest a compromise peace with Germany.

The strains were worse for the Central Powers. In October 1916, the chief minister of Austria was assassinated by a young socialist crying, "Down with Absolutism! We want peace!"[8] The following month, when the feeble old Emperor Francis Joseph died sixty-eight years after his mother Sophia had pushed him onto the throne in 1848 (page 756), a symbol of unity disappeared. In spite of absolute censorship, political dissatisfaction and conflicts among nationalities grew. In April 1917, Austria's chief minister summed up the situation in the gloomiest possible terms. The country and army were exhausted. Another winter of war would bring revolution and disintegration. "If the monarchs of the Central Powers cannot make peace in the coming months," he wrote, "it will be made for them by their peoples."[9] Both

The Fruits of War This photo shows how, in desperation, the people of Vienna decimated the city's beloved forest to get a little firewood to heat their homes. Economic collapse weighed heavily on all classes. *(Bildarchiv d. Osterreichische Nationalbibliothek)*

Czech and Yugoslav leaders demanded autonomous democratic states for their peoples. The allied blockade kept tightening; people were starving.

The strain of total war and the Auxiliary Service Law was also evident in Germany. In the winter of 1916 to 1917, Germany's military position appeared increasingly desperate. Stalemates and losses in the west were matched by temporary Russian advances in the east: hence the military's insistence on the all-or-nothing gamble of unrestricted submarine warfare when the entente refused in December 1916 to consider peace on terms that were favorable to the Central Powers.

Also, the national political unity of the first two years of war was collapsing as the social conflict of prewar Germany re-emerged. A growing minority of socialists in the parliament began to vote against war credits, calling for a compromise "peace without annexations or reparations." In July 1917, a coalition of socialists and Catholics passed a resolution in the parliament to that effect. Such a peace was unthinkable for conservatives and military leaders. So also was the surge in revolutionary agitation and strikes by war-weary workers that occurred in early 1917. When the bread ration was further reduced in April, more than 200,000 workers struck and demonstrated for a week in Berlin, returning to work only under the threat of prison and military discipline. Thus militaristic Germany, like its ally Austria-Hungary (and its enemy France), was beginning to crack in 1917. Yet its was Russia that collapsed first and saved the Central Powers, for a time.

THE RUSSIAN REVOLUTION

The Russian Revolution of 1917 was one of modern history's most momentous events. Directly related to the growing tensions of World War One, its significance went far beyond the wartime agonies of a single European nation. The Russian Revolution opened a new era. For some it was Marx's socialist vision come true; for others, it was the triumph of dictatorship. To all, it presented a radically new prototype of state and society.

The Fall of Imperial Russia

Like its allies and its enemies, Russia embraced war with patriotic enthusiasm in 1914. At the Winter Palace, while throngs of people knelt and sang "God Save the Tsar," Tsar Nicholas II (1894–1917) repeated the oath Alexander I had made in 1812 and vowed never to make peace as long as the enemy stood on Russian soil. Russia's lower house, the Duma, voted war credits. Conservatives anticipated expansion in the Balkans, while liberals and most socialists believed alliance with Britain and France would bring democratic reforms. For a moment, Russia was united.

Soon, however, the strains of war began to take their toll. The unprecedented artillery barrages used up Russia's supplies of shells and ammunition, and better-equipped German armies inflicted terrible losses. For a time in 1915, substantial members of Russian soldiers were sent to the front without rifles; they were told to find their arms among the dead. There were 2 million Russian casualties in 1915 alone. Morale declined among soldiers and civilians. Nonetheless, Russia's battered peasant army did not collapse but continued to fight courageously until early 1917.

Under the shock of defeat, Russia moved toward full mobilization on the home front. The Duma and organs of local government took the lead, setting up special committees to coordinate defense, industry, transportation, and agriculture. These efforts improved the military situation, and Russian factories produced more than twice as many shells in 1916 as in 1915. Yet there were many failures, and Russia mobilized less effectively for total war than the other warring nations.

The great problem was leadership. Under the constitution resulting from the revolution of 1905 (pages 812–813), the tsar had retained complete control over the bureaucracy and the army. Legislation proposed by the Duma, which was weighted in favor of the wealthy and conservative classes, was subject to the tsar's veto. Moreover, Nicholas II fervently wished to maintain the sacred inheritance of supreme royal power, which with the Orthodox church was for him the key to Russia's greatness. A kindly, slightly stupid man, of whom a friend said he "would have been an ideal country gentleman, devoting his life to wife and children, his farms and his sport," Nicholas failed to form a close partnership with his citizens in order to fight the war more effectively. He relied instead on the old bureaucratic apparatus, distrusting the moderate Duma, rejecting popular involvement, and resisting calls to share power.

As a result the Duma, the educated middle classes, and the masses became increasingly critical of the tsar's leadership. Following Nicholas's belated dismissal of the incompetent minister of war, demands for more democratic and responsive government exploded in the Duma in the summer of 1915. "From the beginning of the war," declared one young liberal, "public opinion has understood the character and magnitude of the struggle; it has understood that short of organizing the whole country for war, victory is impossible. But the Government has rejected every offer of help with disdain."[10] In September, parties ranging from conservative to moderate socialist formed the Progressive Bloc, which called for a completely new government responsible to the Duma instead of the tsar. In answer, Nicholas temporarily adjourned the Duma and announced that he was traveling to the front in order to lead and rally Russia's armies.

His departure was a fatal turning point. With the tsar in the field with the troops, control of the government was taken over by the hysterical empress, Tsarina Alexandra, and a debauched adventurer, the monk Rasputin. A minor German princess and granddaughter of England's Queen Victoria, Nicholas's wife was a devoted mother with a sick child, a strong-willed woman with a hatred of parliaments. Having constantly urged her husband to rule absolutely, Alexandra tried to do so herself in his absence. She seated and unseated the top ministers. Her most trusted adviser was "our Friend Grigori," an uneducated Siberian preacher who was appropriately nick-named Rasputin—the "Degenerate."

Rasputin began his career with a sect noted for mixing sexual orgies with religious ecstasies, and his influence rested on mysterious healing powers. Alexis, Alexandra's fifth child and heir to the throne, suffered from a rare disease, hemophilia. The tiniest cut meant uncontrollable bleeding, terrible pain, and possible death. Medical science could do nothing. Only Rasputin could miraculously stop the bleeding, perhaps through hypnosis. The empress's faith in Rasputin was limitless. "Believe more in our Friend," she wrote her husband in 1916. "He lives for you and Russia." In this atmosphere of unreality, the government slid steadily toward revolution.

In a desperate attempt to right the situation and end unfounded rumors that Rasputin was the empress's lover, three members of the high aristocracy murdered Rasputin in December 1916. The empress went into semipermanent shock, her mind haunted by the dead man's prophecy: "If I die or you desert me, in six months you will lose your son and your throne."[11] Food shortages in the cities worsened, morale declined. On March 8, women in Petrograd (formerly St. Petersburg) calling for bread started riots, which spontaneously spread to the factories and throughout the city. From the front the tsar ordered the troops to restore order, but discipline broke down and the soldiers joined the revolutionary crowd. The Duma responded by declaring a provisional government on March 12, 1917. Three days later, Nicholas abdicated without protest.

THE PROVISIONAL GOVERNMENT

The March revolution was the result of an unplanned uprising of hungry, angry people in the capital, but it was joyfully accepted throughout the country. The patriotic upper and middle classes rejoiced at the prospect of a more determined and effective war effort, while workers happily anticipated better wages and more food. All classes and political parties called for liberty and democracy. They were not disappointed. As Lenin said, Russia became the freest country in the world. After generations of arbitrary authoritarianism, the provisional government quickly established equality before the law; freedom of religion, speech, and assembly; the right of unions

Family Portrait With husband Nicholas II standing behind, the beautiful but tense Alexandra shows one of her daughters, who could not inherit the Russian throne, to her grandmother, Queen Victoria of England, and Victoria's son, the future Edward VII. European monarchs were closely related by blood and breeding before 1914. *(Nicholas A. de Basily Collection, Hoover Institution)*

to organize and strike; and the rest of the classic liberal program.

Yet both the liberal and moderate socialist leaders of the provisional government rejected social revolution. The reorganized government formed in May 1917, which included the fiery agrarian socialist Alexander Kerensky, refused to confiscate large landholdings and give them to peasants, fearing that such drastic action in the countryside would only complete the disintegration of Russia's peasant army. For the patriotic Kerensky, as for other moderate socialists, the continuation of war was still the all-important national duty. There would be plenty of time for land reform later, and thus all the government's efforts were directed toward a last offensive in July. Human suffering and war-weariness grew, sapping the limited strength of the provisional government.

From its first day, the provisional government had to share power with a formidable rival—the Petrograd Soviet (or council) of Workers' and Soldiers' Deputies. Modeled on the revolutionary soviets of 1905, the Petrograd Soviet was a huge, fluctuating mass meeting of two to three thousand workers, soldiers, and socialist intellectuals. Seeing itself as a true grass-roots revolutionary democracy, this counter- or half-government suspiciously watched the provisional government and issued its own radical orders, further weakening the provisional government. The most famous of these orders was Army Order No. 1, issued to all Russian military forces as the provisional government was forming.

Order No. 1 stripped officers of their authority and placed power in the hands of elected committees of common soldiers. Designed primarily to protect the revolution from some counter-revolutionary Bonaparte on horseback, Army Order No. 1 instead led to a total collapse of army discipline. Many an officer was hanged for his sins. Meanwhile, following the foolhardy summer offensive, masses of peasant soldiers began "voting with their feet," to use Lenin's graphic phrase. That is, they began returning to their villages to help their families get a share of the land, land that peasants were simply seizing as they settled old scores in a great agrarian upheaval. All across the country, liberty was turning into anarchy in the summer of 1917. It was an unparalleled opportunity for the most radical and most talented of Russia's many socialist leaders, Vladimir Ilyich Lenin (1870–1924).

LENIN AND THE BOLSHEVIK REVOLUTION

From his youth, Lenin's whole life was dedicated to the cause of revolution. Born into the middle class, the seventeen-year-old Lenin became an implacable enemy of imperial Russia when his older brother was executed for plotting to kill the tsar in 1887. As a law student he began searching for a revolutionary faith. He found it in Marxian socialism, which began to win converts among radical intellectuals as industrialization surged forward in Russia in the 1890s. Exiled to Siberia for three years because of socialist agitation, Lenin studied Marxist doctrines with religious intensity. After his release, the young priest of socialism joined fellow believers in western Europe. There he lived for seventeen years and developed his own revolutionary interpretations of the body of Marxian thought.

Three interrelated ideas were central for Lenin. First, turning to the early fire-breathing Marx of 1848 and the *Communist Manifesto* for inspiration, Lenin stressed that capitalism could be destroyed only by violent revolution. He tirelessly denounced all revisionist theories of a peaceful evolution to socialism as betraying Marx's message of unending class conflict. Lenin's second, more original, idea was that, under certain conditions, a socialist revolution was possible even in a relatively backward country like Russia. Though capitalism was not fully developed there and the industrial working class was small, the peasants were poor and thus potential revolutionaries.

Lenin believed that at a given moment revolution was determined more by human leadership than by vast historical laws. Thus Lenin's third basic idea: the necessity of a highly disciplined workers' party, strictly controlled by a dedicated elite of intellectuals and full-time revolutionaries like Lenin himself. Unlike ordinary workers and trade union officials, this elite would never be seduced by short-term gains. It would not stop until revolution brought it to power.

Lenin's theories and methods did not go unchallenged by other Russian Marxists. At the meetings of the Russian Social Democratic Labor party in London in 1903, matters came to a head. Lenin demanded a small, disciplined, elitist party, while his opponents wanted a more democratic party with mass membership. The Russian party of Marxian socialism promptly split into two rival factions. Lenin's camp was called *Bolsheviks,* or "Majority group"; his opponents were *Mensheviks,* or "Minority group." Lenin's majority did not last, but Lenin did not care. He kept the fine-sounding name Bolshevik and developed the party he wanted: tough, disciplined, revolutionary.

Unlike most socialists, Lenin did not rally round the national flag in 1914. Observing events from neutral Switzerland, he saw the war as a product of imperialistic rivalries and a marvelous opportunity for class war and socialist upheaval. The March revolution was, Lenin felt, a step in that direction. Since propaganda and internal subversion were accepted weapons of total war, the German government graciously provided the impatient Lenin, his wife, and about twenty trusted colleagues with safe passage across Germany and back into Russia in April 1917. The Germans hoped that Lenin would undermine the sagging war effort of the world's freest society. They were not disappointed.

Mass Demonstrations in Petrograd in June 1917 showed a surge of working-class support for the Bolsheviks. In this photo a few banners of the Mensheviks and other moderate socialists are drowned in a sea of Bolshevik slogans. *(Sovfoto)*

Arriving triumphantly at Petrograd's Finland Station on April 3, Lenin attacked at once. To the great astonishment of the local Bolsheviks, he rejected all cooperation with the "bourgeois" provisional government of the liberals and moderate socialists. His slogans were radical in the extreme: "All power to the Soviets." "All land to the peasants." "Stop the war now." Never a slave to Marxist determinism, the brilliant but not unduly intellectual Lenin was a superb tactician. The moment was now.

Yet Lenin almost overplayed his hand. An attempt by the Bolsheviks to seize power in July collapsed, and Lenin fled and went into hiding. He was charged with being a German agent, and indeed he and the Bolsheviks were getting money from Germany.[12] But no matter. Intrigue between Kerensky, who became prime minister in July, and his commander in chief General Lavr Kornilov, a popular war hero "with the heart of a lion and the brains of a sheep," resulted in Kornilov's leading a feeble attack against the provisional government in September. In the face of this rightist "counter-revolutionary" threat, the Bolsheviks were rearmed and redeemed. Kornilov's forces disintegrated, but Kerensky lost all credit with the army, the only force that might have saved him and democratic government in Russia.

THE RUSSIAN REVOLUTION

1914	Russia enthusiastically enters the First World War
1915	Two million Russian casualties
	Progressive Bloc calls for a new government responsible to the Duma rather than to the tsar
	Tsar Nicholas adjourns the Duma and departs for the front; control of the government falls to Alexandra and Rasputin
December 1916	Murder of Rasputin
March 8, 1917	Bread riots in Petrograd (St. Petersburg)
March 12, 1917	Duma declares a provisional government
March 15, 1917	Tsar Nicholas abdicates without protest
April 3, 1917	Lenin returns from exile and denounces the provisional government
May 1917	Reorganized provisional government, including Kerensky, continues the war
	Petrograd Soviet issues Army Order no. 1, granting military power to committees of common soldiers
Summer 1917	Agrarian upheavals: peasants seize estates, peasant soldiers desert the army to participate
October 1917	Bolsheviks gain a majority in the Petrograd Soviet
November 6, 1917	Bolsheviks seize power; Lenin heads the new "provisional workers' and peasants' government"
November 1917	Lenin ratifies peasant seizure of land and worker control of factories; all banks nationalized
January 1918	Lenin permanently disbands the Constituent Assembly
February 1918	Lenin convinces the Bolshevik Central Committee to accept a humiliating peace with Germany in order to pursue the revolution
March 1918	Treaty of Brest-Litovsk: Russia loses one-third of its population
	Trotsky as war commissar begins to rebuild the Russian army
	Government moves from Petrograd to Moscow
1918–1920	Great Civil War
Summer 1918	Eighteen competing regional governments; White armies oppose the Bolshevik revolution
1919	White armies on the offensive but divided politically; they receive little benefit from Allied intervention
1920	Lenin and Red armies victorious, retaking Belorussia and the Ukraine

Vladimir Lenin Dramatically displaying both his burning determination and his skill as a revolutionary orator, Lenin addresses the victorious May Day celebration of 1918 in Moscow's Red Square. *(Culver Pictures)*

TROTSKY AND THE SEIZURE OF POWER

Throughout the summer, the Bolsheviks had appealed very effectively to the workers and soldiers of Petrograd, markedly increasing their popular support. Party membership had soared from 50,000 to 240,000 and in October the Bolsheviks gained a fragile majority in the Petrograd Soviet. Moreover, Lenin had found a strong right arm—Leon Trotsky, the second most important person in the Russian Revolution.

A spellbinding revolutionary orator and independent radical Marxist, Trotsky (1877–1940) supported Lenin wholeheartedly in 1917. It was he who brilliantly executed the Bolshevik seizure of power. Painting a vivid but untruthful picture of German and counter-revolutionary plots, Trotsky first convinced the Petrograd Soviet to form a special Military-Revolutionary Committee in October and make him its leader. Military power in the capital passed

into Bolshevik hands. Trotsky's second master stroke was to insist that the Bolsheviks reduce opposition to their coup by taking power in the name, not of the Bolsheviks, but of the more popular and democratic soviets, which were meeting in Petrograd from all over Russia in early November. On the night of November 6, militants from Trotsky's committee joined with trusty Bolshevik soldiers to seize government buildings and pounce on members of the provisional government. Then on to the congress of soviets! There a Bolshevik majority—roughly 390 of 650 turbulent delegates—declared that all power had passed to the soviets and named Lenin head of the new government.

The Bolsheviks came to power for three key reasons. First, by late 1917 democracy had given way to anarchy: power was there for those who would take it. Second, in Lenin and Trotsky the Bolsheviks had an utterly determined and truly superior leadership, which both the tsarist government and the provisional government lacked. Third, in 1917 the Bolsheviks succeeded in appealing to many soldiers and urban workers, people who were exhausted by war and eager for socialism. With time, many workers would become bitterly disappointed, but for the moment they had good reason to believe they had won what they wanted.

DICTATORSHIP AND CIVIL WAR

History is full of short-lived coups and unsuccessful revolutions. The truly monumental accomplishment of Lenin, Trotsky, and the rest of the Bolsheviks was not taking power but keeping it. In the next four years, the Bolsheviks went on to conquer the chaos they had helped to create, and they began to build their kind of dictatorial socialist society. The conspirators became conquerors. How was this done?

Lenin had the genius to profit from developments over which he and the Bolsheviks had no control. Since summer, a peasant revolution had been sweeping across Russia, as the tillers of the soil invaded and divided among themselves the great and not-so-great estates of the landlords and the church. Peasant seizure of the land—a Russian 1789—was not very Marxist, but it was quite unstoppable in 1917. Thus Lenin's first law, which supposedly gave land to the peasants, actually merely approved what peasants were already doing. Urban workers' great demand in November was direct control of individual factories by local workers' committees. This, too, Lenin ratified with a decree in November.

Unlike many of his colleagues, Lenin acknowledged that Russia had lost the war with Germany, that the Russian army had ceased to exist, and that the only realistic goal was peace at any price. The price was very high. Germany demanded in December 1917 that the Soviet government give up all its western territories. These areas were inhabited by Poles, Finns, Lithuanians, and other non-Russians—all those peoples who had been conquered by the tsars over three centuries and put into the "prisonhouse of nationalities," as Lenin had earlier called the Russian Empire.

At first, Lenin's fellow Bolsheviks would not accept such great territorial losses. But when German armies resumed their unopposed march into Russia in February 1918, Lenin had his way in a very close vote in the Central Committee of the party. "Not even his greatest enemy can deny that at this moment Lenin towered like a giant over his Bolshevik colleagues."[13] A third of old Russia's population was sliced away by the German meat ax in the Treaty of Brest-Litovsk in March 1918. With peace, Lenin had escaped the certain disaster of continued war and could uncompromisingly pursue his goal of absolute political power for the Bolsheviks—now renamed Communists—within Russia.

In November 1917, the Bolsheviks had cleverly proclaimed their regime only a "provisional workers' and peasants' government," promising that a freely elected Constituent Assembly would draw up a new constitution. But the freest elections in Russia's history—both before and after 1917—produced a stunning setback for the Bolsheviks, who won less than one-fourth of the elected delegates. The Socialist Revolutionaries—the peasants' party—had a clear majority. The Constituent Assembly met for only one day, on January 18, 1918. It was then permanently disbanded by Bolshevik soldiers acting under Lenin's orders. Thus, even before the peace with Germany, Lenin was forming a one-party government.

The destruction of the democratically elected Constituent Assembly helped feed the flames of civil war. People who had risen up for self-rule in November saw that once again they were getting dictatorship from the capital. For the next three years, "Long live the [democratic] soviets; down with the Bolsheviks" was to be a popular slogan. The officers of the old army took the lead in organizing the so-called White opposition to the Bolsheviks in southern Russia and the Ukraine, in Siberia, and to the west of Petrograd. The Whites came from many social groups and were united only by their hatred of the Bolsheviks—the Reds.

By the summer of 1918, fully eighteen self-proclaimed regional governments—several of which represented minority nationalities—competed with Lenin's Bolsheviks in Moscow. By the end of the year, White armies were on the attack. In October 1919, it appeared they might triumph, as they closed in on Lenin's government from three sides. Yet they did not. By the spring of 1920, the White armies had been almost completely defeated, and the Bolshevik Red Army had retaken Belorussia and the Ukraine. The following year, the Communists also reconquered the independent nationalist governments of the Caucasus. The civil war was over; Lenin had won.

Lenin and the Bolsheviks won for several reasons. Strategically, they controlled the center, while the Whites were always on the fringes and disunited. Moreover, the poorly defined political program of the Whites was vaguely conservative, and it did not unite all the foes of the Bolsheviks under a progressive, democratic banner. For example, the most gifted of the White generals, the nationalistic General Anton Denikin, refused to call for a democratic republic and a federation of nationalities, although he knew that doing so would help his cause. Most important, the Communists quickly developed a better army, an army for which the divided Whites were no match.

Once again, Trotsky's leadership was decisive. The Bolshevik's had preached democracy in the army and elected officers in 1917. But beginning in March 1918, Trotsky as war commissar re-established the draft and the most drastic discipline for the newly formed Red Army. Soldiers deserting or disobeying an order were summarily shot. Moreover, Trotsky made effective use of former tsarist army officers, who were actively recruited and given unprecedented powers of discipline over their troops. In short, Trotsky formed a disciplined and effective fighting force.

The Bolsheviks also mobilized the home front. Establishing "war communism"—the application of the total war concept to a civil conflict—they seized grain from peasants, introduced rationing, nationalized all banks and industry, and required everyone to work. Although these measures contributed to a breakdown of normal economic activity, they also served to maintain labor discipline and to keep the Red Army supplied.

"Revolutionary terror" also contributed to the Communist victory. The old tsarist secret police was re-established as the Cheka, which hunted down and executed thousands of real or supposed foes, like the tsar's family and other "class enemies." At one point, shortly after the government moved from Petrograd to Moscow in March 1918, a circus clown in Moscow was making fun of the Bolsheviks to an appreciative audience. Chekists in the crowd quickly pulled out their guns and shot several laughing people. Moreover, people were shot or threatened with being shot for minor nonpolitical failures. The terror caused by the secret police became a tool of the government. The Cheka sowed fear, and fear silenced opposition.

Finally, foreign military intervention in the civil war ended up helping the Communists. After Lenin made peace with Germany, the Allies (the Americans, British, and Japanese) sent troops to Archangel and Vladivostok to prevent war materiel they had sent the provisional government from being captured by the Germans. After the Soviet government nationalized all foreign-owned factories without compensation and refused to pay all of Russia's foreign debts, Western governments and particularly France began to support White armies. Yet these efforts were small and halfhearted. In 1919 Western peoples were sick of war, and few Western politicians believed in a military crusade against the Bolsheviks. Thus Allied intervention in the civil war did not aid the Whites effectively, though it did permit the Communists to appeal to the patriotic nationalism of ethnic Russians, which was particularly strong among former tsarist army officers. Allied intervention was both too little and too much.

The Russian Revolution and the Bolshevik triumph was, then, one of the reasons why the First World War was such a great turning point in modern history. A radically new government, based on socialism and one-party dictatorship, came to power in a great European state, maintained power, and eagerly encouraged worldwide revolution. Although halfheartedly constitutional monarchy in Russia was undoubtedly headed for some kind of political crisis before 1914, it is hard to imagine the triumph of the most radical proponents of change and reform except in a situation of total collapse. That was precisely what happened to Russia in the First World War.

THE PEACE SETTLEMENT

In 1918 the guns of world war finally fell silent. After winning great concessions from Lenin in the Treaty of Brest-Litovsk in March 1918, the Germans launched their last major attack against France. Yet this offensive failed like those before it. With breathtaking rapidity, the United States, Great Britain, and France decisively defeated Germany militarily. Then, as civil war spread in Russia and as chaos engulfed much of eastern Europe, the victorious Western Allies came together in Paris to establish a lasting peace.

November 1918

The Fall of Monarchy Entitled simply "November 1918," this eloquent drawing from a popular German magazine shows the crowns of Europe scattered like driftwood after the final wave of war and revolution. *(Photo: Caroline Buckler)*

Expectations were high; optimism was almost unlimited. The Allies labored intensively and soon worked out terms for peace with Germany and for the creation of the peace-keeping League of Nations. Nevertheless, the hopes of peoples and politicians were soon disappointed, for the peace settlement of 1919 turned out to be a terrible failure. Rather than creating conditions for peace, it sowed the seeds of another war. Surely this was the ultimate tragedy of the Great War, a war that directly and indirectly cost $332 billion and left 10 million dead and another 20 million wounded. How did it happen? Why was the peace settlement unsuccessful?

THE END OF THE WAR

In early 1917, the strain of total war was showing everywhere. After the Russian Revolution in March, there were major strikes in Germany. In July a coalition of moderates passed a "peace resolution" in the

German parliament, calling for peace without territorial annexations. To counter this moderation born of war-weariness, the German military established a virtual dictatorship and aggressively exploited the collapse of Russian armies after the Bolshevik Revolution. Victory in the east having quieted German moderates, General Ludendorff and company fell on France once more in the great spring offensive of 1918. For a time, German armies pushed forward, coming within thirty-five miles of Paris. But Ludendorff's exhausted, overextended forces never broke through. They were decisively stopped in July at the second battle of the Marne, where 140,000 fresh American soldiers saw action. Adding 2 million men in arms to the war effort by August, the late but massive American intervention decisively tipped the scales in favor of Allied victory.

By September, British, French, and American armies were advancing steadily on all fronts, and a panicky General Ludendorff realized that Germany had lost the war. Yet he insolently insisted that moderate politicians shoulder the shame of defeat, and on October 4, the emperor formed a new, more liberal German government to sue for peace. As negotiations over an armistice dragged on, an angry and frustrated German people finally rose up. On November 3, sailors in Kiel mutinied, and throughout northern Germany, soldiers and workers began to establish revolutionary councils on the Russian soviet model. The same day, Austria-Hungary surrendered to the Allies and began breaking apart. Revolution broke out in Germany, and masses of workers demonstrated for peace in Berlin. With army discipline collapsing, the emperor was forced to abdicate and fled to Holland. Socialist leaders in Berlin proclaimed a German republic on November 9 and simultaneously agreed to tough Allied terms of surrender. The armistice went into effect November 11, 1918. The war was over.

REVOLUTION IN GERMANY

Military defeat brought political revolution to Germany and Austria-Hungary, as it had to Russia. In Austria-Hungary, the revolution was primarily nationalistic and republican in character. Having started the war to preserve an antinationalist dynastic state, the Habsburg Empire had perished in the attempt. In its place, independent Austrian, Hungarian, and Czechoslovakian republics were pro-

Rosa Luxemburg Shown here addressing a party congress, Rosa Luxemburg played a leading role in the socialist movement until her death in 1919. A brilliant theorist, she scorned moderate socialism and stressed the revolutionary character of Marxism. *(Süddeutscher Verlag)*

claimed, while a greatly expanded Serbian monarchy united the south Slavs and took the name of Yugoslavia. The prospect of firmly establishing the new national states overrode class considerations for most people in east central Europe.

The German Revolution of November 1918 resembled the Russian Revolution of March 1917. In both cases, a genuine popular uprising toppled an authoritarian monarchy and established a liberal provisional republic. In both countries, liberals and moderate socialists took control of the central government, while workers' and soldiers' councils formed a counter-government. In Germany, however, the moderate socialists won and the Lenin-like radical revolutionaries in the councils lost. In communist terms, the liberal, republican revolution in Germany in 1918 was only half a revolution: a bourgeois political revolution without a communist second installment. It was Russia without Lenin's Bolshevik triumph.

There were several reasons for the German outcome. The great majority of Marxian socialist leaders in the Social Democratic party were, as before the war, really pink and not red. They wanted to establish real political democracy and civil liberties, and they favored the gradual elimination of capitalism. They were also German nationalists, appalled by the prospect of civil war and revolutionary terror. Moreover, there was much less popular support among workers and soldiers for the extreme radicals than in Russia. Nor did the German peasantry, which already had most of the land, at least in western Germany, provide the elemental force that has driven all great modern revolutions, from the French to the Chinese.

Of crucial importance also was the fact that the moderate German Social Democrats, unlike Kerensky and company, accepted defeat and ended the war the day they took power. This act ended the decline in morale among soldiers and prevented the

The Treaty of Versailles was signed in the magnificent Hall of Mirrors, part of the vast palace that Louis XIV had built to celebrate his glory. The Allies did not allow Germany to participate in the negotiation of the treaty. *(National Archives, Washington)*

regular army with its conservative officer corps from disintegrating. When radicals, headed by Karl Liebknecht and Rosa Luxemburg and their supporters in the councils, tried to seize control of the government in Berlin in January, the moderate socialists called on the army to crush the uprising. Liebknecht and Luxemburg were arrested and then brutally murdered by army leaders, which caused the radicals in the Social Democratic party to break away in anger and form a pro-Lenin German Communist party shortly thereafter. Finally, even if the moderate socialists had followed Liebknecht and Luxemburg on the Leninist path, it is very unlikely they would have succeeded. Civil war in Germany would certainly have followed, and the Allies, who were already occupying western Germany according to the terms of the armistice, would have marched on to Berlin and ruled Germany directly. Historians have often been unduly hard on Germany's moderate socialists.

THE TREATY OF VERSAILLES

The peace conference opened in Paris in January 1919 with seventy delegates representing twenty-seven victorious nations. There were great expectations. A young British diplomat later wrote that the victors "were convinced that they would never commit the blunders and iniquities of the Congress of Vienna [of 1815]." Then the "misguided, reactionary, pathetic aristocrats" had cynically shuffled populations; now "we believed in nationalism, we believed in the self-determination of peoples." Indeed, "we were journeying to Paris . . . to found a new order in Europe. We were preparing not Peace only, but Eternal Peace."[14] The general optimism and idealism had been greatly strengthened by President Wilson's January 1918 peace proposal, the Fourteen Points, which stressed national self-determination and the rights of small countries.

The real powers at the conference were the United States, Great Britain, and France, for Germany was not allowed to participate, and Russia was locked in civil war and did not attend. Italy was considered part of the Big Four, but its role was quite secondary. Almost immediately the three great allies began to quarrel. President Wilson, who was wildly cheered by European crowds as the spokesman for a new idealistic and democratic international cooperation, was almost obsessed with creating a League of Nations. Wilson insisted that this question come first, for he passionately believed that only a permanent international organization could protect member states from aggression and avert future wars. Wilson had his way, although Lloyd George of Great Britain and especially Clemenceau of France were unenthusiastic. They were primarily concerned with punishing Germany.

Playing on British nationalism, Lloyd George had already won a smashing electoral victory in December on the popular platform of making Germany pay for the war. "We shall," he promised, "squeeze the orange until the pips squeak." Personally inclined to make a somewhat moderate peace with Germany, Lloyd George was to a considerable extent a captive of demands for a total victory worthy of the sacrifices of total war against a totally depraved enemy. As Rudyard Kipling summed up the general British feeling at the end of the war, the Germans were "a people with the heart of beasts."[15]

France's Georges Clemenceau, "the Tiger" who had broken wartime defeatism and led his country to victory, wholeheartedly agreed. Like most French people, Clemenceau wanted old-fashioned revenge. He also wanted lasting security for France. This, he believed, required the creation of a buffer state between France and Germany, the permanent demilitarization of Germany, and vast German reparations. He feared that sooner or later Germany with its 60 million people would attack France with its 40 million, unless the Germans were permanently weakened. Moreover, France had no English Channel (or Atlantic Ocean) as a reassuring barrier against German aggression. Wilson, supported by Lloyd George, would hear none of it. Clemenceau's demands seemed vindictive, violating morality and the principle of national self-determination. By April the conference was deadlocked on the German question, and Wilson packed his bags to go home.

Clemenceau's obsession with security reflected his anxiety about France's long-term weakness. In the end, convinced that France should not break with its allies because France could not afford to face Germany alone in the future, he agreed to a compromise. He gave up the French demand for a Rhineland buffer state in return for a formal defensive alliance with the United States and Great Britain. Under the terms of this alliance, both Wilson and Lloyd George promised that their countries would come to France's aid in the event of a German attack. Thus Clemenceau appeared to win his goal of French security, as Wilson had won his of a permanent international organization. The Allies moved quickly to finish the peace settlement, believing that necessary adjustments would later be possible within the dual framework of a strong Western alliance and the League of Nations (see Map 27.4).

The Treaty of Versailles between the Allies and Germany was the key to the settlement, and the terms were not unreasonable as a first step toward reestablishing international order. (Had Germany won, it seems certain that France and Belgium would have been treated with greater severity, as Russia had been at Brest-Litovsk.) Germany's colonies were given to France, Britain, and Japan as League of Nations mandates. Germany's territorial losses within Europe were minor, thanks to Wilson. Alsace-Lorraine was returned to France. Parts of Germany inhabited primarily by Poles were ceded to the new Polish state, in keeping with the principle of national self-determination. Predominantly German Danzig was also placed within the Polish tariff lines, but as a self-governing city under League of Nations protection. Germany had to limit its army to 100,000 men and agree to build no military fortifications in the Rhineland.

More harshly, the Allies declared that Germany (with Austria) was responsible for the war and had therefore to pay reparations equal to all civilian damages caused by the war. This unfortunate and much-criticized clause expressed inescapable popular demands for German blood, but the actual figure was not set and there was the clear possibility that reparations might be set at a reasonable level in the future, when tempers had cooled.

When presented with the treaty, the German government protested vigorously. But there was no alternative, especially in that Germany was still starving

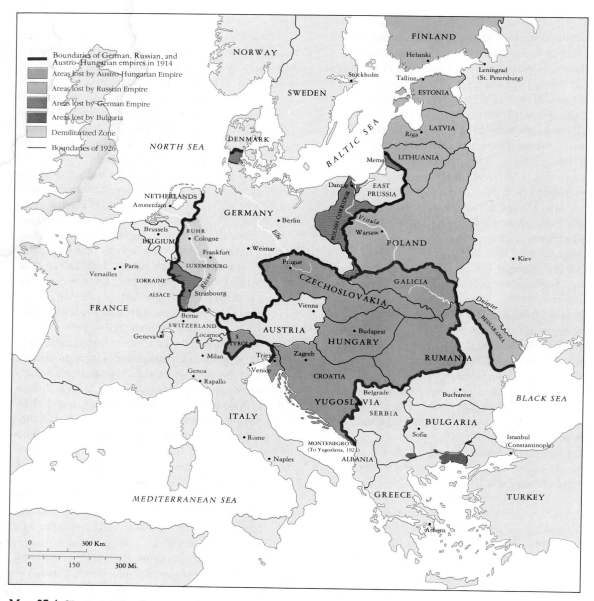

MAP 27.4 Shattered Empires and Territorial Changes After World War One The Great War brought tremendous changes in eastern Europe. New nations were established, and a dangerous power vacuum was created between Germany and Soviet Russia.

Map legend:
- Boundaries of German, Russian, and Austro-Hungarian empires in 1914
- Areas lost by Austro-Hungarian Empire
- Areas lost by Russian Empire
- Areas lost by German Empire
- Areas lost by Bulgaria
- Demilitarized Zone
- Boundaries of 1926

because the Allies had not yet lifted their naval blockade. On June 28, 1919, German representatives of the ruling moderate Social Democrats and the Catholic party signed the treaty in the Sun King's Hall of Mirrors at Versailles, where Bismarck's empire had been joyously proclaimed almost fifty years before.

Separate peace treaties were concluded with the other defeated powers—Austria, Hungary, Bulgaria, and Turkey. For the most part, these treaties merely ratified the existing situation in east central Europe following the breakup of the Austro-Hungarian Empire. Like Austria, Hungary was a particularly big loser, as its "captive" nationalities (and some interspersed Hungarians) were ceded to Rumania, Czechoslovakia, Poland, and Yugoslavia. Italy got some Austrian territory. The Turkish empire was broken up. France received Lebanon and Syria, while Britain took Iraq and Palestine, which was to include a Jewish national homeland first promised by Britain in 1917. Officially League of Nations mandates, these acquisitions of the Western powers were one of the more imperialistic elements of the peace settlement. Another was mandating Germany's holdings in China to Japan. The age of Western imperialism lived on. National self-determination remained a reality only for Europeans and their offspring.

AMERICAN REJECTION OF THE VERSAILLES TREATY

The rapidly concluded peace settlement of early 1919 was not perfect, but within the context of war-shattered Europe it was an acceptable beginning. The principle of national self-determination, which had played such a large role in starting the war, was accepted and served as an organizing framework. Germany had been punished but not dismembered. A new world organization complemented a traditional defensive alliance of satisfied powers. The serious remaining problems could be worked out in the future. Moreover, Allied leaders had seen speed as essential for another reason: they detested Lenin and feared that his Bolshevik Revolution might spread. They realized that their best answer to Lenin's unending calls for worldwide upheaval was peace and tranquillity for war-weary peoples.

There were, however, two great interrelated obstacles to such peace: Germany and the United States. Plagued by communist uprisings, reactionary plots, and popular disillusionment with losing the war at the last minute, Germany's moderate socialists and their liberal and Catholic supporters faced an enormous challenge. Like French republicans after 1871, they needed time (and luck) if they were to establish firmly a peaceful and democratic republic. Progress in this direction required understanding yet firm treatment of Germany by the victorious Western Allies, and particularly by the United States.

However, the United States Senate and, to a lesser extent, the American people rejected Wilson's handiwork. Republican senators led by Henry Cabot Lodge refused to ratify the Treaty of Versailles without changes in the articles creating the League of Nations. The key issue was the league's power—more apparent than real—to require member states to take collective action against aggression.

Lodge and others believed that this requirement gave away Congress's constitutional right to declare war. No doubt Wilson would have been wise to accept some reservations. But, in failing health, Wilson with narrow-minded self-righteousness rejected all attempts at compromise. He instructed loyal Democratic senators to vote against any reservations whatsoever to the Treaty of Versailles. In doing so, Wilson assured that the treaty was never ratified by the United States in any form and that the United States never joined the League of Nations. Moreover, the Senate refused to ratify Wilson's defensive alliance with France and Great Britain. America turned its back on Europe.

Perhaps understandable in the light of American traditions and the volatility of mass politics, the Wilson-Lodge fiasco and the new-found gospel of isolationism nevertheless represented a tragic and cowardly renunciation of America's responsibility. Using America's action as an excuse, Great Britain, too, refused to ratify its defensive alliance with France. Bitterly betrayed by its allies, France stood alone. Very shortly, France was to take actions against Germany that would feed the fires of German resentment and seriously undermine democratic forces in the new republic. The great hopes of early 1919 were turning to ashes by the end of the year. The Western alliance had collapsed, and a grandiose plan for permanent peace had given way to a fragile truce. For this and for what came later, the United States must share a large part of the guilt.

Why did World War One have such revolutionary consequences? Why was it such a great break with the past? World War One was, first of all, a war of committed peoples. In France, Britain, and Germany in particular, governments drew on genuine popular support. This support reflected not only the diplomatic origins of the war but also the way western European society had been effectively unified under the nationalist banner in the later nineteenth century. The relentlessness of total war helps explain why so many died, why so many were crippled physically and psychologically, and why Western civilization would in so many ways never be the same again. More concretely, the war swept away monarchs and multinational empires. National self-determination apparently triumphed, not only in Austria-Hungary but in much of Russia's western borderlands as well. Except in Ireland and parts of Soviet Russia, the revolutionary dream of national unity, born of the French Revolution, had finally come true.

Two other revolutions were products of the war. In Russia, the Bolsheviks established a radical regime, smashed existing capitalist institutions, and stayed in power with a new kind of authoritarian rule. Whether the new Russian regime was truly Marxian or socialist was questionable, but it indisputably posed a powerful, ongoing revolutionary challenge in Europe and Europe's colonial empires.

More subtle, but quite universal in its impact, was an administrative revolution. This revolution, born of the need to mobilize entire societies and economies for total war, greatly increased the power of government. And after the guns grew still, government planning and wholesale involvement in economic and social life did not disappear in Europe. Liberal market capitalism and a well-integrated world economy were among the many casualties of the administrative revolution, and greater social equality was everywhere one of its results. Thus, even in European countries where a communist takeover never came close to occurring, society still experienced a great revolution.

Finally, the "war to end war" did not bring peace but only a fragile truce: in the West the Allies failed to maintain their wartime solidarity. Germany remained unrepentant and would soon have more grievances to nurse. Moreover, the victory of national self-determination in eastern Europe created a power vacuum between a still-powerful Germany and a potentially mighty communist Russia. A vast area lay open to military aggression from two sides.

NOTES

1. M. Beloff, *U.S. News and World Report,* March 8, 1976, p. 53.
2. Quoted by J. Remak, *The Origins of World War I,* Holt, Rinehart & Winston, New York, 1967, p. 84.
3. Quoted by W. E. Mosse, *Alexander II and the Modernization of Russia,* Collier Books, New York, 1962, pp. 125–126.
4. Quoted by Remak, p. 123.
5. Quoted by J. E. Rodes, *The Quest for Unity: Modern Germany 1848–1970,* Holt, Rinehart & Winston, New York, 1971, p. 178.
6. Quoted by F. P. Chambers, *The War Behind the War, 1914–1918,* Faber & Faber, London, 1939, p. 444.
7. Ibid., p. 168.
8. Quoted by R. O. Paxton, *Europe in the Twentieth Century,* Harcourt Brace Jovanovich, New York, 1975, p. 109.
9. Quoted by Chambers, p. 378.
10. Ibid., . 110.
11. Ibid., pp. 302, 304.
12. A. B. Ulam, *The Bolsheviks,* Collier Books, New York, 1968, p. 349.
13. Ibid., p. 405.
14. H. Nicolson, *Peacemaking 1919,* Grosset & Dunlap Universal Library, New York, 1965, pp. 8, 31–32.
15. Ibid., p. 24.

SUGGESTED READING

O. Hale, *The Great Illusion, 1900–1914* (1971), is a thorough account of the prewar era. Both J. Remak, *The Origins of World War I* (1967), and L. Lafore, *The Long Fuse* (1971), are highly recommended studies of the causes of the First World War. A. J. P. Taylor, *The Struggle for Mastery in Europe, 1848–1919* (1954), is an outstanding survey of diplomatic developments with an exhaustive bibliography. V. Steiner, *Britain and the Origins of the First World War* (1978), and G. Kennan, *The Decline of Bismarck's European Order: Franco-Russian Relations, 1875–1890* (1979), are also major contributions. K. Jarausch's *The Enigmatic Chancellor* (1973) is an important recent study on Bethmann-Hollweg and German policy in 1914. C. Falls, *The Great War* (1961), is the best brief introduction to military aspects of the war. B. Tuchman, *The Guns of August* (1962), is a marvelous account of the dramatic first month of the war and the beginning of military stalemate. G. Ritter provides an able study in *The Schlieffen Plan* (1958). A. J. P. Taylor, *The First World War* (1963), is a strikingly illustrated history of the war, and A. Horne, *The Price of Glory: Verdun 1916* (1979), is a moving account of the famous siege. J. Ellis, *Eye-Deep in Hell* (1976), is a vivid account of trench warfare.

F. L. Carsten, *War Against War* (1982), considers radical movements in Britain and Germany. The best single volume on the home fronts is still F. Chambers, *The War Behind the War, 1914–1918* (1939). Chambers drew heavily on the many fine books on the social and economic impact of the war in different countries published by the Carnegie Endowment for International Peace under the general editorship of J. T. Shotwell. A Marwick, *The Deluge* (1970), is a lively account of war and society in Britain, while G. Feldman, *Army, Industry, and Labor in Germany, 1914–1918* (1966), shows the impact of total war and military dictatorship on Germany. Two excellent collections of essays, J. Roth, ed., *World War I* (1967), and R. Albrecht-Carrié, ed., *The Meaning of the First World War* (1965), deftly probe the enormous consequences of the war for people and society. The debate over Germany's guilt and aggression, which has been reopened in recent years, may be best approached through G. Feldman, ed., *German Imperialism, 1914–1918* (1972), and A. Hillgruber, *Germany and the Two World Wars* (1981). M. Fainsod, *International Socialism and the World War* (1935), ably discusses the splits between radical and moderate socialists during the conflict. In addition to Erich Maria Remarque's great novel *All Quiet on the Western Front,* Henri Barbusse, *Under Fire* (1917), and Jules Romains, *Verdun* (1939), are highly recommended for their fictional yet realistic recreations of the war. P. Fussell, *The Great War and Modern Memory* (1975), probes all the powerful literature inspired by the war.

A. Ulam's *The Bolsheviks* (1968), which focuses on Lenin, is a masterful introduction to the Russian Revolution, as is B. Wolfe, *Three Who Made a Revolution* (1955), a collective biography of Lenin, Trotsky, and Stalin. R. Conquest, *V. I. Lenin* (1972), is a good short biography. Leon Trotsky himself wrote the colorful and exciting *History of the Russian Revolution* (1932), which may be compared with the classic eyewitness account of the young, pro-Bolshevik American John Reed, *Ten Days That Shook the World* (1919). R. Daniels, *Red October* (1969), provides a clear account of the Bolshevik seizure of power, and R. Pipes, *The Formation of the Soviet Union* (1968), is recommended for its excellent treatment of the nationality problem during the revolution. A. Wildman, *The End of the Russian Imperial Army* (1980), is a fine account of the soldiers' revolt, and G. Leggett, *The Cheka: Lenin's Secret Police* (1981), shows revolutionary terror in action. Boris Pasternak's justly celebrated *Doctor Zhivago* is a great historical novel of the revolutionary era. R. Massie, *Nicholas and Alexandra* (1971), is a moving popular biography of Russia's last royal family and the terrible health problem of the heir to the throne. H. Nicolson, *Peacemaking 1919* (1965), captures the spirit of the Versailles settlement. T. Bailey, *Woodrow Wilson and the Lost Peace* (1963), and W. Widenor, *Henry Cabot Lodge and the Search for an American Foreign Policy* (1981), are also highly recommended. A. Mayer provocatively stresses the influence of domestic social tensions and widespread fear of further communist revolt in *The Politics and Diplomacy of Peacemaking* (1969).

28

THE AGE OF ANXIETY

**W**HEN ALLIED DIPLOMATS met in Paris in early 1919 with their optimistic plans for building a lasting peace, most people looked forward to happier times. They hoped that life would return to normal. They hoped that once again life would make sense in the familiar prewar terms of peace, prosperity, and progress. These hopes were in vain. The Great Break—the First World War and the Russian Revolution—had mangled too many things beyond repair. Life would no longer fit neatly into the old molds.

Instead, great numbers of men and women felt themselves increasingly adrift in a strange, uncertain, and uncontrollable world. They saw themselves living in an age of anxiety, an age of continuous crisis, which lasted until at least the early 1950s. In almost every area of human experience, people went searching for ways to put meaning back into life. What did the doubts and searching mean for Western thought, art, and culture? How did political leaders try to reestablish real peace and prosperity between 1919 and 1939? And why did they fail? These are questions this chapter will explore.

UNCERTAINTY IN MODERN THOUGHT

A complex revolution in thought and ideas was under way before the First World War, but only small, unusual groups were aware of it. After the war, new and upsetting ideas began to spread through the entire population. Western society began to question and even abandon many cherished values and beliefs that had guided it since the eighteenth-century Enlightenment and the nineteenth-century triumph of industrial development, scientific advances, and evolutionary thought.

Before 1914 most people still believed in progress, reason, and the rights of the individual. Progress was a daily reality, apparent in the rising standard of living, the taming of the city, and the steady increase in popular education. Such developments also encouraged the comforting belief in the logical universe of Newtonian physics, as well as faith in the ability of a rational human mind to understand that universe through intellectual investigation. And just as there were laws of science, so were there laws of society that rational human beings could discover and then wisely act on. Finally, the rights of the individual were not just taken for granted, they were actually increasing. Well-established rights were gradually spreading to women and workers, and new "social rights" like old-age pensions were emerging. In short, before World War One, most Europeans had a moderately optimistic view of the world, and with good reason.

From the 1880s on, however, a small band of serious thinkers and creative writers began to attack these well-worn optimistic ideas. These critics rejected the general faith in progress and the power of the rational human mind. One of the most influential of them was the German philosopher Friedrich Nietzsche (1844–1900).

Nietzsche believed that Western civilization had lost its creativity and decayed into mediocrity. Christianity's "slave morality" had glorified weakness and humility. Furthermore, human beings in the West had overstressed rational thinking at the expense of passion and emotion. Nietzsche viewed the pillars of conventional morality—reason, democracy, progress, respectability—as outworn social and psychological constructs whose influence was suffocating creativity. The only hope of revival was for a few superior individuals to free themselves from the humdrum thinking of the masses and embrace life passionately. Such individuals would become true heroes, supermen capable of leading the dumb herd of inferior men and women. Nietzsche also condemned both political democracy and greater social equality.

The growing dissatisfaction with established ideas before 1914 was apparent in other thinkers. In the 1890s, the French philosophy professor Henri Bergson (1859–1941) convinced many young people through his writing that immediate experience and intuition are as important as rational and scientific thinking for understanding reality. Indeed, according to Bergson, a religious experience or a mystical poem is often more accessible to human comprehension than a scientific law or a mathematical equation.

Another thinker who agreed about the limits of rational thinking was the French socialist Georges Sorel (1847–1922). Sorel frankly characterized

Marxian socialism as an inspiring but unprovable religion rather than a rational scientific truth. Socialism would come to power, he believed, through a great, violent strike of all working people, which would miraculously shatter capitalist society. Sorel rejected democracy and believed that the masses of the new socialist society would have to be tightly controlled by a small revolutionary elite.

In the years after 1918, a growing chorus of thinkers, creative writers, and scientists echoed and enlarged on the themes first expressed by the small band of critics between 1880 and 1914. Many prophets of doom bore witness to the decline and decay of Western civilization. The experience of history's most destructive war suggested to many that human beings certainly were a pack of violent, irrational animals quite capable of tearing the individual and his or her rights to shreds. There was growing pessimism and a general crisis of the mind. People did not know what to think. This disorientation was particularly acute in the 1930s, when the rapid rise of harsh dictatorships and the Great Depression transformed old certainties into bitter illusions.

No one expressed this state of uncertainty better than the French poet and critic Paul Valéry (1871–1945) in the early 1920s. Speaking of the "crisis of the mind," Valéry noted that Europe was looking at its future with dark foreboding:

The storm has died away, and still we are restless, uneasy, as if the storm were about to break. Almost all the affairs of men remain in a terrible uncertainty. We think of what has disappeared, and we are almost destroyed by what has been destroyed; we do not know what will be born, and we fear the future, not without reason. . . . Doubt and disorder are in us and with us. There is no thinking man, however shrewd or learned he may be, who can hope to dominate this anxiety, to escape from this impression of darkness. [1]

In the midst of economic, political, and social disruptions Valéry saw the "cruelly injured mind," besieged by doubts and suffering from anxieties. This was the general intellectual crisis of the twentieth century, which touched almost every field of thought. The implications of new discoveries and ideas in physics, psychology, philosophy, and literature played a central role in this crisis, disturbing "thinking people" everywhere.

THE NEW PHYSICS

Ever since the scientific revolution of the seventeenth century, scientific advances and their implications have greatly influenced the beliefs of thinking people. By the late nineteenth century, science was one of the main pillars supporting Western society's optimistic and rationalistic view of the world. The Darwinian concept of evolution had been accepted and assimilated in most intellectual circles. Progressive minds believed that science, unlike religion and philosophical speculation, was based on hard facts and controlled experiments. Science seemed to have achieved an unerring and almost completed picture of reality. Unchanging natural laws seemed to determine physical processes and permit useful solutions to more and more problems. All this was comforting, especially to people who were no longer committed to traditional religious beliefs. And all this was challenged by the new physics.

An important first step toward the new physics was the discovery at the end of the century that atoms were not like hard, permanent little billiard balls. They were actually composed of many far smaller, fast-moving particles, such as electrons and protons. The Polish-born physicist Marie Curie (1867–1934) and her French husband discovered that radium constantly emits subatomic particles and thus does not have a constant atomic weight. Building on this and other work in radiation, the German physicist Max Planck (1858–1947) showed in 1900 that subatomic energy is emitted in uneven little spurts, which Planck called "quanta," and not in a steady stream as previously believed. Planck's discovery called into question the old sharp distinction between matter and energy; the implication was that matter and energy might be different forms of the same thing. The old view of atoms as the stable, basic building blocks of nature, with a different kind of unbreakable atom for each of the ninety-two chemical elements, was badly shaken.

In 1905 the German-born Jewish genius Albert Einstein (1879–1955) went further than the Curies and Planck in challenging Newtonian physics. His famous theory of special relativity postulated that time and space are not absolute, but relative to the viewpoint of the observer. To clarify Einstein's idea, consider a person riding on a train. From the viewpoint of an observer outside the train, the passenger's

"The War, as I Saw It" This was the title of a series of grotesque drawings that appeared in 1920 in *Simplicissimus,* Germany's leading satirical magazine. Nothing shows better the terrible impact of World War One than this profoundly disturbing example of expressionist art. *(Photo: Caroline Buckler)*

net speed is exactly the same whether the passenger is walking or sitting. From the passenger's viewpoint, walking to the restaurant car is different from sitting in a seat. The closed framework of Newtonian physics was quite limited compared to that of Einsteinian physics, which unified an apparently infinite universe with the incredibly small, fast-moving subatomic world. Moreover, Einstein's theory stated clearly that matter and energy are interchangeable and that all matter contains enormous levels of potential energy.

The 1920s opened the "heroic age of physics," in the apt words of one of its leading pioneers, Ernest Rutherford (1871–1937). Breakthrough followed breakthrough. In 1919 Rutherford showed that the atom could be split. By 1944 seven subatomic particles had been identified, of which the most important was the neutron. The neutron's capacity to pass through other atoms allowed for even more intense experimental bombardment of matter, leading to chain reactions of unbelievable force. This was the road to the atomic bomb.

Although few nonscientists understood the revolution in physics, the implications of the new theories and discoveries, as presented by newspapers and popular writers, were disturbing to millions of men and women in the 1920s and 1930s. The new universe was strange and troubling. It lacked any absolute objective reality. Everything was "relative," that is, dependent on the observer's frame of reference. Moreover, the universe was uncertain and undetermined, without stable building blocks. In 1927 the German physicist Werner Heisenberg (1901–1976) formulated the "principle of uncertainty." Heisenberg's principle postulates that, because it is impossible to know the position and speed of an individual electron, it is therefore impossible to predict its behavior. Instead of Newton's dependable, rational laws, there seemed to be only tendencies and probabilities in an extraordinarily complex and uncertain universe.

Moreover, a universe described by abstract mathematical symbols seemed to have little to do with human experience and human problems. When, for example, Max Planck was asked what science could contribute to resolving conflicts of values, his response was simple: "Science is not qualified to speak to this question." Physics, the queen of the sciences, no longer provided people easy, optimistic answers— or, for that matter, any answers at all.

FREUDIAN PSYCHOLOGY

With physics presenting an uncertain universe so unrelated to ordinary human experience, questions regarding the power and potential of the human mind assumed special significance. The findings and speculations of the leading psychologist, Sigmund Freud (page 786), were particularly disturbing.

Before Freud, poets and mystics had probed the unconscious and irrational aspects of human behavior. But most professional, "scientific" psychologists assumed that a single, unified conscious mind processed sense experiences in a rational and logical way. Human behavior in turn was the result of rational calculation—of "thinking"—by the conscious mind. Basing his insights on the analysis of dreams and of hysteria, Freud developed a very different view of the human psyche beginning in the late 1880s.

According to Freud, human behavior is basically irrational. The key to understanding the mind is the primitive irrational unconscious, which he called the id. The unconscious is driven by sexual, aggressive, and pleasure-seeking desires and is locked in a constant battle with the other parts of the mind: the rationalizing conscious (the ego), which mediates what a person *can* do, and ingrained moral values (the superego), which tell what a person *should* do. Human behavior is a product of fragile compromise between instinctual drives and the controls of rational thinking and moral values. Since the instinctual drives are extremely powerful, the ever-present danger for individuals and whole societies is that unacknowledged drives will overwhelm the control mechanisms in a violent, distorted way. Yet Freud also agreed with Nietzsche that the mechanisms of rational thinking and traditional moral values can be too strong. They can repress sexual desires too effectively, crippling individuals and entire peoples with guilt and neurotic fears.

Freudian psychology and clinical psychiatry had become an international movement by 1910, but only after 1918 did they receive popular attention, especially in the Protestant countries of northern Europe and in the United States. Many opponents and even some enthusiasts interpreted Freud as saying that the first requirement for mental health is an uninhibited sex life. Thus, after the First World War, the popular interpretation of Freud reflected and en-

Freud's Consulting Room in Vienna Freud developed his theories as a therapist while treating mental disorders. He sat in the armchair on the left. His patients lay on the couch and gazed away from him, in part because Freud could not bear being watched all day long. *(Photograph by Edmund Engelman)*

couraged growing sexual experimentation, particularly among middle-class women. For more serious students, the psychology of Freud and his followers drastically undermined the old, easy optimism about the rational and progressive nature of the human mind.

PHILOSOPHY: LOGICAL EMPIRICISM AND EXISTENTIALISM

The intellectual crisis of the twentieth century was fully reflected in philosophy, but in two very different ways. In English-speaking countries, the main development was the acceptance of logical empiricism (or logical positivism) in university circles. In continental countries, where esoteric and remote logical empiricism has never won many converts, the primary development in philosophy was existentialism.

Logical empiricism was truly revolutionary. It quite simply rejected most of the concerns of traditional philosophy, from the existence of God to the meaning of happiness, as nonsense and hot air. This outlook began primarily with the Austrian philosopher Ludwig Wittgenstein (1889–1951), who later emigrated to England, where he trained numerous disciples.

Wittgenstein argued in his pugnacious *Tractatus Logico-Philosophicus (Essay on Logical Philosophy)* in 1922 that philosophy is only the logical clarification of thoughts, and therefore the study of language, which expresses thoughts. The great philosophical issues of the ages—God, freedom, morality, and so on—are quite literally senseless, a great waste of time, for statements about them can neither be tested by scientific experiments nor demonstrated by the logic of mathematics. Statements about such matters reflect only the personal preferences of a given individual. As Wittgenstein put it in the famous last sentence of his work: "Of what one cannot speak, of that one must keep silent." Logical empiricism, which has remained dominant in England and the United States to this day, drastically reduced the scope of philosophical inquiry. Anxious people could find few if any answers in this direction.

Highly diverse and even contradictory, *existential* thinkers were loosely united in a courageous search for moral values in a world of terror and uncertainty. Theirs were true voices of the age of anxiety.

Most existential thinkers in the twentieth century have been atheists. Like Nietzsche, who had already proclaimed that "God is dead," they did not believe a supreme being had established humanity's fundamental nature and given life its meaning. In the words of the famous French existentialist Jean-Paul Sartre (1905–1980), human beings simply exist: "They turn up, appear on the scene." Only after they "turn up" do they seek to define themselves. Honest human beings are terribly alone, for there is no God to help them. They are hounded by despair and the meaninglessness of life. The crisis of the existential thinker epitomized the modern intellectual crisis—the shattering of traditional beliefs in God, reason, and progress.

Existentialists did recognize that human beings, unless they kill themselves, must act. Indeed, in the words of Sartre, "man is condemned to be free." There is, therefore, the possibility—indeed, the necessity—of giving meaning to life through actions, of defining oneself through choices. To do so, individuals must become "engaged" and choose their own actions courageously, consistently, and in full awareness of their inescapable responsibility for their own behavior. In the end, existentialists argued, human beings can overcome the absurdity that existentialists saw in life.

Modern existentialism developed first in Germany in the 1920s , when the philosophers Martin Heidegger and Carl Jaspers found a sympathetic audience among disillusioned postwar university students. But it was in France during the years immediately after World War Two that existentialism came of age. The terrible conditions of the war reinforced the existential view of life and the existential approach to it. On the one hand, the armies of the German dictator Hitler had conquered most of Europe and unleashed a hideous reign of barbarism. On the other, men and women had more than ever to define themselves by their actions. Specifically, each individual had to choose whether to join the Resistance against Hitler or to accept and even abet tyranny. The writings of Sartre, who along with Albert Camus (1913–1960), was the leading French existentialist and himself active in the Resistance, became enormously influential. He and his colleagues offered a powerful answer to profound moral issues and the contemporary crisis.

THE REVIVAL OF CHRISTIANITY

Christianity and religion in general had been on the defensive in intellectual circles since the Enlightenment, especially during the late nineteenth century. The loss of faith in human reason and in continual progress now led to a renewed interest in the Christian view of the world in the twentieth century. A number of thinkers and theologians began to revitalize the fundamentals of Christianity, especially after World War One. They had a powerful impact on society. Sometimes described as Christian existentialists because they shared the loneliness and despair of atheistic existentialists, they revived the tradition of Saint Augustine. They stressed human beings' sinful nature, the need for faith, and the mystery of God's forgiveness.

This development was a break with the late nineteenth century. In the years before 1914, some theologians, especially Protestant theologians, had felt the need to interpret Christian doctrine and the Bible so that they did not seem to contradict science, evolution, and common sense. Christ was therefore seen primarily as the greatest moral teacher, and the "supernatural" aspects of his divinity were strenuously played down. An important if extreme example of this tendency was the young Albert Schweitzer's *Quest of the Historical Jesus* (1906). A theologian and later a famous medical missionary and musician of note, Schweitzer (1875–1965) argued that Christ while on earth was a completely natural man whose teachings had been only temporary rules to prepare himself and his disciples for the end of the world, which they were erroneously expecting. In short, some modern theologians were embarrassed by the miraculous, unscientific aspects of Christianity and turned away from them.

The revival of fundamental Christian belief after World War One was fed by rediscovery of the work of the nineteenth-century Danish religious philosopher Søren Kierkegaard (1813–1855), whose ideas became extremely influential. Kierkegaard had rejected formalistic religion and denounced the worldliness of the Danish Lutheran church. He had eventually resolved his personal anguish over his imperfect nature by making a total religious commitment to a remote and majestic God.

Similar ideas were brilliantly developed by the Swiss Protestant theologian Karl Barth (1886–1968), whose many influential writings after 1920 sought to re-create the religious intensity of the Reformation. For Barth, the basic fact about human beings is that they are imperfect, sinful creatures, whose reason and will are hopelessly flawed. Religious truth is therefore made known to human beings only through God's grace. People have to accept God's word and the supernatural revelation of Jesus Christ with awe, trust, and obedience. Lowly mortals should not expect to "reason out" God and his ways.

Among Catholics, the leading existential Christian thinker was Gabriel Marcel (1889–1973). Born into a cultivated French family, where his atheistic father was "gratefully aware of all that . . . art owed to Catholicism but regarded Catholic thought itself as obsolete and tainted with absurd superstitions,"[2] Marcel found in the Catholic church an answer to what he called the postwar "broken world." Catholicism and religious belief provided the hope, humanity, honesty, and piety for which he hungered. Flexible and gentle, Marcel and his countryman Jacques Maritain (1882–1973) denounced anti-Semitism and supported closer ties with non-Catholics.

After 1914 religion became much more relevant and meaningful to thinking people than it was before the war. In addition to Marcel and Maritain, many other illustrious individuals turned to religion between about 1920 and 1950. The poets T. S. Eliot and W. H. Auden, the novelists Evelyn Waugh and Aldous Huxley, the historian Arnold Toynbee, the Oxford professor C. S. Lewis, the psychoanalyst Karl Stern, and the physicist Max Planck were all either converted to religion or attracted to it for the first time. Religion, often of a despairing, existential variety, was one meaningful answer to terror and anxiety. As another famous Roman Catholic convert, English novelist Graham Greene, wrote: "One began to believe in heaven because one believed in hell."[3]

Twentieth-Century Literature

Literature articulated the general intellectual climate of pessimism, relativism, and alienation. Novelists developed new techniques to express new realities. The great nineteenth-century novelists had typically written as all-knowing narrators, describing realistic characters and their relationship to an understandable if sometimes harsh society. In the twentieth century, most major writers adopted the limited, often confused viewpoint of a single individual. Like Freud, these novelists focused their attention on the complexity and irrationality of the human mind, where feelings, memories, and desires are forever scrambled. The great French novelist Marcel Proust (1871–1922), in his semi-autobiographical *Remembrance of Things Past* (1913–1922), recalled bittersweet memories of childhood and youthful love and tried to discover their innermost meaning. To do so, Proust lived like a hermit in a soundproof Paris apartment for ten years, withdrawing from the present to dwell on the past.

Serious novelists also used the "stream-of-consciousness" technique to explore the psyche. In *Jacob's Room* (1922), Virginia Woolf (1882–1941) turned the novel into a series of internal monologues, in which ideas and emotions from different periods of time bubble up as randomly as from a patient on a psychoanalyst's couch. William Faulkner (1897–1963), perhaps America's greatest twentieth-century novelist, used the same technique in *The Sound and the Fury*, much of whose intense drama is confusedly seen through the eyes of an idiot. The most famous stream-of-consciousness novel—and surely the most disturbing novel of its generations—is *Ulysses*, which the Irish novelist James Joyce (1882–1941) published in 1922. Into *Ulysses'* account of an ordinary day in the life of an ordinary man, Joyce weaves an extended ironic parallel between his hero's aimless wanderings through the streets and pubs of Dublin and the adventures of Homer's hero Ulysses on his way home from Troy. Abandoning conventional grammar and blending foreign words, puns, bits of knowledge, and scraps of memory together in bewildering confusion, the language of *Ulysses* is intended to mirror modern life itself: a gigantic riddle waiting to be unraveled.

As creative writers turned their attention from society to the individual and from realism to psychological relativity, they rejected the idea of progress.

Some even described "anti-utopias," nightmare visions of things to come. In 1918 an obscure German high school teacher named Oswald Spengler (1880–1936) published *Decline of the West,* which quickly became an international sensation. According to Spengler, every culture experiences a life cycle of growth and decline. Western civilization, in Spengler's opinion, was in its old age, and death was approaching in the form of conquest by the yellow race. T. S. Eliot (1888–1965), in his famous poem *The Waste Land* (1922), depicted a world of growing desolation, although after his conversion to Anglo-Catholicism in 1927, Eliot came to hope cautiously for humanity's salvation. No such hope appeared in the work of Franz Kafka (1883–1924), whose novels *The Trial* and *The Castle,* as well as several of his greatest short stories, portray helpless individuals crushed by inexplicably hostile forces. The German-Jewish Kafka died young, at forty-one, and so did not see the world of his nightmares materialize in the Nazi state.

The Englishman George Orwell (1903–1950), however, had seen both that reality and its Stalinist counterpart by 1949 when he wrote perhaps the ultimate in anti-utopian literature: *1984.* The action is set in the future, in 1984. Big Brother—the dictator—and his totalitarian state use a new kind of language, sophisticated technology, and psychological terror to strip a weak individual of his last shred of human dignity. As the supremely self-confident chief of the Thought Police tells the tortured, broken, and framed Winston Smith: "If you want a picture of the future, imagine a boot stamping on a human face—forever."[4] A phenomenal best-seller, *1984* spoke to millions of people in the closing years of the age of anxiety.

MODERN ART AND MUSIC

Throughout the twentieth century, there has been considerable unity in the arts. The "modernism" of the immediate prewar years and the 1920s is still strikingly modern. Manifestations of modernism in art, architecture, and music have of course been highly varied, just as in physics, psychology, and philosophy; yet there are resemblances, for artists, scientists, and original thinkers partake of the same culture. Creative artists rejected old forms and old

Virginia Woolf grew up in a famous literary family to become a leading member of England's intellectual aristocracy. Her novels captured sensations like impressionist paintings, and her home attracted a circle of artists and writers known as the Bloomsbury Group. *(BBC Hulton/The Bettmann Archive)*

values. Modernism in art and music meant constant experimentation and a search for new kinds of expression. And though many people find the modern visions of the arts strange, disturbing, and even ugly, the twentieth century, so dismal in many respects, will probably stand as one of Western civilization's great artistic eras.

ARCHITECTURE AND DESIGN

Modernism in the arts was loosely unified by a revolution in architecture. The architectural revolution not only gave the other arts striking new settings, it intended nothing less than to transform the physical framework of the urban society according to a new

Frank Lloyd Wright: The "Falling Water" House Often considered Wright's masterpiece, Falling Water combines modern architectural concepts with close attention to a spectacular site. Anchored to a high rock ledge by means of reinforced concrete, the house soars out over a cascading waterfall at Bear Run in western Pennsylvania. Built in 1937 for a Pittsburgh businessman, Falling Water is now open to the public and attracts 70,000 visitors each year. *(Art Resource)*

principle: *functionalism.* Buildings, like industrial products, should be useful and "functional": that is, they should serve, as well as possible, the purpose for which they were made. Thus, architects and designers had to work with engineers, town planners, and even sanitation experts. Moreover, they had to throw away useless ornamentation and find beauty and aesthetic pleasure in the clean lines of practical constructions and efficient machinery. The Viennese pioneer Adolf Loos (1870–1933) quite typically equated ornamentation with crime, and the Franco-Swiss genius Le Corbusier (1887–1965) insisted that "a house is a machine for living in."[5]

The United States, with its rapid urban growth and lack of rigid building traditions, pioneered in the new architecture. In the 1890s, the Chicago school of ar-

chitects, led by Louis H. Sullivan (1856–1924), used cheap steel, reinforced concrete, and electric elevators to build skyscrapers and office buildings lacking almost any exterior ornamentation. In the first decade of the twentieth century, Sullivan's student Frank Lloyd Wright (1869–1959) built a series of radically new and truly modern houses featuring low lines, open interiors, and mass-produced building materials. Europeans were inspired by these efforts and by such other American examples of functional construction as the massive, unadorned grain elevators of the Midwest.

Around 1905, when the first really modern buildings were going up in Europe, architectural leadership shifted to the German-speaking countries and remained there until Hitler took power in 1933. In

1911 the twenty-eight-year-old Walter Gropius (1883–1969) broke sharply with the past in his design of the Fagus shoe factory at Alfeld, Germany. A clean, light, elegant building of glass and iron, Gropius's new factory represented a jump right into the middle of the century.

After the First World War, the new German republic gave Gropius the authority to merge the schools of fine and applied arts at Weimar into a single, interdisciplinary school, the Bauhaus. In spite of intense criticism from conservative politicians and university professors, the Bauhaus brought together many leading modern architects, artists, designers, and theatrical innovators, who worked as an effective, inspired team. Throwing out traditional teaching methods, they combined the study of fine art, such as painting and sculpture, with the study of applied art in the crafts of printing, weaving, and furniture making. Throughout the 1920s, the Bauhaus, with its stress on functionalism and good design for everyday life, attracted enthusiastic students from all over the world. It had a great and continuing impact.

Along with Gropius, the architect and town planner Le Corbusier had a revolutionary influence on the development of modern architecture. Often drawing his inspiration from industrial forms, such as ocean liners, automobiles, and airplanes, Le Corbusier designed houses with flat roofs, open interior spaces, and clear, clean lines. His famous Savoy Villa at Poissy rested on concrete pillars and seemed to float on air. A true visionary, Le Corbusier sketched plans for a city of the future, with tall buildings surrounded by playgrounds and parks.

Another leader in the modern or "international" style was Ludwig Mies van der Rohe (1886–1969), who followed Gropius as director of the Bauhaus in 1930 and emigrated to the United States in 1937. His classic Lake Shore Apartments in Chicago, built between 1948 and 1951, symbolize the triumph of steel-frame and glass-wall modern architecture, which had grown out of Sullivan's skyscrapers and German functionalism in the great building boom after the Second World War.

MODERN PAINTING

Modern painting grew out of a revolt against French impressionism (see Color Insert V). The *impressionism* of Monet, Renoir, and Pissarro was, in part, a kind of "superrealism." Leaving exact copying of objects to photography, these artists sought to capture the momentary overall feeling, or impression, of light falling on a real-life scene before their eyes. By 1890, when impressionism was finally established, a few artists known as *post-impressionists,* or *expressionists,* were already striking out in new directions. After 1905 art took on an abstract, nonrepresentational character, which it has generally retained to the present.

Though individualistic in their styles, post-impressionists were united in their desire to know and depict worlds other than the visible world of fact. Like the early nineteenth-century romantics, they wanted to portray unseen, inner worlds of emotion and imagination. Like modern novelists, they wanted to express a complicated psychological view of reality as well as an overwhelming emotional intensity. In *The Starry Night* (1889), for example, the great Dutch expressionist Vincent van Gogh (1853–1890) painted the vision of his mind's eye. Flaming cypress trees, exploding stars, and a cometlike Milky Way swirl together in one great cosmic rhythm (see Color Insert V). Paul Gauguin (1848–1903), the French stockbroker-turned-painter, pioneered in expressionist techniques, though he used them to infuse his work with tranquillity and mysticism. In 1891 he fled to the South Pacific in search of unspoiled beauty and a primitive way of life. Gauguin believed that the form and design of a picture was important in itself and that the painter need not try to represent objects on canvas as the eye actually saw them.

Fascination with form, as opposed to light, was characteristic of post-impressionism and expressionism (see Color Insert VI). Paul Cézanne (1839–1906), who had a profound influence on twentieth-century painting, was particularly committed to form and ordered design. He told a young painter, "You must see in nature the cylinder, the sphere, and the cone."[6] As Cézanne's later work became increasingly abstract and nonrepresentational, it also moved away from the traditional three-dimensional perspective toward the two-dimensional plane, which has characterized so much of modern art. The expressionism of a group of painters led by Henri Matisse (1869–1954) was so extreme that an exhibition of their work in Paris in 1905 prompted shocked critics to call them *les fauves* —"the wild beasts." Matisse and his followers were primarily concerned, not with real objects, but with the arrangement of color, line, and form as an end in itself.

Picasso: Guernica In this rich, complex work a shrieking woman falls from a burning house on the far right. On the left a woman holds a dead child, while toward the center are fragments of a warrior and a screaming horse pierced by a spear. Picasso has used only the mournful colors of black, white, and gray. *(Pablo Picasso, Guernica [1937, May–early June]. Oil on canvas. © SPADEM, Paris/VAGA, New York, 1982)*

In 1907 a young Spaniard in Paris, Pablo Picasso (1881–1973), founded another movement—cubism. Cubism concentrated on a complex geometry of zig-zagging lines and sharp-angled, overlapping planes. About three years later came the ultimate stage in the development of abstract, nonrepresentational art. Artists such as the Russian-born Wassily Kandinsky (1866–1944) turned away from nature completely. "The observer," said Kandinsky, "must learn to look at [my] pictures . . . as form and color combinations . . . as a representation of *mood* and not as a representation of *objects*." [7] On the eve of the First World War, extreme expressionism and abstract painting were developing rapidly not only in Paris but also in Russia and Germany. Modern art had become international.

In the 1920s and 1930s, the artistic movements of the prewar years were extended and consolidated. The most notable new developments were dadaism and surrealism. Dadaism attacked all accepted standards of art and behavior, delighting in outrageous conduct. Its name, from the French word *dada*, meaning "hobbyhorse," is deliberately nonsensical. A famous example of dadaism was a reproduction of Leonardo da Vinci's *Mona Lisa* in which the famous woman with the mysterious smile sports a mustache and is ridiculed with an obscene inscription. After 1924 many dadaists were attracted to surrealism, which became very influential in art in the late 1920s and 1930s. Surrealism was inspired to a great extent by Freudian psychology. Surrealists painted a fantastic world of wild dreams and complex symbols, where watches melted and giant metronomes beat time in precisely drawn but impossible alien landscapes.

Refusing to depict ordinary visual reality, surrealist painters made powerful statements about the age of anxiety. Picasso's twenty-six-foot-long mural *Guernica* (1937) masterfully unites several powerful strands in twentieth-century art. Inspired by the Spanish civil war, the painting commemorates the bombing of the ancient Spanish town of Guernica by fascist planes, an attack that took the lives of a thousand people—one out of every eight inhabitants—in a single night of terror. Combining the free distortion of expressionism, the overlapping planes of cubism, and the surrealist fascination with grotesque subject matter, *Guernica* is what Picasso meant it to be: an unforgettable attack on "brutality and darkness."

MODERN MUSIC

Developments in modern music were strikingly parallel to those in painting. Composers, too, were attracted by the emotional intensity of expressionism. The ballet *The Rite of Spring* by Igor Stravinsky (1882–1971) practically caused a riot when it was first performed in Paris in 1913 by Sergei Diaghilev's famous Russian dance company. The combination of pulsating, barbaric rhythms from the orchestra pit and an earthy representation of lovemaking by the dancers on the stage seemed a shocking, almost pornographic enactment of a primitive fertility rite.

After the experience of the First World War, when irrationality and violence seemed to pervade the human experience, expressionism in opera and ballet flourished. One of the most famous and powerful examples is the opera *Wozzeck* by Alban Berg (1885–1935), first performed in Berlin in 1925. Blending a half-sung, half-spoken kind of dialogue with harsh, atonal music, *Wozzeck* is a gruesome tale of a soldier driven by Kafka-like inner terrors and vague suspicions of unfaithfulness to murder his mistress.

Some composers turned their backs on long-established musical conventions. As abstract painters arranged lines and color but did not draw identifiable objects, so modern composers arranged sounds without creating recognizable harmonies. Led by the Viennese composer Arnold Schönberg (1874–1951), they abandoned traditional harmony and tonality. The musical notes in a given piece were no longer united and organized by a key; instead they were independent and unrelated. Schönberg's twelve-tone music of the 1920s arranged all twelve notes of the scale in an abstract, mathematical pattern, or "tone row." This pattern sounded like no pattern at all to the ordinary listener and could be detected only by a highly trained eye studying the musical score. Accustomed to the harmonies of classical and romantic music, audiences generally resisted modern atonal music. Only after the Second World War did it begin to win acceptance.

MOVIES AND RADIO

Until after World War Two at the earliest, these revolutionary changes in art and music appealed mainly to a minority of "highbrows" and not to the general public. That public was primarily and enthusiastically wrapped up in movies and radio. The long-declining traditional arts and amusements of people in villages and small towns almost vanished, replaced by standardized, commercial entertainment.

Moving pictures were first shown as a popular novelty in naughty peepshows—"What the Butler Saw" —and penny arcades in the 1890s, especially in Paris. The first movie houses date from an experiment in Los Angeles in 1902. They quickly attracted large audiences and led to the production of short, silent action films like the eight-minute *Great Train Robbery* of 1903. American directors and businessmen then set up "movie factories," at first in the New York area and after 1910 in Los Angeles. These factories churned out two short films each week. On the eve of the First World War full-length feature films like the Italian *Quo Vadis* and the American *Birth of a Nation,* coupled with improvements in the quality of pictures, suggested the screen's vast possibilities.

During the First World War the United States became the dominant force in the rapidly expanding silent-film industry. In the 1920s, Mack Sennett (1884–1960) and his zany Keystone Cops specialized in short, slapstick comedies noted for frantic automobile chases, custard-pie battles, and gorgeous bathing beauties. Screen stars such as Mary Pickford and Lillian Gish, Douglas Fairbanks and Rudolph Valentino became household names, with their own "fan clubs." Yet Charlie Chaplin (1889–1978), a funny little Englishman working in Hollywood, was unquestionably the king of the "silver screen" in the 1920s. In his enormously popular role as a lonely tramp, complete with baggy trousers, battered derby, and an awkward, shuffling walk, Chaplin symbolized the "gay spirit of laughter in a cruel, crazy world."[8] Chaplin also demonstrated that, in the hands of a genius, the new medium could combine mass entertainment and artistic accomplishment.

The early 1920s was also the great age of German films. Protected and developed during the war, the

Matinee Idols Fresh and winsome, Canadian-born Mary Pickford was affectionately known as "America's Sweetheart." Starring in sentimental romances like *Poor Little Rich Girl*, she reigned over Hollywood with her husband Douglas Fairbanks. Dark and handsome, Italian-born Rudolph Valentino, shown here in the stirring *Four Horsemen of the Apocalypse*, was Hollywood's original "Latin lover." *(The New York Public Library Picture Collection)*

large German studios excelled in bizarre expressionist dramas, beginning with *The Cabinet of Dr. Caligari* in 1919. Unfortunately, their period of creativity was short-lived. By 1926 American money was drawing the leading German talents to Hollywood and consolidating America's international domination. Film making was big business, and European theater owners were forced to book whole blocks of American films to get the few pictures they really wanted. This system put European producers at a great disadvantage until "talkies" permitted a revival of national film industries in the 1930s, particularly in France.

Whether foreign or domestic, motion pictures became the main entertainment of the masses until after the Second World War. In Great Britain one in every four adults went to the movies twice a week in the late 1930s, and two in five went once a week. Continental countries had similar figures. The greatest appeal of motion pictures was that they offered ordinary people a temporary escape from the hard realities of everyday life. For an hour or two the moviegoer could flee the world of international tensions, uncertainty, unemployment, and personal frustrations. The appeal of escapist entertainment was especially strong during the Great Depression.

Millions flocked to musical comedies featuring glittering stars such as Ginger Rogers and Fred Astaire and to the fanciful cartoons of Mickey Mouse and his friends.

Radio became possible with the transatlantic "wireless" communication of Guglielmo Marconi (1874–1937) in 1901 and the development of the vacuum tube in 1904, which permitted the transmission of speech and music. But only in 1920 were the first major public broadcasts of special events made in Great Britain and the United States. Lord Northcliffe, who had pioneered in journalism with the inexpensive, mass-circulation *Daily Mail,* sponsored a broadcast of "only one artist . . . the world's very best, the soprano Nellie Melba."[9] Singing from London in English, Italian, and French, Melba was heard simultaneously all over Europe on June 16, 1920. This historic event captured the public's imagination. The meteoric career of radio was launched.

Every major country quickly established national broadcasting networks. In the United States, such networks were privately owned and financed by advertising. In Great Britain, Parliament set up an independent, high-minded public corporation, the British Broadcasting Corporation (BBC), which was supported by licensing fees. Elsewhere in Europe, the typical pattern was direct control by the government.

Whatever the institutional framework, radio became popular and influential. By the late 1930s, more than three out of every four households in both democratic Great Britain and dictatorial Germany had at least one cheap, mass-produced radio. In other European countries, radio ownership was not quite so widespread, but the new medium was no less important.

Radio in unscrupulous hands was particularly well suited for political propaganda. Dictators like Mussolini and Hitler controlled the airwaves and could reach enormous national audiences with their frequent, dramatic speeches. In democratic countries, politicians such as President Franklin Roosevelt and Prime Minister Stanley Baldwin effectively used informal "fireside chats" to bolster their support.

Motion pictures also became powerful tools of indoctrination, especially in countries with dictatorial regimes. Lenin himself encouraged the development of Soviet film making, believing that the new medium was essential to the social and ideological transformation of the country. Beginning in the mid-1920s, a series of epic films, the most famous of which were directed by Sergei Eisenstein (1898–1948), brilliantly dramatized the communist view of Russian history.

In Germany, Hitler turned to a young and immensely talented woman film maker, Leni Riefenstahl (b. 1902), for a masterpiece of documentary propaganda, *The Triumph of the Will,* based on the Nazi party rally at Nuremberg in 1934. Riefenstahl combined stunning aerial photography, joyful crowds welcoming Hitler, and mass processions of young Nazi fanatics. Her film was a brilliant and all-too-powerful documentary of Germany's "Nazi rebirth." The new media of mass culture were clearly potentially dangerous instruments of political manipulation.

THE SEARCH FOR PEACE AND POLITICAL STABILITY

The Versailles settlement had established a shaky truce, not a solid peace. Within the general context of intellectual crisis and revolutionary artistic experimentation, politicians and statesmen struggled to create a stable international order.

The pursuit of real and lasting peace proved difficult. Germany hated the Treaty of Versailles, France was fearful and isolated. Britain was undependable, and the United States had turned its back on European problems. Eastern Europe was in ferment, and no one could predict the future of communist Russia. Moreover, the international economic situation was poor and greatly complicated by war debts and disrupted patterns of trade. Yet for a time, from 1925 to late 1929, it appeared that peace and stability were within reach. When the subsequent collapse of the 1930s mocked these hopes, the disillusionment of liberals in the democracies was intensified.

GERMANY AND THE WESTERN POWERS

Germany was the key to lasting peace. Only under the pressure of the Allies' naval blockade and threat to extend their military occupation from the Rhineland to the rest of the country had Germany's new republican government signed the Treaty of Versailles in June 1919. To Germans of all political parties, the treaty represented a harsh, dictated peace, to be revised or repudiated as soon as possible. The treaty had neither broken nor reduced Germany, which was potentially still the strongest country in Europe. Thus the treaty had fallen between two stools: too harsh for a peace of reconciliation, too soft for a peace of conquest.

Moreover, with ominous implications for the future, France and Great Britain did not see eye to eye on Germany. By the end of 1919, France wanted to stress the harsh elements in the Treaty of Versailles. Most of the war in the west had been fought on French soil, and much of rich, industrialized, northern France had been devastated. The expected costs of reconstruction were staggering; like Great Britain, France had also borrowed large sums from the United States during the war, which had to be repaid. Thus French politicians believed that massive reparations from Germany were a vital economic necessity. Moreover, if the Germans had to suffer to make the payments, the French would not be overly concerned. Having compromised with President Wilson only to be betrayed by America's failure to ratify the treaty, many French leaders saw strict implementation of all provisions of the Treaty of Versailles as France's last best hope. Large reparation payments could hold Germany down indefinitely, and France would realize its goal of security.

The British soon felt differently. Prewar Germany had been Great Britain's second-best market in the entire world, and after the war a healthy, prosperous Germany appeared to be essential to the British economy. Indeed, many English people agreed with the analysis of the young English economist John Maynard Keynes (1883–1946), who eloquently denounced the Treaty of Versailles in his famous *Economic Consequences of the Peace* (1919). According to Keynes's interpretation, astronomical reparations and harsh economic measures would indeed reduce Germany to the position of an impoverished second-rate power, but such impoverishment would increase economic hardship in all countries. Only a complete revision of the foolish treaty could save Germany—and Europe. Keynes's attack exploded like a bombshell and became very influential. It stirred deep guilt feelings about Germany in the English-speaking world, feelings that often paralyzed English and American leaders in their relations with Germany and its leaders between the First and Second World Wars.

The British were also suspicious of France's army —momentarily the largest in Europe—and France's foreign policy. Ever since 1890, France had looked to Russia as a powerful ally against Germany. But with Russia hostile and socialist, and with Britain and the United States unwilling to make any firm commitments, France turned to the newly formed states of eastern Europe for diplomatic support. In 1921 France signed a mutual defense pact with Poland and associated itself closely with the so-called Little Entente, an alliance that joined Czechoslovakia, Rumania, and Yugoslavia against defeated and bitter Hungary. The British and the French were also on cool terms because of conflicts relating to their League of Nations mandates in the Middle East.

While French and British leaders drifted in different directions, the Allied reparations commission completed its work. In April 1921, it announced that Germany had to pay the enormous sum of 132 billion gold marks ($33 billion), payable in annual installments of 2.5 billion gold marks. Facing possible occupation of more of its territory, the young German republic, which had been founded in Weimar but moved back to Berlin, made its first payment in 1921. Then in 1922, wracked by rapid inflation and political assassinations, and motivated by hostility and arrogance as well, the Weimar Republic announced its inability to pay more. It proposed a moratorium on reparations for three years, with the clear implication that thereafter reparations would either be drastically reduced or eliminated entirely.

The British were willing to accept this offer, but the French were not. Led by their tough-minded, legalistic prime minister, Raymond Poincaré, they decided they either had to call Germany's bluff or see the entire peace settlement dissolve to France's great disadvantage. So, despite strong British protests, France and its ally Belgium decided to pursue a firm policy. In early January 1923, French and Belgian armies began to occupy the Ruhr district, the heartland of industrial Germany, creating the most serious international crisis of the 1920s.

THE OCCUPATION OF THE RUHR

The strategy of Poincaré and his French supporters was simple. Since Germany would not pay reparations in hard currency or gold, France and Belgium would collect reparations in kind—coal, steel, and

"Hands Off the Ruhr" The French occupation of the Ruhr to collect reparations payments raised a storm of patriotic protest, including this anti-French poster of 1923. *(Internationaal Instituut voor Sociale Geschiedenis)*

The Fruits of Germany's Inflation In the end, currency had value only as waste paper. Here bank notes are being purchased by the bail for paper mills, along with old rags *(Lumpen)* and bones *(Knochen)*. *(Archiv für Kunst u. Geschichte/Katherine Young)*

machinery. If forcible collection proved impossible, France would use occupation to paralyze Germany and force it to accept the Treaty of Versailles.

Strengthened by a wave of patriotism, the German government ordered the people of the Ruhr to stop working and start resisting—passively—the French occupation. The coal mines and steel mills of the Ruhr grew silent, leaving 10 percent of Germany's total population in need of relief. The French answer to passive resistance was to seal off, not only the Ruhr, but the entire Rhineland from the rest of Germany, permitting only enough food to prevent starvation. They also revived plans for a separate state in the Rhineland.

By the summer of 1923, France and Germany were engaged in a great test of wills. As the German government had anticipated, French armies could not collect reparations from striking workers at gunpoint. But French occupation was indeed paralyzing Germany and its economy, for the Ruhr district normally produced 80 percent of Germany's steel and coal. Moreover, the occupation of the Ruhr turned rapid German inflation into runaway inflation. Faced with the need to support the striking Ruhr workers and their employers, the German government began to print money to pay its bills. Prices soared. People went to the store with a big bag of paper money; they returned home with a handful of groceries. German money rapidly lost all value, and so did anything else with a stated fixed value.

Runaway inflation brought about a social revolution. The accumulated savings of many retired and middle-class people were wiped out. The old middle-class virtues of thrift, caution, and self-reliance were cruelly mocked by catastrophic inflation. People told themselves that nothing had real value any more, not even money. The German middle and lower-middle classes felt cheated and burned with resentment. Many hated and blamed the Western governments, their own government, big business, the Jews, the workers, the communists for their misfortune. They were psychologically prepared to follow radical leaders in a moment of crisis.

In August 1923, as the mark fell and political unrest grew throughout Germany, Gustav Stresemann assumed leadership of the government. Stresemann adopted a compromising attitude. He called off passive resistance in the Ruhr and in October agreed in principle to pay reparations, but asked for a re-examination of Germany's ability to pay. Poincaré accepted. His hard line was becoming increasingly unpopular with French citizens, and it was hated in Britain and the United States. Moreover, occupation was dreadfully expensive, and France's own currency was beginning to lose value on foreign exchange markets.

More generally, in both Germany and France power was finally passing to the moderates, who realized that continued confrontation was a destructive, no-win situation. Thus, after five long years of hostility and tension culminating in a kind of undeclared war in the Ruhr in 1923, Germany and France decided to give compromise and cooperation a try. The British, and even the Americans, were willing to help. The first step was a reasonable compromise on the reparations question.

HOPE IN FOREIGN AFFAIRS, 1924–1929

The Reparations Commission appointed an international committee of financial experts headed by an American banker, Charles G. Dawes, to re-examine reparations from a broad perspective. The committee made a series of recommendations known as the Dawes Plan (1924), which was accepted by France, Germany, and Britain. German reparations were reduced and placed on a sliding scale, like an income tax, whereby yearly payments depended on the level of German economic prosperity. The Dawes Plan also recommended large loans to Germany, loans that could come only from the United States. These loans were to help Stresemann's government put its new currency on a firm basis and promote German recovery. In short, Germany would get private loans from the United States and pay reparations to France and Britain, thus enabling those countries to repay the large sums they owed the United States.

This circular flow of international payments was complicated and risky. For a time, though, it worked. The German republic experienced a spectacular economic recovery. By 1929 Germany's wealth and income were 50 percent greater than in 1913. With prosperity and large, continuous inflows of American capital, Germany easily paid about $1.3 billion in reparations in 1927 and 1928, enabling France and Britain to pay the United States. In 1929 the Young Plan, named after an American businessman, further reduced German reparations and formalized the link between German reparations and French-British debts to the United States. In this way the Americans, who did not have armies but who did have money, belatedly played a part in the general economic settlement, which though far from ideal facilitated the worldwide recovery of the late 1920s.

The economic settlement was matched by a political settlement. In 1925 the leaders of Europe signed a number of agreements at Locarno, Switzerland. Stresemann, who guided German's foreign policy until his death in 1929, had suggested a treaty with France's conciliatory Aristide Briand, who had returned to office in 1924 after French voters rejected the bellicose Poincaré. By this treaty Germany and France solemnly pledged to accept their common border, and both Britain and Italy agreed to fight either country if it invaded the other. Stresemann also agreed to settle boundary disputes with Poland and Czechoslovakia by peaceful means, and France promised those countries military aid if they were attacked by Germany. For their efforts Stresemann and Briand shared the Nobel Peace Prize in 1926. The effect of the treaties of Locarno was far-reaching. For several years, a "spirit of Locarno" gave Europeans a sense of growing security and stability in international affairs.

Hopes were strengthened by other developments. In 1926 Germany joined the League of Nations, where Stresemann continued his "peace offensive."

In 1928 fifteen countries signed the Kellogg-Briand Pact, which "condemned and renounced war as an instrument of national policy." The signing states agreed to settle international disputes peacefully. Often seen as idealistic nonsense because it made no provisions for action in case war actually occurred, the pact was nevertheless a hopeful step. It grew out of a suggestion by Briand that France and the United States renounce the possibility of war between their two countries. Briand was gently and subtly trying to draw the United States back into involvement with Europe. When Secretary of State Frank B. Kellogg proposed a multinational pact, Briand appeared close to success. Thus the cautious optimism of the late 1920s also rested on the hope that the United States would accept its responsibilities as a great world power and consequently contribute to European stability.

HOPE IN DEMOCRATIC GOVERNMENT

Domestic politics also offered reason to hope. During the occupation of the Ruhr and the great inflation, republican government in Germany had appeared on the verge of collapse. In 1923 communists momentarily entered provincial governments, and in November an obscure nobody named Adolf Hitler leaped on a table in a beer hall in Munich and proclaimed a "national socialist revolution." But Hitler's plot was poorly organized and easily crushed, and Hitler was sentenced to prison, where he outlined his theories and program in his book *Mein Kampf* (*My Struggle*). Throughout the 1920s, Hitler's National Socialist party attracted support only from a few fanatical anti-Semites, ultranationalists, and disgruntled ex-servicemen. In 1928 his party had an insignificant twelve seats in the national parliament. Indeed, after 1923 democracy seemed to take root in Weimar Germany. A new currency was established, and the economy boomed.

The moderate businessmen who tended to dominate the various German coalition governments were convinced that economic prosperity demanded good relations with the Western powers, and they supported parliamentary government at home. Stresemann himself was a man of this class, and he was the key figure in every government until his death in 1929. Elections were held regularly, and republican democracy appeared to have growing support among a majority of the German people.

There were, however, sharp political divisions in the country. Many unrepentant nationalists and monarchists populated the right and the army. Germany's Communists were noisy and active on the left. The Communists, directed from Moscow, reserved their greatest hatred and sharpest barbs for their cousins the Social Democrats, whom they endlessly accused of betraying the revolution. The working classes were divided politically, but most supported the nonrevolutionary but socialist Social Democrats.

The situation in France had numerous similarities to that in Germany. Communists and Socialists battled for the support of the workers. After 1924 the democratically elected government rested mainly in the hands of coalitions of moderates, and business interests were well represented. France's great accomplishment was rapid rebuilding of its war-torn northern region. The expense of this undertaking led, however, to a large deficit and substantial inflation. By early 1926, the franc had fallen to 10 percent of its prewar value, causing a severe crisis. Poincaré was recalled to office, while Briand remained minister for foreign affairs. The Poincaré government proceeded to slash spending and raise taxes, restoring confidence in the economy. The franc was "saved," stabilized at about one-fifth of its prewar value. Good times prevailed until 1930.

Despite its political shortcomings, France attracted artists and writers from all over the world in the 1920s. Much of the intellectual and artistic ferment of the times flourished in Paris. As the writer Gertrude Stein (1874–1946), a leader of the large colony of American expatriates living in Paris, later recalled: "Paris was where the twentieth century was."[10] More generally, France appealed to foreigners and the French as a harmonious combination of small businesses and family farms, of bold innovation and solid traditions.

Britain, too, faced challenges after 1920. The wartime trend toward greater social equality continued, however, helping to maintain social harmony. The great problem was unemployment. Many of Britain's best markets had been lost during the war. In June 1921, almost 2.2 million people—23 percent of the labor force—were out of work, and throughout the 1920s unemployment hovered around 12 percent. Yet the state provided unemployment benefits of equal size to all those without jobs and supplemented those payments with subsidized housing, medical

An American in Paris The young Josephine Baker suddenly became a star when she brought an exotic African eroticism to French music halls in 1925. American blacks and Africans had a powerful impact on entertainment in Europe in the 1920s and 1930s. *(BBC Hulton/The Bettmann Archive)*

aid, and increased old-age pensions. These and other measures kept living standards from seriously declining, defused class tensions, and pointed the way toward the welfare state Britain established after World War Two.

Relative social harmony was accompanied by the rise of the Labour party as a determined champion of the working classes and of greater social equality. Committed to the kind of moderate, "revisionist" socialism that had emerged before World War One (pages 818–819), the Labour party replaced the Lib-

eral party as the main opposition to the Conservatives. The new prominence of the Labour party reflected the decline of old liberal ideals of competitive capitalism, limited government control, and individual responsibility. In 1924 and 1929, the Labour party under Ramsay MacDonald governed the country with the support of the smaller Liberal party. Yet Labour moved toward socialism gradually and democratically, so that the middle classes were not overly frightened as the working classes won new benefits.

The Conservatives under Stanley Baldwin showed

the same compromising spirit on social issues. The last line of Baldwin's greatest speech in March 1925 summarized his international and domestic programs: "Give us peace in our time, O Lord." Thus, in spite of such conflicts as the 1926 strike by hard-pressed coal miners, which ended in an unsuccessful general strike, social unrest in Britain was limited in the 1920s and in the 1930s as well. In 1922 Britain granted southern, Catholic Ireland full autonomy after a bitter guerrilla war, thus removing another source of prewar friction. In summary, developments in both international relations and in the domestic politics of the leading democracies gave cause for cautious optimism in the late 1920s.

THE GREAT DEPRESSION, 1929–1939

Like the Great War, the Great Depression must be spelled with capital letters. Economic depression was nothing new. Depressions occurred throughout the nineteenth century with predictable regularity, as they recur in the form of recessions and slumps to this day. What was new about this depression was its severity and duration. It struck with ever-greater intensity from 1929 to 1933, and recovery was uneven and slow. Only with the Second World War did the depression disappear in much of the world (see Map 28.1).

The social and political consequences of prolonged economic collapse were enormous. The depression shattered the fragile optimism of political leaders in the late 1920s. Mass unemployment made insecurity a reality for millions of ordinary people, who had paid little attention to the intellectual crisis or to new directions in art and ideas. In desperation, people looked for leaders who would "do something." They were willing to support radical attempts to deal with the crisis by both democratic leaders and dictators.

THE ECONOMIC CRISIS

There is no agreement among historians and economists about why the Great Depression was so deep and lasted so long. Thus, it is best to trace the course of the great collapse before trying to identify what caused it.

Though economic activity was already declining moderately in many countries by early 1929, the crash of the stock market in the United States in October of that year really started the Great Depression. The American stock market boom, which had seen stock prices double between early 1928 and September 1929, was built on borrowed money. Many wealthy investors, speculators, and people of modest means had bought stocks by paying only a small fraction of the total purchase price and borrowing the remainder from their stockbrokers. Such buying "on margin" was extremely dangerous. When prices started falling, the hard-pressed margin buyers either had to put up more money, which was often impossible, or sell their shares to pay off their brokers. Thus thousands of people started selling all at once. The result was a financial panic. Countless investors and speculators were wiped out in a matter of days or weeks.

The general economic consequences were swift and severe. Stripped of their wealth and confidence, battered investors and their fellow citizens started buying fewer goods. Production began to slow down, and unemployment began to rise. Soon the entire American economy was caught in a vicious, spiraling decline.

The financial panic in the United States triggered a worldwide financial crisis, and that crisis resulted in a drastic decline in production in country after country. Throughout the 1920s American bankers and investors had lent large amounts of capital not only to Germany but to many countries. Many of these loans were short term, and once panic broke, New York bankers began recalling them. Gold reserves thus began to flow out of European countries, particularly Germany and Austria, toward the United States. It became very hard for European businessmen to borrow money, and the panicky public began to withdraw its savings from the banks. These banking problems eventually led to the crash of the largest bank in Austria in 1931 and then to general financial chaos. The recall of private loans by American bankers also accelerated the collapse in world prices, as businessmen around the world dumped industrial goods and agricultural commodities in a frantic attempt to get cash to pay what they owed.

The financial crisis led to a general crisis of production: between 1929 and 1933, world output of goods fell by an estimated 38 percent. As this happened, each country turned inward and tried to go it alone.

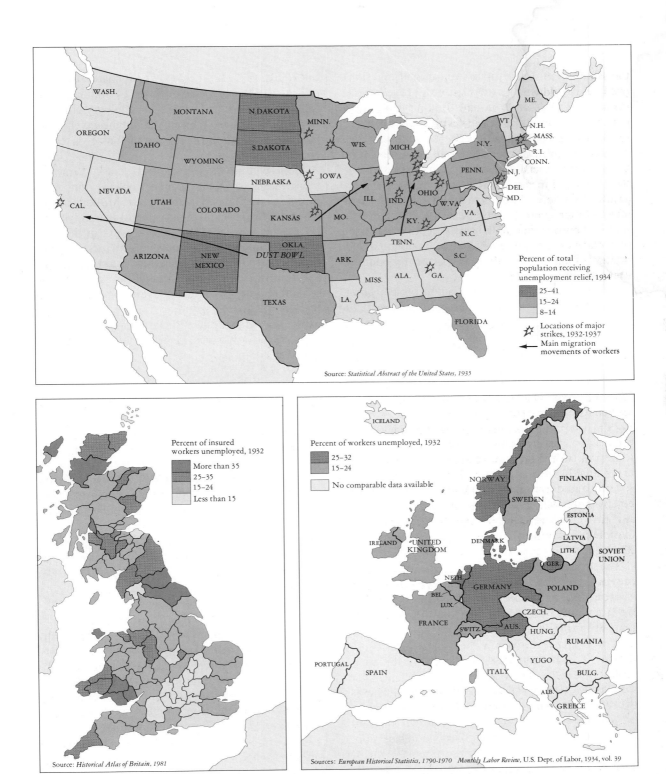

Map 28.1 The Great Depression in the United States, Britain, and Europe National and regional differences were substantial. Germany, industrial northern Britain, and the American Middle West were particularly hard-hit.

In 1931, for example, Britain went off the gold standard, refusing to convert bank notes into gold, and reduced the value of its money. Britain's goal was to make its goods cheaper and therefore more salable in the world market. But because more than twenty nations, including the United States in 1934, also went off the gold standard, no country gained a real advantage. Similarly, country after country followed the example of the United States when it raised protective tariffs to their highest levels ever in 1930 and tried to seal off shrinking national markets for American producers only. Within this context of fragmented and destructive economic nationalism, recovery finally began in 1933.

Although opinions differ, two factors probably best explain the relentless slide to the bottom from 1929 to early 1933. First, the international economy lacked a leadership able to maintain stability when the crisis came. Specifically, as a noted American economic historian concludes, the seriously weakened British, the traditional leaders of the world economy, "couldn't and the United States wouldn't" stabilize the international economic system in 1929.[11] The United States, which had momentarily played a positive role after the occupation of the Ruhr, cut back its international lending and erected high tariffs.

The second factor was poor national economic policy in almost every country. Governments generally cut their budgets and reduced spending when they should have run large deficits in an attempt to stimulate their economies. Since World War Two, such a "counter-cyclical policy," advocated by John Maynard Keynes, has become a well-established weapon against depression. But in the 1930s Keynes's prescription was generally regarded with horror by orthodox economists.

Mass Unemployment

The need for large-scale government spending was tied to mass unemployment. As the financial crisis led to cuts in production, workers lost their jobs and had little money to buy goods. This led to still more cuts in production and still more unemployment, until millions were out of work. In Britain, unemployment had averaged 12 percent in the 1920s; between 1930 and 1935, it averaged more than 18 percent. Far worse was the case of the United States, where unemployment had averaged only 5 percent in

the 1920s. In 1932 unemployment soared to about *one-third* of the entire labor force: 14 million people were out of work (see Map 28.1). Only by pumping new money into the economy could the government increase demand and break the vicious cycle of decline.

Along with its economic effects, mass unemployment posed a great social problem that mere numbers cannot adequately express. Millions of people lost their spirit and dignity in an apparently hopeless search for work. Homes and ways of life were disrupted in millions of personal tragedies. Young people postponed marriages they could not afford, and birthrates fell sharply. There was an increase in suicide and mental illness. Poverty or the threat of poverty became a grinding reality. In 1932 the workers of Manchester, England, appealed to their city officials—a typical appeal echoed throughout the Western world:

We tell you that thousands of people . . . are in desperate straits. We tell you that men, women, and children are going hungry. . . . We tell you that great numbers are being rendered distraught through the stress and worry of trying to exist without work. . . .

If you do not do this—if you do not provide useful work for the unemployed—what, we ask, is your alternative? Do not imagine that this colossal tragedy of unemployment is going on endlessly without some fateful catastrophe. Hungry men are angry men.[12]

Mass unemployment was a terrible time bomb preparing to explode.

The New Deal in the United States

Of all the major industrial countries, only Germany was harder hit by the Great Depression, or reacted more radically to it, than the United States. Depression was so traumatic in the United States because the 1920s had been a period of complacent prosperity. The Great Depression and the response to it was a major turning point in American history.

President Herbert Hoover and his administration initially reacted to the stock market crash and economic decline with dogged optimism and limited action. In May 1930, Hoover told a group of business and farm leaders, "I am convinced that we have now passed the worst and with continued unity of effort we shall rapidly recover." When, however, the full force of the financial crisis struck Europe in the summer of 1931 and boomeranged back to the United States, people's worst fears became reality. Banks failed; unemployment soared. In 1932 industrial production fell to about 50 percent of its level in 1929. In these tragic circumstances Franklin Delano Roosevelt, an inspiring wheelchair aristocrat previously crippled by polio, won a landslide electoral victory with grand but vague promises of a "New Deal for the forgotten man."

Roosevelt's basic goal was to reform capitalism in order to preserve it. In his words, "A frank examination of the profit system in the spring of 1933 showed it to be in collapse; but substantially everybody in the United States, in public office and out of public office, from the very rich to the very poor, was as determined as was my Administration to save it."[13] Roosevelt rejected socialism and government ownership of industry in 1933. To right the situation, he chose forceful government intervention in the economy.

In this choice, Roosevelt and his advisers were greatly influenced by American experience in World War One. During the wartime emergency, the American economy had been thoroughly planned and regulated. Roosevelt and his "brain trust" of advisers adopted similar policies to restore prosperity and reduce social inequality. Roosevelt was flexible, pragmatic, and willing to experiment. Government intervention and experimentation were combined in some of the New Deal's most significant measures.

The most ambitious attempt to control and plan the economy was the National Recovery Administration (NRA), established by Congress right after Roosevelt took office. The key idea behind the NRA was to reduce competition and fix prices and wages for everyone's benefit. This goal required government, business, and labor to hammer out detailed regulations for each industry. Along with this kind of national planning in the private sector of the economy, the government believed it could sponsor enough public works projects to assure recovery. Because the NRA broke with the cherished American tradition of free competition and aroused conflicts among businessmen, consumers, and bureaucrats, it did not work well. By the time the NRA was declared unconstitutional in 1935, Roosevelt and the New Deal were already moving away from government efforts to plan and control the entire economy.

Instead, Roosevelt and his advisers attacked the

Middle-Class Unemployment An English office worker's unusual sandwich board poignantly summarizes the bitter despair of the unemployed in the 1930s. *(BBC Hulton/The Bettmann Archive)*

key problem of mass unemployment directly. The federal government accepted the responsibility of employing directly as many people as financially possible, something Hoover had consistently rejected. Thus, when it became clear in late 1933 that the initial program of public works was too small, new agencies were created to undertake a vast range of projects.

San Francisco, 1934 Standing on the corner, waiting for something to do: this classic photograph by Dorothea Lange captures the frustration and waste of unemployment in the Depression years. *(Dorothea Lange, The Oakland Museum)*

The most famous of these was the Works Progress Administration (WPA), set up in 1935. At its peak in late 1938, this government agency employed more than 3 million individuals. One-fifth of the entire labor force worked for the WPA at some point in the 1930s. To this day thousands of public buildings, bridges, and highways built by the WPA stand as monuments to energetic government efforts to provide people with meaningful work. The WPA was enormously popular in a nation long schooled in self-reliance and the work ethic. The hope of a job with the government helped check the threat of social revolution in the United States.

Other social measures aimed in the same direction. Following the path blazed by Germany's Bismarck in the 1880s, the U.S. government in 1935 established a national social security system, with old-age pensions and unemployment benefits, to protect many workers against some of life's uncertainties. The National Labor Relations Act of 1935 gave union organizers the green light by declaring collective bargaining to be the policy of the United States. Following some bitter strikes, such as the sit-down strike at General Motors in early 1937, union membership more than doubled, from 4 million in 1935 to 9 million in 1940. In general, between 1935 and 1938 government rulings and social reforms chipped away at the privileges of the wealthy and tried to help ordinary people.

Yet, despite its undeniable accomplishments in social reform, the New Deal was only partly successful as a response to the Great Depression. At the height of the recovery, in May 1937, 7 million workers were still unemployed. The economic situation then worsened seriously in the recession of 1937 and 1938. Production fell sharply, and although unemployment never again reached the 15 million mark of 1933, it hit 11 million in 1938 and was still a staggering 10 million when war broke out in Europe in September 1939.

The New Deal never did pull the United States out of the Depression. This failure frustrated Americans then, and it is still puzzling today. Perhaps, as some have claimed, Roosevelt should have used his enormous popularity and prestige in 1933 to nationalize the banks, the railroads, and some heavy industry, so that national economic planning could have been successful. On the other hand, Roosevelt's sharp attack on big business and the wealthy after 1935 had popular appeal but also damaged business confidence and made the great capitalists uncooperative. Given the low level of profit and the underutilization of many factories, however, it is questionable whether business would have behaved much differently even if the New Deal had catered to it.

Finally, it is often argued that the New Deal did not put enough money into the economy through deficit financing. Like his predecessors in the White House, Roosevelt was attached to the ideal of the balanced budget. His largest deficit was only $4.4 billion in 1936. Compare this figure with deficits of $21.5 billion in 1942 and $57.4 billion in 1943, when the nation was prosperously engaged in total war and unemployment had vanished. By 1945 many

ART: A MIRROR OF SOCIETY

Art reveals the interests and values of society and frequently gives intimate and unique glimpses of how people actually lived. In portraits and statues, whether of saints, generals, philosophers, popes, poets, or merchants, it preserves the memory and fame of men and women who shaped society. In paintings, drawings, and carvings, it also shows how people worked, played, relaxed, suffered, and triumphed. Art, therefore, is extremely useful to the historian, especially when written records are scarce. Every work of art and every part of it has meaning and has something of its own to say.

Art also manifests the changes and continuity of European life; as values changed in Europe, so did major artistic themes. In the nineteenth century, the impressionists, seeking to capture a given moment as the eye perceives it, gloried in the vibrant diversity of urban society. In their wholehearted embrace of modern life, they reflected western Europe's faith in science, progress, and democracy in the late nineteenth century. Though the twentieth century witnessed the dissipation of such optimism, the impressionists, by valuing color and abstract design for their own sake, served as the crucial bridge between traditional representational and modern art. The career of Cézanne (overleaf), in particular, exemplifies this artistic progression: after rejecting as too light and frivolous his early impressionistic work, Cézanne adopted a style characterized by greater form and solidity.

Artists of the early and mid-twentieth century anticipated and then gave poignant expression to the anxieties and terrors that have plagued modern times. Some continued Cézanne's experimentation with form, a process that found its ultimate expression in cubism. The cubist works of artists like Picasso reflect the distorted and multiple viewpoints of a society that lacked nineteenth-century certitudes. Others such as Gustave Klimt (also represented here) retreated from realistic depiction by conveying their ideas and emotions indirectly through symbols. Still other artists participated in the movement known as expressionism, which emphasized the subjective portrayal of inner experience. In *The Dance of Life,* below, Edvard Munch, a leading proponent of expressionism, tries to show the whole range of human emotions at once. Solitary figures struggling fitfully with terror and uncertainty—a favorite twentieth-century theme—dominate Munch's work. Here the girl in white represents innocence, the tense women in black stand for mourning and rejection, and the women in red evoke the joy of passing pleasure. (Nasjonalgalleriet, Oslo.)

The Card Players *(above)* Paul Cézanne (1839–1906). An immensely important and revolutionary painter, Cézanne rejected his early impressionistic style as too light and delicate. In this 1892 masterpiece he shows the dignity of all human existence and experience, no matter how ordinary or commonplace. One can also sense the devotion to form and solidity that made Cézanne the father of modern abstract painting. *(The Metropolitan Museum of Art: Bequest of Stephen C. Clark, 1960)*

The Starry Night *(above)* Vincent van Gogh (1853–1890). The distorted visions of van Gogh anticipated the widespread tension and torment that marked the age of anxiety. The tragic Dutchman absorbed impressionism in Paris, but under the burning sun of southern France he went beyond portraying the world of external reality. He feverishly painted his own inner world of intense emotion and wild imagination, thereby contributing greatly to modern expressionism. *(Museum of Modern Art, New York. Acquired through the Lillie P. Bliss Bequest)*

Judith I *(left)* Gustave Klimt (1862–1918). Men (and women) were firm believers in the elemental power of female seduction at the beginning of this century. This 1901 painting by a leading Viennese symbolist retells the biblical story of Judith, who slept with a Babylonian general for many nights in order to cut off his head and save her people. The symbolists' fascination with exotic sensations harkened back to romanticism. *(Osterreichische Galerie, Vienna)*

The Three Dancers *(right)* Pablo Picasso (1881–1973). A child prodigy, Picasso turned from realism to the fractured, shifting, multiple point of view known as cubism. With this immensely influential innovation Picasso shattered the continuity of composition that had prevailed since the Renaissance, and merged time and space in the relativity of an Einsteinian world. In this 1925 painting Picasso mourns in rage a friend's death through the frenzied contortions and cruciform image of the dancers. *(Tate Gallery, London/S.P.A.D.E.M., Paris/ V.A.G.A., New York)*

Birthday *(above)* Marc Chagall (1889–1985). No modern artist has expressed more joyfully the enduring mystery of love than the highly original, Russian-born Jewish painter Chagall. In this 1915 painting the prospect of a birthday bouquet from his beloved Bella sends the young husband soaring in bliss. Love and fantasy go hand in hand, Chagall seems to say. *(Solomon R. Guggenheim Museum, New York; Photo: Carmelo Guadagno)*

The Grand Constructors *(right)* Fernard Léger (1881–1955). The twentieth-century fascination with urban life, the machine, and workers dominate the work of Léger. Like most ordinary people, Léger is thoroughly enchanted with the creations of technology and mass culture. Yet the robot-like action of the workers in this 1950 picture also suggests that dehumanization often accompanies our modern marvels. *(Musée National Fernand Léger, Bot/S.P.A.D.E.M., Paris/V.A.G.A., New York)*

Christmas Night *(left)* Henri Matisse (1869–1954). In his youth Matisse led avant-garde artists who delighted in breaking with tradition and shocking the public. This joyous design for a church stained-glass window, however, glows with cultural continuity and the spiritual peace of the artist's last years. Its beauty inspired by that of medieval masterpieces (see insert II), Matisse's stained-glass window proclaims the good tidings of Christmas to our time. *(Museum of Modern Art, New York. Gift of Time, Inc.)*

economists concluded that the New Deal's deficit-financed public works had been too small a step in the right direction. These Keynesian views were to be very influential in economic policy in Europe and America after the Second World War.

THE SCANDINAVIAN RESPONSE TO DEPRESSION

Of all the Western democracies, the Scandinavian countries under Socialist leadership responded most successfully to the challenge of the Great Depression. Having grown steadily in the late nineteenth century, Socialists became the largest political party in Sweden and then in Norway after the First World War. In the 1920s they passed important social reform legislation for both peasants and workers, gained practical administrative experience, and developed a unique kind of socialism. Flexible and nonrevolutionary, Scandinavian socialism grew out of a strong tradition of cooperative community action. Even before 1900, Scandinavian agricultural cooperatives had shown how individual peasant families could join together for everyone's benefit. Labor leaders and capitalists were also inclined to work together.

When the economic crisis struck in 1929, Socialist governments in Scandinavia built on this pattern of cooperative social action. Sweden in particular pioneered in the use of large-scale deficits to finance public works and thereby maintain production and employment. Scandinavian governments also increased social welfare benefits, from old-age pensions and unemployment insurance to subsidized housing and maternity allowances. All this spending required a large bureaucracy and high taxes, first on the rich and then on practically everyone. Yet both private and cooperative enterprise thrived, as did democracy. Some observers saw Scandinavia's welfare socialism as an appealing "middle way" between sick capitalism and cruel communism or fascism.

RECOVERY AND REFORM IN BRITAIN AND FRANCE

In Britain, MacDonald's Labour government and then, after 1931, the Conservative-dominated coalition government followed orthodox economic theory. The budget was balanced, but unemployed workers received barely enough welfare to live. Despite government lethargy, the economy recovered considerably after 1932. By 1937 total production was about 20 percent higher than in 1929. In fact, for Britain the years after 1932 were actually somewhat better than the 1920s had been, quite the opposite of the situation in the United States and France.

This good, but by no means brilliant, performance reflected the gradual reorientation of the Britain economy. After going off the gold standard in 1931 and establishing protective tariffs in 1932, Britain concentrated increasingly on the national rather than the international market. The old export industries of the Industrial Revolution, such as textiles and coal, continued to decline, but the new industries like automobiles and electrical appliances grew in response to British home demand. Moreover, low interest rates encouraged a housing boom. By the end of the decade there were highly visible differences between the old, depressed industrial areas of the north and the new, growing areas of the south. These developments encouraged Britain to look inward and avoid unpleasant foreign questions.

Because France was relatively less industrialized and more isolated from the world economy, the Great Depression came late. But once the depression hit France, it stayed and stayed. Decline was steady until 1935, and the short-lived recovery never brought production or employment back up to predepression levels. Economic stagnation both reflected and heightened an ongoing political crisis. There was no stability in government. As before 1914, the French parliament was made up of many political parties, which could never cooperate for very long. In 1933, for example, five coalition cabinets formed and fell in rapid succession.

The French lost the underlying unity that had made governmental instability bearable before 1914. Fascist-type organizations agitated against parliamentary democracy and looked to Mussolini's Italy and Hitler's Germany for inspiration. In February 1934, French fascists and semifascists rioted and threatened to overturn the republic. At the same time the Communist party and many workers opposed to the existing system were looking to Stalin's Russia for guidance. The vital center of moderate republicanism was sapped from both sides.

Frightened by the growing strength of the Fascists at home and abroad, the Communists, the Socialists, and the Radicals formed an alliance—the Popular Front—for the national elections of May 1936. Their clear victory reflected the trend toward polarization.

The number of Communists in the parliament jumped dramatically from 10 to 72, while the Socialists, led by Léon Blum, became the strongest party in France with 146 seats. The really quite moderate Radicals slipped badly, and the conservatives lost ground to the semifascists.

In the next few months, Blum's Popular Front government made the first and only real attempt to deal with the social and economic problems of the 1930s in France. Inspired by Roosevelt's New Deal, the Popular Front encouraged the union movement and launched a far-reaching program of social reform, complete with paid vacations and a forty-hour workweek. Popular with workers and the lower-middle class, these measures were quickly sabotaged by rapid inflation and cries of revolution from fascists and frightened conservatives. Wealthy people sneaked their money out of the country, labor unrest grew, and France entered a severe financial crisis. Blum was forced to announce a "breathing spell" in social reform.

The fires of political dissension were also fanned by civil war in Spain. The Communists demanded that France support the Spanish republicans, while many French conservatives would gladly have joined Hitler and Mussolini in aiding the attack of Spanish fascists. Extremism grew, and France itself was within sight of civil war. Blum was forced to resign in June 1937, and the Popular Front quickly collapsed. An anxious and divided France drifted aimlessly once again, preoccupied by Hitler and German rearmament.

After the First World War, Western society entered a complex and difficult era—truly an age of anxiety. Intellectual life underwent a crisis marked by pessimism, uncertainty, and fascination with irrational forces. Rejection of old forms and ceaseless experimentation characterized art and music, while motion pictures and radio provided a new, standardized entertainment for the masses. Intellectual and artistic developments that had been confined to small avant-garde groups before 1914 gained wider currency along with the insecure state of mind they expressed.

Politics and economics were similarly disrupted. In the 1920s, statesmen groped to create an enduring peace and rebuild the prewar prosperity, and for a brief period late in the decade, they even seemed to have succeeded. Then the Great Depression shattered the fragile stability. Uncertainty returned with redoubled force in the 1930s. The international economy collapsed, and unemployment struck millions. The democracies turned inward as they sought to cope with massive domestic problems and widespread disillusionment. Generally speaking, they were not very successful. The old liberal ideals of individual rights and responsibilities, elected government, and economic freedom seemed ineffective and outmoded to many, even when they managed to survive. And in many countries they were abandoned completely.

NOTES

1. P. Valéry, *Variety,* trans. Malcolm Cowley, Harcourt, Brace, New York, 1927, pp. 27–28.
2. G. Marcel, as quoted by S. Hughes, *The Obstructed Path: French Social Thought in the Years of Desperation, 1930–1960,* Harper & Row, New York, 1967, p. 82.
3. G. Greene, *Another Mexico,* Viking Press, New York, 1939, p. 3.
4. G. Orwell, *1984,* New American Library, New York, p. 220.
5. C. E. Jeanneret-Gris (Le Corbusier), *Towards a New Architecture,* J. Rodker, London, 1931, p. 15.
6. Quoted by A. H. Barr, Jr., *What Is Modern Painting?,* 9th ed., Museum of Modern Art, New York, 1966, p. 27.
7. Ibid., p. 25.
8. R. Graves and A. Hodge, *The Long Week End: A Social History of Great Britain, 1918–1939,* Macmillan, New York, 1941, p. 131.
9. Quoted by A. Briggs, *The Birth of Broadcasting,* Oxford University Press, London, 1961, 1.47.
10. Quoted by R. J. Sontag, *A Broken World, 1919–1939,* Harper & Row, New York, 1971, p. 129.
11. C. P. Kindleberger, *The World in Depression, 1929–1939,* University of California Press, Berkeley, 1973, p. 292.
12. Quoted by S. B. Clough et al., eds., *Economic History of Europe: Twentieth Century,* Harper & Row, New York, 1968, pp. 243–245.

13. Quoted by D. Dillard, *Economic Development of the North Atlantic Community,* Prentice-Hall, Englewood Cliffs, N.J., 1967, p. 591.

SUGGESTED READING

Among general works, R. Sontag, *A Broken World, 1919–1939* (1971), and E. Wiskema, *Europe of the Dictators, 1919–1945* (1966), are particularly recommended. The former has an excellent bibliography. A. Bullock, ed., *The Twentieth Century* (1971), is a lavish visual feast combined with penetrating essays on major developments since 1900. Two excellent accounts of contemporary history—one with a liberal and the other with a conservative point of view—are R. Paxton, *Europe in the Twentieth Century* (1975), and P. Johnson, *Modern Times: The World from the Twenties to the Eighties* (1983). Crucial changes in thought before and after World War One are discussed in three rewarding intellectual histories: G. Masur, *Prophets of Yesterday* (1961); H. S. Hughes, *Consciousness and Society* (1956); and M. Biddiss, *Age of the Masses: Ideas and Society Since 1870* (1977). R. Stromberg, *European Intellectual History Since 1789,* 4th ed. (1986), and F. Baumer, *Modern European Thought: Continuity and Change in Ideas, 1600–1950* (1970), are recommended general surveys.

J. Rewald, *The History of Impressionism,* rev. ed. (1961) and *Post-Impressionism* (1956), are excellent, as are the works of A. H. Barr, Jr., cited in the Notes. P. Collaer, *A History of Modern Music* (1961), and H. R. Hitchcock, *Architecture: 19th and 20th Centuries* (1958), are good introductions, while T. Wolfe, *From Bauhaus to My House* (1981), is a lively critique of modern architecture. L. Barnett, *The Universe and Dr. Einstein* (1952), is a fascinating study of the new physics. P. Rieff, *Freud* (1956), and M. White, ed., *The Age of Analysis* (1955), open up basic questions of twentieth-century psychology and philosophy. P. Gay, *Weimar Culture* (1970), is a brilliant exploration of the many-sided artistic renaissance in Germany in the 1920s. M. Marrus, ed., *Emergence of Leisure* (1974), is a pioneering inquiry into an important aspect of mass culture. H. Daniels-Rops, *A Fight for God,* 2 vols. (1966), is a sympathetic history of the Catholic church between 1870 and 1939.

C. Maier, *Recasting Bourgeois Europe* (1975), is an ambitious comparative study of social classes and conflicts in France, Germany, and Italy after World War One. R. Wohl, *The Generation of 1914* (1979); R. Kuisel, *Capital and State in Modern France: Renovation and Economic Management* (1982); and W. McDougall, *France's Rhineland Diplomacy, 1914–1924* (1978), are three more important studies on aspects of the postwar challenge. M. Childs, *Sweden: The Middle Way* (1961), applauds Sweden's efforts at social reform. W. Neuman, *The Balance of Power in the Interwar Years, 1919–1939* (1968), perceptively examines international politics after the Locarno treaties of 1925. In addition to the contemporary works discussed in the text, the crisis of the interwar period comes alive in R. Crossman, ed., *The God That Failed* (1950), in which famous Western writers tell why they were attracted to and later repelled by communism; Ortega y Gassett's renowned *The Revolt of the Masses* (1932); and F. A. Hayek's *The Road to Serfdom* (1944), a famous warning of the dangers to democratic freedoms.

In addition to C. Kindleberger's excellent study of the Great Depression cited in the Notes, there is J. Galbraith's very lively and understandable account of the stock market collapse, *The Great Crash* (1955). J. Garraty, *Unemployment in History* (1978), is noteworthy, though novels best portray the human tragedy of economic decline. W. Holtby, *South Riding* (1936), and W. Greenwood, *Love on the Dole* (1933), are moving stories of the Great Depression in England; H. Fallada, *Little Man, What Now?* (1932), is the classic counterpart for Germany. Also highly recommended as commentaries on English life between the wars are R. Graves, *Goodbye to All That,* rev. ed. (1957), and G. Orwell, *The Road to Wigan Pier* (1972). Among French novelists, André Gide painstakingly examines the French middle class and its values in *The Counterfeiters,* while Albert Camus, the greatest of the existential novelists, is at his unforgettable best in *The Stranger* and *The Plague.*

29

DICTATORSHIPS AND THE SECOND WORLD WAR

*T*HE ERA OF ANXIETY and economic depression was also a time of growing strength for political dictatorship. Popularly elected governments and basic civil liberties declined drastically in Europe. On the eve of the Second World War, liberal democratic government survived only in Great Britain, France, the Low Countries, the Scandinavian nations, and neutral Switzerland. Elsewhere in Europe, various kinds of "strong men" ruled. Dictatorship seemed the wave of the future. Thus the decline in liberal political institutions and the intellectual crisis were related elements in the general crisis of European civilization.

The era of dictatorship is a highly disturbing chapter in the history of Western civilization. The key development was not simply the resurgence of dictatorship but the rise of a new kind of tyranny—the modern totalitarian state. Modern totalitarianism reached its fullest realization in Communist Russia and Nazi Germany in the 1930s. Stalin and Hitler mobilized their peoples for enormous undertakings and ruled with unprecedented severity.

Today we want to believe that the era of totalitarian dictatorship was a terrible accident, that Stalin's slave labor camps and Hitler's gas chambers "can't happen again." But one cannot be sure: it was all very recent and very powerful. What was the nature of the twentieth-century totalitarian state? How did totalitarianism affect ordinary people, and why did it lead to another world war? These are the questions this chapter will seek to answer.

AUTHORITARIAN AND TOTALITARIAN STATES

The modern totalitarian state differed from the old-fashioned authoritarian state. Completely rejecting liberal values and drawing on the experience of total war, the totalitarian state exercised much greater control over the masses and mobilized them for constant action. The nature of this control may be examined by comparing the old and new forms of dictatorship in a general way, before entering the strange worlds of Stalin's Russia and Hitler's Germany.

CONSERVATIVE AUTHORITARIANISM

The traditional form of antidemocratic government in European history has been conservative authoritarianism. Like Catherine the Great in Russia and Metternich in Austria, the leaders of such governments have tried to prevent major changes that would undermine the existing social order. To do so, they have relied on obedient bureaucracies, vigilant police departments, and trustworthy armies. Popular participation in government has been forbidden or else severely limited to such natural allies as landlords, bureaucrats, and high church officials. Liberals, democrats, and socialists have been persecuted as radicals, often to find themselves in jail or exile.

Yet old-fashioned authoritarian governments were limited in their power and in their objectives. Lacking modern technology and communications, they had not the power to control many aspects of their subjects' lives. Nor did they wish to do so. Preoccupied with the goal of mere survival, these governments' demands were largely limited to taxes, army recruits, and passive acceptance. As long as the people did not try to change the system, they often had considerable personal independence.

After the First World War, this kind of authoritarian government revived, especially in the less-developed eastern part of Europe. There, the parliamentary regimes that had been founded on the wreckage of empires in 1918 fell one by one. By early 1938 only economically and socially advanced Czechoslovakia remained true to liberal political ideals. Conservative dictators also took over in Spain and Portugal.

There were several reasons for this development. These lands lacked a strong tradition of self-government, with its necessary restraint and compromise. Moreover, many of these new states were torn by ethnic conflicts that threatened their very existence. Dictatorship appealed to nationalists and military leaders as a way to repress such tensions and preserve national unity. Large landowners and the church were still powerful forces in these largely agrarian areas, and they often looked to dictators to save them from progressive land reform or communist agrarian upheaval. So did some members of the middle class, which was small and weak in eastern Europe. Finally, though some kind of democracy managed to stagger through the 1920s in Austria, Bulgaria, Rumania, Greece, Estonia, and Latvia, the Great Depression delivered the final blow in those countries in 1936.

Nazi Mass Rally, 1936 This picture captures the spirit of modern totalitarianism. The uniformed members of the Nazi party have willingly merged themselves into a single force and await the command of the godlike leader. *(Wide World Photos)*

Although some of the authoritarian regimes adopted certain Hitlerian and fascist characteristics in the 1930s, their general aims were not totalitarian. They were concerned more with maintaining the status quo than with forcing society into rapid change or war. This tradition lives on today, especially in some of the military dictatorships in Latin America.

Hungary was a good example of conservative authoritarianism. In the chaos of collapse in 1919, Béla Kun formed a Lenin-like government, but communism in Hungary was soon crushed by foreign troops, large landowners, and hostile peasants. Thereafter, a combination of great and medium-sized landowners instituted a semi-authoritarian regime, which maintained the status quo in the 1920s. Hungary had a parliament, but elections were carefully controlled. The peasants did not have the right to vote, and an upper house representing the landed aristocracy was re-established. There was no land reform, no major social change. In the 1930s, the Hungarian government remained conservative and nationalistic. Increasingly, it was opposed by a Nazi-like fascist movement, the Arrow Cross, which demanded radical reform and totalitarian measures.

Another example of conservative authoritarianism was newly independent Poland, where democratic government was overturned in 1926 when General Joseph Pilsudski established a military dictatorship. Poland was torn by bitter party politics and sandwiched between Russia and Germany. Pilsudski silenced opposition and tried to build a strong state. His principal supporters were the army, major industrialists, and dedicated nationalists.

In Yugoslavia, King Alexander (1921–1934) proclaimed a centralized dictatorship in 1929 to prevent ethnic rivalries among Serbs, Croats, and Slovenes from tearing the country apart. An old-style authoritarian, Alexander crushed democracy, jailed separatists, and ruled through the bureaucracy.

Another example of conservative authoritarianism was Portugal, at the westernmost end of the European peninsula. Constantly shaken by military coups and uprisings after a republican revolution in 1910, very poor and backward Portugal finally got a strong dictator in Antonio de Oliveira Salazar in 1932. A devout Catholic, Salazar gave the church the strongest possible position in the country, while controlling the press and outlawing most political activity. Yet there was no attempt to mobilize the masses or to accomplish great projects. The traditional society was firmly maintained, and that was enough.

MODERN TOTALITARIANISM

Although both are dictatorships, modern totalitarianism and conservative authoritarianism differ. They may be thought of as two distinct types of political organization that in practice sometimes share certain elements.

Modern totalitarianism burst on the scene with the revolutionary total war effort of 1914 to 1918. The war called forth a tendency to subordinate all institutions and all classes to one supreme objective: victory. Nothing, absolutely nothing, had equal value. People were called to make ever-greater sacrifices, and their personal freedom was constantly reduced by ever-greater government control. As the outstanding French thinker Elie Halévy put it in 1936, the varieties of modern totalitarian tyranny—fascism, nazism, and communism—may be thought of as "feuding brothers" with a common father, the nature of modern war.[1]

The crucial experience of World War One was carried further by Lenin and the Bolsheviks during the Russian civil war. Lenin showed how a dedicated minority could make a total effort and achieve victory over a less-determined majority. Lenin also demonstrated how institutions and human rights might be subordinated to the needs of a single group—the Communist party—and its leader, Lenin. Thus Lenin provided a model for single-party dictatorship, and he inspired imitators.

Building on its immediate origins in World War One and the Russian civil war, modern totalitarianism reached maturity in the 1930s in Stalinist Russia and Nazi Germany. Both had several fundamental characteristics of modern totalitarianism.

Armed with modern technology and communications, the true totalitarian state began as a dictatorship exercising complete political power, but it did not stop there. Increasingly, the state took over and tried to control just as completely the economic, social, intellectual, and cultural aspects of life. Although such unlimited control could not be fully realized, the individual's freedom of action was greatly reduced. Deviation from the norm even in art or family behavior could become a crime. In theory, nothing was politically neutral, nothing was outside the scope of the state.

This grandiose vision of total state control broke decisively not only with conservative authoritarianism but also with nineteenth-century liberalism and democracy. Indeed, totalitarianism was a radical revolt against liberalism. Liberalism sought to limit the power of the state and protect the sacred rights of the individual. Moreover, liberals stood for rationality, harmony, peaceful progress, and a strong middle class. All of that disgusted totalitarians as sentimental slop. They believed in will power, preached conflict, and worshiped violence. They believed that the individual was infinitely less valuable than the state and that there were no lasting rights, only temporary rewards for loyal and effective service. Only a single powerful leader and a single party, both unrestrained by law or tradition, determined the destiny of the totalitarian state.

Unlike old-fashioned authoritarianism, modern totalitarianism was based not on an elite but on the masses. As in the First World War, the totalitarian state sought and sometimes won the support and even the love of ordinary people. Modern totalitarianism built on politically alert masses, on people who had already become engaged in the political process, most notably through commitment to nationalism and socialism. Its character as a mass movement gave totalitarianism much of its elemental force.

The final shared characteristic of real totalitarian states was their boundless dynamism. The totalitarian society was a fully mobilized society, a society moving toward some goal. It was never content merely to survive, like an old-fashioned military dictatorship or a decaying democracy. Paradoxically, totalitarian regimes never reached their goals. Or, more precisely, as soon as one goal was achieved at the cost of enormous sacrifice, another arose at the leader's command to take its place. Thus totalitarianism was in the end a *permanent* revolution, an *unfinished* revolution, in which rapid, profound change imposed from on high went on forever.

TOTALITARIANISM OF THE LEFT AND THE RIGHT

The two most-developed totalitarian states—Stalin's Communist Russia and Hitler's Nazi Germany— shared all the central characteristics of totalitarianism. But although those regimes may seem more alike than not, there were at least two major differences between them.

Communism as practiced in Soviet Russia grew out of Marxian socialism. Nazism in Germany grew out of extreme nationalism and racism. This distinction meant that private property and the middle class received very different treatment in the two states. In Soviet Russia, the socialist program of the radical left was realized: all large holdings of private property were taken over by the state, and the middle class lost its wealth and status. In Germany, big landowners and industrialists on the conservative right were sharply criticized but managed to maintain their private wealth. This difference in property and class relations has led some scholars to speak of "totalitarianism of the left"—Stalinist Russia—and "totalitarianism of the right"—Nazi Germany.

More important were the differing possibilities for regeneration. Socialism, with its concetn for social justice and human progress, is linked to the living core of Western civilization and the Judeo-Christian tradition. Stalin's communism was an ugly perversion of socialism, but even in its darkest moments it

Vicious Anti-Semitism was visible in all European countries before World War One. This 1898 French cartoon shows the Jewish banker Rothschild worshipping gold and exploiting the whole world. Jews were also denounced as revolutionary socialists intent upon destroying private property and the middle class. *(Historical Pictures Service, Chicago)*

had the potential for reforming itself and creating a more humane society. Nazism, however, had no such potential. Based on the claptrap phobias of anticapitalism, anti-Semitism, and racism, its elements could be found in many a European city before the First World War. Totally negative and devoid of even perverted truth, it promised only destruction and never rebirth.

STALIN'S RUSSIA

Lenin established the basic outlines of a modern totalitarian dictatorship in Russia after the Bolshevik Revolution and during the civil war. Joseph Stalin (1879–1953) finished the job. A master of political infighting, Stalin cautiously consolidated his power and eliminated his enemies in the mid-1920s. Then in 1928, as undisputed leader of the ruling Communist party, he launched the first five-year plan—the "revolution from above," as he so aptly termed it.

The five-year plans were extremely ambitious. Often incorrectly considered a mere set of economic measures to speed up Soviet Russia's industrial development, the five-year plans actually marked the beginning of a renewed attempt to mobilize and transform Soviet society along socialist lines. The goal was to create a new way of life and to generate new attitudes and new loyalties. The means Stalin and the small Communist party elite chose were constant propaganda, enormous sacrifice, and unlimited violence and state control. Thus the Soviet Union in the 1930s became a dynamic, modern totalitarian state.

FROM LENIN TO STALIN

By spring 1921, Lenin and the Bolsheviks had won the civil war, but they ruled a shattered and devastated land. Many farms were in ruins, and food supplies were exhausted. In southern Russia, drought combined with the ravages of war to produce the worst famine in generations. By 1920, according to the government, from 50 to 90 percent of the population in seventeen provinces was starving. Industrial production also broke down completely. In 1921, for example, output of steel and cotton textiles was only about 4 percent of what it had been in 1913. The revolutionary Trotsky later wrote that the "collapse of the productive forces surpassed anything of the kind history had ever seen. The country, and the government with it, were at the very edge of the abyss."[2] The Bolsheviks had destroyed the economy as well as their foes.

In the face of economic disintegration and rioting by peasants and workers, as well as an open rebellion by previously pro-Bolshevik sailors at Kronstadt, which had to be quelled with machine guns, the tough but ever-flexible Lenin changed course. In March 1921, he announced the New Economic Policy (NEP), which re-established limited economic freedom in an attempt to rebuild agriculture and industry. During the civil war, the Communists had simply seized grain without payment. Lenin in 1921 substituted a grain tax on the country's peasant producers, who were permitted to sell their surpluses in free markets. Peasants were also encouraged to buy as many goods as they could afford from private traders and small handicraft manufacturers, both of whom were allowed to reappear. Heavy industry, railroads,

and banks, however, remained wholly nationalized. Thus NEP saw only a limited restoration of capitalism.

Lenin's New Economic Policy was shrewd and successful, from two points of view. Politically, it was a necessary but temporary compromise with Russia's overwhelming peasant majority. Flushed with victory after their revolutionary gains of 1917, the peasants would have fought to hold onto their land. With fond hopes of immediate worldwide revolution fading by 1921, Lenin realized that his government was not strong enough to take it from them. As he had accepted Germany's harsh terms at Brest-Litovsk in 1918, Lenin made a deal with the only force capable of overturning his government.

Economically, NEP brought rapid recovery. In 1926 industrial output had surpassed the level of 1913, and Russian peasants were producing almost as much grain as before the war. Counting shorter hours and increased social benefits, workers were living somewhat better than they had in the past.

As the economy recovered and the government somewhat relaxed its censorship and repression, an intense struggle for power began in the inner circles of the Communist party, for Lenin had left no chosen successor when he died in 1924. The principal contenders were the stolid Stalin and the flamboyant Trotsky.

The son of a shoemaker, Joseph Dzhugashvili—later known as Stalin—studied for the priesthood but was expelled from his theological seminary, probably for rude rebelliousness. By 1903 he had joined the Bolsheviks. In the years before the First World War, he engaged in many revolutionary activities in the Transcaucasian area of southern Russia, including a daring bank robbery to get money for the Bolsheviks. This raid gained Lenin's attention and approval. Ethnically a Georgian and not a Russian, Stalin in his early writings focused on the oppression of minority peoples in the Russian Empire. Stalin was a good organizer but a poor speaker and writer, with no experience outside of Russia.

Leon Trotsky, a great and inspiring leader who had planned the 1917 takeover (pages 883–884) and then created the victorious Red Army, appeared to have all the advantages. Yet it was Stalin who succeeded Lenin. Stalin won because he was more effective at gaining the all-important support of the party, the only genuine source of power in the one-party state.

Lenin and Stalin in 1922 Lenin re-established limited economic freedom throughout Russia in 1921, but he ran the country and the Communist party in an increasingly authoritarian way. Stalin carried the process much further and eventually built a regime based on harsh dictatorship. *(Sovfoto)*

Rising to general secretary of the party's Central Committee just before Lenin's first stroke in 1922, Stalin used his office to win friends and allies with jobs and promises. Stalin also won recognition as commissar of nationalities, a key position in which he governed many of Russia's minorities.

The "practical" Stalin also won because he appeared better able than the brilliant Trotsky to relate Marxist teaching to Russian realities in the 1920s. First, as commissar of nationalities, he built on Lenin's idea of granting minority groups a certain degree of freedom in culture and language while maintaining rigorous political control through carefully selected local Communists. Stalin could loudly claim, therefore, to have found a way to solve the ancient problem of ethnic demands for independence in the multinational state. And of course he did.

Second, Stalin developed a theory of "socialism in one country," which was more appealing to the majority of Communists than Trotsky's doctrine of "permanent revolution." Stalin argued that Russia had the ability to build socialism on its own. Trotsky maintained that socialism in Russia could succeed only if revolution occurred quickly throughout Europe. To many communists, Trotsky's views seemed to sell Russia short and to promise risky conflicts with capitalist countries by recklessly encouraging revolutionary movements around the world. Stalin's willingness to break with NEP and push socialism at home appealed to young militants. In short, Stalin's theory of socialism in one country provided many in the party with a glimmer of hope in the midst of the capitalist-appearing NEP, which they had come to detest.

With cunning skill Stalin gradually achieved absolute power between 1922 and 1927. First he allied with Trotsky's personal enemies to crush Trotsky, who was expelled from the Soviet Union in 1929 and eventually was murdered in Mexico in 1940, undoubtedly on Stalin's order. Stalin then aligned with the moderates, who wanted to go slow at home, to suppress Trotsky's radical followers. Finally, having defeated all the radicals, he turned against his allies, the moderates, and destroyed them as well. Stalin's final triumph came at the Party Congress of December 1927, which condemned all "deviation from the general party line" formulated by Stalin. The dictator was then ready to launch his "revolution from above"—the real Russian revolution for millions of ordinary citizens.

The Five-Year Plans

The Party Congress of 1927, which ratified Stalin's seizure of power, marked the end of the New Economic Policy and the beginning of the era of socialist five-year plans. The first five-year plan had staggering economic objectives. In just five years, total industrial output was to increase by 250 percent. Heavy industry, the preferred sector, was to grow even faster;

steel production, for example, was to jump almost 300 percent. Agricultural production was slated to increase by 150 percent, and one-fifth of Russia's peasants were scheduled to give up their private plots and join socialist collective farms. In spite of warnings from moderate Communists that these goals were unrealistic, Stalin raised them higher as the plan got under way. By 1930 a whirlwind of economic and social change was sweeping the country.

Stalin unleashed his "second revolution" for a variety of interrelated reasons. There were, first of all, ideological considerations. Like Lenin, Stalin and his militant supporters were deeply committed to socialism as they understood it. Since the country had recovered economically and their rule was secure, they burned to stamp out NEP's private traders, independent artisans, and few well-to-do peasants. Purely economic motivations were also important. Although the economy had recovered, it seemed to have stalled in 1927 and 1928. A new socialist offensive seemed necessary if industry and agriculture were to grow rapidly.

Political considerations were most important. Internationally, there was the old problem, remaining from prerevolutionary times, of catching up with the advanced and presumably hostile capitalist nations of the West. As Stalin said in 1931, when he pressed for ever-greater speed and sacrifice: "We are fifty or a hundred years behind the advanced countries. We must make good this distance in ten years. Either we do it, or we shall go under."[3]

Domestically, there was what Communist writers of the 1920s called the "cursed problem"—the problem of the Russian peasants. For centuries, Russian peasants had wanted to own the land, and finally they had it. Sooner or later, the Communists reasoned, the peasants would become conservative little capitalists and pose a threat to the regime. Therefore, Stalin decided on a preventive war against the peasantry, in order to bring it under the absolute control of the state.

That war was *collectivization*—the forcible consolidation of individual peasant farms into large, state-controlled enterprises. Beginning in 1929, peasants all over the Soviet Union were ordered to give up their land and animals and to become members of collective farms, although they continued to live in their own homes. As for the *kulaks,* the better-off peasants, Stalin instructed party workers to "liquidate them as a class." Stripped of their land and livestock, the kulaks were generally not even permitted to join the collective farms. Many starved or were deported to forced-labor camps for "re-education."

Since almost all peasants were in fact poor, the term *kulak* soon meant any peasant who opposed the new system. Whole villages were often attacked. One conscience-stricken colonel in the secret police confessed to a foreign journalist: "I am an old Bolshevik. I worked in the underground against the Tsar and then I fought in the Civil War. Did I do all that in order that I should now surround villages with machineguns and order my men to fire indiscriminately into crowds of peasants? Oh, no, no!"[4]

Forced collectivization of the peasants led to economic and human disaster. Large numbers of peasants slaughtered their animals and burned their crops in sullen, hopeless protest. Between 1929 and 1933, the number of horses, cattle, sheep, and goats in the Soviet Union fell by at least half. Nor were the state-controlled collective farms more productive. The output of grain barely increased between 1928 and 1938, when it was almost identical to that of 1913. Communist economists had expected collectivized agriculture to pay for new factories. Instead, the state had to invest heavily in agriculture, building thousands of tractors to replace slaughtered draft horses. Collectivized agriculture was unable to make any substantial financial contribution to Soviet industrial development in the first five-year plan. The human dimension of the tragedy was shocking. Collectivization created man-made famine in 1932 and 1933, and many perished. Indeed, Stalin confided to Churchill at Yalta in 1945 that 10 million people had died in the course of collectivization.

Yet collectivization was a political victory of sorts. By the end of 1932, fully 60 percent of Russian peasant families had been herded onto collective farms; by 1938, 93 percent. Regimented and indoctrinated as employees of an all-powerful state, the peasants were no longer even a potential political threat to Stalin and the Communist party. Moreover, the state was assured of grain for bread for urban workers, who were much more important politically than the peasants. Collective farmers had to meet their grain quotas first and worry about feeding themselves second. Many collectivized peasants drew much of their own food from tiny, grudgingly tolerated garden plots that they worked in their off hours. No wonder some peasants joked, with that grim humor peculiar to the totalitarian society, that the initials then used by the

Communist party actually stood for "The Second Serfdom, That of the Bolsheviks."

The industrial side of the five-year plans was more successful—indeed, quite spectacular. The output of industry doubled in the first five-year plan and doubled again in the second. Soviet industry produced about four times as much in 1937 as it had in 1928. No other major country had ever achieved such rapid industrial growth. Heavy industry led the way; consumer industry grew quite slowly. Steel production—a near-obsession with Stalin, whose name fittingly meant "man of steel" in Russian—increased roughly 500 percent between 1928 and 1937. A new heavy industrial complex was built almost from scratch in western Siberia. Industrial growth also went hand in hand with urban development. Cities rose where nomadic tribes had grazed their flocks. More than 25 million people migrated to cities during the 1930s.

The great industrialization drive, concentrated between 1928 and 1937, was an awe-inspiring achievement purchased at enormous sacrifice. The sudden creation of dozens of new factories required a great increase in investment and a sharp decrease in consumption. Few nations had ever invested more than one-sixth of their yearly net national income. Soviet planners decreed that more that one-third of net income go for investment. This meant that only two-thirds of everything being produced could be consumed by the people *and* the increasingly voracious military. The money was collected from the people by means of heavy, hidden sales taxes.

There was, therefore, no improvement in the average standard of living. Indeed, the most careful studies show that the average nonfarm wage apparently purchased only about *half* as many goods in 1932 as in 1928. After 1932 real wages rose slowly, so that in 1937 workers could buy about 60 percent of what they had bought in 1928. Thus rapid industrial development went with an unprecedented decline in the standard of living for ordinary people.

Two other factors contributed importantly to rapid industrialization: firm labor discipline and foreign engineers. Between 1930 and 1932, trade unions lost most of their power. The government could assign workers to any job anywhere in the country, and individuals could not move without the permission of the police. When factory managers needed more hands, they called on their counterparts on the collective farms, who sent them millions of "unneeded" peasants over the years.

Foreign engineers were hired to plan and construct many of the new factories. Highly skilled American engineers, hungry for work in the depression years, were particularly important until newly trained Soviet experts began to replace them after 1932. The gigantic mills of the new Siberian steel industry were modeled on America's best. Those modern mills were eloquent testimony to the ability of Stalin's planners to harness even the skill and technology of capitalist countries to promote the surge of socialist industry.

LIFE IN STALINIST SOCIETY

The aim of Stalin's five-year plans was to create a new kind of society and human personality, as well as a strong industrial economy and a powerful army. Stalin and his helpers were good Marxian economic determinists. Once everything was owned by the state, they believed, a socialist society and a new kind of human being would inevitably emerge. They were by no means totally successful, but they did build a new society, whose broad outlines exist to this day. For the people, life in Stalinist society had both good and bad aspects.

The most frightening aspect of Stalinist society was brutal, unrestrained police terrorism. First directed primarily against the peasants after 1929, terror was increasingly turned on leading Communists, powerful administrators, and ordinary people for no apparent reason. As one Soviet woman later recalled: "We all trembled because there was no way of getting out of it. Even a Communist himself can be caught. To avoid trouble became an exception."[5] A climate of fear fell on the land.

In the early 1930s, the top members of the party and government were Stalin's obedient servants, but there was some grumbling in the party. At a small gathering in November 1932, even Stalin's wife complained bitterly about the misery of the people. Stalin showered her with insults, and she died that same night, apparently by her own hand. In late 1934 Stalin's number-two man, Sergei Kirov, was suddenly and mysteriously murdered. Although Stalin himself probably ordered Kirov's murder, he used the incident to launch a reign of terror.

In August 1936 sixteen prominent old Bolsheviks confessed to all manner of plots against Stalin in spectacular public trials in Moscow. Then, in 1937, lesser party officials and newer henchmen were arrested. In addition to party members, union officials, managers, intellectuals, army officers, and countless ordinary citizens were struck down. Local units of the secret police were even ordered to arrest a certain percentage of the people in their district. In all, at least 8 million people were probably arrested, and millions never returned from prisons and forced labor camps.

Stalin's mass purges were truly baffling, and many explanations have been given for them. Possibly Stalin believed that the old Communists, like the peasants under NEP, were a potential threat to be wiped out in a preventive attack. Yet why did leading Communists willingly confess to crimes they could not possibly have committed? Their lives had been devoted to the party and the socialist revolution. In the words of the German novelist Arthur Koestler, they probably confessed "in order to do a last service to the Party," the party they loved even when it was wrong. Some of them were subjected to torture and brainwashing. It has been argued that the purges indicate that Stalin was sadistic or insane, for his bloodbath greatly weakened the government and the army. Others see the terror as an aspect of the fully developed totalitarian state, which must by its nature always be fighting real or imaginary enemies. At the least, the mass purges were a message to the people: no one was secure. Everyone had to serve the party and its leader with redoubled devotion.

Another aspect of life in the 1930s was constant propaganda and indoctrination. Party activists lectured workers in factories and peasants on collective farms, while newspapers, films, and radio broadcasts endlessly recounted socialist achievements and capitalist plots. Art and literature became highly political. Whereas the 1920s had seen considerable experimentation in modern art and theater, the intellectual elite were ordered by Stalin to become "engineers of human minds." Writers and artists who could effectively combine genuine creativity and political propaganda became the darlings of the regime. They often lived better than top members of the political elite. It became increasingly important for the successful writer and artist to glorify Russian nationalism. Russian history was rewritten so that early tsars like Ivan the Terrible and Peter the Great became worthy forerunners of the greatest Russian leader of all—Stalin.

Adult Education Illiteracy, especially among women, was a serious problem after the Russian Revolution. This early photo shows how adults successfully learned to read and write throughout the Soviet Union. *(Sovfoto/Eastfoto)*

Stalin seldom appeared in public, but his presence was everywhere—in portraits, statues, books, and quotations from his "sacred" writings. Although the government persecuted religion and turned churches into "museums of atheism," the state had both an earthly religion and a high priest—Marxian socialism and Joseph Stalin.

Life was hard in Stalin's Soviet Russia. The standard of living declined substantially in the 1930s. The masses of people lived primarily on black bread and wore old, shabby clothing. There were constant shortages in the stores, although very heavily taxed vodka was always readily available. A shortage of housing was a particularly serious problem. Millions were moving into the cities, but the government built few new apartments. In 1940 there were approximately 4 people per room in every urban dwelling, as opposed to 2.7 per room in 1926. A relatively lucky family received one room for all its members and shared both a kitchen and a toilet with others on the floor. Less-fortunate workers, kulaks, and class enemies built scrap-lumber shacks or underground dugouts in shantytowns.

Life was hard, but by no means hopeless. Idealism and ideology had real appeal for many Russians, who saw themselves heroically building the world's first socialist society while capitalism crumbled in the West. This optimistic belief in the future of Soviet Russia also attracted many disillusioned Western liberals to communism in the 1930s.

On a more practical level, Soviet workers did receive some important social benefits, such as old-age pensions, free medical services, free education, and day-care centers for children. Unemployment was almost unknown. Finally, there was the possibility of personal advancement.

The keys to improving one's position were specialized skills and technical education. Rapid industrialization required massive numbers of trained experts, such as skilled workers, engineers, and plant managers. Thus the state provided tremendous incentives to those who could serve its needs. It paid the mass of unskilled workers and collective farmers very low wages, but it dangled high salaries and many special privileges before its growing technical and managerial elite. This elite joined with the political and artistic elites in a new upper class, whose members were rich, powerful, and insecure, especially during the purges. Yet the possible gains of moving up outweighed the risks. Millions struggled bravely in universities, institutes, and night schools for the all-important specialized education. One young man summed it up: "In Soviet Russia there is no capital except education. If a person does not want to become a collective farmer or just a cleaning woman, the only means you have to get something is through education."[6]

WOMEN IN SOVIET RUSSIA

Women's lives were radically altered by Stalinist society. Marxists had traditionally believed that both capitalism and the middle-class husband exploited women. The Russian Revolution of 1917 immediately proclaimed complete equality of rights for women. In the 1920s, divorce and abortion were made very easy, and women were urged to work outside the home and liberate themselves sexually. A prominent and influential Bolshevik feminist, Alexandra Kollontai, went so far as to declare that the sexual act had no more significance than "drinking a glass of water." This observation drew a sharp rebuke from the rather prudish Lenin, who said that "no sane man would lie down to drink from a puddle in the gutter or even drink from a dirty glass."[7] After Stalin came to power, sexual and familial liberation was played down, and the most lasting changes for women involved work and education.

The changes were truly revolutionary. Young women were constantly told that they must be fully equal with men, that they could and should do anything men could do. Russian peasant women had long experienced the equality of backbreaking physical labor in the countryside, and they continued to enjoy that equality on collective farms. With the advent of the five-year plans, millions of women also began to toil in factories and on heavy construction, building dams, roads, and steel mills in summer heat and winter frost. Yet most of the opportunities open to men through education were also opened to women. Determined women pursued their studies and entered the ranks of the better-paid specialists in industry and science. Medicine practically became a woman's profession. By 1950, 75 percent of all doctors in Soviet Russia were women.

Thus Stalinist society gave women great opportunities but demanded great sacrifices as well. The vast majority of women simply *had* to work outside the home. Wages were so low that it was almost impossible for a family or couple to live only on the husband's earnings. Moreover, the full-time working woman had a heavy burden of household tasks in her off hours, for most Soviet men in the 1930s still considered the home and the children the woman's responsibility. Finally, rapid change and economic hardship led to many broken families, creating further physical, emotional, and mental strains for women. In any event, the often-neglected human resource of women was ruthlessly mobilized in Stalinist society. This, too, was an aspect of the Soviet totalitarian state.

MUSSOLINI'S ITALY

Before turning to Hitler's Germany, it is necessary to look briefly at Mussolini's role in Italy. Like all the other emerging dictators, Mussolini hated liberalism, and he destroyed it in Italy. But that was not all. Mussolini and his supporters were the first to call themselves "fascists"—revolutionaries determined to create a certain kind of totalitarian state. As Mussolini's famous slogan of 1926 put it: "Everything in the state, nothing outside the state, nothing against the state." But Mussolini in power, unlike Stalin and Hitler, did not in fact create a real totalitarian state.

His dictatorship was rather an instructive hybrid, a halfway house between conservative authoritarianism and modern totalitarianism.

THE SEIZURE OF POWER

Before the First World War, Italy was a liberal state moving gradually toward democracy. But there were serious problems. Much of the Italian population was still poor, and class differences were extreme. Many peasants were more attached to their villages and local interests than to the national state. Moreover, the papacy and many devout Catholics, as well as the socialists, were strongly opposed to the heirs of Cavour and Garibaldi, middle-class lawyers and politicians who ran the country largely for their own benefit. Relations between church and state were often tense.

The war worsened the political situation. Having fought on the side of the Allies almost exclusively for purposes of territorial expansion, Italian nationalists were bitterly disappointed with Italy's modest gains at Versailles. Workers and peasants also felt cheated: to win their support during the war, the government had promised social and land reform, which it did not deliver after the war.

Encouraged by the Russian Revolution of 1917, radical workers and peasants began occupying factories and seizing land in 1920. These actions scared and radicalized the property-owning classes. The Italian middle classes were already in an ugly mood, having suffered from inflation during the war. Moreover, after the war, the pope lifted his ban on participation by Catholics in Italian politics, and a strong Catholic party quickly emerged. Thus by 1922 almost all the major groups in Italian society were opposed—though for different reasons—to the liberal parliamentary government.

Into these cross-currents of unrest and frustration stepped the blustering, bullying Benito Mussolini (1883–1945). Son of a village schoolteacher and a poor blacksmith, Mussolini began his political career as a Socialist leader and radical newspaper editor before World War One. In 1914, powerfully influenced by antiliberal cults of violent action, the young Mussolini urged that Italy join the Allies, for which he was expelled from the Italian Socialist party by its antiwar majority. Later Mussolini fought at the front and was wounded in 1917. Returning home, he began organizing bitter war veterans like himself into a band of Fascists—from the Italian word for "a union of forces."

At first, Mussolini's program was a radical combination of nationalist and socialist demands, including territorial expansion, benefits for workers, and land reform for peasants. As such, it competed with the better-organized Socialist party and failed to get off the ground. When Mussolini saw that his violent verbal assaults on the rival Socialists won him growing support from the frightened middle class, he shifted gears in 1920. In thought and action, Mussolini was a striking example of the turbulence of the age of anxiety.

Mussolini and his growing private army of Black Shirts began to grow violent. Typically, a band of Fascist toughs would roar off in trucks at night and swoop down on a few isolated Socialist organizers, beating them up and force-feeding them almost deadly doses of castor oil. Few people were killed, but Socialist newspapers, union halls, and local Socialist party headquarters were destroyed. Mussolini's toughs pushed Communists and Socialists out of the city governments of northern Italy.

Mussolini, a skillful politician, refused to become a puppet of frightened conservatives and capitalists. He allowed his followers to convince themselves that they were not just opposing the "reds," but making a real revolution of their own. Many believed that they were not only destroying parliamentary government, but forming a strong, dynamic movement that would help the little people against the established interests.

With the government breaking down in 1922, largely because of the chaos created by his direct-action bands, Mussolini stepped forward as the savior of order and property. Striking a conservative note in his speeches and gaining the sympathetic neutrality of army leaders, Mussolini demanded the resignation of the existing government and his own appointment by the king. In October 1922, to force matters a large group of Fascists marched on Rome to threaten the king and force him to call on Mussolini. The threat worked. Victor Emmanuel III (1900–1946), who had no love for the old liberal politicians, asked Mussolini to form a new cabinet. Thus, after widespread violence and a threat of armed uprising, Mussolini seized power "legally." He was immediately granted dictatorial authority for one year by the king and the parliament.

Mussolini loved to swagger and bluster. Here he strikes a theatrical pose while reviewing his troops in Rome. *(BBC Hulton/The Bettmann Archive)*

THE REGIME IN ACTION

Mussolini became dictator on the strength of Italians' rejection of parliamentary government, coupled with fears of Russian-style revolution. Yet what he intended to do with his power was by no means clear until 1924. Some of his dedicated supporters pressed for a "second revolution." Mussolini's ministers, however, included old Conservatives, Moderates, and even two reform-minded Socialists. A new electoral law was passed giving two-thirds of the representatives in the parliament to the party that won the most votes, which allowed the Fascists and their allies to win an overwhelming majority in 1924. Shortly thereafter, five of Mussolini's Fascist thugs kidnapped and murdered Giacomo Matteotti, the young leader of the Socialists in the parliament. In the face of this outrage, the opposition demanded that Mussolini's armed squads be dissolved and all violence be banned.

Although he may or may not have ordered Matteotti's murder, Mussolini stood at the crossroads of a severe political crisis. After some hesitation, he charged forward. Declaring his desire to "make the nation Fascist," he imposed a series of repressive measures. Freedom of the press was abolished, elections were fixed, and the government ruled by decree. Mussolini arrested his political opponents, disbanded all independent labor unions, and put dedicated Fascists in control of Italy's schools. Moreover, he created a Fascist youth movement, Fascist labor unions, and many other Fascist organizations. By the end of 1926, Italy was a one-party dictatorship under Mussolini's unquestioned leadership.

Yet Mussolini did not complete the establishment of a modern totalitarian state. His Fascist party never became all-powerful. It never destroyed the old power structure, as the Communists did in Soviet Russia, or succeeded in dominating it, as the Nazis did in Germany. Membership in the Fascist party was more a sign of an Italian's respectability than a commitment to radical change. Interested primarily in personal power, Mussolini was content to compromise with the old conservative classes that controlled the army, the economy, and the state. He never tried to purge these classes or even move very vigorously against them. He controlled and propagandized labor, but left big business to regulate itself, profitably and securely. There was no land reform.

Mussolini also came to draw on the support of the Catholic church. In the Lateran Agreement of 1929, he recognized the Vatican as a tiny independent state, and he agreed to give the church heavy financial support. The pope expressed his satisfaction and urged Italians to support Mussolini's government.

Nothing better illustrates Mussolini's unwillingness to harness everyone and everything for dynamic action than his treatment of women. He abolished divorce and told women to stay at home and produce children. To promote that goal, he decreed a special tax on bachelors in 1934. In 1938 women were limited by law to a maximum of 10 percent of the better-paying jobs in industry and government. Italian women, as women, appear not to have changed their attitudes or behavior in any important way under Fascist rule.

It is also noteworthy that Mussolini's government did not persecute Jews until late in the Second World War, when Italy was under Nazi control. Nor did Mussolini establish a truly ruthless police state. Only twenty-three political prisoners were condemned to death between 1926 and 1944. In spite of much pompous posing by the chauvinist leader and in spite of mass meetings, salutes, and a certain copying of Hitler's aggression in foreign policy after 1933, Mussolini's Italy—though undemocratic—was never really totalitarian.

HITLER'S GERMANY

The most frightening totalitarian state was Nazi Germany. A product of Hitler's evil genius as well as of Germany's social and political situation and the general attack on liberalism and rationality in the age of anxiety, Nazi Germany emerged rapidly after Hitler came to power in 1933. The Nazis quickly smashed or took over most independent organizations, mobilized the economy, and began brutally persecuting the Jewish population. From the start, all major decisions were in the hands of the aggressive dictator Adolf Hitler.

Adolf Hitler A lonely, unsuccessful misfit before 1914, Hitler found his mission during World War One and its aftermath. He emerged as a spellbinding speaker and a master of the politics of hate and violence. *(UPI/Bettmann Newsphotos)*

THE ROOTS OF NAZISM

Nazism grew out of many complex developments, of which the most influential were extreme nationalism and racism. These two ideas captured the mind of the young Hitler, and it was he who dominated Nazism for as long as it lasted.

Born the fourth child of a successful Austrian customs official and an indulgent mother, Adolf Hitler (1889–1945) spent his childhood happily in small towns in Austria. A good student in grade school, Hitler did poorly on reaching high school and dropped out at age fourteen after the death of his father. After four years of unfocused loafing, Hitler finally left for Vienna to become an artist. Denied admission to the Imperial Academy of Fine Arts because he lacked talent, the dejected Hitler stayed on in Vienna. There he lived a comfortable, lazy life on his generous orphan's pension and found most of the perverted beliefs that guided his life.

In Vienna Hitler soaked up extreme German nationalism, which was particularly strong there. Austro-German nationalists, as if to compensate for their declining position in the Austro-Hungarian Empire, believed Germans to be a superior people and the natural rulers of central Europe. They often advocated union with Germany and violent expulsion of "inferior" peoples as the means of maintaining German domination of the Austro-Hungarian Empire.

Hitler was deeply impressed by Vienna's mayor, Karl Lueger, whom he called the "mightiest mayor of all times." Lueger claimed to be a "Christian socialist." With the help of the Catholic trade unions, he had succeeded in winning the support of the little people of Vienna for an attack on capitalism and liberalism, which he held responsible for un-Christian behavior and excessive individualism. A master of mass politics in the urban world, Lueger showed Hitler the enormous potential of anticapitalist and antiliberal propaganda.

From Lueger and others, Hitler eagerly absorbed virulent anti-Semitism, racism, and hatred of Slavs. He was particularly inspired by the racist ravings of an ex-monk named Lanz von Liebenfels. Preaching the crudest, most exaggerated distortions of the Darwinian theory of survival, Liebenfels stressed the superiority of Germanic races, the inevitability of racial conflict, and the inferiority of the Jews. Liebenfels even anticipated the breeding and extermination policies of the Nazi state. He claimed that the master race had to multiply its numbers by means of polygamy and breeding stations, while it systematically sterilized and liquidated inferior races. Anti-Semitism and racism became Hitler's most passionate convictions, his explanation for everything. He believed inferior races—the Slavs and the Jews in particular—were responsible for Austria's woes. The Jews, he claimed, directed an international conspiracy of finance capitalism and Marxian socialism against German culture, German unity, and the German race. Hitler's belief was totally irrational, but he never doubted it.

Although he moved to Munich in 1913 to avoid being drafted in the Austrian army, the lonely Hitler greeted the outbreak of the First World War as a salvation. He later wrote in his autobiography, *Mein Kampf,* that, "overcome by passionate enthusiasm, I fell to my knees and thanked heaven out of an overflowing heart." The struggle and discipline of war gave life meaning, and Hitler served bravely as a dispatch carrier on the western front.

When Germany was suddenly defeated in 1918, Hitler's world was shattered. Not only was he a fanatical nationalist, but war was his reason for living. Convinced that Jews and Marxists had "stabbed Germany in the back," he vowed to fight on. And in the bitterness and uncertainty of postwar Germany, his wild speeches began to attract attention.

In late 1919 Hitler joined a tiny extremist group in Munich called the German Workers' party. In addition to denouncing Jews, Marxists, and democrats, the German Workers' party promised unity under a uniquely German "national socialism," which would abolish the injustices of capitalism and create a mighty "people's community." By 1921 Hitler had gained absolute control of this small but growing party. Moreover, Hitler was already a master of mass propaganda and political showmanship. Party members sported badges and uniforms, gave victory salutes, and marched like robots through the streets of Munich. But Hitler's most effective tool was the mass rally, a kind of political revival meeting. Songs, slogans, and demonstrations built up the tension until Hitler finally arrived. He then often worked his audience into a frenzy with wild, demagogic attacks on the Versailles treaty, the Jews, the war profiteers, and Germany's Weimar Republic.

Party membership multiplied tenfold after early 1922. In late 1923, when the Weimar Republic seemed on the verge of collapse, Hitler decided on an armed uprising in Munich. Inspired by Mussolini's recent easy victory, Hitler had found an ally in General Ludendorff of First World War fame. After Hitler had overthrown the Bavarian government, Ludendorff was supposed to march on Berlin with Hitler's support. The plot was poorly organized, however, and it was crushed by the police, backed up by the army, in less than a day. Hitler was arrested, tried, and sentenced to five years in prison. He had failed for the moment. But Nazism had been born, and it did not die.

HITLER'S ROAD TO POWER

At his trial, Hitler violently denounced the Weimar Republic and skillfully presented his own program. In doing so he gained enormous publicity and attention. Moreover, he learned from his unsuccessful

"Hitler, Our Last Hope" So reads the very effective Nazi campaign poster, which is attracting attention with its gaunt and haggard faces. By 1932 almost half of all Germans, like these in Berlin, had come to agree. *(Bildarchiv Preussischer Kulturbesitz)*

revolt. Hitler concluded that he had to undermine rather than overthrow the government, that he had to use its tolerant democratic framework to intimidate the opposition and come to power through electoral competition. He forced his more violent supporters to accept his new strategy. Finally, Hitler used his brief prison term—he was released in less than a year—to dictate *Mein Kampf.* There he expounded on his basic themes—"race," with the stress on anti-Semitism; "living space," with a sweeping vision of war and conquered territory; and the leader-dictator (*Führer*) with unlimited, arbitrary power. Hitler's followers had their bible.

In the years of prosperity and relative stability between 1924 and 1929, Hitler concentrated on building his National Socialist German Workers' party, or Nazi party. By 1928 the party had a hundred thousand highly disciplined members under Hitler's absolute control. To appeal to the middle class, Hitler de-emphasized the anticapitalist elements of national socialism and vowed to fight Bolshevism.

The Nazis were still a small splinter group in 1928, when they received only 2.6 percent of the vote in the general elections and twelve Nazis won seats in the parliament. There the Nazi deputies pursued the legal strategy of using democracy to destroy democracy. As Hitler's talented future minister of propaganda Joseph Goebbels (1897–1945) explained in 1928 in the party newspaper: "We become Reichstag deputies in order to paralyze the spirit of Weimar with its own aid. . . . We come as enemies! As the wolf breaks into the sheepfold, so we come."[8]

In 1929 the Great Depression began striking down economic prosperity, one of the barriers that had kept the wolf at bay. Unemployment jumped from 1.3 million in 1929 to 5 million in 1930; that year Germany had almost as many unemployed as all the other countries of Europe combined. Industrial production fell by one-half between 1929 and 1932. By the end of 1932, an incredible 43 percent of the labor force was unemployed, and it was estimated that only one in every three union members was working full time. No factor contributed more to Hitler's success than the economic crisis. Never very interested in economics before, Hitler began promising German voters economic as well as political and military salvation.

Hitler focused his promises on the middle and lower-middle class—small businessmen, office workers, artisans, and peasants. Already disillusioned by the great inflation of 1923, these people were seized by panic as bankruptcies increased, unemployment soared, and the dreaded Communists made dramatic election gains. The middle and lower-middle classes deserted the Conservative and Moderate parties for the Nazis in great numbers.

The Nazis also appealed strongly to German youth. Indeed, in some ways the Nazi movement was a mass movement of young Germans. Hitler himself was only forty in 1929, and he and most of his top aides were much younger than other leading German politicians. "National Socialism is the organized will of the youth," proclaimed the official Nazi slogan, and the battle cry of Gregor Strasser, a leading Nazi organizer, was, "Make way, you old ones."[9] In 1931 almost 40 percent of Nazi party members were under thirty, compared to 20 percent of Social Democrats. Two-thirds of Nazi members were under forty. National recovery, exciting and rapid change, and personal advancement: these were the appeals of Nazism to millions of German youths.

In the election of 1930, the Nazis won 6.5 million votes and 107 seats, which made them second in strength only to the Social Democrats, the moderate socialists. The economic situation continued to deteriorate, and Hitler kept promising he would bring re-

covery. In 1932 the Nazi vote leaped to 14.5 million, and the Nazis became the largest party in the Reichstag.

Another reason Hitler came to power was the breakdown of democratic government as early as May 1930. Unable to gain support of a majority in the Reichstag, Chancellor (chief minister) Heinrich Brüning convinced the president, the aging war hero General Hindenburg, to authorize rule by decree. The Weimar Republic's constitution permitted such rule in emergency situations, but the rather authoritarian, self-righteous Brüning intended to use it indefinitely. Moreover, Brüning was determined to overcome the economic crisis by cutting back government spending and ruthlessly forcing down prices and wages. Brüning's ultraorthodox policies not only intensified the economic collapse in Germany, they also convinced the lower-middle classes that the country's republican leaders were stupid and corrupt. These classes were pleased rather than dismayed by Hitler's attacks on the republican system. After President Hindenburg forced Brüning to resign in May 1932, the new government headed by Franz von Papen continued to rule by decree.

The continuation of the struggle between the Social Democrats and Communists, right up until the moment Hitler took power, was another aspect of the breakdown of democratic government. The Communists foolishly refused to cooperate with the Social Democrats, even though the two parties together outnumbered the Nazis in the Reichstag, even after the elections of 1932. German Communists (and the complacent Stalin) were blinded by their ideology and their hatred of the Socialists. They were certain that Hitler's rise represented the last agonies of monopoly capitalism and that a Communist revolution would quickly follow his taking power. The Socialist leaders pleaded, even at the Russian embassy, for at least a temporary alliance with the Communists to block Hitler, but to no avail. Perhaps the Weimar Republic was already too far gone, but this disunity on the left was undoubtedly another nail in its coffin.

Finally, there was Hitler's skill as a politician. A master of mass propaganda and psychology, he had written in *Mein Kampf* that the masses were the "driving force of the most important changes in this world" and were themselves driven by hysterical fanaticism and not by knowledge. To arouse such hysterical fanaticism, he believed that all propaganda had to be limited to a few simple, endlessly repeated

The Mobilization of Young People was a prime objective of the Nazi leadership. Here boys in a Nazi youth group, some of whom are only children, are disciplined and conditioned to devote themselves to the regime. *(BBC Hulton/The Bettmann Archive)*

slogans. Thus, in the terrible economic and political crisis, he harangued vast audiences with passionate, irrational oratory. Men moaned and women cried, seized by emotion. And many uncertain individuals, surrounded by thousands of entranced listeners, found security and a sense of belonging.

At the same time, Hitler excelled at dirty, backroom politics. That, in fact, brought him to power. In 1932 he cleverly succeeded in gaining the support of key people in the army and big business. These people thought they could use Hitler for their own advantage, to get increased military spending, fat contracts, and tough measures against workers. Conservative and nationalistic politicians like Papen thought similarly. They thus accepted Hitler's demand to join the government only if he became chancellor. There would be only two other National Socialists and nine solid Conservatives as ministers, and in such a coalition government, they reasoned, Hitler could be used and controlled. On January 30, 1933, Hitler was legally appointed chancellor by President Hindenburg.

THE NAZI STATE AND SOCIETY

Hitler moved rapidly and skillfully to establish an unshakable dictatorship. His first step was to continue using terror and threats to gain more power while maintaining legal appearances. He immediately called for new elections and applied the enormous power of the government to restrict his opponents. In the midst of a violent electoral campaign, the Reichstag building was partly destroyed by fire. Although the Nazis themselves may have set the fire, Hitler screamed that the Communist party was responsible. On the strength of this accusation, he convinced President Hindenburg to sign dictatorial emergency acts that practically abolished freedom of speech and assembly, in addition to most personal liberties.

When the Nazis won only 44 percent of the vote in the elections, Hitler immediately outlawed the Communist party and arrested its parliamentary representatives. Then, on March 23, 1933, the Nazis pushed through the Reichstag the so-called Enabling Act, which gave Hitler absolute dictatorial power for four years. Only the Social Democrats voted against this bill, for Hitler had successfully blackmailed the Center party by threatening to attack the Catholic church.

Armed with the Enabling Act, Hitler and the Nazis moved to smash or control all independent organizations. Meanwhile, Hitler and his propagandists constantly proclaimed that their revolution was legal and constitutional. This deceitful stress on legality, coupled with the divide-and-conquer technique, disarmed the opposition until it was too late for effective resistance.

The systematic subjugation of independent organizations and the creation of a totalitarian state had massive repercussions. The Social Democrat and Center parties were soon dissolved, and Germany became a one-party state. Only the Nazi party was legal. Elections were farces. The Reichstag was jokingly referred to as the most expensive glee club in the country, for its only function was to sing hymns of praise to the Führer. Hitler and the Nazis took over the government bureaucracy intact, installing many Nazis in top positions. At the same time, they created a series of overlapping Nazi party organizations, responsible solely to Hitler. Thus Hitler had both an established bureaucracy for normal business and a private, personal "party government" for special duties.

In the economic sphere, strikes were forbidden and labor unions were abolished, replaced by a Nazi Labor Front. Professional people—doctors and lawyers, teachers and engineers—also saw their previously independent organizations swallowed up in Nazi associations. Nor did the Nazis neglect cultural and intellectual life. Publishing houses were put under Nazi control, and universities and writers were quickly brought into line. Democratic, socialist, and Jewish literature was put on ever-growing blacklists. Passionate students and pitiful professors burned forbidden books in public squares. Modern art and architecture were ruthlessly prohibited. Life became violently anti-intellectual. As Hitler's cynical minister of propaganda, Joseph Goebbels, put it: "When I hear the word 'culture' I reach for my gun."[10] By 1934 a totalitarian state characterized by frightening dynamism and obedience to Hitler was already largely in place.

By 1934 only the army retained independence, and Hitler moved brutally and skillfully to establish his control there, too. He realized that the army, as well as big business, was suspicious of the Nazi storm troopers (the SA), the quasi-military band of 3 million toughs in brown shirts who had fought Communists and beaten up Jews before the Nazis took power. These unruly storm troopers expected top positions in the army and even talked of a "second revolution" against capitalism. Needing the support of the army and big business, Hitler decided that the SA leaders had to be eliminated. On the night of June 30, 1934, he struck.

Hitler's elite personal guard—the SS—arrested and shot without trial roughly a thousand SA leaders and assorted political enemies. While his propagandists spread lies about SA conspiracies, the army leaders and President Hindenburg responded to the purge with congratulatory telegrams. Shortly thereafter, the army leaders swore a binding oath of "unquestioning obedience . . . to the Leader of the German State and People, Adolf Hitler." The purge of the SA was another decisive step toward unlimited totalitarian terror. The SS, the elite guard that had loyally murdered the SA leaders, grew rapidly. Under its methodical, inhuman leader, Heinrich Himmler (1900–1945), the SS joined with the political police, the Gestapo, to expand its network of special courts and concentration camps. Nobody was safe.

From the beginning, the Jews were a special object of Nazi persecution. By the end of 1934, most Jewish lawyers, doctors, professors, civil servants, and musicians had lost their jobs and right to practice their professions. In 1935 the infamous Nuremberg Laws classified as Jewish anyone having one or more Jewish grandparents and deprived Jews of all rights of citizenship. By 1938 roughly one-quarter of Germany's half-million Jews had emigrated, sacrificing almost all their property in order to leave Germany.

Following the assassination of a German diplomat in Paris by a young Jewish boy trying desperately to strike out at persecution, the attack on the Jews accelerated. A well-organized wave of violence destroyed homes, synagogues, and businesses, after which German Jews were rounded up and made to pay for the damage. It became very difficult for Jews to leave Germany. Some Germans privately opposed these outrages, but most went along or looked the other way. Although this lack of response partly reflected the individual's helplessness in the totalitarian state, it was also a sign of the strong popular support Hitler's government enjoyed.

HITLER'S POPULARITY

Hitler had promised the masses economic recovery —"work and bread"—and he delivered. Breaking with Brüning's do-nothing policies, Hitler immedi-ately launched a large public works program to pull Germany out of the depression. Work began on superhighways, offices, gigantic sports stadia, and public housing. In 1936, as Germany rearmed rapidly, government spending began to concentrate on the military. The result was that unemployment dropped steadily, from 6 million in January 1933 to about 1 million in late 1936. By 1938 there was a shortage of workers, and women eventually took many jobs previously denied them by the antifeminist Nazis. Thus everyone had work, and between 1932 and 1938 the standard of living for the average employed worker rose more than 20 percent. The profits of business also increased. For millions of people, economic recovery was tangible evidence in their daily lives that the excitement and dynamism of Nazi rule were based on more than show.

For the masses of ordinary German citizens, who were not Jews, Slavs, gypsies, Jehovah's Witnesses, or Communists, Hitler's government meant greater equality and exceptional opportunities. It must be remembered that in 1933 the position of the traditional German elites—the landed aristocracy, the wealthy capitalists, and the well-educated professional classes —was still very strong. Barriers between classes were generally high. Hitler's rule introduced vast changes in this pattern. For example, stiff educational requirements, which favored the well-to-do, were greatly relaxed. The new Nazi elite was composed largely of young and poorly educated dropouts, rootless lower-middle-class people like Hitler, who rose to the top with breathtaking speed.

More generally, the Nazis, like the Russian Communists, tolerated privilege and wealth only as long as they served the needs of the party. Big business was constantly ordered around, to the point that "probably never in peacetime has an ostensibly capitalist economy been directed as non- and even anti-capitalistically as the German economy between 1933 and 1939."[11] Hitler brought about a kind of social revolution, which was enthusiastically embraced by millions of modest middle- and lower-middle-class people and even by many workers.

Hitler's extreme nationalism, which had helped him gain power, continued to appeal to Germans after 1933. Ever since the wars against Napoleon, many Germans had believed in a special mission for a superior German nation. The successes of Bismarck had furthered such feelings, and near-victory in World War One made nationalists eager for re-

Events Leading to World War Two

1919	Treaty of Versailles
	J. M. Keynes, *Economic Consequences of the Peace*
1919–1920	U.S. Senate rejects the Treaty of Versailles
1921	Germany is billed $35 billion in reparations
1922	Mussolini seizes power in Italy
	Germany proposes a moratorium on reparations
January 1923	France and Belgium occupy the Ruhr
	Germany orders passive resistance to the occupation
October 1923	Stresemann agrees to reparations with re-examination of Germany's ability to pay
1924	Dawes Plan: German reparations reduced and put on a sliding scale; large U.S. loans to Germany recommended to promote German recovery; occupation of the Ruhr ends
	Adolf Hitler, *Mein Kampf*
1924–1929	Spectacular German economic recovery; circular flow of international funds enables sizable reparations payments
1925	Treaties of Locarno promote European security and stability
1926	Germany joins the League of Nations
1928	Kellogg-Briand Pact renounces war as an instrument of international affairs
1929	Young Plan further reduces German reparations
	Crash of U.S. stock market
1929–1933	Depths of the Great Depression
1931	Japan invades Manchuria
1932	Nazis become the largest party in the Reichstag
January 1933	Hitler appointed chancellor
March 1933	Reichstag passes the Enabling Act, granting Hitler absolute dictatorial power
October 1933	Germany withdraws from the League of Nations
July 1934	Nazis murder Austrian chancellor
March 1935	Hitler announces German rearmament
June 1935	Anglo-German naval agreement
October 1935	Mussolini invades Ethiopia and receives Hitler's support
1935	Nuremburg Laws deprive Jews of all rights of citizenship
March 1936	German armies move unopposed into the demilitarized Rhineland
July 1936	Outbreak of civil war in Spain
1937	Japan invades China
	Rome-Berlin Axis
March 1938	Germany annexes Austria
September 1938	Munich Conference: Britain and France agree to German seizure of the Sudetenland from Czechoslovakia
March 1939	Germany occupies the rest of Czechoslovakia; the end of appeasement in Britain
August 1939	Russo-German nonaggression pact
September 1, 1939	Germany invades Poland
September 3, 1939	Britain and France declare war on Germany

newed expansion in the 1920s. Thus, when Hitler went from one foreign triumph to another and a great German empire seemed within reach, the majority of the population was delighted and praised the Führer's actions.

By no means all Germans supported Hitler, however, and a number of German groups actively resisted him after 1933. Tens of thousands of political enemies were imprisoned, and thousands were executed. Opponents of the Nazis pursued different goals, and under totalitarian conditions they were never unified, which helps account for their ultimate lack of success. In the first years of Hitler's rule, the principal resisters were the Communists and the Social Democrats in the trade unions. But the expansion of the SS system of terror after 1935 smashed most of these leftists. A second group of opponents arose in the Catholic and Protestant churches. However, their efforts were directly primarily at preserving genuine religious life, not at overthrowing Hitler. Finally, in 1938 (and again in 1942–1944), some high-ranking army officers, who feared the consequences of Hitler's reckless aggression, plotted against him, unsuccessfully.

NAZI EXPANSION AND THE SECOND WORLD WAR

Although economic recovery and increased opportunities for social advancement won Hitler support, they were only by-products of Nazi totalitarianism. The guiding concepts of Nazism remained space and race—the territorial expansion of the superior German race. As Germany regained its economic strength and as independent organizations were brought under control, Hitler formed alliances with other dictators and began expanding. German expansion was facilitated by the uncertain, divided, pacific Western democracies, which tried to buy off Hitler to avoid war. Yet war was inevitable, in both the West and the East, for Hitler's ambitions were essentially unlimited. On both war fronts the Nazi soldiers scored enormous successes until late 1942, establishing a horrifyingly vast empire of death and destruction.

AGGRESSION AND APPEASEMENT, 1933–1939

Hitler's tactics in international politics after 1933 strikingly resembled those he used in domestic politics between 1924 and 1933. When Hitler was weak, he righteously proclaimed that he intended to overturn the "unjust system" established by the treaties of Versailles and Locarno—but only by legal means. As he grew stronger, and as other leaders showed their willingness to compromise, he increased his demands and finally began attacking his independent neighbors (see Map 29.1).

Hitler realized that his aggressive policies had to be carefully camouflaged at first, for Germany's army was limited by the Treaty of Versailles to only a hundred thousand men. As he told a group of army commanders in February 1933, the early stages of his policy of "conquest of new living space in the East and its ruthless Germanization" had serious dangers. If France had real leaders, Hitler said, "it will not give us time but attack us, presumably with its eastern satellites."[12] Thus Hitler loudly proclaimed his peaceful intentions to all the world. Nevertheless, he felt strong enough to walk out of a sixty-nation disarmament conference and withdraw from the League of Nations in October 1933. Stresemann's policy of peaceful cooperation was dead; the Nazi determination to rearm was out in the open.

Following this action, which met with widespread approval at home, Hitler moved to incorporate independent Austria into a Greater Germany. Austrian Nazis climaxed an attempted overthrow by murdering the Austrian chancellor in July 1934. They were unable to take power, however, because a worried Mussolini, who had initially greeted Hitler as a fascist little brother, massed his troops on the Brenner Pass and threatened to fight. When, in March 1935, Hitler established a general military draft and declared the "unequal" disarmament clauses of the Treaty of Versailles null and void, other countries appeared to understand the danger. With France taking the lead, Italy and Great Britain protested strongly and warned against future aggressive actions.

Yet the emerging united front against Hitler quickly collapsed. Of crucial importance, Britain adopted a policy of appeasement, granting Hitler everything he could reasonably want (and more) in order to avoid war. The first step was an Anglo-German naval agreement in June 1935, which broke

MAP 29.1 The Growth of Nazi Germany, 1933–1939 Until March 1939, Hitler brought ethnic Germans into the Nazi state; then he turned on the Slavic peoples he had always hated.

Germany's isolation. The second step came in March 1936, when Hitler suddenly marched his armies into the demilitarized Rhineland, brazenly violating the treaties of Versailles and Locarno. This was the last good chance to stop the Nazis, for Hitler had ordered his troops to retreat if France resisted militarily. But an uncertain France would not move without British support, and the occupation of German soil by Ger-

man armies seemed right and just to Britain. Its strategic position greatly improved, Germany had handed France a tremendous psychological defeat.

British appeasement, which practically dictated French policy, lasted far into 1939. It was motivated by British feelings of guilt toward Germany and the pacifism of a population still horrified by the memory of the First World War. Like many Germans,

Cartoonist David Low's biting criticism of appeasing leaders appeared shortly after Hitler remilitarized the Rhineland. Appeasement also appealed to millions of ordinary citizens, who wanted to avoid at any cost another great war. *(Cartoon by David Low supplied by permission of* The London Standard*)*

British statesmen seriously underestimated Hitler. They believed that they could use him to stop Russian communism. A leading member of Britain's government personally told Hitler in November 1937 that it was his conviction that Hitler "not only had accomplished great things in Germany itself, but that through the total destruction of Communism in his own country . . . Germany rightly had to be con-sidered as a Western bulwark against Commu-nism."[13] Such rigid anticommunist feelings made an alliance between the Western powers and Stalin against Hitler very unlikely.

As Britain and France opted for appeasement and Russia watched all developments suspiciously, Hitler found powerful allies. In 1935 the bombastic Musso-lini decided that imperial expansion was needed to revitalize fascism. From Italian colonies on the east coast of Africa he attacked the independent African kingdom of Ethiopia. The Western powers and the League of Nations piously condemned Italian aggression, which angered Mussolini, without saving Ethiopia from defeat. Hitler, who had secretly supplied Ethiopia with arms to heat up the conflict, supported Italy energetically and thereby overcame Mussolini's lingering doubts about the Nazis. The result was an agreement on close cooperation in 1936 between Italy and Germany, the so-called Rome-Berlin Axis. Japan, which had been expanding into Manchuria since 1931, soon joined the alliance between Italy and Germany.

At the same time, Germany and Italy intervened in the long, complicated Spanish civil war, where their support eventually helped General Francisco Franco's fascist movement defeat republican Spain. Spain's only official aid came from Soviet Russia, for public opinion in Britain and especially in France was hopelessly divided on the Spanish question.

By late 1937, as he was proclaiming his peaceful intentions to the British and their gullible prime minister, Neville Chamberlain, Hitler told his generals his real plans. His "unshakable decision" was to crush Austria and Czechoslovakia at the earliest possible moment, as the first step in his long-contemplated drive to the east for "living space." By threatening Austria with invasion, Hitler forced the Austrian chancellor in March 1938 to put local Nazis in control of the government. The next day, German armies moved in unopposed, and Austria became two more provinces of Greater Germany (see Map 29.1).

Simultaneously, Hitler began demanding that the pro-Nazi, German-speaking minority of western Czechoslovakia—the Sudetenland—be turned over to Germany. Yet democratic Czechoslovakia was prepared to defend itself. Moreover, France had been Czechoslovakia's ally since 1924; and if France fought, Soviet Russia was pledged to help. As war appeared inevitable—for Hitler had already told the leader of the Sudeten Germans that "we must always ask so much we cannot be satisfied"—appeasement triumphed again. In September 1938, Chamberlain flew to Germany three times in fourteen days. In these negotiations, to which Russia was deliberately not invited, Chamberlain and the French agreed with Hitler that the Sudetenland should be ceded to Germany immediately. Returning to London from the Munich Conference, Chamberlain told cheering crowds that he had secured "peace with honor . . . peace for our time." Sold out by the Western powers, Czechoslovakia gave in.

Confirmed once again in his opinion of the Western democracies as weak and racially degenerate, Hitler accelerated his aggression. In a shocking violation of his solemn assurances that the Sudetenland was his last territorial demand, Hitler's armies occupied the Czech lands in March 1939, while Slovakia became a puppet state. The effect on Western public opinion was electrifying. For the first time, there was no possible rationale of self-determination for Nazi aggression, since Hitler was seizing Czechs and Slovaks as captive peoples. Thus, when Hitler used the question of German minorities in Danzig as a pretext to smash Poland, a suddenly militant Chamberlain declared that Britain and France would fight if Hitler attacked his eastern neighbor. Hitler did not take these warnings seriously, and he pressed on.

In an about-face that stunned the world, Hitler offered and Stalin signed a ten-year Russo-German nonaggression pact in August 1939, whereby each dictator promised to remain neutral if the other became involved in war. Even more startling was the attached secret protocol, which ruthlessly divided eastern Europe into German and Russian zones, "in the event of a political territorial reorganization." Although this top-secret protocol sealing the destruction of Poland and the Baltic states became known only after the war, the nonaggression pact itself was enough to make Britain and France cry treachery, for they too had been negotiating with Stalin. But Stalin had remained distrustful of Western intentions. Moreover, Britain and France had offered him military risk without gain, while Hitler had offered territorial gain without risk. For Hitler, everything was set. He told his generals on the day of the nonaggression pact: "My only fear is that at the last moment some dirty dog will come up with a mediation plan." On September 1, 1939, German armies and warplanes smashed into Poland from three sides. Two days later, finally true to their word, Britain and France declared war on Germany. The Second World War had begun.

HITLER'S EMPIRE, 1939–1942

Using planes, tanks, and trucks in the first example of the *Blitzkrieg,* or "lightning war," Hitler's armies crushed Poland in four weeks. While Soviet Russia quickly took its part of the booty—the eastern half of Poland and the Baltic states of Lithuania, Estonia, Latvia—French and British armies dug in in the west. They expected another war of attrition and economic blockade.

In spring 1940, the lightning war struck again. After quickly occupying Denmark, Norway, and Holland, German motorized columns broke through southern Belgium, split the Franco-British forces, and trapped the entire British army on the beaches of Dunkirk. By heroic efforts the British managed to withdraw their troops but not their equipment to England.

France was taken by the Nazis. The aging marshal Henri-Philippe Pétain formed a new French government—the so-called Vichy government—to accept defeat, and German armies occupied most of France. By July 1940, Hitler ruled practically all of western continental Europe; Italy was an ally; and the Soviet Union a friendly neutral. Only Britain, led by the uncompromising Winston Churchill (1874–1965), remained unconquered. Churchill proved to be one of history's greatest wartime leaders, rallying his fellow citizens with stirring speeches, infectious confidence, and bulldog determination.

Germany sought to gain control of the air, the necessary first step for an amphibious invasion of Britain. In the Battle of Britain, up to a thousand German planes attacked British airfields and key factories in a single day, dueling with British defenders high in the skies. Losses were heavy on both sides. Then in September Hitler angrily and foolishly changed his strategy, turning from military objectives to indiscriminate bombing of British cities in an attempt to break British morale. British factories increased production of their excellent fighter planes; antiaircraft defense improved with the help of radar; and the heavily bombed people of London defiantly dug in. In September–October 1940, Britain was beating Germany three to one in the air war. There was no possibility of immediate German invasion of Britain.

In these circumstances, the most reasonable German strategy would have been to attack Britain through the eastern Mediterranean, taking Egypt and the Suez Canal and pinching off Britain's supply of oil. Moreover, Mussolini's early defeats in Greece had drawn Hitler into the Balkans, where Germany quickly conquered Greece and Yugoslavia while

forcing Hungary, Rumania and Bulgaria into alliances with Germany by April 1941. This reinforced the logic of a thrust into the eastern Mediterranean. But Hitler was not a reasonable person. His lifetime obsession with a vast eastern European empire for the master race irrationally dictated policy. By late 1940, he had already decided on his next move, and in June 1941, German armies suddenly attacked the Soviet Union along a vast front. With Britain still unconquered, Hitler's decision was a wild, irrational gamble, epitomizing the violent, unlimited ambitions of modern totalitarianism.

Faithfully fulfilling all his obligations under the Nazi-Soviet Pact and even ignoring warnings of impending invasion, Stalin was caught off guard. Nazi armies moved like lightning across the Russian steppe. By October 1941, Leningrad was practically surrounded, Moscow beseiged, and most of the Ukraine conquered; yet the Russians did not collapse. When a severe winter struck German armies outfitted in summer uniforms, the invaders were stopped.

While Hitler's armies dramatically expanded the war in Europe, his Japanese allies did the same in Asia. Engaged in a general but undeclared war against China since 1937, Japan's rulers had increasingly come into diplomatic conflict with the Pacific Basin's other great power, the United States. When the Japanese occupied French Indochina in July 1941, the United States retaliated by cutting off sales of vital rubber, scrap iron, oil, and aviation fuel. Tension mounted further, and on December 7, 1941, Japan attacked the U.S. naval base at Pearl Harbor in Hawaii. Hitler immediately declared war on the United States, even though his treaty obligations with Japan did not require him to initiate this course of action.

As Japanese forces advanced swiftly into southeast Asia after the crippling surprise attack at Pearl Harbor, Hitler and his European allies continued the two-front war against the Soviet Union and Great Britain. Not until late 1942 did the Nazis suffer their first major defeats, as will be shown in Chapter 30. In the meantime, Hitler ruled a vast European empire stretching from the outskirts of Moscow to the English Channel. Hitler and the top Nazi leadership began building their "New Order," and they continued their efforts until their final collapse in 1945. In doing so, they showed what Nazi victory would have meant.

Hitler's New Order was based firmly on the guiding principle of Nazi totalitarianism: racial imperialism. Within this New Order, the Nordic peoples—the Dutch, the Norwegians, and Danes—received preferential treatment, for they were racially related to the Germans. The French, an "inferior" Latin people, occupied the middle position. They were heavily taxed to support the Nazi war effort, but were tolerated as a race. Once Nazi reverses began to mount in late 1942, however, all the occupied territories of western and northern Europe were exploited with increasing intensity. Material shortages and both mental and physical suffering afflicted millions of people.

Slavs in the conquered territories to the east were treated with harsh hatred as "subhumans." At the height of his success in 1941 to 1942, Hitler painted for his intimate circle the fantastic details of a vast eastern colonial empire, where the Poles, Ukrainians, and Russians would be enslaved and forced to die

Prelude to Murder This photo captures the terrible inhumanity of Nazi racism. Frightened and bewildered families from the soon-to-be destroyed Warsaw ghetto are being forced out of their homes by German soldiers for deportation to concentration camps. There they face murder in the gas chambers. *(Collection Viollet)*

out, while Germanic peasants resettled their abandoned lands. Himmler and the elite corps of SS volunteers struggled loyally, sometimes against the German army, to implement part of this general program even before victory was secured. In parts of Poland, the SS arrested and evacuated Polish peasants to create a German "mass settlement space." Polish workers and Russian prisoners of war were transported to Germany, where they did most of the heavy labor and were systematically worked to death. The conditions of Russian slave labor in Germany were so harsh that four out of five Russian prisoners did not survive the war.

Finally, Jews were condemned to extermination, along with gypsies, Jehovah's Witnesses, and captured Communists. By 1939 German Jews had lost all their civil rights, and after the fall of Warsaw the Nazis began deporting them to Poland. There they and Jews from all over Europe were concentrated in ghettos, compelled to wear the Jewish star, and turned into slave laborers. But by 1941, Himmler's SS was carrying out the "final solution of the Jewish question"—the murder of every single Jew. All over Hitler's empire, Jews were arrested, packed like cattle onto freight trains, and dispatched to extermination camps.

There the victims were taken by force or deception to "shower rooms," which were actually gas chambers. These gas chambers, first perfected in the quiet, efficient execution of 70,000 mentally ill Germans between 1938 and 1941, permitted rapid, hideous, and thoroughly bureaucratized mass murder. For fifteen to twenty minutes there came the terrible screams and gasping sobs of men, women, and children choking to death on poison gas. Then, only silence. Special camp workers quickly tore the victims' gold teeth from their jaws and cut off their hair for use as chair stuffings. The bodies were then cremated, or sometimes boiled for oil to make soap, while the bones were crushed to produce fertilizers. At Auschwitz, the most infamous of the Nazi death factories, as many as 12,000 human beings were slaughtered each day. On the turbulent Russian front, the SS death squads forced the Jewish population to dig giant pits, which became mass graves as the victims were lined up on the edge and cut down by machine guns. The extermination of the European Jews was the ultimate monstrosity of Nazi racism and racial imperialism. By 1945, 6 million Jews had been murdered in cold blood.

The tremendous practical and spiritual maladies of the age of anxiety led in many lands to the rise of dictatorships. Many of these dictatorships were variations on conservative authoritarianism, but there was also a fateful innovation—the modern totalitarian regime, most fully developed in Communist Russia and Nazi Germany. The totalitarian regimes utterly rejected the liberalism of the nineteenth century. Inspired by the lessons of total war and Lenin's one-party rule, they tried to subordinate everything to the state. Although some areas of life escaped them, state control increased to a staggering, unprecedented degree. The totalitarian regimes trampled on basic human rights with unrestrained brutality and police terror. Moreover, they were armed with the weapons of modern technology, rendering opposition almost impossible.

Both Communist Russia and Nazi Germany tried to gain the *willing* support of their populations. Monopolizing the means of expression and communication, they claimed to represent the masses and to be building new, more equal societies. Many people believed them. Both regimes also won enthusiastic supporters by offering tough, ruthless people from modest backgrounds enormous rewards for loyal and effective service. Thus these totalitarian dictatorships rested on considerable genuine popular support, as well as on police terror. This combination gave them their awesome power and dynamism. That dynamism was, however, channeled in quite different directions. Stalin and the Communist party aimed at building their kind of socialism and the new socialist personality at home. Hitler and the Nazi elite aimed at unlimited territorial and racial aggression on behalf of a master race; domestic recovery was only a means to that end. Unlimited aggression made war inevitable, first with the Western democracies and then with Germany's totalitarian neighbor. It plunged Europe into the ultimate nightmare.

NOTES

1. E. Halévy, *The Era of Tyrannies,* Doubleday, Garden City, N.Y., 1965, pp. 265–316, esp. p. 300.

2. Quoted by P. C. Roberts, " 'War Communism': A Re-examination," *Slavic Review* 29 (June 1970): 257.

3. Quoted by A. G. Mazour, *Soviet Economic Development: Operation Outstrip, 1921–1965,* Van Nostrand, Princeton, N.J., 1967, p. 130.

4. Quoted by I. Deutscher, *Stalin: A Political Biography,* 2nd ed., Oxford University Press, New York, 1967, p. 325.

5. Quoted by H. K. Geiger, *The Family in Soviet Russia,* Harvard University Press, Cambridge, 1968, p. 123.

6. Ibid., p. 156.

7. Quoted by B. Rosenthal, "Women in the Russian Revolution and After," in *Becoming Visible: Women in European History,* ed., R. Bridenthal and C. Koonz, Houghton Mifflin, Boston, 1976, p. 383.

8. Quoted by K. D. Bracher, in T. Eschenburg et al., *The Path to Dictatorship, 1918–1933,* Doubleday, Garden City, N.Y., 1966, p. 117.

9. Quoted by K. D. Bracher, *The German Dictatorship: The Origins, Structure and Effects of National Socialism,* Praeger, New York, 1970, pp. 146–147.

10. Quoted by R. Stromberg, *An Intellectual History of Modern Europe,* Appleton-Century-Crofts, New York, 1966, p. 393.

11. D. Schoenbaum, *Hitler's Social Revolution: Class and Status in Nazi Germany, 1933–1939,* Doubleday, Garden City, N.Y., 1967, p. 114.

12. Quoted by Bracher, *German Dictatorship,* p. 289.

13. Ibid, p. 306.

SUGGESTED READING

The historical literature on totalitarian dictatorships is rich and fascinating. H. Arendt, *The Origins of Totalitarianism* (1951), is a challenging interpretation. E. Weber, *Varieties of Fascism* (1964), stresses the radical social aspirations of fascist movements all across Europe. F. L. Carsten, *The Rise of Fascism,* rev. ed. (1982), and W. Laqueur, ed., *Fascism* (1976), are also recommended.

Richard Stites, *The Women's Liberation Movement in Russia: Feminism, Nihilism, and Bolshevism, 1860–1930* (1978); S. Fitzpatrick, *Cultural Revolution in Russia, 1928–1931* (1978); K. Geiger, *The Family in Soviet Russia* (1968); and I. Deutscher, *Stalin: A Political Biography* (1967), are all highly recommended, as is Deutscher's sympathetic three-volume study of Trotsky. S. Cohen, *Bukharin and the Bolshevik Revolution* (1973), examines the leading spokesman of moderate communism, who was destroyed by Stalin. R. Conquest, *The Great Terror* (1968), is an excellent account of Stalin's purges of the 1930s. A. Solzhenitsyn, *The Gulag Archipelago* (1964), passionately condemns Soviet police terror, which Solzhenitsyn tracks back to Lenin. A. Koestler, *Darkness at Noon* (1956), is a famous fictional account of Stalin's trials of the Old Bolsheviks. R. Medvedev, *Let History Judge* (1972), is a penetrating and highly recommended history of Stalinism by a Russian dissident. Three other remarkable books are J. Scott, *Behind the Urals* (1942, 1973), an eyewitness account of an American steelworker in Russia in the 1930s; S. Alliluyeva, *Twenty Letters to a Friend* (1967), the amazing reflections of Stalin's daughter, who has twice chosen to live in the United States; and M. Fainsod, *Smolensk Under Soviet Rule* (1958), a unique study based on Communist records captured first by the Germans and then by the Americans.

E. R. Tannebaum, *The Fascist Experience* (1972), is an excellent study of Italian culture and society under Mussolini. I. Silone, *Bread and Wine* (1937), is a moving novel by a famous opponent of dictatorship in Italy. Two excellent books on Spain are H. Thomas, *The Spanish Civil War* (1961), and E. Malefakis, *Agrarian Reform and Peasant Revolution in Spain* (1970). In the area of foreign relations, G. Kennan, *Russia and the West Under Lenin and Stalin* (1961), is justly famous, while A. L. Rowse, *Appeasement* (1961), powerfully denounces the policies of the appeasers. R. Paxton, *Vichy France* (1973), tells a controversial story extremely well, and J. Lukac, *The Last European War* (1976), skillfully—and infuriatingly—argues that victory by Hitler could have saved Europe from both Russian and American domination.

On Germany, F. Stern, *The Politics of Cultural Despair* (1963), and G. Mosse, *The Crisis of German Ideology* (1964), are excellent complementary studies on the origins of Nazism. The best single work on Hitler's Germany is K. Bracher, *The German Dictatorship: The Origins, Structure and Effects of National Socialism* (1970), while W. Shirer, *The Rise and Fall of the Third Reich* (1960), is the best-selling account of an American journalist who experienced Nazi Germany firsthand. J.

Fest, *Hitler* (1974), and A. Bullock, *Hitler* (1953), are engrossing biographies of the Führer. In addition to *Mein Kampf, Hitler's Secret Conversations, 1941–1944* (1953) reveals the dictator's wild dreams and beliefs. Among countless special studies, E. Kogon, *The Theory and Practice of Hell* (1958), is a chilling examination of the concentration camps; M. Mayer, *They Thought They Were Free* (1955), probes the minds of ten ordinary Nazis and why they believed Hitler was their liberator; and A. Speer, *Inside the Third Reich* (1970), contains the fascinating recollections of Hitler's wizard of the armaments industry. G. Mosse, *Toward the Final Solution* (1978), is a powerful history of European racism, and L. Dawidowicz, *The War Against the Jews, 1933–1945* (1975), is a superb account of the Holocaust. Jørgen Haestrup, *Europe Ablaze* (1978), is a monumental account of wartime resistance movements throughout Europe, and *The Diary of Anne Frank* is a remarkable personal account of a young Jewish girl in hiding during the Nazi occupation of Holland.

30

THE RECOVERY OF EUROPE AND THE AMERICAS

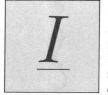 *N 1942*, when Hitler's empire stretched across Europe and the Nazi "New Order" was taking shape, Western civilization was in danger of dying. A terrible, triumphant barbarism was striking at the hard-won accomplishments and uneven progress of many generations. From this low point, European society staged a truly astonishing recovery.

The Nazis and their allies were utterly defeated. Battered western Europe then experienced a great renaissance in the postwar era, which lasted into the late 1960s. The western hemisphere, with its strong European heritage, also made exemplary progress. Soviet Russia eventually became more humane and less totalitarian. Yet there was also a tragic setback. The Grand Alliance against Hitler gave way to an apparently endless cold war, in which conflict between East and West threatened world peace and troubled domestic politics.

How and why did Europe recover from the depths of despair in one of the most extraordinary periods of rebirth in its long history? What were the causes of the cold war, the most disappointing development of the postwar era? These are some of the more important questions this chapter will seek to answer.

ALLIED VICTORY AND THE COLD WAR, 1942–1950

The recovery of Western society depended on the defeat of the Nazis and their Italian, Balkan, and Japanese allies. On this point the twenty-six allied nations, led by Britain, the United States, and Soviet Russia, were firmly agreed. The Grand Alliance—to use Winston Churchill's favorite term—functioned quite effectively in military terms to achieve this overwhelming objective. By the summer of 1943, the tide of battle had turned, and Allied victory was only a matter of time.

Yet victory was flawed. The Allies could not cooperate politically when it came to peacemaking. Motivated by different goals and hounded by misunderstandings, the United States and Soviet Russia soon found themselves at loggerheads. By the end of 1947, Europe was rigidly divided. It was West versus East in the cold war.

Chance, rather than choice, brought together the anti-Axis coalition. Stalin had been cooperating fully with Hitler between August 1939 and June 1941, and only the Japanese attack on Pearl Harbor in December 1941 and Hitler's immediate declaration of war had overwhelmed powerful isolationism in the United States. The Allies' first task was to try to overcome their mutual suspicions and build an unshakable alliance on the quicksand of accident. By means of two interrelated policies they succeeded.

First, President Roosevelt accepted Churchill's contention that the United States should concentrate first on defeating Hitler. Only after victory in Europe would the United States turn toward the Pacific for an all-out attack on Japan, the lesser threat. Therefore, the United States promised and sent large amounts of military aid to Britain and Russia, and American and British forces in each combat zone were tightly integrated under a single commander. America's policy of "Europe first" helped solidify the anti-Hitler coalition.

Second, within the European framework, the Americans and the British put immediate military needs first. They consistently postponed tough political questions relating to the eventual peace settlement. Thus, in December 1941 and again in May 1942, Stalin asked the United States and Britain to agree to Russia's moving its western border of 1938 farther west at the expense of Poland, in effect ratifying the gains Stalin had made from his deal with Hitler in 1939.

Stalin's request ran counter to the moralistic Anglo-American Atlantic Charter of August 1941. In good Wilsonian fashion, the Atlantic Charter had called for peace without territorial expansion or secret agreements, and free elections and self-determination for all liberated nations. Stalin thus received only a military alliance and no postwar commitments in 1942. Yet the United States and Britain did not try to take advantage of Russia's precarious position in 1942, promising an invasion of continental Europe as soon as possible. They feared that hard bargaining would anger Stalin and encourage him to consider making a separate peace with Hitler.

Both sides found it advantageous to paper over their long-standing differences by stressing military operations and the total defeat of the Axis. At a January 1943 conference in Casablanca, Morocco, to plan a massive Allied offensive, Churchill and Roosevelt adopted the principle of the "unconditional surrender" of Germany and Japan. Stalin agreed to it shortly thereafter. The policy of unconditional surrender had profound implications. It cemented the Grand Alliance, denying Hitler any hope of dividing his foes. It probably also discouraged Germans and Japanese who might have tried to overthrow their dictators in order to make a compromise peace. And, most important, it meant that Russian and Anglo-American armies would almost certainly come together to divide all of Germany, and all of Europe, among themselves.

The military resources of the Grand Alliance were awesome. The strengths of the United States were its mighty industry, its large population, and its national unity. Even before Pearl Harbor, President Roosevelt had called America the "arsenal of democracy" and given military aid to Britain and Russia. Now the United States geared up rapidly for all-out war production and drew heavily on a generally cooperative Latin America for resources. It not only equipped its own armies but eventually gave its allies about $50 billion of arms and equipment. Britain received by far the most, but about one-fifth of the total went to Russia in the form of badly needed trucks, planes, and munitions.

Too strong to lose and too weak to win when it stood alone, Britain, too, continued to make a great contribution. The British economy was totally and effectively mobilized, and the sharing of burdens through rationing and heavy taxes on war profits maintained social harmony. Moreover, as 1942 wore on, Britain could increasingly draw on the enormous physical and human resources of its empire and the United States. By early 1943, the Americans and the British combined small aircraft carriers with radar-guided bombers to rid the Atlantic of German submarines. Britain, the impregnable floating fortress, became a gigantic front-line staging area for the decisive blow to the heart of Germany.

As for Soviet Russia, so great was its strength that it might well have defeated Germany without Western help. In the face of the German advance, whole factories and populations were successfully evacuated to eastern Russia and Siberia. There, war production was reorganized and expanded, and the Red Army was increasingly well supplied. The Red Army was

The Siege of Leningrad lasted almost three years, but the Russians heroically defended their city, which was never taken. These women are sawing poles for anti-tank defenses beside a bomb-battered building on what was once Leningrad's most stylish thoroughfare. *(Süddeutscher Verlag)*

also well led, for a new generation of talented military leaders quickly arose to replace those so recently purged. Most important of all, Stalin drew on the massive support and heroic determination of the Soviet people. Broad-based Russian nationalism, as opposed to narrow communist ideology, became the powerful unifying force in what was appropriately called the "Great Patriotic War of the Fatherland."

Finally, the United States, Britain, and Soviet Russia were not alone. They had the resources of much of the world at their command. And, to a greater or lesser extent, they were aided by a growing resistance movement against the Nazis throughout Europe, even in Germany. Thus, although Ukrainian peasants often welcomed the Germans as liberators, the barbaric occupation policies of the Nazis quickly drove them to join and support behind-the-lines guerrilla forces. More generally, after Russia was invaded in June 1941, Communists throughout Europe took the lead in the underground resistance,

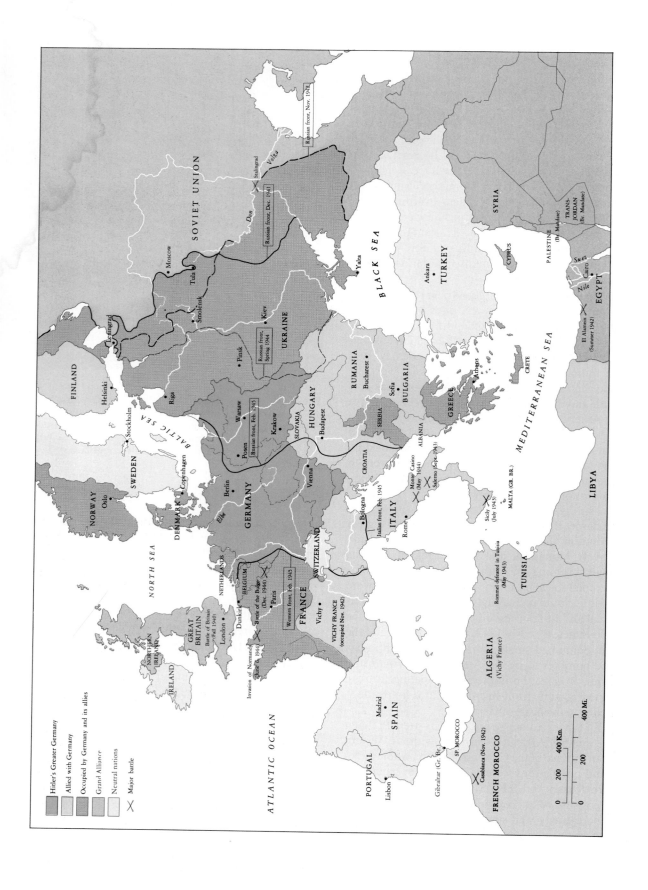

Legend:

- Hitler's Greater Germany
- Allied with Germany
- Occupied by Germany and its allies
- Grand Alliance
- Neutral nations
- ✕ Major battle

ATLANTIC OCEAN

NORTH SEA

BALTIC SEA

NORTH SEA

MEDITERRANEAN SEA

BLACK SEA

SOVIET UNION

FINLAND

SWEDEN

NORWAY
• Oslo

DENMARK
• Copenhagen

GREAT BRITAIN
• London
Battle of Britain (Fall 1940)

NORTHERN IRELAND

IRELAND

NETHERLANDS

BELGIUM
Battle of the Bulge (Dec. 1944) ✕

Dunkirk •

Invasion of Normandy (June 6, 1944) ✕

Western front, Feb. 1945

Paris •

FRANCE

Vichy •

VICHY FRANCE (occupied Nov. 1942)

SWITZERLAND

GERMANY
Elbe
Berlin •

Vienna •

AUSTRIA

Posen •
Russian front, Feb. 1945

Warsaw •

Kraków •

SLOVAKIA

HUNGARY
Budapest •

CROATIA

SERBIA

ALBANIA

Monte Cassino (May 1944) ✕

Salerno (Sept. 1943) ✕

ITALY
Rome •
Bologna •
Italian front, Feb. 1945

Sicily (July 1943) ✕

MALTA (GR. BR.)

GREECE
Athens •

CRETE

BULGARIA
Sofia •

RUMANIA
Bucharest •

Yalta •

TURKEY
Ankara •

CYPRUS

SYRIA

PALESTINE (Br. Mandate)

TRANS-JORDAN (Br. Mandate)

EGYPT
Cairo •
Nile
Suez

El Alamein (Summer 1942) ✕

LIBYA

TUNISIA
Rommel defeated in Tunisia (May 1943)

ALGERIA (Vichy France)

FRENCH MOROCCO
Casablanca (Nov. 1942) ✕

SP. MOROCCO

Gibraltar (Gr. Br.) ✕

SPAIN
Madrid •

PORTUGAL
Lisbon •

Leningrad •

Moscow •
Tula •

Smolensk •

Riga •

Pinsk •

Kiev •
Russian front, Spring 1944

UKRAINE

Don

Volga

Stalingrad
Russian front, Dec. 1941

Russian front, Nov. 1942

Helsinki •

Stockholm •

400 Mi.
400 Km.
200
200
0
0

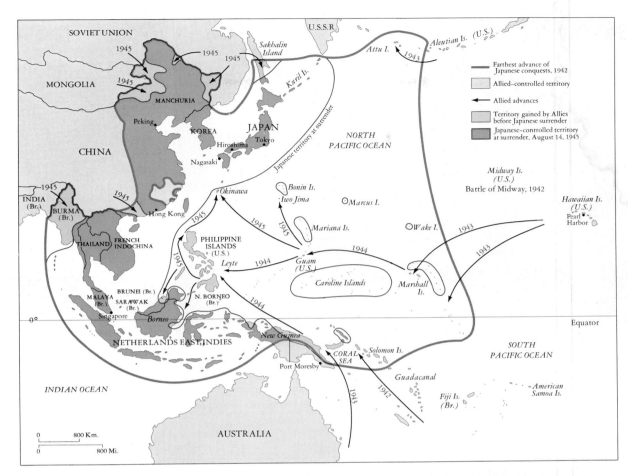

Map labels (within image):

SOVIET UNION
MONGOLIA
1945   1945   1945
Sakhalin Island
U.S.S.R.
Attu I.   1943   Aleutian Is. (U.S.)
MANCHURIA
Peking
KOREA
CHINA
JAPAN
Hiroshima   Tokyo
Nagasaki
NORTH PACIFIC OCEAN
Midway Is. (U.S.)
Battle of Midway, 1942
Japanese territory at surrender
1945
INDIA (Br.)
BURMA (Br.)
Hong Kong
THAILAND   FRENCH INDOCHINA
Okinawa
Bonin Is.
Iwo Jima
Marcus I.
Mariana Is.
Wake I.   1943
1944
1943
Hawaiian Is. (U.S.)
Pearl Harbor
PHILIPPINE ISLANDS (U.S.)
Leyte   1944
Guam (U.S.)
1944
Caroline Islands
Marshall Is.
MALAYA (Br.)   BRUNEI (Br.)   SARAWAK (Br.)   N. BORNEO (Br.)
Singapore   Borneo
0°
NETHERLANDS EAST INDIES
1944
Equator
New Guinea
Port Moresby
CORAL SEA
Solomon Is.
SOUTH PACIFIC OCEAN
Guadacanal
1942
1943
Fiji Is. (Br.)
American Samoa Is.
INDIAN OCEAN
800 Km.
800 Mi.
AUSTRALIA

Legend:
— Farthest advance of Japanese conquests, 1942
☐ Allied-controlled territory
← Allied advances
☐ Territory gained by Allies before Japanese surrender
☐ Japanese-controlled territory at surrender, August 14, 1945

MAP 30.1 World War Two in Europe The map shows the extent of Hitler's empire at its height, before the battle of Stalingrad in late 1942, and the subsequent advances of the Allies until Germany surrendered on May 7, 1945.

MAP 30.2 World War Two in the Pacific Japanese forces also overran an enormous territory in 1942, which the Allies slowly recaptured in a long bitter struggle. As this map shows, Japan still held a large Asian empire in August 1945, when the unprecedented devastation of atomic warfare suddenly forced it to surrender.

joined by a growing number of patriots and Christians. Anti-Nazi leaders from occupied countries established governments-in-exile in London, like that of the "Free French" under the intensely proud General Charles de Gaulle. These governments gathered valuable secret information from resistance fighters and even organized armies to help defeat Hitler.

THE TIDE OF BATTLE

Barely halted at the gates of Moscow and Leningrad in 1941, the Germans renewed their Russian offensive in July 1942. This time they drove toward the southern city of Stalingrad, in an attempt to cripple communications and seize the crucial oil fields of Baku. Reaching Stalingrad, the Germans slowly occupied most of the ruined city in a month of incredibly savage house-to-house fighting.

Then, in November 1942, Soviet armies counterattacked. They rolled over Rumanian and Italian troops to the north and south of Stalingrad, quickly closing the trap and surrounding the entire German Sixth Army of 300,000 men. The surrounded Germans were systematically destroyed, until by the end of January 1943 only 123,000 soldiers were left to surrender. Hitler, who had refused to allow a retreat,

B-17 Pilots These American women are returning from a training flight in their Flying Fortress, nicknamed "Pistol Packin' Mama." Women pilots ferried the planes for the U.S. Air Corps in support missions during the second World War. *(U.S. Air Force Photo)*

had suffered a catastrophic defeat. In the summer of 1943, the larger, better-equipped Soviet armies took the offensive and began moving forward (see Map 30.1).

In late 1942 the tide also turned in the Pacific and North Africa. By early summer 1942, Japan had established a great empire in east Asia (see Map 30.2). Unlike the Nazis, the Japanese made clever appeals to local nationalists, who hated European imperial domination and preferred Japan's so-called Greater Asian Co-Prosperity Sphere.

Then, in the Battle of the Coral Sea in May 1942, Allied naval and air power stopped the Japanese advance and also relieved Australia from the threat of invasion. This victory was followed by the Battle of Midway Island, in which American pilots sank all four of the attacking Japanese aircraft carriers and established American naval superiority in the Pacific. In August 1942, American marines attacked Guadalcanal in the Solomon Islands. Badly hampered by the policy of "Europe first"—only 15 percent of Allied resources were going to fight the war in the Pacific in early 1943—the Americans, under General Douglas

MacArthur and Admiral Chester Nimitz, and the Australians nevertheless began "island hopping" toward Japan. Japanese forces were on the defensive.

In North Africa, the war had been seesawing back and forth since 1940. In May 1942, combined German and Italian armies, under the brilliant General Erwin Rommel, attacked British-occupied Egypt and the Suez Canal for the second time. After a rapid advance, they were finally defeated by British forces at the Battle of El Alamein, only seventy miles from Alexandria. In October, the British counter-attacked in Egypt, and almost immediately thereafter, an Anglo-American force landed in Morocco and Algeria. These French possessions, which were under the control of Pétain's Vichy French goverment, quickly went over to the Allies.

Having driven the Axis powers from North Africa by the spring of 1943, Allied forces maintained the initiative by invading Sicily and then mainland Italy. Mussolini was deposed by a war-weary people, and the new Italian government publicly accepted unconditional surrender in September 1943. Italy, it seemed, was liberated. Yet Mussolini was rescued by

War in the Pacific A Japanese ship burns off the coast of New Guinea as an attacking B-25 roars overhead. The lights along the shoreline are fires caused by United States bombers. *(Air Force Photo)*

German commandos in a daring raid and put at the head of a puppet government. German armies seized Rome and all of northern Italy. Fighting continued in Italy.

Indeed, bitter fighting continued in Europe for almost two years. Germany, less fully mobilized for war than Britain in 1941, applied itself to total war in 1942 and enlisted millions of prisoners of war and slave laborers from all across occupied Europe in that effort. Between early 1942 and July 1944, German war production actually tripled. Although British and American bombing raids killed many German civilians, they were surprisingly ineffective from a military point of view. Also, German resistance against Hitler failed. After an unsuccessful attempt on Hitler's life in July 1944, thousands of Germans were brutally liquidated by SS fanatics. Terrorized at home and frightened by the prospect of unconditional surrender, the Germans fought on with suicidal stoicism.

On June 6, 1944, American and British forces under General Dwight Eisenhower landed on the beaches of Normandy in history's greatest naval invasion. Having tricked the Germans into believing that the attack would come near the Belgian border, the Allies secured a foothold on the coast of Normandy. In a hundred dramatic days, more than 2 million men and almost a half-million vehicles pushed inland and broke through German lines. Rejecting proposals to strike straight at Berlin in a massive attack, Eisenhower moved forward cautiously on a broad front. Not until March 1945 did American troops cross the Rhine and enter Germany.

The Russians, who had been advancing steadily since July 1943, reached the outskirts of Warsaw by August 1944. For the next six months they moved southward into Rumania, Hungary, and Yugoslavia. In January 1945, Red armies again moved westward through Poland, and on April 26 they met American forces on the Elbe River. The Allies had closed their vise on Nazi Germany and overrun Europe. As Soviet forces fought their way into Berlin, Hitler committed suicide in his bunker, and on May 7 German commanders capitulated.

Three months later the United States dropped atomic bombs on Hiroshima and Nagasaki. Mass

Hiroshima, August 1945 A single atomic bomb leveled 90 percent of this major city and claimed 130,000 casualties. Hiroshima has never regained its earlier prosperity. *(U.S. Army Air Forces)*

bombing of cities and civilians, one of the terrible new practices of World War Two, had ended in the final nightmare—unprecedented human destruction in a single blinding flash. The Japanese surrendered. The Second World War, which had claimed the lives of more than 50 million soldiers and civilians, was over.

THE ORIGINS OF THE COLD WAR

Total victory was not followed by genuine peace. The most powerful allies—Soviet Russia and the United States—began to quarrel as soon as the unifying threat of Nazi Germany disappeared. Though the hostility between the eastern and western superpowers was a tragic disappointment for millions of people, it was not really surprising. It grew sadly but logically out of military developments, wartime agreements, and long-standing political and ideological differences.

The conference Stalin, Roosevelt, and Churchill had held in the Iranian capital of Teheran in November 1943 was of crucial importance in determining subsequent events. There, the Big Three had jovially reaffirmed their determination to crush Germany and searched for the appropriate military strategy. Churchill, fearful of the military dangers of a direct attack and anxious to protect Britain's political interests in the eastern Mediterranean, argued that American and British forces should follow up their North African and Italian campaigns with an indirect attack on Germany through the Balkans. Roosevelt, however, agreed with Stalin that an American-British frontal assault through France would be better. This agreement was part of Roosevelt's general effort to meet Stalin's wartime demands whenever possible. As Roosevelt reportedly told his friend William Bullitt, formerly American ambassador to the Soviet Union, before the Teheran conference, "I have just a hunch that Stalin doesn't want anything but security

The Big Three In 1945 a triumphant Winston Churchill, ailing Franklin Roosevelt, and determined Joseph Stalin met at Yalta in southern Russia to plan for peace. Cooperation soon gave way to bitter hostility. *(National Archives, Washington)*

for his country, and I think that if I give him everything I possibly can and ask nothing from him in return, *noblesse oblige,* he won't try to annex anything and will work for a world of democracy and peace."[1]

At Teheran, the Normandy invasion had been set for the spring of 1944. Although military considerations probably largely dictated this decision, it had momentous political implications: it meant that the Russian and the American-British armies would come together in defeated Germany along a north-south line and that only Russian troops would liberate eastern Europe. Thus the basic shape of postwar Europe was already emerging. Real differences over questions like Poland were carefully ignored.

When the Big Three met again at Yalta on the Black Sea in southern Russia in February 1945, rapidly advancing Soviet armies were within one hundred miles of Berlin. The Red Army had occupied not only Poland but also Bulgaria, Rumania, Hungary, part of Yugoslavia, and much of Czecho-

slovakia. The temporarily stalled American-British forces had yet to cross the Rhine into Germany. Moreover, the United States was far from defeating Japan. Indeed, it was believed that the invasion and occupation of Japan would cost a million American casualties—an estimate that led to the subsequent decision to drop atomic bombs in order to save American lives. In short, Russia's position was strong and America's weak.

There was little the increasingly sick and apprehensive Roosevelt could do but double his bet on Stalin's peaceful intentions. It was agreed at Yalta that Germany would be divided into zones of occupation and would pay heavy reparations to the Soviet Union in the form of agricultural and industrial goods, though many details remained unsettled. At American insistence, Stalin agreed to declare war on Japan after Germany was defeated. He also agreed to join the proposed United Nations, which the Americans believed would help preserve peace after the war; it was founded in April 1945 in San Francisco. For Poland and eastern Europe—"that Pandora's Box of infinite troubles," according to American Secretary of State Cordell Hull—the Big Three struggled to reach an ambiguous compromise at Yalta: East European governments were to be freely elected but pro-Russian. As Churchill put it at the time, "The Poles will have their future in their own hands, with the single limitation that they must honestly follow in harmony with their allies, a policy friendly to Russia."[2]

The Yalta compromise over eastern Europe broke down almost immediately. Even before the Yalta Conference, Bulgaria and Poland were in the hands of Communists, who arrived home in the baggage of the Red Army. Minor concesssions to non-Communist groups thereafter did not change this situation. Elsewhere in eastern Europe, pro-Russian "coalition" governments of several parties were formed, but the key ministerial posts were reserved for Moscow-trained Communists.

At the postwar Potsdam Conference of July 1945, the long-ignored differences over eastern Europe finally surged to the fore. The compromising Roosevelt had died and been succeeded by the more determined President Harry Truman, who demanded immediate free elections throughout eastern Europe. Stalin refused pointblank. "A freely elected government in any of these East European countries would be anti-Soviet," he admitted simply, "and that we cannot allow."[3]

Here, then, is the key to the much-debated origins of the cold war. American ideals, pumped up by the crusade against Hitler, and American politics, heavily influenced by millions of voters from eastern Europe, demanded free elections in Soviet-occupied eastern Europe. On the other hand, Stalin, who had lived through two enormously destructive German invasions, wanted absolute military security from Germany and its potential Eastern allies, once and for all. Suspicious by nature, he believed that only Communist states could truly be devoted allies, and he feared that free elections would result in independent and quite possibly hostile governments on his western border. Moreover, by the middle of 1945 there was no way short of war that the United States and its Western allies could really influence developments in eastern Europe, and war was out of the question. Stalin was bound to have his way.

West Versus East

The American response to Stalin's exaggerated conception of security was to "get tough." In May 1945, Truman abruptly cut off all aid to Russia. In October, he declared that the United States would never recognize any government established by force against the free will of its people. In March 1946, former British Prime Minister Churchill ominously informed an American audience that an "iron curtain" had fallen across the continent, dividing Germany and all of Europe into two antagonistic camps. Soon emotional, moralistic denunciations of Stalin and Communist Russia re-emerged as part of American political life. Yet the United States also responded to the popular desire to "bring the boys home" and demobilized with incredible speed, though some historians have argued that American leaders believed that the atomic bomb gave the United States all the power it needed. When the war against Japan ended in September 1945, there were 12 million Americans in the armed forces; by 1947 there were only 1.5 million, as opposed to 6 million for Soviet Russia. "Getting tough" really meant "talking tough."

Stalin's agents quickly reheated the "ideological struggle against capitalist imperialism." Moreover, the large, well-organized Communist parties of France and Italy obediently started to uncover American plots to take over Europe and aggressively challenged their own governments with violent criticisms and large strikes. The Soviet Union also put pressure on Iran and Turkey, and while Greek Communists battled Greek royalists, another bitter civil war raged in China. By the spring of 1947, it appeared to many Americans that Stalin wanted much more than just puppet regimes in Soviet-occupied eastern Europe. He seemed determined to export communism by subversion throughout Europe and around the world.

The American response to this challenge was the Truman Doctrine, which was aimed at "containing" communism to areas already occupied by the Red Army. Truman told Congress in March 1947: "I believe it must be the policy of the United States to support free people who are resisting attempted subjugation by armed minorities or by outside pressure." To begin, Truman asked Congress for military aid to Greece and Turkey. Then in June, Secretary of State George C. Marshall offered Europe economic aid—the "Marshall Plan"—to help it rebuild.

The Berlin Air Lift Standing in the rubble of their bombed-out city, a German crowd in the American sector awaits the arrival of a U.S. transport plane flying in over the Soviet blockade in 1948. The crisis over Berlin was a dramatic indication of growing tensions among the Allies, which resulted in the division of Europe into two hostile camps. *(Walter Sanders,* Life © *Time Inc.)*

Stalin refused Marshall Plan assistance for all of eastern Europe. He purged the last remaining non-Communist elements from the coalition governments of eastern Europe and established Soviet-style, one-party Communist dictatorships. The seizure of power in Czechoslovakia in February 1948 was particularly brutal and antidemocratic, and it greatly strengthened Western fears of limitless Communist expansion, beginning with Germany. Thus, when Stalin blocked all traffic through the Soviet zone of Germany to the former capital of Berlin, which had also been divided into sectors at the end of the war by the occupying powers, the Western allies responded firmly but not provocatively. Hundreds of planes began flying over the Russian roadblocks around the clock, supplying provisions to the people of West Berlin and thwarting Soviet efforts to swallow them up. After 324 days, the Russians backed down: containment seemed to work. In 1949, therefore, the United States formed an anti-Soviet military alliance of western governments, the North Atlantic Treaty Organization (NATO); in response, Stalin tightened his hold on his satellites, later united in the Warsaw Pact. Europe was divided into two hostile blocs.

In late 1949, the Communists triumphed in China, frightening and infuriating many Americans, who saw an all-powerful worldwide communist conspiracy extending even into the upper reaches of the American government. When the Russian-backed Communist forces of northern Korea invaded southern Korea in 1950, President Truman's response was swift. American-led United Nations armies intervened. The cold war had spread around the world and become very hot.

It seems clear that the rapid descent from victorious Grand Alliance to bitter cold war was intimately connected with the tragic fate of eastern Europe. When the eastern European power vacuum after 1932 had lured Nazi racist imperialism, the appeasing Western democracies had quite mistakenly done nothing. They had, however, had one telling insight: how, they had asked themselves, could they unite with Stalin to stop Hitler without giving Stalin great gains on his western borders? After Hitler's invasion of Soviet Russia, the Western powers preferred to ignore this question and hope for the best. But when Stalin later began to claim the spoils of victory, a helpless but moralistic United States refused to cooperate and professed outrage. One cannot help but feel that Western opposition immediately after the war came too late and quite possibly encouraged even more aggressive measures by the always-suspicious Stalin. And it helped explode the quarrel over eastern Europe into a global confrontation, which became institutionalized and lasts to this day despite intermittent periods of relaxation.

THE WESTERN EUROPEAN RENAISSANCE

As the cold war divided Europe into two blocs, the future appeared bleak on both sides of the Iron Curtain. Economic conditions were the worst in generations, and millions of people lived on the verge of starvation. Politically, Europe was weak and divided, a battleground for cold war ambitions. Moreover, long-cherished European empires were crumbling in the face of Asian and African nationalism. Yet Europe recovered, and the Western nations led the way. In less than a generation, western Europe achieved unprecedented economic prosperity and regained much of its traditional prominence in world affairs. It was an amazing rebirth—a true renaissance.

THE POSTWAR CHALLENGE

After the war, economic conditions in western Europe were terrible. Simply finding enough to eat was a real problem. Runaway inflation and black markets testified to severe shortages and hardship. The bread ration in Paris in 1946 was little more than it had

been in 1942 under the Nazi occupation. Rationing of bread had to be introduced in Britain in 1946 for the first time. Both France and Italy produced only about half as much in 1946 as before the war. Many people believed that Europe was quite simply finished. The prominent British historian Arnold Toynbee felt that, at best, western Europeans might seek to civilize the crude but all-powerful Americans, somewhat as the ancient Greeks had civilized their Roman conquerors.

Suffering was most intense in defeated Germany. The major territorial change of the war had moved Soviet Russia's border far to the west. Poland was in turn compensated for this loss to Russia with land taken from Germany (see Map 30.3). To solidify these boundary changes, 13 million people were driven from their homes in eastern Germany (and other eastern countries) and forced to resettle in a greatly reduced Germany. The Russians were also seizing factories and equipment as reparations, even tearing up railroad tracks and sending the rails to the Soviet Union. The command "Come here, woman," from a Russian soldier was the sound of terror, the prelude to many a rape.

In 1945 and 1946, conditions were not much better in the Western zones. There was the same soul-numbing devastation. Walking through Munich, a survivor wrote that

You could often see for miles, and then you went through canyons, as in the mountains, the rubble towering up on both sides. . . . I wandered like a sleepwalker through this wasteland. . . . There was no city. There was only the ghost, the feeling, the sensation of a devastated, stunned wasteland. The creatures in this wasteland resembled ghosts. . . . Their faces were without expression, their eyes sunken and listless. . . . A huge solitude and despair seized me.[4]

The Western allies also treated the German population with great severity at first. By February 1946, the average daily diet of a German in the Ruhr had been reduced to two slices of bread, a pat of margarine, a spoonful of porridge, and two small potatoes. Countless Germans sold many of their possessions to American soldiers to buy food. Cigarettes replaced worthless money as currency. The winter of 1946 to 1947 was one of the coldest in memory, and there were widespread signs of actual starvation. By the spring of 1947, refugee-clogged, hungry, prostrate

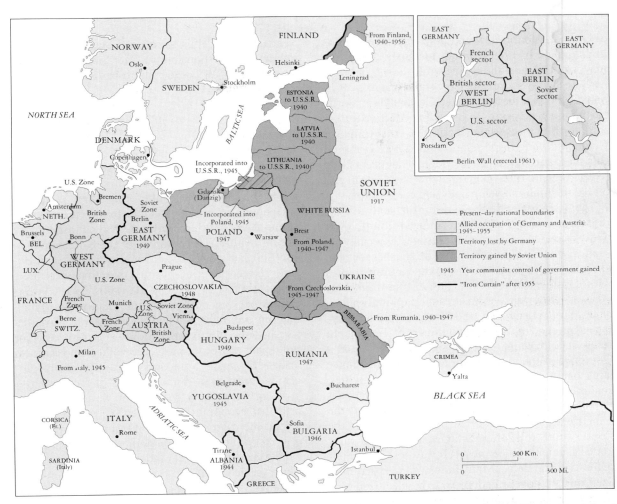

MAP 30.3 Europe After World War Two Both the Soviet Union and Poland took land from Germany, which the Allies partitioned into occupation zones. Those zones subsequently formed the basis of the East and the West German states, as the Iron Curtain fell to divide both Germany and Europe.

Germany was on the verge of total collapse and threatening to drag down the rest of Europe.

Yet western Europe was not finished. The Nazi occupation and the war had discredited old ideas and old leaders. All over Europe, many people were willing to change and experiment in hopes of building a new and better Europe out of the rubble. New groups and new leaders were coming to the fore to guide these aspirations. Progressive Catholics and revitalized Catholic political parties—the Christian Democrats—were particularly influential.

In Italy the Christian Democrats emerged as the leading party in the first postwar elections in 1946,

and in early 1948 they won an absolute majority in the parliament in a landslide victory. Their very able leader was Alcide De Gasperi, a courageous antifascist and former Vatican librarian, firmly committed to political democracy, economic reconstruction, and moderate social reform. In France, too, the Catholic party provided some of the best postwar leaders, like Robert Schuman. This was particularly true after January 1946, when General De Gaulle, the inspiring wartime leader of the Free French, resigned after having re-established the free and democratic Fourth Republic. As Germany was partitioned by the cold war, a radically purified Federal Republic of Germany found new and able leadership among its Catholics. In 1949 Konrad Adenauer, the former mayor of Cologne and a long-time anti-Nazi, began his long, highly successful democratic rule; the Christian Democrats became West Germany's majority party for a generation. In providing effective leadership for their respective countries, the Christian Democrats were inspired and united by a common Christian and European heritage. They steadfastly rejected totalitarianism and narrow nationalism and placed their faith in democracy and cooperation.

The Socialists and the Communists, active in the resistance against Hitler, also emerged from the war with increased power and prestige, especially in France and Italy. They, too, provided fresh leadership and pushed for social change and economic reform with considerable success. Thus, in the immediate postwar years, welfare measures such as family allowances, health insurance, and increased public housing were enacted throughout much of Europe. In Italy social benefits from the state came to equal a large part of the average worker's wages. In France large banks, insurance companies, public utilities, coal mines, and the Renault auto company were nationalized by the government. Britain followed the same trend. The voters threw out Churchill and the Conservatives in 1945, and the socialist Labour party under Clement Attlee moved toward establishment of the "welfare state." Many industries were nationalized, and the government provided each citizen with free medical service and taxed the middle and upper classes heavily. Thus, all across Europe, social reform complemented political transformation, providing solid foundations for a great European renaissance.

The United States also provided strong and creative leadership. Frightened by fears of Soviet expansion, the United States provided western Europe with both massive economic aid and ongoing military protection. Economic aid was channeled through the Marshall Plan, which required that the participating countries coordinate their efforts for maximum effectiveness and which led to the establishment of the Organization of European Economic Cooperation (OEEC). Over the next five years, the United States furnished foreign countries roughly $22.5 billion, of which seven-eighths was in the form of outright gifts rather than loans. Military protection was provided through NATO, established as a regional alliance for self-defense and featuring American troops stationed permanently in Europe as well as the American nu-

clear umbrella. Thus the United States assumed its international responsibilities after the Second World War, exercising the leadership it had shunned in the tragic years after 1919.

ECONOMIC "MIRACLES"

As Marshall Plan aid poured in, the battered economies of western Europe began to turn the corner in 1948. Impoverished West Germany led the way with a spectacular advance after the Allies permitted Adenauer's government to reform the currency and stimulate private enterprise. Other countries were not far behind. The outbreak of the Korean War in 1950 further stimulated economic activity, and Europe entered a period of rapid, sustained economic progress that lasted into the late 1960s. By 1963 western Europe was producing more than two-and-one-half times as much as it had before the war. Never before had the European economy grown so fast. For politicians and economists, for workers and business leaders, it was a time of astonishing, loudly proclaimed economic "miracles."

There were many reasons for western Europe's brilliant economic performance. American aid helped the process get off to a fast start. Europe received equipment to repair damaged plants and even whole new specialized factories when necessary. Thus, critical shortages were quickly overcome. Moreover, since European nations coordinated the distribution of American aid, many barriers to European trade and cooperation were quickly dropped. Aid from the United States helped, therefore, to promote both a resurgence of economic liberalism with its healthy competition and an international division of labor.

As in most of the world, economic growth became a basic objective of all western European governments, for leaders and voters were determined to avoid a return to the dangerous and demoralizing stagnation of the 1930s. Governments generally accepted Keynesian economics (see page 918) and sought to stimulate their economies, and some also adopted a number of imaginative strategies. Those in Germany and France were particularly successful and influential.

Under Minister of Economy Ludwig Erhard, a roly-poly, cigar-smoking ex-professor, postwar West Germany broke decisively with the totally regulated, strait-jacketed Nazi economy. Erhard bet on the free-

Berlin Digs Out What was once a great newspaper building stands as a ghostly gutted-out shell in this altogether typical postwar scene from 1945. But the previously impassable street has been partially cleared of rubble and traffic has begun to move again. In the midst of ruins life refuses to die. *(U.S. Army Signal Corps)*

market economy, while maintaining the extensive social welfare network inherited from the Hitler era. He and his teachers believed, not only that capitalism was more efficient, but also that political and social freedom could thrive only if there were real economic freedom. Erhard's first step was to reform the currency and abolish rationing and price controls in 1948. He boldly declared, "The only ration coupon is the Mark."[5] At first, profits jumped sharply, prompting businessmen to quickly employ more people and produce more. By the late 1950s, Germany had a prospering economy and full employment, a strong currency and stable prices. Germany's success aroused renewed respect for free-market capitalism and encouraged freer trade among other European nations.

In France the major innovation was a new kind of planning. Under the guidance of Jean Monnet, an economic pragmatist and apostle of European unity, a planning commission set ambitious but flexible goals for the French economy. It used Marshall aid money and the nationalized banks to funnel money into key industries, several of which were state owned. At the same time, the planning commission and the French bureaucracy encouraged private enterprise to "think big." The often-cautious French business community responded, investing heavily in new equipment and modern factories. Thus France combined flexible planning and a "mixed" state and private economy to achieve the most rapid economic development in its long history. Throughout the 1950s and 1960s, there was hardly any unemployment in France. The average person's standard of living improved dramatically. France, too, was an economic "miracle."

Other factors also contributed to western Europe's economic boom. In most countries after the war, there were large numbers of men and women ready to work hard for low wages and the hope of a better future. Germany had millions of impoverished refugees, while France and Italy still had millions of poor peasants. Expanding industries in those countries thus had a great asset to draw on. More fully urbanized Britain had no such rural labor pool; this lack, along with a welfare socialism that stressed "fair shares" rather than rapid growth, helps account for its fairly poor postwar economic performance.

In 1945 impoverished Europe was still rich in the sense that it had the human skills of an advanced industrial society. Skilled workers, engineers, managers, and professionals knew what could and should be done, and they did it.

Many consumer products had been invented or perfected since the late 1920s, but few Europeans had been able to buy them during the depression and war. In 1945 the electric refrigerator, the washing machine, and the automobile were rare luxuries. There was, therefore, a great potential demand, which the economic system moved to satisfy.

Finally, ever since 1919 the nations of Europe had suffered from high tariffs and small national markets, which made for small and therefore inefficient factories. In the postwar era European countries junked many of these economic barriers and gradually created a large unified market—the Common Market. This action, which stimulated the economy, was part of the postwar search for a new European unity.

TOWARD EUROPEAN UNITY

Western Europe's political recovery was spectacular. Republics were re-established in France, West Germany, and Italy. Constitutional monarchs were restored in Belgium, Holland, and Norway. These democratic governments took root once again and thrived. To be sure, only West Germany established a two-party system on the British-American model; states like France and Italy returned to multiparty politics and shifting parliamentary coalitions. Yet the middle-of-the-road parties—primarily the Christian Democrats and the Socialists—dominated and provided continuing leadership. National self-determination was accompanied by civil liberties and great individual freedom. All of this was itself an extraordinary achievement.

Even more remarkable was the still-unfinished, still-continuing movement toward a united Europe. The Christian Democrats with their shared Catholic heritage were particularly committed to "building Europe," and other groups shared their dedication. Many Europeans believed that narrow, exaggerated nationalism had been a fundamental cause of both

MAP 30.4 **European Alliance Systems** After the Cold War divided Europe into two hostile military alliances, six Western European countries formed the Common Market in 1957. The Common Market grew later to include most of Western Europe, while the Communist states organized their own economic association—COMECON.

world wars, and that only through unity could European conflict be avoided in the future. Many western Europeans also realized how very weak their countries were in comparison with the United States and the Soviet Union, the two superpowers that had divided Europe from outside and made it into a cold war battleground. Thus, the cold war encouraged some visionaries to seek a new "European nation," a superpower capable of controlling western Europe's destiny and reasserting its influence in world affairs.

The close cooperation among European states required by the Marshall Plan led to the creation of both the OEEC and the Council of Europe in 1948. European federalists hoped that the Council of Europe would quickly evolve into a true European parliament with sovereign rights, but this did not happen. Britain, with its empire and its "special relationship" with the United States, consistently opposed giving any real political power—any sovereignty—to the council. Many old-fashioned continental nationalists and communists felt similarly. The Council of Europe became little more than a multinational debating society.

Frustrated in the direct political approach, European federalists turned toward economics. As one of them explained, "Politics and economics are closely related. Let us try, then, for progress in economic matters. Let us suppress those obstacles of an economic nature which divide and compartmentalize the nations of Europe."[6] In this they were quite successful.

Two far-seeing French statesmen, the planner Jean Monnet and Foreign Minister Robert Schuman, courageously took the lead in 1950. The Schuman Plan called for a special international organization to control and integrate all European steel and coal production. West Germany, Italy, Belgium, the Netherlands, and Luxembourg accepted the French idea in 1952; the British would have none of it. The immediate economic goal—a single competitive market without national tariffs or quotas—was rapidly realized. By 1958 coal and steel moved as freely among

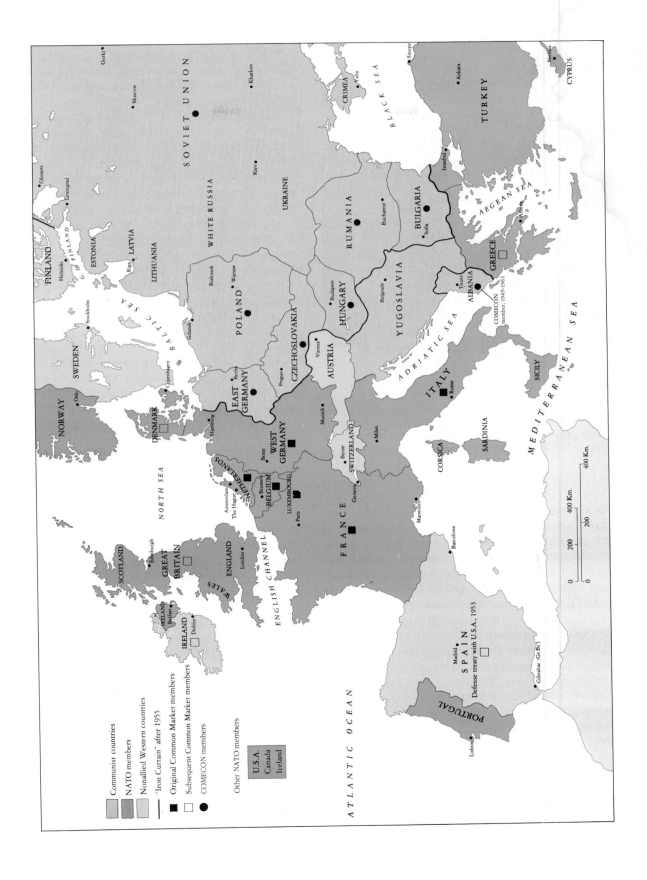

Communist countries

NATO members

Nonallied Western countries

"Iron Curtain" after 1955

Original Common Market members

Subsequent Common Market members

COMECON members

Other NATO members

U.S.A.
Canada
Iceland

French President De Gaulle and his wife bid farewell to President and Mrs. Kennedy at the presidential palace in Paris in 1961. A proud statesman who never forgot the snubs received from his American and British allies during the war, De Gaulle challenged American leadership in Western Europe. *(Wide World Photos)*

the six nations of the European Coal and Steel Community as among the states of the United States. The more far-reaching political goal was to bind the six member nations so closely together economically that war among them would become unthinkable and virtually impossible. This brilliant strategy did much to reduce tragic old rivalries, particularly that of France and Germany, which practically disappeared in the postwar era.

The coal and steel community was so successful that it encouraged further technical and economic cooperation among "the Six." In 1957 the same six nations formed Euratom to pursue joint research in atomic energy; they also signed the Treaty of Rome, which created the European Economic Community, generally known as the Common Market (see Map 30.4). The first goal of the treaty was gradual reduction of all tariffs among the Six to create a large free-trade area. Others were the free movement of capital and labor and common economic policies and institutions.

An epoch-making stride toward unity, the Common Market was a tremendous success. Tariffs were rapidly reduced, and the European economy was stimulated. Companies and regions specialized in what they did best. Western Europe was being united in a single market almost as large as that of the United States. Many medium-sized American companies rushed to Europe, for a single modern factory in, say, Belgium or southern Italy had a vast potential market of 170 million customers.

The development of the Common Market fired imaginations and encouraged hopes of rapid progress toward political as well as economic union. In the 1960s, however, these hopes were frustrated by a resurgence of more traditional nationalism. Once again, France took the lead. Mired in a bitter colonial war in Algeria, the country turned in 1958 to General De Gaulle, who established the Fifth French Republic and ruled as its president until 1969. A towering giant both literally and figuratively, De Gaulle was the last of the bigger-than-life wartime leaders. A complex man who aroused a strong and sometimes negative response, especially in the United States, De Gaulle was at heart a romantic nationalist dedicated to reasserting France's greatness and glory. Once he had resolved the Algerian conflict, he labored to recreate a powerful, truly independent France, which would lead and even dictate to the other Common Market states.

De Gaulle personified the political resurgence of the leading nations of western Europe, as well as declining fears of the Soviet Union in the 1960s. Viewing the United States as the main threat to genuine French (and European) independence, he withdrew all French military forces from the "American-controlled" NATO command, which had to move from Paris to Brussels. De Gaulle tried to create financial difficulties for the United States by demanding gold for the American dollars France had accumulated. France also developed its own nuclear weapons. Within the Common Market, De Gaulle in 1963 and again in 1967 vetoed the application of the pro-American British, who were having second thoughts and wanted to join. More generally, he refused to permit the scheduled advent of majority rule within the Common Market, and he forced his partners to accept many of his views. Thus, throughout the 1960s the Common Market thrived economically, but it did not transcend deep-seated nationalism and remained a union of sovereign states.

Decolonialization

The postwar era saw the total collapse of colonial empires. Between 1947 and 1962, almost every colonial territory gained independence. Europe's long expansion, which had reached a high point in the late nineteenth century, was completely reversed (see Map 30.5). The spectacular collapse of Western political empires fully reflected old Europe's eclipsed power after 1945. Yet the new nations of Asia and Africa have been so deeply influenced by Western ideas and achievements that the "westernization" of the world has continued to rush forward.

Modern nationalism, with its demands for political self-determination and racial equality, spread from intellectuals to the masses in virtually every colonial territory after the First World War. Economic suffering created bitter popular resentment, and thousands of colonial subjects had been unwillingly drafted into French and British armies. Nationalist leaders stepped up their demands. By 1919 one high-ranking British official mournfully wrote: "A wave of unrest is sweeping over the Empire, as over the rest of the world. Almost every day brings some disturbance or other at our Imperial outposts."[7] The Russian Revolution also encouraged the growth of nationalism, and Soviet Russia verbally and militarily supported nationalist independence movements.

Furthermore, European empires had been based on an enormous power differential between the rulers and the ruled, a difference that had declined almost to the vanishing point by 1945. Not only was western Europe poor and battered immediately after the war, but Japan had demonstrated that whites were not invincible. With its political power and moral authority in tatters, Europe's only choice was either to submit gracefully or to enter into risky wars of reconquest.

Most Europeans regarded their empires very differently after 1945 than before 1914, or even before 1939. Empire had rested on self-confidence and a sense of righteousness; Europeans had believed their superiority to be not only technical and military but spiritual and moral as well. The horrors of the Second World War and the near-destruction of Western civilization destroyed such complacent arrogance and gave opponents of imperialism the upper hand in Europe. After 1945 most Europeans were willing to let go of their colonies more or less voluntarily and to concentrate on rebuilding at home.

India played a key role in decolonialization and the end of empire. India was Britain's oldest, largest, and most lucrative nonwhite possession, and Britain had by far the largest colonial empire. Nationalist opposition to British rule coalesced after the First World War under the leadership of the British-educated lawyer Mahatma Gandhi (1869–1948), who preached nonviolent "noncooperation" against the British. Indian intellectuals effectively argued the old liberal case for equality and self-determination. In response, Britain's rulers gradually introduced political reforms and limited self-government. When the war ended, independence followed very rapidly. The new Labour government was determined to leave India; radicals and socialists had always opposed imperialism, and the heavy cost of governing India had become an intolerable financial burden. The obstacle posed by conflict between India's Hindu and Muslim populations was resolved in 1947 by creating two states, predominantly Hindu India and Muslim Pakistan.

If Indian nationalism drew on Western parliamentary liberalism, Chinese nationalism developed and triumphed in the framework of Marxist-Leninist totalitarianism. In the turbulent early 1920s, a broad alliance of nationalist forces within the Russian-supported Kuomintang—the National People's party—was dedicated to unifying China and abolishing European concessions. But in 1927 Chiang Kai-shek (1887–1975), the successor to Sun Yat-Sen (page 856) and the leader of the Kuomintang, broke with his more radical Communist allies, headed by Mao Tse-tung.

In 1931 Mao Tse-tung (1893–1976) led his followers on an incredible five-thousand-mile march to remote northern China and dug in. Even war against the Japanese army of occupation could not force Mao and Chiang to cooperate. By late 1945 the longstanding quarrel erupted in civil war. Stalin gave Mao some aid, and the Americans gave Chiang much more. Winning the support of the peasantry by promising to expropriate the big landowners, the tougher, better-organized Communists forced the Nationalists to withdraw to the island of Taiwan in 1949.

Mao and the Communists united China's 550 million inhabitants in a strong centralized state, expelled foreigners, and began building a new society along Soviet lines, with mass arrests, forced-labor camps, and ceaseless propaganda. The peasantry was collectivized, and the inevitable five-year plans concentrated quite successfully on the expansion of heavy industry.

Most Asian countries followed the pattern of either India or China. Britain quickly gave Sri Lanka (Ceylon) and Burma independence in 1948; the Philippines became independent of the United States in 1946. The Dutch attempt to reconquer the Netherlands East Indies was unsuccessful, and in 1949 Indonesia emerged independent.

The French similarly sought to re-establish colonial rule in Indochina, but despite American aid, they were defeated in 1954 by forces under the Communist and nationalist guerrilla leader Ho Chi Minh (1890–1969), supported by Russia and China. At the subsequent international peace conference in Geneva, French Indochina gained independence. Vietnam was divided into two hostile zones, one communist and one anticommunist, pending unification on the basis of internationally supervised free elections. But the elections were never held, and civil war soon broke out between the North and the South.

In Africa, Arab nationalism was an important factor in the ending of empire. Sharing a common lan-

MAP 30.5 The New States in Africa and Asia India led the way to political independence as European empires passed away.

guage and culture, Arab nationalists were also loosely united by their opposition to the colonial powers and to the migration of Jewish refugees to Palestine. The British, whose occupation policies in Palestine were condemned by Arabs and Jews, by Russians and Americans, announced their withdrawal from Palestine in 1948. The United Nations voted for the creation of two states, one Arab and one Jewish. The Arab countries immediately attacked the new Jewish nation and suffered a humiliating defeat. In the course of the fighting, thousands of Arab refugees fled from the territory that became the Jewish state of Israel.

Many of these Arab refugees refused to accept defeat. They vowed to fight on, for generations if necessary, until the state of Israel was destroyed or until they established their own independent Palestinian

Chinese Red Guards line up before a giant picture of Mao Tse-tung in about 1967. They are waving the "Little Red Book," which contains a collection of Mao's slogans and teachings. *(Wide World Photos)*

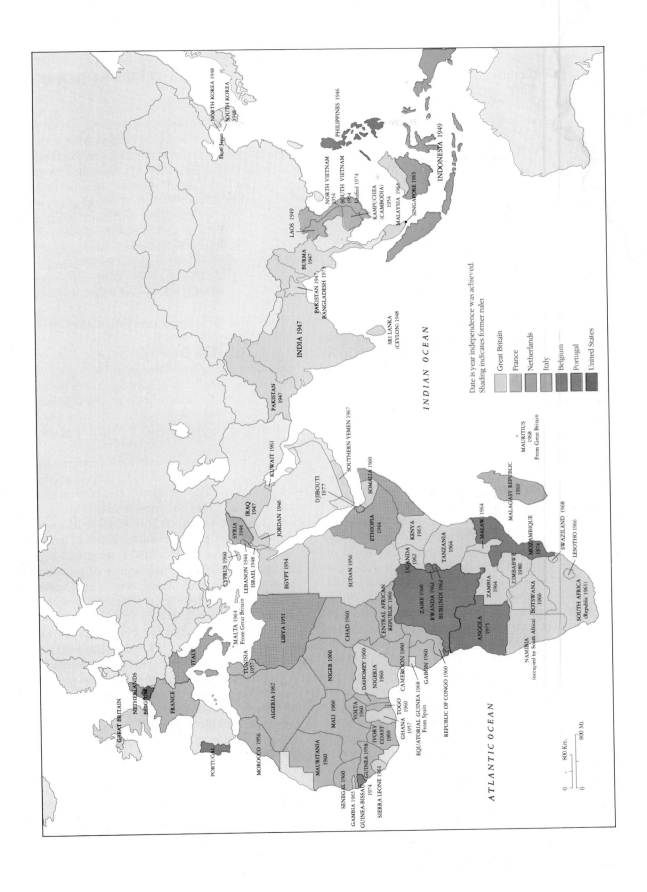

NORTH KOREA 1948
SOUTH KOREA 1948
From Japan

PHILIPPINES 1946

INDONESIA 1949

NORTH VIETNAM 1954
SOUTH VIETNAM 1954
Unified 1974

KAMPUCHEA (CAMBODIA) 1954

MALAYSIA 1963

SINGAPORE 1965

LAOS 1949

BURMA 1947

PAKISTAN 1947
BANGLADESH 1973

INDIA 1947

SRI LANKA (CEYLON) 1948

PAKISTAN 1947

INDIAN OCEAN

Date is year independence was achieved.
Shading indicates former ruler

- Great Britain
- France
- Netherlands
- Italy
- Belgium
- Portugal
- United States

SOUTHERN YEMEN 1967

KUWAIT 1961

DJIBOUTI 1977

SOMALIA 1960

MAURITIUS 1968
From Great Britain

IRAQ 1947

JORDAN 1946

SYRIA 1944

CYPRUS 1960

LEBANON 1944

ISRAEL 1948

ETHIOPIA 1944

KENYA 1963

TANZANIA 1964

MALAWI 1964

MALAGASY REPUBLIC 1960

MOZAMBIQUE 1974

SWAZILAND 1968

LESOTHO 1966

EGYPT 1954

SUDAN 1956

UGANDA 1962

ZAIRE 1960

RWANDA 1962

BURUNDI 1962

ZAMBIA 1964

ZIMBABWE 1980

BOTSWANA 1966

SOUTH AFRICA (Republic 1961)

CENTRAL AFRICAN REPUBLIC 1960

ANGOLA 1975

NAMIBIA (occupied by South Africa)

*MALTA 1964
From Great Britain

LIBYA 1951

CHAD 1960

TUNISIA 1957

GREAT BRITAIN

NETHERLANDS

BELGIUM

FRANCE

ITALY

PORTUGAL

ALGERIA 1962

NIGER 1960

MALI 1960

VOLTA 1960

DAHOMEY 1960

NIGERIA 1960

CAMEROON 1960

GABON 1960

MOROCCO 1956

MAURITANIA 1960

SENEGAL 1960

GAMBIA 1965

GUINEA-BISSAU 1974

SIERRA LEONE 1961

GUINEA 1958

IVORY COAST 1960

GHANA 1957

TOGO 1960

EQUATORIAL GUINEA 1968
From Spain

REPUBLIC OF CONGO 1960

ATLANTIC OCEAN

0   800 Km.
0   800 Mi.

state. The Palestinian refugees also sought the support of existing Arab states, claiming that Israel was the great enemy of Arab interests and Arab nationalism. The Arab-Israeli conflict was destined to outlive the postwar era, enduring—like Soviet-American antagonism—to this day.

The Arab defeat in 1948 triggered a nationalist revolution in Egypt in 1952, where a young army officer named Gamal Abdel Nasser (1918–1970) drove out the pro-Western king. In 1956 Nasser abruptly nationalized the Suez Canal, the last symbol and substance of Western power in the Middle East. Infuriated, the British and French, along with the Israelis, invaded Egypt. This was, however, to be the dying gasp of imperial power: the moralistic, anti-imperialist Americans joined with the Russians to force the British, French, and Israelis to withdraw.

The failure of the Western powers to unseat Nasser in 1956 in turn encouraged Arab nationalists in Algeria. Algeria's large French population considered Algeria an integral part of France. It was this feeling that made the ensuing war so bitter and so atypical of decolonialization. In the end, General De Gaulle, who had returned to power as part of a movement to keep Algeria French, accepted the principle of Algerian self-determination. In 1962, after more than a century of French rule, Algeria became independent and the European population quickly fled.

In most of Africa south of the Sahara, decolonialization proceeded much more smoothly. Beginning in 1957, Britain's colonies won independence with little or no bloodshed. In 1960 the clever De Gaulle offered the leaders of French black Africa the choice of a total break with France or immediate independence within a kind of French commonwealth. Heavily dependent on France for economic aid and technology, all but one of the new states chose association with France. Throughout the 1960s France (and its western European partners) successfully used economic and cultural ties with former colonies, such as special trading privileges with the Common Market and heavy investment in French-based education, to maintain a powerful European presence in black Africa. Radicals charged France (and Europe generally) with "neocolonialism," designed to perpetuate European economic domination indefinitely. In any event, enduring aid and influence in black Africa was an important manifestation of western Europe's political recovery and even of its possible emergence as a genuine superpower.

SOVIET EASTERN EUROPE

While western Europe surged ahead economically, regaining political independence as American influence gradually waned, eastern Europe followed a different path. Soviet Russia first tightened its grip on the "liberated" nations of eastern Europe under Stalin and then refused to let go. Economic recovery in eastern Europe proceeded, therefore, along Soviet lines, and political and social developments were largely determined by changes in the Soviet Union. Thus one must look primarily at Soviet Russia to understand the achievements and failures of eastern European peoples after the Second World War.

STALIN'S LAST YEARS

The unwillingness of the United States to accept what Stalin did to territories occupied by the triumphant Red Army was at least partly responsible for the outbreak and institutionalization of the cold war. Yet Americans were not the only ones who felt disappointed and even betrayed by Stalin's postwar actions.

The Great Patriotic War of the Fatherland had fostered Russian nationalism and a relaxation of totalitarian terror. It also produced a rare but real unity between Soviet rulers and most Russian people. When an American correspondent asked a distinguished sixty-year-old Jewish scientist, who had decided to leave Russia for Israel in 1972, what had been the best period in Russian history, he received a startling answer: the Second World War. The scientist explained: "At that time we all felt closer to our government than at any other time in our lives. It was not *their* country then, but *our* country. . . . It was not *their* war, but *our* war."[8] Having made such a heroic war effort, the vast majority of the Soviet people hoped in 1945 that a grateful party and government would grant greater freedom and democracy. Such hopes were soon crushed.

Even before the war ended, Stalin was moving his country back toward rigid dictatorship. As early as 1944, the leading members of the Communist party were being given a new motivating slogan: "The war on Fascism ends, the war on capitalism begins."[9] By early 1946, Stalin was publicly singing the old tune that war was inevitable as long as capitalism existed. Stalin's invention of a new foreign foe was mainly an

Lenin Avenue, Volgograd Devastated Stalingrad was completely rebuilt and then re-named Volgograd as part of Khrushchev's de-Stalinization campaign. Seen here are the massive apartment blocks, the gigantic boulevard, and the stress on public transportation as opposed to private automobiles, which are all quite characteristic of Soviet urban style. *(Sovfoto/Eastfoto)*

excuse for re-establishing totalitarian measures, for the totalitarian state cannot live without enemies. Unfortunately, as dissident Russian historians have argued, Stalin's language at home and his actions in eastern Europe were so crudely extreme that he managed to turn an imaginary threat into a real one, as the cold war took hold.

One of Stalin's first postwar goals was to repress the millions of Soviet citizens who were outside Soviet borders when the war ended. Many had been captured by the Nazis; others were ordinary civilians who had been living abroad. Many were opposed to Stalin; some had fought for the Germans. Determined to hush up the fact that large numbers of Soviet citizens hated his regime so much that they had willingly supported the Germans and refused to go home, Stalin demanded that all these "traitors" be returned to him. At Yalta, Roosevelt and Churchill agreed, and they kept their word. American and British military commanders refused to recognize the right of political asylum under any circumstances.

Roughly 2 million people were delivered to Stalin against their will. Most were immediately arrested and sent to forced-labor camps, where about 50 percent perished. The revival of many forced-labor camps, which had accounted for roughly one-sixth of all new construction in Soviet Russia before the war, was further stimulated by large-scale purges of many people who had never left the Soviet Union, particularly in 1945 and 1946.

Culture and art were also purged. Rigid anti-Western ideological conformity was reimposed in violent campaigns led by Stalin's trusted henchman, Andrei Zhdanov. Zhdanov denounced many artists, including the composers Sergei Prokofiev and Dimitri Shostakovich and the outstanding film director Sergei Eisenstein. The great poet Anna Akhmatova was condemned as "a harlot and nun who mixes harlotry and prayer" and, like many others, driven out of the writers' union, which practically ensured that her work would not be published. In 1949 Stalin launched a savage verbal attack on Soviet Jews, who were accused of being pro-Western and antisocialist.

In the political realm, Stalin reasserted the Communist party's complete control of the government and his absolute mastery of the party. Five-year plans were reintroduced to cope with the enormous task of economic reconstruction. Once again, heavy and military industry were given top priority, and consumer goods, housing, and still-collectivized agriculture were neglected. Everyday life was very hard: in 1952 the wages of ordinary people still bought 25 to 40 percent *less* than in 1928. In short, it was the 1930s all over again in Soviet Russia, although police terror was less intense than during that era's purges.

Stalin's prime postwar innovation was to export the Stalinist system to the countries of eastern Europe. The Communist parties of eastern Europe had established one-party states by 1948, thanks to the help of the Red Army and the Russian secret police. Rigid ideological indoctrination, attacks on religion, and a lack of civil liberties were soon facts of life. Industry was nationalized, and the middle class was stripped of its possessions. Economic life was then faithfully recast in the Stalinist mold. Forced industrialization, with five-year plans and a stress on heavy industry, lurched forward without regard for human costs. For the sake of ideological uniformity, agriculture had to be collectivized; this process went much faster in Bulgaria and Czechoslovakia than in Hungary and Poland. Finally, the satellite countries were forced to trade heavily with Soviet Russia on very unfavorable terms, as traditional economic ties with western Europe were forcibly severed.

Only Josip Tito (1892–1980), the popular resistance leader and Communist chief of Yugoslavia, was able to resist Russian economic exploitation successfully. Tito openly broke with Stalin in 1948, and since there was no Russian army in Yugoslavia, he got away with it. Tito's successful proclamation of Communist independence led the infuriated and humiliated Stalin to purge the Communist parties of eastern Europe. Hundreds of thousands who had joined the party after the war were expelled. Popular Communist leaders who, like Tito, had led the resistance against Germany, were made to star in reruns of the great show trials of the 1930s, complete with charges of treason, unbelievable confessions, and merciless executions. Thus did history repeat itself as Stalin sought to create absolutely obedient instruments of domination in eastern Europe.

REFORM AND DE-STALINIZATION

In 1953 the aging Stalin finally died, and a new era slowly began in Soviet eastern Europe. Even as they struggled for power, Stalin's heirs realized that change

and reform were necessary. There was, first of all, widespread fear and hatred of Stalin's political terrorism, which had struck both high and low with its endless purges and unjust arrests. Even Stalin's secret-police chief, Lavrenti Beria, publicly favored a relaxation of controls in an unsuccessful attempt to seize power. Beria was arrested and shot, after which the power of the secret police was curbed and many of its infamous forced-labor camps were gradually closed. Change was also necessary for economic reasons. Agriculture was in bad shape, and shortages of consumer goods were discouraging hard work and initiative. Finally, Stalin's aggressive foreign policy had led directly to an ongoing American commitment to western Europe and a strong Western alliance. Soviet Russia was isolated and contained.

On the question of just how much change should be permitted, the Communist leadership was badly split. The conservatives led by Stalin's long-time foreign minister, the stone-faced Vyacheslav Molotov, wanted to make as few changes as possible. The reformers, led by Nikita Khrushchev, argued for major innovations. Khrushchev (1894–1971), who had joined the party as an uneducated coal miner in 1918 at twenty-four and had risen steadily to a high-level position in the 1930s, was emerging as the new ruler by 1955.

To strengthen his position and that of his fellow reformers within the party, Khrushchev launched an all-out attack on Stalin and his crimes at a closed session of the Twentieth Party Congress in 1956. In gory detail he described to the startled Communist delegates how Stalin had tortured and murdered thousands of loyal Communists, how he had trusted Hitler completely and bungled the country's defense, and how he had "supported the glorification of his own person with all conceivable methods." For hours Soviet Russia's top leader delivered an attack whose content would previously have been dismissed as "anti-Communist hysteria" in many circles throughout the Western world.

Khrushchev's "secret speech" was read to Communist party meetings throughout the country and strengthened the reform movement. The liberalization—or "de-Stalinization," as it was called in the West—of Soviet Russia was genuine. The Communist party jealously maintained its monopoly on political power, but Khrushchev shook it up and brought in new blood. The economy was made more responsive to the needs and even some of the desires of the people, as some resources were shifted from heavy industry and the military toward consumer goods and agriculture. Stalinist controls over workers were relaxed, and independent courts rather than the secret police judged and punished nonpolitical crimes.

Russia's very low standard of living finally began to improve and continued to rise throughout the 1960s. By 1970 Russians were able to buy twice as much food, three times as much clothing, and twelve times as many appliances as in 1950. (Even so, the standard of living in Soviet Russia was only about half that of the wealthier western European countries in 1970 and well below that of east European countries as well.)

De-Stalinization created great ferment among writers and intellectuals, who hungered for cultural freedom. The poet Boris Pasternak (1890–1960), who survived the Stalinist years by turning his talents to translating Shakespeare, finished his great novel *Doctor Zhivago* in 1956. Published in the West but not in Russia, *Doctor Zhivago* is both a literary masterpiece and a powerful challenge to communism. It tells the story of a prerevolutionary intellectual who rejects the violence and brutality of the revolution of 1917 and the Stalinist years. Even as he is destroyed, he triumphs because of his humanity and Christian spirit. Pasternak was forced by Khrushchev himself to refuse the Nobel prize in 1958—but he was not shot. Other talented writers followed Pasternak's lead, and courageous editors let the sparks fly.

The writer Alexander Solzhenitsyn (b. 1918) created a sensation when his *One Day in the Life of Ivan Denisovich* was published in Russia in 1962. Solzhenitsyn's novel portrays in grim detail life in a Stalinist concentration camp—a life to which Solzhenitsyn himself had been unjustly condemned—and is a damning indictment of the Stalinist past.

Khrushchev also de-Stalinized Soviet foreign policy. "Peaceful coexistence" with capitalism was possible, he argued, and great wars were not inevitable. Khrushchev made positive concessions, meeting with U.S. President Dwight Eisenhower at the first summit meeting since Potsdam and agreeing in 1955 to real independence for a neutral Austria after ten long years of Allied occupation. Thus there was considerable relaxation of cold war tensions between 1955 and 1957. At the same time, Khrushchev began wooing the new nations of Asia and Africa—even if they were not communist—with promises and aid.

He also proclaimed that there could be different paths to socialism, thus calling a halt to the little cold war with Tito's Yugoslavia.

De-Stalinization stimulated rebelliousness in the eastern European satellites. Having suffered in silence under Stalin, Communist reformers and the masses were quickly emboldened to seek much greater liberty and national independence. Poland took the lead in March 1956: riots there resulted in the release of more than nine thousand political prisoners, including the previously purged Wladyslaw Gomulka. Taking charge of the government, Gomulka skillfully managed to win greater autonomy for Poland while calming anti-Russian feeling.

Hungary experienced a real and very tragic revolution. Led by students and workers—the classic urban revolutionaries—the people of Budapest installed a liberal Communist reformer as their new chief in October 1956. Soviet troops were forced to leave the country. One-party rule was abolished, and the new government promised free elections, freedom of expression, and massive social changes. Worst of all from the Russian point of view, the new government declared Hungarian neutrality and renounced Hungary's military alliance with Moscow. As in 1849, the Russian answer was to invade Hungary with a large army and to crush, once again, a national, democratic revolution.

Fighting was bitter until the end, for the Hungarians hoped that the United States would fulfill its earlier propaganda promises and come to their aid. When this did not occur because of American unwillingness to risk a general war, the people of eastern Europe realized that their only hope was to strive for small domestic gains while following Russia obediently in foreign affairs. This cautious approach produced some results. In Poland, for example, the peasants were not collectivized, and Catholics were allowed to practice their faith. Thus eastern Europe profited, however modestly, from Khrushchev's policy of de-Stalinization and could hope for still greater freedom in the future.

THE FALL OF KHRUSHCHEV

In October 1962, a remarkable poem entitled "Stalin's Heirs," by the popular young poet Yevgeny Yevtushenko (b. 1933), appeared in *Pravda,* the official newspaper of the Communist party and the most important one in Soviet Russia. Yevtushenko wrote:

Some of his heirs are in retirement pruning their rose-
   bushes,
   and secretly thinking that their time will come again.
Others even attack Stalin from the rostrum but at
   home, at night-time, think back to bygone days.[10]

Like Solzhenitsyn's novel about Stalin's concentration camps, published a month later, this very political poem was authorized by Communist party boss Khrushchev himself. It was part of his last, desperate offensive against the many well-entrenched conservative Stalinists in the party and government, who were indeed "secretly thinking that their time will come again." And it did.

Within two years Khrushchev had fallen in a bloodless palace revolution. Under Leonid Brezhnev (1906–1982), Soviet Russia began a period of limited "re-Stalinization." The basic reason for this development was that Khrushchev's Communist colleagues saw de-Stalinization as a dangerous, two-sided threat. How could Khrushchev denounce the dead dictator without eventually denouncing and perhaps even arresting his still-powerful henchmen? In a heated secret debate in 1957, when the conservatives had tried without success to depose the menacing reformer, Khrushchev had pointed at two of Stalin's most devoted followers, Molotov and Kaganovich, and exclaimed: "Your hands are stained with the blood of our party leaders and of innumerable innocent Bolsheviks!" "So are yours!" Molotov and Kaganovich shouted back at him. "Yes, so are mine," Khrushchev replied. "I admit this. But during the purges I was merely carrying out your order. . . . I was not responsible. You were."[11] Moreover, the widening campaign of de-Stalinization posed a clear threat to the dictatorial authority of the party. It was producing growing, perhaps uncontrollable, criticism of the whole Communist system. The party had to tighten up while there was still time. It was clear that Khrushchev had to go.

Another reason for conservative opposition was Khrushchev's foreign policy. Although he scored some diplomatic victories, notably with Egypt and India, Khrushchev's policy toward the West was highly erratic and ultimately unsuccessful. In 1958 he ordered the Western allies to evacuate West Berlin within six months, which led only to a reaffirmation of allied unity and to Khrushchev's backing down. Then in 1961, as relations with Communist China deteriorated dramatically, Khrushchev ordered the East Germans to build a wall between East and West Berlin, thereby sealing off West Berlin in clear violation of existing access agreements between the Great Powers. The recently elected U.S. president, John F. Kennedy, acquiesced. Emboldened and seeing a chance to change the balance of military power decisively, Khrushchev ordered missiles with nuclear warheads installed in Fidel Castro's Communist Cuba. President Kennedy countered with a naval blockade of Cuba, and after a tense diplomatic crisis, Khrushchev was forced to remove the Russian missiles in return for American pledges not to disturb Castro's regime. Khrushchev looked like a bumbling buffoon; his influence, already slipping, declined rapidly after the Cuban fiasco.

After Brezhnev and his supporters took over in 1964, they started talking cautiously of Stalin's "good points" and ignoring his crimes. Their praise of the whole Stalinist era, with its rapid industrialization and wartime victories, informed Soviet citizens that no fundamental break with the past had occurred at home. Russian leaders also launched a massive arms buildup, determined never to suffer Khrushchev's humiliation in the face of American nuclear superiority. And they began building the large navy and air force necessary for intervention in faraway places, like Cuba, around the globe. Yet Brezhnev and company proceeded cautiously in the mid-1960s. They avoided direct confrontation with the United States and seemed more solidly committed to peaceful coexistence than the deposed Khrushchev—to the great relief of people in the West.

THE WESTERN HEMISPHERE

One way to think of what historians used to call the New World is as a vigorous offshoot of Western civilization, an offshoot that has gradually developed its own characteristics while retaining European roots. From this perspective, one can see many illuminating parallels and divergences in the histories of Europe and the Americas. So it was after the Second World War. The western hemisphere experienced a many-faceted postwar recovery, somewhat similar to that of Europe, though it began earlier, especially in Latin America.

POSTWAR PROSPERITY IN THE UNITED STATES

The Second World War cured the depression in the United States and brought about the greatest boom in American history. Unemployment practically vanished, as millions of new workers, half of them women, found jobs. Personal income doubled and the well-being of Americans increased dramatically. Yet the experience of the 1930s weighed heavily on people's minds, feeding fears that peace would bring renewed depression.

In fact, conversion to a peacetime economy went smoothly, marred only by a spurt of inflation accompanying the removal of government controls. Moreover, the U.S. economy continued to advance fairly steadily for a long generation. Though cold-war fears marked American relations with the rest of the world, economic prosperity satisfied at home.

This helps explain why postwar domestic politics consisted largely of modest adjustments to the status quo until the 1960s. After a flurry of unpopular postwar strikes, a conservative Republican Congress chopped away at the power of labor unions by means of the Taft-Hartley Act of 1947. But Truman's upset victory in 1948 demonstrated that Americans had no interest in undoing Roosevelt's social and economic reforms. The Congress proceeded to increase social security benefits, subsidize middle- and lower-class housing, and raise the minimum wage. These and other liberal measures consolidated the New Deal. But true innovations, whether in health or civil rights, were rejected, and in 1952 the Republican party and the voters turned to General Eisenhower, a national hero and self-described moderate.

The federal government's only major new undertaking during the "Eisenhower years" was the interstate highway system, a suitable symbol of the basic satisfaction of the vast majority. Some Americans feared that the United States was becoming a "blocked society," obsessed with stability and incapable of wholesome change. This feeling contributed in 1960 to the election of the young, attractive John F. Kennedy, who promised to "get the country moving again." President Kennedy captured the popular imagination with his flair and rhetoric, revitalized the old Roosevelt coalition, and modestly expanded existing liberal legislation before he was struck down by an assassin's bullet in 1963.

THE CIVIL RIGHTS REVOLUTION

Belatedly and reluctantly, complacent postwar America experienced a genuine social revolution: after a long and sometimes bloody struggle, blacks (and their white supporters) threw off a deeply entrenched system of segregation, discrimination, and repression. This movement for civil rights advanced on several fronts. Eloquent lawyers from the National Association for the Advancement of Colored People (NAACP) challenged school segregation in the courts and in 1954 won a landmark decision in the Supreme Court that "separate educational facilities are inherently unequal." While state and local governments in the South were refusing to comply, blacks were effectively challenging institutionalized inequality with bus boycotts, sit-ins, and demonstrations. As Martin Luther King told the white power structure, "We will not hate you, but we will not obey your evil laws."[12]

Blacks also used their growing political power in key northern states to gain the support of the liberal wing of the Democratic party. All these efforts culminated after the liberal landslide that elected Lyndon Johnson in 1964. The Civil Rights Act of 1964 categorically prohibited discrimination in public services and on the job. In the follow-up Voting Rights Act of 1965, the federal government firmly guaranteed all blacks the right to vote. By the 1970s, substantial numbers of blacks had been elected to public and private office throughout the southern states, proof positive that dramatic changes had occurred in American race relations.

Black voters and political leaders enthusiastically supported the accompanying surge of new liberal social legislation in the mid-1960s. President Johnson, reviving the New Deal approach of his early congressional years, solemnly declared "unconditional war on poverty." Congress and the administration created a host of antipoverty projects, such as the domestic peace corps, free preschools for slum children, and community-action programs. Although these programs were directed to all poor Americans—the majority of whom are white—they were also intended to extend greater equality for blacks to the realm of economics. More generally, the United States promoted in the mid-1960s the kind of fundamental social reform that western Europe had em-

The March on Washington in August 1963 marked a dramatic climax in the civil rights struggle. More than 200,000 people gathered at the Lincoln Memorial to hear the young Martin Luther King deliver his greatest address, his "I have a dream" speech. *(UPI/ Bettmann Newsphotos)*

braced immediately after World War Two. The United States became much more of a welfare state, as government spending for social benefits rose dramatically and approached European levels.

ECONOMIC NATIONALISM IN LATIN AMERICA

Although the countries of Latin America share a European heritage, specifically a Spanish-Portuguese heritage, their striking differences make it difficult to generalize meaningfully about modern Latin American history. Yet a growing economic nationalism

seems unmistakable. As the early nineteenth century saw Spanish and Portuguese colonies win wars of political independence, recent history has been an ongoing quest for genuine economic independence through local control and industrialization, which has sometimes brought Latin American countries into sharp conflict with Europe and the United States.

To understand the rise of economic nationalism, one must remember that Latin American countries developed as producers of foodstuffs and raw materials, which were exported to Europe and the United States in return for manufactured goods and capital investment. This exchange was mutually beneficial, especially in the later nineteenth century, and the countries that participated most actively, like Argentina and southern Brazil, became the wealthiest and most advanced. There was, however, a heavy price to pay. Latin America became very dependent on foreign markets, products, and investments. Industry did not develop and large landowners profited most, further enhancing their social and political power.

The old international division of labor, disrupted by the First World War but re-established in the 1920s, was finally destroyed by the Great Depression —a historical turning point as critical for Latin America as for the United States. Prices and exports of Latin American commodities collapsed as Europe and the United States drastically reduced their purchases and raised tariffs to protect domestic procedures. With foreign sales plummeting, Latin American countries could not buy industrial goods abroad. Latin America suffered the full force of the global economic crisis.

The result in the larger, more important Latin American countries was a profound shift in the direction of economic nationalism after 1930. The more popularly based governments worked to reduce foreign influence and gain control of their own economies and natural resources. They energetically promoted national industry by means of high tariffs, government grants, and even state enterprise. They favored the lower-middle and urban working classes with social benefits and higher wages in order to increase their purchasing power and gain their support. These efforts at recovery were fairly successful. By the late 1940s, the factories of Argentina, Brazil, and Chile could generally satisfy domestic consumer demand for the products of light industry. In the 1950s, some countries began moving into heavy industry. Economic nationalism and the rise of industry are particularly striking in the two largest and most influential countries, Mexico and Brazil, which together account for half the population of Latin America.

MEXICO. Overthrowing the elitist, upper-class rule of the tyrant Porfirio Díaz, the spasmodic, often-chaotic Mexican Revolution of 1910 culminated in 1917 in a new constitution. This radical nationalistic document called for universal suffrage, massive land reform, benefits for labor, and strict control of foreign capital. Actual progress was quite modest until 1934, when a charismatic young Indian from a poor family, Lazaro Cárdenas, became president and dramatically revived the languishing revolution. Under Cárdenas, many large estates were divided up among small farmers or returned undivided to Indian communities.

Meanwhile, because foreign capitalists were being discouraged, Mexican businessmen built many small factories and managed to thrive. The government also championed the cause of industrial workers. In 1938, when Mexican workers became locked in a bitter dispute with British and American oil companies, Cárdenas nationalized the petroleum industry—to the astonishment of a world unaccustomed to such actions. Finally, the 1930s saw the flowering of a distinctive Mexican culture, which proudly embraced its long-despised Indian past and gloried in the modern national revolution.

In 1940 the official, semiauthoritarian party that has governed Mexico continuously since the revolution selected the first of a series of more moderate presidents. Steadfast in their radical, occasionally anti-American rhetoric, these presidents used the full power of the state to promote industrialization through a judicious mixture of public, private, and even foreign enterprise. The Mexican economy grew rapidly, at about 6 percent per year from the early 1940s and the late 1960s, with the upper and middle classes reaping the lion's share of the benefits.

BRAZIL. After the fall of Brazil's monarchy in 1889, politics was largely dominated by the coffee barons and by regional rivalries. These rivalries and deteriorating economic conditions allowed a military revolt led by Getulio Vargas, governor of one of Brazil's larger states, to seize control of the federal government in 1930. Vargas, who proved to be a consummate politician, fragmented the opposition and established a mild dictatorship that lasted until 1945. Vargas's rule was generally popular, combining as it did effective economic nationalism and moderate social reform.

Somewhat like President Franklin Roosevelt in the United States, Vargas decisively tipped the balance of political power away from the Brazilian states to the ever-expanding federal government, which became a truly national government for the first time. Vargas and his allies also set out to industrialize Brazil and gain economic independence. While the national coffee board used mountains of surplus coffee beans to fire railroad locomotives, the government supported Brazilian manufacturers with high tariffs, gen-

José Clemente Orozco (1883–1949) was one of the great and committed painters of the Mexican Revolution. Orozco believed that art should reflect the "new order of things" and inspire the common people—the workers and the peasants. This vibrant central mural in the National Palace in Mexico City, one of Orozco's many great wall paintings, depicts a brutal Spanish conquest and a liberating revolution. *(Reproduction authorized by The Instituto Nacional de Bellas Artes)*

986

erous loans, and labor peace. This probusiness policy did not prevent new social legislation: workers received shorter hours, pensions, health and accident insurance, paid vacations, and other benefits. Finally, Vargas shrewdly upheld the nationalist cause in his relations with the giant to the north. Early in the Second World War, for example, he traded U.S. military bases in Brazil for American construction of Brazil's first huge steel-making complex. By 1945, when the authoritarian Vargas fell in a bloodless military coup that called for greater political liberty, Brazil was modernizing rapidly.

Modernization continued for the next fifteen years. The economy boomed. Presidential politics were re-established, while the military kept a watchful eye for extremism among the civilian politicians. Economic nationalism was especially vigorous under the flamboyant President Kubitschek (1956–1960), a doctor of German-Czech descent. The government borrowed heavily from international bankers to promote industry and built the extravagant new capital of Brasília in the midst of a wilderness. When Brazil's creditors demanded more conservative policies to stem inflation, Kubitschek delighted the nationalists with his firm and successful refusal. His slogan was "Fifty Years' Progress in Five," and he seemed to mean it.

The Brazilian and Mexican formula of national economic development, varying degrees of electoral competition, and social reform was shared by some other Latin American countries, notably Argentina and Chile. By the late 1950s, optimism was widespread, if cautious. Economic and social progress seemed to promise less violent, more democratic politics. These expectations were profoundly shakened by the Cuban revolution.

THE CUBAN REVOLUTION

Although many aspects of the Cuban revolution are obscured by controversy, certain background conditions are clear. First, after achieving independence in 1898, Cuba was for many years virtually an American protectorate. The Cuban constitution gave the United States the legal right to intervene in Cuban affairs, a right that was frequently exercised until Roosevelt renounced it in 1934. Second, and partly because the American army had often been the real power, Cuba's political institutions were weak and its politicians were extraordinarily corrupt. Under the strongman Fulgencio Batista, an opportunistic ex-sergeant who controlled the government almost continually from 1933 to 1958, graft and outright looting were a way of life. Third, Cuba was one of Latin America's most prosperous and advanced countries by the 1950s, but its sugar-and-tourist economy was dependent on the United States. Finally, the enormous differences between rich and poor in Cuba were typical of Latin America. But Cuba also had a strong Communist party, which was highly unusual.

Fidel Castro, a magnetic leader with the gift of oratory and a flair for propaganda, managed to unify anti-Batista elements in a revolutionary front. When Castro's guerrilla forces triumphed in late 1958, the new government's goals were unclear. Castro had promised a "real" revolution but had always laughed at charges that he was a communist. As the regime consolidated its power in 1959 and 1960, it became increasingly clear that "real" meant "communist" in Castro's mind. Wealthy Cubans, who owned three-quarters of the sugar industry and many profitable businesses, fled to Miami. Soon the middle class began to follow.

Meanwhile, relations with the Eisenhower administration—which had indirectly supported Castro by refusing to sell arms to Batista after March 1958—deteriorated rapidly. Thus, in April 1961, newly elected President Kennedy went ahead with a pre-existing CIA plan to use Cuban exiles to topple Castro. But the Kennedy administration lost its nerve and abandoned the exiles as soon as they were put ashore at the Bay of Pigs. This doomed the invasion, and the exiles were quickly captured, to be ransomed later for $60 million.

The Bay of Pigs invasion—a triumph for Castro and a humiliating, roundly criticized fiasco for the United States—had significant consequences. It freed Castro to build his version of a communist society, and he did. Political life in Cuba featured "anti-imperialism," an alliance with the Soviet bloc, the dictatorship of the party, and a vigorously promoted Castro cult. Revolutionary enthusiasm was genuine among party activists, much of Cuba's youth, and some of the masses some of the time. Prisons and emigration silenced opposition. The economy was characterized by all-pervasive state ownership, collective farms, and Soviet trade and aid. Early efforts to industrialize ran aground, and sugar production at pre-Castro levels continued to dominate the economy.

Socially, the regime pursued equality and the creation of a new socialist personality. In short, revolutionary totalitarianism came to the Americas.

The failure of the United States' halfhearted effort to derail Castro probably encouraged Khrushchev to start putting nuclear missiles in Cuba, leading directly to the most serious East-West crisis since the Korean war. And, although the Russians backed down (page 982), Castro's survival heightened both hopes and fears that the Cuban revolution could spread throughout Latin America. As leftists were emboldened to try guerrilla warfare, conservatives became more rigid and suspicious of calls for change. In the United States, fear of communism aroused heightened cold war–style interest in Latin America. Using the Organization of American States to isolate Cuba, the United States in 1961 pledged $10 billion in aid over ten years to a new hemispheric "Alliance for Progress." The alliance was intended to promote long-term economic development and social reform, which American liberals typically assumed would immunize Latin America from the Cuban disease.

U.S. aid did contribute modestly to continued Latin America economic development in the 1960s, although population growth canceled out two-thirds of the increase on a per capita basis. Democratic social reforms—the other half of the Alliance for Progress formula—proceeded slowly, however. Instead, the period following the Cuban revolution saw the rise of extremism and a revival of conservative authoritarianism in Latin America. These developments marked the turbulent beginnings of a new era in the late 1960s.

The recovery of Europe and the Americas during and after World War Two is one of the most remarkable chapters in the long, uneven course of Western civilization. Although the dangerous tensions of the cold war frustrated fond hopes for a truly peaceful international order, the transition from imperialism to decolonialization proceeded rapidly, surprisingly smoothly, and without serious damage to western Europe. Instead, genuine political democracy gained unprecedented strength in the West, and economic progress quickened the pace of ongoing social and cultural transformation. Thus the tremendous promise inherent in Western society's fateful embrace of the "dual revolution," which had begun in France and England in the late eighteenth century and which had momentarily halted the agonies of the Great Depression and the horrors of Nazi totalitarianism, was largely if perhaps only temporarily realized in the shining achievements of the postwar era.

NOTES

1. William Bullitt, "How We Won the War and Lost the Peace," *Life,* XXV (30 August 1948): 94.
2. Quoted by N. Graebner, *Cold War Diplomacy, 1945–1960,* Van Nostrand, Princeton, N.J., 1962, p. d17.
3. Ibid.
4. Quoted by F. Prinz, ed., *Trümmerzeit in Munchen,* Münchner Stadtmuseum, Munich, 1984, p. 273; trans. by J. Buckler.
5. Quoted in J. Hennessy, *Economic "Miracles,"* André Deutsch, London, 1964, p. 5.
6. P. Van Zeeland, in *European Integration,* ed. C. G. Haines, John Hopkins Press, Baltimore, 1957, p. xi.
7. Lord Milner, quoted by R. von Albertini, "The Impact of Two World Wars on the Decline of Colonialism," *Journal of Contemporary History* 4 (January 1969):17.
8. Quoted by H. Smith, *The Russians,* Quadrangle/New York Times, New York, 1976, p. 303.
9. Quoted by D. Treadgold, *Twentieth Century Russia,* Houghton Mifflin, Boston, 5th ed., 1981, p. 442.
10. Quoted by M. Tatu, *Power in the Kremlin: From Khrushchev to Kosygin,* Viking Press, New York, 1968, p. 248.
11. Quoted by I. Deutscher, in *Soviet Society,* ed. A. Inkeles and K. Geiger, Houghton Mifflin, Boston, 1961, p. 41.
12. Quoted by S. E. Morison et al., *A Concise History of the American Republic,* Oxford University Press, New York, 1977, p. 697.

SUGGESTED READING

G. Wright, *The Ordeal of Total War, 1939–1945* (1968), is the best comprehensive study on World War Two, while B. H. Liddell Hart, *The History of the Second*

World War (1971), is a good overview of military developments. Three dramatic studies of special aspects of the war are A. Dallin, *German Rule in Russia, 1941–1945* (1957), which analyzes the effects of Nazi occupation policies on the Soviet population; L. Collins and D. La Pierre, *Is Paris Burning?* (1965), a best-selling account of the liberation of Paris and Hitler's plans to destroy the city; and J. Toland, *The Last 100 Days* (1966), a lively account of the end of the war. Great leaders and matchless stylists, Winston Churchill and Charles de Gaulle have both written histories of the war in the form of memoirs. Other interesting memoirs are those of Harry Truman (1958); Dwight Eisenhower, *Crusade in Europe* (1948); and Dean Acheson, *Present at the Creation* (1969), a beautifully written defense of American foreign policy in the early cold war. W. A. Williams, *The Tragedy of American Diplomacy* (1962), and W. La Feber, *America, Russia, and the Cold War* (1967), claim, on the contrary, that the United States was primarily responsible for the conflict with the Soviet Union. Two other important studies focusing on American policy are J. Gaddis, *The United States and the Origins of the Cold War* (1972), and D. Yergin, *Shattered Peace: The Origins of the Cold War and the National Security Council* (1977). A. Fontaine, a French journalist, provides a balanced general approach in his *History of the Cold War*, 2 vols. (1968). V. Mastny's thorough investigation of Stalin's war aims, *Russia's Road to the Cold War* (1979), is highly recommended.

R. Mayne, *The Recovery of Europe, 1945–1973*, rev. ed. (1973), and N. Luxenburg, *Europe Since World War II*, rev. ed. (1979), are recommended general surveys, as are two important works: W. Laqueur, *Europe Since Hitler*, rev. ed. (1982), and P. Johnson, *Modern Times: The World from the Twenties to the Eighties* (1983). T. White, *Fire in the Ashes* (1953), is a vivid view of European resurgence and Marshall Plan aid by an outstanding journalist. Postwar economic and technological developments are carefully analyzed by D. S. Landes, *The Unbound Prometheus: Technological Change and Industrial Development in Western Europe from 1750 to the Present* (1969). A Shonfield, *Modern Capitalism* (1965), provides an engaging, optimistic assessment of the growing importance of government investment and planning in European economic life. F. R. Willis, *France, Germany, and the New Europe, 1945–1967* (1968), is useful for postwar European diplomacy. Three outstanding works on France are J. Ardagh, *The New French Revolution* (1969), which puts the momentous social changes since 1945 in human terms; G. Wright, *Rural Revolution in France: The Peasantry in the Twentieth Century* (1964); and D. L. Hanley et al., eds., *France: Politics and Society Since 1945* (1979). R. Dahrendorf, *Society and Democracy in Germany* (1971), and H. S. Hughes, *The United States and Italy* (1968), are excellent introductions to recent German and Italian history. A. Marwick, *British Society Since 1945* (1982), and A. H. Halsey, *Change in British Society*, 2nd ed. (1981), are good on postwar developments.

H. Seton-Watson, *The East European Revolution* (1965), is a good history of the communization of eastern Europe, and S. Fischer-Galati, ed., *Eastern Europe in the Sixties* (1963), discusses major developments. P. Zinner, *National Communism and Popular Revolt in Eastern Europe* (1956) and *Revolution in Hungary* (1962), are excellent on the tragic events of 1956. Z. Brzezinski, *The Soviet Bloc: Unity and Conflict* (1967), is a major inquiry. W. Connor, *Socialism, Politics and Equality: Hierarchy and Change in Eastern Europe and the USSR* (1979), and J. Hough and M. Fainsod, *How the Soviet Union is Governed* (1978), are important general studies. A. Amalrik, *Will the Soviet Union Survive Until 1984?* (1970), is a fascinating interpretation of contemporary Soviet society and politics by a Russian who paid for his criticism with prison and exile. A. Lee, *Russian Journal* (1981), and H. Smith, *The Russians* (1976), are excellent journalistic yet comprehensive reports by perceptive American observers.

R. von Albertini, *Decolonialization* (1971), is a good history of the decline and fall of European empires. The tremendous economic problems of the newly independent countries of Asia and Africa are discussed sympathetically by B. Ward, *Rich Nations and Poor Nations* (1962), and R. Heilbroner, *The Great Ascent* (1953). Two excellent general studies on Latin America are J. E. Fagg, *Latin America: A General History*, 3rd ed. (1977), and R. J. Shafer, *A History of Latin America* (1978). Both contain detailed suggestions for further reading.

31

LIFE IN THE POSTWAR ERA

HILE EUROPE staged its astonishing political and economic recovery from the Nazi nightmare, the patterns of everyday life and the structure of Western society were changing no less rapidly and remarkably. Epoch-making inventions and new technologies—the atomic bomb, television, computers, jet planes, and contraceptive pills, to name only a few—profoundly affected human existence. Important groups in society formulated new attitudes and demands, which were reflected in such diverse phenomena as the ever-expanding role of government, the revolt of youth in the late 1960s, and the women's movement. Rapid social change was clearly a fact of life in the Western world.

It was by no means easy to make sense out of all these changes while they were happening. Many "revolutions" and "crises" proved to be merely passing fads, sensationally ballyhooed by the media one day and forgotten the next. Some genuinely critical developments, such as those involving the family, were complex and contradictory, making it hard to understand what was really happening, much less explain why. Yet, by the 1980s, the great changes in social structure and everyday life that took place after the Second World War were coming into sharper focus. Above all, the historian was gaining vital perspective, for it became increasingly clear that the years from about 1968 to 1974 marked the end of the postwar period, as shall be seen in Chapter 32. Thus the startling postwar renaissance emerged in its turn as a separate era in the long evolution of the West, an era with its own distinctive social characteristics but still linked to what came before and after.

How, then, did Western society and everyday life change in the postwar era, and why? What did these changes mean to people? These are the questions this chapter will seek to answer.

SCIENCE AND TECHNOLOGY

Ever since the scientific revolution of the seventeenth century and the Industrial Revolution at the end of the eighteenth century, scientific and technical developments have powerfully influenced attitudes, soci-

ety, and everyday life. Never was this influence stronger than after about 1940. Fantastic pipe dreams of science fiction a brief century ago became realities. Submarines passed under the North Pole, and astronauts walked on the moon. Skilled surgeons replaced their patients' failing arteries with plastic tubing. Millions of people around the world simultaneously watched a historic event on television. The list of wonders seemed endless.

The reason science and technology proved so productive and influential was that, for the first time in history, they were effectively joined together on a massive scale. This union of "pure theoretical" science with "applied" science or "practical" technology had already made possible striking achievements in the late nineteenth century in some select fields, most notably organic chemistry, electricity, and preventive medicine. Generally, however, the separation of science and technology still predominated in the late 1930s. Most scientists were university professors, who were little interested in such practical matters as building better machines and inventing new products. Such problems were the concern of tinkering technicians and engineers, who were to a large extent trained on the job. Their accomplishments and discoveries owed more to careful observation and trial-and-error experimentation than to theoretical science.

During World War Two, however, scientists and technicians increasingly marched to the sound of the same drummer. Both scientific research and technical expertise began to be directed at difficult but highly practical military problems. The result was a number of spectacular breakthroughs, such as radar and the atomic bomb, which had immediate wartime applications. After the war, this close cooperation between pure science and applied technology continued with equal success. Indeed, the line between science and technology became harder and harder to draw.

The consequences of the new, intimate link between science and technology were enormous. Seventeenth-century propagandists for science, such as Francis Bacon, had predicted that scientific knowledge of nature would give human beings the power to control the physical world. With such control, they believed, it would be possible to create material abundance and genuine well-being. The successful union of science and technology created new industries and spurred rapid economic growth after 1945, making this prediction finally come true for the great majority of people in Europe and North America in the postwar era.

At the same time, however, the unprecedented success of science in controlling and changing the physical environment produced unexpected and unwanted side effects. Chemical fertilizers poisoned rivers in addition to producing bumper crops. A great good like the virtual elimination of malaria-carrying mosquitoes by DDT dramatically lowered the death rate in tropical lands, but it also contributed to a population explosion in those areas. The list of such unwelcome side effects became very long. By the late 1960s, concern about the undesirable results of technological change had brought into being a vigorous environmental movement. The ability of science and technology to control and alter nature was increasingly seen as a two-edged sword, which had to be wielded with great care and responsibility.

THE STIMULUS OF WORLD WAR TWO

Just before the outbreak of World War Two, a young Irish scientist and Communist named John Desmond Bernal wrote a book entitled *The Social Function of Science*. Bernal argued that the central government should be the source of funds for scientific research and that these funds should be granted on the basis of the expected social and political benefits. Most scientists were horrified by Bernal's proposals, which were contradictory to their cherished ideals. Scientists were committed to designing their own research without regard for its immediate usefulness. As late as 1937, the great physicist Ernest Rutherford could state that the work he and his colleagues were doing in nuclear physics at Cambridge University had no conceivable practical value for anyone, and he expressed delight that such was the case. Nor did university scientists concern themselves with government grants, since many had independent incomes to help finance their still-inexpensive experiments.

The Second World War changed this pattern. Pure science lost its impractical innocence. Most leading university scientists went to work on top-secret projects to help their governments fight the war. The development of radar by British scientists was a particularly important outcome of this new kind of sharply focused research.

Lord Rutherford The great British physicist Ernest Rutherford split the atom in 1919 with a small device he could hold in his hands. Here he is seen with a colleague in Cambridge University's renowned Cavendish Laboratory in 1932, when pure science was still relatively small-scale and unconcerned with practical applications. *(Cavendish Laboratory, University of Cambridge)*

As early as 1934, the British Air Ministry set up a committee of scientists and engineers to study the problem of air defense systematically. A leading British expert's calculations on radio waves suggested that the idea of a "death ray" so powerful it could destroy an attacking enemy aircraft was nonsense, but that detection of enemy aircraft by radio waves was theoretically possible. Radio waves emitted at intervals by a transmitter on the ground would bounce off flying aircraft, and a companion receiver on the ground would hear this echo and detect the approaching plane. Experiments went forward, and by 1939 the British had installed a very primitive radar system along the southern and eastern coasts of England.

Immediately after the outbreak of war with Germany in September 1939, the British military enlisted leading academic scientists in an all-out effort to improve the radar system. The basic problem was developing a high-powered transmitter capable of sending very short wavelengths, which could be precisely focused in a beam sweeping the sky like a searchlight. In summer 1940, British physicists made the dramatic technical breakthrough that solved this problem of short-wave transmission. The new and radically improved radar system, which was quickly installed, played a key role in Britain's victory in the battle for air supremacy in the fall of 1940. During the war, many different types of radar were developed—for fighter planes, for bombers, for detection of submarines.

After 1945, war-born microwave technology generated endless applications, especially in telecommunications. Microwave transmission very conveniently carried long-distance telephone conversations, television programs, and messages to and from satellites.

The air war also greatly stimulated the development of jet aircraft and computers. Although the first jet engines were built in the mid-1930s, large-scale government-directed research did not begin until immediately before the war. The challenge was to build a new kind of engine—a jet engine—capable of burning the low-grade "leftovers" of petroleum refining, thereby helping to overcome the desperate shortage of aviation fuel. The task proved extremely difficult and expensive. Only toward the end of the war did fast, high-flying jet fighters become a reality. Quickly adopted for both military and peacetime purposes after the war, jet airplanes contributed to the enormous expansion of commercial aviation in the 1950s.

The problems of air defense also spurred further research on electronic computers, which had barely come into existence before 1939. Computers calculated the complex mathematical relationships between fast-moving planes and antiaircraft shells, to increase the likelihood of a hit.

Wartime needs led to many other major technical breakthroughs. Germany had little oil and was almost completely cut off from foreign supplies. But Germany's scientists and engineers found ways to turn coal into gasoline so that the German war machine did not sputter to a halt.

The most spectacular result of directed scientific research during the war was the atomic bomb. In August 1939, Albert Einstein wrote to President Franklin Roosevelt, stating that recent work in physics suggested that

it may become possible to set up a nuclear chain reaction in a large mass of uranium, by which vast amounts of power and large quantities of new radium-like elements would be generated. . . . This new phenomenon would also lead to the construction of bombs, and it is conceivable—though much less certain—that extremely powerful bombs of a new type may thus be constructed.[1]

This letter and ongoing experiments by nuclear physicists led to the top-secret Manhattan Project and the decision to build the atomic bomb.

The American government spared no expense to turn a theoretical possibility into a practical reality. A mammoth crash program went forward in several universities and special laboratories, the most important of which was the newly created laboratory at Los Alamos in the wilds of New Mexico. The Los Alamos laboratory was masterfully directed from 1942 by J. Robert Oppenheimer (1904–1967), a professor and theoretical physicist. Its sole objective was to design and build an atomic bomb. Toward that end Oppenheimer assembled a team of brilliant American and European scientists and managed to get them to cooperate effectively. After three years of intensive effort, the first atomic bomb was successfully tested in July 1945. In August 1945, two bombs were dropped on Hiroshima and Nagasaki, ending the war with Japan.

Atomic Weapons were the ultimate in state-directed scientific research. In this awesome photo the mushroom cloud of an American atomic bomb rises over the Pacific island of Bikini. *(Joint Army Navy Task Force)*

The atomic bomb showed the world both the awesome power and the heavy moral responsibilities of modern science and its high priests. As one of Oppenheimer's troubled colleagues exclaimed while he watched the first mushroom cloud rise over the American desert: "We are all sons-of-bitches now!"[2]

THE RISE OF BIG SCIENCE

The spectacular results of directed research during World War Two inspired a new model for science—"Big Science." By combining theoretical work with sophisticated engineering in a large organization, Big Science could attack extremely difficult problems. Solution of these problems led to new and better products for consumers and to new and better weapons for the military. In any event, the assumption was that almost any conceivable technical goal might be attained. Big Science was extremely expensive. Indeed, its appetite for funds was so great that it could be financed only by governments and large corporations. Thus the ties between science and taxpaying society grew very close.

Science became so "big" largely because its equipment grew ever more complex and expensive. Because many advances depended directly on better instruments, the trend toward bigness went on unabated. This trend was particularly pronounced in atomic physics, perhaps the most prestigious and influential area of modern science. When Rutherford first "split the atom" in 1919, his equipment cost only a few dollars. In the 1930s, the price of an accelerator, or "atom smasher," reached $10,000, and the accelerators used in high-energy experiments while the atomic bomb was being built were in the $100,000 range. By 1960, however, when the western European nations pooled their resources in the European Council for Nuclear Research (CERN) to build an accelerator outside of Geneva—an accelerator with power in billions rather than millions of electron volts—the cost had jumped to $30 million. These big accelerators did an amazingly good job of prying atoms apart, and over two hundred different particles have been identified so far. Yet new answers produced new questions, and the logic of ever-more-sophisticated observations demanded ever-more-powerful and ever-more-costly accelerators in the postwar period.

Astronomers followed physicists in the ways of Big Science. Their new eye was the radio telescope, which picked up radio emissions rather than light. In the 1960s the largest of these costly radio telescopes sat atop a mountain and had a bowl a thousand feet wide to focus the radio signals from space. Aeronautical research and development also attained mammoth proportions. The cost of the Anglo-French *Concorde,* the first supersonic passenger airliner, went into the billions. Even ordinary science became big and expensive by historical standards. The least costly laboratory capable of doing useful research in either pure or applied science required around $200,000 a year in the 1960s.

Populous, victorious, and wealthy, the United States took the lead in Big Science after World War Two. Between 1945 and 1965, spending on scientific research and development in the United States grew five times as fast as the national income. By 1965 fully 3 percent of all income in the United States was spent on science. While large American corporations maintained impressive research laboratories, fully three-quarters of all funds spent on scientific research and development in the United States was coming from the government by 1965. It was generally accepted that government should finance science heavily. One wit pointed out that by the mid-1960s the "science policy" of the supposedly conservative Republican party in the United States was almost identical to that of the supposedly revolutionary Communist party of the Soviet Union.

One of the reasons for the similarity was that science was not demobilized in either country after the war. Indeed, scientists remained a critical part of every major military establishment and, after 1945 as during World War Two, a large portion of all scientific research went for "defense." Jet bombers gave way to rockets, battleships were overtaken by submarines with nuclear warheads, and spy planes were replaced with spy satellites. All such new weapons demanded breakthroughs no less remarkable than those of radar and the first atomic bomb. After 1945, roughly one-quarter of all men and women trained in science and engineering in the West—and perhaps more in the Soviet Union—were employed full-time in the production of weapons to kill other humans.

The Apollo Program Astronauts Neil Armstrong, Michael Collins, and Edwin Aldrin, Jr., took off from Florida on July 16, 1969 in the Apollo II spacecraft. Astronaut Armstrong was the first man to set foot on the moon, four days later, on July 20. His footprint in the lunar dust brought to reality another fantasy of science fiction. The astronauts splashed down in the Pacific Ocean, and recovery was made by the U.S.S. *Hornet* on July 24. *(National Aeronautics and Space Administration)*

Sophisticated science, lavish government spending, and military needs all came together in the space race of the 1960s—the most sensational example of Big Science in action after the creation of the atomic bomb. In 1957 the Russians used long-range rockets developed in their nuclear weapons program to put a satellite in orbit. In 1961 they sent the world's first cosmonaut circling the globe. Breaking with President Eisenhower's opposition to an expensive space program, President Kennedy made an all-out U.S. commitment to catch up with the Russians and land a manned spacecraft on the moon "before the decade was out." Harnessing pure science, applied technology, and up to $5 billion a year, the Apollo Program achieved its ambitious objective in 1969. Four more moon landings followed by 1972.

The rapid expansion of government-financed research in the United States attracted many of Europe's best scientists during the 1950s and 1960s. Thoughtful Europeans lamented this "brain drain." In his best seller *The American Challenge* (1967), the French journalist Jean-Jacques Servan-Schreiber

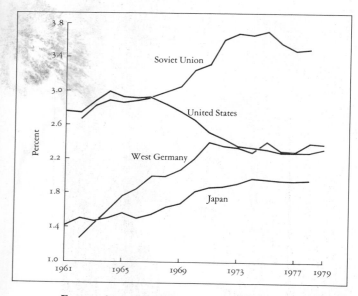

FIGURE 31.1 Research and Development Expenditures as a Percentage of GNP in the United States, Soviet Union, West Germany, and Japan, 1961–1979 While the United States spent less of its national income on research and development after the early 1960s, European nations and Japan spent more. This helped Europe and Japan narrow or even close the technological gap that had existed after the end of World War Two. *(Source: Data Resources, Inc.)*

warned that Europe was falling hopelessly behind the United States in science and technology. The only hope was to copy American patterns of research before the United States achieved an absolute stranglehold on computers, jet aircraft, atomic energy, and indeed most of the vital dynamic sectors of the late twentieth-century economy.

In fact, a revitalized Europe was already responding to the American challenge. European countries were beginning to pool their efforts and spend more on science and engineering, as they concentrated on big projects like the *Concorde* supersonic passenger airliner and the peaceful uses of atomic energy. Thus European countries created their own Big Science. By 1974 many European nations were devoting a substantial percentage of their income to research and development and were in the process of achieving equality with the United States in many fields of scientific endeavor (see Figure 31.1).

THE LIFE OF SCIENTISTS AND TECHNOLOGISTS

The rise of Big Science and of close ties between science and technology greatly altered the lives of scientists. The scientific community grew much larger than ever before: of all the scientists who have ever lived, nine out of ten are still alive today. The astonishing fact is that the number of scientists has been doubling every fifteen years for the past three centuries. There were, therefore, about four times as many scientists in 1975 as in 1945, just as there were a *million times* as many scientists as there were in 1670. Scientists, technologists, engineers, and medical specialists counted in modern society, in part because there were so many of them.

One important consequence of the bigness of science was its high degree of specialization. With close to a hundred thousand scientific journals being published by the 1970s, no one could possibly master a broad field like physics or medicine. Instead, a field like physics was constantly dividing and subdividing into new specialties and subdisciplines. The fifty or one hundred men and women who were truly abreast of the latest developments in a highly specialized field formed an international "invisible college." Cooperating and competing, communicating through special journals and conferences, the leading members of these invisible colleges kept the problems of the subdiscipline under constant attack. Thus intense specialization undoubtedly increased the rates at which both basic knowledge was acquired and practical applications were made.

Highly specialized modern scientists and technologists normally had to work as members of a team. The problems and equipment of Big Science were simply too complicated and expensive for a person to work effectively as an individual researcher. The collaborative "team" character of much of modern scientific research—members of invisible colleges were typically the leaders of such teams—completely changed the work and lifestyle of modern scientists. Old-fashioned, prewar scientists were like professional golfers—lonely individuals who had to make all the shots themselves. Modern scientists and technologists were more like players on American professional football teams. There were owners and directors, coaches and assistant coaches, overpaid stars and unsung heroes, veterans and rookies, kickoff specialists and substitutes, trainers and water boys.

James Watson and Harry Crick won the 1962 Nobel Prize in Medicine. Their path-breaking work on DNA, the molecule of heredity, helped open exciting possibilities for gene-splicing and biological engineering. *(UPI/Bettmann Newsphotos)*

If this parallel seems fanciful, consider the research group of Luis Alvarez at the high-energy physics Radiation Laboratory of the University of California at Berkeley in the late 1960s. This group consisted of more than two hundred people. At the top were Alvarez and about twenty Ph.D.'s, followed by twenty graduate research assistants and fourteen full-time engineers. Almost fifty people were categorized as "technical leadership"—computer programmers, equipment operators, and so on. Finally, there were more than a hundred "technical assistants"—primarily scanners who analyzed photographs showing the tracks of particles after various collisions. A laboratory like that of CERN outside Geneva resembled a small city of several thousand people—scientists, technicians, and every kind of support personnel. A great deal of modern science and technology went on, therefore, in large, well-defined bureaucratic organizations. The individual was very often a small cog in a great machine, a member of a scientific army.

The advent of large-scale scientific bureaucracies led to the emergence of a new group, science managers and research administrators. Such managers generally had scientific backgrounds, but their main tasks were scheduling research, managing people, and seeking money from politicians or financial committees of large corporations. This last function was particularly important, for there were limits to what even the wealthiest governments and corporations would spend for research. Competition for funds was always intense, even in the fat 1960s.

Many science managers were government bureaucrats. These managers doled out funds and "refereed" the scientific teams that were actually playing on the field. Was the *Concorde* supersonic jet too noisy to land in New York City? Did saccharin cause cancer, and should it be banned? The list of potential questions was endless. Beginning in the late 1960s, the number of such referees and the penalties they were imposing seemed to explode, driven forward by public alarm about undesirable side effects of technological advance. More generally, the growth of the scientific bureaucracy suggested how scientists and technologists permeated the entire society and many aspects of life.

Two other changes in the lives of scientists should be noted briefly. One was the difficulty of appraising an individual's contribution to a collaborative team effort. Who deserved the real credit (or blame) for a paper coauthored by a group of twenty-five physicists? Even in a field like chemistry, which remained relatively "small" in its research techniques, more than two-thirds of all papers had two or more authors by the 1970s. Questions of proper recognition within the team effort were thus very complicated and preoccupying to modern scientists.

A second, related change was that modern science became highly, even brutally, competitive. This competitiveness is well depicted in Nobel Prize winner James Watson's fascinating book *The Double Helix,* which tells how in 1953 Watson and an Englishman, Francis Crick, discovered the structure of DNA, the molecule of heredity. A brash young American Ph.D. in his twenties, Watson seemed almost obsessed by the idea that some other research team would find the solution first and thereby deprive him of the fame and fortune he desperately wanted. With so many thousands of like-minded researchers in the wealthy countries of the world, it was hardly surprising that scientific and technical knowledge rushed forward in the postwar era.

TOWARD A NEW SOCIETY

The prodigious expansion of science and technology greatly affected the peoples of the Western world. By creating new products and vastly improved methods of manufacturing and farming, it fueled rapid economic growth and rising standards of living. Moreover, especially in Europe, scientific and technological progress, combined with economic prosperity, went a long way toward creating a whole new society after World War Two.

This new society was given many catchy titles. Some called it the "technocratic society," a society of highly trained specialists and experts. For others, fascinated by the great increase in personal wealth, it was the "affluent society" or the "consumer society."

For those struck by the profusion of government-provided social services, it was simply the "welfare state." For still others, it was the "permissive society," where established codes of conduct no longer prevailed. In fact, Western society in the postwar era was all of these: technocratic, affluent, welfare-oriented, and permissive. These characteristics reflected changes in the class structure and indicated undeniable social progress.

THE CHANGING CLASS STRUCTURE

After 1945 European society became more mobile and more democratic. Old class barriers relaxed, and class distinctions became fuzzier.

Changes in the structure of the middle class, directly related to the expansion of science and technology, were particularly influential in the general drift toward a less rigid class structure. The model for the middle class in the nineteenth and early twentieth centuries was the independent, self-employed individual who owned a business or practiced a liberal profession like law or medicine. Many businesses and professional partnerships were tightly held family firms. Marriage into such a family often provided the best opportunity for an outsider to rise to the top. Ownership of property—usually inherited property—and strong family ties were often the keys to wealth and standing within the middle class.

This traditional pattern, which first changed in the United States and the Soviet Union (for very different reasons) before the Second World War, declined drastically in western Europe after 1945. A new breed of managers and experts rose to replace traditional property owners as the leaders of the middle class. Within large bureaucratic corporations and government, men and women increasingly advanced as individuals and on the basis of merit (and luck). Ability to serve the needs of a large organization, which usually depended on special expertise, largely replaced inherited property and family connections in determining an individual's social position in the middle and upper-middle class. Social mobility, both upward and downward, increased. At the same time, the middle class grew massively and became harder to define.

There were a number of reasons for these developments. Rapid industrial and technological expansion created in large corporations and government agen-

A Modern Manager Despite considerable discrimination, women were increasingly found in the expanding middle class of salaried experts after World War Two, working in business, science, and technology. *(Niépce-Rapho)*

cies a powerful demand for technologists and managers capable of responding effectively to an ever-more-complicated world. This growing army of specialists—the backbone of the new middle class—could be led effectively only by like-minded individuals, of whom only a few at best could come from the old owning families.

Second, the old propertied middle class lost control of many of its formerly family-owned businesses. Even very wealthy families had to call on the general investing public for capital, and heavy inheritance taxes forced sales of stock, further diluting family influence. Many small businesses (including family

farms) simply passed out of existence, and their ex-owners joined the ranks of salaried employees. In Germany in 1950, for example, 33 percent of the labor force was self-employed and 20 percent was white-collar workers. By 1962 the percentages for these two groups were exactly reversed. Moreover, the wave of nationalization in western and eastern Europe after the Second World War automatically replaced capitalist owners with salaried managers and civil servants in state-owned companies.

Top managers and ranking civil servants therefore represented the model for a new middle class of salaried specialists. Well paid and highly trained, often with backgrounds in science or engineering or accounting, these experts increasingly came from all social classes, even the working class. Pragmatic and realistic, they were primarily concerned with efficiency and practical solutions to concrete problems. Generally, they were not very interested in the old ideological debates about capitalism and socialism, confidently assuming that their skills were indispensable in either system or any combination of the two.

Indeed, the new middle class of experts and managers was an international class, not much different in socialist eastern Europe than in capitalist western Europe and North America. Everywhere successful managers and technocrats passed on the opportunity for all-important advanced education to their children, but only in rare instances could they pass on the positions they had attained. Thus the new middle class, which was based largely on specialized skills and high levels of education, was more open, democratic, and insecure than the old propertied middle class.

The structure of the traditional lower classes also became more flexible and open. There was a mass exodus from farms and the countryside. One of the most traditional and least mobile groups in European society drastically declined: after 1945 the number of peasants declined by more than 50 percent in almost every European country. Meanwhile, because of rapid technological change, the industrial working class ceased to expand, stabilizing at slightly less than one-half of the labor force in wealthy advanced countries. Job opportunities for white-collar and service employees, however, expanded rapidly. Such employees bore a greater resemblance to the new middle class of salaried specialists than to industrial workers, who were themselves better educated and more specialized. Developments within the lower classes contributed, therefore, to the breakdown of rigid social divisions.

Social Security Reforms and Rising Affluence

While the demands of modern technology and big bureaucracies broke down rigid class divisions, European governments, with their new and revitalized political leadership (pages 968–970), reduced class tensions with a series of social security reforms. Many of these reforms simply strengthened social security measures first pioneered in Bismarck's Germany before World War One. Unemployment and sickness benefits were increased and extended, as were retirement benefits and old-age pensions. Other programs were new.

Britain's Labour government took the lead immediately after the Second World War in establishing a comprehensive national health system; other European governments followed the British example. Depending on the system, patients either received completely free medical care or paid only a very small portion of the total cost.

Most countries also introduced family allowances —direct government grants to parents to help them raise their children. Lower-paid workers generally received the largest allowances, and the rate per child often kept increasing until the third or fourth child. These allowances helped many poor families make ends meet. Most European governments also gave maternity grants and built inexpensive public housing for low-income families and individuals. Other social welfare programs ranged from cash bonuses for getting married in Belgium and Switzerland to subsidized vacations for housewives in Sweden.

It would be wrong to think that the expansion of social security services after World War Two provided for every human need "from cradle to grave," as early advocates of the welfare state hoped and its critics feared. But these social reforms did provide a humane floor of well-being, below which very few individuals could fall in the advanced countries of northern and western Europe. (Social benefits were greatest in the wealthiest nations, such as Sweden, West Germany, Britain, and less in poorer areas of southern and eastern Europe.)

These reforms also promoted greater social and economic equality. They were expensive, paid for in part by high taxes on the rich. In Britain, for example, where social security benefits for the population at large and taxes on the rich have both become quite high, the top 5 percent of the population received about 14 percent of national income after taxes in 1957, as opposed to fully 43 percent in 1913. Thus extensive welfare measures leveled society both by raising the floor and by lowering the ceiling.

The rising standard of living and the spread of standardized, mass-produced consumer goods also worked to level Western society. A hundred years ago, food and drink cost roughly two-thirds of the average family's income in western and northern Europe; by the mid-1960s, they took only about one-third to two-fifths of that family's income. Consumption of traditional staples like bread and potatoes actually declined almost everywhere in Europe after 1945; yet because incomes have risen rapidly, people eat more meat, fish, and dairy products. The long-elusive goal of adequate and good food was attained almost universally in advanced countries.

But progress introduced new problems. People in Europe and North America were eating too much rather than too little, giving rise to an endless proliferation of diet foods and diet fads. Another problem was that modern consumers often appeared remarkably ignorant of basic nutrition. They stuffed themselves with candy, soft drinks, French fries, and spongy white bread, and frequently got poor value for their money. Finally, the traditional pleasures of eating good food well prepared suffered catastrophic declines in the postwar age of fast-food franchises and mass-produced, hopelessly standardized burgers and buns.

The phenomenal expansion of the automobile industry exemplified even more strikingly the emergence of the consumer society. In the United States, automobile ownership was commonplace far down the social scale by the mid-1920s, whereas only the rich could generally afford cars in Europe before the Second World War. In 1948 there were only 5 million cars in western Europe, and most ordinary people dreamed at most of stepping up from a bicycle to a motorcycle. With the development of cheaper, mass-produced cars, this situation changed rapidly. By 1957 the number of cars had increased to 15 million, and automobiles had become a standard item of middle-class consumption. By 1965 the number of cars in western Europe had tripled again to 44 million, and car ownership had come well within the range of better-paid workers.

Europeans took great pleasure in the products of the "gadget revolution" as well. Like Americans, Europeans filled their houses and apartments with washing machines, vacuum cleaners, refrigerators, dishwashers, radios, TVs, and stereos. The purchase of these and other consumer goods was greatly facilitated by installment purchasing, which allowed people to buy on credit. Before World War Two, Europeans had rarely bought "on time." But with the expansion of social security safeguards, reducing the need to accumulate savings for hard times, ordinary people were increasingly willing to take on debt. This change had far-reaching consequences.

Household appliances became necessities for most families. Middle-class women had to do much of their own housework, for young girls avoided domestic service like the plague. Moreover, more women than ever before worked outside the home, and they needed machines to help do household chores as quickly as possible. The power tools of "do-it-yourself" work also became something of a necessity, for few dependable artisans were available for household repairs.

Leisure and recreation occupied an important place in consumer societies. Indeed, with incomes rising and the workweek shrinking from roughly forty-eight hours right after the war to about forty-one hours by the early 1970s, leisure became big business. In addition to ever-popular soccer matches and horse races, movies, and a growing addiction to television, individuals had at their disposal a vast range of commercialized hobbies, most of which could soak up a lot of cash. Newsstands were full of specialized magazines about everything from hunting and photography to knitting and antique collecting. Interest in "culture," as measured by attendance at concerts and exhibitions, also increased. Even so, the commercialization of leisure through standardized manufactured products was striking.

The most astonishing leisure-time development in the consumer society was the blossoming of mass travel and tourism. Before the Second World War, travel for pleasure and relaxation remained a rather aristocratic pastime. Most people had neither the time nor the money for it. But with month-long paid vacations required by law in most European countries, and widespread automobile ownership, beaches and ski resorts came within the reach of the middle class and many workers. At certain times of year, hordes of Europeans surged to the sea or the mountains, and woe to the traveler who had not made arrangements well in advance. By the late 1960s packaged tours with cheap group flights and bargain hotel accommodations had made even distant lands easily accessible. One-fifth of West Germany's population traveled abroad each year. A French company, the Club Méditerranée, grew rich building imitation Tahitian paradises around the world. At Swedish nudist colonies on secluded west African beaches, secreta-

Sports Fans developed fierce tribal loyalties, finding comradeship and a sense of belonging cheering for their teams. Here Liverpool's famous rooting section goes wild with delight after its team clinches the English soccer championship in 1977. Soccer matches have occasionally degenerated into pitched battles between rival fans. *(Wide World Photos)*

ries and salesmen from Stockholm fleetingly worshiped the sun in the middle of the long northern winter. Truly, consumerism had come of age.

RENEWED DISCONTENT AND THE STUDENT REVOLT

For twenty years after 1945, Europeans were largely preoccupied with the possibilities of economic progress and consumerism. The more democratic class structure also helped to reduce social tension, and ideological conflict went out of style. In the late 1960s, however, sharp criticism and discontent re-emerged. It was a common complaint that Europeans were richer but neither happier nor better. Social conflicts re-emerged.

Simmering discontent in eastern Europe was not hard to understand. The gradual improvement in the standard of living stood in stark contrast to the ongoing lack of freedom in political and intellectual life and made that lack of freedom all the more distasteful. As will be shown in the next chapter, such dissatisfaction found eloquent expression once again, despite the refinement of techniques of repression in eastern Europe and the willingness of the Soviet Union to crush reform efforts in Czechoslovakia with military might in 1968.

The reappearance of discontent in western Europe was not so easily explained. From the mid-1950s on, western European society was prosperous, democratic, and permissive. Yet this did not prevent growing hostility to the existing order among some children of the new society. Radical students in particular rejected the materialism of their parents and claimed that the new society was repressive and badly flawed. Though these criticisms and the movements they sparked were often ridiculed by the older generation, they reflected some real problems of youth, education, and a society of specialists. They deserve closer attention.

In contrast to the United States, high school and university educations in Europe were limited for centuries to a small elite. That elite consisted mainly of young men and women from the well-to-do classes, along with a sprinkling of scholarship students from humble origins. Whereas 22 percent of the American population was going on to some form of higher education in 1950, only 3 to 4 percent of west European

youths were doing so. Moreover, European education was still directed toward traditional fields: literature, law, medicine, and pure science. Its basic goal was to pass on culture and pure science to an elite, and with the exception of law and medicine, applied training for specialists was not considered very important.

After World War Two, public education in western Europe began to change dramatically. Enrollments exploded. By 1960 there were at least three times as many students going to some kind of university as there had been before the war, and the number continued to rise sharply until the 1970s. Holland had ten thousand university students in 1938 and a hundred thousand in 1960. In France 14 percent of young people went to a university in 1965, as opposed to 4.5 percent in 1950. With an increase in scholarships and a growing awareness that higher education was the key to success, European universities became more democratic, opening their doors to more students from the lower-middle and lower classes. Finally, in response to the prodigious expansion of science and technology, the curriculum gradually changed. All sorts of new, "practical" fields —from computer science to business administration —appeared alongside the earlier liberal arts and sciences.

The rapid expansion of higher education created problems as well as opportunities for students. Classes were badly overcrowded, and there was little contact with professors. Competition for grades became intense. Moreover, although more "practical" areas of study were added, they were added less quickly than many students wanted. Thus many students felt that they were not getting the kind of education they needed for the modern world and that basic university reforms were absolutely necessary. The emergence of a distinctive "youth culture" also brought students into conflict with those symbols of the older generation and parental authority—professors and school officials.

These tensions within the exploding university population came to a head in the late 1960s and early 1970s. Following in the footsteps of their American counterparts, who pioneered with large-scale student protests in the mid-1960s, European university students rose to challenge their university administrations and even their governments. The most far-reaching of these revolts occurred in France in 1968.

Student Protest in Paris These rock-throwing students in the Latin Quarter of Paris are trying to force educational reforms, or even to topple De Gaulle's government. Throughout May 1968 students clashed repeatedly with France's tough riot police in bloody street fighting. *(Bruno Barbey/Magnum Photos, Inc.)*

It began at the stark new University of Nanterre in the gloomy industrial suburbs of Paris. Students demanded both changes in the curriculum and a real voice in running the university. The movement spread to the hallowed halls of the medieval Sorbonne in the heart of Paris. Students occupied buildings and took over the university. This takeover led to violent clashes with police, who were ordered in to break up a demonstration that was fast becoming an uprising.

The student radicals appealed to France's industrial workers for help. Rank-and-file workers ignored the advice of their cautious union officials, and a more or less spontaneous general strike spread across France in May 1968. It seemed certain that President De Gaulle's Fifth Republic would collapse. In fact, De Gaulle stiffened, declaring he was in favor of reforms but would oppose "bedwetting." Securing the firm support of French army commanders in West Germany, he moved troops toward Paris and called

for new elections. Thoroughly frightened by the protest-turned-upheaval and fearful that a successful revolution could lead only to an eventual Communist takeover, the masses of France voted for a return to law and order. De Gaulle and his party scored the biggest electoral victory in modern French history, and the mini-revolution collapsed.

Yet the proud De Gaulle and the confident, if old-fashioned, national political revival he represented had been cruelly mocked. In 1969 a tired and discouraged President De Gaulle resigned over a minor issue, and within a year he was dead. For much of the older generation in France, and indeed throughout western Europe, the student revolution of 1968 signaled the end of illusions and the end of an era. Social stability and material progress had resulted in conflict and uncertainty. Under such conditions, all schemes for western European equality with the external superpowers—the United States and the Soviet Union—would have an air of unreality.

The student protest of the 1960s, which peaked in 1968 but echoed well into the 1970s, was due to more than overcrowded classrooms and outdated courses. It reflected a rebirth of romantic revolutionary idealism, which repudiated the quest for ever more consumer goods as stupid and destructive. Student radicalism was also related to the Vietnam War, which led many students in Europe and America to convince themselves that Western civilization was immoral and imperialistic. Finally, the students of the late 1960s were a completely new generation: they had never known anything but prosperity and tranquillity, and they had grown bored with both.

The student revolt was also motivated by new perceptions about the new society of highly trained experts. Some reflective young people feared that universities would soon do nothing but turn out docile technocrats both to stock and to serve "the establishment." Others saw the class of highly trained specialists they expected to enter as the new exploited class in society. The remedy to this situation, both groups believed, was "participation"—the democratization of decision making *within* large, specialized bureaucratic organizations. Only in this way would such organizations serve real human needs and not merely exploit the individual and the environment. Thus the often unrealistic and undisciplined student radicals tried to answer a vital question: how was the complex new society of specialized experts to be made humane and responsive?

WOMEN AND THE FAMILY

The growing emancipation of women in Europe and North America was unquestionably one of the most important developments after the Second World War. This development gathered speed in the 1960s and reached a climax in the mid-1970s. Women demanded and won new rights. Having shared fully in the postwar education revolution, women were better educated than ever before. They took advantage of the need for trained experts in a more fluid society and moved into areas of employment formerly closed to them. Married women in particular became much more likely to work outside the home than they were a few short years earlier. Women no longer had to fatalistically accept childbearing and child-

rearing, for if they wished they could use modern techniques of contraception to control the number and spacing of their offspring. In short, women became more equal and independent, less confined and stereotyped. A major transformation was in process.

The changing position of women altered the modern family. Since the emancipation of women is still incomplete, it is impossible to say for certain whether some major revolution has occurred within the family. Nevertheless, as women today consolidate and expand the breakthroughs of the 1960s and early 1970s, it seems clear that the family has experienced some fundamental reorientations at the very least. This becomes apparent if we examine women's traditional role in the home and then women's new roles outside the home in the postwar era.

MARRIAGE AND MOTHERHOOD

Before the Industrial Revolution, most men and women married late, and substantial numbers never married at all. Once a woman was married, though, she normally bore several children, of whom a third to a half would not survive to adulthood. Moreover, many women died in childbirth. With the growth of industry and urban society, people began to marry earlier, and fewer remained unmarried. As industrial development led to higher incomes and better diets, more children survived to adulthood, and population grew rapidly in the nineteenth century. By the late nineteenth century, contraception within marriage was spreading.

In the twentieth century, and especially after World War Two, these trends continued. In the postwar era, women continued to marry earlier. In Sweden, for example, the average age of first marriage dropped steadily from twenty-six in the early 1940s to twenty-three in the late 1960s. Moreover, more than nine out of ten women were marrying at least once, usually in their early twenties. Marriage was never more in vogue than in the generation after the Second World War. The triumph of romantic attraction over financial calculation seemed complete, and perhaps never before had young couples expected so much emotional satisfaction from matrimony.

After marrying early, the typical woman in Europe, the United States, and Canada had her children quickly. Whereas women in the more distant past very often had children as long as they were fertile, women in Europe and North America were having about 80 percent of their children before they were thirty. As for family size, the "baby boom" that lasted several years after 1945 made for fairly rapid population growth of 1 to 1.5 percent per year in many European countries. In the 1960s, however, the long-term decline in birthrates resumed. Surveys in northern and western Europe began to reveal that most women believed that two instead of three children were ideal.

Women must have 2.1 children on the average if total population is to remain constant over the long term. Indeed, the number of births fell so sharply in the 1960s that total population practically stopped growing in many European countries. By the mid-1970s, more people were dying each year than were being born in Austria, East Germany, West Germany, and Luxembourg, where total numbers actually declined. The United States followed the same trend; the birthrate declined from 25 per thousand in 1957 to 15 per thousand in 1973, and it recovered slightly thereafter only because the baby boomers were reaching childbearing age, not because individual women were having more children. Since the American death rate has remained practically unchanged, the rate of population growth from natural increase (that is, excluding immigration) dropped by two-thirds, from 1.5 percent to .6 percent per year between the 1950s and the 1970s. The population of Africa, Asia, and Latin America was still growing very rapidly from natural increase, but that was certainly not true for most European countries and countries of predominantly European ancestry.

The culmination of the trends toward early almost-universal marriage and small family size in wealthy societies had revolutionary implications for women. An examination of these implications suggests why the emancipation of women—sooner or later—was almost assuredly built into the structure of modern life.

The main point is that motherhood occupied a much smaller portion of a woman's life than at the beginning of this century. The average woman's life expectancy at birth increased from about fifty years in 1900 to about seventy-five years in 1970. At the same time, women were increasingly compressing childbearing into the decade between their twentieth and thirtieth birthdays, instead of bearing children until they were in their late thirties. By the early

1970s about half of Western women, and more than half in some nations, were having their last baby by the age of twenty-six or twenty-seven. When the youngest child trooped off to kindergarten, the average mother still had more than forty years of life in front of her.

This was a momentous change. Throughout history, most married women had been defined to a considerable extent as mothers. Motherhood was very demanding: pregnancy followed pregnancy, and there were many children to nurse, guide, and bury. Now, however, the years devoted to having babies and caring for young children represented at most a seventh of the average woman's life. Motherhood had become a relatively short phase in most women's total life span. Perhaps a good deal of the frustration that many women felt in the 1960s and 1970s was due to the fact that their traditional role as mothers no longer absorbed the energies of a lifetime, and new roles in the male-dominated world outside the family were opening up slowly.

A related revolutionary change for women was that the age-old biological link between sexual intercourse and motherhood was severed. As is well known, beginning in the early 1960s many women chose to gain effective control over pregnancy with oral contraceptives and intrauterine devices. They no longer relied on undependable males and their undependable methods. Less well known are certain physiological facts, which help explain why many women in the advanced countries did elect to practice birth control at some point in their lives.

Women in the postwar era were capable of having children for many more years than their forebears. The age of *menarche*—the age at which girls begin to menstruate and become fertile—had dropped from about seventeen years in the early nineteenth century to about thirteen years by the 1970s. At the same time, the age at onset of menopause rose. At the beginning of the eighteenth century, menopause occurred at about age thirty-six, on average; it now occurred at about fifty. These physiological changes over time are poorly understood, but they were apparently due to better diets and living standards, which also substantially increased people's height and size. In any event, many modern women chose to separate their sexual lives from their awesome reproductive power, which had increased with the lengthening of the time in which they were capable of

A Modern Family This scene sums up some important changes taking place within the family in the postwar era. The young father feeds and talks with the baby, while the student-mother concentrates on the education essential for successful employment. *(Niépce-Rapho)*

bearing children. In doing so, these women became free to pursue sensual pleasure for its own sake. The consequences of this revolutionary development will continue to work themselves out for a long time.

WOMEN AT WORK

For centuries before the Industrial Revolution, ordinary women were highly productive members of society. They often labored for years before marriage to accumulate the necessary dowry. Once married, women worked hard on farms and in home industries while bearing and caring for their large families. With the growth of modern industry and large cities, young women continued to work as wage earners. But once a poor woman married, she typically stopped working in a factory or a shop, struggling in-stead to earn money at home by practicing some low-paid craft as she looked after her children. In the middle classes, it was a rare and tough-minded woman who worked outside the home for wages, although charity work was socially acceptable.

Since the beginning of the twentieth century and especially after World War Two, the situation has changed dramatically once again. Opportunities for women of modest means to earn cash income within the home practically disappeared. Piano teachers, novelists, and part-time typists still worked at home as independent contractors, but the ever-greater complexity of the modern wage-based economy and its sophisticated technology meant that almost all would-be wage earners had to turn elsewhere. Moreover, motherhood took less and less time, so that the full-time mother-housewife had less and less eco-

Day-Care Centers have gradually developed to meet the needs of working women. This center at a Chicago high school is open to children of teachers and of teen-aged mothers who are continuing their schooling. *(Wide World Photos)*

nomic value for families. Thus the reduction of home-centered work and child care resulted in a sharp rise across Europe and North America in the number of married women who were full-time wage earners.

In communist countries, the trend went the furthest. In the Soviet Union, most married women worked outside the home; there women accounted for almost half of all employed persons in the postwar era. In noncommunist western Europe and North America there was a good deal of variety, depending

on whether married women had traditionally worked outside the home, as in France or Sweden, or stayed at home, as in Belgium and Switzerland. Nevertheless, the percentage of married women who worked rose sharply in all countries, from a range of roughly 20 to 25 percent in 1950 to a range of 35 to 60 percent in the 1970s. This rise was particularly dramatic in the United States, where married women were twice as likely to be employed in 1979 as they were in 1952.

The dramatic growth of employment among married women was a development whose ultimate effects are still unknown. Nevertheless, it seems clear that the rising employment of married women was a powerful force in the drive for women's equality and emancipation. Take the critical matter of widespread discrimination between men and women in pay, occupation, and advancement. The young unmarried woman of eighty years ago generally accepted such injustices. She thought of them as temporary nuisances and looked forward to marriage and motherhood for fulfillment. In the postwar era, a married wage earner in her thirties developed a totally different perspective. Employment became a permanent condition within which she, like her male counterpart, sought not only income but psychological satisfaction as well. Sexism and discrimination quickly became increasingly loathsome and evoked that sense of injustice that drives revolutions and reforms. The "movement" spread, winning converts among the young and newly awakened.

Rising employment for married women was a factor in the decline of the birthrate (see Figure 31.2). Women who worked had significantly fewer children than women of the same age who did not. Moreover, survey research showed that young women who had worked and intended to work again revised downward the number of children they expected to have after the first lovable but time-consuming baby was born. One reason was obvious: raising a family while holding down a full-time job was a tremendous challenge and often resulted in the woman being grossly overworked. The fatiguing, often frustrating multiple demands of job, motherhood, and marriage simply became more manageable with fewer children.

Another reason for the decline of the birthrate was that motherhood interrupted a woman's career. The majority of women in Western countries preferred or were forced to accept—interpretations varied—staying at home for a minimum of two or three years while their children were small. The longer the break in employment, the more a woman's career suffered. Women consistently earned less than men partly because they were employed less continuously and thus did not keep moving steadily up the bureaucratic ladders of large organizations.

Because most Western countries did little to help women in the problem of re-employment after their children were a little older, some women came to advocate the pattern of career and family typically found in communist eastern Europe. There, women

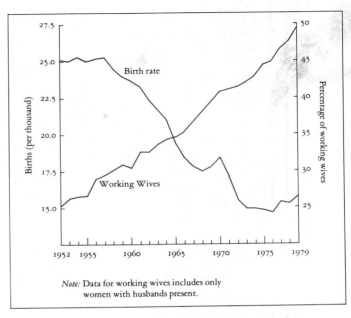

Note: Data for working wives includes only women with husbands present.

FIGURE 31.2 The Decline of the Birthrate and the Increase of Working Wives in the United States, 1952–1979 The challenge of working away from home encouraged American wives to prefer fewer children and helped to lower the birthrate.

were usually employed continuously until they retired. There were no career-complicating interruptions for extended mothering. Instead, a woman in a communist country received as her right up to three months of maternity leave to care for her newborn infant and recover her strength. Then she returned to her job, leaving her baby in the care of a state-run nursery or, more frequently, a retired relative or neighbor. By the 1970s some western European countries were beginning to provide well-defined maternity leaves as part of their social security systems. The United States lagged far behind in this area.

What the increasing numbers of career-minded women with independent, self-assertive spirits meant for marriage and relations between the sexes was by no means clear. As we have seen, marriage remained an almost universal experience. Moreover, the decline of informal village and neighborhood socializing with the advent of the automobile and suburban living made most wives and husbands more dependent than ever on their mates (and their children) for their emotional needs. Never was more being demanded from hearth and home.

The great increase in life expectancy for males and females by itself made marriage more stable, at least in one sense. The average couple was living together for forty years before the death of one dissolved the union, as opposed to less than twenty years together at the beginning of the century. And husbands were slowly getting the message that the old rule of leaving the dishes and diapers exclusively to wives needed rewriting, especially in two-income families. In short, the nuclear family showed great strength, adapting itself once again to changing values and changing conditions.

At the same time, contrary trends clearly emerged in the late 1960s, which carried over strongly into the 1970s and 1980s. Everywhere the divorce rate kept moving up: it doubled in the United States between 1970 and 1980. Nearly everywhere in Western countries, except in southern Europe, over one-quarter of marriages ended in divorce by the early 1980s: in Sweden, it was one in two. Studies of marriage consistently showed that working women were considerably more likely to get divorced than nonworking women. The independent working woman could more easily afford to leave if dissatisfied, while the no-income career housewife was more nearly locked into her situation.

Beginning in the very late 1960s, the marriage rate also began to plunge in a number of Western countries, and it continued to decline throughout the 1970s before stabilizing in the 1980s. Both women and men married progressively later, and those who never married grew as a portion of the population. As the number of singles grew, there was also a considerable increase in the number of unmarried couples living together, reminiscent of patterns among the European working classes in the early days of industrialization. Some observers argued that young women and men were only postponing marriage because of less robust economic conditions. Others contended that marriage, after its long rise, was finally in retreat in the face of growing careerism and acceptance of new, less structured relations between (and within) the sexes. More fundamentally, falling birthrates, more married women in the workplace, later marriage, and increased divorce (and remarriage) rates were all related to the growing emancipation of women. They were all part of a complicated

constellation of striking changes, which strongly suggested that a major break with the past had already taken place in marriage patterns and family relationships.

_____

This chapter has examined the major postwar social changes that accompanied the political recovery and economic expansion discussed in Chapter 30. These social changes were profound. Science combined with technology, often under government direction, to fulfill the loftiest hopes of its enthusiasts and achieve amazing success. The triumphs of applied science contributed not only to economic expansion but also to a more fluid, less antagonistic class structure, in which specialized education was the high road to advancement, regardless of political system. Within the prosperous, increasingly technocratic society, women asserted themselves. Beginning in the 1960s, they moved increasingly into the labor market and gave birth to fewer children. In doing so, women began striking off in a new direction, which has continued to this day. Their greater commitment to employment and decision to raise fewer children—a social pattern in sharp contrast to that of the late 1940s and 1950s—foretold the more general break in Western history that occurred shortly thereafter, as will be shown in Chapter 32.

NOTES

1. Quoted by J. Ziman, *The Force of Knowledge: The Scientific Dimension of Society,* Cambridge University Press, Cambridge, Eng., 1976, p. 128.
2. Quoted by S. Toulmin, *The Twentieth Century: A Promethean Age,* ed. A. Bullock, Thames & Hudson, London, 1971, p. 294.

SUGGESTED READING

J. Ziman, *The Force of Knowledge: The Scientific Dimension of Society* (1976), which has an excellent bibliography, is a penetrating look at science by a leading physicist. C. P. Snow, *The Two Cultures and the Scientific Revolution,* rev. ed. (1963), explores the gap between scientists and nonscientists in a widely discussed book. A Toffler, *Future Shock* (1970), is an interesting but exaggerated best-seller, which claims that many contemporary psychological problems are due to overly rapid technical and scientific development. J. Ellul, *The Technological Society* (1964), is also highly critical of technical progress, while D. S. Landes, *The Unbound Prometheus: Technological Change and Industrial Development in Western Europe from 1750 to the Present* (1969), remains enthusiastic. Two more stimulating works on technology are J. J. Servan-Schreiber, *The World Challenge* (1981), and H. Jacoby, *The Bureaucratization of the World* (1973).

In addition to studies cited in the Suggested Reading for Chapter 30, A. Simpson, *The New Europeans* (1968), is a good guide to contemporary Western society. Two engaging books on recent intellectual developments are J. Barzun, *The House of Intellect* (1959), and R. Stromberg, *After Everything: Western Intellectual History Since 1945* (1970). L. Wylie, *Village in the Vauclause,* rev. ed. (1964), and P. J. Hélias, *The Horse of Pride* (1980), provide fascinating pictures of life in the French village. A. Kriegel, *The French Communists* (1972) and *Eurocommunism* (1978), are also recommended. A. Touraine, *The May Movement* (1971), is sympathetic toward the French student revolt, while the noted sociologist R. Aron, *The Elusive Revolution* (1969), is highly critical. F. Zweig, *The Worker in an Affluent Society* (1961), probes family life and economic circumstances in the British working class on the basis of extensive interviews. R. E. Tyrrell, ed., *The Future That Doesn't Work* (1977), is a polemical but absorbing attack on British socialism. W. Hollstein, *Europe in the Making* (1973), is a fervent plea to integrate Europe by a former top official of the Common Market. The magazines *Encounter, Commentary,* and *The Economist* often carry interesting articles on major social and political trends, as do *Time* and *Newsweek.*

E. Sullerot, *Women, Society and Change* (1971), is an outstanding introduction to women's evolving role. R. Patia, ed., *Women in the Modern World* (1967), compares women's situations in many countries. Two other influential books on women and their new awareness are S. de Beauvoir, *The Second Sex* (1962), and B. Friedan, *The Feminine Mystique* (1963). These may be compared with C. Lasch, *Haven in a Heartless World* (1977), and A. Cherlin, *Marriage, Divorce, Remarriage* (1981), which interpret changes in the American family.

32

**THE RECENT PAST,
1968 TO THE PRESENT**

*S*OMETIME DURING the late 1960s or early 1970s, the postwar era came to an end. With fits and starts, a new age opened, as postwar certitudes like domestic political stability, social harmony, and continuous economic improvement evaporated. In any event, that is how this historian reads the most recent past. Others may form different judgments, for we are simply too close to the postwar era to gain vital perspective on the period that has succeeded it. As Voltaire once said, "The man who ventures to write contemporary history must expect to be attacked for everything he has said and everything he has not said."[1]

Yet the historian must take a stand. We have already examined some indications of the end of the postwar era. Fundamental changes within the family, featuring new roles for women, gathered momentum in the late 1960s. The minirevolution of 1968 was a fundamental turning point in recent French history, symptomatic of a general rebirth of political instability and even crisis in several leading nations. Major changes in East-West relations also marked a real, if more ambiguous, turning point. Most important of all, the astonishing postwar economic advance, unparalleled in its rapidity and consistency, came to an abrupt halt. Old, almost forgotten, problems like high unemployment, expensive energy, and international monetary instability suddenly re-emerged. Throughout the Western world, the general mood changed; stylish opinion leaders traded in facile optimism for equally superficial pessimism. There was clearly no going back to the buoyant self-confidence of the postwar era.

In an attempt to make sense out of a turbulent recent past, which merges with an uncertain present, this chapter will focus on three questions of fundamental importance. First, why, after a generation, did the world economy shift into reverse gear, and what were some of the social consequences of that shift? Second, what were the most striking political developments within the nations of the Atlantic alliance? Specifically, how did West Germany take the initiative in trying to negotiate an enduring reconciliation with its Communist neighbors, and why did the United States enter into a time of troubles before seeking to reassert its strength and leadership in the 1980s? Third, how did these changes interact with the evolution of the Soviet bloc? Finally, the chapter will close with some reflections on the future.

THE TROUBLED ECONOMY

The energy crisis looms large in the sudden transition from almost automatic postwar growth to serious economic difficulties in the 1970s and 1980s. The first surge in oil prices in 1973 stunned the international economy, and the second surge in 1979 led to the deepest recession since the 1930s. The collapse of the postwar monetary system in 1971 and the rapid accumulation of international debts also caused heavy long-term damage. The social consequences of harder times were profound and many-sided.

MONEY AND OIL

During the Second World War, British and American statesmen were convinced that international financial disorder after 1918 had contributed mightily to economic problems, the Great Depression, and renewed global warfare. They were determined not to repeat their mistakes, and in the Bretton Woods Agreement of 1944, they laid the foundations for a new international monetary system, which proved instrumental in the unprecedented postwar boom.

The new system, operating through the World Bank and the International Monetary Fund, was based on the American dollar, which was supposed to be "as good as gold" because foreign governments could always exchange dollars for gold at $35 an ounce. The United States proceeded to make needed dollars readily available to the rest of the world, first by giving Marshall Plan aid to Europe and then by constantly spending more abroad than it earned in the 1950s and 1960s. However, by early 1971, the United States had overspent to the point where it had only $11 billion in gold left in Fort Knox and Europe had accumulated 50 billion American dollars. The result was a classic, long-overdue "run on the bank" in 1971, as foreigners panicked and raced to exchange their dollars for gold. President Richard Nixon was forced to stop the sale of American gold. The price of gold then soared on world markets, and the value of the dollar declined. Moreover, fixed rates of exchange were abandoned, and all major currencies began to fluctuate rapidly against each other. The American dollar, for example, lost 40 percent of its value against the German mark between February

An OPEC Meeting Begins As this picture suggests, the Organization of Petroleum Exporting Countries (OPEC) took on many aspects of an international political alliance, through which ministers of member states met periodically to fix the price of world trade's most vital commodity. The OPEC alliance rode high in the 1970s as the industrialized nations failed to make a concerted response. *(Wide World Photos)*

and March 1973. Great uncertainty replaced postwar predictability in international finance, which also complicated trade and foreign investment.

Even more serious was the dramatic reversal in the price and availability of energy. As described in Chapter 22, coal-fired steam engines broke the bottleneck of chronically inadequate energy in the late eighteenth-century economy, making possible the Industrial Revolution and improved living standards in the nineteenth century. In the twentieth century, petroleum proved its worth, and the great postwar

boom was fueled by cheap oil, especially in western Europe. Cheap oil from the Middle East permitted energy-intensive industries—automobiles, chemicals, and electric power—to expand rapidly and lead other sectors of the economy forward. More generally, cheap oil and cheap energy encouraged businesses to invest massively in machinery and improved technology. This investment enabled workers to produce more—quite typically, productivity per worker in the United States grew handsomely at more than 3 percent a year between 1950 and 1973

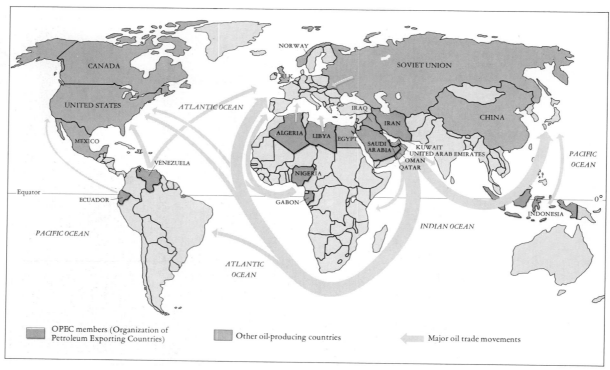

MAP 32.1 OPEC and the World Oil Trade Though much of the world depends on imported oil, Western Europe and Japan are OPEC's biggest customers. What major oil exporters remain outside of OPEC?

—and allowed a steady rise in the standard of living without much inflation.

In the 1950s and 1960s, the main oil-exporting countries, grouped together in the Arab-dominated Organization of Petroleum Exporting Countries (OPEC), had watched the price of crude oil decline consistently compared to the price of manufactured goods, as the Western oil companies vigorously expanded production and kept prices low to win users of coal to petroleum (see Map 32.1). The Egyptian leader Nasser argued that Arab countries should manipulate oil prices to further increase their revenues and also to strike at Israel and its Western allies. But Egypt lacked oil and Nasser failed. Colonel Muammar Khadafy of Libya proved more successful. He won important concessions from Western nations and oil companies in the early 1970s, and his example activated the OPEC countries. In 1971 OPEC for the first time presented a united front against the oil companies and obtained a solid price increase. The

stage was set for the revolution in energy prices during the fourth Arab-Israeli war in October 1973.

The war began on the solemn sabbath celebration of Yom Kippur, or the Day of Atonement, the holiest day in the Jewish calendar. Egypt and Syria launched a surprise attack on an unsuspecting Israel, breaking through defense positions and destroying a large part of the Israeli air force. In response to urgent pleas, the United States airlifted $2.2 billion of its most sophisticated weapons to Israel, which accepted a cease-fire after its successful counterattack had encircled much of the Egyptian army. Surprisingly, the Yom Kippur War eventually led to peace between Egypt and Israel. Egypt's initial military victories greatly enhanced the power and prestige of General Anwar Sadat (1918–1981), Nasser's successor. This advantage enabled the realistic Sadat to achieve in 1979 the negotiated settlement with Israel that he had long desired.

In the first days of the war, the Arab (and non-

The Egyptian-Israeli Peace Treaty of 1979 is celebrated by the men who made it possible, Egypt's President Anwar al-Sadat, U.S. President Jimmy Carter, and Israeli Prime Minister Menachem Begin. Egypt recognized Israel's right to exist and established normal diplomatic relations, while Israel agreed to withdraw from Egyptian territory occupied in the Six-Day War of 1967. *(National Archives and Records Administration)*

Arab) oil producers in OPEC placed an embargo on oil shipments to the United States and the Netherlands, in retaliation for their support of Israel. They also cut production and raised prices by 70 percent, ostensibly to prevent Europe from sharing oil with the United States. In reality, greed and a desire for revenge against the West took over: a second increase in December, after the cease-fire, meant that crude oil prices quadrupled in less than a year. It was widely realized that OPEC's brutal action was economically destructive, but the world's major powers did nothing. The Soviet Union was a great oil exporter and benefited directly, while a cautious western Europe looked to the United States for leadership. But the United States was immobilized, its attention absorbed by the Watergate crisis (see page 1026). Thus governments, companies, and individuals were left to deal piecemeal and manage as best they could with the so-called oil shock—a "shock" that was really an earthquake.

INFLATION, DEBT, AND UNEMPLOYMENT

Coming close on the heels of upheaval in the international monetary system, the price revolution in energy sources plunged the world into its worst economic decline since the 1930s. The energy-intensive industries that had driven the economy up in the 1950s and 1960s now dragged it down in the mid-1970s. Yet, while industrial output fell, soaring energy costs sent prices surging. "Stagflation"—the unexpected combination of economic stagnation and rapid inflation—appeared, to bedevil the public and baffle economists. Unemployment rose, while productivity and living standards declined.

But no cycle lasts forever, and by 1976 a modest recovery was in progress. People were learning to save energy, turning down thermostats, and buying smaller cars. Optimists argued that the challenge of redesigning life styles to cope with expensive energy actually represented a great opportunity.

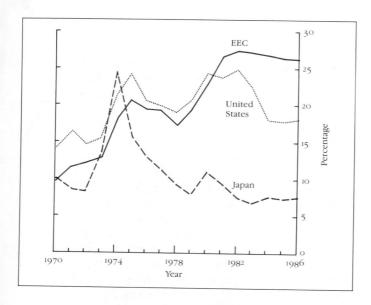

FIGURE 32.1 The Misery Index, 1970–1985 Combining rates of unemployment and inflation provided a simple but effective measure of economic hardship. This particular index represents the sum of two times the unemployment rate plus the inflation rate, reflecting the widespread belief that joblessness causes more suffering than higher prices. EEC = European Economic Community, or Common Market countries. *(Source: OECD data, as given in* The Economist, *June 15, 1985, p. 69.)*

Iran's Islamic revolution in 1978 and 1979 confounded these hopes, at least in the short run. Iranian oil production collapsed, OPEC again doubled the price of crude oil, and the world economy succumbed to its second oil shock. Once again, unemployment and inflation rose dramatically before another recovery began in 1982, driven by a reversal in oil prices, falling interest rates, and large U.S. trade and budget deficits. But the recovery was very uneven. In the summer of 1985, the unemployment rate in western Europe rose to its highest levels since the Great Depression. Fully 19 million people were unemployed.

Many means were devised in the 1970s to measure the troubled economy, but perhaps none was more telling than the "misery index." First used with considerable effect by candidate Jimmy Carter in the 1976 U.S. presidential debates, the misery index combined rates of inflation and unemployment in a single, powerfully emotional number. Figure 32.1 presents a comparison of misery indexes for the

United States and the Common Market countries between 1970 and 1985. As may be seen, "misery" increased on both sides of the Atlantic, but the increase was substantially greater in western Europe. This helps explain why these hard times—often referred to by Europeans simply as "the crisis"—probably had an even greater psychological impact on Europeans than on Americans.

Nor was the Soviet bloc spared. Both the Soviet Union and the satellite states of its eastern European empire did less and less well: annual rates of economic growth fell from 6 to 7 percent in the late 1960s to 2 to 3 percent in 1980. This performance was no worse than that of most Western countries, but it mocked the long-standing propaganda boast to "catch and surpass the capitalistic West," which was quietly dropped in favor of less humorous slogans.

The revolution in energy prices had major consequences for economic and political relations between East bloc members. Eastern Europe is generally poor in energy resources, especially petroleum, whereas the Soviet Union has enormous gas deposits and is the world's largest oil producer. Thus the explosion of oil prices greatly increased the economic leverage of the Soviet Union over eastern Europe, and it strengthened trade ties within Comecon, the economic "club" formed by the Soviet Union and its allies. The Russians supplied more desperately needed oil and raw materials, and they took in return the pick of eastern European manufacturers. Eastern European hopes of closer commercial (and cultural) ties with their Western neighbors necessarily faded.

Debts and deficits piled up quickly in the troubled economy of the 1970s and 1980s. In the first place, the price hikes of 1973 required a massive global transfer of wealth to the OPEC countries from both rich and poor nations. Like individual consumers suddenly faced with a financial emergency, countries scrambled to borrow to pay their greatly increased fuel bills. Poor countries, especially, turned to the big private international banks. These banks received deposits—the so-called petrodollars—from OPEC members and lent them back out to poor countries so that these nations could pay their oil bills. This circular flow averted total collapse. But there was a high price to pay in the form of a rapid expansion of international debt, which bounded higher after the second oil shock and posed a serious long-term threat to the world economy in the 1980s.

Rich nations also went on a borrowing binge. Almost everywhere they ran up big debts to pay for imported oil and also to maintain social welfare services, as their economies declined and tax receipts fell. Even West Germany, justly famous for its commitment to low inflation and sound money, ran up a huge increase. By 1981 interest on Germany's national debt consumed one quarter of all government spending and was the largest single item in Germany's budget.

Western consumers also joined the race for ever-higher levels of debt. Borrowing to buy before prices rose seemed smart in the 1970s, and that attitude carried over into the 1980s. Like burgeoning government debt, a record-high level of consumer debt was a two-edged sword. It sustained current economic activity but quite possibly posed serious repayment problems, an appropriately ambiguous reflection of the troubled economy.

SOME SOCIAL CONSEQUENCES

The most pervasive consequences of recent economic stagnation was probably psychological and attitudinal. Optimism gave way to pessimism; romantic utopianism yielded to sober realism. This drastic change in mood—a complete surprise only to those who had never studied history—affected states, institutions, and individuals in countless ways.

To be sure, there were heartbreaking human tragedies—lost jobs, bankruptcies, and mental breakdowns. But, on the whole, the welfare system fashioned in the postwar era prevented mass suffering and degradation. Extended benefits for the unemployed, pensions for the aged, free medical care for the needy, surplus food and special allowances for parents with children—all these and a host of lesser supports did their part. The responsive, socially concerned national state undoubtedly contributed to the preservation of political stability and democracy in the face of economic difficulties, difficulties that might have brought revolution and dictatorship in earlier times.

The energetic response of governments to social needs helps explain the sharp increase in total government spending in most countries during the 1970s and 1980s. In 1982 western European governments spent an average of more than one-half of gross national income, as compared to only 37 per-

cent fifteen years earlier. In the United States, the combined share of federal, state, and local governments rose from 31 to 35 percent in the same years. The role of government in everyday life became more important.

In all countries, people were much more willing to see their governments increase spending than raise taxes. This imbalance contributed to the rapid growth of budget deficits, national debts, and inflation discussed earlier. By the late 1970s, a powerful reaction to government's ever-increasing role set in, and Western governments were gradually forced to introduce austerity measures to slow the seemingly inexorable growth of public spending and the welfare state. The partially successful efforts of Margaret Thatcher in Britain and Ronald Reagan in the United States to limit the growth of social programs absorbed the attention of the English-speaking world, but François Mitterand of France was the temporary exception who proved the general rule. After his election as president in 1981, Mitterand led his Socialist party and Communist allies on a vast program of nationalization and public investment designed to spend France out of economic stagnation. By 1983 this attempt had clearly failed. Mitterand's Socialist government was then compelled to impose a wide variety of austerity measures fully worthy of Reagan and Thatcher, until elections in 1986 brought a conservative coalition to power by a narrow margin.

When governments were eventually forced to restrain spending, Big Science was often singled out for cuts, unless its ties to the military were very direct. The problems of CERN were a good example. Formed to pool western European efforts in high-energy particle physics (page 996), CERN succeeded admirably in stealing the lead from the United States in this exciting but esoteric and uncommercial field. But the costs were so enormous—$400 million for construction of the latest electron-smashing accelerator—that some governments, such as Great Britain's, were budgeting 10 percent of all their spending for scientific research on particle physics alone. In the 1980s, CERN was increasingly attacked as an extravagant misallocation of scarce resources at a time when new fields, such as computers and genetic research, were bursting with scientific opportunities that offered mouth-watering commercial applications. More generally, tighter funding for Big Science accelerated the ongoing computer revolution. That

"The New Poor" Economic crisis and prolonged unemployment in the early 1980s reduced many from modest affluence to harsh poverty, creating a class of new poor. This photo captures that human tragedy. After two years of unemployment, this homeless French office worker must sleep each night in a makeshift shelter for the destitute. *(Magnum)*

revolution thrived on the diffusion of unprecedented computational and informational capacity to small research groups and private businesses, which were both cause and effect of the revolution itself.

Individuals felt the impact of austerity even earlier, for unlike governments, they could not pay their bills by printing money and going ever further into debt. The energy crisis forced them to re-examine not only their fuel bills, but the whole pattern of self-indulgent materialism in the postwar era as well. The result was a leaner, tougher lifestyle, featuring more attention to nutrition and a passion for exercise. Correspondingly, there was less blind reliance on medical science for good health and a growing awareness that individuals must accept a large portion of the responsibility for illness and disease. More people began to realize that they could substantially increase their life spans simply by eating regular meals, sleeping seven or

eight hours each night, exercising two or three times a week, maintaining moderate weight, forgoing smoking, and using alcohol only in moderation. A forty-five-year-old American male who practiced three or fewer of these habits could expect to live to be sixty-seven; one who adhered to five or six could expect to live eleven more years, to age seventy-eight.

Yet it was the very real threat of unemployment that probably had the most profound impact. A good job promised pride and well-being, while the most generous unemployment benefits only prevented catastrophe. The increased focus on jobs continued the 1960s trend of more married women working. It also encouraged both men and women to postpone marriage until they had put their careers on a firm foundation, so that the age of marriage rose sharply for both sexes in many Western countries.

Indeed, the employment question seemed to shape

the outlook of a whole generation. The students of the 1980s were serious, practical, and often conservative. As one young woman at a French university told a reporter in 1985, "Jobs are the big worry now, so everyone wants to learn something practical." In France, as elsewhere, it was an astonishing shift from the romantic visions and political activism of the late 1960s. Speaking of the French student revolution of 1968, another undergraduate handed down a tough judgment for the same reporter. "It was a search for a Utopia that can't exist. It just doesn't mean a thing to us anymore."[2]

THE ATLANTIC ALLIANCE

Forged in the late 1940s to rebuild Europe and prevent possible Soviet expansion beyond the iron curtain, the Atlantic alliance remained an enduring reality in the face of economic difficulties. But the alliance was neither static nor monolithic, and its evolution reflected major developments within the member states. Those in West Germany and the United States were of critical importance.

GERMANY AND THE EUROPEAN SETTLEMENT

The turning points of history are sometimes captured in dramatic moments rich in symbolism. So it was in December 1970, when West German Chancellor Willy Brandt flew to Poland for the signing of a historic treaty of reconciliation. Brandt laid a wreath at the tomb of the Polish unknown soldier and another at the monument commemorating the armed uprising of Warsaw's Jewish ghetto against occupying Nazi armies, after which the ghetto was totally destroyed and the Jewish survivors sent to the gas chambers. Standing before the ghetto memorial, a somber Brandt fell to his knees and knelt as if in prayer. "I wanted," Brandt said later, "to ask pardon in the name of our people for a million-fold crime which was committed in the misused name of the Germans."[3]

Brandt's gesture at the Warsaw ghetto memorial and the treaty with Poland were part of his policy of reconciliation with eastern Europe, which aimed at nothing less than a comprehensive peace settlement for central Europe and a new resolution of the "German question." That weighty question had first burst on the European scene with the modern nationalism of the French Revolution. How could fragmented Germany achieve political unity, and what role would a powerful, unified Germany play in the international order? "Resolved" in a certain fashion by Bismarck's wars of unification, the question was posed again in the twentieth century when an aggressive Germany tried twice to conquer Europe. Agreed on crushing Hitler and denazifying Germany during the Second World War, the wartime Allies then found themselves incapable of working together and imposing a general peace treaty on defeated Germany (pages 964–966). Instead, Germany was divided into two antagonistic states by 1949, and the German question continued to fester as national unity disappeared.

The Federal Republic of Germany—commonly known as West Germany—was the larger of the two, with 45 million inhabitants as opposed to 18 million in East Germany. Formed out of the American, British, and French zones of occupation and based on freely expressed popular sovereignty, the Federal Republic claimed that the Communist dictatorship installed by the Russians lacked free elections and hence all legal basis. While concentrating on completing its metamorphosis from defeated enemy to invaluable ally within NATO and the Common Market, West Germany also sought with some success to undermine the East German Communist regime. Between 1949 and 1954, it welcomed with open arms 2.3 million East German refugees seeking political freedom and economic opportunity, and it refused to have diplomatic relations with any state (except the Soviet Union) that recognized East Germany as a legal government. East Germany, first looted by the Soviets and then constantly losing its best workers to West Germany, limped along while the Federal Republic boomed. But the building of the Berlin Wall in 1961 (page 982) changed all that. It sealed the refugees' last escape route through West Berlin and allowed East Germany to stabilize and eventually become the world's most prosperous Communist country.

As the popular socialist major of West Berlin, Willy Brandt understood the significance of the Berlin Wall and the lack of an energetic U.S. response to

Willy Brandt in Poland, 1970 Chancellor Brandt's gesture at the Warsaw memorial to the Jewish victims of Nazi terrorism was criticized by some West Germans but praised by many more. This picture reached an enormous audience, appearing in hundreds of newspapers in both the East and the West. *(Süddeutscher Verlag)*

its construction. He saw the painful limitations of West Germany's official hard line when the Allies had, in fact, accepted the postwar status quo. Thus Brandt became convinced that a revitalized West Germany needed a new foreign policy, just as the German Social Democratic party he headed had abandoned doctrinaire Marxian socialism to become a broad-based opposition party after the Second World War. After a long battle and two bitter electoral defeats in the 1960s, Brandt became foreign minister in a coalition government in 1966 and won the chancellorship in 1969.

Brandt's victory marked the Federal Republic's political coming of age. First, it brought the Social Democrats to national power for the first time since the 1920s and showed that genuine two-party political democracy had taken firm hold. Second, it was a graphic indication of West Germany's new-found liberalism and political tolerance, for the gravel-voiced Brandt was a very unconventional German. Illegitimate son of a poor, unwed shop-girl, and a fire-breathing Socialist in his youth, Brandt had fled to Norway in the 1930s and had fought against Nazi Germany in the Second World War. Yet the electorate judged the man himself, turning a deaf ear to smears and innuendoes about treason and low birth. Third, Brandt showed that West Germany, postwar Europe's economic giant and political dwarf, was now both prepared and willing to launch major initiatives in European affairs.

The essence of Brandt's policy was to seek genuine peace and reconciliation with the communist East, as Adenauer had already done with France and the West. He negotiated treaties with the Soviet Union, Poland, and Czechoslovakia, which accepted existing state boundaries in return for a mutual renunciation of force or the threat of force. Thus West Germany abandoned the fiction that the "provisional" loss of eastern territory to Poland and the Soviet Union (see Map 30.3), agreed to by the Big Four at the Potsdam Conference in 1945, might some day be altered in Germany's favor in the final peace treaty that would never come. In addition, Brandt shrewdly made German ratification of these bilateral treaties conditional on a new agreement between the wartime Big Four, an agreement that solemnly guaranteed the freedom of West Berlin, that perennial source of bitter cold war conflict. Finally, using the imaginative formula of "two German states within one German nation," Brandt's government broke decisively with the past and entered into direct relations with East Germany, aiming for modest practical improvements rather than unattainable reunification.

Since all his initiatives required both American and Russian consent, Brandt constantly reiterated that none of these changes affected the respective military alliances of NATO and the Warsaw Pact. Yet, by boldly establishing "normal relations" with the communist East, West Germany seemed not only to turn another page on its ever-more-distant Nazi past, but on many bitter cold war conflicts as well. Thus West Germany's eastern peace settlement contributed to a general reduction in East-West tensions, which included a limited agreement on nuclear arms control between the United States and the Soviet Union in 1972. And with the German question apparently resolved, West Germany had freed itself to assume without reservations a leading role in Europe. In the future, it would often join with its Common Market partners in an attempt to insulate East-West relations within Europe from the enduring Soviet-American power struggle that characterized the rest of the world.

POLITICAL CRISIS IN THE UNITED STATES

The late 1960s and early 1970s also marked the end of the postwar era in the United States. The natural leader of the Atlantic alliance fell into a long and self-destructive political crisis, which weakened the nation at home and abroad and echoed throughout the 1970s.

The crisis in the United States had numerous manifestations, ranging from apparently uncontrollable annual summer riots to brutal political assassinations, which struck down Martin Luther King and both President John F. Kennedy and his younger brother Robert. But it first reached vast proportions in connection with President Johnson's leadership during the undeclared Vietnam War. Thus President Johnson, who wanted to go down in history as a master reformer and healer of old wounds (pages 983–984), left new ones as his most enduring legacy.

American involvement in Vietnam had its origins in the cold war and the ideology of containment (page 966). From the late 1940s on, most Americans and their leaders viewed the world in terms of a constant struggle to stop the spread of communism, although they were not prepared to try to roll back communism where it already existed. As Europe began to revive and China established a Communist government in 1949, efforts to contain communism shifted to Asia. The bloody Korean War (1950–1953) ended in stalemate, but the United States did succeed in preventing a Communist government in South Korea. After the defeat of the French in Indochina in 1954, the Eisenhower administration refused to sign the Geneva accords that temporarily divided the country into two zones pending national unification by means of free elections. President Eisenhower then proceeded to acquiesce in the refusal of the anti-communist South Vietnamese government to accept the verdict of elections and provided it with military aid. President Kennedy greatly increased the number of American "military advisers," to 16,000, and had the existing South Vietnamese leader deposed in 1963 when he refused to follow American directives.

After successfully portraying his opponent, Barry Goldwater, as a trigger-happy extremist in a nuclear age and resoundingly winning the 1964 election on a peace platform, President Johnson proceeded to expand the American role in the Vietnam conflict. As Johnson explained to his ambassador in Saigon, "I am not going to lose Vietnam. I am not going to be the President who saw Southeast Asia go the way China went."[4] American strategy was to "escalate" the war sufficiently to break the will of the North Vietnamese and their southern allies, without resorting to "overkill" that might risk war with the entire communist bloc. Thus the South received massive military aid, American forces in South Vietnam gradually grew to a half-million men, and the United States bombed North Vietnam with ever-greater intensity. But there was no invasion of the North, nor were essential seaborne military supplies from the Soviet Union ever disrupted. In the end, the strategy of limited war backfired. It was the Americans themselves who grew weary, and the American leadership that cracked.

The undeclared war in Vietnam, fought nightly on American television, eventually divided the nation. Initial support was strong. The politicians, the media, and the population as a whole saw the war as part of a legitimate defense against communist totalitarianism in all poor countries. But in 1966 and 1967, influential opinion leaders like the *New York Times* and the *Washington Post* turned hostile, and the television networks soon followed. A growing number of critics denounced the war as an immoral and unsuccessful intrusion into a complex and distant civil war. There were major protests, often led by college students. Criticism reached a crescendo after the Vietcong "Tet Offensive" in January 1968. This, the Communists' first major attack with conventional weapons on major cities, failed militarily: the Vietcong suffered heavy losses and the attack did not spark a mass uprising. But U.S. critics of the Vietnam War interpreted the bloody battle as a decisive American defeat, clear proof that a Vietcong victory was inevitable. And although public opinion polls never showed more than 20 percent of the people supporting American withdrawal before that became the announced policy after the November 1968 elections, America's leaders now lost all heart. After an ambiguous defeat in the New Hampshire primary, President Johnson tacitly admitted defeat: he called for negotiations with North Vietnam and announced that he would not stand for re-election.

Elected by a razor-slim margin in 1968, President Richard Nixon sought to gradually disengage America from Vietnam and the accompanying national crisis. He restated the long-standing American objective of containment in Vietnam, of aiding the "South Vietnamese people to determine their own political future without outside interference."[5] Using American military power more effectively, while simultaneously pursuing peace talks with the North Vietnamese, Nixon cut American forces in Vietnam from 550,000 to 24,000 in four years. The cost of the war dropped from $25 billion a year under Johnson to $3 billion under Nixon. Moreover, President Nixon launched a daring flank attack in diplomacy. He journeyed to China in 1971 and reached a spectacular if limited reconciliation with Communist China, which took advantage of China's growing fears of the Soviet Union and undermined North Vietnam's position. In January 1973, fortified by the overwhelming endorsement of the people in his 1972 electoral triumph, President Nixon and Secretary of State Henry Kissinger finally reached a peace agreement with North Vietnam. The agreement allowed remaining American forces to complete their withdrawal, while the United States reserved the right to resume bombing if the accords were broken. South Vietnamese forces seemed to hold their own, and the storm of crisis seemed past.

Instead, as the Arab oil embargo unhinged the international economy, the United States reaped the Watergate whirlwind. Like some other recent American presidents, Nixon authorized spying activities that went beyond the law. But in an atmosphere in which a huge series of secret government documents —later known as the "Pentagon Papers"—could be stolen and then given to the country's most influential newspaper for publication as part of its anti–Vietnam War campaign, Nixon went further than his predecessors. He authorized special units to use various illegal means to stop the leaking of government secrets to the press. One such group broke into the Democratic party headquarters in Washington's Watergate complex in June 1972 and was promptly arrested. Eventually, the media and the machinery of Congressional investigation turned the breakin and later efforts to hush up the bungled job into a great moral issue. In 1974 a beleaguered Nixon was forced to resign in disgrace, as the political crisis in the United States reached its culmination.

The consequences of renewed political crisis during the Watergate affair were profound. First, it resulted in a major shift of power away from the presidency toward Congress, especially in foreign affairs.

Nixon in China, 1972 Shown here toasting U.S.–China friendship with Chinese Premier Chou En-lai in Peking in February 1972, President Nixon took advantage of Chinese fears of the Soviet Union to establish good relations with Asia's Communist giant. Arriving after twenty-five years of mutual hostility, reconciliation with China was Nixon's finest achievement. *(UPI/Bettmann Newsphotos)*

Therefore, as American aid to South Vietnam diminished in 1973 and as an emboldened North Vietnam launched a general invasion against South Vietnamese armies in early 1974, first President Nixon and then President Gerald Ford stood by because Congress refused to permit any American response. After more than thirty-five years of battle, the Vietnamese Communists unified their country in 1975 as a totalitarian state—a second consequence of the U.S. crisis. Third, the belated fall of South Vietnam in the wake of Watergate shook America's postwar pride and confidence. Generally interpreted as a disastrous American military defeat, the Vietnam aftermath left the United States divided and uncertain about its proper role in world affairs. The long-dominant belief that the interests of the United States required an unending global struggle against the spread of communism was seriously damaged. In the 1970s, however, no alternative concept received general support, unless it was a narrow preoccupation with the multiplying problems of the troubled international economy.

The Helsinki Agreement, 1975 President Ford signs the historic accord guaranteeing European borders and calling for improvements in human rights. On the far left is Helmut Schmidt of West Germany, flanked by a jovial Erich Honecker savoring the fullest possible diplomatic recognition of his East German Communist state. *(UPI/Bettmann Newsphotos)*

RECENT DEVELOPMENTS

The complex political crisis in the United States during the Vietnam War and West Germany's reconciliation with eastern Europe under Willy Brandt were clearly major turning points in recent history. The power and prestige of the United States had suffered a serious decline, while West Germany had opened the door to major diplomatic agreements regarding Europe. Or so it seemed to many at the time. Yet the ultimate significance of these turning points remains uncertain, as may be seen by examining the often contradictory course of recent developments.

Brandt's Eastern initiatives and Nixon's phased withdrawal from Vietnam were part of many-sided Western efforts to reduce East-West tensions in the early 1970s. This policy of *détente,* or progressive relaxation of cold war tensions, reached its apogee with the Conference on Security and Cooperation in Europe, a thirty-five nation summit that opened negotiations in Helsinki, Finland, in 1973 and reached a final agreement in 1975. Including all European nations (except isolationist Albania), the United States, and Canada, the Final Act of the Helsinki Conference had certain elements of a general European peace treaty, like those signed at Vienna in 1815 and at Versailles in 1919. It formally agreed that Europe's existing political frontiers, including those separating the two Germanies, could not be changed by force and provided for increased East-West economic and cultural relations as well. Thus the Atlantic alliance solemnly accepted the territorial status quo in eastern Europe, as well as the Soviet Union's gains from World War Two. In return for this major concession, the Soviet Union and its allies agreed to numerous provisions guaranteeing the human rights and political freedoms of their peoples. The Final Act was a compromise embodying Western concerns for human rights and Soviet preoccupations with military security and control of eastern Europe. Optimists saw a bright new day breaking in international relations.

These hopes gradually faded in the later 1970s. The Soviet Union and its allies would ignore the human rights provisions of the Helsinki agreement (see above). Moreover, East-West political competition remained very much alive outside Europe. Many Americans became convinced that the Soviet Union was taking advantage of détente, steadily building up its military might and pushing for political gains in Africa, Asia, and Latin America. Having been expelled from Egypt by Anwar Sadat after the 1973 war with Israel, the Soviets sought and won toeholds in South Yemen, Somalia, and later Ethiopia. Having supported guerrilla wars against the Portuguese in Angola and Mozambique, the Soviet Union was rewarded with Marxian regimes in both countries. The spectacular 1975 airlift of 20,000 Cubans to Angola to help the new Marxian government consolidate its power rattled Americans' nerves and increased their suspicions.

But it was in Afghanistan that Soviet action seemed most contrary to the spirit of détente. The Soviet Union had long been interested in its Islamic neighbor, and in April 1978, a pro-Soviet coup established a Marxist regime there. This new government soon made itself unpopular, and rebellion spread through the countryside. To preserve Communist rule, the Soviet Union in December 1979 suddenly airlifted crack troops to Kabul, the capital, and occupied Afghanistan with 100,000 men. Alarmed by the scale and precision of the Soviet invasion, many Americans feared that the oil-rich states of the Persian Gulf would be next and searched for an appropriate response.

President Carter tried to lead the Atlantic alliance beyond verbal condemnation. He ordered a halt to extra sales of American grain—one of the few commodities the Soviet Union really needed from the United States—to the Soviet Union. But among its European allies only Great Britain supported the American policy of economic sanctions. France, and especially West Germany, argued that the Soviets' deplorable action in Afghanistan should not be turned into an East-West confrontation and tried to salvage as much as possible of détente within Europe. President Carter, they implied, had overreacted. The Afghanistan crisis again revealed serious differences within the Atlantic alliance, differences that had been surfacing periodically ever since General De Gaulle's independent course in the 1960s.

The alliance showed the same lack of concerted action when an independent trade union rose in Poland (see page 1037), most notably when western Europe again refused to follow the United States in imposing economic sanctions against Poland and the Soviet Union after the declaration of martial law in Poland in December 1981. Some observers concluded that the alliance had lost the will to think and act decisively in relations with the Soviet bloc. They saw inaction as part of a larger problem of growing disunity within the Western democracies, where debate and dissent were so pervasive that consistent and courageous action was virtually impossible and decline almost inevitable. Others noted that occasional dramatic differences within the alliance reflected the fact that the Common Market and the United States had drifted apart and become economic rivals.

Yet, despite its very real difficulties, the Atlantic alliance, formed in the late 1940s to check Soviet expansion in Europe, endured and remained true to its original purpose in the 1980s. The U.S. military buildup launched by Jimmy Carter in his last years in office was accelerated by President Ronald Reagan, who was swept into office in 1980 by the wave of patriotism following an agonizing hostage crisis in Iran. The new American leadership was convinced that the military balance had tipped in favor of the Soviet Union. Increasing defense spending rapidly, the Reagan administration concentrated especially on nuclear arms and an expanded navy as keys to a resurgence of American power in the post-Vietnam era. Somewhat reluctantly, and in the face of large protest demonstrations, European governments agreed that

American Hostages in Iran Blindfolded and hands tied, American employees at the U.S. embassy in Teheran are threatened and humiliated by their militant Iranian captors on the first day of their ordeal. In their anguish over the hostages, Americans tended to blame President Carter for weakness, though all the hostages eventually did return to the United States. *(UPI/Bettmann Newsphotos)*

NATO's forces had to be strengthened. They also reluctantly agreed to install medium-range American cruise missiles with nuclear warheads on their soil, in response to the vast arsenal of medium-range "European" missiles that the Soviet Union had targeted to destroy all important targets in western Europe without even calling on Soviet bombers or missile-launching submarines. Thus western Europeans accepted the need to maintain some kind of rough nuclear and general military balance in Europe to guarantee their freedom and genuine independence (see Map 32.2). Increasingly unable to act as a unit in local conflicts in Africa, Asia, the Middle East, or Central America because of different perceptions and interests, the Atlantic alliance, reinforced by a rich network of common cultural and political values, remained a powerful force defending the heartland of Western civilization.

THE SOVIET BLOC

The fluctuations in Western response to the Soviet bloc were tied in part to puzzling ambiguities within the Soviet system itself. Ever since Lenin, and certainly since Stalin, the Soviet Union has combined political dictatorship with egalitarian ideology, for example; and there has been a strong tendency in the West to see the Soviet Union in terms of black or white, of archvillain or great hero.

MAP 32.2 The Use of Nuclear Power in the 1980s One major consequence of the growing use of nuclear power to generate electricity is that many countries have developed the expertise necessary to make nuclear weapons should they so choose.

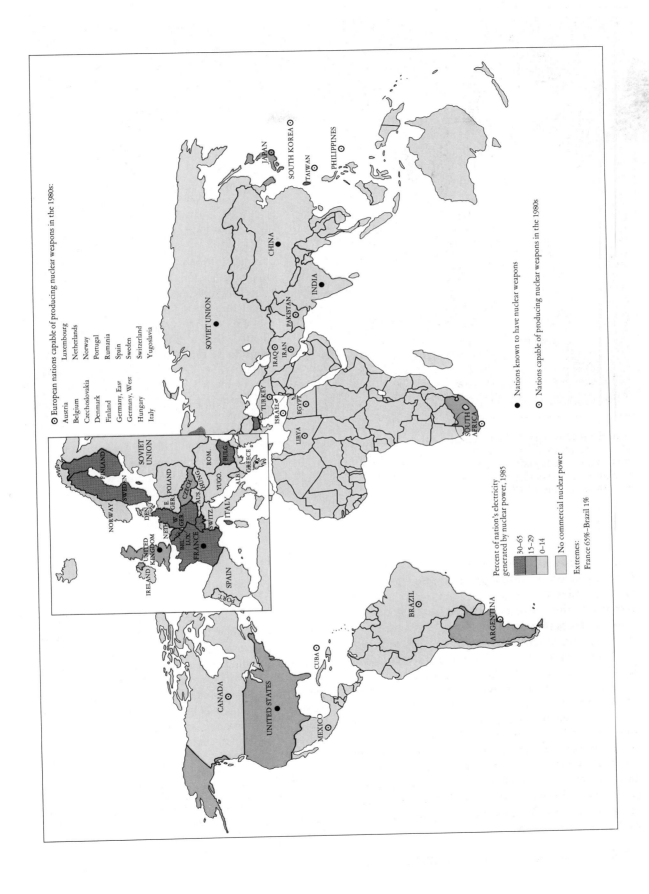

European nations capable of producing nuclear weapons in the 1980s:

Austria	Luxembourg
Belgium	Netherlands
Czechoslovakia	Norway
Denmark	Portugal
Finland	Rumania
Germany, East	Spain
Germany, West	Sweden
Hungary	Switzerland
Italy	Yugoslavia

● Nations known to have nuclear weapons

◉ Nations capable of producing nuclear weapons in the 1980s

Percent of nation's electricity generated by nuclear power, 1985

30–65
15–29
0–14
No commercial nuclear power

Extremes:
France 65%–Brazil 1%

In fact, and at the risk of oversimplification, these extremes may be regarded as equally inappropriate. The Soviet Union has consistently remained a somber gray in its behavior. First, the Communist party in the Soviet Union has steadfastly sought to maintain its monopoly of political power, which has not been difficult because communism is wrapped in Russian nationalism and traditional authoritarianism. Second, there has been an equally strong desire to preserve the Communist system throughout eastern Europe, where it has much less support than in the Soviet Union and is therefore subject to liberation efforts, which have been unsuccessful thus far. Third, military power has held the system together, providing a firm basis for continuous but cautious efforts to expand the Soviet sphere of influence. These enduring realities dominate the recent past, as may be seen by looking at the invasion of Czechoslovakia, the Brezhnev era, and the fate of Solidarity in Poland.

The Czechoslovak Experiment

In the wake of Khrushchev's reforms in the Soviet Union (pages 980–981), the 1960s brought modest liberalization and more consumer goods to eastern Europe, as well as somewhat greater national autonomy, especially in Poland and Rumania. Czechoslovakia moved more slowly than its Communist neighbors, but in January 1968, it began making up for lost time. The reform elements in the Czechoslovak Communist party gained a majority and voted out the long-time Stalinist leader in favor of Alexander Dubček. The new government launched a series of major economic and political reforms that fascinated observers around the world.

Educated in Moscow, Dubček was a dedicated Communist. But he and his allies within the party were also idealists, who believed that they could reconcile genuine socialism with personal freedom and internal party democracy. Thus local decision making by trade unions, managers, and consumers replaced rigid bureaucratic planning. Censorship was relaxed, and mindless ideological conformity gave way to exciting free expression. People responded enthusiastically, and the reform program proved enormously popular. Czechoslovakia had been eastern Europe's only advanced industrial state before the Second World War, and Dubček was reviving traditions that were still deeply cherished.

Although Dubček remembered the lesson of the Hungarian revolution (page 981) and constantly proclaimed his loyalty to the Warsaw Pact of Communist states, the determination of the Czech reformers to build "socialism with a human face" frightened hard-line Communists. In March 1968, Polish students took to the streets shouting, "We want a Polish Dubček" and "Long Live Czechoslovakia!" Czechoslovakia was obviously setting a dangerous example for the peoples of eastern Europe, tempting them to challenge the Communist party's absolute monopoly of political power. These fears were particularly strong in Poland and East Germany, where the leaders knew full well that they lacked popular support. Moreover, the Soviet Union attached great military significance to Czechoslovakia because of its strategic geographical position, and Moscow feared that a liberalized Czechoslovakia would eventually be drawn to neutralism, or even to the democratic West. Thus the East bloc countries launched a concerted campaign of intimidation against the Czech leaders, warning ominously of "counter-revolutionary tendencies" in public statements and demanding a restoration of Soviet orthodoxy in private meetings. Dubček made minor concessions on defense, but his regime was unwilling to knuckle under. The Soviet response was brutal. In August 1968, 500,000 Russian and allied eastern European troops suddenly occupied Czechoslovakia.

The Czechs made no attempt to resist militarily. The Soviets immediately arrested Dubček and the other top leaders, but to their chagrin, they found no collaborators to form a new government. Thus, instead of being shot, the arrested Czech leaders were flown to Moscow, where they surrendered to demands after they and their country had been threatened by Brezhnev with the most severe punishments. The Czech Communists agreed to reimpose censorship and accepted an indefinite stationing of Soviet troops on their soil. Gradually but inexorably, the reform program was abandoned and its supporters removed from office. Thus the Czechoslovak experiment in humanizing communism and making it serve the needs of ordinary citizens failed.

Shortly after the Czechoslovak invasion, Brezhnev declared the so-called Brezhnev Doctrine, according to which Soviet Russia and its allies had the right to intervene in any socialist country whenever they saw the need. The Chinese drew the reasonable conclu-

The End of Reform In August 1968 Soviet tanks rumbled into Prague to extinguish Czechoslovakian efforts to build a humane socialism. Here people watch the massive invasion from the sidewalks, knowing full well the suicidal danger of armed resistance. *(Magnum)*

sion that they might be next, which encouraged them to seek the reconciliation with the United States that helped Richard Nixon obtain a Vietnam agreement with Hanoi. Predictably, the occupation of Czechoslovakia raised a storm of protest. Many Communist parties in western Europe were harshly critical, partly out of conviction and partly to limit their electoral losses. But the occupation did not seriously alter ongoing Western efforts—mostly notably, those of West Germany's Willy Brandt—to secure better relations with the East-bloc countries. The reason was simple. The West considered Czechoslovakia to be part of Russia's sphere of influence, for better or worse. Thus Stalin's empire remained solidly in place, and it

seemed that change in eastern Europe could only continue to follow developments in the Soviet Union for years to come.

THE SOVIET UNION

The 1968 invasion of Czechoslovakia was probably the crucial event of the Brezhnev era, which really lasted beyond the aging leader's death in 1982, until the emergence in 1985 of Mikhail Gorbachev (see page 1036). The invasion demonstrated unmistakably the intense conservatism of Russia's ruling elite and its determination to maintain the status quo in the Soviet bloc. It showed that Russia's Communist leaders were less inclined to accept fundamental reforms than were their Western counterparts. Thus the failure of both the Czechoslovak experiment and the student revolution in France proved that similar hopes of reconciling socialism with freedom were illusive on both sides of the iron curtain in the late 1960s. But whereas the aftermath of 1968's romantic upheaval in France brought a number of social and political reforms, notably for women and in higher education, the aftermath of 1968 in Czechoslovakia witnessed only a long step backward to the Stalinist regime.

Intervention in Czechoslovakia also brought further re-Stalinization of Soviet Russia, though with collective rather than personal dictatorship and without uncontrolled terror. This compromise seemed to suit the leaders and most of the people. Whether Westerners liked it or not, Soviet Russia appeared quite stable in the 1970s and early 1980s.

A gradually rising standard of living for ordinary people contributed greatly to stability. By 1974 two-thirds of the nation's families had television sets, almost 60 percent had sewing and washing machines, and about half had some kind of refrigerator. The economic crisis of the 1970s markedly slowed the rate of improvement, and long lines and innumerable shortages persisted. But long-suffering Soviet consumers compared the present with the recent past and not with conditions abroad. The enduring differences between the life of the elite and the life of ordinary people also reinforced the system. Ambitious individuals still had tremendous incentive to do as the state wished, in order to gain access to special, well-stocked stores, attend special schools, and travel abroad.

Another source of stability was that ordinary Russians remained more intensely nationalistic than almost any other people in the world. The party leaders successfully identified themselves with this patriotism, stressing their role in saving the motherland during the Second World War and protecting it now from foreign foes, including eastern European "counter-revolutionaries." By playing on nationalist feelings, de-Stalinization was very easily reversed. Many ordinary Russians considered an attack on Stalin to be an attack on the great sacrifices they had willingly made for their nation. Similarly, ordinary Russians took enormous pride in their country's military power, and young men accepted an inescapable three-year hitch in the army without question. The cult of Lenin, which replaced the cult of Stalin, also had nationalistic overtones, which neutralized the general cynicism about Communist ideology.

The weight of history also contributed to the preservation of the status quo. For centuries, the tsars were uncompromising absolutists, who taught their subjects that undivided and hence unquestioned authority was essential for the good of the state. Moreover, the politically dominant Great Russians constitute only half of the total Soviet population. As their action in Czechoslovakia showed, the Great Russian leaders feared that greater freedom and open political competition might result in demands for autonomy and even independence, not only by eastern European nationalities, but by non-Russian nationalities within the Soviet Union itself. Thus Western-style liberalism and democracy appeared as alien and divisive political philosophies that would undermine Russia's power and achievements.

The strength of the government was expressed in the re-Stalinization of culture and art. Free expression and open protest disappeared. In 1968, when a small group of dissenters appeared in Red Square to protest the invasion of Czechoslovakia, they were arrested before they could unfurl their banners. This proved to be the high point of dissent, for in the 1970s Brezhnev and company made certain that public dissent did not infect Soviet intellectuals. The slightest acts of open nonconformity and protest were severely punished, but with sophisticated, cunning methods.

Most frequently, dissidents were blacklisted and thus rendered unable to find a decent job, since the government was the only employer. This fate was enough to keep most in line. More determined but unrenowned protesters were quietly imprisoned in jails or mental institutions. Celebrated nonconformists such as Solzhenitsyn were permanently expelled from the country. Once again, Jews were persecuted as a "foreign" element, though some were eventually permitted to emigrate to Israel.

As the distinguished Russian dissident historian Roy Medvedev summed it up:

The technology of repression has become more refined in recent years. Before, repression always went much farther than necessary. Stalin killed millions of people when arresting 1000 would have enabled him to control the people. Our leaders ... found out eventually that you don't have to put people in prison or in a psychiatric hospital to silence them. There are other ways.[6]

POLITICAL DEVELOPMENTS WITHIN THE ATLANTIC ALLIANCE AND SOVIET EASTERN EUROPE, 1961–1985

Aug 1961	Construction of the Berlin Wall
Nov 1963	Assassination of U.S. President John F. Kennedy
Aug 1964	Tonkin Gulf Resolution: escalation of American involvement in Vietnam
Nov 1964	Re-election of U.S. President Lyndon B. Johnson
Jan 1968	Tet Offensive of Vietcong in Vietnam
Aug 1968	Soviet invasion of Czechoslovakia: Dubček forced to abandon liberal reform program
Nov 1968	Election of U.S. President Richard M. Nixon
1969–1973	Chancellor Willy Brandt negotiates reconciliation between West Germany and Communist eastern Europe
Dec 1970	Strikes in Poland in protest against large price rises; fall of government of Wladyslaw Gomulka
Feb 1972	Nixon visits Premier Chou En-lai in Peking; re-establishes good relations with Communist China
May 1972	Salt I Treaty between the United States and the Soviet Union
Jan 1973	Paris Accords between the United States and North Vietnam
Oct 1973	Fourth Arab-Israeli War; OPEC quadruples price of oil
Aug 1974	Nixon resigns from presidency over the Watergate scandal; Gerald R. Ford takes over as U.S. president
April 1975	Fall of Saigon to the Communists; reunification of North and South Vietnam
July 1975	Helsinki Agreement: Atlantic alliance accepts eastern European status quo in return for Soviet human-rights guarantees
Nov 1976	Election of U.S. President Jimmy Carter
1978–1979	Islamic revolution in Iran: oil production collapses, OPEC doubles the price of oil
March 1979	Camp David Accords between Israel and Egypt
May 1979	Election of British Prime Minister Margaret Thatcher
June 1979	Salt II Treaty between the United States and the Soviet Union
Nov 1979–Jan 1981	Iranian hostage crisis
Dec 1979	Soviet invasion of Afghanistan
Aug 1980	Occupation of the Lenin Shipyards in Gdansk: Polish government accedes to Solidarity's demands
Nov 1980	Election of U.S. President Ronald Reagan
May 1981	Election of French President François Mitterand
Dec 1981	General Jaruzelski proclaims martial law in Poland; Solidarity leaders arrested
1982	Death of Soviet First Secretary Leonid Brezhnev
1983	Installation of American cruise and Pershing missiles in western Europe
March 1985	Mikhail Gorbachev becomes First Secretary of the Soviet Communist Party
Nov 1985	Reagan-Gorbachev summit in Geneva

Superpower Summit, 1985 At their Geneva meeting U.S. President Reagan and Soviet leader Gorbachev vigorously debated arms control and the many issues that separated their governments. Smiling frequently for the press and locked in an intense campaign for public support, especially in western Europe, they agreed only to meet again. *(Wide World Photos)*

Thus the worst aspects of Stalin's totalitarianism had been eliminated, but rule by a self-perpetuating Communist elite in the Soviet Union appeared as solid as ever throughout the 1970s.

That elite seemed equally secure in the 1980s, as far as any challenge from below was concerned. The long-established system of administrative controls continued to stretch downward from the central ministries and state committees to provincial cities, and from there to factories, neighborhoods, and villages. At each level of this massive state bureaucracy, the overlapping hierarchy of the Communist party, with its 17.5 million members, continued to watch over all decisions and manipulate every aspect of national life. Organized opposition was simply impossible, and the average Soviet citizen left politics to the bosses.

Yet the massive state and party bureaucracy was a mixed blessing. It discouraged economic efficiency and personal initiative as well as political dissent and intellectual innovation. It safeguarded the elite, but it also promoted apathy in the masses. Therefore, when

the ailing Brezhnev finally died in 1982, his successor, the long-time chief of the secret police, Yuri Andropov, tried to invigorate the system. Andropov introduced modest reforms to improve economic performance and campaigned against worker absenteeism and high-level corruption. Relatively little came of these efforts, for both Andropov and his successor died in office in little more than a year. But Andropov's efforts combined with the dreary procession of state funerals in Red Square to set the stage for the emergence in March 1985 of Mikhail Gorbachev, the most vigorous Soviet leader in a generation.

The fifty-four-year-old Gorbachev was smart, charming, and tough. As long-time Soviet foreign minister Andrei Gromyko reportedly said, "This man has a nice smile, but he has got iron teeth."[7] In his first year in office, Gorbachev attacked corruption and incompetence in the upper reaches of the bureaucracy. Gorbachev launched a strong campaign against alcoholism and drunkenness, which were also deadly scourges of Soviet society. He seemed determined to use tough measures to make both the elite and the masses "shape up," so that the economy would perform better while the Communist party as a whole maintained firm control.

The new Soviet leader also seemed tough and determined in international affairs. He and his colleagues made clear that they would not permit any major deviation from the Communist model in eastern Europe, like the one that had only recently occurred in Poland (see discussion below). Gorbachev repeatedly attacked President Reagan's plan to build a space shield against nuclear missiles, popularly known as "Star Wars," and tried to exploit existing differences between the United States and its European allies on defense matters. The outcome of all these initiatives was uncertain in early 1986, but Mikhail Gorbachev seemed firmly in command and a leader to be reckoned with.

THE SOLIDARITY REVOLUTION

While Soviet leaders seemed quite secure in the last years of the Brezhnev era, their satellite empire witnessed a spectacular resurgence of popular protest. Polish workers joined together en masse to fight peacefully for freedom and self-determination, while the world watched in amazement.

Poland was an unruly satellite from the beginning. Stalin said that introducing communism to Poland was like putting a saddle on a cow. Efforts to saddle the cow—really a spirited stallion—led to widespread riots in 1956 (see page 981). As a result, the Polish Communists dropped efforts to impose Soviet-style collectivization on the peasants and to break the Roman Catholic church. Most agricultural land remained in private hands as the Catholic church thrived. Long a symbol of Poland's powerful patriotism, the Catholic church succeeded in holding the allegiance of rural people as they poured into the new industrial centers. With an independent agriculture and a vigorous church, the Communists failed to monopolize society.

They also failed to manage the economy effectively. The 1960s saw little economic improvement. When the government suddenly announced large price increases right before Christmas in 1970, Poland's working class rose again in angry protest. Factories were occupied and strikers were shot, but Wladyslaw Gomulka fell from power. Edward Gierek, the new Communist leader, then wagered that massive inflows of Western capital and technology, especially from a now-friendly West Germany, could produce a Polish "economic miracle" that would win popular support for the regime. Instead, bureaucratic incompetence coupled with worldwide recession put the economy into a nose dive by the mid-1970s. Workers, intellectuals, and the church became increasingly restive. Then the real "Polish miracle" occurred: Cardinal Karol Wojtyla, archbishop of Krakow, was elected pope in 1978. In June 1979, he returned for an astonishing pilgrimage across his native land. Preaching love of Christ and country and the "inalienable rights of man," Pope John Paul II electrified the Polish nation. The economic crisis became a spiritual crisis as well.

In August 1980, as scattered strikes to protest higher meat prices spread, the 16,000 workers at the gigantic Lenin Shipyards in Gdansk (formerly known as Danzig), laid down their tools and occupied the showpiece plant. As other workers along the Baltic coast joined "in solidarity," the strikers advanced truly revolutionary demands: the right to form free trade unions, the right to strike, freedom of speech, release of political prisoners, and economic reforms. After eighteen days of shipyard occupation, as families brought food to the gates and priests said mass daily amid huge overhead cranes, the government gave in and accepted the workers' demands in the Gdansk Agreement. In a state where the Communist party claimed to rule on behalf of the proletariat, a working-class revolt had won an unprecedented victory.

Led by a feisty Lenin Shipyards electrician and devout Catholic named Lech Walesa, the workers proceeded to organize their free and democratic trade union. They called it "Solidarity." Joined by intellectuals and supported by the Catholic church, Solidarity became the union of a nation. By March 1981, it had a membership of 9.5 million, of 12.5 million who were theoretically eligible. A full-time staff of 40,000 linked the union members and their sections together with modern communications technology and vital information. Solidarity created its own press service and published newspapers, as cultural and intellectual freedom blossomed in Poland. Solidarity's leaders had tremendous well-organized support, and the threat of calling a nationwide strike gave them real power in ongoing negotiations with the Communist bosses who replaced Gierek.

But if Solidarity had power, it did not try to take power. History, the Brezhnev Doctrine, and virulent

The Rise of Solidarity This photo shows the determination and mass action that allowed Polish workers to triumph in August 1980. Backed by a crowd of enthusiastic supporters, leader Lech Walesa announces the historic Gdansk Agreement to striking workers at the main gate of the Lenin Shipyards. *(Jean Gaumy/Magnum)*

attacks from Communist neighbors all guaranteed the intervention of the Red Army if Polish Communists "lost control." And since Poland's 35 million population had a long tradition of fierce patriotism and romantic revolt against both Russians and Germans, a terrible bloodbath would be the inevitable tragic consequence. Thus the Solidarity revolution was always a "self-limiting revolution," aiming at defending the cultural and trade union freedoms won in the Gdansk Agreement, without directly challenging the Communist monopoly of political power.

Solidarity's combination of strength and moderation explains why it lasted so long before it was crushed. The Soviet Union, already condemned worldwide for its invasion of Afghanistan, decided to play a waiting game of threats and pressure. After a crisis in March 1981 that followed police beatings of

Solidarity activists, Walesa settled for minor government concessions, and Solidarity again dropped plans for a massive general strike. It was a turning point. Criticism of Walesa's moderate leadership and calls for local self-government in unions and factories grew. Solidarity lost its cohesiveness. The worsening economic crisis also encouraged grassroots radicalism and frustration: a hunger-march banner proclaimed that "A hungry nation can eat its rulers."[8] With an eye on Western public opinion, the Polish Communist leadership shrewdly denounced Solidarity for promoting economic collapse and provoking Russian invasion. In December 1981, the Communist leader General Jaruzelski suddenly struck in the dead of subfreezing night, proclaiming martial law and cutting all communications, arresting Solidarity's leaders and "saving" the nation.

The rise and fall of Solidarity was a major historical development. Jaruzelski's "invasion by proxy" again showed the Soviet Union's determination to maintain communist orthodoxy in its Eastern empire, which clearly rested on fear and old-fashioned military might. But the Solidarity revolution also showed the enduring appeal of other old-fashioned values—cultural freedom, trade union rights, patriotic nationalism, and Catholic piety. And the fact that Poland lived enthusiastically by these values for sixteen months meant that General Jaruzelski proceeded cautiously with communist "normalization." Solidarity failed, but only in part.

THE FUTURE IN PERSPECTIVE

What about the future? For centuries, astrologers and scientists, experts and ordinary people, have been trying to answer this question. Although it may seem that the study of what has been has little to say about what will be, the study of history over a long period is actually very useful in this regard. It helps put the future in perspective.

In 1931 a distinguished Harvard professor of genetics examined the prospects for the human race in an article read by millions. Among his predictions was that "in the year 2500 the population of the world should be about 3,500 millions, or about twice the figures of today."[9] In fact, the population of the world reached 4 billion in the 1970s and, outside the highly developed countries of Europe and North America, is still growing rapidly. The six-century projection of the learned expert was proved dead wrong in less than fifty years (see Map 32.3).

History is full of such erroneous predictions, a few of which we have mentioned in this book. Yet lack of success has not diminished the age-old desire to look into the future. Self-proclaimed experts even pretend that they have created a new science of futurology. With great pomposity they often act as if their hunches and guesses about future human developments were inescapable realities. Yet the study of history teaches healthy skepticism regarding such predictions, however scientific they may appear. Past results suggest that most such predictions will simply not come true, or not in the anticipated way. Thus history provides some psychological protection from the fantastic visions of modern astrologers.

This protection is particularly valuable today, because a great many projections into the future are quite pessimistic, just as they were very optimistic in the 1950s and 1960s. Many people in the Western world seem convinced that conditions are going to get worse rather than better. They fear, for example, that trade wars will permanently cripple the world economy, that pollution will destroy the environment, and that the traditional family will disappear. Until very recently, many experts and politicians were predicting that the energy crisis—in the form of skyrocketing oil prices—meant disaster, in the form of lower standards of living at best and the collapse of civilization at worst. Now some of these same experts worry that the unexpected sharp decline in oil prices will bankrupt both Third World oil producers, such as Mexico, and the large American banks that have lent them so much money. It is heartening to know that most such predictions will almost certainly not prove true, just as the same knowledge of likely error is sobering in more optimistic ages.

One of the more frightening and pessimistic predictions currently in vogue is that the northern nations of Europe and North America will increasingly find themselves locked in a life-and-death struggle with the poor, overpopulated southern nations of Africa, Asia, and South America. This North-South conflict, it is predicted, will replace the cold war struggle of East and West with a much more dangerous international class and race conflict of rich versus poor, white versus colored. Such, it is said, is the bitter legacy of Western imperialism.

As Map 32.4 shows, there is indeed an enormous gap between the very wealthy nations of noncommunist western Europe and North America and the very poor nations of much of Africa and Asia. Yet closer examination does not reveal a growing split between two sharply defined economic camps. On the contrary, there are five or six distinct categories of nations in terms of income level. The communist

MAP 32.3 World Population Density Population densities vary enormously. The highest densities are in western Europe and east Asia. The United States and the Soviet Union are both sparsely populated, with most people concentrated in a few large urban areas.

MAP 32.4 Estimated World per Capita Income in the Early 1980s

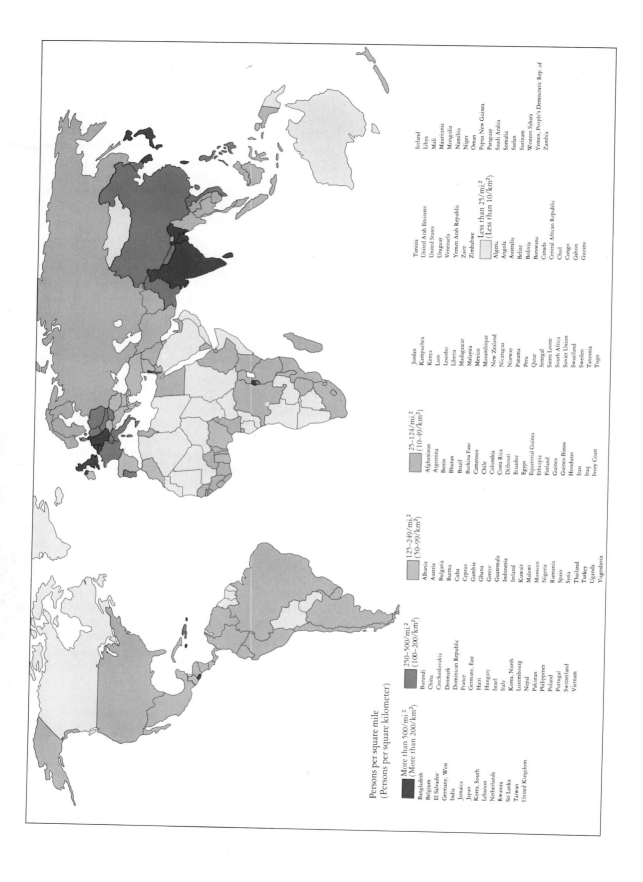

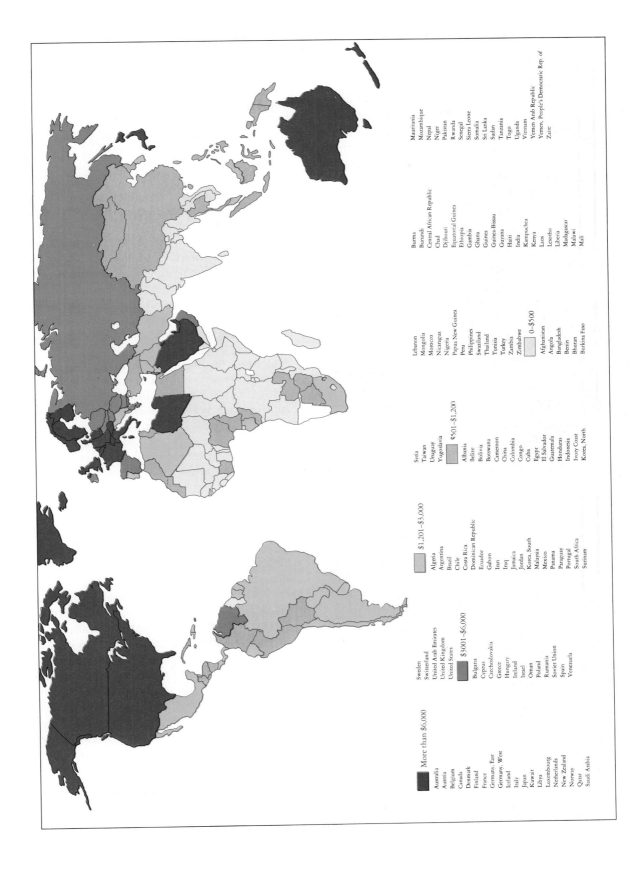

countries of eastern Europe form something of a middle-income group, as do the major oil-exporting states, which, contrary to common belief, are still behind the wealthier countries of western Europe. Poverty in parts of Latin America is severe, but as the map shows, standards of living are substantially higher there than in much of Africa and Asia, both of which encompass considerable variation.

When one considers differences in culture, religion, politics, and historical development, the supposed split between "rich" and "poor" nations breaks down still further. Thus a global class war between rich and poor appears unlikely in the foreseeable future. A more reasonable expectation is continuing pressure to reduce international economic differences through taxation and welfare measures, as has already occurred domestically in the wealthy nations. Such pressure may well bring at least modest success, for the wealthy nations generally realize that an exclusively Western viewpoint on global issues is unrealistic and self-defeating. The true legacy of Western imperialism is one small world.

It is this that makes the nuclear arms race so ominous. Not only do the United States and the Soviet Union possess unbelievably destructive, ever-expanding nuclear arsenals, but Great Britain, France, China, and India all have "the bomb," and probably Israel and South Africa do as well. Other countries are equipped or desire to "go nuclear" (see Map 32.2). Thus some gloomy experts have predicted that twenty or thirty states will have nuclear weapons in the 1990s. In a world increasingly plagued by local wars and ferocious regional conflicts, they have concluded that nuclear war is almost inevitable and have speculated that the human race is an "endangered species."

Such predictions and the undeniable seriousness of the arms race appear to have jolted Western populations out of their customary fatalism regarding nuclear weapons, at least temporarily. Efforts to reduce or even halt the nuclear buildup in the Soviet Union and the NATO alliance have blossomed again. Moreover, the recent revival of the antinuclear movement has drawn broad popular support and enlisted creditable mainstream leaders, such as Catholic bishops in the United States and Protestant clergy in West Germany. An optimist can hope that comparable concern in non-Western areas may yet develop to help create the global political will necessary to control nuclear proliferation before it is too late.

Whatever does or does not happen, the study of history puts the future in perspective in other ways. We have seen that every age has its problems and challenges. Others before us have trod these paths of crisis and uncertainty. This knowledge helps save us from exaggerated self-pity in the face of our own predicaments.

Perhaps our Western heritage may even inspire us with pride and measured self-confidence. We stand, momentarily, at the end of the long procession of Western civilization winding through the ages. Sometimes the procession has wandered, or backtracked, or done terrible things. But it has also carried the efforts and sacrifices of generations of toiling, struggling ancestors. Through no effort of our own, we are the beneficiaries of those sacrifices and achievements. Now that it is our turn to carry the torch onward, we may remember these ties with our forebears.

To change the metaphor, we in the West are like a card player who has been dealt many good cards. Some of them are obvious, like our technical and scientific heritage or our commitments to human rights and the individual. Others are not so obvious, sometimes half-forgotten or even hidden up the sleeve. One thinks, for example, of the Christian Democrats, the moderate Catholic party, which emerged after World War Two to play such an important role in the western European renaissance. Or one thinks of the dismantling of colonial empires, which was a victory of Western ideals of liberty and nationhood as well as a defeat for Western imperialism. We hold a good hand.

Our study of history, of mighty struggles and fearsome challenges, of shining achievements and tragic failures, gives a sense of what is the essence of life itself: the process of change over time. Again and again we have seen how peoples and societies evolve, influenced by ideas, human passions, and material conditions. As sure as anything is sure, this process of change over time will continue, as the future becomes the present and then the past. And students of history are better prepared to make sense of this unfolding process because they have already observed it. They know how change goes forward, on the basis of existing historical forces, and their projections will probably be as good as those of the futurologists. Students of history are also prepared for the new and unexpected in human development, for they have already seen great breakthroughs and revolutions.

They have an understanding of how things really happen.

NOTES

1. Quoted by W. Laqueur, *Europe Since Hitler,* Penguin Books, Baltimore, 1972, p. 9.
2. *Wall Street Journal,* June 25, 1985, pp. 1, 20.
3. Quoted by Kessing's Research Report, *Germany and East Europe Since 1945: From the Potsdam Agreement to Chancellor Brandt's "Ostpolitik,"* Charles Scribner's Sons, New York, 1973, pp. 284–285.
4. Quoted by S. E. Morison et al., *A Concise History of the American Republic,* Oxford University Press, New York, 1977, p. 735.
5. Richard Nixon, *Public Papers, 1969,* U.S. Government Printing Office, Washington, D.C., 1971, p. 371.
6. Quoted by H. Smith, *The Russians,* Quadrangle/New York Times, New York, 1976, pp. 455–456.
7. Quoted in *Time,* January 6, 1986, p. 66.
8. T. G. Ash, *The Polish Revolution: Solidarity,* Charles Scribner's Sons, New York, 1983, p. 186.
9. E. M. East, in *Scientific Monthly,* April 1931; also in *Reader's Digest* 19 (May 1931): 151.

SUGGESTED READING

Many of the studies cited in the Suggested Reading for Chapters 30 and 31 are also of value for the years since 1968. Journalistic accounts in major newspapers and magazines are also invaluable tools for an understanding of recent developments. Among general works W. Laqueur, *Europe Since Hitler,* rev. ed. (1982), and W. Keylor, *The Twentieth Century: An International History* (1984), are particularly helpful with their extensive, up-to-date bibliographies. B. Jones, *The Making of Contemporary Europe* (1980), is a good brief account, while G. Parker, *The Logic of Unity* (1975), analyzes the forces working for and against European integration. D Swann, *The Economics of the Common Market,* 5th ed. (1984), carries developments into the 1980s. L. Barzini, *The Europeans* (1983), draws engaging group portraits of the different European peoples today and is strongly recommended. On West Germany since 1968, L. Whetten, *Germany's Ostpolitik* (1971), and W. Patterson and G. Smith, eds., *The West German Model: Perspectives on a Stable State* (1981), are good introductions. Willy Brandt eloquently states his case for reconciliation with the East in *A Peace Policy for Europe* (1969). The spiritual dimension of West German recovery is probed by G. Grass in his world-famous novel *The Tin Drum* (1963), as well as in the novels of H. Böll. W. Laqueur, *The Germans* (1985), is a highly recommended contemporary report by a famous historian doubling as a journalist.

Among the many books to come out of the Czechoslovak experience in 1968, three are particularly recommended: H. Schwartz, *Prague's 200 Days: The Struggle for Democracy in Czechoslovakia* (1969); I. Svitak, *The Czechoslovak Experiment, 1968–1969* (1971); and Z. Zeman, *Prague Spring* (1969). T. Ash, *The Polish Revolution: Solidarity* (1983), is the best book on the subject and is highly recommended. It may be compared with a less sympathetic account by N. Ascherson, *The Polish August: The Self-Limiting Revolution* (1982). A. Bramberg, ed., *Poland: Genesis of a Revolution* (1983), is a valuable collection of documents with extensive commentary, while R. Leslie, *The History of Poland Since 1863* (1981), provides long-term perspective. On the Soviet Union, in addition to works cited in Chapter 30, D. Shipler, *Russia: Broken Idols, Solemn Dreams* (1983), is a solid report by an American journalist, while A. Shevchenko, *Breaking with Moscow* (1985), is the altogether fascinating autobiography of a top Russian diplomat who defected to the United States. A. De Porte, *Europe Between the Superpowers: The Enduring Balance* (1979), and J. Hough and M. Fainsod, *How the Soviet Union Is Governed* (1979), are major scholarly studies.

Among innumerable works on recent economic developments, L. Thurow, *The Zero-Sum Society* (1981), is an interesting example of early 1980s pessimism in the United States, and it may be compared with the engaging and informative work by J. Eatwell, *Whatever Happened to Britain? The Economics of Decline* (1982). W. Rostow, *The World Economy: History and Prospect* (1977), is a massive scholarly tome by a perennial optimist, and P. Hawkins, *The Next Economy* (1983), contains intelligent insights that merit consideration by the ordinary citizen. Three major intellectual works, which are rather somber in their projections, are R. Heilbroner, *An Inquiry into the Human Prospect* (1974), and J. Revel, *The Totalitarian Temptation* (1977) and *How Democracies Perish* (1983).

CHAPTER OPENER CREDITS

NOTES ON THE ILLUSTRATIONS

CHAPTER OPENER CREDITS

NOTES ON THE ILLUSTRATIONS

Page 506   A senior merchant of the Dutch East India Company pointing out the Company's ships in Batavia Bay (now Djakarta, Indonesia) to his wife. Detail of a painting by Albert Cuyp (1620–1691).

Page 511   Philippe de Champaigne (French, 1602–1674), *Cardinal Richelieu Swearing the Order of the Holy Ghost.*

Page 512   Antoine Coysevox (French, 1640–1730), *Louis XIV,* statue for the Town Hall of Paris, 1687–1689.

Page 517   "The Noble Is the Spider," from Jacques Lagniet, *Receuil des Proverbes,* 1657–1663.

Page 518   *The Rape of the Sabine Women,* ca 1636–1637, by Nicolas Poussin, French painter (1594–1665). Oil on canvas.

Page 523   *Las Meninas* (The Maids of Honor), 1656, by Diego Rodriguez de Silva y Velasquez (1599–1660), leading painter of the Spanish school.

Page 527   Title page of *The Lamentable Complaints of Nick Froth the Tapster and Rulerost the Cooke,* 1641, in The British Library.

Page 528   Second Great Seal of the Commonwealth, 1651.

Page 533   Johannes Vermeer (Dutch, 1632–1675), known as Jan Vermeer van Delft, *Young Woman with a Water Jug.* Oil on canvas, height 18 inches, width 16 inches.

Page 534   Engraving by Dapper.

Page 538   Coronation of Frederick I of Prussia (1701–1713).

Page 545   From A. Thevet, *Cosmographie universelle,* 1575.

Page 557   Feast of the Trinity at St. Basil's, Moscow. St. Basil's is important in two respects: it is the culmination of the Russian tradition of sixteenth-century centralized churches and it is the most sculptural work of Russian architecture.

Page 563   Peter Paul Rubens (Dutch, 1577–1640), *The Education of Marie de' Medici.*

Page 564   The Monastery of Melk, situated on a promontory on the Danube, is a masterpiece of Austrian baroque. It was begun by Jakob Prandtauer in 1702 and completed by his pupil Joseph Munggenast after 1738. Today the monastery's library has an important art collection and more than 1,800 manuscripts dating from the ninth century on.

Page 566   The Winter Palace (left), designed for Peter the Great by Domenico Trezzini and refurbished for Elizabeth by Bartolomeo Rastrelli (1700–1771), and the Old Admiralty (right), St. Petersburg, from an engraving by M. I. Makhaev, 1761.

Page 570   *Hall's Library at Margate,* aquatint by T. Malton, 1789. The British Library.

Page 573   Ptolemy's system according to Regiomontanus.

Page 574   Engraving by Joannes Blaeu from his *Atlas Major,* 1662, in the Map Library at The British Library.

Page 576   Tito Lessi (Italian, 1858–1917), *Galileo detta al figlio i discorsi sulle due nuove scienze.*

Page 579   Louis XIV and Colbert visiting the Académie des Sciences, from C. Perrault's *Mémoires pour servir à l'histoire naturelle des animaux,* 1671.

Page 581   Frans Hals (Dutch, 1581/85–1666), *René Descarte,* 1649. Oil on panel, 19 by 14 cm.

Page 586   Jean Antoine Houdon (French, 1741–1828), *Voltaire,* 1781. Marble bust, 20 inches high. The Fine Arts Museums of San Francisco, Mr. and Mrs. E. John Magnin gift.

Page 588   Huber, *Le lever de Voltaire à Ferney,* Musée Carnavelet, Paris.

Page 592   *Une Soirée chez Madame Geoffrin* by A. Ch. G. Lemonnier, French painter (1793–1824).

Page 595   Marten Meytens (alternate spelling: Mijtens; Swedish-Austrian, 1695–1770), *Kaiseria Maria Theresie mit Familie.* Meytens was an active court painter; in 1759 he was made director of the Vienna Academy of Art.

Page 596   Engraving after Borovikovsky, in the British Museum.

Page 602   After Adolf Von Menzel (German, 1815–1905), *Frederick II Playing the Flute at Sans Souci,* one of a series of large historical works illustrating the life of Frederick the Great (1852; Berlin, former State Museums).

Page 606   Joseph Vernet (1714–1789), *The Port of Dieppe in 1754,* one of fourteen in a famous series of port scenes commissioned by Louis XV.

Page 611   *Les Glaneuses* by Jean François Millet (1814–1875), French genre and landscape painter of the Barbizon school. The original can be seen in the Louvre.

Page 614   Peter Brueghel, the younger (1564–1637), *Harvesting Scene.* Oil on panel, 23⅛ by 17¼ inches. William Rockhill Nelson Gallery of Art, Atkins Museum of Fine Arts, K. C. Nelson Fund.

Page 615   Painting by Thomas Weaver, engraved by William Ward and published July 21, 1812. Mezzotint, 23⁷⁄₁₀ by 17⅘ inches.

Page 619   Colored engraving, 1746.

Page 626   Samuel Scott (English, 1702–1772), *Old East India Quay, London,* Victoria and Albert Museum. Samuel Scott was the most distinguished native English topographical view painter in the eighteenth century. Such painting was popularized in England by Canaletto during his residence there from 1746–1755.

Page 630   Frontispiece from a map of "the most Inhabited part of Virginia containing the whole province of Maryland with part of Pennsylvania, New Jersey and North Carolina drawn by Joshua Fry and Peter Jefferson in 1775," in Thomas Jeffrey's *America Atlas,* 1776, in The British Library.

Page 636   William Hogarth (1697–1764), English painter and engraver. Final scene from his series *The Idle Apprentice,* with the wayward boy on his way to his execution by hanging. Harsh physical punishment for children and teenagers was an eighteenth-century fact of life. Hangings were popular events, a spectator sport for rowdy crowds.

Page 644   After an engraving by R. Lehman of the foundlings' home called La Rota.

Page 649   *Famille de paysans,* ca 1640, by Louis Le Nain, French painter (1593–1648). The original can be seen in the Louvre.

Page 656   "The Remarkable Effects of Vaccination,"

an anonymous nineteenth-century Russian cartoon in the Clements C. Fry Collection of Medical Prints and Drawings, Yale Medical Library.

Page 659   From *L'Illustration*, 1855 (1ᵉ semester), p. 309.

Page 660   W. W. Wheatley, "Dancing around the Church," 1848.

Page 666   Jacques-Louis David (French, 1748–1825), *The Tennis Court Oath*.

Page 673   John Trumbull (American, 1756–1843), *The Declaration of Independence*. Oil on canvas, 1786. 21⅛ by 31⅛ inches.

Page 674   E. C. Mills, *Signing of Treaty of Amity and Commerce and of Alliance between France and the United States*.

Page 675   This portrait of Louis XVI by Joseph-Siffrein Duplessis, French portrait painter (1725–1802), hangs in the Marie Antoinette Gallery at Versailles.

Page 679   This drawing by Persin de Prieur, "Premier assaut contre La Bastille," can be seen in the Musée Carnavalet, Paris.

Page 685   "Un Comité révolutionnaire sous la Terreur," after Alexandre Évariste Fragonard, French historical painter (1780–1850).

Page 689   Jacques-Louis David (French, 1748–1825), *Napoleon Crossing the Alps*. Oil on canvas.

Page 699   Fritz the giant steam hammer at the Krupp steelworks in Germany, photographed on 16 September 1861.

Page 702   James Hargreaves (d. 1778), English inventor, weaver, and mechanic, invented the spinning jenny about 1765.

Page 705   Engraving by Henry Beighton, 1717, of the atmospheric steam engine invented about 1705 by Thomas Newcomen, English blacksmith (1663–1729).

Page 707   The Northern locomotive *Fire Fly* on a narrow field bridge. Photo by Matthew Brady (American, 1823–1896), famous photographer of the Civil War.

Page 708   Honoré Daumier (1808–1879), *The Third-Class Carriage*. Oil on canvas. Daumier was both a caricaturist and a serious painter.

Page 712   The Cockerill works at Seraing, Belgium, at night. Lithograph by E. Toovey, Brussels, 1852.

Page 713   Royal visit to steelworks in Crewe, Cheshire: the tire-expanding machine, February 1866.

Page 718   The textile factory of Messrs Swainson, Birley and Co. near Manchester, extant until 1966: 7 stories high, 158 yards long, 18 yards wide, 660 windows, 32,500 panes of glass. The building was subsequently taken over by Horrock, Crewdson and renamed Fishwich Mills.

Page 719   From *Parliamentary Papers*, 1842, vol. XV.

Page 726   "Proclamation of the Roman Republic," 1848 lithograph by Bertarelli, Milan.

Page 731   Yohann Hochle, *Ball in the Winter Riding School*, 1815.

Page 733   *Count Clemens von Metternich* (1773–1859) by Sir Thomas Lawrence, English painter (1769–1830).

Page 740   Left to right: K. Marx, F. Engels (rear), with Marx's daughters: Jenny, Eleanor, and Laura, photographed in the 1860s.

Page 742   Eugene Delacroix (1798–1863), French painter and leader of the Romantic school.

Page 745   *Liszt am Klavier*, 1840, by Josef Danhauser, German painter (1805–1845).

Page 747   Eugene Delacroix (French, 1798–1863), *Les Massacres de Scio*. Louvre. This dramatic interpretation of a contemporary event scandalized Paris Salon visitors in 1824.

Page 749   From *Punch*, 1846. The humorous weekly *Punch*—founded in 1841 by the British journalist and sociologist Henry Mayhew (1812–1887) and others—is the most famous of its kind. Its cartoons and caricatures became a powerful vehicle of political and social comment.

Page 752   *The Legislative Belly*, lithograph by Honoré Daumier (1808–1879).

Page 760   Paul Gustav Doré (French illustrator and painter, 1833–1883), *Over London by Rail* from his *London*, published in 1872.

Page 764   "The Court for King Cholera," cartoon from *Punch*, XXIII (1852), 139.

Page 768   Cross-section of a Parisian house, about 1850, from Edmund Texier, *Tableauade Paris*, Paris, 1852, vol. I, p. 65.

Page 770   Opening of steam-propelled tramways by the locomotive *Harding* in Paris between the railroad stations of Montparnasse and Austerlitz. From *L'Illustration*, 19 August 1876.

Page 774   *Un Coin de Table*, 1904, by Paul-Émile Chabas, French painter (1869–1937). Oil on canvas.

Page 778   Market for servants, situated just outside the ancient boundary wall (the Kitai Yard) of Moscow and open every day of the year, Sundays being the busiest. From *The Illustrated London News*, 1 November 1850, p. 458. England had no fully illustrated newspaper until the first number of the weekly *Illustrated London News* appeared on 14 May 1842, with 16 printed pages and 32 woodcuts.

Page 791   Sir Frederick William Burton (Irish watercolorist, 1816–1900), portrait of George Eliot (Mary Anne Cross), 1865.

Page 794   From *Album of Photographic Views, 1890–1899, for the Construction of the Novoselitsa Branches of the Southwestern Railway in the Ukraine.*

Page 798   Demolition of part of the Latin Quarter in 1860. Engraving from a drawing by Félix Thorigny.

Page 810   Merchants of Nijni-Novgorod drinking tea. From *L'Illustration,* 29 August 1905.

Page 816   Assassination of 62 hostages in Haxo Road, Belville, France, by the Communards, 1872.

Page 826   Sir Benjamin Stone's photograph of a steamer on the Aswan Dam in 1907. Giant statues of Ramses II guard the ancient Egyptian rock temples he built at Abu Simbel. These were preserved at vast expense when the Aswan Dam was rebuilt in the 1960s and its rising water level threatened to flood them.

Page 836   Ellis Island pens, photographed in 1907.

Page 855   Min-Chiang-Chek, prisoner number 7 who was condemned to death for murdering missionaries at Kucheng. *The Graphic,* 23 November 1895.

Page 861   *The Congress at Berlin in 1878* by Anton von Werner, German painter of portraits and historical subjects (1843–1915).

Page 876   Panoramic view of Sackville Street and wharf area heavily shelled by British gunboat on Liffey River during the Easter Rising. *The Graphic,* 1916.

Page 894   Berlin family living in railway boxcar after World War I.

Page 900   Edmund Engelmann took this and other photographs secretly in May 1938 while Freud's apartment was under surveillance by the Gestapo. His chance for survival was about 50 percent. When leaving Vienna it was too dangerous for him to take the negatives, so he left them with an acquaintance. After the war this acquaintance had died, and Engelmann recovered these unique photographs only with great difficulty.

Page 904   Frank Lloyd Wright (American architect, 1869–1959), Falling Water, Bear Run, Pennsylvania—perhaps the greatest modern house in America, 1936. The largely self-taught Wright was an exponent of what he called "organic architecture": the idea that a building should blend in with its setting and be harmonious with nature.

Page 906   *Guernica,* 1937, by Pablo Picasso, Spanish painter and sculptor (1881–1973). The original oil on canvas, 11 feet, 5½ inches high by 25 feet, 5¾ inches wide, is in the Museo del Prado, Madrid.

Page 908   Mary Pickford (1893–1979) photographed by Hartsook in 1918. Rudolph Valentino (1895–1926) as he appeared in *Four Horsemen of the Apocalypse* (1921).

Page 920   Scene in San Francisco in 1934, photographed by Dorothea Lange.

Page 927   100,000 Nazi Storm Troopers gathered in the Luitpodarena in Nuremberg, Germany, to hear Adolf Hitler on Brown Shirt Day at the Nazi Party convention, 20 September 1936.

Page 929   French caricature by C. Leavdre, 1898.

Page 949   The cartoon "Stepping Stones to Glory" by Sir David Low (1891–1963) appeared in the London *Evening Standard* on 8 July 1936.

Page 956   East German troops supervising construction workers at the Berlin Wall, photographed from West Berlin.

Page 963   Rabaul Harbor, New Britain. U.S. Air Force North American B-25 passing over Japanese ship.

Page 971   The *Deutscher Verlag* building in Berlin after impassable street had been cleared of rubble, photographed on 6 July 1945.

Page 986   Muro Central in the Palacio Nacional, Mexico City, painted 1929–1935 by José Clemente Orozco (1883–1949), Mexican painter of the modernist school.

Page 990   Demonstrators link arms across Boulevard St. Michel on Left Bank during Paris riots of May 1968.

Page 995   First atomic bomb test at Bikini Atoll, in photograph released 26 July 1946.

Page 997   Astronaut Edwin E. Aldrin, Jr., leaving the lunar module. Apollo II was launched in Florida on 16 July 1969. Astronauts Neil A. Armstrong and Aldrin landed on the moon on 20 July while Michael Collins circled in the main spacecraft until rejoined by the others on 21 July. The astronauts returned to Earth on 24 July, when they were picked up in the Pacific Ocean.

Page 1006   Students in the Boulevard Saint Michel in Paris protesting the closing of the surburban Nanterre University, photographed on 3 May 1968.

Page 1014   Nuclear plant in the Loire Valley of France.

INDEX

Menarche, age of, 1008
Mendeleev, Dmitri, 787
Menopause, age of, 1008
Mental illness, 654–655, 786–787, 899–900
Mercantilism: as practiced by Colbert, 515, 624; as colonial economic warfare, 624–633; Adam Smith's criticism of, 735–736
Merchants: in cottage industry, 621–623
Metternich, Klemens von, 747; and Napoleon, 694; and balance of power, 730–731; conservative policies of, 732–734; opposes Greek national war, 746; flees in 1848, 754
Mexico, 631–632, 833, 985
Miasmatic theory of disease, 765–766
Michael, tsar of Russia, 558
Michelet, Jules, 643, 737
Mickey Mouse, 909
Microwave technology, 994
Middle class: and Calvinist values, 526; new industrial, 716; rise of in France, 676–677; effect on representative government, 728; as political factor in England, 749–750; in 19th–century reform efforts, 750–751; in cities of 1900, 771, 772–775; changes in modern, 1000–1002
Middlemarch (Eliot), 791
Midway Island, battle of, 962
Mies van der Rohe, Ludwig, 905
Migrants, 837–840
Migrations: of Irish to America, 723, 724; of 19th–century Europeans, 835–840; of 19th–century Asians, 840
Milan: in Revolutions of 1848, 756
Militarism: of Prussians, 550–552
Mill, John Stuart, 817
Millet, Jean François, 610, 611 (illus.)
Mines Act of 1842, 719
Mining: use of steam in, 704–705, 706; use of women, children in, 718, 719
Missionaries, 847–848
Mitterrand, François, 1021
Modern life: science and technology, 992–1000; emergence of a new society, 1000–1007; women and family in, 1007–1012; perspectives on future, 1039–1043
Modern society: movies and radio in, 907–909; changing class structure, 1000–1002; social security, welfare reforms, 1002; rising affluence, 1002–1005; discontent, student revolts, 1005–1007; postwar roles of women and marriage, 1007–1012; lifespans in, 1012, 1022
Modern thought: uncertainty in, 896–903; the new physics, 897–899; Freudian psychology, 899–900; modern philosophies, 900–901; revival of Christianity, 901–902; modern literature, art, music, 902–907
Mohammed Ali, 834
Mohammedanism. *See* Islam
Molière, 519
Molotov, Vyacheslav, 980, 982
Moltke, Helmuth von, 866
Mona Lisa, 906
Monarchy: absolutist, 508–515, 519–524, 525; development of modern English, 529–532; influence on east, west systems, 542–543; Enlightenment's influence on, 596–603; fall of in France, 675–688

Monasteries: in Spain, 522; contemplative orders abolished, 658
Monet, Claude, 709
Monetary systems: international, 1016–1017
Mongols, 553–555
Monks. *See* Monasteries
Monnet, Jean, 971, 972
Monroe Doctrine, 732
Montague, Lady Mary Wortley, 655
Montesquieu, Charles–Louis, Baron de, 585–586, 593, 669
Morality: 1900 middle–class code of, 775; working class code of, 776, 777
Morocco, 863
Mortality rates, 767, 836
Moscow, 694; rise of, 555–556; uprising in, 812
Motherhood. *See* Family; Women
Motion: Galileo's work on, 555–557; Newton's synthesis of findings on, 577–578
Motion pictures, 907–909
Mountain (French political group), 684
Movies. *See* Motion pictures
Mozambique, 842, 1029
Mr., Mrs., and Baby (Droz), 784
Mun, Thomas, 624
Munich, 940
Music: French classicism, 519; baroque, 562; romanticism, 744–746; modern, 907
Music halls, 778
Muslims: at battle of Omdurman, 844; and British in India, 852–853
Mussolini, Benito, 909; in power, 936–939; opposes, then joins Hitler, attacks Ethiopia, 947, 950; deposed, 962–963
My Secret Life (anonymous), 781–782

Nagasaki, bombing of, 963
Nanking, Treaty of, 832
Naples: and unification of Italy, 799, 803
Napoleon I, emperor of France: rules France, 688–690; England defeats at Trafalgar, 693; becomes emperor, 693; European wars of, 693–695; defeated in Russia, abdicates, 694; defeated at Waterloo, 695, 731; reappears, exiled again, 731; in Egypt, 834
Napoleon III, emperor of France (Louis Napoleon): wins election of 1848, 754, 796; and rebuilding of Paris, 767, 797; reasons for election, 796–797; as president of Second Republic, 797; as emperor, 797–799; and Cavour, 801; and Bismarck, 805, 807
Napoleonic Ideas (Napoleon), 796
Nasser, Gamal Abdel, 978, 1018
National Assembly of France, 677–678, 680, 681, 682, 797, 798, 815–816
National Association for the Advancement of Colored People, 983
National Convention (France), 684, 687–688
Nationalism: in Hungary, 547; and French Republic's success in war, 687, 737; concept of, 736–737; triumphs in Europe, 796–824; in France, 796–799; in Italy, 799–803; in Germany, 803–808; and the modernizing of Russia,